T0180752

Lecture Notes in Artificial Intelligence 13818

Subseries of Lecture Notes in Computer Science

More information about this subseries at https://link.springer.com/bookseries/1244

Filippo Cavallo · John-John Cabibihan ·
Laura Fiorini · Alessandra Sorrentino ·
Hongsheng He · Xiaorui Liu ·
Yoshio Matsumoto · Shuzhi Sam Ge (Eds.)

Social Robotics

14th International Conference, ICSR 2022
Florence, Italy, December 13–16, 2022
Proceedings, Part II

 Springer

Editors
Filippo Cavallo
University of Florence
Florence, Italy

John-John Cabibihan 🔟
Qatar University
Doha, Qatar

Laura Fiorini
University of Florence
Florence, Italy

Alessandra Sorrentino
University of Florence
Florence, Italy

Hongsheng He 🔟
Wichita State University
Wichita, KS, USA

Xiaorui Liu
Qingdao University
Qingdao, China

Yoshio Matsumoto
National Institute of Advanced Industrial
Science and Technology
Tsukuba, Japan

Shuzhi Sam Ge 🔟
National University of Singapore
Singapore, Singapore

ISSN 0302-9743   ISSN 1611-3349 (electronic)
Lecture Notes in Artificial Intelligence
ISBN 978-3-031-24669-2   ISBN 978-3-031-24670-8 (eBook)
https://doi.org/10.1007/978-3-031-24670-8

LNCS Sublibrary: SL7 – Artificial Intelligence

This Springer imprint is published by the registered company Springer Nature Switzerland AG
The registered company address is: Gewerbestrasse 11, 6330 Cham, Switzerland

Preface

The 14th International Conference on Social Robotics (ICSR 2022) was held as a traditional in-person conference in Florence, Italy on December 13th–16th, 2022. The theme of ICSR 2022 was Social Robots for Assisted Living and Healthcare, emphasizing on the increasing importance of social robotics in human daily living and society.

The International Conference on Social Robotics brings together researchers and practitioners working on the interaction between humans and intelligent robots and on the integration of robots into the fabric of our society. Out of a total of 143 submitted manuscripts reviewed by a dedicated international team of editors, associate editors and reviewers, 111 full papers were selected for inclusion into the proceedings in this book and presented during the technical and special sessions and the conference. In addition to paper presentation sessions, ICSR 2021 also featured three keynote talks, twelve workshops, two robot design competitions, and exhibitions. The keynote talks were delivered by three renowned researchers – Professor Kerstin Dautenhahn from University of Waterloo, Canada, Professor Maria Chiara Carrozza, Italian National Research Council (CNR), Italy, and Professor Oussama Khatib, Stanford University, United States.

We would like to express our sincere gratitude to all members of the Steering Committee, International Advisory Committee, Organizing Committee, and volunteers for their dedication in making the conference a great success. We are indebted to the associate editors and reviewers for their hard work in the rigorous review of the papers. We are also very grateful to the authors, participants, and sponsors, for the continued support to ICSR.

December 2022

Filippo Cavallo
John-John Cabibihan
Laura Fiorini
Alessandra Sorrentino
Hongsheng He
Xiaorui Liu
Yoshio Matsumoto
Shuzhi Sam Ge

Organization

General Chair

Cavallo, Filippo   University of Florence, Italy

Co-general Chair

Cabibihan, John-John   Qatar University, Qatar

Honorary Chair

Ge, Shuzhi Sam   National University of Singapore, Singapore

Program Chairs

Fiorini, Laura   Università degli studi di Firenze, Italy
Liu, Xiaorui   Qingdao University, China
Matsumoto, Yoshio   National Institute of Advanced Industrial Science
                                and Technology, Japan

Workshop Chairs

Sorrentino, Alessandra   University of Florence, Italy

Local Arrangement Chairs

La Viola, Carlo   University of Florence, Italy
Mancioppi, Gianmaria   Scuola Superiore Sant'Anna, Italy

Competition Chair

Kumar Pandey, Amit   beingAI Limited, Hong Kong, China; Socients AI
                                and Robotics, Paris, France

Publication Chair

He, Hongsheng   Wichita State University, USA
Rovini, Erika   University of Florence, Italy

Publicity Chairs

Trovato, Gabriele   Shibaura Institute of Technology, Tokyo, Japan
Zhao, Xiaopeng   University of Tennessee, USA

Standing Committee

Ge, Shuzhi Sam   National University of Singapore, Singapore

International Program Committee

Alhaddad, Ahmad Yaser   Qatar University, Qatar
Belpaeme, Tony   Ghent University, Belgium
Borghese, N. Alberto   University of Milan, Italy
Cangelosi, Angelo   University of Manchester, UK
Chi, Wenzheng   Soochow University, China
Cortellessa, Gabriella   ISTC-CNR, Italy
D'Onofrio, Grazia   IRCSS Ospedale Casa Sollievo della Sofferenza,
                                              Italy
De Oliveira, Ewerton   Universidade Federal da Paraiba, Brazil
Esposito, Anna   University of Campania, Italy
Fortunati, Leopoldina   University of Udine, Italy
Greco, Claudia   University of Campania, Italy
Greer, Julienne   University of Texas at Arlington, USA
Hu, Yue   University of Waterloo, Canada
Jiang, Wanyue   Qingdao University, China
Katsanis, Ilias   University of the Aegean, Greece
Li, Dongyu   Beihang University, China
Liu, Xiaorui   Qingdao University, China
Louie, Wing-Yue (Geoffrey)   Oakland University, USA
Luperto, Matteo   Università degli Studi di Milano, Milano, Italy
Mastrogiovanni, Fulvio   University of Genoa, Italy
Menezes, Paulo   University of Coimbra, Portugal
Perugia, Giulia   Eindhoven University of Technology,
                                              The Netherlands
Rossi, Alessandra   University of Naples Federico II, Italy
Rossi, Silvia   University of Naples Federico II, Italy
Sciutti, Alessandra   Italian Institute of Technology, Italy
Trigili, Emilio   Scuola Superiore Sant'Anna, The BioRobotics
                                              Institute, Pontedera, Italy
Wang, Wei   Beihang University, China
Wing Chee So, Catherine   Chinese University of Hong Kong, China

Marques-Villarroya, Sara
Marra, Alessandra
Mentasti, Simone
Morillo-Mendez, Lucas
Morreale, Luca
Ning, Mang
Oddi, Angelo
Orlandini, Andrea
Perugia, Giulia
Pipino, Vanessa
Proietti, Tommaso
Ragab, Abdelrahman Mohamed
Raimo, Gennaro
Rawal, Niyati
Rezaei Khavas, Zahra
Riches, Lewis
Rodriguez Leon, Jhon Freddy

Rogers, Kantwon
Romeo, Marta
Rossi, Silvia
Rossi, Alessandra
Rovini, Erika
Santos Assunção, Gustavo Miguel
Saveriano, Matteo
Scotto di Luzio, Francesco
Semeraro, Francesco
Shahverdi, Pourya
Shangguan, Zhegong
Sharma, Vinay Krishna
Shatwell, David
Sorrentino, Alessandra
Sun, Zhirui
Tang, Zhihao

Contents – Part II

Social Robots as Advanced Educational Tool

Social Robot Applications in Clinical and Assistive Scenarios

Collaborative Social Robots Through Dynamic Game

Contents – Part I

Social Robot Perception and Control Capabilities

Investigating Non Verbal Interaction with Social Robots

Foster Attention and Engagement Strategies in Social Robots

**Special Session 1: Social Robotics Driven by Intelligent Perception
and Endogenous Emotion-Motivation Core**

**Special Session 2: Adaptive Behavioral Models of Robotic Systems
Based on Brain-Inspired AI Cognitive Architectures**

Advanced HRI Capabilities for Interacting with Children

A Model Child? Behavior Models for Simulated Infant-Robot Interaction

Ameer Helmi[(✉)], Kristen M. Koenig, and Naomi T. Fitter

Oregon State University (OSU), Corvallis, OR 97331, USA
{helmia,koenigkr,naomi.fitter}@oregonstate.edu

Abstract. Simulated child-robot interaction offers ways to test robot behaviors before real-world trials with vulnerable populations. At the same time, this type of simulation requires realistic models of child behavior. We combined cognitive science research on infant attention with real-world child-robot interaction data to develop two behavior tree-based models of child behavior (i.e., robot-interested and robot-uninterested). We evaluated these models through a video-based study ($N = 60$). Participants rated the proposed models as more familiar, humanlike, and natural than a control (random behavior) model. This work can support related work on child-robot interaction, as well as broader efforts on using technology to support infant development.

1 Introduction

Worldwide, approximately half of children between the ages of two and six achieve the recommended amounts of physical activity [24]. Early interventions that encourage physical activity and motor exploration are vital to promoting the interrelated development of physical, cognitive, and social skills [6,15]. Assistive child-robot interventions are gaining attention due to the potential of robots to dovetail with early intervention services. For example, a NAO and Dash robot were combined with a body-weight support harness to encourage movement by a child with Down's Syndrome [11]. Other teams used robots to encourage leg motion practice in infants [3,5]. We designed a custom assistive robot to encourage motor exploration in children [25]. The robot, shown in Fig. 1, comprises a TurtleBot2 base and a custom-designed reward module capable of supplying developmentally appropriate stimuli for young children.

In past work, we conducted an exploratory study with children in free ambulatory play and discovered that our assistive robot effectively encouraged children to stand up and move [25,26]. We plan to build on these promising findings by studying a range of robot planning strategies for encouraging infant motion; however, young children are a vulnerable population. Further, work in the space of infant-robot mobility interventions often involves brief studies (i.e., as short at eight minutes per session) with small numbers of participants due to challenges keeping very young children on task. Thus, situated child-robot interaction data is extremely limited, and we require methods for simulating sufficiently realistic child-robot interactions to ensure that assistive robots are as safe, reliable, and viable as possible before real-world deployments [20]. In the limited work

F. Cavallo et al. (Eds.): ICSR 2022, LNAI 13818, pp. 3–12, 2022.
https://doi.org/10.1007/978-3-031-24670-8_1

  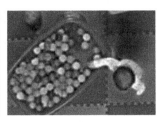

Fig. 1. Child behavior from past studies. *Left:* Custom assistive robot with light, sound, and bubble stimulus hardware. *Center:* Robot-interested child interacting with our assistive robot. *Right:* Robot-uninterested child playing with toys.

addressing models of child-robot interaction, one framework that has been used is ACT-R, which is similar to a programming language for designing models of simulated human cognition [2]. In past work, ACT-R modeled a single child's actions during hide-and-seek with a robot [23]. Other efforts used Hidden Markov Models to model infant free-play behavior, focusing on toy selection [14]. Our method builds on this past work by combining psychology research on child attention with annotated child-robot interaction video data to construct more realistic models of child behavior. The key research goal of this work was to *design and evaluate a beginning set of child behavior models that can help us vet robot interaction strategies for early mobility interventions.*

In this paper, we first describe the two proposed infant behavior models (i.e., robot-interested and robot-uninterested) and how we constructed the behavior trees for each model (Sect. 2). In Sect. 3, we discuss our online video-based evaluation of the models, and the results of the evaluation appear in Sect. 3.2. Section 4 discusses the implications of our models and offers directions for future research. The main contribution of this paper is the design and initial validation of two data-driven behavior tree models for infant behavior in simulated child-robot interaction.

2   Infant Behavior Models

Cognitive science research informed our methodology for creating infant behavior models. We annotated video data from a prior exploratory playgroup and constructed behavior tree models for two simulated infants.

2.1   Cognitive Science Foundations

Cognitive science methods for video coding and past findings related to child attention informed our efforts to model infant behavior. Lansink et al. performed seminal work on annotating child attention during interactions with objects [12]. Video annotators in the study used behavioral labels of casual and focused attention to note the child's attention. Casual attention was marked by general inattentiveness and a high frequency of looking away from objects [13,18]. Focused attention was marked by a decrease in heart rate, longer glances, and a lower likelihood of looking away from the object of interest [12,19]. In our own video coding, as described further in Sect. 2.2, we adopted these types of attention as the core of our annotation strategy.

Additionally, past cognitive science work shows that infants cycle between casual attention and focused attention and spend measurable characteristic durations attuned to different objects of interest (e.g., toys) [12]. When a child is in focused attention, Lansink et al. found that the child will stay focused on an object 96.5% of the time and look away 3.5% of the time [12]. We formed our models, as further explained in Sect. 2.3, partly based on this information from past literature and partly from our own annotations.

2.2   Playgroup Data Annotation

Our team previously recorded overhead video data from a study during which children interacted with our assistive robot and developmentally appropriate toys in an open play space, as further reported in [25]. The assistive robot is composed of a TurtleBot2 base (a common mobile robotic platform capable of non-holonomic base motion in 2D) and a custom reward module for delivering stimuli (e.g., LED light patterns, sounds, bubbles) to child users of the system. We selected the 30-min video of the children's initial play behaviors with our robot for analysis since this segment captured ad-hoc interaction; the robot is intended for early interventions that may be one-time sessions.

Specifically, we annotated the behaviors of the two youngest children in the study (1.5 and 2 years of age), as these participants best fit the age range for the types of early interventions that our robot was designed for (i.e., below 3 years of age). We observed that the younger child displayed a limited amount of time with the robot, and accordingly, formed the *robot-uninterested* model based on this infant. The older child spent a moderate amount of time playing with the robot and thus provided the foundation for the *robot-interested* model. Example interactions by these two children appear in Fig. 1.

From the video of these two children, we annotated periods of casual and focused attention, as well as the duration of time focused on the robot and toys. We excluded coding times when either child was out of the camera field of view. Based on the cognitive science groundings from the previous subsection, we used the following codebook to annotate the video:

- *Casual attention:* shifting gaze continually or failing to focus on clear target.
- *Focused attention on a toy:* performing primarily long glances at toy(s) or playing directly with toy(s).
- *Focused attention on the robot:* performing primarily long glances at robot or playing directly with robot.
- *Interaction duration:* length of time that one of the above states lasted.

The results of our video annotation for each child appear in Table 1. The robot-interested child spent a larger proportion of time in focused attention with both the robot and toys in the play space. Additionally, the robot-interested child spent a higher mean time playing with the robot and toys. We applied these results to the designed behavior tree models of infant behavior, as further explained in the following subsection.

Table 1. Video annotation results including percentages of infant casual and focused attention, as well as mean and standard deviation time spent with items of interest when in focused attention.

Behavior Code	Robot-interested	Robot-uninterested
Casual attention	51.7%	81.1%
Focused attention - Toy	17.5%	11.4%
Focused attention - Robot	30.8%	6.8%
Interaction duration - Toy (s)	19.1 ± 15.9	12.5 ± 10.4
Interaction duration - Robot (s)	35.1 ± 34.0	15.0 ± 10.1

2.3 Behavior Trees

Behavior trees have been used to control autonomous agents in video games [7] and for supporting robot decision-making [1,16], but have yet to be applied to modeling infant behavior. We identified behavior trees to be a viable model option since they are easy to interpret and allow for flexibility in incorporating future data [4]. In this subsection, we outline background on behavior trees and describe our proposed behavior tree models of child behavior. When discussing the basic functions of behavior trees, we use the standard terminology of parent and child node, not to be confused with a human parent and human child.

A behavior tree operates as a top-down left-to-right hierarchical tree that evaluates true or false *condition* nodes in the tree and determines an *action* node to activate. Internal nodes, such as *fallback* and *sequence* nodes, are used to control the flow of the tree [4]. Branches of the behavior tree will return one of three statuses to the root node: *success* if a node completes, *failure* if a condition or action fails, or *running* if an action is in progress. *Fallback* nodes, represented with a ?, are used when only one branch underneath the fallback node should be active. If one child node of the fallback returns *success* or *running*, the fallback node will return *success* to its parent node. *Sequence* nodes, represented with an arrow (→), are used when all child nodes under the sequence node should return *success* or *running*. A sequence node returns *success* to its parent node only if all child nodes return *success*; otherwise, it will return *running* or *failure*. Statuses are returned by child nodes to parent nodes until reaching the root (topmost) node, which indicates the current status of the entire behavior tree. Other node types, such as parallel nodes, exist in behavior trees broadly but are not used in our implementation.

We developed two behavior trees (robot-interested and robot-uninterested models) for determining a simulated child's actions while interacting with toys and our robot. All branches of the behavior trees are available for viewing on our public repository [9]. Our behavior trees operates in three distinct layers: the *visual field* layer, the *attention type* layer, and the *action* layer. Each layer has conditions which determine which branch of the next layer to proceed to. We outline each layer and the associated condition or action options below:

– Visual field layer
  • See robot + toy(s), See toy(s), See robot, or See neither robot nor toy(s)
– Attention type layer

- Focused attention on toy, Focused attention on robot, or Casual attention
- Action layer
  - Play with toy, Play with robot, Stand still, or Move random direction

Each branch of the tree begins by evaluating what objects are visible to the child, e.g., if the child sees only the robot, then the probability of focused attention on the toy is removed. The conditions in the *attention type* layer are probabilities based on the percentages from Table 1. The conditions in the *action* layer are probabilities based on percentages described previously in [12], i.e., a child will stay focused on an object 96.5% of the time and look away 3.5% of the time. Each action (e.g., Play - Toy) in the *action* layer is performed for a specific length of time (based on the mean lengths of time shown in Table 1) and returns a status of *running* during the action. A child that is not playing with either a toy or the robot will move in a random direction for two seconds or stay still for two seconds. Once an action is completed, the node returns *success* and the tree is re-evaluated for a new action.

3   Model Evaluation

We conducted an online within-subjects study to assess how the child behavior models were perceived relative to one another, as well as relative to a control (random behavior) model. All study procedures were approved by Oregon State University under protocol #IRB-2019-0172.

3.1   Methods

The evaluation presented participants with three different videos depicting interactions between a simulated child and surroundings including multiple toys and a robot. Each video represented one condition in our evaluation:

- *Robot-Interested:* child behavior followed robot-interested model.
- *Robot-Uninterested:* child behavior followed robot-uninterested model.
- *Random:* child has an equal probability of each type of attention described previously, and time spent in each action is randomized.

Video Stimuli: We developed a custom simulation using Python3 and ROS Noetic. The simulated child was placed in a virtual play space with three randomly placed static toys and the assistive robot. A blue line originating from the child indicated gaze direction to participants. The child's field of view was 60° from each side of the blue line and determined which objects were visible at each time step; this field of view was not conveyed to participants. The simulated child's image would flip between facing left or right to match the gaze direction, as shown in Fig. 2. The simulated child acted according to one of the conditions and could move in the environment and interact with toys or the robot. Each condition, including random, was programmed in Python3 as a behavior tree which evaluated and chose actions during each time step. ROS Noetic was used to control the timings of behaviors during the simulation and to allow for future

Fig. 2. *Left:* Stimulus frame depicting the location of the mock infant, toys, and robot. The blue line originating from the child indicates gaze direction. *Right:* Stimulus frame showing the robot bubbles action. The child image orientation has flipped to match the gaze direction.

integration with behavior tree packages. The robot behaved according to a uniform behavior tree across conditions, the purpose of which is to stay near the child to encourage play. The generated video stimuli were 45 s on average. Fig. 2 shows two frames from one stimulus video.

Procedure: Participants were recruited via a university student pool. Respondents completed the study online via a Qualtrics survey that began with an informed consent page. Next, participants completed demographic questions and read introductory information that explained the simulated interaction scenario. In each of the following survey blocks, respondents watched one of the three randomly ordered video stimuli and responded to questions about the simulated child after the video concluded. Finally, participants completed an attention-check question and described the factors influencing their survey responses via a free-responses question requiring a minimum of 200 characters. Participants received course credit for completing the study.

Measures: The survey included questions about the simulated infant's behavior and apparent interests, as well as basic demographic questions. Five survey questions were administered on a seven-point Likert scale, as described below:

- *Familiarity* of child behavior, "Very Strange" (1) to "Very Familiar" (7)
- *Humanlikeness*, "Very Non-Humanlike" (1) to "Very Humanlike" (7)
- *Naturalness* of behavior, "Very Artificial" (1) to "Very Natural" (7)
- Whether the child was *interested in the toys*, "Strongly Disagree" (1) to "Strongly Agree" (7)
- Whether the child was *interested in the robot*, "Strongly Disagree" (1) to "Strongly Agree" (7)

The first two questions above came from inventories on the uncanny valley [10], and the *naturalness* question is our own exploratory addition. The final scales sought to capture perceived differences in the simulated infants' interests. Further demographic questions gathered information on participant age, identity, profession, experience with children, and experience with robots.

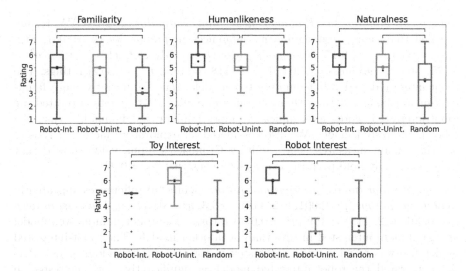

Fig. 3. Survey responses to video stimuli. Boxplots include boxes from the 25th to the 75th percentiles, center lines with a circle marker for medians, asterisks for means, whiskers up to 1.5 times the inter-quartile range, and "+" marks for outliers. Brackets above the boxplots indicate significant pairwise differences.

Hypotheses: Our two main hypotheses were as follows:

- **H1**: Participants will rate the robot-interested and robot-uninterested conditions as higher in familiarity, naturalness, and humanlikeness than the random condition. In other words, we expect the models founded on real observations of human behavior to seem more lifelike.
- **H2**: Participants will rate the robot-interested condition as most interested in the robot and the robot-uninterested condition as most interested in toys.

These hypotheses arose from the foundation of the model design in cognitive science and annotation of two real children's interactions with our robot.

Participants: The study was completed by $N = 60$ students from Oregon State University between the ages of 18 and 41 ($M = 19.8$ and $SD = 3.3$), including 17 cisgender men, 42 cisgender women, and one non-binary individual. One participant was a parent/guardian and 25 participants indicated experience interacting with children in our early intervention age range of interested (6–36 months). 53 participants indicated little or no experience with robots.

Analysis: We analyzed stimulus video ratings using repeated-measures ANOVA (rANOVA) tests with $\alpha = 0.05$. Tukey's HSD Test for multiple comparisons were conducted for significant main effects. We report effect sizes using η^2, where $\eta^2 = 0.010$ is considered a small effect, $\eta^2 = 0.040$ a medium effect, and $\eta^2 = 0.090$ a large effect [8]. Statistical analyses were conducted using jamovi [17,21,22].

3.2 Results

We compared ratings across the study conditions. Response distributions and rANOVA results are shown in Fig. 3.

Ratings of Familiarity, Humanlikeness, and Naturalness: rANOVA results revealed that there were significant differences in *familiarity* ($p< 0.001$, $F(2, 118) = 25.4$, $\eta^2 = 0.171$), *humanlikeness* ($p< 0.001$, $F(2, 118) = 18.6$, $\eta^2 = 0.125$), and *naturalness* ($p< 0.001$, $F(2, 118) = 16.4$, $\eta^2 = 0.112$) ratings. The robot-interested and robot-uninterested models were significantly more familiar, humanlike, and natural than the random model. Participants also rated the robot-interested model as significantly more familiar and humanlike than the robot-uninterested model. We also conducted an exploratory factor analysis of our three main measures. The resulting Cronbach's alpha value showed that these scales may hold promise as a realism construct ($\alpha = 0.92$).

Ratings of Child Interest in Toys and Robot: Significant differences appeared in the *interest in toys* ($p< 0.001$, $F(2, 118) = 89.3$, $\eta^2 = 0.477$), and *interest in robot* ($p< 0.001$, $F(2, 118) = 169$, $\eta^2 = 0.646$) ratings. The robot-uninterested model appeared more interested in toys than both other models. The robot-interested model also was rated as more interested in toys than the random model. Participants rated the robot-interested model as significantly more interested in the robot than any other model. The random model also appeared to be more interested in the robot than the robot-uninterested model.

4   Discussion

This paper proposed and evaluated two models of infant behavior based on insights from cognitive science and analysis of real-world interaction data. The model evaluation results support **H1**; participants rated the robot-interested and robot-uninterested conditions higher in familiarity, humanlikeness, and naturalness when compared to the random condition. Likewise, we found support for **H2**. Participants rated the robot-interested model as more interested in the robot and the robot-uninterested model as more interested in the toys, and both findings had very large effect sizes.

Free-text responses further elucidated respondents' model expectations and perceptions. Most participants noted that they focused on what objects drew child interest and how long object interactions lasted. One participant wrote "if the child was playing with toys and the robot, I saw that as less artificial." Another respondent mentioned that "in [one] video, the child seemed scared of the robot and appeared to seek the bear for comfort, [which] seemed like an appropriate response." A comment on the random condition labeled it as "strange" and mentioned that the child "wandered all over the place with maybe a couple of glances towards objects." A further participant noted that "[their] experience [led them] to believe that a child that age should be mesmerized by the toys and especially moving ones such as the robot." Consistently with the cognitive science literature, written feedback supported the idea that it is natural for children to fixate on and engage with items in the environment.

The *strengths* of this work include the extension of related work to effectively simulate infant behaviors during interactions with toys and a robot. The models fuse research in infant attention and video-annotated data of real child-robot interactions. The model evaluation supported that these models function as intended. The current robot-interested and robot-uninterested models, in addition to future models to be created using similar methods, will allow us (and others with similar interests) to vet robot planning algorithms before deploying these strategies in resource-intensive child-robot interactions in the real world.

Limitations of this work include the current scope; namely, the models represent ad hoc interactions with a robot, and the model evaluation centered on just one set of video stimuli. We could follow the same process as used in this paper to annotate further types of child behavior, such as interactions with parents or other children, and build and test similar models more broadly. Other limitations arose from the demographics of respondents. Most participants did not have children of their own, although nearly half of the group had experience with children below three years of age. We could recruit a broader set of participants, including more parents, in future model evaluations. We also plan to use our model to compare real vs. simulated child behavior in future study trials.

In conclusion, this paper presents infant behavior models that use methods from cognitive science, are data-driven, and employ easy-to-read and flexible behavior trees. We demonstrated that our models can produce more realistic-seeming infant behavior than a random model. This work can inform assistive robot designers and others who are interested in modeling infant behavior.

Acknowledgments. We thank Emily Scheide and Ryan Quick for helping to create the study stimuli.

References

1. Abiyev, R.H., Günsel, I., Akkaya, N., Aytac, E., Çağman, A., Abizada, S.: Robot soccer control using behaviour trees and fuzzy logic. Procedia Comput. Sci. **102**, 477–484 (2016)
2. Anderson, J.R., Matessa, M., Lebiere, C.: ACT-R: a theory of higher level cognition and its relation to visual attention. Hum.-Comput. Interact. **12**(4), 439–462 (1997)
3. Boyd, J., et al.: An infant smart-mobile system to encourage kicking movements in infants at-risk of cerebral palsy. In: Proceedings of the IEEE Workshop Advanced Robotics and Its Social Impacts (ARSO), pp. 1–5 (2017)
4. Colledanchise, M., Ögren, P.: Behavior Trees in Robotics and AI: an Introduction. CRC Press (2018)
5. Fitter, N.T., et al.: Socially assistive infant-robot interaction: Using robots to encourage infant leg-motion training. IEEE Robot. Autom. Mag. **26**(2), 12–23 (2019)
6. Fox, S.E., Levitt, P., Nelson III, C.A.: How the timing and quality of early experiences influence the development of brain architecture. Child Dev. **81**(1), 28–40 (2010)
7. Fu, Y., Qin, L., Yin, Q.: A reinforcement learning behavior tree framework for game AI. In: Proceedings of the International Conference on Economics, Social Science, Arts, Education and Management Engineering, pp. 573–579 (2016)
8. Funder, D.C., Ozer, D.J.: Evaluating effect size in psychological research: sense and nonsense. Adv. Meth. Pract. Psychol. Sci. **2**(2), 156–168 (2019)

9. Helmi, A., Koenig, K.M., Fitter, N.T.: Infant behavior trees repository (2022). https://github.com/shareresearchteam/infant_simulation_behavior_trees

10. Kamide, H., Kawabe, K., Shigemi, S., Arai, T.: Development of a psychological scale for general impressions of humanoid. Adv. Robot. **27**(1), 3–17 (2013)

11. Kokkoni, E., et al.: GEARing smart environments for pediatric motor rehabilitation. J. Neuroeng. Rehabil.**17**(1), 1–15 (2020)

12. Lansink, J.M., Mintz, S., Richards, J.E.: The distribution of infant attention during object examination. Dev. Sci. **3**(2), 163–170 (2000)

13. Lansink, J.M., Richards, J.E.: Heart rate and behavioral measures of attention in six-, nine-, and twelve-month-old infants during object exploration. Child Dev. **68**(4), 610–620 (1997)

14. Le, H., Hoch, J.E., Ossmy, O., Adolph, K.E., Fern, X., Fern, A.: Modeling infant free play using hidden markov models. In: Proceedings of the IEEE International Conference on Development and Learning (ICDL), pp. 1–6 (2021)

15. Logan, S.W., Schreiber, M., Lobo, M., Pritchard, B., George, L., Galloway, J.C.: Real-world performance: Physical activity, play, and object-related behaviors of toddlers with and without disabilities. Pediatric Phys. Ther. **27**(4), 433–441 (2015)

16. Paxton, C., Ratliff, N., Eppner, C., Fox, D.: Representing robot task plans as robust logical-dynamical systems. In: Proceedings of the IEEE/RSJ International Conference on Intelligent Robots and Systems (IROS), pp. 5588–5595 (2019)

17. R Core Team: R: A language and environment for statistical computing (Version 4.0) [Computer software] (2020). https://cran.r-project.org/

18. Ruff, H.A.: Components of attention during infants' manipulative exploration. Child Dev. 105–114 (1986)

19. Ruff, H.A., Lawson, K.R.: Development of sustained, focused attention in young children during free play. Dev. Psychol. **26**(1), 85 (1990)

20. Salem, M., Lakatos, G., Amirabdollahian, F., Dautenhahn, K.: Towards safe and trustworthy social robots: ethical challenges and practical issues. In: ICSR 2015. LNCS (LNAI), vol. 9388, pp. 584–593. Springer, Cham (2015). https://doi.org/10.1007/978-3-319-25554-5_58

21. Singmann, H.: afex: Analysis of factorial experiments [R package] (2018). https://cran.r-project.org/package=afex

22. The jamovi project: jamovi (Version 1.6) [Computer software] (2020). https://www.jamovi.org

23. Trafton, J.G., et al.: Children and robots learning to play hide and seek. In: Proceedings of the ACM SIGCHI/SIGART Conference on Human-Robot Interaction, pp. 242–249 (2006)

24. Tucker, P.: The physical activity levels of preschool-aged children: a systematic review. Early Child. Res. Q. **23**(4), 547–558 (2008)

25. Vinoo, A., et al.: Design of an assistive robot for infant mobility interventions. In: Proceedings of the IEEE International Conference Robot and Human Interactive Communication (RO-MAN), pp. 604–611 (2021)

26. Vora, J.R., et al.: Influence of a socially assistive robot on physical activity, social play behavior, and toy-use behaviors of children in a free play environment: a within-subjects study. Front. Robot. AI (2021)

Children Perceived Perception of a Mini-Humanoid Social Robot Based on a Psychometric Scale: A Pilot Study in Greece

Ilias Katsanis[1], Ahmad Yaser Alhaddad[2], John-John Cabibihan[2(✉)], and Vassilis Moulianitis[1]

[1] Department of Product and Systems Design Engineering, University of the Aegean, 84100 Syros, Greece
[2] Department of Mechanical and Industrial Engineering, Qatar University, Doha, Qatar
john.cabibihan@qu.edu.qa

Abstract. There is a growing interest in the integration of social robots in different applications in our daily lives. However, it can be challenging to design a social robot that is perceived positively among the target end-users. Psychometric scales can be used to give insights and assist in the designing of an acceptable social robot. In this study, the Greek adaptation of the Human-Robot Interaction Evaluation Scale (HRIES) has been considered to evaluate the attitude of children toward a developed social robot. Questionnaires were used to collect data from 40 neurotypical children before and after interacting with the social robot. The results showed no statistical differences due to gender. The analysis of the questionnaire scores revealed changes in the children's perceptions after the session with the robot. This implies that direct interactions with a social robot helped in altering existing perceived attitudes toward social robots. Assessment tools, such as psychometric scales, are necessary to evaluate the acceptability of social robots.

Keywords: Social robots acceptability · Psychometric scales · Robot design for children

1 Introduction

The advances in technology are allowing the rapid integration of new methods and techniques in healthcare, such as using wearable devices to monitor health and robots to provide assistance in surgery [1–3]. These advances have allowed the rapid integration of robots in many aspects of human lives, such as elderly care and autism therapy [4,5]. Additionally, the advancements in hardware and sensor fusion technologies are enabling the execution of various tasks which can be performed by social robots during interactions [6–8].

Social robots are developed to aid users through social interaction, creating strong communication bonds, and perceive and display emotions [9]. In recent

F. Cavallo et al. (Eds.): ICSR 2022, LNAI 13818, pp. 13–22, 2022.
https://doi.org/10.1007/978-3-031-24670-8_2

years, there has been a great interest in the design and deployment of social
robots that meet the requirements of autism therapy and interventions [10–14].
Robots' morphological characteristics such as shape, size, and form factor were
reported to affect intervention [15]. Hence, more research is needed to investigate critical areas in social robots for autism therapy, such as safety and user
perceptions [16–18].

Fig. 1. The developed mini-humanoid robot that was considered in this study.

Due to the presence of a social robot in personal environments and their
direct interaction with people, the impressions, attitudes of users, and their perceptions toward social robots require assessment [19]. User acceptance is affected
by robots' design and thus different psychometric scales were developed based
on various behavioral and psychological attributes [18]. The idea of how individuals perceive robots is crucial not only to better understand the interactions
with robots, but also to design and develop robots that are considered to be
acceptable among the target end-users.

A previous study with children with autism showed that a relatively smaller
social robot compared to the children could play a role in its acceptance and
it was hypothesized that it gives the children more sense of control over it [20].
Hence, in this study, children's perceived perception toward a developed mini-
humanoid social robot (i.e., in Fig. 1) are evaluated using the HRIES scale. The

study acquired the responses from neurotypical children before and after presenting the social robot.

The rest of the paper is structured as follows. Section 2 describes related work and theoretical background while Sect. 3 presents the adopted methods. Section 4 provides the results and Sect. 5 discusses the findings.

2   Background

There are many methods that were considered to measure the effects of a robot's design and its acceptability among the target end-users. The Godspeed questionnaire is one example of an assessment tool that used Likert scale to measure the perceptions of users toward robots in terms of perceived safety, animacy, likability, intelligence, and anthropomorphism [21]. A recent study proposed a new scale that accurately measures the perceptions of robots and the willingness of humans to interact with them [22]. Another work focused on investigating the negative attitudes toward robots (i.e., NARS) based on 5-Point Likert scale questions that explored users' negative attitudes and the factors influencing their interactions with robots [23]. The assessment of ethical issues pertaining to the use of robots in therapy sessions for children with autism was the main focus of another scale [24].

Several studies investigated the perceptions and attitudes toward robots [19] [25, 26]. For example, a study investigated the effects of robot types and cultural backgrounds on the attitudes toward robots [27]. Results revealed that robots with high mental abilities elicited more hesitant attitudes. The social impact of comfort and negative attitudes toward robots between young, middle-aged, and older adults were explored in another study [28]. The findings showed that there were no significant differences between young and middle-aged adults responses. Another study investigated 49 participants' first impressions during an interaction scenario with a robot [29]. The study measured their perception changes over three sessions. The results showed that different perceptual dimensions stabilized and that perceptual differences persisted for robots with varying levels of humanlikeness across the sessions.

3   Methods

3.1   Participants

The data were collected from 40 typically developed children (45% females and 55% males) aged between 4–6 years old attending a kindergarten in Athens, Greece. A written consent was obtained from the parent of each child prior to conducting the study. The procedures of this work did not include invasive or potential hazardous methods and were in accordance with the Code of Ethics of the Declaration of Helsinki.

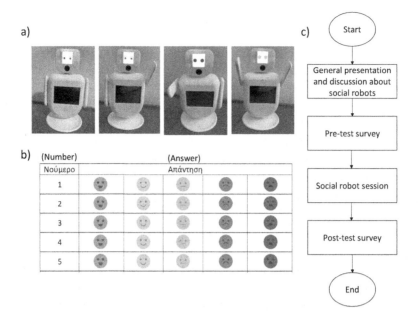

Fig. 2. The adopted methods in this study. a) The developed mini-humanoid robot performing different behaviors. b) The 5-Point Likert scale answer sheet. c) The flowchart of the procedures.

3.2   The Social Robot

The evaluation in this study considered a newly developed mini-humanoid social robot [6]. The robot is equipped with different sensors and actuators that allows the execution of various tasks such as speech recognition, motion classification, face detection, and the display of different gestures and moves (Fig. 2a). Furthermore, the robot is optimized to have low power consumption and it is 3D-printed with removable parts that enable customization and personalization.

3.3   Questionnaire Items

The questionnaire of the study included the 16 items listed in the Human Robot Interaction Evaluation Scale (HRIES) to study the perceived perception of the children toward the developed robot. The items in HRIES were presented in the form of questions and were translated to Greek. Uncanny, warm, and intentional items were translated to the closest meanings in Greek. To make it more convenient for the children, the answer sheet contained five emojis representing the 5-Point Likert scale (Fig. 2b). Pre-test questionnaire was considered to measure children's bias and perception toward social robots while post-test questionnaires were used to identify and measure possible changes to their perception after the interaction session with the mini-humanoid social robot. The 16 items of the questionnaire are presented in Table 1. The four subscales are based on the sum of their respective items. For example, the score for Sociability is the sum of the individual scores for items N. 2, 5, 7, and 12.

Table 1. The 16 questionnaire items and their corresponding Greek translation. Sociability subscale comprises items N. 2, 5, 7, and 12. Animacy subscale comprises items N. 3, 9, 13, and 16. Agency subscale comprises items N. 4, 6, 11, and 14. Disturbance subscale comprises items N. 1, 8, 10, and 15.

N.	HRIES Question	Greek Translation
1	Is the robot weird?	Μοιάζουν τα ρομπότ περίεργα·
2	Is the robot likeable?	Συμπαθείτε τα ρομπότ·
3	Is the robot alive?	Είναι ένα ρομπότ ζωντανό·
4	Is the robot intelligent?	Είναι ένα ρομπότ έξυπνο·
5	Is the robot warm?	Είναι ένα ρομπότ ευγενικό·
6	Is the robot self-reliant?	Μπορεί ένα ρομπότ να κάνει πράγματα μόνο του·
7	Is the robot trustworthy?	Μπορείς να εμπιστευτείς ένα ρομπότ·
8	Is the robot creepy?	Σας προκαλεί φόβο το ρομπότ·
9	Is the robot human-like?	Μοιάζει σαν ένας άνθρωπος το ρομπότ·
10	Is the robot uncanny?	Προκαλεί απέχθεια το ρομπότ·
11	Is the robot rational?	Μπορεί να σκεφτεί ένα ρομπότ·
12	Is the robot friendly?	Είναι ένα ρομπότ φιλικό·
13	Is the robot real?	Είναι ένα ρομπότ πραγματικό·
14	Is the robot intentional?	Κάνει κάτι το ρομπότ σκόπιμα·
15	Is the robot scary?	Είναι ένα ρομπότ πραγματικό·
16	Is the robot natural?	Είναι ένα ρομπότ φυσικό αντικείμενο

3.4 Procedures

Participants were divided into 3 groups based on their classes at the school and each group took part in a two-fold survey: pre-test and post-test. In the pre-test survey, children prior to interacting with the social robot discussed with the teachers about robots in general and then they were shown a presentation about social robots as the conversation continued (Fig. 2c). This step was necessary as part of the introduction to the study and then to initiate the survey. Next, the children filled in the pre-test questionnaire sheets. In the post-test survey, the social robot was first presented to the children for around three min to explore and examine it. Next, the robot performed a short demo showing different set of behaviors. The demo of the robot was simple and limited to the requirements of the study and according to the guidelines of the teachers. Finally, the children filled in the post-test questionnaire.

3.5 Analysis

Cronbach's alpha test was used to measure the internal consistency of the questionnaire items. Mann-Whitney U tests were conducted to study the effect of gender and to evaluate the developed social robot on the perceived perception of the children before (i.e., Pre-test) and after (i.e., Post-test) the interactions in terms of the four subscales of HRIES, namely, Sociability, Animacy, Agency, and Disturbance. The statistical significance was set at p<.05.

4   Results

4.1   Internal Consistency

A reliability test using Cronbach's alpha test was conducted on all the question-naire items and achieved an acceptable score of 0.72 [21].

4.2   Gender's Effect

To identify the differences, if any, of children's perceptions toward the robot due to gender, a Mann-Whitney U test was used on all the responses of males and females. The median response score for females (4.0) was not statistically significantly different compared to males (4.0), $p = 0.825$.

4.3   Questionnaire Items

The outcomes of the questionnaire items in pre-test and post-test were plot-ted in terms of the 5-Point Likert scale (Fig. 3). The pre-test plot shows that the agreement (i.e., Agree and Strongly Agree) responses scored the highest for the questions about natural, intentional, real, friendly, trustworthy, self-reliant, warm, intelligent, and likeable features of social robots. As for the disagreement, the highest scores were for the questions about scary, uncanny, creepy, and weird features of social robots. The post-test plot shows that most agreement responses were similar to that of pre-test, but with addition of rational feature of the pre-sented social robot. As for the disagreement, the questions about scary, uncanny, creepy, and weird features of the social robot scored the highest. Direct compar-ison between the two plots reveals noticeable changes in the scores, such as in the questions about the natural, intentional, rational, and likeable features of the social robot.

4.4   Pre-test vs Post-test

To determine the effect of interacting with the social robot on the children's per-ception, Mann-Whitney U tests were conducted on the four subscales of HRIES before and after the interactions at p<.05. For sociability, the results showed no statistical significant difference between pre-test median (16) before the interac-tion and post-test median (17) after the interaction, $p = 0.064$. As for Animacy, there was no statistical significant difference between pre-test (14.5) and post-test (15), $p = 0.504$. The results for Agency showed no statistical significant difference between before (15) and after (15) interaction, $p = 0.823$. Similarly for Disturbance, there was no significant difference between pre-test scores (8) and post-test scores (8), $p = 0.984$.

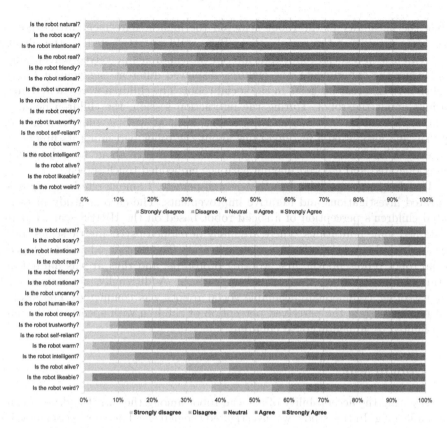

Fig. 3. The plots for the 5-Point Likert scale responses of the participants for the 16 questions. a) Pre-test survey. b) Post-test survey.

5 Discussion

Investigating the design features of a social robot and how they are perceived by the target end-users is an essential part to ensure its acceptability. Psychometric scales can be used to give insights about how different design choices are being perceived. In this study, the HRIES scale was considered to investigate children's perceived perception of a developed social robot. Two sets of the same questionnaire were considered before and after interacting with the social robot to identify any significant differences. Gender has been reported to affect the preferences toward humanoid robots [30]. However, in our study the statistical tests revealed no significant difference between the responses of males and females in their perception of the presented robot, which is aligned with a previous study [19].

The inspection of the questionnaire questions score in both tests revealed some changes in the children's perceptions of social robots (Fig. 3). The natural feature of the social robot achieved the highest agreement score in the pre-test while the likeability of the robot achieved the highest agreement in the post-test after presenting the social robot. This could be attributed to the direct interaction with a social robot that altered the children's perceived perception.

During the experiments, the children displayed different engagement levels and showed different interests in the social robot. The children were excited and curious about the robot. During the interaction session, the children demonstrated physical interactions and imitations, such as waving, movements, and speech, and also asked a few questions about the robot pertaining its functionalities and behaviors. The children also showed curiosity about how the robot being operated and enjoyed playing with the embedded touch screen.

The design of a social robot that is well-perceived among children requires repeated investigations and iterative improvements. The current study investigated children's perception of a social robot based on the HRIES scale, but it contained some limitations. There are many developed psychometric scales, but the study evaluated the robot based on one scale. The considered and developed social robot represents the first working prototype, and thus, it was limited in terms of functionalities, design, and appearance. Additionally, no comparison against other commercially-available social robots was conducted. The study did not investigate the perceived perception of children with special needs and was limited to 40 neurotypical children.

6   Conclusion

Investigating the acceptability of a social robot among the target end-users can be challenging. In this study, we investigated the perceived perception of a developed social robot among 40 children. Questionnaires based on the HRIES scale were used twice to collect data before and after the session with the social robot. The children's interactions with the robot provided important insights about the robot. The analysis of the questionnaire items showed changes in the children's perceived perception of social robots. The statistical analysis of the two tests (i.e., pre-test vs post-test) showed no statistical significant difference for the subscales of HRIES. Additionally, no statistical differences were found due to gender.

Future work should consider the integration of children with special needs and compare their perceived perception of the social robot to that of neurotypical children. Additionally, other psychometrics scales and social robots should be considered in the evaluation of the developed social robot. Finally, a follow-up work should use an improved design of the social robot with more functionalities and a refined appearance.

References

1. Alhaddad, A.Y., et al.: Sense and learn: recent advances in wearable sensing and machine learning for blood glucose monitoring and trend-detection. Front. Bioeng. Biotechnol. 699 (2022)

2. Alhaddad, A.Y.: Toward 3D printed prosthetic hands that can satisfy psychosocial needs: grasping force comparisons between a prosthetic hand and human hands. In: International Conference on Social Robotics, pp. 304–313. Springer (2017)
3. Cabibihan, J.-J., Alhaddad, A.Y., Gulrez, T., Yoon, W.J.: Influence of visual and haptic feedback on the detection of threshold forces in a surgical grasping task. IEEE Robot. Autom. Lett. **6**(3), 5525–5532 (2021)
4. Broekens, J., Heerink, M., Rosendal, H., et al.: Assistive social robots in elderly care: a review. Gerontechnology **8**(2), 94–103 (2009)
5. Alhaddad, A.Y., Cabibihan, J.J., Bonarini, A.: Influence of reaction time in the emotional response of a companion robot to a child's aggressive interaction. Int. J. Soc. Robot. 1–13 (2020)
6. Katsanis, I.A., Moulianitis, V.C., Panagiotarakos, D.T.: Design, development, and a pilot study of a low-cost robot for child-robot interaction in autism interventions. Multimodal Technol. Interact. **6**(6), 43 (2022)
7. Alban, A.Q., et al.: Detection of challenging behaviours of children with autism using wearable sensors during interactions with social robots. In: 2021 30th IEEE International Conference on Robot & Human Interactive Communication (RO-MAN), pp. 852–857. IEEE (2021)
8. Alhaddad, A.Y., Cabibihan, J.-J., Bonarini, A.: Real-time social robot's responses to undesired interactions between children and their surroundings. Int. J. Soc. Robot. 1–9 (2022)
9. Feil-Seifer, D., Mataric, M.J.: Defining socially assistive robotics. In: 9th International Conference on Rehabilitation Robotics, 2005. ICORR 2005, pp. 465–468. IEEE (2005)
10. Alhaddad, A.Y., Cabibihan, J.-J., Hayek, A., Bonarini, A.: Safety experiments for small robots investigating the potential of soft materials in mitigating the harm to the head due to impacts. SN Appl. Sci. **1**(5), 1–10 (2019). https://doi.org/10.1007/s42452-019-0467-7
11. Begum, M., Serna, R.W., Yanco, H.A.: Are robots ready to deliver autism interventions? a comprehensive review. Int. J. Soc. Robot. **8**(2), 157–181 (2016)
12. Alhaddad, A.Y., Cabibihan, J.-J., Hayek, A., Bonarini, A.: Influence of the shape and mass of a small robot when thrown to a dummy human head. SN Appl. Sci. **1**(11), 1–9 (2019). https://doi.org/10.1007/s42452-019-1447-7
13. Bogue, R.: Rehabilitation robots. Ind. Robot Int. J. **45**(3), 301–306 (2018)
14. Alhaddad, A.Y., Cabibihan, J.-J., Bonarini, A.: Recognition of aggressive interactions of children toward robotic toys. In: 2019 28th IEEE International Conference on Robot and Human Interactive Communication (RO-MAN), pp. 1–8. IEEE (2019)
15. Cabibihan, J.J.: Social robots and wearable sensors for mitigating meltdowns in autism - a pilot test. In: Ge, S.S., et al. (eds.) ICSR 2018. LNCS (LNAI), vol. 11357, pp. 103–114. Springer, Cham (2018). https://doi.org/10.1007/978-3-030-05204-1_11
16. Katsanis, I.A., Moulianitis, V.C.: An architecture for safe child-robot interactions in autism interventions. Robotics **10**(1), 20 (2021)
17. Alhaddad, A.Y., Cabibihan, J.-J., Bonarini, A.: Head impact severity measures for small social robots thrown during meltdown in autism. Int. J. Soc. Robot. **11**(2), 255–270 (2019)
18. Spatola, N., Kühnlenz, B., Cheng, G.: Perception and evaluation in human-robot interaction: the human-robot interaction evaluation scale (hries)-a multicomponent approach of anthropomorphism. Int. J. Soc. Robot. **13**(7), 1517–1539 (2021)

19. Alhaddad, A.Y., Mecheter, A., Wadood, M.A., Alsaari, A.S., Mohammed, H., Cabibihan, J.-J.: Anthropomorphism and its negative attitudes, sociability, animacy, agency, and disturbance requirements for social robots: a pilot study. In: Li, H., et al. (eds.) ICSR 2021. LNCS (LNAI), vol. 13086, pp. 791–796. Springer, Cham (2021). https://doi.org/10.1007/978-3-030-90525-5_73

20. Alhaddad, A.Y., Javed, H., Connor, O., Banire, B., Al Thani, D., Cabibihan, J.J.: Robotic trains as an educational and therapeutic tool for autism spectrum disorder intervention. In: International Conference on Robotics and Education RiE 2017, pp. 249–262. Springer (2018)

21. Bartneck, C., Kulić, D., Croft, E., Zoghbi, S.: Measurement instruments for the anthropomorphism, animacy, likeability, perceived intelligence, and perceived safety of robots. Int. J. Soc. Robot. 1(1), 71–81 (2009)

22. Carpinella, C.M., Wyman, A.W., Perez, M.A., Stroessner, S.J.: The robotic social attributes scale (rosas) development and validation. In: Proceedings of the 2017 ACM/IEEE International Conference on Human-Robot Interaction, pp. 254–262 (2017)

23. Nomura, T., Suzuki, T., Kanda, T., Kato, K.: Measurement of negative attitudes toward robots. Interact. Stud. 7(3), 437–454 (2006)

24. Peca, A., et al.: Robot enhanced therapy for children with autism disorders: measuring ethical acceptability. IEEE Technol. Soc. Mag. 35(2), 54–66 (2016)

25. Sheba, J.K., Mohan, R.E., García, E.A.M.: Easiness of acceptance metric for effective human robot interactions in therapeutic pet robots. In: 2012 7th IEEE Conference on Industrial Electronics and Applications (ICIEA), pp. 150–155. IEEE (2012)

26. Young, J.E., Hawkins, R., Sharlin, E., Igarashi, T.: Toward acceptable domestic robots: applying insights from social psychology. Int. J. Soc. Robot. 1(1), 95–108 (2009)

27. Dang, J., Liu, L.: Robots are friends as well as foes: ambivalent attitudes toward mindful and mindless AI robots in the United States and China. Comput. Hum. Behav. 115, 106612 (2021)

28. Backonja, U., et al.: Comfort and attitudes towards robots among young, middle-aged, and older adults: a cross-sectional study. J. Nurs. Sch. 50(6), 623–633 (2018)

29. Paetzel, M., Perugia, G., Castellano, G.: The persistence of first impressions: the effect of repeated interactions on the perception of a social robot. In: Proceedings of the 2020 ACM/IEEE International Conference on Human-Robot Interaction, pp. 73–82 (2020)

30. Tung, F.-W.: Influence of gender and age on the attitudes of children towards humanoid robots. In: Jacko, J.A. (ed.) HCI 2011. LNCS, vol. 6764, pp. 637–646. Springer, Heidelberg (2011). https://doi.org/10.1007/978-3-642-21619-0_76

Computational Audio Modelling for Robot-Assisted Assessment of Children's Mental Wellbeing

Nida Itrat Abbasi[1]([✉]), Micol Spitale[1]([✉]), Joanna Anderson[2]([✉]),
Tamsin Ford[2]([✉]), Peter B. Jones[2]([✉]), and Hatice Gunes[1]([✉])

[1] Department of Computer Science and Technology, University of Cambridge,
15 JJ Thomson Ave, Cambridge CB3 0FD, UK
{nia22,ms2871,hg410}@cam.ac.uk
[2] Department of Psychiatry, University of Cambridge, Herchel Smith Bldg,
Robinson Way, Cambridge CB2 0SZ, UK
{jpa44,tjf52,pbj21}@cam.ac.uk

Abstract. Robots endowed with the capability of assessing the mental wellbeing of children have a great potential to promote their mental health. However, very few works have explored the computational modeling of children's mental wellbeing, which remains an open research challenge. This paper presents the first attempt to computationally assess children's wellbeing during child-robot interactions via audio analysis. We collected a novel dataset of 26 children (8–13 y.o.) who interacted with a Nao robot to perform a verbal picture-based task. Data was collected by audio-video recording of the experiment session. The Short Mood and Feelings Questionnaire (SMFQ) was used to label the participants into two groups: (1) "higher wellbeing" (child SMFQ score <= SMFQ median), and (2) "lower wellbeing" (child SMFQ score > SMFQ median). We extracted audio features from these HRI interactions and trained and compared the performances of eight classical machine learning techniques across three cross-validation approaches: (1) 10 repetitions of 5-fold, (2) leave-one-child-out, and (3) leave-one-picture-out. We have also computed and analysed the sentiment of the audio transcriptions using the ROBERTa model. Our experimental results show that: (i) speech features are reliable for assessing children's mental wellbeing, but they may not be sufficient on their own, and (ii) verbal information, specifically the sentiment that a picture elicited in children, may impact the children's responses.

Keywords: Children · Wellbeing assessment · Affective computing · Robots · Speech features

1 Introduction

Affective robots are defined as "robots that can recognize human emotions and show affective behaviors" [26]. Past works have largely explored the use of

---

N. I. Abbasi and M. Spitale—Equal Contribution.

F. Cavallo et al. (Eds.): ICSR 2022, LNAI 13818, pp. 23–35, 2022.
https://doi.org/10.1007/978-3-031-24670-8_3

affective robotics, either with virtual or physical agents, to promote the mental wellbeing of people, such as improving communication skills during therapy for children with autism [28] and reducing the feeling of loneliness in elderly people [6]. In addition, with the recent advances in affective computing [24], computer scientists investigated how to automatically assess human affect, specifically concerning promoting mental wellbeing in adults (e.g., recognizing depression and anxiety) using speech markers [16]. However, to the best of our knowledge, none of them explored how to automatically assess the mental wellbeing of children in a robot-aided interaction.

This paper presents the first step towards the automatic robot-assisted assessment of children's wellbeing from speech using the child-robot interaction (cHRI) dataset introduced in [1]. To assess children's mental wellbeing, this work focuses on speech features because they have been shown to be good indicators to recognize depression in people [10]. We ran multiple experiments with eight classical machine learning techniques (e.g., logistic regression, decision tree), and we cross-validated them using three approaches: i) 10 repetitions of 5-fold, ii) leave-one-child-out, and iii) leave-one-picture-out cross-validations. These experiments were conducted specifically on a picture task (Task 3 introduced in [1], inspired by the Children Apperception Test (CAT) [4]) because this was one of the tasks in the study with free-flowing conversation. These evaluations enabled us to understand how speech markers can be informative in assessing children's wellbeing computationally. In our earlier paper [1], we introduced the experimental design of the cHRI study to evaluate mental wellbeing in children. We also compared the robotised administration of psychological questionnaires with the established standards of self-report and parent-report modes of questionnaire administration. Our results show that robotised mode of test administration is more effective in identifying cases with wellbeing related concerns in children. Differently from this previous work [1], in this paper, we undertake the following: (1) the implementation of computational models to assess children's mental wellbeing in a robot-aided interaction, utilising speech features (not yet explored in the literature); and
(2) the interpretation of these models in light of the validation methods utilised that can inform future research on automatic assessment of children's wellbeing.

2   Background

Children's psychological distress can impact their mental wellbeing, negatively influencing the academic outcome and relationships. Socially Assistive Robots (SARs) have been effectively used in children to provide companionship [9], clinical related support [25], and academic assistance [22]. In the last decade, many health-related initiatives ("ALIZ-E" project for diabetes management [5], "DREAM" project for providing robot therapy for Autism [14]) have been set up where child-robot interaction has shown promising results. SARs have also been instrumental in enabling children to be more open about their "true feelings" [13] and have been employed successfully not just to interview children regarding abuse, violence and bullying but also to change their perspectives on some of their formerly carried out misdemeanours [7,13,23]. Thus, child-robot interaction can help make children talk about their thoughts and feelings without fear of being intimidated or that they are doing something wrong. To this end, in this work, we have utilised SARs to automatically identify children with wellbeing-related concerns using speech.

With the advance of machine learning, many computational models have been used to learn representations from speech data. Specifically, past works have investigated the use of speech signals for recognizing mental wellbeing disorders, such as depression and anxiety of humans because from a clinical point of view, speech markers usually inform the diagnosis of distress (e.g., duration of the speech, speech tone, pitch) and also the speech signals are very easy to record via non-intrusive devices [27]. In fact, in [10], the authors reviewed the state of the art of speech analysis to assess depression and suicide risk. They highlighted the importance of identifying and using speech markers in automatic model design that are interpretable from a clinical standpoint. Analogously, researchers in [19] conducted a literature review on speech analysis to assess psychiatric disorders automatically (e.g., depression, bipolar, anxiety). They presented a set of limitations to overcome in this field, and they suggested that comprehensive transdiagnostic and longitudinal studies are needed to further advance in the automatic assessment of those disorders. In [32], the authors investigated the relationship between emotion and depression affected speech. Their results showed that speech-based emotional information contributes to the classification of depressed individuals. Also, previous work [21] investigated how noise and reverberation affected depression detection from speech. Finally, the authors of [3] focused on the cross-cultural and cross-linguistic characteristics and how those aspects played a role in depressed speech using verbal biomarkers.

3   Methodology

This section discusses the methodology followed during the study: participants recruited, protocol, experiment tasks and data annotation.

Participants: We collected a dataset of 26 children between 8–13 years old (mean age = 9.6 y.o., SD = 1.5. y.o., 19 females and 7 males) - who were interacting with a Nao robot as shown in Fig. 1. We recruited the participants via school advertising and/or through contacts in the research team in the Cambridgeshire area, United Kingdom. We did not include children with neurological and psychological disorders declared by their guardians.

Protocol: We recorded the sessions using the Jabra disc microphone placed on the table where the robot was seated and two cameras. The robot followed a pre-programmed script and asked children to perform a picture task inspired by the Child Appperception Test (CAT). We opted for this specific task because it enables the assessment of the personality and wellbeing traits of children [4], and

Fig. 1. Experimental setup with the Nao robot and the display screen while performing (a) the SMFQ test and (b) the picture task (images from the actual cHRI sessions are not displayed to protect the children's privacy).

variations of this task have been used previously in HRI [8].

Experimental Tasks: The task consisted of 3 images which correspond to card 7 (a tiger with claws and fangs is seen jumping towards a monkey, Picture 1), card 9 (a rabbit seats on a bed and looks through an open door of a dark room, Picture 2) and card 10 (baby dog lying on another bigger dog, both exhibiting minimum expressions, in the background of a bathroom, Picture 3) respectively from the CAT [4] as they were most related to our goal (task duration: 5–10 mins). Children were asked to tell a story related to the pictures displayed on a computer screen placed behind the robot (as shown in Fig. 1). Specifically, the robot asked the following questions for each of the displayed images: (1) Picture 1: "What do you see in this picture?", "What do you think happened before in this picture?", "What do you think happened after in this picture?"; (2) Picture 2: "What do you think is happening here? Do you notice anything unusual about the picture?", "Do you think it was something that happened for real, or is this made-up?"; (3) Picture 3: "What do you see in this picture?", "What do you think happened before in this picture?", "What do you think happened after in this picture?". Prior to the picture-based task, the robot administered the Short Mood and Feelings Questionnaire (SMFQ) [30] asking children to verbally answer the questionnaire statements, choosing among the options available displayed on the screen (i.e., "True", "Sometimes", or "Not true").

Data Annotation: In our previous work [1], we divided the participants in the study into three groups (lower tertile, medium tertile and higher tertile). However, in this work, we decided to split the participants into two groups ("lower wellbeing" and "higher wellbeing") based on the median of the SMFQ score because our preliminary analysis - which is out of the scope of this paper - showed no differences in speech features of the three clusters. Note that the SMFQ is typically used for assessing wellbeing over the last two weeks and not for detecting momentary changes during or after a task. Therefore, we used the SMFQ for labelling the population based on their general wellbeing, prior to the task. The resulting groups are (1) low quantile category (child's SMFQ score <= median SMFQ score) that we labeled as "higher wellbeing", and (2) high quantile category (child's SMFQ score > median SMFQ score), that we labeled as "lower wellbeing". For example, if a child has scored 2 (below 3, SMFQ median) in the SMFQ test, we assigned them to the "higher wellbeing" group; while if a child scored 17 (above 3, SMFQ median), we assigned them to the "lower wellbeing" group. This resulted in the following grouping: 14 participants belonged to the "higher wellbeing" category, and 12 belonged to the "lower wellbeing" category.

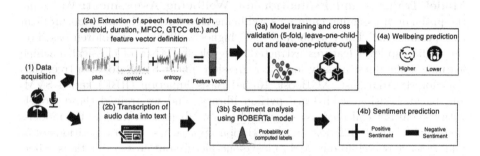

Fig. 2. The experimental methodology consists of (1) dataset acquisition during the cHRI sessions, where audio was recorded using a Jabra mic. (2a) Speech features were extracted and combined as feature vectors that were the input of the (3a) classification algorithms across 3 cross-validation approaches in parallel for (4a) prediction of wellbeing. (2b) Sentiment analysis was also performed on the transcribed text (from the recorded audio files) (3b) using the ROBERTa model for extraction of the sentiment label and the probability of attaining the label for (4b) sentiment prediction.

4   Computational Assessment of Children's Wellbeing

This section describes the modeling approach used to automatically assess children's wellbeing from picture task-based interactions with the robot.

Speech Feature Extraction: As children performed the task with the robot via speech-based interaction, we decided to focus only on auditory signals. In addition, speech features [27] (e.g., pitch, speaking rate) have been identified as promising non-verbal cues to recognize depression in patients. In [10], authors reported abnormalities in speech features of patients with depression. For example, monotony in the pitch and toneless voice are often associated with a depressed voice. Thus, our paper focuses only on the speech features of children. For each child's response clip to each picture task (see Fig. 2), we extracted clip-level audio features using a state-of-the-art Matlab audio toolbox[1]. Specifically, we extracted 91 audio features, including interpretable features such as the duration of children's speech and pitch, and lower-level auditory features, such as MFCC, GTCC and spectral centroid. We first removed constant and null features to prepare the speech features for the machine learning models. Then, we decided to condense the temporal information of each child's response clip to each picture task into statistical descriptors as in [20], computing a fixed-length vector for each feature of each clip that consists of mean, median, standard deviation, minimum, maximum, and auto-correlation with 1-second lag (resulting in a feature vector with size $26 \times 91 \times 6$).

Model Training and Evaluation for Wellbeing Assessment: We define the problem of assessing children's wellbeing as a binary classification problem that predicts the "lower wellbeing" and "higher wellbeing" of children based on the audio-clip-level features extracted. We selected a set of classical machine learning techniques, namely logistic regression, linear SVM, decision tree, random forest, AdaBoost, XGBoost, Radial Basis Function (RBF) kernel SVM, and bagging, using scikit-learn python library[2] and we trained those models with the dataset collected to assess children's wellbeing. To validate the models, we exploited three different cross-validation approaches: 1) 10 repetitions of 5-fold, 2) leave-one-child-out, and 3) leave-one-picture-out cross-validations. First, we implemented a 5-fold stratified cross-validation repeated 10 times, resulting in 50 folds. We repeated the 5-fold cross-validation to improve the model results since different dataset splits can result in very different model estimations. We opted for stratified cross-validation to guarantee the same numbers of "higher wellbeing" and "lower wellbeing" labeled data in each fold. Second, we cross-validated our models, leaving one child out to ensure subject-independent predictions, commonly used in [11,12]. Our dataset contains multiple observations of the same child (for each child, we collected 3 data points, one for each picture task) and using the same subject in both training and test sets can affect the model's generalization capabilities. This results in 26 folds (the number of children involved in the dataset). Third, our dataset contains 26 observations of the same picture, thus we evaluated our models also exploiting a leave-one-picture-out approach to investigate the effect introduced by the different pictures (3-fold cross-validation). All three validation approaches have been optimized by tuning their hyper-parameters during training with the Optuna framework [2]. To evaluate the models, we computed the classifiers' accuracy, recall, and precision and then we compared those evaluation metrics to select the best model for each cross-validation approach. Once we obtained the best-performing model, we ran a feature importance analysis to understand which features contributed most to the model.

---

[1] https://uk.mathworks.com/help/audio/ref/audiofeatureextractor.html.
[2] https://scikit-learn.org/stable/.

Sentiment and Speech Feature Analyses: To extract verbal information, we manually transcribed the children's speech. We ran a sentiment analysis of the transcribed text, exploiting the ROBERTa model [18]. We extracted the predicted sentiment label (positive and negative) and the probability of attaining the computed label. For the categorical predicted labels (positive and negative), we ran Chi square tests to evaluate the differences between population groups ("higher wellbeing" and "lower wellbeing") and between pictures (Picture 1 vs. Picture 2 vs. Picture 3) for each population group. In order to investigate group-level changes ("higher wellbeing" vs. "lower wellbeing") in speech features, we conducted a Wilcoxon rank sum test between the probability of prediction of the negative sentiment and the top 25 most discriminative speech features. Further, we conducted a Friedman's test to understand the effect of pictures across the "higher wellbeing" and "lower wellbeing" groups. Post-hoc analysis Wilcoxon sign rank tests were conducted across pictures (Picture 1 vs. Picture 2 vs. Picture 3) for the predicted probability of negative sentiment and the top 25 most discriminative features.

5 Results and Discussion

This section reports the results obtained from the training of the models described in Sect. 4, including the comparison of the models explored and the statistical analyses conducted to interpret the models' results.

Model Predictions: The models that performed best are respectively the random basis function SVM with a mean accuracy of 83% for the 5-fold (recall $= 75\%$, precision $= 87\%$, and F1 $= 79\%$) and 90% for the leave-one-picture-out validations (recall $= 83\%$, precision $= 94\%$, and F1 $= 88\%$), and the decision tree with a mean accuracy of 70% (recall $= 36\%$, precision $= 46\%$, and F1 $= 39\%$) for leave-one-child-out case. For the sake of clarity, we report in Table 1 the performance of the models in terms of accuracy with the three validation techniques. Our results show that speech features can be promising in investigating children's mental wellbeing-related concerns. This suggests that speech features may be used for the automatic assessment of children's wellbeing. As expected, the model validated using the leave-one-child-out has a lower accuracy with respect to others because the training set and the test set contain different subject data (i.e., if the data of a child is included in the training set, this child's data are not included in the test set), making the model subject-independent. It is also worth noting that the precision of the leave-one-child-out decision tree model is 46%, resulting in a very low performance (i.e., a high number of False positives) that cannot be yet used to assess child wellbeing in cHRI settings, given the importance of the model prediction's precision. To understand and interpret these results, we looked into the folds of the leave-one-child-out and leave-one-picture-out cross-validations. The folds are depicted in Fig. 3. As shown in Fig. 3(a), the model accuracy varied between 70% and 80% across the folds, except for children 1 and 2, who behave very differently with respect to the other data points of the sample, resulting in respectively 100% and around 60% of model's accuracy. Analogously, Fig. 3(b) shows that fold 2, corresponding to Picture 2, results in around 92% of accuracy while the other two folds that represent respectively Picture 1 and Picture 3 have around 90% of accuracy.

Table 1. Mean accuracy between folds of the models implemented with the three cross-validation approaches.

Models	5-fold	Leave-One-Child-Out	Leave-One-Picture-Out
Logistic regression	0.74	0.56	0.79
Linear SVM	0.73	0.59	0.82
Random forest tree	0.68	0.41	0.75
Bagging	0.75	0.50	0.82
XGBoost	0.73	0.51	0.81
AdaBoost	0.72	0.50	0.77
Decision tree	0.70	**0.70**	0.60
RBF SVM	**0.83**	0.55	**0.90**

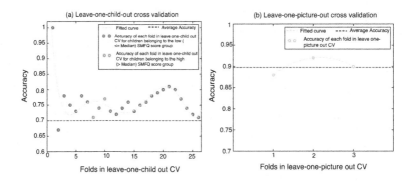

Fig. 3. Visualisation of the best performing classifiers. (a) Leave-one-child-out Decision Tree mean accuracy (x-axis is the fold indicating the child whose data was left out as the test set). (b) Leave-one-picture-out Radial Basis Function Kernel SVM mean accuracy (x-axis is the fold indicating the picture whose data was left out as the test set).

Analysis: From the sentiment analysis, our results suggest that, in both "lower wellbeing" and "higher wellbeing" groups, all the pictures elicited a more negative sentiment than a positive one in children, as depicted in Fig. 4. This result is in line with the CAT test goal that aims to trigger specific feelings in children, such as loneliness in Picture 2. Specifically, Picture 2 shows a higher

negative sentiment in the "lower wellbeing" group than in the "higher wellbeing" group. However, when we conducted a Chi-square test between pictures
for the two groups, we did not find the results significantly different. For this
reason, instead of only using the labels of the predictions (i.e., positive and
negative), we decided to analyse the probability of those predictions. Thus, we
conducted a Friedman's test between the picture conditions (Picture 1, Picture
2 and Picture 3) of the "higher wellbeing" and the "lower wellbeing" groups.
Within the "higher wellbeing" group, we found that there was a significant difference between the probability of the negative sentiment between the three
pictures ($X_F^2(2) = 7, p = 0.03$). We then ran a post-hoc Wilcoxon signed rank
tests analysis with a Bonferroni adjusted alpha level of $0.017(0.05/3)$, and we
found that the probability of negative sentiment was not significantly different
between the conditions (Picture 1, Picture 2, Picture 3). For the group with
"lower wellbeing", another Friedman's test showed that there was a significant
difference between the probability of negative sentiment between the three pictures ($X_F^2(2) = 7.17, p = 0.03$). Post-hoc Wilcoxon signed rank tests with a
Bonferroni adjusted alpha level of $0.017(0.05/3)$ showed that there was no statistically significant difference in terms of the probability of negative sentiment
between the conditions (Picture 1, Picture 2 and Picture 3).

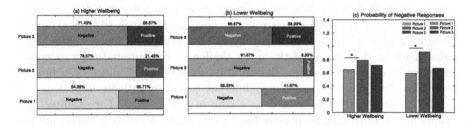

Fig. 4. Sentiment analysis was performed using ROBERTa model to determine the sentiment labels (positive, negative) for "higher wellbeing" (a) and "lower wellbeing" (b)
groups. (c) Negative sentiment prediction probability compared between the pictures
and the groups ("higher wellbeing" and "lower wellbeing"). *$p < 0.05$ uncorrected.

Alongside the sentiment analysis, we also conducted a feature importance
analysis to compute the top 25 features from a 5-fold cross-validation analysis of
the RBF SVM model. We observed that the feature that contributed the most
to the model prediction was the duration of the children's speech, followed by
the Delta GTCC. To further investigate the contribution of the most important
feature, we conducted a Friedman's test between the conditions (Picture 1, Picture 2 and Picture 3) of the "higher wellbeing" and the "lower wellbeing" groups
for the speech duration. Within the "higher wellbeing" group, we found that a
Friedman's test showed that there was a significant difference in the duration
of the speech feature between the three conditions (Picture 1, Picture 2 and
Picture 3) ($X_F^2(2) = 19, p < 0.001$). We then ran the post-hoc Wilcoxon signed

rank tests with a Bonferroni adjusted alpha level of $0.017(0.05/3)$ and we found a statistical significant difference of the speech duration($W = 105, p < 0.001$ corrected) between Picture 1 ($Mdn = 51.5$) and Picture 2 ($Mdn = 18.5$). Post-hoc Wilcoxon signed rank tests with a Bonferroni adjusted alpha level of $0.017(0.05/3)$ also resulted in a statistically significant difference of the duration of the speech($W = 12, p = 0.02$ corrected) between Picture 2 ($Mdn = 18.5$) and Picture 3 ($Mdn = 35$). For the "lower wellbeing" population, another Friedman's test showed that there was a significant difference between the three conditions (Picture 1, Picture 2 and Picture 3) ($X_F^2(2) = 10.085, p = 0.006$). Analogously, we found that the post-hoc Wilcoxon signed rank tests with a Bonferroni adjusted alpha level of $0.017(0.05/3)$ showed a statistically significant difference in terms of speech duration ($W = 66, p = 0.003$ corrected) between Picture 1 ($Mdn = 49.5$) and Picture 2 ($Mdn = 30$). The other feature tests (e.g., GTCC, Delta GTCC) that resulted in being significant are not reported because they are out of the scope of this paper that only focused on interpretable features.

Discussion: Our results show that the mean accuracy of the models in leave-one-child-out and leave-one-picture-out evaluations varied across folds. Specifically, we observe that for the leave-one-child-out evaluation, the mean accuracy varied between 70% and 80%, meaning that a set of additional child-specific features have a key role in the model learning. The model should consider child-specific characteristics that, for instance, can emerge from non-auditory behaviors (e.g., visual cues) or personal characteristics (e.g., personality). Such additional factors can further inform the model, resulting in child-specific model training. Past works highlighted that one of the main challenges for automatically assessing mental wellbeing is the need for personalized models [33]. Children can behave very differently (e.g., talk more, use different tones), negatively impacting the models' training and performance, as shown in our findings. For example, the authors in [29] implemented personalized modeling of depression using multiple modalities of data. To qualitatively interpret our results, we watched the videos of children corresponding to the non-average points in the model (child 1 and child 2, see Fig. 3(a)). We observed that child 1 was very talkative and used a wide spectrum of intonations to describe the pictures, while child 2 didn't speak that long, and their pitch was monotonous. Such behavioral differences could be attributed to other factors, such as the children's personalities. Child 1 appears to be more extroverted and talkative than child 2. Within the psychology literature, many studies [15,17] have reported a strong relationship between personality and mental health as well as how personality attributes impact the detection of depression in adults [16]. However, to the best of our knowledge, none of them have yet explored the influence of personality on the detection of mental disorders in children. From our sentiment analysis, our results show that experiment stimuli (Picture 1, Picture 2 and Picture 3) have an impact on the responses of children. From leave-one-picture-out validation, we found that the mean accuracy was higher for Picture 2. This could be due to the sentiment of children's speech. As shown in Fig. 4, Picture 2 was the most negative perceived picture, triggering negative feelings in children. The picture conveys a sentiment of loneliness that elicited stronger negative reactions in children[3].

6   Conclusion

This paper presents the audio analysis of a cHRI dataset for robot-assisted assessment of children's mental wellbeing. Our results showed that speech features are reliable indicators for assessing children's mental wellbeing, but they are insufficient for accurate and precise prediction. This suggests that personalised modeling can be the most suitable approach for this assessment task. Limitations of this work include an imbalanced population sample (more girls than boys), novelty effect [31] and the conservative approach in categorisation of the population groups ("lower wellbeing" and "higher wellbeing") using the median SMFQ score. In future works, we aim to address these limitations to gain further insights into speech-based modeling of robot-assisted assessment of children's mental wellbeing.

Open Access Statement: For the purpose of open access, the authors have applied a Creative Commons Attribution (CC BY) licence to any Author Accepted Manuscript version arising.

Data Access Statement: Overall statistical analysis of research data underpinning this publication is available in the text of this publication. Additional raw data related to this publication cannot be openly released; the raw data contains transcripts of interviews, but none of the interviewees consented to data sharing.

Acknowledgments. This work was supported by the University of Cambridge's OHMC Small Equipment Funding. N. I. Abbasi is supported by the W.D. Armstrong Trust PhD Studentship and the Cambridge Trusts. M. Spitale and H. Gunes are supported by the EPSRC project ARoEQ under grant ref. EP/R030782/1. All research at the Department of Psychiatry in the University of Cambridge is supported by the NIHR Cambridge Biomedical Research Centre (BRC-1215-20014, particularly T. Ford) and NIHR Applied Research Collaboration East of England (P. Jones, J. Anderson). The views expressed are those of the authors and not necessarily those of the NIHR or the Department of Health and Social Care.

References

1. Abbasi, N.I., et al.: Can robots help in the evaluation of mental wellbeing in children? an empirical study. In: 2022 31st IEEE International Conference on Robot and Human Interactive Communication (RO-MAN), pp. 1459–1466. IEEE (2022)
2. Akiba, T., et al.: Optuna: a next-generation hyperparameter optimization framework. In: Proceedings of the 25th ACM SIGKDD International Conference on Knowledge Discovery & Data Mining, pp. 2623–2631 (2019)

---

[3] https://childmind.org/article/help-children-manage-fears/.

3. Alghowinem, S., et al.: Cross-cultural depression recognition from vocal biomarkers. In: Interspeech, pp. 1943–1947 (2016)
4. Bellak, L., Bellak, S.S.: Children's apperception test (1949)
5. Belpaeme, T., et al.: Multimodal child-robot interaction: building social bonds. J. Hum.-Robot Interact. **1**(2) (2012)
6. Bemelmans, R., et al.: Socially assistive robots in elderly care: a systematic review into effects and effectiveness. J. Am. Med. Directors Assoc. **13**(2), 114–120 (2012)
7. Bethel, C.L., et al.: Using robots to interview children about bullying: lessons learned from an exploratory study. In: RO-MAN 2016, pp. 712–717. IEEE (2016)
8. Bremner, P., et al.: Personality perception of robot avatar tele-operators. In: HRI 2016, pp. 141–148. IEEE (2016)
9. Crossman, M.K., et al.: The influence of a socially assistive robot on mood, anxiety, and arousal in children. Prof. Psychol. Res. Pract. **49**(1), 48 (2018)
10. Cummins, N., et al.: A review of depression and suicide risk assessment using speech analysis. Speech Commun. **71**, 10–49 (2015)
11. Fernandez, R., Picard, R.W.: Modeling drivers' speech under stress. Speech Commun. **40**(1–2), 145–159 (2003)
12. Gholamiangonabadi, D., et al.: Deep neural networks for human activity recognition with wearable sensors: Leave-one-subject-out cross-validation for model selection. IEEE Access **8**, 133982–133994 (2020)
13. Godoi, D., et al.: Proteger: a social robotics system to support child psychological evaluation. In: 2020 Latin American Robotics Symposium (LARS), 2020 Brazilian Symposium on Robotics (SBR) and 2020 Workshop on Robotics in Education (WRE), pp. 1–6. IEEE (2020)
14. Gómez Esteban, P., et al.: A multilayer reactive system for robots interacting with children with autism. arXiv e-prints pp. arXiv-1606 (2016)
15. Hettema, J.M., et al.: A population-based twin study of the relationship between neuroticism and internalizing disorders. Am. J. Psychiatry **163**(5), 857–864 (2006)
16. Jaiswal, S., et al.: Automatic prediction of depression and anxiety from behaviour and personality attributes. In: ACII 2019, pp. 1–7. IEEE (2019)
17. Klein, D.N., et al.: Personality and depression: explanatory models and review of the evidence. Ann. Rev. Clin. Psychol. **7**, 269 (2011)
18. Liao, W., et al.: An improved aspect-category sentiment analysis model for text sentiment analysis based on roberta. Appl. Intell. **51**(6), 3522–3533 (2021)
19. Low, D.M., et al.: Automated assessment of psychiatric disorders using speech: a systematic review. Laryngoscope Invest. Otolaryngol. **5**(1), 96–116 (2020)
20. Mathur, L., et al.: Modeling user empathy elicited by a robot storyteller. In: ACII 2021, pp. 1–8. IEEE (2021)
21. Mitra, V., et al.: Noise and reverberation effects on depression detection from speech. In: ICASSP 2016, pp. 5795–5799. IEEE (2016)
22. Papadopoulos, I., et al.: A systematic review of the literature regarding socially assistive robots in pre-tertiary education. Comput. Educ. **155**, 103924 (2020)
23. Peter, J., et al.: Can social robots affect children's prosocial behavior? an experimental study on prosocial robot models. Comput. Hum. Behav. **120**, 106712 (2021)
24. Poria, S., et al.: A review of affective computing: from unimodal analysis to multimodal fusion. Inform. Fus. **37**, 98–125 (2017)
25. Raigoso, D., et al.: A survey on socially assistive robotics: clinicians' and patients' perception of a social robot within gait rehabilitation therapies. Brain Sci. **11**(6), 738 (2021)
26. Rhim, J., et al.: Investigating positive psychology principles in affective robotics. In: ACII 2019, pp. 1–7. IEEE (2019)

27. Ringeval, F., et al.: Avec 2019 workshop and challenge: state-of-mind, detecting depression with AI, and cross-cultural affect recognition. In: Proceedings of the 9th International on Audio/visual Emotion Challenge and Workshop, pp. 3–12 (2019)
28. Scassellati, B., et al.: Robots for use in autism research. Ann. Rev. Biomed. Eng. **14**(1), 275–294 (2012)
29. Shah, R.V., et al.: Personalized machine learning of depressed mood using wearables. Transl. Psychiatry **11**(1), 1–18 (2021)
30. Sharp, C., et al.: The short mood and feelings questionnaire (SMFQ): a unidimensional item response theory and categorical data factor analysis of self-report ratings from a community sample of 7-through 11-year-old children. J. Abnorm. Child Psychol. **34**(3), 365–377 (2006)
31. Smedegaard, C.V.: Reframing the role of novelty within social HRI: from noise to information. In: 2019 14th ACM/IEEE International Conference on Human-Robot Interaction (HRI), pp. 411–420. IEEE (2019)
32. Stasak, B., et al.: An investigation of emotional speech in depression classification. In: Interspeech, pp. 485–489 (2016)
33. Xu, X., et al.: Leveraging collaborative-filtering for personalized behavior modeling: a case study of depression detection among college students. In: Proceedings of the ACM on Interactive, Mobile, Wearable and Ubiquitous Technologies, vol. 5, no. 1, pp. 1–27 (2021)

The Sound of Actuators in Children with ASD, Beneficial or Disruptive?

Melanie Jouaiti[1], Eloise Zehnder[2(✉)], and François Charpillet[2]

[1] Electrical and Computer Engineering Department, University of Waterloo,
200 University Ave, Waterloo, ON N2L3G1, Canada
`mjouaiti@uwaterloo.ca`
[2] Université de Lorraine, CNRS, Inria, LORIA, 54000 Nancy, France
`eloise.zehnder@univ-lorraine.fr`, `francois.charpillet@inria.fr`

Abstract. It is often overlooked in human-robot gestural interactions that, robot produce sound when they move. That aspect might be either beneficial or detrimental to the interaction, but it should be taken into account, especially in the context of robot-assisted therapy.

In this paper, we therefore considered sensory perception in the case of typically developing children and children with Autistic Spectrum Disorders and designed a pilot study with twenty participants to evaluate the impact the sound of actuators has on a rhythmic gestural interaction. Participants were asked to perform a waving-like gesture back at a robot in three different conditions: with visual perception only, auditory perception only and both perceptions. We analyze coordination performance and focus of gaze in each condition. Preliminary results indicate that the sound of actuators might be beneficial for children with autism and only slightly disruptive for typically developing children.

Keywords: ASD · Motor coordination · Sensory processing

1 Introduction

During robot assisted therapy, sensory and cognitive aspects of the interaction can influence it to the detriment of its use and effectiveness.

Interpersonal interactions are inherently multimodal but in the case of gestural human-robot interactions, the human partner perceives the movements from the robot but also the sound produced by the robot motors. In that case, these two modalities (visual and auditory) are congruent, which, according to research in neuroscience, might be confusing for the human perception system. Moreover, research also shows that the human brain has different ways of processing different sensory stimuli and that sensory dominance may appear. Sensory processing also depends on the context:

M. Jouaiti and E. Zehnder—These authors contributed equally.

F. Cavallo et al. (Eds.): ICSR 2022, LNAI 13818, pp. 36–44, 2022.
https://doi.org/10.1007/978-3-031-24670-8_4

- **Vision may be dominant over audition in spatial localization.** A modality-appropriateness hypothesis suggests that "the human perceptual system is cognizant of the fact that vision is a more trustworthy modality for spatial localization than audition and proprioception and, for this reason, it is more closely attended" [28]. Moreover, visual information does not have the strong alerting capacity of auditory signals and therefore people are predisposed to direct their attention towards visual stimulation predominantly [21].
- **Audition may be dominant for temporal judgments.** [12] showed that the auditory perception can severely alter or even remove the visual perception when the stimuli are spatially and temporally congruent. They produced white noise bursts through headphones and observed decreased visual orientation discrimination performance. However, suppression occurs only if the sound and visual stimuli are presented in an ipsilateral, spatially congruent manner and in a temporally congruent manner.

This co-existence of two sensory stimuli is particularly a concern for rhythmic interactions. Rhythmic interactions trigger the emergence of involuntary movement coordination when two humans interact with each other (walking, clapping, drumming...). Synchrony is pervasive in biological systems and unconsciously facilitates the creation of emotional connections. Human-Robot coordination or imitation is a promising research subject in socially assistive robotics as several neurological disorders such as Parkinson's, cerebral palsy, autism do not affect synchronization abilities. It has therefore been widely used with a therapeutic goal, particularly for children with autism [5,25], but also for motor rehabilitation [9].

Gault et al. showed that the auditory modality facilitates discrimination and reproduction of rhythmic patterns [6]. Besides, Repp et al. conducted a study on sensorimotor coordination where participants were required to tap their finger in rhythm with an auditory or visual sequence and report whether a time-shifted event was present [23]. Results showed that the visual information yielded greater variability of movement, smaller involuntary phase correction response and poorer time-shifted event detection than the auditory information. After that, participants were subjected simultaneously to both auditory and visual sequences and were instructed to ignore the auditory information. Analysis evidenced that involuntary phase correction response depended more on auditory than on visual information and that variability was similar to the auditory sequences. Moreover, other research also showed that people have greater difficulty synchronizing finger taps with a visual signal compared to an auditory signal [1,3,4]. It has also been argued that the motor system is more responsive to auditory than to visual input [4], which has been confirmed by [13,27] and suggested that there are different timing mechanisms in the two modalities [15].

Beyond the disruptive aspect of combining sensory modalities, it has also proved to be useful, for example, [26], in a Parkinson gait rehabilitation study, showed that auditory and visual perception and both perceptions all improve different aspects of gait. This evidences that, in some cases, the auditory and visual perception can reinforce each other.

We also showed in [14] that the sound of robot actuators disturbs the motor coordination of neurotypical adult subjects in a waving rhythmic task. The sensory processing of children with ASD is however different and this sound may affect them in other ways. Besides, this is a relevant question since robot actuators always produce a sound and this may be perturbing in a therapeutic setting.

The development of sensory systems in children appears to be related to their developmental process [22,29]. In young children, proximal receptors (touch, taste, smell) are more developed than distal receptors which gradually supersede the former with age.

ASD is usually associated with abnormal sensory processing where a stimulus can either trigger no reaction or a disproportionate/exaggerated response [8]. Contrary to neurotypical children, children with autism are known to prefer the use of proximal receptors (touch, taste) rather than distal receptors (vision, audition) [7,24]. However, both neurotypical and children with autism respond more to a visual stimulus than to an auditory stimulus [11,17,18]. In a multi-sensory study, [10] subjected children to multi-sensory stimuli. When combining visual and auditory stimuli, neurotypical children and children with ASD reacted predominantly to vision. However, for the combination of touch and sound, neurotypical children responded more to sound while children with ASD responded more to touch.

Children with autism may exhibit an unpredictable or inconsistent motor response to sensory stimuli, that is either an inhibited or facilitated motor response [19]. Moreover, [11] showed that a visual stimulus is more likely to elicit a movement stimulation than an auditory stimulus.

In this paper, we therefore considered sensory perception in the case of typically developing children and children with Autistic Spectrum Disorders and designed a pilot study to evaluate the impact the sound of actuators has on a rhythmic gestural interaction.

2 Materials and Methods

The goal of this study is to study the sensory dominance of neurotypical children and children with ASD during a human-robot rhythmic interaction. This will allow us to better understand sensory processing in such interactions and thus to better design motor therapies involving a robot.

2.1 Study Design

This study replicates the sensory dominance study introduced in [14]. Participants were asked to wave back at the Pepper[1] robot [20] (Softbanks Robotics) depending on three conditions that subjected the participants to various sensory stimuli. The study session lasted about one hour.

---

[1] https://www.softbankrobotics.com/emea/en/pepper.

Parent was asked to fill in the Bogdashina sensory profile [2] for their child beforehand. This questionnaire allowed us to assess the sensory dominance of each child.

During the study session, the child and their parent were first asked to answer some questionnaires. Afterwards, the robot was switched on and the child and his or her parent were free to interact with it in its built-in interaction mode. This part could last between ten and twenty minutes depending on the interest the child exhibited.

Then, the child was equipped with TEA[2] Motion sensors on the right arm. The sensors are calibrated at the beginning of the session with the resting pose of the child (standing, arms straight against the body). They provides us with quaternions. The child was seated in front of the robot, their arm resting on a pillow. The child was instructed to wave back at the robot under various conditions:

- a baseline condition where the child could hear and see the robot (AV)
- a condition where the child could not see but hear the robot due to a removable panel (A)
- a condition with white noise through headphones where the child could not hear the robot (V)

The child was videotaped during the interaction.

Finally, the child and their parent were asked again to answer questionnaires. Those questionnaires are out of the scope of this paper and we will, therefore, not report on those results here.

2.2 Participants

Twenty children participated in the study. Five children were autistic (only boys, 9.6 ± 2.07 years old). The other fifteen were neurotypical (including 7 girls, 9.1 ± 2.0 years old). Two neurotypical children were excluded from the study results due to a motion sensor malfunction. Moreover, due to the COVID-19 outbreak, we had to cancel additional studies and recruitment was interrupted. This study was approved by Inria ethical committee. The accompanying parent of each child gave a written informed consent.

2.3 Materials

The Robot. The Pepper robot was programmed to wave according to a sinusoidal signal. The signal frequency varied from one interaction to the other (0.9 Hz, 1.0 Hz or 1.1 Hz) to avoid frequency acclimatisation. The robot woke up from its rest state at the beginning of each series of interactions. Waving periods were indicated by an auditory stimulus and by the robot eyes becoming green, they were unlit otherwise. At the end of each series, the robot returned to its rest state. Each condition consisted of a series of nine waving interactions.

---

[2] https://www.teaergo.com/products/tea-captiv-t-sens-motion-imu/.

Gaze Analysis. Using the video of the child, we can extract gaze direction (See Fig. 1). The program[3] first detects the face in the picture, then identifies face landmarks to extract the eyes. Applying a threshold on the image allows to extract the pupil coordinates.

Coordination Analysis. The coordination performance is computed using the Phase Locking Value (PLV), which provides a score between 0 and 1 (1 being fully coordinated).

The Phase Locking Value (PLV) has been introduced by [16] to measure coordination in brain signals. It relies on the assumption that both signals are locked with a constant phase difference but the PLV allows for deviations and evaluates this spread. First, the Hilbert transform is computed, providing the instantaneous phase ϕ for each signal, then the instantaneous PLV can be obtained:

$$PLV(t) = \frac{1}{N} \left| \sum_{i=0}^{N} e^{j(\phi_1(i) - \phi_2(i))} \right| \tag{1}$$

with N the sliding window size, $j = \sqrt{-1}$, ϕ_k the instantaneous phase of signal k.

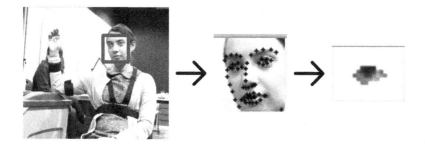

Fig. 1. Illustration of the gaze extraction process: Face detection → landmarks detection → eye extraction. The subject is equipped with motion sensors in the first image: one on the arm, one on the forearm and one in the back placed on a harness

3 Experimental Results

3.1 Coordination Performance

To ascertain that the child was actually looking at the robot when required, we extracted the gaze direction from the video. Interactions where the child's gaze direction varied too much were excluded from the data analysis. It is worth mentioning that children's gaze was more focused on the robot in the V condition (ASD: 48.2%, neurotypical: 52.8%) than in the AV condition (ASD: 22.2%, neurotypical: 26.9%).

---

[3] https://github.com/antoinelame/GazeTracking.

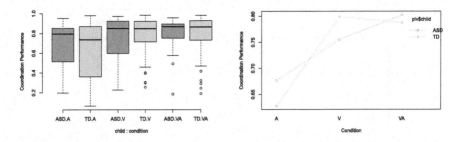

Fig. 2. Coordination performance results. Up: boxplot representation of the coordination performance according to condition (AV, V, A) and child diagnosis (ASD, neurotypical). Down: Interaction effect between the conditions

Preliminary results show that autistic children were more coordinated in the AV condition while neurotypical children were similarly coordinated in the AV and V conditions. See Table 1 and Fig. 2 for an overview of the results.

Table 1. Average coordination performance (AV: auditory-visual condition, A: auditory condition, V: visual condition)

Condition	AV	A	V
Neurotypical	0.79 ± 0.20	0.63 ± 0.27	0.80 ± 0.17
ASD	0.80 ± 0.17	0.76 ± 0.23	0.68 ± 0.23

A two-way ANOVA reveals a significant difference between the conditions ($p < 0.001$) but not between the different children diagnosis ($p = 0.28$). A post-hoc Tukey test on the conditions showed a significant difference between the AV and A conditions ($p < 0.001$) and between the V and A conditions ($p < 0.001$), but not between the AV and V conditions ($p = 0.99$).

A two-way ANOVA also reveals a significant difference between age groups ($p < 0.001$) (See Fig. 3). A post-hoc Tukey test on the age groups showed a significant difference between six year-olds and every other age group ($p < 0.001$).

3.2 Sensory Profile

The sensory profile revealed that most children with ASD appear to be more sensitive to visual stimuli (See Table 2).

For the neurotypical children, only two appear to be more sensitive to visual stimuli and five to auditory stimuli. A statistical analysis reveals no correlation between sensory profile results and coordination performance

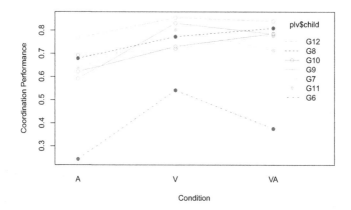

Fig. 3. Coordination performance for each age group, G*X* indicates age group X, for example G6 comprises 6 years old. (See details in text)

Table 2. Summary table with Coordination performance scores and sensory profile scores (PSV: visual sensory profile; PSA: auditory sensory profile) for the 5 children with ASD in the study

AV	V	A	PSV	PSA
0.69	**0.80**	0.70	**8**	4
0.66	**0.83**	0.66	11	**12**
0.92	**0.93**	0.86	**13**	**13**
0.82	0.63	0.64	**8**	5
0.68	0.48	0.53	**9**	7

4 Discussion and Conclusion

Preliminary results showed that both neurotypical children and children with ASD coordinated better with a visual signal or with a visual-auditory combination than with an auditory signal alone. This predominance of vision over audition is in concordance with previous studies [10,11,17,18]. Besides, we observed that the children tend to look less at the robot when they can also hear the sound of the robot motors than when they cannot. While this should obviously be confirmed with a higher number of children, the children results appear to differ from the ones from the adults. While adults were perturbed in their coordination when subjected to both visual and auditory stimuli, this combination may reinforce the children's interaction and lead to better coordination.

This study encountered a few limitations, the main being the limited number of participants, particularly children with autism, which makes the comparison between the neurotypical sample and the autistic spectrum disorder sample somewhat unbalanced. While these preliminary results already give us interesting information, we would expect the overall results would have been more significant with more participants.

While the results are preliminary and need to be validated with more children, they are encouraging as children enjoyed interacting with the robot and the sound of actuators appears to facilitate coordination, at least for children with ASD.

Acknowledgements. We thank all the children and parents who willingly took part in this study and filled in so many questionnaires.

References

1. Bartlett, N.R., Bartlett, S.C.: Synchronization of a motor response with an anticipated sensory event. Psychol. Rev. **66**(4), 203 (1959)
2. Bogdashina, O.: Sensory Perceptual Issues in Autism and Asperger Syndrome: Different Sensory Experiences-different Perceptual Worlds. Jessica Kingsley Publishers (2016)
3. Dunlap, K.: Reaction to rhythmic stimuli with attempt to synchronize. Psycholog. Rev. **17**(6), 399 (1910)
4. Fraisse, P.: Auditory rhythms and visual rhythms. Ann. Psychol. **49**, 21–42 (1948)
5. Fujimoto, I., Matsumoto, T., De Silva, P.R.S., Kobayashi, M., Higashi, M.: Mimicking and evaluating human motion to improve the imitation skill of children with autism through a robot. Int. J. Soc. Robot. **3**(4), 349–357 (2011)
6. Gault, R.H., Goodfellow, L.D.: An empirical comparison of audition, vision, and touch in the discrimination of temporal patterns and ability to reproduce them. J. Gen. Psychol. **18**(1), 41–47 (1938)
7. Goldfarb, W.: Receptor preferences in schizophrenic children. AMA Arch. Neurol. Psychiatry **76**(6), 643–652 (1956)
8. Goldfarb, W.: Self-awareness in schizophrenic children. Arch. Gen. Psychiatry **8**(1), 47–60 (1963)
9. Guneysu, A., Siyli, R.D., Salah, A.A.: Auto-evaluation of motion imitation in a child-robot imitation game for upper arm rehabilitation. In: The 23rd IEEE International Symposium on Robot and Human Interactive Communication, 2014 RO-MAN, pp. 199–204. IEEE (2014)
10. Hermelin, B., O'Connor, N.: Effects of sensory input and sensory dominance on severely disturbed, autistic children and on subnormal controls. Br. J. Psychol. **55**(2), 201–206 (1964)
11. Hermelin, B., O'connor, N.: Psychological experiments with autistic children (1970)
12. Hidaka, S., Ide, M.: Sound can suppress visual perception. Tech. rep., Sci. Rep. **5**, 10483 (2015)
13. Jaśkowski, P., Jaroszyk, F., Hojan-Jezierska, D.: Temporal-order judgments and reaction time for stimuli of different modalities. Psychol. Res. **52**(1), 35–38 (1990)
14. Jouaiti, M., Henaff, P.: The sound of actuators: disturbance in human-robot interactions? In: Joint IEEE International Conference on Development and Learning and Epigenetic Robotics (ICDL-EpiRob), pp. 75–80 (2019)
15. Kolers, P.A., Brewster, J.M.: Rhythms and responses. J. Exper. Psychol. Hum. Percept. Perform. **11**(2), 150 (1985)
16. Lachaux, J.P., Rodriguez, E., Martinerie, J., Varela, F.J., et al.: Measuring phase synchrony in brain signals. Hum. brain Mapp. **8**(4), 194–208 (1999)

17. O'Connor, N., Hermelin, B.: Sensory dominance: in autistic imbecile children and controls. Arch. Gen. Psychiatry **12**(1), 99–103 (1965)
18. O'Connor, N.: Visual perception in autistic children. Infantile autism: Concepts, characteristics and treatment. London: Churchill Livingstone (1971)
19. Ornitz, E.M., Ritvo, E.R.: Perceptual inconstancy in early infantile autism: the syndrome of early infant autism and its variants including certain cases of childhood schizophrenia. Arch. Gen. Psychiatry **18**(1), 76–98 (1968)
20. Pandey, A.K., Gelin, R.: A mass-produced sociable humanoid robot: pepper: the first machine of its kind. IEEE Robot. Autom. Mag. **25**(3), 40–48 (2018)
21. Posner, M.I., Nissen, M.J., Klein, R.M.: Visual dominance: an information-processing account of its origins and significance. Psychol. Rev. **83**(2), 157 (1976)
22. Renshaw, S.: The errors of cutaneous localization and the effect of practice on the localizing movement in children and adults. Pedagog. Seminary J. Gen. Psychol. **38**(1–4), 223–238 (1930)
23. Repp, B.H., Penel, A.: Auditory dominance in temporal processing: new evidence from synchronization with simultaneous visual and auditory sequences. J. Exper. Psychol. Hum. Percept. Perform. **28**(5), 1085 (2002)
24. Schopler, E.: Early infantile autism and receptor processes. Arch. Gen. Psychiatry **13**(4), 327–335 (1965)
25. Srinivasan, S.M., Lynch, K.A., Bubela, D.J., Gifford, T.D., Bhat, A.N.: Effect of interactions between a child and a robot on the imitation and praxis performance of typically devloping children and a child with autism: A preliminary study. Percept. Motor Skills **116**(3), 885–904 (2013)
26. Suteerawattananon, M., Morris, G., Etnyre, B., Jankovic, J., Protas, E.: Effects of visual and auditory cues on gait in individuals with parkinson's disease. J. Neurolog. Sci. **219**(1–2), 63–69 (2004)
27. Vroomen, J., Gelder, B.D.: Sound enhances visual perception: cross-modal effects of auditory organization on vision. J. Exper. Psychol. Hum. Perception Perform. **26**(5), 1583 (2000)
28. Welch, R.B.: Meaning, attention, and the unity assumption in the intersensory bias of spatial and temporal perceptions. In: Advances in psychology, vol. 129, pp. 371–387. Elsevier (1999)
29. Zaporozhets, A.: The origin and development of the conscious control of movements in man. In: Recent Soviet Psychology. Liveright New York (1961)

Evaluating Robot Acceptance in Children with ASD and Their Parents

Eloise Zehnder[1]([⊠]), Melanie Jouaiti[2], and François Charpillet[1]

[1] Université de Lorraine, CNRS, Inria, LORIA, 54000 Nancy, France
eloise.zehnder@univ-lorraine.fr, francois.charpillet@inria.fr
[2] Electrical and Computer Engineering Department, University of Waterloo,
200 University Ave, N2L3G1 Waterloo, ON, Canada
mjouaiti@uwaterloo.ca

Abstract. Acceptance is an important ergonomic matter for an effective use of technologies, especially in the case of assistive robots. Work on acceptance with children with autistic spectrum disorder, including their parents, is still lacking. Therefore, this study aims at evaluating robots' acceptance with parents and children with and without autistic spectrum disorder. We proceeded by evaluating acceptance and anthropomorphism before and after a free interaction with the Pepper robot, for neurotypical children (N = 13) and children with autism (N = 5) and their parents. Preliminary results indicate that acceptance metrics showed a rather positive appreciation of the robot by the children but less positive for their parents. Limitations and recommendations are proposed at the end of the study.

1 Introduction

While parents' and children's overall acceptance is important for further use of any technology, only a few studies report on children with autistic spectrum disorder (ASD) and their parents' involvement with robot acceptance [1,12]. Children are generally influenced by their parents' attitudes [20] and parental involvement in robot assisted therapies is important to continue monitoring therapeutic work outside of sessions [3].

Technology acceptance is required to facilitate the use and effectiveness of assistive technologies. Assistive robots' acceptance by social actors in childrens' lives such as teachers or parents have been reported as essential [7,8]. However, only a few studies with parents have been done in this area [1,12] although they are important for the overseeing and the involvement in assisted therapies with children [3,20].

In the study of [1], parents' acceptance has been evaluated with rather unconventional scales in acceptance fields (Session Rating Scale, Treatment adherence) neglecting essential factors in acceptance models such as the perceived ease of use (Technology Acceptance Model [5]) or social influence (Unified Theory of

---

E. Zehnder, M. Jouaiti—These authors contributed equally.

F. Cavallo et al. (Eds.): ICSR 2022, LNAI 13818, pp. 45–53, 2022.
https://doi.org/10.1007/978-3-031-24670-8_5

Acceptance and Use of Technology [26]). This also excludes interesting factors such as familiarity with technology or robots [2], technology and robot anxiety [19] or user experience [6], which can also influence user acceptance. While this type of evaluation method allows comparison between parents and children acceptance scores, more measurement tools could be relevant to better encompass of the parents' perception and acceptance of potential assistive robots. So far, there are only a few assessment methods to measure acceptance for younger children and perception of robots as relational agents. As stated by [13], these will often be used by older children or adults while neglecting the comprehension or attention abilities of younger children around 5 years old [13]. Using picture-based scales appears as a potentially efficient evaluation method to evaluate the acceptance and anthropomorphism of robots [13]. Indeed, it appears that children will show anthropomorphism towards robots by applying social rules the same way they may respond to humans [4] while being conscious that robots remain objects [27]. Anthropomorphism in general has been shown to improve perceived self-efficacy in users and their attitude towards the system [16]. In children, anthropomorphism affects their attitudes towards the robot but seem to prefer moderately realistic robots [25]. While it is assumed that individuals with autism prefer less human-like robots [22], a study by [14] showed that children with higher functioning autism preferred the more human-like robot. Anthropomorphism can also increase robot acceptance in general [24], especially in younger adults compared to middle-aged adults. [17]. Thus, the exploration comparison of acceptance and attributed anthropomorphism in children with autism represents an aspect that deserves further exploration.

2   Materials and Methods

The goal of this study is to explore how acceptance can evolve before and after interacting with a social robot for parents and children with autism.

2.1   Study Overview

For each study session, the child and their parent were first asked to answer robot acceptance questionnaires about the Pepper robot. The robot was visible but turned off during this time. It was made clear to the parent that despite the lack of preliminary interaction with the robot, the parent was asked to answer the acceptance and user experience questionnaire according to their attitudes and representations. The parent and the child, seated at the same table, could see the robot, switched off, during this first phase of the questionnaire. Afterwards, the robot was switched on and the child and his or her parent were free to interact with it in its built-in interaction mode (e.g. waving, imitating animals, telling the time...). This part could last between ten and twenty minutes depending on the interest the child exhibited. Then, the child was equipped with motion sensors on the right arm for a coordination task, which is out of the scope of this study. Finally, the child and their parent were asked again to answer the same acceptance questionnaires while still being able to interact with the robot. The whole study session lasted about one hour.

2.2   Participants

Eighteen children participated in the study. Five children had autism spectrum disorder (only boys, 9.6 ± 2.07 years old). The thirteen other were neurotypical (including 7 girls, 9.1 ± 2.0 years old). Due to the COVID-19 outbreak, we had to cancel additional studies and recruitment was interrupted. This study was approved by the Inria ethical committee. The accompanying parent of each child gave a written informed consent.

2.3   Measures

Children

At the beginning and at the end of the session, the robot acceptance was evaluated for the child with a picture-sorting task (PST) composed of 8 pictures (a baby, a cat, Pepper, a frog, a robotic arm, a movie robot, a computer and a teddy bear) to rank from the most to the less human-like for them, and a social acceptance questionnaire (SAQ) (scaling: 2 = yes, 1 = maybe, 0 = no) with questions such as (1) "would you like to be good friend with a robot who can't see?", (2) "would you like to be good friend with a robot who can't hear well?", (3) "would you play with a robot even if they had special needs?" and (4) "would you be friend with a robot who has special needs?". As reported by [13], the usual tests with Likert scales may not work for younger children or the ones who may be lacking attention. We therefore assumed that these tools may be more appropriate. For the questions used in the SAQ, the authors also explain that robots often have limited interactions regarding automatic speech and language recognition for example and asking children if they would be friends with a robots with "special needs" was originally a way to compare the robots results with human peers with similar limitations. In our case, the SAQ can help us verify if these limitations constitute an issue for accepting robots.

Parents

General acceptance was also evaluated before and after the study for the parent with a combination of four questionnaires to encompass more factors contributing to the robots' acceptance:

- The Almere Model [10] (40 items, 4 points Likert scale), derived from the UTAUT [26] acceptance model which is composed of new components related to the social aspect of assistive agents such as perceived sociability or social presence.
- A technology Anxiety scale from [9,18] (adapted from [21])
- A technological familiarity scale from [9,23].
- The French version of the Attrakdiff, a standardized user experience questionnaire (28 items and 7 points Osgood scale) [15] with 4 subscales: Pragmatic Quality (PQ), Hedonic Quality (subdivided into Hedonic-Stimulation (HQS) and Hedonic-Identification (HQI)), and finally Attractiveness (ATT).

3 Results

Summary of the Results

In a first analysis (See Table 1), it appears that children scores in all groups demonstrated an increased acceptance of robots and an increased anthropomorphism towards Pepper after the interaction with Pepper and the experiment (see Fig. 1). For parents, we observe that acceptance (see Fig. 2) and user experience scores (see Fig. 3) overall decreased after the interaction with Pepper and the experiment, while technology anxiety scores raised for parents of TD children and technology familiarity scores increased.

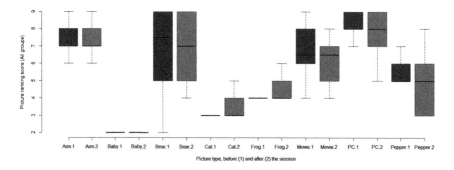

Fig. 1. PST ranks for all the pictures for all children

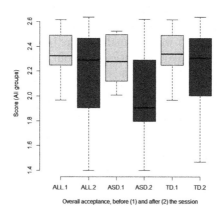

Fig. 2. Overall acceptance scores by parent groups

Effect of the Interaction with Pepper

To explore if the study and the free interaction with Pepper had an effect on our different evaluation scales, we ran paired Wilcoxon tests.

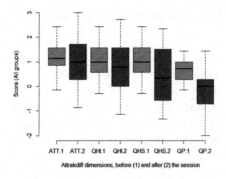

Fig. 3. Attrakdiff scores by dimension for all parents

The Attrakdiff scores (See Table 1) for all parents revealed that pragmatic quality medians changed significantly (p = 0.009, effect size r = 0.714291) as well as the hedonic quality (stimulation) (p = 0.026, r = 0.39). In particular, the items "Predictable-Unpredictable" (p = 0.009, r = 1.99), "Uncontrollable-Manageable" (p = 0.006, r = 1.99), and "Conservative-Innovative" (p = 0.007, r = 1.49), "Boring-Captivating" (p = 0.029, r = 1.50) significantly changed, meaning Pepper appears more unpredictable, uncontrollable, conservative and boring after the study.

Overall acceptance scores didn't significantly change (p = 0.257, r = 0.10), except for the Facilitating conditions (p = 0.007, r = −0.75), Perceived adaptativeness (p = 0.001, r = 0.79) and Perceived usefulness items (p = 0.0006, r = 0.80).

Group Differences
ASD and TD groups scores were compared with Welch t-tests. We observed no significant differences in the two group scores, except for the Hedonic Quality (Identification) scores of the Attrakdiff, after the study. The 5 parents of children with autism (M = −0.37, SD = 0.71) compared to the 13 parents of neurotypical children (M = 0.714, SD = 0.716) demonstrated significantly lower scores, (t(7.35) = 2.89, p = 0.02) indicating that they could generally relate less to Pepper.

4   Discussion and Conclusion

The experiment setup lead to a broad set of results, with the purpose of understanding better how the acceptance of children and their parents with robots is situated, and if the interaction with a robot improves its acceptance.

First of all, all children showed a slightly increased acceptance of robots (from 1,31 to 1,41) and an slightly increased anthropomorphism towards Pepper after the study (from 5,44 on the PST scale on average to 5). However, these differences are not significant. This may be due to the small number of participants (5 in one group and 13 in the other), or simply, the interaction did not change their

Table 1. Summary table of the different questionnaire scores with means(standard deviations)

Questionnaire	Group					
	All (N = 18)		ASD (N = 5)		TD (N = 13)	
	Before	After	Before	After	Before	After
SAQ (robot)	1.31 (0.5)	1.41 (0.67)	1.4 (0.34)	1.5 (0.47)	1.3 (0.7)	1.4 (0.8)
PST (Pepper)	5.44 (1.38)	5 (1.49)	6.2 (2.17)	5 (2.12)	5.15 (0.89)	5 (1.29)
Acceptance	2.29 (0.29)	2.16 (0.39)	2.28 (0.22)	2.00 (0.46)	2.29 (0.29)	2.22 (0.36)
Attrakdiff (PQ)	0.78 (0.86)	−0.07 (1.07)	1.31 (1.04)	−0.6 (1.36)	0.58 (0.73)	0.12 (0.92)
Attrakdiff (QHI)	0.76 (0.65)	0.41 (0.85)	0.97 (0.79)	−0.37 (0.7)	0.69 (0.60)	0.71 (0.71)
Attrakdiff (ATT)	1.30 (0.94)	1.24 (1.26)	1.8 (1.31)	0.85 (1.65)	1.12 (0.73)	1.39 (1.13)
Attrakdiff (QHS)	1.07 (0.83)	0.64 (0.96)	1.34 (0.98)	0.4 (0.80)	0.97 (0.79)	0.74 (1.02)
Technology anxiety	1.66 (0.7)	1.7 (0.6)	1.9 (0.8)	1.7 (0.8)	1.6 (0.7)	1.7 (0.6)
Technology familiarity	4.14 (1.54)	4.29 (1.64)	3.67 (1.73)	3.53 (1.69)	4.3 (1.5)	4.6 (1.6)

perception much. Pepper might be perceived as slightly more acceptable and anthropomorphic after the experiment. As in [13], children tended to place each entity in a reasonable position during the picture sorting task. It is hard to conclude anything for children with ASD, due to the size of the sample.

The use of the SAQ scale had some limitations. As it includes questions about the social acceptance of children with disabilities and robots described as having bugs, children were sometimes hesitant when answering the questions as their parents were present and expecting them to answer socially appropriate responses. A more relevant question would have been to ask the children if they would like to have a Pepper at home, which would perhaps have shown more acceptance of it. This question was sometimes spontaneously asked to the children by the parents or experimenters. As observed during the experiment, the most enthusiastic children generally answered "yes" while the older children did not necessarily see what to do with Pepper. Younger children who were afraid of it did not want it. These observations are valid for typically developing and children with autistic spectrum disorder. Thus, the presence or absence of parents sometimes has an important influence on the answers given by the children, although they have a reassuring presence for some. This is a bias to be taken into account and it is important to be able to adapt further experiments accordingly. As interventions are recommended for children with ASD as early as possible [11], these results tell us that interactions with a robot for younger children have an impact that seems positive on its acceptance for further therapy purposes.

For parents, acceptance and user experience scores overall decreased after the interaction. Pragmatic and Hedonic quality (stimulation) scores decreased significantly which is coherent with the context of the experiment. In particular, the items "Predictable-Unpredictable", "Uncontrollable-Manageable", and "Conservative-Innovative", "Boring-Captivating", significantly changed. Pepper was indeed perceived as more unpredictable, uncontrollable, conservative and boring after the study. Overall acceptance scores did not significantly change, except for the Facilitating conditions, Perceived adaptativeness and Perceived usefulness items. No significant difference was found between group scores of parents of children with ASD and children with TD, except for the Hedonic Quality (Identification) scores. Where parents from children with typical development obtained significantly higher scores after the interaction. For them, technology anxiety scores raised and technology familiarity scores increased while it had the opposite effect for parents of children with ASD. These results are interesting because they seem to show that parents of children with special needs (in this case, parents of children with ASD) have more expectations of and reliance on Pepper which could explain these score differences. Also, Pepper was proposed with its basic and limited interactions (such as waving, saying hello, telling the time, imitating animals, dancing...) which are not representative of a fully-functioning assistive and companion robot. We assume that Peppers' limited abilities may have greatly influenced the results, especially since they are not intended for the assistance of children with special needs, which may explain the lower acceptance and user experience scores for the parents of children with ASD, but also the higher technology anxiety and lower technology familiarity scores. Pepper also presented some start-up delays as well as delays or absence of responses to voice commands, presenting it as a poorly functioning robot and generally disappointing to parents who may have had higher expectations of Pepper. We thus assume that a fully functional, ready to-use robot would have led to different results for parents, especially those of children with ASD. Whether for children or parents, an authority bias must be considered, as it can influence the interactions. A social desirability bias was sometimes observed when children were answering the questionnaires and had their parents watching them. As these first results are interesting, more participants may provide more significant results. Although the parents' questionnaires provided broad and comprehensive information, they took 15 to 20 min to complete before and after the session, which can seem long and tedious for some participants. Open-ended questions might be more appropriate and enjoyable for the participants during the study.

To conclude, it seems that children, in general, show a good acceptance of the studied robot (Pepper robot with its basic interactions), especially if they are younger and less disenchanted with the limited skills of the robot. Parents of children with autistic spectrum disorder have greater expectations of robots that could potentially be assistive ones, as acceptance and user experience has lower scores after the interaction. It is thus likely that effectiveness, usability and utility are of a greater importance for these parents. This study has obviously some limitations but the results remain interesting and give leads for agents acceptance studies with children with or without special needs, with or without their parents.

Acknowledgements. We thank all the children and parents who willingly took part in this study and filled in so many questionnaires.

References

1. van den Berk-Smeekens, I., et al.: Adherence and acceptability of a robot-assisted pivotal response treatment protocol for children with autism spectrum disorder. Sci. Rep. **10**(1), 1–11 (2020)
2. Bishop, L., van Maris, A., Dogramadzi, S., Zook, N.: Social robots: the influence of human and robot characteristics on acceptance. Paladyn J. Behav. Robot. **10**(1), 346–358 (2019)
3. Boccanfuso, L., Scarborough, S., Abramson, R.K., Hall, A.V., Wright, H.H., O'Kane, J.M.: A low-cost socially assistive robot and robot-assisted intervention for children with autism spectrum disorder: field trials and lessons learned. Autonom. Robots **41**(3), 637–655 (2017)
4. Breazeal, C., Harris, P.L., DeSteno, D., Kory Westlund, J.M., Dickens, L., Jeong, S.: Young children treat robots as informants. Topics Cogn. Sci. **8**(2), 481–491 (2016)
5. Davis, F.D.: Perceived usefulness, perceived ease of use, and user acceptance of information technology. MIS Q. 319–340 (1989)
6. De Graaf, M.M., Allouch, S.B.: Exploring influencing variables for the acceptance of social robots. Robot. Autonom. Syst. **61**(12), 1476–1486 (2013)
7. Fridin, M., Angel, H., Azery, S.: Acceptance, interaction, and authority of educational robots: an ethnography study of child-robot interaction. In: IEEE Workshop on Advanced Robotics and Its Social Impacts, California (2011)
8. Fridin, M., Belokopytov, M.: Acceptance of socially assistive humanoid robot by preschool and elementary school teachers. Comput. Hum. Behav. **33**, 23–31 (2014)
9. Goudey, A., Bonnin, G.: Must smart objects look human? study of the impact of anthropomorphism on the acceptance of companion robots. Recherche et Appl. en Mark. (Engl. Ed.) **31**(2), 2–20 (2016)
10. Heerink, M., Kröse, B., Evers, V., Wielinga, B.: Assessing acceptance of assistive social agent technology by older adults: the almere model. Int. J. Soc. Robot. **2**(4), 361–375 (2010)
11. Huijnen, C.A., Lexis, M.A., Jansens, R., de Witte, L.P.: Roles, strengths and challenges of using robots in interventions for children with autism spectrum disorder (ASD). J. Autism Dev. Disord. **49**(1), 11–21 (2019)
12. Huskens, B., Palmen, A., Van der Werff, M., Lourens, T., Barakova, E.: Improving collaborative play between children with autism spectrum disorders and their siblings: the effectiveness of a robot-mediated intervention based on lego® therapy. J. Autism Dev. Disord. **45**(11), 3746–3755 (2015)
13. Kory-Westlund, J.M., Breazeal, C.: Assessing children's perceptions and acceptance of a social robot. In: Proceedings of the 18th ACM International Conference on Interaction Design and Children, pp. 38–50 (2019)
14. Kumazaki, H., et al.: A pilot study for robot appearance preferences among high-functioning individuals with autism spectrum disorder: implications for therapeutic use. PloS One **12**(10), e0186581 (2017)
15. Lallemand, C., Gronier, G.: Méthodes de design UX: 30 méthodes fondamentales pour concevoir et évaluer les systèmes interactifs. Editions Eyrolles (2015)
16. Liu, B., Markopoulos, P., Tetteroo, D.: How anthropomorphism affects user acceptance of a robot trainer in physical rehabilitation. In: HEALTHINF, pp. 30–40 (2019)
17. Liu, K., Tao, D.: The roles of trust, personalization, loss of privacy, and anthropomorphism in public acceptance of smart healthcare services. Comput. Hum. Behav. **127**, 107026 (2022)

18. Meuter, M.L., Bitner, M.J., Ostrom, A.L., Brown, S.W.: Choosing among alternative service delivery modes: an investigation of customer trial of self-service technologies. J. Mark. **69**(2), 61–83 (2005)
19. Nomura, T., Shintani, T., Fujii, K., Hokabe, K.: Experimental investigation of relationships between anxiety, negative attitudes, and allowable distance of robots. In: Proceedings of the 2nd IASTED International Conference on Human Computer Interaction, Chamonix, France. ACTA Press, pp. 13–18. Citeseer (2007)
20. Oros, M., Nikolić, M., Borovac, B., Jerković, I.: Children's preference of appearance and parents' attitudes towards assistive robots. In: 2014 IEEE-RAS International Conference on Humanoid Robots, pp. 360–365. IEEE (2014)
21. Raub, A.C.: Correlates of Computer Anxiety in College Students (1981)
22. Ricks, D.J., Colton, M.B.: Trends and considerations in robot-assisted autism therapy. In: 2010 IEEE International Conference on Robotics and Automation (ICRA), pp. 4354–4359. IEEE (2010)
23. Thompson, D.V., Hamilton, R.W., Rust, R.T.: Feature fatigue: when product capabilities become too much of a good thing. J. Mark. Res. **42**(4), 431–442 (2005)
24. Troshani, I., Rao Hill, S., Sherman, C., Arthur, D.: Do we trust in AI? role of anthropomorphism and intelligence. J. Comput. Inf. Syst. **61**(5), 481–491 (2021)
25. Tung, F.W.: Child perception of humanoid robot appearance and behavior. Int. J. Hum.-Comput. Interact. **32**(6), 493–502 (2016)
26. Venkatesh, V., Morris, M.G., Davis, G.B., Davis, F.D.: User acceptance of information technology: toward a unified view. MIS Q. 425–478 (2003)
27. Westlund, J.M.K., Martinez, M., Archie, M., Das, M., Breazeal, C.: Effects of framing a robot as a social agent or as a machine on children's social behavior. In: 2016 25th IEEE International Symposium on Robot and Human Interactive Communication (RO-MAN), pp. 688–693. IEEE (2016)

Living with *Haru4Kids*: Child and Parent Perceptions of a Co-Habitation Robot for Children

Leigh Levinson[1]([⊠]) [iD], Gonzalo A. Garcia[2] [iD], Guillermo Perez[2] [iD],
Gloria Alvarez-Benito[4] [iD], J. Gabriel Amores[4] [iD], Mario Castaño-Ocaña[2] [iD],
Manuel Castro-Malet[2] [iD], Randy Gomez[3] [iD], and Selma Šabanović[1] [iD]

[1] Indiana University Bloomington, Bloomington, IN 47401, USA
lmlevins@iu.edu
[2] 4i Intelligent Insights, Seville, Spain
[3] Honda Research Institute Japan, Wako, Japan
[4] Universidad de Sevilla, Sevilla, Spain

Abstract. *Haru4Kids* (H4K) is an app-based robot designed to co-habitate with children in their home. Seven families interacted with H4K for about two weeks each, and expressed their general feedback on the platform and their preferred activities with it, as well as their comfort levels with keeping H4K in different spaces of the home. Pre- and Post-interviews with at least one parent and all participating children allowed us to gauge familial comfort with sharing different kinds of information with the platform, and to assess how their experiences living with the robot changed their comfort levels. Children's most preferred robot jokes and requested more diverse educational and entertainment activities. Their comfort sharing information changed after cohabitation, though they were most risk averse to sharing their conversations with others and information generally with teachers and robot creators. Parents also thought children would be more open to sharing with the robot than children actually were. Our work suggests co-habitation robots need to incorporate rich narrative-based activities and a wide variety of content to keep children's attention over time. Child-centered, robotic design must incorporate children's feedback, as parents may not be aware of children's preferences.

Keywords: In-home social robotics · Long-term interactions · Information sharing

1 Introduction

Robots are becoming increasingly accessible to children and impacting many aspects of their lives, including education [17] and therapy [4]. However, research on child-robot interaction often occurs in controlled settings, in part due to

This work has been supported by *Honda Research Institute*.

a lack of robust robotic platforms that can be studied *in the wild* without researcher supervision. Understanding children's perceptions of a social robot in their dynamic, everyday environment is necessary to develop context-appropriate technologies. This study, inspired by UNICEF's *Policy Guidance on AI for children*, aims at understanding children's voluntary use and perception of child-centered AI and robotics in the natural context of the home [14].

This work builds on previous studies which introduced a table-top social robot *Haru* to children and explored how to align its design with UNICEF's Policy Guidance, particularly recognizing children's concerns about privacy when engaging with robots [6]. Since the Haru prototype is still not robust enough for extended home use, here we introduce *Haru4Kids* (H4K), a platform that integrates an app-based avatar of Haru with a table-top rotating stand. H4K was designed to test the feasibility of an in-home social robot for children's use.

We deployed H4K in the homes of seven families as a pilot study with the following research goals in mind: (1) to identify the *patterns of children's free use of the robot* over an extended period of time (2 weeks), and (2) to explore the *perceptions of children and caregivers regarding the robot*. This work therefore starts to uncover how a social robot can fit into the dynamics of home life.

2 Related Work: Long-Term Adoption of Social Robot Companions

A *co-habitating* robot must establish companionship and foster long-term interactions with children and their families. What defines an interaction as *long-term* depends on the quantity and quality of interactions, the variety of capabilities, the scope of the interaction [1], and the novelty effect has worn off [11].

In terms of what makes a *fulfilling* interaction, children may report hedonic, or pleasurable, reasons for using a robot along with more utilitarian beliefs, such as to study and learn with it [8]. Fulfillment can also rely on interesting activities, robot commentary, and immediacy in routines [5]. However, factors that lead to fulfilling interactions can vary depending on children's individual needs [5]. Overall, creating a wide variety of developmentally-appropriate activities can support engaging and long-term child-robot interactions.

Perception of embodied social presence can also affect children's adoption of social robotic companions [12], and has been found to produce more enjoyable interactions than a virtual agent [16]. Furthermore, expressive motion can influence user perceptions of a robot's emotions; even a few degrees of freedom can lead users to connect the motion trajectory, intention, and communication of the agent [10]. Our addition of a rotating-tabletop stand elevates the sense of embodiment and social presence of H4K and differentiates our platform from voice-activated assistants like Alexa and other onscreen social agents.

3   Methods

3.1   Haru4Kids Platform

The H4K platform consists of a Haru avatar displayed on an iPad supported by a rotating stand (Fig. 1a) which spoke using Spanish Text-To-Speech. The app works on the iPad and uses several Apple-specific libraries. At the highest level of abstraction, the application is divided into seven main modules: User Interface, Conversation Manager, Vision Manager, Central Controller, Settings Manager, Logging, and Stand Manager (Fig. 1b). In addition, the Conversation Manager makes use of some services from the *Cloud*. The Central Controller acts as the coordinator of the app behavior, interacting with other modules and accessing the cloud as needed.

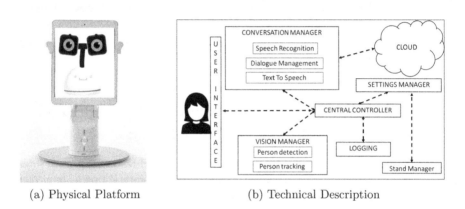

(a) Physical Platform   (b) Technical Description

Fig. 1. *Haru4Kids*: iPad supported by rotating-tabletop stand and high-level technical description of the system

3.2   Participants

In total, seven families from the South of Spain co-habitated with the robot for two weeks. Consent was collected from caregivers and written assent was collected from children ages 7 or older. Across the participating families, Haru engaged with 14 children ($n_{male} = 9$) between the ages of 6 and 13 ($\mu_{age} = 9.6$). One family had an only child, while the other six had at least two children. Three families had two-parent households where pairs of parents were interviewed together. In the other four, either single mothers or where parents had shared custody, only the mothers were interviewed (7 caregiver interviews total). Accounting for the periods of time when children were away from the home, such as on vacation or living in multiple households, the robot was in the home for up to an average of 20 days ($\sigma = 5.9$, max $= 27$).

3.3   Data Collection Instruments

To understand caregiver and child experiences and concerns with a co-habitating robot, we utilized pre- and post- interviews and user logs from the app.

Interviews: The interviews blended closed and open questions to collect user's feedback about Haru and understand their comfort with sharing information with and through the robot. In a 30 min pre-interview, researchers asked children about their first impressions and expectations for interactions with the robot, taking into account that some of the children had experience with the platform in a previous pilot study (e.g. *"What are you most excited to try with Haru?"*). All family members were all asked to express their comfort levels with keeping Haru in different spaces of the home, (e.g., *"On a scale from 1 to 7, how comfortable are you keeping Haru in your kitchen?"*). These questions were adapted to each family's space by using an apartment floor plan to visualize the placement of the robot. All members were asked 2 open questions about the space they were most and least comfortable keeping Haru. We also asked one multiple-item question about information sharing with a social robot (e.g. *"What kind of information would you feel comfortable showing or telling with a robot?"*) and 5 multi-item questions about sharing information with different third parties through the robot (e.g. *"What information would you feel comfortable having the robot share with your teacher?"*). All 12 information items and 5 third parties are referenced in Table 1. Parents were asked about their own comfort with sharing information with the robot, as well as their comfort with their child interacting and sharing information with the robot and third parties (total of 7 closed, information sharing questions with 12 items each).

At the end of the trial period, a researcher returned and conducted a 30–45 min post-interview with family members. Adults were presented with 5 likert-style questions about keeping Haru in the home, then 5 open questions about future activities, their favorite and least favorite aspects of the co-habitation, and their impression of their children's favorite and least favorite activities. Children were asked 8 likert-style questions utilizing emoji's rather than just numbers to identify their excitement about certain activities with Haru. They were also asked 3 open questions to further explore what they enjoyed, didn't enjoy, or would like Haru to do in the future. As a control, we wanted to see whether the children were perceiving the platform as more than just an on-screen app. Therefore, we asked each participating child to draw Haru from memory. Following these questions, all family members were given the opportunity to answer the same comfort level questions about their home (room-specific) and about information sharing (same 6 or 7 questions for children and adults respectfully).

User Logs: App logs recorded through **Cloudwatch** (from *AWS Cloud*) were used to register the main events (all logins and all interactions with the H4K platform) as they occurred during the execution of the application. No personal information (e.g., images or audio) were stored on the cloud, respecting the privacy of the children and their families. A detailed analysis of these logs is out of scope of this paper and will be conducted as part of future work.

3.4 *Haru4Kids* In-home Setup and Activities

Prior to H4K placement, the researcher recorded the pre-interview with at least one caregiver and with each child. Interviews were conducted with parents and children independently to allow them to provide their own feedback. Then, researchers set up the platform in a location specified by the parents. Families were given an explanation of H4K's capabilities, shown how to quit the H4K, and allowed to enable cloud logging which by default was off. All image and audio were recorded locally on the iPad. Researchers asked the children to engage with the robot a few times a week, but parents were asked to help motivate the children if they were not engaging with H4K on their own.

Once H4K was deployed, the children were greeted with small talk by the robot at the beginning of every interaction. Then, the children could directly ask for an activity, were prompted to play an activity, or the robot chose one at random. This version of H4K features the following is the list of activities:

- *Storytelling*: Once the user selects a story, or H4K randomly chooses one of the seven available, Haru tells the story while displaying related illustrations.
- *Gusano Loco ("Crazy Worms")*: H4K asks the user to suggest a word from within different categories (*e.g.*, colors, shapes, school subjects). After acquiring a list of words, H4K uses them to fill in missing words of an incomplete story and recites the humorous resulting narrative out loud.
- *Detective*: A list of words is given. Within the list there is a word that does not match the others; for example: "apple, *chair*, banana, peach". The user has to identify which word does not match the rest.
- *Would you rather ...?*: H4K presents two silly options from which the user chooses which option they prefer (*e.g.*, "Would you rather have three eyes or two noses?"). Then, H4K makes a comment related to their choice.
- *Jokes*: H4K shares three child-friendly jokes in a row.

4 Results

4.1 Takeaways from the Children

General Feedback: All children, regardless of previous exposure to a prototype, had high initial expectations for the robot's capabilities, such as user recognition, robust dialogues, and legs for playing sports. Of all activities, children interacted with jokes the most (Fig. 2a). This aligned with children's pre-interview answers when asked what they were most excited to try (6 specifically mentioned jokes, 5 mentioned games). Their least favorite part was often the stories (mentioned by 6 participants) with children reporting that the content was repetitive and limited, yet storytelling was the second most frequently started activity across families (Fig. 2a). Of all storytelling, 98.5% of stories were chosen at random by H4K rather than requested by the child. Beyond limited content, the biggest reason shared by children for lack of use was disappointment that H4K did not always

Table 1. Child Comfort with Sharing Information. ↓= number of children who changed to discomfort in the post-interview. ↑= number of children who changed to comfort in the post-interview. White = 100% Comfort, Dark Purple = ≥50% comfortable, Light Orange = < 50% comfortable

Info Category	General	Third Parties				
		Teacher	Friends	Siblings/ Cousins	Parents	Robot Creators
Third Party		74%	80%	83%	86%	40%
School Grades	57% ↓3	100%	50%	50%	50%	21% ↓3
Hobbies	100%	79% ↓1	100%	93% ↓1	86% ↓1	86%
Conversations with Others	14% ↓2	7% ↑1	14% ↓1↑1	14% ↓3↑1	29% ↓3↑1	14% ↓1
Name	100%	100%	100%	100%	100%	42% ↓3
Birthday	86% ↓2	93% ↓1	100%	100%	100%	21% ↓5
Pets	100%	93%	100%	100%	100%	71% ↓1
Family Info	43% ↓1	35% ↓1	50% ↓1	100%	93% ↓1	14% ↓2↑1
Friend's Info	64% ↓3	93% ↓1	100%	50% ↓3	79% ↓2	42% ↓4
Location	43% ↓3	36% ↓1	76% ↓1	100%	100%	21%
Voice Recognition	100%	100%	100%	100%	100%	71% ↓4
Face Recognition	93%	100%	100%	100%	100%	42% ↓3
Images of family	57% ↓2	42% ↓3	57% ↓3↑1	83% ↓1	93% ↓1	21% ↓2

understand what they said. On average, families used H4K less throughout the second half of the trial period as is represented by the number of recorded verbal interactions expressed by H4K or the user (See Fig. 2b).

When asked, children expressed interest in playing with Haru again in their home ($\mu = 6.14$ (7-point likert scale)). Diverse, interactive activities they suggested for the future included a "Freeze Dance" game, or a board-game like "3-in-a-row." Children were positive about adding learning components, or a "funny way to study" with Haru, such as receiving math help ($\mu = 5.8$ (7-point likert scale)) and language learning ($\mu = 6.4$ (7-point likert scale)). Many also wanted Haru to be a more holistic companion (e.g. personal alarms to help keep track of time, give advice/a book recommendation, provide recipes for cooking).

In their drawings of Haru from memory, five children drew just the avatar of Haru, one drew the avatar and iPad, one drew just the iPad stand, one drew the stand and the iPad, and six children drew Haru as the integrated stand, iPad and avatar. Therefore, while most interpreted H4K as a holistic platform, there were some children who focused on the avatar alone.

Information Sharing: The pre- and post- interview allowed us to assess if the children's comfort with sharing information with a social robot changed after the interactions (Table 1). A paired t-test conducted on the score out of 72 of their comforts, determined that there was a significant difference before and after the cohabitation period ($t = 5.303$, $p < 0.001$). The following discusses more specific percentages: only 14% of children felt comfortable sharing their conversations

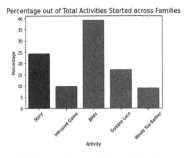

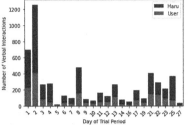

(a) Breakdown of Activity Use   (b) Overall Number of Verbal Interactions

Fig. 2. Frequency of activities & Verbal Interactions between H4K and the User

with others with a robot and only 42% of children felt comfortable sharing their location or family information with a robot. The information they felt most comfortable sharing were their name, their pets, and their voice (100%). The third party they felt less comfortable sharing with and were most likely to change their comfort level about were robot creators. See Table 1 for the percentage of children who felt comfortable sharing information with different third parties.

4.2 Adult and Familial Takeaways

General Feedback: Notable benefits mentioned by parents during the post-interview included that their children were spending less time watching TV, were collaboratively playing with H4K, and took on a sense of responsibility when establishing sibling turn-taking. However, some parents said it was a burden to force children to interact with H4K by the end. Others mentioned concern that they were going to break the robot or that it was just another device to keep track of. All parents and most children (71%) felt most comfortable keeping the robot in the living room and most uncomfortable with the idea of keeping Haru in a bathroom. Furthermore, parents were usually able to identify their children's favorite and least favorite activities with H4K.

Information Sharing: Like their children, adults felt least comfortable sharing conversations with others through Haru (29%). They felt most comfortable sharing their hobbies, birthday, pet information, and friend's information (all 100%) and their voice (86%). In terms of third parties, adults felt most comfortable with their child sharing information with themselves, *the parents* (98%), and the child's siblings or cousins (89%). They were least comfortable with the child sharing information with the child's teacher (69%) and the robot creators (67%). However, parents felt comfortable with their children sharing more categories with robots than children were willing to share themselves. Additionally, a paired t-test of the adult's pre- and post-interview responses about information sharing was not significant (t = 1.387, p = 0.22). Therefore, children were more likely than parents to change their answers post interaction than their caregivers.

5   Discussion

Our study shows that children were open to using a co-habitation robot, though the average number of verbal interactions decreased from the first through the second week. However, the second week of the trial also coincided with the first week of summer vacation, which introduced different family routines and activities. In a future analysis, we will look more closely at sustained use to understand more about how the user engaged throughout each activity.

There are many reasons a family may accept, diminish use, or reject a robot after a co-habitation period of two weeks, including disenchantment, restrictions, and problems with the technology [7]. The expectancy confirmation model [3] can help explain children's diminished satisfaction and thus disenchantment when initially high expectations are not met. Beyond disenchantment, children's lack of interest in the stories may have been related to their relevance. The appropriate age was set to the age of family's youngest child, so older children's interest may have been diminished. Additionally, aspects of perception such as perceived competence can stabilize after the first two minutes and can affect long-term attitudes [15] increasing the stakes of first impressions which can be affected by the robot's aesthetics (e.g. appearance, voice), not just content.

In future deployments, it will be important to mitigate expectations by providing children with transparency statements and adaptable content that can tailor to multiple users' ages and interests. We are also looking forward to targeting different populations of children who suffer from long-term illness. Beyond being educational and fun for typically-developing children, those with long-term illness can benefit from cognitive tasks that can improve their quality of life [2].

In relation to privacy, there is limited research on children's concerns surrounding biometric data such as *voiceprints*. However, research identifies that consumers are comfortable with, yet less aware that, they are using biometrics [9]. Some think people may not consider *giving* their voice to the technology the same as giving it to an organization [9]. This may support why a high percentage of children were still willing to share their voices with the robot creator (71%). With the expected increase in use of biometric data, child-centered researchers should be transparent about how children's data are used in the technology. Additionally, it is known that current child speech recognition is less robust than adult speech recognition [13]. Given children's disappointment when not understood by the robot and simultaneous comfort with being recognized by their voice, researchers should prioritize developing platforms with robust natural language processing that can disambiguate child speech.

Finally, our results reveal that children's preferences for sharing information are not so different from those of their parents. This supports research that identifies how children are increasingly aware of privacy risks, such as cyber risks online [18]. Furthermore, while some children could gain a false sense of security from increased familiarity with a robot platform [18], our child participants' comforts were more malleable and conservative after the interaction. This promises that more studies with cohabitation will help researchers understand children's comfort levels after first-hand experience with a robot. It is also imperative to continue developing education for children surrounding personal information privacy with AI so they can make informed decisions.

6   Conclusion

This study reveals that children are excited about the possibilities of a co-habitating robot and may change their comfort with sharing information with the robot and other third parties over time. Overall, Haru4Kids was able to facilitate long-term, productive interactions with children. Our study represents one of few that integrates the experiences of children and their parents throughout a period of co-habitation with a robot. In reflecting on family member feedback, it is important to remember that parents and children are both stakeholders in the adoption of social robots in the home, and taking both of their feedback into consideration is necessary for developing a child-centered robot that will fit into a family context. With this study as a foundation, we are planning to expand the content and length of co-habitation and the number of families involved across countries to compare how the platform performs cross-culturally.

Acknowledgment. We would like to thank all the participating families and Sol Benitez Casaccia for helping with the translations throughout the process. Authors thank the following persons for their technical essential contributions: Marta López, Ricardo Durán, Iván Delgado, José Andrés Millán, and Douwe Gelling. We would also like to thank Honda Research Institute for supporting this initiative.

References

1. Ahmad, M.I., Mubin, O., Orlando, J.: Adaptive social robot for sustaining social engagement during long-term children-robot interaction. Int. J. Hum.-Comput. Interact. **33**(12), 943–962 (2017). https://doi.org/10.1080/10447318.2017.1300750
2. Alvarez-Benito, G., Suarez, C., Marquez, C.: Hello I am a robot and my name is Curro: Design. Development and Evaluation of a robot solution for Linguistic. Cogn. Phys. Rehab. Children Cancer Treat. (2019)
3. Bhattacherjee, A.: Understanding information systems continuance: an expectation-confirmation model. MIS Quarterly **25**(3), 351–370 (2001). https://doi.org/10.2307/3250921
4. Cabibihan, J.-J., Javed, H., Ang, M., Aljunied, S.M.: Why Robots? A Survey on the Roles and Benefits of Social Robots in the Therapy of Children with Autism. Int. J. Soc. Robot. **5**(4), 593–618 (2013). https://doi.org/10.1007/s12369-013-0202-2
5. Cagiltay, B., White, N., Ibtasar, R., Mutlu, B., Michaelis, J.: Understanding Factors that Shape Children's Long Term Engagement with an In-Home Learning Companion Robot (May 2022)
6. Charisi, V., Imai, T., Rinta, T., Nakhayenze, J.M., Gomez, R.: Exploring the concept of fairness in everyday, imaginary and robot scenarios: a cross-cultural study with children in Japan and Uganda. In: Interaction Design and Children, IDC 2021, pp. 532–536. Association for Computing Machinery, New York (June 2021). https://doi.org/10.1145/3459990.3465184

7. De Graaf, M., Allouch, S.B., Van Diik, J.: Why do they refuse to use my robot?: reasons for non-use derived from a long-term home study. In: 2017 12th ACM/IEEE International Conference on Human-Robot Interaction, HRI, pp. 224–233 (March 2017)

8. De Jong, C., Peter, J., Kühne, R., Van Straten, C., Barco, A.: exploring children's beliefs for adoption or rejection of domestic social robots. In: 2021 30th IEEE International Conference on Robot & Human Interactive Communication (RO-MAN), pp. 598–603 (August 2021). https://doi.org/10.1109/RO-MAN50785.2021.9515438

9. German, R.L., Barber, S.K.: Consumer attitudes about biometric authentication (2018)

10. Knight, H., Simmons, R.: Expressive motion with x, y and theta: Laban Effort Features for mobile robots. In: The 23rd IEEE International Symposium on Robot and Human Interactive Communication, pp. 267–273 (August 2014). https://doi.org/10.1109/ROMAN.2014.6926264

11. Leite, I., Martinho, C., Paiva, A.: Social robots for long-term interaction: a survey. Int. J. Soc. Robot. 5(2), 291–308 (2013). https://doi.org/10.1007/s12369-013-0178-y

12. Leite, I., Martinho, C., Pereira, A., Paiva, A.: As time goes by: Long-term evaluation of social presence in robotic companions. In: RO-MAN 2009 - The 18th IEEE International Symposium on Robot and Human Interactive Communication, pp. 669–674. IEEE, Toyama (September 2009). https://doi.org/10.1109/ROMAN.2009.5326256

13. Liu, W., Li, J., Lee, T.: An Investigation on Applying Acoustic Feature Conversion to ASR of Adult and Child Speech (May 2022). https://doi.org/10.48550/arXiv.2205.12477

14. Office of Global Insight and Policy: Pilot testing 'Policy Guidance on AI for Children' Case studies — Gathering real experiences from the field. http://www.unicef.org/globalinsight/policy-guidance-ai-children-pilot-testing-and-case-studies

15. Paetzel, M., Perugia, G., Castellano, G.: The persistence of first impressions: the effect of repeated interactions on the perception of a social robot. In: Proceedings of the 2020 ACM/IEEE International Conference on Human-Robot Interaction, pp. 73–82. Association for Computing Machinery, New York (March 2020)

16. Pereira, A., Martinho, C., Leite, I., Paiva, A.: iCat, the chess player: the influence of embodiment in the enjoyment of a game (Short Paper). Proceedings of the 7th International Joint Conference On Autonomous Agents And Multiagent Systems, vol. 3, pp. 1253–1256 (May 2008)

17. Toh, L.P.E., Causo, A., Tzuo, P.W., Chen, I.M., Yeo, S.H.: A review on the use of robots in education and young children. J. Educ. Technol. Soc. 19(2), 148–163 (2016)

18. Zhao, J., et al.: 'I make up a silly name': understanding children's perception of privacy risks online. In: Proceedings of the 2019 CHI Conference on Human Factors in Computing Systems, pp. 1–13. ACM, Glasgow (May 2019). https://doi.org/10.1145/3290605.3300336

Towards Developing Adaptive Robot Controllers for Children with Upper Limb Impairments - Initial Data Collection and Analysis

Melanie Jouaiti[1]([✉]), Negin Azizi[1], Steven Lawrence[2], and Kerstin Dautenhahn[1]

[1] Electrical and Computer Engineering Department, University of Waterloo,
200 University Ave, N2L3G1 Waterloo, ON, Canada
{mjouaiti,negin.azizi,kerstin.dautenhahn}@uwaterloo.ca
[2] David R. Cheriton School of Computer Science, University of Waterloo,
200 University Ave, N2L3G1 Waterloo, ON, Canada
s7lawren@uwaterloo.ca

Abstract. Between 2% to 5% of children are affected by Development Coordination Disorders in Canada and have been diagnosed with upper limb impairments, which affect their daily life by reducing their autonomy. The vast diversity of motor impairments and their severity make adaptive solutions imperative when children use a joystick. However, currently those joystick need to be manually tuned and there exists no off-the-shelf affordable adaptive joystick that those children could use to play computer games. The long term of our project is to develop such a joystick. The first step towards that goal consists in collecting joystick data from children with upper limb impairments. In this paper, children with upper limb impairments played a computer game where they navigated a simulated robot through a maze. We analyzed their joystick data and observed a great heterogeneity and variability in the data which made it difficult for the classifier we trained to distinguish between them. This highlights challenges for machine learning techniques that would require fine granularity in terms of the statistical features of each joystick axis as well as temporal variation. These results provide crucial insights for the future development of adaptive robot controllers to support robot-assisted play for children with upper limb challenges.

Keywords: Upper limb impairments · Assistive technology · Adaptive controllers

1 Introduction

Between 2% to 5% of children are affected by Development Coordination Disorders in Canada [1] and have been diagnosed with upper limb impairments, which affect their daily life by reducing their autonomy. Our research focuses on

F. Cavallo et al. (Eds.): ICSR 2022, LNAI 13818, pp. 64–73, 2022.
https://doi.org/10.1007/978-3-031-24670-8_7

children with upper limb impairments and especially on, but not restricted to, cerebral palsy (CP).

Besides, children with upper limb impairments face several types of barriers when it comes to play, including the lack of appropriate equipment. Indeed, for example, there exists no off-the shelf solution in terms of joystick controller that can compensate movement distortion for this population.

As Palisano et al. mentioned, there is great degree of individual variation in upper limb development and abilities, mirroring the large variety of motor and cognitive impairments present in CP and the different levels of severity [13]. Different works in movement or kinematics analysis reported on different aspects of movement characteristics. In general, children with CP display slowness of movement and muscular weakness [14]. There is also, often, a lack of appropriate force control which leads to goal-directed movements often undershooting or overshooting their target [3,4]. Movement variability is also higher in individuals with CP with lower signal-to-noise ratio and higher jerk [15]. Finally, a higher proximal movement drift is usually associated with increased muscle weakness and a distal drift is correlated with increased muscle weakness and tone [11].

For those children, motor impairments can be part of progressive disorders, so despite regular therapy, progress remains fleeting. Individuals affected, therefore consistently face barriers to entertainment opportunities, as off-the-shelf inclusive technology is lacking. In our work, we endeavour to bridge that gap by developing an adaptive joystick controller that can compensate for individual deficits, as well as monitor movement statistics to determine if re-calibration is necessary. These difficulties impair the use of joysticks for games, thus creating barriers to enjoyment and play experience, but also impair the control of devices, such as power-wheelchair. Power wheelchairs already include a compensation mechanism where the user's characteristics are hard-coded[1] and therefore need to be regularly and manually re-calibrated to take progress or regression into account [6]. Those systems are therefore very expensive and there is no affordable off-the-shelf solution for this demographics.

Moreover, play is especially important in the context of therapy as it allows to increase motivation and engagement. In the upper limb rehabilitation literature, few studies use robots that are "social" and make the interaction with the robot an integral part of the therapy. One study [17] used the CosmoBot robot. The children could trigger a robot reaction when the required gesture was performed correctly. Another one [7], designed a Pacman-like game with small graspable mobile robots. Tasevski et al. designed a robot meant to address the motivation issues children face [16]. They reported that their robot facilitated non-verbal communication and gestures, but also verbal production. Fridin et al. reported increased motivation of children with CP and a good involvement in the exercises when using the Nao robot to carry out repetitive training, provide feedback and adapt the exercises based on performance [5]. Calderita et al. used the Ursus

---

[1] https://www.albertahealthservices.ca/assets/hospitals/grh/grh-programs-and-services-i-can-centre-resources-maximizing-use-of-standard-power-wheelchair-joystick.pdf.

robot which adapted the exercises to each participant, while monitoring and learning from the interaction thanks to a novel cognitive architecture [2]. They reported increased collaborative behaviours from the children interacting with the robot.

The over-arching goal of this work is two-fold: Developing an adaptive robot joystick controller that can compensate for individual motor impairments, such as drift, force asymmetry and movement variability, and that can also continuously adapt over time to support the user's skills, as well as using this adaptive controller to enhance the MyJay robot as a robotic play mediator [10]. The first step in this project involved collecting data from healthy participants which we carried out in a separate study, results can be found in [8]. The second step, which we report on this paper, focuses on collecting data from children with upper limb impairments, so that we can identify which adaptations would be suitable and necessary. To do so, we designed a maze navigation computer game, where the children could navigate a virtual robot, using the same commands that our MyJay robot will require in future studies. To our knowledge no data sets exist in the context of our specific target population and envisaged application. We therefore do not have any research questions or hypotheses related to this study. Note, due to COVID-19 restrictions we were not able to run experiments using the physical MyJay robot and thus developed a virtual maze game which could be used more easily in the off-campus premises where the study took place.

2   Material and Methods

2.1   Participants

Children were recruited from an outpatient rehabilitation center in Ontario, Canada. Five children (C0-C4) took part in the study (See Table 1).

Our first participant had type I Spinal muscular atrophy, which is a genetic neuromuscular disease that causes muscles to become weak and atrophied. Affected patients lose a specific type of nerve cell (motor neurons) in the spinal cord that control muscle movement. The second participant had chromosome deletion, which can affect many parts of the body, including weak muscle tone (hypotonia), mild to severe intellectual disability; delayed development of motor skills, such as sitting and walking; and behavioral problems. The next two participants had cerebral palsy (CP). CP is the most common movement disorder in children with a prevalence ranging between 1 and 4 per 1,000 live births across the world [12]. According to the Centers for Disease Control and Prevention (CDC) in the US, 1 in 345 children has been diagnosed with CP[2]. The term CP describes a group of motor impairments and is associated with lesions in areas of the brain that manage movement control, balance and posture. CP occurs when that part of the brain does not develop as it should congenitally (antepartum), or when it is damaged during birth (intrapartum) or post-natally (postpartum). Finally, our last participant was diagnosed with ataxia-telangiectasia, which is

---

[2] https://www.cdc.gov/ncbddd/cp/data.html.

a rare inherited condition that affects the nervous system, the immune system and other body systems. It is characterized by: ataxia (lack of coordination) due to a defect in the cerebellum, oculomotor apraxia, Choreoathetosis (abnormal movements such as involuntary jerky movements of the arms, legs and face along with slow, writhing movements of the hands, feet and other body parts), etc.

2.2   Study Overview

In this study, the child started by pushing the joystick in each of four directions (reporting on this baseline data is out of the scope of this paper). Next, the child controlled a robot navigating a maze in a computer game, using an adaptive XBox controller with a custom joystick. There were 5 levels of difficulty. Each child started with level 1 as a warm up and was then free to decide which level to play (they could skip levels, or play the same level multiple times) and to stop whenever they wanted. The parent was also instructed to let us know if they could see that the child was getting fatigued, in which case the study was stopped. There was no pressure or expectations for them to complete all the levels. Each child afterwards got a small gift (monetary value $< 5C\$$ to thank them for their participation). The study took place at the premises of an organization which specifically provides services for children with disabilities. This study was approved by the University of Waterloo Human Research Ethics Board.

Table 1. Overview of 5 children who participated in the study

id	Age	Gender	Medical diagnostic	Levels played
C0	4	M	Spinal muscular atrophy type I	1, 2
C1	9	F	Chromosone deletion	1
C2	17	M	Cerebral palsy	1, 2
C3	12	M	Cerebral palsy	1, 2, 3
C4	7	M	Ataxia-telangiectasia	1, 2, 3, 1, 4, 5

2.3   Iterative Design

Due to the difficulty in recruiting children with motor impairments, we could not test the system with our target population beforehand and we therefore carried out an iterative design, taking participants' feedback into account.

Participant 0 had difficulties grasping the joystick, as it was too thin for him and too hard to push. He had had a busy day and as he was very tired, we ended the session shortly after starting level 2.

For participants 1 and 2, the robot's speed was too fast and the joystick was too sensitive to their drift. We then modified the game, so that the robot can either only rotate or only move forward/backward and is not able to do both at the same time. Those two participants got frustrated with the speed and the high sensitivity and were not interested in playing after completing levels 1 and 2, respectively.

For the third participant, the speed was still a little too fast. He had problems grasping the joystick as well. But he enjoyed the game and requested to stop after level 3. The motion speed which was too high for this particular participant caused him to often overshoot his goal, which in turn, lead to an increased completion time (See Fig. 2).

For our fourth participant, the speed was too slow in the first two levels. This participant played all the levels and even played the warm-up level twice. After this participant, we modified the game, so that the children can freely modify the speed of the robot, by pressing the XBox buttons.

Table 2. Number of joystick commands required by each child to complete each level. (U) indicates an unfinished level

id	Level 1	Level 2	Level 3	Level 4	Level 5
C0	235575	363390 (U)			
C1	838606				
C2	547957	3255893			
C3	537189	804069	253791		
C4	218035	706262	394729	289414	330635 (U)
	202687				

Fig. 1. The five levels of difficulty of the maze game and a picture of the physical MyJay robot

2.4   Materials

Joystick. We employed an adaptive XBox controller linked to a custom joystick. The XBox controller has two big control buttons.

Maze Game. The maze game was programmed with PyGame. It was designed so that the levels would increase in complexity. For each game, the goal was to navigate the robot to reach the treasure. Once reached, a congratulatory message was displayed and the game returned to the level selection page.

3   Results

3.1   Maze Navigation

Some children were sometimes confused between rotating and going forward and the rotating speed was too high for them, which lead to some overshooting the intended goal and some back and forth to put the robot in the correct orientation. This is especially visible for child 3 (in red on the maze).

Fig. 2. Maze navigation trajectories for each child (child 0: green, child 1: blue, child 2: child 3: pink child 4: yellow (Color figure online)

3.2   Exploratory Analysis of Joystick Commands

We define the range as the 90th percentile in each of the four joystick directions. We define the dispersion value as the number of commands outside the expected command range ($|x| < 0.1$ & $|y| < 0.1$) divided by the total number of commands for each joystick quadrant. To calculate the drift, we transform the x,y

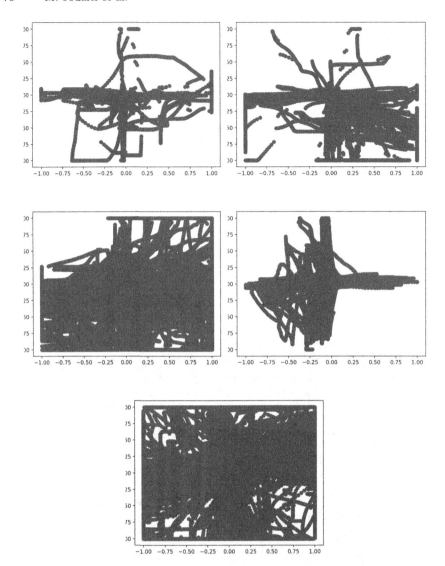

Fig. 3. Player profile for our 5 participants. On the x axis, the left/right command of the joystick is shown; The y axis shows the forward/backward command of the joystick

coordinates to polar coordinates and compute the peak of the theta histogram around 0, $\frac{\pi}{2}$, $\frac{-\pi}{2}$ and $2 \cdot \pi$, this gives us the drift of the four joystick directions. Table 3 gives an overview of those extracted features for each child. It is noticeable that theses values vary a lot from one child to the next and also that impairments affect the four joystick directions differently. For example, child 3 has high dispersion in the third and fourth quadrant of the joystick but very low in the second one and no dispersion in the first one.

Table 3. Extracted joystick characteristics for each child. Drift in radians, min/max value: –0.79/0.79; Dispersion min/max values: 0/1; Range min/max values: –1/1; Variance min/max values: 0/1.

Child id	C0	C1	C2	C3	C4
range F/B	0.085–0.76	0.43–0.85	0.68–1.0	0.93–0.75	0.95–1.0
range L/R	0.73–0.52	1.0–1.0	1.0 –1.0	0.81–0.88	1.0–1.0
var F/B	0.08	0.11	0.16	0.15	0.22
var L/R	0.09	0.25	0.32	0.19	0.30
drift F	–0.01	0	-0.4	0	0.1
drift B	–0.2	–0.1	–0.1	0.1	–0.1
drift L	–0.1	–0.1	-0.1	–0.1	–0.1
drift R	0	0	0	0	0
disp 1	0.36	0.33	0.35	0.0	0.42
disp 2	0.07	0.12	0.43	0.04	0.38
disp 3	0.04	0.14	0.24	0.34	0.26
disp 4	0.12	0.26	0.56	0.24	0.25

3.3 Classifier

We calculated a heat map of the joystick commands to create 64x64 images over non-overlapping windows of 20 data points ($\approx 1s$) (See Fig. 4). Those images are the input features of our network.

We trained a LeNet classifier [9] to see if we could discriminate players. The architecture of the network is as follows: a 2D convolutional layer with 20 filters of size (5x5) with ReLu activation, followed by 2D max pooling with pooling size and stride of size 2x2; a 2D convolutional layer with 50 filters of size (5x5) with ReLu activation, followed by 2D max pooling. The flattened output then goes through a fully connected layer with 500 neurons and ReLu activation and a fully connected layer with 5 neurons and softmax activation. The network was trained with a learning rate of 0.001 for 200 epochs.

For the children's data, the trained network reached a macro precision of 84%, recall of 91% and F1-score of .87 (child 0: 89% precision, 96% recall, 0.93 F1-score; child 1: 60% precision, 89% recall, 0.71 F1-score; child 2: 91% precision, 84% recall, 0.87 F1-score; child 3: 87% precision, 98% recall, 0.92 F1-score; child 4: 88% precision, 85% recall, 0.87 F1-score). See Fig. 4 for the confusion matrix. The heterogeneity and quick variability of the children's movements makes it difficult for the network to learn properly how to classify them. However, if we increase the length of the windows to 200 (10 seconds), the network is able to reach 100% as well.

We also previously collected joystick data from healthy adult participants teleoperating the real MyJay robot for 10 minutes. The analysis of this data is presented in [8]. We also trained a classifier on this data and the network reached 100% accuracy, recall and F1-score for each participant.

Fig. 4. Two examples of the joystick heatmaps that are used as input features for the classifier over a 200 data point window (Left, Center) and confusion matrix of the classification for the children's data

Moreover, this network can also be trained to classify healthy and impaired data and reaches 100% accuracy, 100% recall and 1.0 F1-score

4   Discussion and Conclusion

In this paper, children with upper limb challenges navigated a virtual robot through a maze as part of a computer game. This data collection was necessary, since this kind of data is lacking and hard to acquire. We had to adopt an iterative design as our participants had very different individual characteristics and some features, such as the speed of the robot movements was too high for some children but too low for others. The analysis of this data also revealed a great heterogeneity and variability in the data for each child. Indeed, the variability of the children's commands made it difficult for a neural network to learn properly how to classify them.

The asymmetry and variability of impairments confirmed that adaptive solutions are required, but also highlighted that we need solutions that have a fine granularity, such as taking into account the dispersion of each joystick axis, and not only global dispersion, but also temporally as the extracted features vary over time.

This work is a major stepping stone in our over-arching goal of developing an adaptive joystick controller that can compensate individual motor impairments, such as drift, force asymmetry and movement variability, but also continuously adapt over time to support the user's skills. Future steps will involve training a neural network capable of correcting impaired joystick commands and capable of detecting if the player's statistics varied and if new adaptations are necessary. Finally, we will experimentally validate the adaptive joystick controller in a game setting, mediated by a robot such as MyJay.

Acknowledgments. We would like to sincerely thank all the participants who willingly participated, as well as the organization who made this possible (not named in order to preserve the privacy of the children). This research was undertaken, in part, thanks to funding from the Canada 150 Research Chairs Program.

References

1. Cairney, J., et al.: Cohort profile: the canadian coordination and activity tracking in children (catch) longitudinal cohort. BMJ Open **9**(9), e029784 (2019)
2. Calderita, L.V., et al.: Therapist: towards an autonomous socially interactive robot for motor and neurorehabilitation therapies for children. JMIR Rehab. Assistive Technol. **1**(1), e3151 (2014)
3. Chakerian, D.L., Larson, M.A.: Effects of upper-extremity weight-bearing on hand-opening and prehension patterns in children with cerebral palsy. Developm. Med. Child Neurol. **35**(3), 216–229 (1993)
4. Eliasson, A.C., Gordon, A.M., Forssberg, H.: Impaired anticipatory control of isometric forces during grasping by children with cerebral palsy. Developm. Med. Child Neurol. **34**(3), 216–225 (1992)
5. Fridin, M., Belokopytov, M.: Robotics agent coacher for cp motor function (rac cp fun). Robotica **32**(8), 1265–1279 (2014)
6. Gillham, M., Pepper, M., Kelly, S., Howells, G.: Feature determination from powered wheelchair user joystick input characteristics for adapting driving assistance. Wellcome Open Res. **2** (2017)
7. Guneysu Ozgur, A., et al.: Iterative design of an upper limb rehabilitation game with tangible robots. In: Proceedings of the 2018 ACM/IEEE International Conference on Human-Robot Interaction, pp. 241–250 (2018)
8. Jouaiti, M., Dautenhahn, K.: What kind of player are you? continuous learning of a player profile for adaptive robot teleoperation. In: IEEE International Conference on Development and Learning (ICDL). IEEE (2022)
9. LeCun, Y., Bengio, Y., et al.: Convolutional networks for images, speech, and time series. Handbook Brain Theory Neural Netw. **3361**(10), 1995 (1995)
10. Mahdi, H., Saleh, S., Shariff, O., Dautenhahn, K.: Creating MyJay: A new design for robot-assisted play for children with physical special needs. In: Wagner, A.R., et al. (eds.) ICSR 2020. LNCS (LNAI), vol. 12483, pp. 676–687. Springer, Cham (2020). https://doi.org/10.1007/978-3-030-62056-1_56
11. Mailleux, L., et al.: Clinical assessment and three-dimensional movement analysis: an integrated approach for upper limb evaluation in children with unilateral cerebral palsy. PLoS ONE **12**(7), e0180196 (2017)
12. Oskoui, M., Coutinho, F., Dykeman, J., Jetté, N., Pringsheim, T.: An update on the prevalence of cerebral palsy: a systematic review and meta-analysis. Developm. Med. Child Neurol. **55**(6), 509–519 (2013)
13. Palisano, R.J., et al.: Validation of a model of gross motor function for children with cerebral palsy. Phys. Ther. **80**(10), 974–985 (2000)
14. Rönnqvist, L., Rösblad, B.: Kinematic analysis of unimanual reaching and grasping movements in children with hemiplegic cerebral palsy. Clin. Biomech. **22**(2), 165–175 (2007)
15. Sanger, T.D.: Arm trajectories in dyskinetic cerebral palsy have increased random variability. J. Child Neurol. **21**(7), 551–557 (2006)
16. Tasevski, J., Gnjatović, M., Borovac, B.: Assessing the children's receptivity to the robot marko. Acta Polytechnica Hungarica **15**(5), 47–66 (2018)
17. Wood, K.C., Lathan, C.E., Kaufman, K.R.: Feasibility of gestural feedback treatment for upper extremity movement in children with cerebral palsy. IEEE Trans. Neural Syst. Rehabil. Eng. **21**(2), 300–305 (2012)

A Framework for Assistive Social Robots for Detecting Aggression in Children

Ahmad Yaser Alhaddad[1(✉)], Abdulaziz Al-Ali[2], Amit Kumar Pandey[3,4], and John-John Cabibihan[1]

[1] Department of Mechanical and Industrial Engineering, Qatar University, Doha, Qatar
ahmadyaser.alhaddad@polimi.it, john.cabibihan@qu.edu.qa
[2] KINDI Computing Research Center, Qatar University, Doha, Qatar
[3] beingAI Limited, Seattle, Hong Kong
[4] Socients AI and Robotics, Paris, France

Abstract. Children during their early years might exhibit different forms of aggression against others. Aggression can be physical or relational. Physical aggression can take on different forms such as hitting, pushing, and kicking. The integration of technology, such as social robots, can be used to address aggression among children during childhood. In this study, we present a framework consisting of using sensory modules to detect undesirable physical interactions and social robots to provide a feedback once a behavior is detected. The framework has been demonstrated using a commercially-available social robot (i.e., Professor Einstein) with Raspberry Pi as the sensory module. Experiments with the social robot showed a promising performance of this integration. The outcomes can be used to teach children how to interact with others in an acceptable manner. The proposed framework can be integrated by social roboticists into their designs to create more dynamic interactions targeting aggressive and unwanted interactions.

Keywords: Social robots · Safety · Aggression · Challenging behaviors · Autism

1 Introduction

Behaviors that are meant to hurt or harm another person are considered a form of aggression [1,2]. Based on the classification of the American Psychological Association (APA), aggression can be hostile (i.e., intentional), instrumental (i.e., not intentional), or affective (i.e., emotional) [3]. Different types of aggression are exhibited by preschool children such as physical aggression (e.g., pushing, kicking, and hitting) and relational aggression (e.g., bullying, slandering, and intimidation) [4–6]. In a study investigating the relationship between emotion regulation and children's aggression, results showed the importance of emotion regulation role and the need to develop emotion-regulation skills during early

F. Cavallo et al. (Eds.): ICSR 2022, LNAI 13818, pp. 74–84, 2022.
https://doi.org/10.1007/978-3-031-24670-8_8

childhood [7]. Aggression during early childhood has been found to be linked to behavioral problems, academic decline, and the likelihood of committing a crime [8–11].

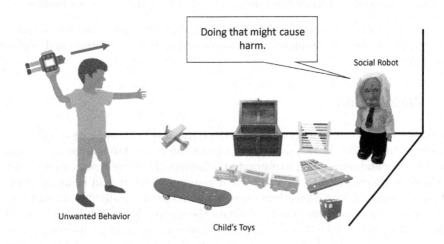

Fig. 1. A graphical representation of the proposed framework showing the social robot reacting to an unwanted behavior exhibited by a child.

Applications of technology in healthcare have lead to an unprecedented accomplishments. One notable example is using robots to assist, monitor, and improve the quality of patients' lives [12]. Service robots were developed to support the elderly and make them more independent in their lives [13–15]. Rehabilitation robots are playing an important role in restoring the limbs functionality of patients with paralysed upper or lower limbs [16,17]. Overcoming the limitations of certain surgeries were made possible thanks to the integration of surgical robots [18].

Social robots are another form of technology that garnered great interest in healthcare [19]. There have been many reported positive outcomes to using social robots in autism therapy. Previous studies reported positive outcomes such as imitation and increased attention [20]. Using a social robot provides flexibility as it can be used alone as an intervention tool or in conjunction with a human therapist [21]. With the integration of wearable technology and other sensors, social robots could potentially be used to address negative interactions, challenging behaviors, and meltdowns [22–25]. The application of social robots can be extended and address aggression among neurotypical children. However, limited research has been conducted to address this issue.

In this study, we propose a framework to integrate social robots and sensory modules to detect and address aggression among children (Fig. 1. We also demonstrate the proposed framework using a social robot and a Raspberry Pi device.

The contributions are summarized as follows:

1. Presenting a framework to target aggression among children.
2. Providing recommendations to properly implement the framework.
3. Demonstrating the framework using a social robot and a sensory module.

This paper is organized as follows. Section 2 describes the background. Section 3 describes the framework. Section 4 presents the prototype and Sect. 5 concludes the paper.

2   Background

A robotic system can be used to adapt to its environment through its reactions to external stimuli [26]. These reactions of a robot can be used to address aggression by detecting and responding to unwanted behaviors. There were some robots that demonstrated reactions to direct physical manipulations. Roball is one example of a robot that displayed reactions once manipulated physically [27]. Roball uses tilt sensors and accelerometers to navigate the environment and display several interaction modes. PARO is a seal-like therapeutic toy that emits voices once it is stroked or touched [28]. The robot uses different sensors to interact with its environment and display reactions by making sounds and moving some body parts (e.g., eyelid).

Different aspects and nuances of emotional, verbal, and behavioral interactions with social robots have been investigated. One study explored the possibility of enabling robots to recognize speech patterns to distinguish between aggressive and non-aggressive (i.e., sarcastic) scenarios [29]. The study collected data from 16 participants displaying different attitudes toward robots. Using extracted quality and prosodic features, a machine learning model was developed to measure the perceived level of seriousness in speech that was reported to be comparable to that of humans. Another work considered investigating the effects of a robot's emotional state (i.e., frustration) on the behaviors and emotions of children to develop a robot's cognitive model [30]. The study proposed a scenario where a robot and a child take turns in playing a game, which requires receiving instructions from the other player. The emotional response (i.e., frustration) of the robot to the received instructions from the child is the variable to be manipulated. Depending on interactions, a suitable cognitive model can be selected to adapt to the child's perspective and responses. Another study investigated the perceived mistreatment in scenarios where two forms of technologies (i.e., robots and computers) are being treated aggressively [31]. The study recruited 80 participants that worked with either of the two technologies while the experimenter performed the aggressive or neutral behavior toward the machines. The findings revealed that the participants sympathized with the robots more compared to computers as they felt that robots are more capable of displaying emotions.

Sensors and wearable devices are being used to detect activities and have been integrated in healthcare to monitor, diagnose, and assist in therapy [32,33]. Limited studies were conducted to classify the interactions between a child and a robot [24,34,35]. In a previous study, the reactions of children to different

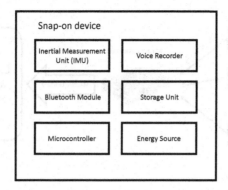

Fig. 2. The main components of the proposed sensory module (snap-on) device. The IMU device consists of a gyroscope and an accelerometer to measure angular rate and accelerations. The voice recorder is an optional part which can be used to detect instances of screaming. The Bluetooth module is used to communicate with other devices wirelessly. The storage unit is used to store collected data offline and the energy source to power up the device. The microcontroller is used to integrate the components, control operations, and handle sensory data.

robots' reactions during unwanted interactions were examined [25]. Three different robotic toys were embedded with a recognition device that detects unwanted physical interactions such as hitting, throwing, and shaking. Once an unwanted behavior was detected, a sound was produced by a speaker near the robotic toys. The participants displayed curiosity, surprised expressions, and astonished looks once they heard the robots' reactions. The results demonstrated the importance of selecting the right reaction time (i.e., around 1 s) for a robot's response.

3   The Framework

3.1   Overview

Children interactions with their environment are dynamic and take on different forms. During playtime, children might take objects, such as toys, and manipulate them. Some of these movements could be considered undesirable or aggressive, especially if targeting other children. For example, children might throw their toys during tantrums. A robotic system that is meant to address aggression must account for the occurrence of such behaviors in its surrounding. This can be achieved in different ways such as using a distributed network of connected sensory modules. The proposed framework in this paper suggests having more than one component as part of the recognition. The main component is the social robot that detects directly or indirectly unwanted behaviors and then responds accordingly to address the behavior of the child. The second component is the sensory module that can be one or multiple connected devices spread across the surroundings and connected to the social robot. Additionally, a wearable device can be included to be a part of the connected devices.

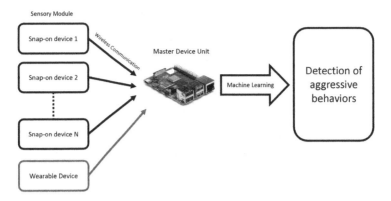

Fig. 3. A network of sensory module (snap-on) devices can be integrated along with a wearable device to detect aggressive behaviors. All the devices can be connected to a master device unit that has access to a processing power used to classify behaviors using machine learning techniques.

A sensory module should at least contain one sensor or more, such as an accelerometer and/or gyroscope, to detect any unwanted physical interactions. Additionally, it could be a snap-on device that contains a voice module to analyse screams (Fig. 2). A group of devices can be distributed within a given room in objects to maximize the detection of aggressive behaviors (Fig. 3). With the integration of a social robot and sensory modules in a child's room, different physical interactions can be detected and addressed (Fig. 4).

3.2   Design Considerations

In a system consisting of a social robot and sensory modules that are meant to detect aggression, there are specific design considerations to account for unwanted behaviors. The social robot used must be made robust to withstand any potential damage to its structure and to be soft to mitigate any harm due to impact [36]. The selection of a robot's mass and shape or the embedding of a soft material layer could be considered as a starting point in designing a safe and robust social robot [37,38]. The appearance of a robot should be evaluated with the target children to identify their attitudes toward it and their perceived perceptions [39]. As for the capabilities, the robot should be equipped with multiple modalities to display reactions such as voice, sounds, movements, gestures, and facial expressions. The set of reactions can be customized to address children of different age groups. Additionally, the selected reactions should be clear to be understood by the children and to be generated properly to establish causality due to unwanted interactions [25].

As for the sensory module, the device should also be robust to withstand aggressive behaviors. Advances in flexible electronics can be adopted to increase the robustness and to provide more freedom in designing the sensory module. The design should be minimized in terms of size to make it easier to embed in the

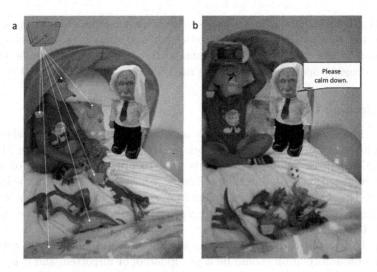

Fig. 4. A child displaying unwanted behaviors while interacting with his surrounding. (a) Possible locations of the Smart, Snap-on devices on the child's cap, shirt, pillow, blanket, and toys. (b) A social companion robot will say calm messages when the sensors detect aggressive behaviors.

surroundings while not being obtrusive or salient to the children. Additionally, placement locations for the sensory modules should also be investigated. The devices should be optimized and energy efficient to ensure a long battery life and less frequent charging.

4 Prototype

This section describes the selected components used to construct a prototype to demo the envisioned framework.

4.1 Social Robot

Professor Einstein (Hanson Robotics, Hong Kong) was considered as the social robot in this framework. The robot uses an ARM7 processor and contains three mics in the chest and head, a camera in the chest to establish eye contact and track faces, infrared sensors to assist in walking, and motors to establish movements. The robot can talk, display expressions, point, and move. A dedicated Python library can be used to program the robot to display specific movements, facial expressions, and to say custom phrases. The camera of the robot was not used in the experiments.

4.2 Sensory Module

The sensory module considered for testing purposes was based on Raspberry (Raspberry Pi 3 Model B+, Raspberry Pi Foundation, UK) equipped with a

Sense Hat board that contains sensors such as an accelerometer and gyroscope. The Pi 3 is powered by a quad-core processor and contains a wireless module, which can be used to connect and command the social robot. Raspbian (V5.10, Debian Project) operating system was installed on a 16 GB micro SD card.

4.3 Machine Learning Model

The machine learning model that was adopted in our work is an architecture based on the Recurrent Neural Network (RNN), the Long Short-term Memory Cell (LSTM) proposed by [40], that is used to process a sequence of inputs. History information is used in the prediction, which is stored within the internal memory. The structure of LSTM differs from standard RNN as it deals with the vanishing gradient problem and aggregates the state information in a memory cell [41,42].

The LSTM cell consists of input gate, forget gate, and output gate that control what information should be kept, updated, or forgotten, and it is defined as follows [43]:

$$i_t = \sigma \left(W_{xi} x_t + W_{hi} h_{t-1} + W_{ci} c_{t-1} + b_i \right)$$

$$f_t = \sigma \left(W_{xf} x_t + W_{hf} h_{t-1} + W_{cf} c_{t-1} + b_f \right)$$

$$c_t = f_t c_{t-1} + i_t tanh \left(W_{xc} x_t + W_{hc} h_{t-1} + b_c \right)$$

$$o_t = \sigma \left(W_{xo} x_t + W_{ho} h_{t-1} + W_{co} c_t + b_o \right)$$

$$h_t = o_t \ tanh \left(c_t \right)$$

where i is the input gate, f is the forget gate, o is the output gate, σ is the logistic sigmoid function, and c is the cell activation vectors.

The model was evaluated and developed using data generated from earlier work [24]. Unwanted interactions between participants and robotic toys were captured using an accelerometer. The interactions included aggressive behaviors such as hitting, throwing, shaking, and dropping. More details about the data acquisition procedures, data format, and model evaluation can be found in our earlier work [25].

4.4 Reactions

A social robot should provide a timely response to an undesired action (Fig. 5). To achieve this goal, an exploratory experiment with the best achieved model was conducted. The model was exported to the detection device and a simple script was written. The detection device was configured to automatically connect to the social robot as it gets turned on. The script starts by loading the stored machine learning model then it continuously reads the data from the sensors of the Sense Hat board. The script then processes the acquired samples and converts them to a format suitable for the machine learning algorithm to make predictions. In these evaluations, the robot provided a timely response within 1–3 seconds of detecting an undesired behavior.

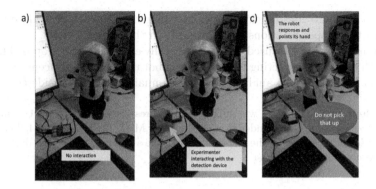

Fig. 5. Part of the exploratory experiments with the social robot (See supplementary material). a) The social robot does not show any response during the no interaction case. b) The experimenter starts interacting with the detection device by shaking it. c) The social robot reacts physically and verbally to the detected behavior.

5 Concluding Remarks

Aggression takes on different forms and can be complex to characterize. The dynamics of physical interactions during an aggressive behavior (e.g., hitting) can be detected with the right sensors and proper machine learning algorithms. The integration of a social robot to respond to an undesirable behavior could potentially be used to address aggression among children. However, there are design considerations that need to be addressed prior to establishing a proper rehabilitation system.

In terms of hardware design, the social robots considered must be robust to withstand unwanted physical aggressive behaviors (e.g., due to throwing) while also being soft not to cause harm to the user or others. The embedded sensors within the robot itself or using sensory modules in objects must also be placed and designed to account for the dynamics of such interactions to prevent damage and losing effectiveness due to repeated impacts.

Investigating the effectiveness of a robot's response in teaching children is another important factor. Repetitive and similar responses might render the interaction dull and boring while more frequent responses will make the interaction feel unnatural. Conveying a message to a child through a social robot can take on different forms such as gestures, sounds, and expressions. Developers might need to investigate the proper frequency and modalities of a robot's responses that provide the most effective messages to children.

The selection of the prediction algorithm plays an important role during children and robot interactions, especially during aggressive scenarios. Due to the intricate and complex dynamics of aggressive behaviors, a machine learning model should provide quick and accurate predictions. Investigating different sensors and their features (e.g., raw vs extracted) can help in finding the best combination to provide the best overall performance [35]. Having a fast algorithm that provides quick predictions will give the developers more leeway to design the proper reactions to incorporate in their social robots.

Future work will be focused on experimentally evaluating the proposed framework with children interacting with a social robot under different scenarios. Data collection based on video analysis and questionnaires will be considered.

Acknowledment. The work was supported by a research grant from QU Marubeni Concept to Prototype Grant under the grant number M-CTP-CENG-2020-4. The statements made herein are solely the responsibility of the authors. The authors declare that they have no conflict of interest.

References

1. Anderson, C.A., Bushman, B.J.: Human aggression. Annu. Rev. Psychol. **53**(1), 27–51 (2002)
2. Krahé, B.: The social psychology of aggression. Routledge (2020)
3. American Psychological Association, Apa dictionary of psychology (2018). https://dictionary.apa.org/aggression. (Accessed 24 Jan 2022)
4. Crick, N.R., Ostrov, J.M., Burr, J.E., Cullerton-Sen, C., Jansen-Yeh, E., Ralston, P.: A longitudinal study of relational and physical aggression in preschool. J. Appl. Dev. Psychol. **27**(3), 254–268 (2006)
5. Taylor, A.J.G., Jose, M.: Physical aggression and facial expression identification. Eur. J. Psychol. **10**(4), 650–659 (2014)
6. Ostrov, J.M.: Psychological science agenda— august 2013. Psychol. Sci. (2013)
7. Ersan, C.: Physical aggression, relational aggression and anger in preschool children: The mediating role of emotion regulation. J. Gen. Psychol. **147**(1), 18–42 (2020)
8. Evans, S.C., Frazer, A.L., Blossom, J.B., Fite, P.J.: Forms and functions of aggression in early childhood. J. Clin.Child Adolescent Psychol. **48**(5), 790–798 (2019)
9. Huitsing, G., Monks, C.P.: Who victimizes whom and who defends whom? a multivariate social network analysis of victimization, aggression, and defending in early childhood. Aggressive Behav. **44**(4), 394–405 (2018)
10. Turney, K., McLanahan, S.: The academic consequences of early childhood problem behaviors. Soc. Sci. Res. **54**, 131–145 (2015)
11. Pingault, J.-B., Côté, S.M., Lacourse, E., Galéra, C., Vitaro, F., Tremblay, R.E.: Childhood hyperactivity, physical aggression and criminality: a 19-year prospective population-based study. PLoS ONE **8**(5), e62594 (2013)
12. Robinson, H., MacDonald, B., Broadbent, E.: The role of healthcare robots for older people at home: A review. Int. J. Soc. Robot. **6**(4), 575–591 (2014)
13. Broekens, J., Heerink, M., Rosendal, H., et al.: Assistive social robots in elderly care: a review. Gerontechnology **8**(2), 94–103 (2009)
14. W.H. Organization, World report on ageing and health. World Health Organization (2015)
15. Marek, K.D., Rantz, M.J.: Aging in place: a new model for long-term care. Nurs. Adm. Q. **24**(3), 1–11 (2000)
16. Bogue, R.: Rehabilitation robots. Indust. Robot: Int. J. (2018)
17. Alhaddad, A.Y.: Toward 3d printed prosthetic hands that can satisfy psychosocial needs: grasping force comparisons between a prosthetic hand and human hands In: International Conference on Social Robotics, pp. 304–313. Springer (2017). https://doi.org/10.1007/978-3-319-70022-9_30

18. Cabibihan, J.-J., Alhaddad, A.Y., Gulrez, T., Yoon, W.J.: Influence of visual and haptic feedback on the detection of threshold forces in a surgical grasping task. IEEE Robot. Automat. Lett. **6**(3), 5525–5532 (2021)

19. Breazeal, C.: Social robots for health applications. In: Annual international Conference of the IEEE Engineering in Medicine And Biology Society, vol. 2011, pp. 5368–5371. IEEE (2011)

20. Cabibihan, J.-J., Javed, H., Ang, M., Jr., Aljunied, S.M.: Why robots? a survey on the roles and benefits of social robots in the therapy of children with autism. Int. J. Soc. Robot. **5**(4), 593–618 (2013)

21. Begum, M., Serna, R.W., Yanco, H.A.: Are robots ready to deliver autism interventions? a comprehensive review. Int. J. Soc. Robot. **8**(2), 157–181 (2016)

22. Cabibihan, J.-J., et al.: Social robots and wearable sensors for mitigating meltdowns in autism - a pilot test. In: Ge, S.S., et al. (eds.) ICSR 2018. LNCS (LNAI), vol. 11357, pp. 103–114. Springer, Cham (2018). https://doi.org/10.1007/978-3-030-05204-1_11

23. Alban, A.Q., et al.: Detection of challenging behaviours of children with autism using wearable sensors during interactions with social robots. In: 2021 30th IEEE International Conference on Robot & Human Interactive Communication (RO-MAN), pp. 852–857. IEEE (2021)

24. Alhaddad, A.Y., Cabibihan, J.-J., Bonarini, A.: Recognition of aggressive interactions of children toward robotic toys. In: 28th IEEE International Conference on Robot and Human Interactive Communication (RO-MAN), vol. 2019, pp. 1–8. IEEE (2019)

25. Alhaddad, A.Y., Cabibihan, J.-J., Bonarini, A.: Influence of reaction time in the emotional response of a companion robot to a child's aggressive interaction. Int. J. Soc. Robot. 1–13 (2020)

26. Alhaddad, A.Y., Cabibihan, J.-J.: Reflex system for intelligent robotics. In: Qatar Foundation Annual Research Conference Proceedings, vol. 2016(1), p. HBSP2914. Hamad bin Khalifa University Press (HBKU Press) (2016)

27. Salter, T., Michaud, F., Létourneau, D., Lee, D., Werry, I.P.: Using proprioceptive sensors for categorizing human-robot interactions. In: Human-Robot Interaction (HRI), 2007 2nd ACM/IEEE International Conference on IEEE, pp. 105–112 (2007)

28. Shibata, T.: Therapeutic seal robot as biofeedback medical device: Qualitative and quantitative evaluations of robot therapy in dementia care. Proc. IEEE **100**(8), 2527–2538 (2012)

29. Maehama, K., Even, J., Ishi, C.T., Kanda, T.: Enabling robots to distinguish between aggressive and joking attitudes. IEEE Robot. Autom. Lett. **6**(4), 8037–8044 (2021)

30. Yadollahi, E., Johal, W., Dias, J., Dillenbourg, P., Paiva, A.: Studying the effect of robot frustration on children's change of perspective. In: 2019 8th International Conference on Affective Computing and Intelligent Interaction Workshops and Demos (ACIIW), pp. 381–387. IEEE (2019)

31. Carlson, Z., Lemmon, L., Higgins, M., Frank, D., Salek Shahrezaie, R., Feil-Seifer, D.: Perceived mistreatment and emotional capability following aggressive treatment of robots and computers. Int. J. Soc. Robot. **11**(5), 727–739 (2019)

32. Ann, O.C., Theng, L.B.: Human activity recognition: a review. In: 2014 IEEE International Conference on Control System, Computing and Engineering (ICCSCE), pp. 389–393. IEEE (2014)

33. Alhaddad, A.Y., et al.: Sense and learn: Recent advances in wearable sensing and machine learning for blood glucose monitoring and trend-detection. Front. Bioeng. Biotechnol. **22**, 699 (2022)

34. Boccanfuso, L., et al.: Emotional robot to examine differences in play patterns and affective response of children with and without asd. In: The Eleventh ACM/IEEE International Conference on Human Robot Interaction, pp. 19–26. IEEE Press (2016)

35. Alhaddad, A.Y., Cabibihan, J.-J., Bonarini, A.: Real-time social robot's responses to undesired interactions between children and their surroundings. Int. J. Soc. Robot. 1–9 (2022)

36. Alhaddad, A.Y., Cabibihan, J.-J., Bonarini, A.: Head impact severity measures for small social robots thrown during meltdown in autism. Int. J. Soc. Robot. **11**(2), 255–270 (2019)

37. Alhaddad, A.Y., Cabibihan, J.-J., Hayek, A., Bonarini, A.: Influence of the shape and mass of a small robot when thrown to a dummy human head. SN Appli. Sci. **1**(11), 1–9 (2019). https://doi.org/10.1007/s42452-019-1447-7

38. Alhaddad, A.Y., Cabibihan, J.-J., Bonarini, A.: Safety experiments for small robots investigating the potential of soft materials in mitigating the harm to the head due to impacts. SN Appl. Sci. **1**(5), 1–10 (2019)

39. Alhaddad, A.Y., Mecheter, A., Wadood, M.A., Alsaari, A.S., Mohammed, H., Cabibihan, J.-J.: Anthropomorphism and Its negative attitudes, sociability, animacy, agency, and disturbance requirements for social robots: a pilot study. In: Li, H., et al. (eds.) ICSR 2021. LNCS (LNAI), vol. 13086, pp. 791–796. Springer, Cham (2021). https://doi.org/10.1007/978-3-030-90525-5_73

40. Zhao, Y., Yang, R., Chevalier, G., Xu, X., Zhang, Z.: Deep residual bidir-lstm for human activity recognition using wearable sensors. Mathem. Prob. Eng. **2018** (2018)

41. Hochreiter, S., Schmidhuber, J.: Long short-term memory. Neural Comput. **9**(8), 1735–1780 (1997)

42. Xingjian, S., Chen, Z., Wang, H., Yeung, D.-Y., Wong, W.-K., Woo, W.-C.: Convolutional lstm network: A machine learning approach for precipitation nowcasting. In: Advances in Neural Information Processing Systems, pp. 802–810 (2015)

43. Graves, A., Jaitly, N., Mohamed, A.-R.: Hybrid speech recognition with deep bidirectional lstm. In: IEEE Workshop on Automatic Speech Recognition and Understanding, vol. 201, pp. 273–278. IEEE (2013)

Kaspar Causally Explains

Hugo Araujo[1][(✉)], Patrick Holthaus[2], Marina Sarda Gou[2], Gabriella Lakatos[2],
Giulia Galizia[2], Luke Wood[2], Ben Robins[2], Mohammad Reza Mousavi[1],
and Farshid Amirabdollahian[2]

[1] King's College London, London, UK
hugo.lds.araujo@gmail.com
[2] University of Hertfordshire, Hatfield, UK

Abstract. The Kaspar robot has been used with great success to work
as an education and social mediator with children with autism spectrum
disorder. Enabling the robot to automatically generate causal explanations is key to enrich the interaction scenarios for children and promote
trust in the robot. We present a theory of causal explanation to be
embedded in Kaspar. Based on this theory, we build a causal model
and an analysis method to calculate causal explanations. We implement
our method in Java with inputs provided by a human operator. This
model automatically generates the causal explanation that are then spoken by Kaspar. We validate our explanations for user satisfaction in an
empirical evaluation.

1 Introduction

Causality has intrigued philosophers since ancient times. Modern theories of
causality were put forward by philosophers such as Hume and Lewis, and they
found applications in engineering, particularly in explaining the results of testing
and verification [1].

A formal logical theory that has been proved useful in engineering practice is
the theory of actual causality by Halpern and Pearl [7]. This theory specifies the
environment as a set of variables and a set of structural equations that describe
the relation between them. Then, given a logical effect (represented as a Boolean
predicate on the variables), a potential cause (also a Boolean predicate) through
analysing counter-factuals in the causal model, i.e., parallel worlds in which the
cause and effect may or may not have occurred.

This theory of causality has been proven useful both in analysing the results
of testing and verification [2], as well as in providing explanations for complex
systems such as neural networks [5]. In this paper, we apply Halpern and Pearl's
theory of actual causality to provide explanations in educational scenarios for
children in the autistic spectrum disorder. In particular, we equip Kaspar, which
is a state-of-the-art humanoid robot primed for interaction with children with
autism spectrum disorder (ASD) [15], with causal explanations. Enabling Kaspar
to generate causal explanations is considered a key to enrich the interaction
scenarios for children and thereby could promote additional trust in the robot.

© The Author(s), under exclusive license to Springer Nature Switzerland AG 2022
F. Cavallo et al. (Eds.): ICSR 2022, LNAI 13818, pp. 85–99, 2022.
https://doi.org/10.1007/978-3-031-24670-8_9

As the main contribution of this work, we implement a tool that automatically builds a causal model and conducts a causal analysis to provide explanations behind certain events during interaction between children and Kaspar. We implement our method in a Java implementation that, given inputs from a human operator, automatically generates the causal explanation that are spoken by Kaspar. Finally, we validate our explanations for user satisfaction in an empirical evaluation with healthy adults.

The rest of this paper is structured as follows. In Sect. 2, we discuss related work. In Sect. 3, we present an overview of Kaspar and the approach to its interaction with children. In Sect. 4, we present the discrete theory of actual causality by Halpern and Pearl. In Sects. 5 and 6, we apply the theory to our context and present the mechanisation of our strategy, respectively. In Sect. 7, we present the explanations provided by Kaspar and our validation experiment. Lastly, in Sect. 8, we provide our conclusions and discuss future work.

2   Related Work

Our context is the theory of actual causality [7], where, in a given scenario leading to an outcome, the events are analysed in order to find causes. This is in contrast with type-level causality where general causal rules governing a system are sought. To our knowledge, no theory of causality has been applied to interactions with robots. Baier et al. [1] have conducted a survey on published approaches that utilise Halpern's notion of causality. We summarise some of the most prominent related work below.

Leitner-Fischer and Leue [11] define a theory of causality that considers the temporal order as well as the non-occurrence of events. They also provide a search-based on-the-fly causality assessment that does not require the counterexamples to be generated in advance. In our work however, the order of events does not play a role: whether a particular event occurred before or after other events does not impact on what we consider cause.

Beer et al. [2] use causal analysis to explain counterexamples in hardware verification. The proposed algorithm is implemented in the IBM RuleBase PE tool. Also, Chockler, Grumberg, and Yadgar [3] employ a notion of responsibility (degree of causality) [4] to improve the quality of abstraction refinement by producing mode efficient counterexamples. Besides the continuous aspects, our approach incorporates the modelling of platform (hardware), controllers (software) and environment into a single model that considers a high-level abstraction of the system. Considering a notion of responsibility is one of the directions for our future work to rank the explanations provided.

3   Application Domain: Kaspar

The Kaspar robot [13] has been used to work with children with autism to help break their social isolation by acting as a social mediator with great success. A skill that children with ASD often struggle with is visual perspective taking (VPT), which is the ability to see the world from another person's view-point, making use of both spatial and social information [8]. Robot-mediated intervention has already been shown to be efficient in teaching autistic children perspective-taking skills [10]. Enabling the robot to automatically generate causal explanations in such scenarios could be key to enrich the interaction scenarios for autistic children [14] and thereby promote additional trust in the education medium. This may in turn make the robot-mediation more successful.

With this purpose in mind, we designed 4 VPT interactive games for the children to play with Kaspar (discussed in Sect. 5.1). In these games, Kaspar asks the child to show a particular interactive object. In each of the scenarios, when Kaspar cannot see the animal that he has requested, he explains the reason why he cannot see it; for example: "I cannot see it because you are holding it too high" or "this is not the animal I have asked to see." By doing that, we expect the children to understand Kaspar's point of view and show the animals to Kaspar in the correct way.

4   Theory of Causal Explanation

In this section, we present Halpern and Pearl's theory of actual causality [7] and demonstrate its application through the following running example; the example is to illustrate the theory and the actual VPT games will follow.

Example 1. Consider a simple scenario where the Kaspar robot and a picture of a lion are sitting on a table. The picture is in Kaspar's line of sight. However, two things prevent Kaspar from actually seeing the lion: (i) Kaspar's eyes are shut (due to the press of a button by the teacher) and (ii) the picture falls off the table (due to the wind blowing from an open window). In this simple scenario, if Kaspar's eyes are closed then this is a cause for Kaspar not seeing the lion. Analogously, if the picture has fallen off the table, that is also a cause.

Mathematical assessments of causality require formal modelling. As a precondition to a model, a signature provides the set of variables and their admissible valuations. The formal definitions in this section are taken from those by Chockler and Halpern [4].

Definition 1 (Signature). *A signature is a tuple*

$$\mathcal{S} = (\mathcal{U}, \mathcal{V}, \mathcal{R}),$$

where $\mathcal{U}$ is a finite set of exogenous variables, $\mathcal{V}$ is a finite set of endogenous variables, and $\mathcal{R}$ associates with every variable $Y \in \mathcal{U} \cup \mathcal{V}$ a finite and nonempty set $\mathcal{R}(Y)$ of possible values for Y.

Exogenous variables are determined by factors outside of the model while endogenous variables are affected by exogenous ones and also by other endogenous variables. For instance, going back to the example, the state of Kaspar's eyes and the state of the picture can be seen as *endogenous* variables, but the presence of lighting that allows for Kaspar to see at all, whether the button was pressed, and whether the window is open are *exogenous* variable.

Example 2. A signature of our running example has the following variables. Below, we describe the variables for each set ($\mathcal{U}$ and $\mathcal{V}$) and their possible values that form $\mathcal{R}$.

In the exogenous set $\mathcal{U}$, we have that:

- u_b represents the button: 0 if it is not pressed and 1 if it is.
- u_w represents the window: 0 it is closed and 1 if it is open.

As for the endogenous set $\mathcal{V}$, we have:

- KE for Kaspar's eyes: 0 if they are open, and 1 if they are shut.
- PS for the picture: 0 if it is on the table and 1 if it has fallen off.
- KS for Kaspar's sight: 1 if Kaspar can see the lion and 0 if it cannot.

Definition 2 (Causal Model). *A causal model over a signature $\mathcal{S}$ is a tuple*

$$M = (\mathcal{S}, \mathcal{F}),$$

where $\mathcal{F}$ associates with each variable $X \in \mathcal{V}$ a function denoted by F_X, such that:

$$F_X : (\times_{U \in \mathcal{U}} \mathcal{R}(U)) \times (\times_{Y \in \mathcal{V} \setminus \{X\}} \mathcal{R}(Y)) \rightarrow \mathcal{R}(X)$$

F_X describes how the value of the endogenous variable X is determined by the values of all other variables in $\mathcal{U} \cup \mathcal{V}$. The indexed Cartesian products $\times_{U \in \mathcal{U}} \mathcal{R}(U)$ and $\times_{Y \in \mathcal{V} \setminus \{X\}} \mathcal{R}(Y)$ consider each possible values of the variables in $\mathcal{U}$ and $\mathcal{V} \setminus \{X\}$, respectively.

As mentioned, the set $\mathcal{U}$ of exogenous variables includes things we need to assume so as to render all relationships deterministic (such as the presence of light, wind conditions and whether someone has pressed the button). We denote $\vec{u}$ (i.e., a set of valuations in $\mathcal{R}(\mathcal{U})$) as the context behind a cause. That is, the context is a mapping of exogenous values to their variables that induce the value of the endogenous variables. Typically, the context can define the value of certain endogenous variables, which, in conjunction with the functions in $\mathcal{F}$, are used to determine the value of the remaining endogenous variables.

Consider that, in our example, the context comprises the unmodelled variables $u_w \in \mathcal{U}$ and $u_b \in \mathcal{U}$. They represent whether the window is open and whether someone has pressed the button that control Kaspar's eyes, respectively. These variables can be seen as inputs that are not controlled by the system.

Example 3. Given the signature of our running example (see Example 2), a causal model for this system can be defined with the following structural equations $\mathcal{F}$.

- $F_{KE}(\vec{u}, PS, KS) = u_b$
- $F_{PS}(\vec{u}, KE, PS) = u_w$
- $F_{KS}(\vec{u}, KE, PS) = 1 - max(KE, PS)$

In summary, the context affects whether Kaspar's eyes are shut or whether the picture is still on the table (i.e., KE and PS, respectively). Then, these variables affect whether Kaspar can see the lion (KS). As defined in the functions ($\mathcal{F}$) above, Kaspar can only see the lion if both KE and PS are 0.

Finally, to make the definition of cause precise, we first need a syntax for causal events. Given a signature $\mathcal{S} = (\mathcal{U}, \mathcal{V}, \mathcal{R})$, a formula of the form $X = x$, for $X \in \mathcal{V}$ and $x \in \mathcal{R}(X)$, is called a primitive event.

Definition 3 (Causal Formula). *A causal formula is of the form*

$$[X_1 \leftarrow x_1, ..., X_k \leftarrow x_k]\Phi, where$$

- *$X_1, ..., X_k$ are distinct variables in $\mathcal{V}$.*
- *$x_i \in \mathcal{R}(X_i)$. And,*
- *Φ is a Boolean combination of primitive events.*

The formula $[X_1 \leftarrow x_1, ..., X_k \leftarrow x_k]\Phi$ states that Φ holds in a system where X_i is set to x_i for $i = 1, ..., k$. Such a formula can be abbreviated as $[\vec{X} \leftarrow \vec{x}]\Phi$. An assignment of the type $X \leftarrow x$ (called an *intervention* by Halpern) can be interpreted as an update in $\mathcal{F}$ where the function for X is set just to x. In our Kaspar example, a valid causal formula is $[KE \leftarrow 1](KS = 0)$. This says that if Kaspar's eyes have been shut, then Kaspar cannot see the picture.

Thus, given a context $\vec{u} \in \mathcal{R}(\mathcal{U})$, we write $(M, \vec{u}) \models [\vec{X} \leftarrow \vec{x}](Y = y)$ if the variable $Y \in \mathcal{V}$ has the value y in a causal model M where X_i is set to x_i for $i = 1, ..., k$. The notation can also be used in the presence of a Boolean combination of primitive events: $(M, \vec{u}) \models [\vec{X} \leftarrow \vec{x}]\Phi$. Furthermore, in the special case where $k = 0$, we write $(M, \vec{u}) \models (Y = y)$ if the variable $Y \in \mathcal{V}$ has the value y given the context $\vec{u} \in \mathcal{R}(\mathcal{U})$ and the causal model M. This notation can also be used in the presence of a Boolean combination of primitive events: $(M, \vec{u}) \models \Phi$.

The types of events that are allowed as causes are of the form $(X_1 = x_1 \wedge ... \wedge X_k = x_k)$, that is, a conjunction of primitive events that can be abbreviated as $\vec{X} = \vec{x}$. Then, cause is formally defined as follows.

Definition 4 (Cause). *We say that $\vec{X} = \vec{x}$ is a cause of Φ in $(M, \vec{u})$ if the following three conditions hold:*

- *AC1. $(M, \vec{u}) \models (\vec{X} = \vec{x}) \wedge \Phi$*
- *AC2. There exists a partition $(\vec{Z}, \vec{W})$ of $\mathcal{V}$ with $\vec{X} \subseteq \vec{Z}$ and some setting $(\vec{x'}, \vec{w'})$ of the variables in $(\vec{X}, \vec{W})$, such that*
  - *a) $(M, \vec{u}) \models [\vec{X} \leftarrow \vec{x'}, \vec{W} \leftarrow \vec{w'}]\neg\Phi$ and,*
  - *b) $(M, \vec{u}) \models [\vec{X} \leftarrow \vec{x}, \vec{W'} \leftarrow \vec{w'}]\Phi$ for all subsets $\vec{W'}$ of $\vec{W}$.*
- *AC3. $(\vec{X} = \vec{x})$ is minimal, that is, no subset of $\vec{X}$ satisfies AC2.*

Statement AC1 checks whether X and Φ are true at the same time, i.e., the cause has actually led to the effect; AC2 examines counterfactual dependence, i.e., given contingencies, changing other variables while keeping X intact brings about Φ and vice versa, changing X removes the effect, and AC3 checks whether everything in X is actually necessary for Φ to be true (that is, whether X is minimal). An important aspect of this definition, which is also relevant to our application, is that the set of endogenous variables is split in two disjoint sets $\vec{W}$ and $\vec{Z}$, where $\vec{X} \subseteq \vec{Z}$. The variables in the set $\vec{W}$ allow for the cause to be tested under certain circumstances (called structural contingencies [4]) where the variables in $\vec{W}$ are set to $\vec{w}'$. The set $\vec{Z}$, however, comprises the variables that mediate the situation that makes Φ hold, when $\vec{X} \leftarrow \vec{x}$. That is, changing the values of variables in $\vec{X}$ might result in changing the values of other variables (i.e., $\vec{Z} - \vec{X}$), which then leads to Φ.

Example 4. Consider the scenario in our Kaspar example where $KE = 1, PS = 1, KS = 0$. We would like to assess whether the fact that the picture has fallen off ($PS = 1$) is the cause of Kaspar not seeing the lion ($KS = 0$).

ACl states that $(\vec{X} = \vec{x})$ cannot be a cause of Φ, unless both the primitive causal events $(\vec{X} = \vec{x})$ and the effect Φ are true in the causal model M, given the context $\vec{u}$. That is, it states that for $PS = 1$ to be the cause of $KS = 0$, then both need to be true in $(M, \vec{u})$; thus, in this scenario, ACl holds. Conversely, if we were trying to assess whether $KE = 0$ is the cause of $KS = 0$ then, ACl could not be satisfied, as $KE = 0$ is not true in $(M, \vec{u})$ and, therefore, it could not be considered a cause.

AC2 is the most complex clause and is divided into two parts. AC2(a) says that for $(\vec{X} = \vec{x})$ to be a cause of Φ, there must be a setting $(\vec{X} \leftarrow \vec{x}')$ where Φ does not hold (under the contingency $\vec{W} \leftarrow \vec{w}'$). Contingencies are necessary since, for instance, Kaspar still cannot see the lion ($KS = 0$) even if we apply the intervention where the picture is still on the table ($PS \leftarrow 0$) because Kaspar's eye would have been shut anyway ($KE = 0$). We can see that $(M, \vec{u}) \models [PS \leftarrow 0] \neg (KS = 0)$ does not hold whilst $(M, \vec{u}) \models [PS \leftarrow 0, KE \leftarrow 0] \neg (KS = 0)$ does. Clearly, the contingency where $KE \leftarrow 0$ (represented by $\vec{W} \leftarrow \vec{w}$ in Definiton 4) is necessary.

AC2(b) exists to counteract some of the "permissiveness" of AC(a) by ruling out variables in the contingency as part of the actual cause. It states that the contingency $\vec{W} \leftarrow \vec{w}'$ should have no effect on Φ as long as we have the assignment $\vec{X} \leftarrow \vec{x}$. In our example, the contingency $(KE \leftarrow 0)$ alone has no effect on Φ: Kaspar still cannot see the lion. The definition states that this should be true for all subsets W' of $\vec{W}$, including the empty set[1].

Finally, AC3 asserts that the identified cause is minimal. In our scenario, it prevents $(PS = 1 \land KE = 1)$ from being a cause, since $(PS = 1)$ suffices to satisfy AC2. Thus, AC3 also holds and we can say that, in $(M, \vec{u})$, $(PS = 1)$ is a cause of $(KS = 0)$. A similar explanation can be made to show that $(KE = 1)$ is also a cause of $(KS = 0)$.

---

[1] There's a slight abuse of notation since w' might not be the same size as W'.

5   Causal Explanation for Kaspar

To analyse actual causality, we need to define a causal model for Kaspar. The model comprises variables, a state space (with all possible variable valuations), and a set of equations that describe the interaction between variables. In this section, we first explain the context of Kaspar interactive games and subsequently define our model of Kaspar's interaction with its surroundings during the said games. This representation (i.e., our causal model) allows us to find the actual causes for an effect by modifying variable values and observing whether the effect persists.

5.1   Interactive Games

In the experiments, children and Kaspar interact with each other during games that have been found to require explanations regarding the robot's visual perspective [6]. The goal of each game is to assess whether a child can put themselves in Kaspar's shoes; we ask if they realise whether Kaspar can or cannot see something. For instance, we cover Kaspar's eyes with a blindfold and then ask the child if Kaspar can or cannot see a picture of a lion that sits in front of the robot. The correct is answer is that Kaspar cannot see the lion. If the child answer that Kaspar can see the lion, then we'd like to automatically generate an explanation as to why this is incorrect; in that case, it is because of the blindfold.

Explanations can be generated by building a causal model of the game, defining the Φ (that states, for example, that Kaspar cannot see the chosen animal) and determining causes for it. There are four distinct games that can be played: (i) *Picture game*: Several pictures of different animals are spread around the room. Kaspar chooses an animal and asks the child to show him its picture. (ii) *Head game*: Several pictures of different animals are spread around the room. Kaspar chooses an animal and asks the child to move the robot's head in the direction of the chosen animal. (iii) *Rotate game*: Different pictures of animals are spread around a turntable. Walls are put in between animals such that Kaspar can only see one animal at a time. The robot chooses an animal and asks the child to spin the table so that the correct animal is visible. (iv) *Cube game*: A cube that contains pictures of different animal on each facet is given to the child. Kaspar chooses an animal depicted in the cube and asks the child to show the correct animal.

In all of these four games, a button can be pressed by a human which causes Kaspar to fall asleep (by closing his eyes). Furthermore, a blindfold can also be used to cover Kaspar's eyes. After the child has acted on Kaspar's instruction, a human asks the child two questions: "Is Kaspar seeing or not seeing any animal?" and "Is Kaspar seeing or not seeing the chosen animal". The first questions assesses whether the child realises that Kaspar cannot see the animal because, for example, he's asleep or he's wearing a blindfold. The second checks whether the child realises that Kaspar is not seeing the chosen animal, since for instance the picture of the animal is too far away or to the left of Kaspar's field of vision. If the child answers the questions correctly Kaspar plays a sound of the chosen animal as a reward. Otherwise, an explanation is given to the child.

5.2   Causal Model

We can cover all of the four games above with a single causal model. Table 1 shows the variables in our model. During the games where Kaspar asks the child to show a picture of a certain animal, there may be multiple pictures of different animals and even other objects placed around the room. However, in our model we are only interested in asking questions about one particular object, i.e., the chosen animal. Given the situation where the child picks up an object, our model captures whether the chosen object is the correct animal. Further, we also make note of its position relative to Kaspar's line of sight (to the left or right, above or below, too far or too close), and whether the animal is in the correct orientation (e.g., not upside down).

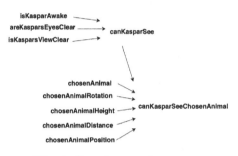

Fig. 1. Causal network

Table 1. Model variables

Variables	Possible Values
chosenAnimal	correct	wrong
chosenAnimalPosition	correct	left	right
chosenAnimalRotation	correct	wrong
chosenAnimalHeight	correct	high	low
chosenAnimalDistance	correct	far	close
isKasparAwake	correct	asleep
areKasparsEyesClear	correct	covered
isKasparsViewClear	correct	obstructed
canKasparSee	true	false
canKasparSeeChosenAnimal	true	false

Furthermore, Kaspar's eyes can be covered by a blindfold, or Kaspar can be asleep (eyes closed), or there can be wall blocking Kaspar from seeing an animal. Any of these situations can prevent Kaspar from seeing the chosen animal. We assume that Kaspar can only see the chosen animal, if Kaspar's line of sight is clear and the animal is correctly aligned in all four senses (position, rotation, height, and distance).

A causal network is a graphical representation that displays variable dependency. In this work, we can only determine cause for acyclic models. That is, if the value of variable A depends on the value of variable B, then the opposite must not be true. Figure 1 depicts the causal network of our system. Furthermore, the structural equations that define values of the variables in the model can be seen below.

- $\mathcal{F}_{canKasparSee}() == isKasparAwake = correct \land$
  $areKasparsEyesClear = correct \land$
  $isKasparsViewClear = correct$
- $\mathcal{F}_{canKasparSeeChosenAnimal}() = canKasparSee \land$
  $chosenAnimal = correct \land$
  $chosenAnimalPosition = correct \land$

$$chosenAnimalRotation = correct \wedge$$
$$chosenAnimalHeight = correct \wedge$$
$$chosenAnimalDistance = correct$$

In our model, we have that the variable $canKasparSee$ is true if, and only if, $isKasparAwake$, $areKasparsEyesClear$, and $isKasparViewClear$ are all set to $correct$. The value of the variable $canKasparseeChosenAnimal$ is true if, and only if, $canKasparSee$ is true and the chosen animal is correctly positioned.

As for effects, to put it simply, in Halpern and Pearl's theory, they are represented via a Boolean combination of variable values. In this work, we are particularly interested in the effects that describe instances of Kaspar not seeing the chosen animal. This directly correlates to the two questions that can be asked to the children: "Is Kaspar seeing or not seeing any animal?" and "Is Kaspar seeing or not seeing the chosen animal". The effects we are interested in observing are (i) "Kaspar is not able to see any animal" and (ii) "Kaspar is not seeing the chosen animal". Their mathematical representation in our causal analysis syntax is: (i) $canKasparSee = false$ and (ii) $canKasparSeeChosenAnimal = false$, respectively.

Example 5 (Covered Eyes). Consider the scenario where the chosen animal is positioned correctly, however, Kaspar's eyes are covered (see Table 2). In this case, we have that our effect is $canKasparSee = false$.

We then ask the child "Is Kaspar seeing or not seeing any animal?". If the child answers the question incorrectly (in this case, by saying that Kaspar is able to see them), then we provide the explanation of why this is incorrect.

An actual cause of the type $(\vec{X} \leftarrow \vec{x})$ can only be determined if the three clauses hold. For this example, the only possible cause is $(areKasparsEyesClear = covered)$. AC1 and AC3 are trivially satisfied. The former, because both the cause $(areKasparsEyesClear = covered)$ and the effect $(canKasparSee = false)$ are true in our model. The latter, because the causal explanation is minimal as there is only one variable involved. The remaining clause, AC2, is satisfied because if the value of the variable $areKasparsEyesClear$ is changed to $correct$ $(areKasparsEyesClear \leftarrow correct)$, we have that $\neg(canKasparSee = false)$, thus AC2. No contingency is necessary for this example.

Example 6 (Animal out of sight and Kaspar is asleep). Now, consider a second scenario. This time, Kaspar is asleep and the chosen animal is too far away. Table 3 depicts the variables and their values in this causal model. We then ask the child "Is Kaspar seeing or not seeing the lion?". The correct answer to this questions is "Kaspar is not seeing the lion", and, thus, our effect is "$canKasparseeChosenAnimal = false$". We now present the cause behind it.

Similarly to the previous example, the actual cause needs to satisfy the three clauses. This time, there are two separate causes: $(isKasparAwake = asleep)$ and $(chosenAnimalDistance = far)$. The explanations for both cases are similar and, thus, we'll only focus on explaining the latter case. The first clause, AC1, is satisfied because both the cause $(chosenAnimalDistance = far)$ and

Table 2. Example 1

Variables	Value
chosenAnimal	correct
chosenAnimalPosition	correct
chosenAnimalRotation	correct
chosenAnimalHeight	correct
chosenAnimalDistance	correct
isKasparAwake	correct
areKasparsEyesClear	covered
isKasparsViewClear	correct
canKasparSee	false
canKasparSeeChosenAnimal	false

Table 3. Example 2

Variables	Value
chosenAnimal	correct
chosenAnimalPosition	correct
chosenAnimalRotation	correct
chosenAnimalHeight	correct
chosenAnimalDistance	far
isKasparAwake	asleep
areKasparsEyesClear	correct
isKasparsViewClear	correct
canKasparSee	false
canKasparSeeChosenAnimal	false

the effect ($canKasparseeChosenAnimal = false$) are true in our model. The third clause, AC3, is also satisfied since ($chosenAnimalDistance = far$) is minimal.

Finally, AC2 is satisfied with the use of the contingencies. We apply the intervention where ($isKasparAwake \leftarrow correct$) as a contingency and we assess the parts a and b of clause AC2. The AC2(a) clause, which checks whether changes to the cause negates the effect, is satisfied since the causal formula $(M, \vec{u}) \models [chosenAnimalDistance \leftarrow correct, isKasparAwake \leftarrow correct] \neg(canKasparseeChosenAnimal = false)$ holds. Similarly, AC2(b), which checks whether the contingencies applied in AC2(a) do not negate the effect, is satisfied since, for instance, $(M, \vec{u}) \models [chosenAnimalDistance \leftarrow far, isKasparAwake \leftarrow correct](canKasparseeChosenAnimal = false)$ also holds.

6 Mechanisation

We mechanise the process of causal analysis using an automated rule based system that produces a proof of causality. Our approach is advantageous over a search-based approach for causal analysis, because the latter involves building the state-space of all counterfactuals and searching through them. The process for determining causes is represented in Fig. 2.

The user running the experiment selects the values of the variables in the user interface. This is done via specific key presses on a keyboard which are fed into our JAVA program (available at: https://bit.ly/ke-vs1-code). Then, a form that contains the values for the variables in the causal model is generated. The program builds a causal model, and evaluates whether the two effects hold (i.e., whether Kaspar is able to see and whether it is currently seeing the chosen animal). In case either of them hold, we determine the causes, which are then fed back into the user interface and mapped to the voice-based explanations played by Kaspar to the child. Even though multiple causes can be determined (e.g., the picture is both too far away and the wrong way around), during the games, only one explanation is provided to the child to avoid overwhelming the

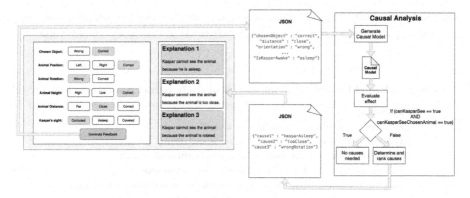

Fig. 2. Kaspar causally explains process

participant. The chosen explanation is decided using an internal ranking system decided by experts; that is, in case there are multiple explanations, only the top ranked one is provided. Then, the child has a chance to correct the behaviour and the explanations are determined again, if necessary.

The rule-based system for causal analysis is proven correct for the four Kaspar games; however, it can be extend to additional games, if required. The proofs of soundness are omitted due to space limitation and are included in an extended version available online: https://bit.ly/KasparCausallyExplains.

7   Explanations and Their Validation

We carried out an initial survey to be able to assess explanations generated by the presented system in terms of their general usefulness. For that purpose, we asked 20 adult participants (10 PhD students or staff members from research groups based at King's College London and 10 PhD students or staff members from the University of Hertfordshire) to watch videos of Kaspar providing an explanation and then rate each explanation using the explanation satisfaction (ES) scale [9]. This survey is based on several key attributes of explanations such as whether they are understandable, satisfying, sufficiently detailed, complete, informative about the interaction, useful, accurate, and trustworthy. These attributes are used to assess suitability of an explanation provided by an autonomous system. We used "what Kaspar can see" as the construct for the ES scale, which were shown to the participants for each video (cf. Table 4).

We have additionally employed the Negative Attitude towards Robots Scale (NARS) [12] to calibrate the obtained results against potential biases against robots. That allows us to later compare the current study with future studies targeting different user groups such as children. No other data has been collected and the study has been approved by the University of Hertfordshire's ethics committee for studies involving human participants, protocol number: SPECS/SF/UH/04944. Participants were provided with an information sheet describing the study. Implied consent was obtained at the beginning of the survey, giving participants the option to withdraw from the study at any time.

Table 4. Adapted ES scale that was shown to study participants for each video.

#	Question
1	From the explanation, I **understand** what Kaspar can see.
2	This explanation of what Kaspar can see is **satisfying**.
3	This explanation of what Kaspar can see has **sufficient detail**.
4	This explanation of what Kaspar can see seems **complete**.
5	This explanation of what Kaspar can see tells me **how to interact** with it.
6	This explanation of what Kaspar can see is **useful to my goals**.
7	This explanation of what Kaspar can see shows me how **accurate** it is.
8	This explanation lets me judge when I should **trust and not trust** Kaspar.

In total, we have shown 16 videos (available at: https://bit.ly/ke-vs1-videos) to participants that contain all possible explanations for the variables of the causal network (Table 1) of the games identified in [6] and described in Sect. 5.1. Table 5 provides an overview of the videos and describes the utterance that Kaspar uses, which may be accompanied by disambiguation gestures.

Table 5. Video recordings of explanations for the variables of the causal network that have been shown to the participants. In this table, "..." at beginning of utterances stands for "I cannot see the animal, because".

#	Variables	Game	Utterance
1	chosenAnimal: wrong	Picture	That is not the animal I have asked to see
12	chosenAnimal: wrong	Rotate	That is not the animal I have asked to see
14	chosenAnimal: wrong	Cube	That is not the animal I have asked to see
2	chosenAnimalPosition: left	Cube	...you are holding it too far left
5	chosenAnimalPosition: right	Cube	...you are holding it too far right
10	chosenAnimalPosition: left	Head	...my head is too far right
7	chosenAnimalPosition: right	Head	...my head is too far left
9	chosenAnimalDistance: far	Picture	...you are holding it too far
13	chosenAnimalDistance: close	Picture	...you are holding it too close
4	chosenAnimalHeight: low	Picture	...you are holding it too low
15	chosenAnimalHeight: high	Picture	...you are holding it too high
6	chosenAnimalRotation: wrong	Cube	...you are holding it the wrong way around
3	isKasparsViewClear: obstructed	Rotate	...the wall is in front of it
11	isKasparsViewClear: obstructed	Cube	...there is something in the way
8	areKasparsEyesClear: covered	Cube	...my eyes are covered
16	canKasparSeeAnimal: false	Cube	...you are not holding it in front of my eyes

Because participant ratings were not normally distributed, we used the non-parametric one-sample Wilcoxon rank-sum test [16] to test whether ratings on the Explanation Satisfaction (ES) scale were greater than the mean value. Results attest that, when averaging across all the videos, each of the explanation is rated significantly above the neutral value (all $p < 0.001$), cf. Fig. 3a. Likewise, rating across the explanations are rated above neutral for each of the videos (all $p < 0.001$) as shown in Fig. 3b. Participant ratings on NARS attested a low negative attitude towards robots with mean values for $\overline{S1} \approx 1.78$ (interaction subscale), $\overline{S2} \approx 2.7$ (social subscale), and $\overline{S3} \approx 1.48$ (emotion subscale). S1 and S3 are rated significantly below the neutral value (both $p < 0.001$) whereas S2 can not be reliably distinguished from neutral ($p \approx 0.053$).

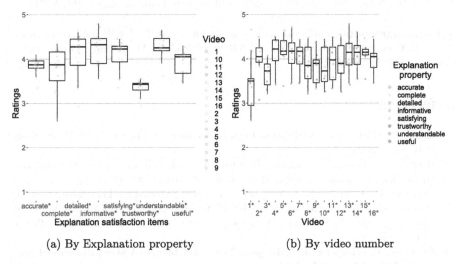

(a) By Explanation property   (b) By video number

Fig. 3. Results of the ES scale (5-point Likert scale) grouped by explanation property (3a) as highlighted in Table 4 and grouped by video number (3b) as listed in Table 5. Coloured points indicate the mean values of the other dimension. Asterisks mark items significantly greater than the average value.

These results confirm that, with healthy adults, the explanations that the system can generate are beneficial to relate cause and effect. Participants consistently rate them as accurate, complete, sufficiently detailed, satisfying, understandable, useful to their goals, and informative about the interaction. They further help to determine when to trust the robot. Knowing that adults find the generated explanations useful gives us an estimate whether the generated explanations have a potential to help autistic children in our future experiments.

8 Conclusions

We employ causal analysis as the key ingredient in providing explanations during interaction between the Kaspar robot and children. To that end, we make use of the theory of actual causation by Halpern and Pearl; outline the scenarios in which Kaspar interacts with the children; and build a causal model that covers these scenarios. We mechanised the strategy as a Java program to automatically generate causal explanations that are provided by Kaspar in order to enrich the interactions and improve trust. We validated the explanations via a controlled survey to show that they clarify and enhance the games.

For more complex interactions, we believe alternative causal explanations can be automatically ranked, e.g., in terms of their brevity. Developing theories of ranked explanations and empirically evaluating them in this context are worthwhile avenues of future work. Moreover, we are currently preparing extensive user studies at our partner schools to further evaluate our results for user groups involving children with ASD. Subsequently, we plan to perform iterative experiments to measure the effectiveness of explanations in improving VPT.

Acknowledgements. This work has been supported by the UKRI TAS Hub, Grant Award Reference EP/V00784X/1 and UKRI TAS Node in Verifiability, Grant Award Reference EP/V026801/2.

References

1. Baier, C., et al.: From verification to causality-based explications. In: Proceedings of ICALP (2021)
2. Beer, I., Ben-David, S., Chockler, H., Orni, A., Trefler, R.J.: Explaining counterexamples using causality. Formal Meth. Syst. Des. **40**(1), 20–40 (2012)
3. Chockler, H., Grumberg, O., Yadgar, A.: Efficient automatic STE refinement using responsibility. In: Ramakrishnan, C.R., Rehof, J. (eds.) TACAS 2008. LNCS, vol. 4963, pp. 233–248. Springer, Heidelberg (2008). https://doi.org/10.1007/978-3-540-78800-3_17
4. Chockler, H., Halpern, J.Y.: Responsibility and blame: A structural-model approach. JAIR **22**, 93–115 (2004)
5. Chockler, H., Kroening, D., Sun, Y.: Explanations for occluded images. In: Proceedings of ICCV 2021, pp. 1214–1223. IEEE (2021)
6. Gou, M.S., et al.: Towards understanding causality-a retrospective study of using explanations in interactions between a humanoid robot and autistic children. In: Proceedings of (RO-MAN). IEEE (2022)
7. Halpern, J.Y.: Actual Causality. MIT Press (2016)
8. Hamilton, A.F.C., Brindley, R., Frith, U.: Visual perspective taking impairment in children with autistic spectrum disorder. Cognition **113**(1), 37–44 (2009)
9. Hoffman, R.R., Mueller, S.T., Klein, G., Litman, J.: Metrics for explainable AI: Challenges and prospects. arXiv preprint arXiv:1812.04608 (2018)
10. Lakatos, G., Wood, L.J., Syrdal, D.S., Robins, B., Zaraki, A., Dautenhahn, K.: Robot-mediated intervention can assist children with autism to develop visual perspective taking skills. J. Behav. Robot. **12**(1), 87–101 (2021)
11. Leitner-Fischer, F., Leue, S.: Causality checking for complex system models. In: Giacobazzi, R., Berdine, J., Mastroeni, I. (eds.) VMCAI 2013. LNCS, vol. 7737, pp. 248–267. Springer, Heidelberg (2013). https://doi.org/10.1007/978-3-642-35873-9_16

12. Nomura, T., Kanda, T., Suzuki, T.: Experimental investigation into influence of negative attitudes toward robots on human-robot interaction. AI Soc. **20**(2), 138–150 (2006)

13. Robins, B., Dautenhahn, K., Te Boekhorst, R., Billard, A.: Robotic assistants in therapy and education of children with autism. Univ. Access Inf. Soc. **4**(2), 105–120 (2005)

14. Rutherford, M.D., Subiaul, F.: Children with autism spectrum disorder have an exceptional explanatory drive. Autism **20**(6), 744–753 (2016)

15. Wood, L.J., Zaraki, A., Robins, B., Dautenhahn, K.: Developing Kaspar: a Humanoid Robot for Children with Autism. Int. J. Soc. Robot. **13**(3), 491–508 (2021)

16. Woolson, R.F.: Wilcoxon signed-rank test. Wiley encyclopedia of clinical trials, pp. 1–3 (2007)

Social Robots as Advanced Educational Tool

Training School Teachers to Use Robots as an Educational Tool: The Impact on Robotics Perception

Giulia Pusceddu[1,2]([✉]), Francesca Cocchella[3,4], Michela Bogliolo[2,5],
Giulia Belgiovine[4], Linda Lastrico[1,2], Maura Casadio[2], Francesco Rea[1],
and Alessandra Sciutti[4]

[1] Robotics, Brain and Cognitive Science Department (RBCS), Italian Institute of
Technology, Genoa, Italy
giulia.pusceddu@iit.it
[2] Department of Informatics, Bioengineering, Robotics, and Systems Engineering
(DIBRIS), University of Genoa, Genoa, Italy
[3] Department of Educational Science (DISFOR), University of Genoa,
Genoa, Italy
[4] Cognitive Architecture for Collaborative Technologies Unit (CONTACT),
Italian Institute of Technology, Genoa, Italy
[5] Scuola di Robotica, Genoa, Italy

Abstract. This study investigates whether an educational robotics
training program for kindergarten, primary, and secondary teachers
causes them to change their impressions of a robotic platform. Questionnaires submitted before and after a 3-month training program were
used to assess the opinions of 40 teachers. The training program aided in
bringing teachers' expectations closer to the actual potential of the robot.
The course seems to level participants' impressions: differences between
STEM and literary teachers before the program are no longer detected
after it. Although those with a wider technological background have more
willingness to use the robot, all the teachers, in the end, perceived the
robotic platform as appreciated and beneficial for the education of students. Our findings highlight the crucial benefit of a training program in
robotics for teachers: it not only provides the knowledge to use a robotic
platform but also helps form a more informed vision of the possibilities
afforded by robotics platforms for education.

Keywords: Robots in education · Technology at school · Robotics
acceptance

1 Introduction

The use of social robots is growing in the educational field, especially for children,
to enhance and support their learning. In this context, robots can positively

The NaoToKnow project was funded under the PNSD Italian national call for proposals STEAM Methodologies and implemented by the network of school institutes
ARETE+4NAO.

affect both cognitive and affective aspects [1]. Most studies concerning robots in education focus on students, even if they are not the only stakeholders involved. Teachers represent a relevant portion of users of educational robotics. They are experts in designing and evaluating pupils' learning; therefore, assessing their opinions, expectations, and concerns about robots in education may be crucial to improving the modalities of use of robots at school.

In the last decades, researchers started investigating teachers' impressions of educational robots using surveys. In the works of Kim et al. [16] and Reich et al. [20], teachers reported negative attitudes about teaching and learning with educational robots; in Lee et al. [17], they also demonstrated to be more critical about integrating robots into schools than students and parents. However, teachers with greater technology commitment reported more positive attitudes towards educational robots [20]. A similar result was evidenced in a survey administered to elementary school teachers after a robotics workshop, in which the intention of use of the robot in educational activities positively correlated with the teachers' attitude to technology, other than with the perceived usefulness of the robot [9]. Interestingly, elementary school teachers seem to have more negative attitudes and less eagerness to use educational robots than their middle-school colleagues [20]; they appear apprehensive about the impact of robots on younger school children's social skills that might suffer from the use of artificial agents. Similar concerns were expressed in focus groups analyzed by Serholt et al. [22], where teachers were worried that robots not able to interact on the same emotional plan as humans might lead children to develop impaired emotional intelligence. Besides, they feared that children might become over-reliant on robots and lose the capacity to be critical. Additionally, in both [20] and [21], teachers believed that the limited access to the robots could cause competitiveness among students and had the impression that pupils would quickly lose their interest in the robots. In the same works, other teachers' concerns regarded the extra workload that robots would bring to them and the possibility of robots taking their place in the future. Thanks also to science fiction literature and filmography (e.g., Blade Runner [6], Terminator [2]), the idea that robots will soon replace humans in their jobs is widespread in the collective naive imagination. People without experience in robotics are often exposed to the concept of a robot as a threat. Experts in robotics know that it is most likely not the case: in the following years, in social settings, robots will probably be used just as tools or simple helpers and will not be completely autonomous. To fill the gap between naive imagination and reality, we believe that users - teachers in our case - could benefit from learning first-hand the functioning of these robotics devices to understand their potential and limits fully. In this way, they can integrate them effectively into the learning programs. Despite all their concerns, in [22], even teachers themselves emphasized the need for adequate training so that they could comprehend a robot's functioning.

The above-reported works represent suitable indicators of teachers' opinions on educational robots, even if they do not include robotics activity in authentic learning contexts. Incorporating HRI in real-world learning scenarios represents a promising chance to gain a more comprehensive overview of educational robotics, but only a few studies consider teachers' points of view. Among those, Westlund et al. [25] carried out a two-month study in a kindergarten in which children interacted with a Tega robot. They administered pre and post-questionnaires to the teachers who supervised the activity. From before to after the study, their enthusiasm for employing a social robot in their classrooms declined together with their belief that the Tega robot would benefit students' education. They also would have used it differently than how proposed by the researchers. This finding suggests once again that educators may benefit from learning robotics skills to make the device behave as they deem appropriate.

The previous studies highlight a need to provide robotics training programs for teachers to promote the deployment of educational robotics in schools. At the same time, it would be necessary to understand whether and how a training program affects the perception of robotics of teachers with different backgrounds and in different school types. To this aim, in this work, we questioned teachers before and after a robotics training program that included theoretical and practical aspects of using the NAO robot.

2   Research Questions

We formulated three research questions by drawing inspiration from previous work related to teachers' opinions about robots in education. Considering that, in the media, robots are mostly portrayed as autonomous, error-proof machines endowed with self-consciousness, we expect teachers to project these expectations on NAO at the beginning of the training program; we assume that the training would help them to be aware of the real potential of the robot. Thus we asked:

RQ1: Will the training program aid in lowering teachers' naive expectations of robots' skills and thus help them become aware of the true potential of the robot? Will this positively or negatively affect the intentions of using the device?

RQ2: Are teachers' age, previous knowledge about technology, the subject taught (STEM or literary), and the type of school they teach in (kindergarten, primary, secondary) correlated with their impression of NAO and their will to use it in class?

RQ3: At the end of the training program, how will teachers evaluate the enjoyment and participation of the class in the robotics activities? Will they find these activities useful for the education of their students?

3   Robotics Training Program

The NaoToKnow project was funded under a call for proposals of the Italian Ministry of Education and implemented by the national network of educational institutes ARETE+4NAO[1]. The project involves twenty-three schools in Italy

---

[1] https://www.icmamelipalestrina.edu.it/arete4nao/.

engaged in training their teachers on the topics of educational robotics and advanced coding, with the aim of the implementation of inclusive educational activities through the use of humanoid robotics and innovative teaching methodologies within sample classes. The educational training was delivered by Scuola di Robotica[2] and the primary objective was to provide the necessary skills for teachers to introduce humanoid robotics within curricular lessons and laboratory activities. The training involved 106 teachers from kindergarten, primary and secondary schools. The course lasted three months and involved teachers participating in thirty hours of online training dedicated to developing skills for the use of humanoid robotics in the classroom. Every school owned a NAO robot at the teachers' disposal to perform the practical activities proposed in the course. First of all, teachers were familiarized with programming using Open Roberta[3] an online simulator for programming the NAO; then, the training included the fundamentals of how to program the robot NAO on Choreographe[4] through block programming (a visual and intuitive programming method). Specifically, the course included the following teachings:

1. Introduction to humanoid robotics;
2. Introduction and familiarization with NAO;
3. How to connect NAO to a router;
4. Building dialogues, using blocks set up on Choregraphe and programming in Python;
5. How to make NAO walk;
6. Creating personalized movements, using the Timeline on Choregraphe;
7. Creating a synchronized movement with Coregraphe;
8. Face and object recognition, using NAO's camera;
9. Programming NAO's touch sensors;
10. How to acquire data with NAO's sensors.

At the end of the program, teachers participating in the course built a final project with their students: each class made a short video presentation of the activities completed during the training and prepared a live demonstration of them using NAO. The projects were presented at a final in-person event, where Scuola di Robotica's instructors revised them: all the projects were evaluated positively.

During the training course, the teachers had the possibility to participate in a research project coordinated by Scuola di Robotica, the University of Genoa, and the Italian Institute of Technology, focused on understanding students' and teachers' robot perception, by replying to a series of questionnaires at the beginning and at the end of the course.

---

[2] https://www.scuoladirobotica.it/.

[3] https://lab.open-roberta.org/.

[4] https://www.softbankrobotics.com/emea/en/support/nao-6/downloads-softwares.

4   Methods

4.1   Participants

Participants were recruited from the 106 teachers that joined the NAO To Know project. The study was approved by the University of Genoa's ethical committee (n. 20220317, 03/17/2022). Teachers signed an informed consent form and completed two sets of questionnaires: one after the first lesson of the project and another after the last one. The first set of questionnaires (Q1) was fully completed by 71 teachers, while 52 participants fully completed the second one (Q2). For both Q1 and Q2, 12 participants were excluded from further analysis because they failed to answer correctly to the attention-bump item (i.e., "to demonstrate your attention, answer 5 to this question") that was inserted in the survey to prevent random responses. In the questionnaires, teachers were asked to insert a personal anonymous code, self-created according to our indications, to connect the two questionnaire answers. 40 participants fully completed both questionnaires ($n_1 = 40$, 7 males, 33 females; age: $M = 47.9, SD = 8.13$); 10% of the sample comprises teachers from kindergarten, 37.5% of primary school teachers, and the remaining 52.5% of secondary school teachers.

4.2   Questionnaires

The questionnaires were administered in Italian, using Survey Monkey[5] and required about 15 min to be completed. The surveys were created ad hoc using items previously utilized in HRI and educational contexts to assess the teachers' impression of the robot NAO. Q1 consisted in:

- Twelve items to assess *Agency and Patiency* i.e., the attributed capacity to act and to feel, and six items of *Mind Attribution* i.e., the tendency to attribute a mind to other agents, from Gray et al. [12] (e.g., "I believe the robot NAO is able to feel pain ";"...to act morally";"...to think").
- Nine items from the scale *Warmth and Competence* i.e., the attribution of being heartfelt and intelligent to an agent, by Fiske et al. [8] (e.g., "I believe the robot Nao is independent";"...sincere").
- Six items from *Human-like appearance* scale i.e., the level of physical similarity with the humans, by Ferrari et al. [7] (e.g., "In my opinion NAO looks like a human).
- Three items from a short version of scale by Spaccatini et al. [23] to assess the *Likeability* i.e., the degree of liking the NAO (e.g., "I think NAO is nice").
- *UTAUT Unified Theory Of Acceptance And Use Of Technology* scale, already used for NAO by Vega et al. [24]. The scale is composed of the following sub-scale: *Intention of Use* (three items, e.g., "I think I will use NAO during classes"); *Perceived Enjoyment* (six items, e.g., "I like to do stuff with NAO"); Perceived Sociability (three items, e.g., "I believe the robot understands me;;"); *Trust* (two items, e.g., "I would follow the robot's advice");

---

[5] https://it.surveymonkey.com.

Performance Expectancy (four items, e.g., "NAO's technology is useful for education in general"); *Effort Expectancy* (two items, e.g., "NAO's technology is easy to use").

Moreover, teachers answered the following ad hoc created items: "How familiar are you with educational robotics?"; "How familiar are you with technology at school?". To assess their confidence level in technology and robotics, they had to choose one of these options: "Very much"(5) "Much"(4), "Enough"(3), "A few"(2), or "'At all"(1). Participants evaluated all items on a 5-point Likert scale (1 = "I strongly disagree", 5 = "I strongly agree"). Finally, demographic information (age, gender, education), including details about their job (school, type of subject taught), were collected. In Q2, the same scales administrated in Q1 were used, with the addition of the following scales:

– Three items from *Class Enjoyment scale* by D'Amico et al. [5] (e.g., "Activities with NAO have been funny for the class").
– Items from *Performance Expectancy* scale by Moore and Benbasat [19], composed of the two following sub-scales: *Ease of Use* (six items, "using NAO makes my work easier"); *Public Image* i.e. image in school derived from using the robot (4 items, e.g., "The fact that I used NAO improved my image at school").

4.3 Statistical Analyses

The statistical analyses were realized using Jamovi[6]. First, items initially formulated negatively to avoid participants' acquiescence in their answers were appropriately reversed. Then, for each scale, we computed the descriptive statistics and internal consistency using Chronbach's α (Table 1). All the scales with $\alpha > 0.6$ were considered consistent [3]. In our sample, female teachers were prevalent: thirty-three out of forty participants declared to be female (82.5%). The sample thus reflects the national average in Italy; according to the Italian Ministry of Education, 83.2% of teachers in public education are female [18]. Since the male population in this study is not adequately represented, no observations about gender are reported. Relating to RQ1, we conducted within-subject analyses (Wilcoxon signed-rank tests) to confront the answers between the two questionnaires.

In an effort to answer RQ2, we ran Spearman's correlation tests to verify whether teachers' age, their confidence in school technology, and educational robotics are correlated with Intention of Use, Perceived Enjoyment, Performance Expectation, and Effort Expectations. We then checked for possible differences between teachers of STEM disciplines and literary ones running independent sample T-tests. Mann-Whitney tests were carried out to look for possible differences based on teachers' type of school (kindergarten, primary, secondary).

With regard to RQ3, we ran a post-analysis on data of Public Image, Ease of Usage, and Class Enjoyment scales, which were solely evaluated in Q2. We

---

[6] https://www.jamovi.org/.

conducted Wilcoxon rank tests against the neutral scale mid-point (3 "Neither agree nor disagree", on a 5-point Likert scale).

5 Results

In connection with RQ1, we found that, with respect to Q1, answers to Q2 show a significant decrement on the majority of the scales: Agency ($p < .001$), Patiency ($p = 0.005$), Mind Attribution ($p < .001$), Competence ($p < .001$), Warmth ($p = 0.012$), Intention of Use ($p < .001$), Perceived Enjoyment ($p = 0.001$), Performance Expectation ($p < .001$), and Trust ($p < .001$). No significant differences between Q1 and Q2 were evidenced for the Human-likeness ($p = 0.514$), the Likeability ($p = 0.955$), and the Effort Expectation ($p = 0.200$) scales.

Concerning the second research question, results reveal that teachers' confidence in Educational Robotics and School Technology correlates positively with Effort Expectancy (Q1): respectively $\rho = 0.378, p = 0.016$; $\rho = 0.429, p = 0.006$. In Q2, confidence in Educational Robotics showed again positive link with Effort Expectancy ($\rho = 0.387, p = 0.014$), as well as with Ease of Usage ($\rho = 0.571, p < .001$).

A significant correlation concerning Age with Agency was observed in Q1 ($\rho = -0.315, p = 0.037$). Age is also positively correlated with the Performance Expectancy expressed in Q2 ($\rho = 0.354, p = 0.025$). No significant correlation of Age with Intention of Use was found in Q1 ($\rho = 0.212, p = 0.189$), while it was present in Q2 ($\rho = 0.507, p < 0.001$). Moreover, Intention of Use presents significant positive correlations with Performance Expectations ($\rho = 0.564, p < .001$) and Perceived Enjoyment ($\rho = 0.371, p = 0.018$) in Q1.

We then checked for possible differences between teachers of STEM disciplines ($n_1 = 22$) and literary ones ($n_2 = 17$). For Q1, it was observed a difference between the two groups regarding robot's Competence, evaluated significantly higher by STEM teachers ($M_1 = 3.03, M_2 = 2.34$; $p = 0.047$). In Q2, after the training program, no significant difference regarding Competence was detected ($M_1 = 2.15, M_2 = 1.87$; $p = 0.420$). Analyses regarding teachers working in different schools (i.e., kindergarten, primary or secondary) did not evidence significant differences between these groups.

Relating to RQ3, we found that levels of all the scales significantly differ from the neutral value. In particular, Public Image ($M = 2.52, SD = 0.85; p < .001$) and Ease of Usage ($M = 2.73, SD = 0.80; p = 0.015$) levels resulted significantly lower mid-point; conversely teachers' opinion on Class Enjoyment resulted significantly positive ($M = 3.48, SD = 0.98; p = 0.005$).

6 Discussion and Conclusion

In this work, we have tried to study how a training program on robotics may affect teachers' expectations and impressions of the robot. After the training program, participants decreased their levels of expectancy about the robot's

Table 1. Descriptive statistics and internal consistencies of data from questionnaires Q1 (M_1, SD_1, α_1) and Q2 (M_2, SD_2, α_2) are reported.

Scale (1-to-5-point Likert)	M_1	SD_1	α_1	M_2	SD_2	α_2
Agency (i.e. capacity of acting, doing)	2.70	1.01	.81	2.04	0.81	.75
Patiency (i.e. capacity of feeling)	1.64	0.81	.90	1.27	0.59	.94
Mind attribution (i.e. having a mind)	2.64	0.97	.86	1.88	0.85	.81
Competence (i.e. being competent, intelligent)	2.77	1.09	.81	2.04	1.03	.85
Warmth (i.e. being heartfelt, sympathetic)	2.80	1.42	.91	2.33	1.18	.84
Human-like Appearance	2.76	0.74	.73	2.66	0.69	.64
Likeability (i.e. degree of liking of the robot)	4.18	0.84	.85	4.19	0.95	.93
Intention of Use	4.01	0.80	.90	3.36	1.11	.89
Perceived Enjoyment (in using the robot)	4.24	0.57	.68	3.82	0.77	.80
Performance Expectation	3.83	0.80	.84	3.38	0.89	.90
Effort Expectation	2.44	0.91	.95	2.21	0.95	.83
Trust	2.49	1.20	.86	1.73	0.91	.71
Perceived Sociability*	–	–	–	2.56	0.97	.59
Public Image* (i.e. for using the robot at school)	–	–	–	2.52	0.85	.76
Ease of Usage*	–	–	–	2.73	0.80	.77
Class Enjoyment* (in using the robot)	–	–	–	3.48	0.98	.83

* Scales present in Q2 only.

capabilities and autonomous skills (RQ1). This suggests that educating participants on how to use a robot results in a more realistic comprehension of the potential of the robot itself. Also, the Perceived Enjoyment of the robot lowered; this could be due to the novelty effect [15]: humans tend to be more curious and engage more with a new person, artificial agent, or object the first times they see it; then, after a few interactions, they start losing interest. This phenomenon is a well-known problem of HRI [11]. Conversely, teachers did not change their minds about the robot's human-like appearance or about how much they liked it. Probably in evaluating these constructs, they are more influenced by the appearance of the robot and not by the interaction with it.

Furthermore, results show that the background of participants influences to a different extent, some aspects of the perception of NAO (RQ2). Specifically, our results suggest that the more teachers are confident with robotics, the more they are aware of the effort needed to interact with it. Additionally, a difference in the perception of NAO according to the subject taught by the participants is evidenced. STEM teachers tend to believe the robot is more competent compared to literature teachers, but this difference only occurs in the first moment. This could imply that the training program may have a role in leveling the robot's perception regardless of their teaching domain. The age of participants seems to have an impact on the evaluation of the agency of the robot and performance expectancy. This result is consistent with previous findings in the literature.

As evidenced by [4] the advancement of technology may be considered new and unfamiliar to older users. Such unfamiliarity might be a concern because some researchers found that older users showed little interest and motivation in learning novel technologies ([10]. However, research also suggests that consumers starting with higher technology discomfort show a positive level of enthusiasm about their user experience in the end.

Outcomes of questionnaire Q2 show that teachers' evaluated the experience with NAO as positive for their classes (RQ3). The mean value is above the mean point of the scale (corresponding to a neutral judgment) but not to a great extent ($M = 3.48, SD = 0.98$). As reported by [3], usually, when participants are not sure how to respond, they tend to settle their responses on the mid-point of the scale. Furthermore, participants' difficulty in using the robots might have influenced their opinion in evaluating their students. Future works should put students' observations together with the ones from the teachers for a more comprehensive overview. Moreover, participants reported low levels of perceived Ease of Usage of the robot: this is in line with previous studies' observations. Teachers reported low levels also in the Public Image scale, which refers to a possible improvement of their reputation at school thanks to the use of NAO. This could be a sign that employing a robot at school is not considered prestigious: maybe, more incentives should be given to teachers to employ robots at school in order to improve their motivation and promote innovative ways of learning.

In light of the above-discussed results, we believe the present work makes some noteworthy contributions to the existing literature. We think that a course such as the one described in this study not only provides teachers with new skills but also gives them a more accurate view of the current possibilities and limits of educational robotics. This could be meaningful because it might allow teachers to become active and aware actors in robotics education. Besides, they would be able to adapt teaching methods often rigidly delivered by researchers to convey concepts to students appropriately.

In the future, it would be necessary to run more studies to gain a wider overview of teachers' impressions of educational robots also comparing to the students' ones. For example, as some works suggest that cultural background influences humans' perception of robots [13,14], it may be interesting running a cross-cultural study involving teachers from different countries to investigate whether this effect applies to educational robotics.

Acknowledgements. The "NaoToKnow" project was funded under the PNSD national call for proposals "STEAM Methodologies" and implemented by the national network of school Institutes "ARETE+4NAO, of which the Istituto Comprensivo "Goffredo Mameli" of Palestrina (RM) directed by DS Professor Ester Corsi is the leader, involving twenty-three Comprehensive Institutes in the Italian regions of Lazio, Abruzzo, Campania, Sardinia, Lombardy, Piedmont and Emilia-Romagna. The authors wish to thank Scuola di Robotica for the support, with particular reference to Filippo Bogliolo, Gianluca Pedemonte and Emanuele Micheli. A special thank to Dr. Joshua Zonca for the support in the statistical analysis.

References

1. Belpaeme, T., Kennedy, J., Ramachandran, A., Scassellati, B., Tanaka, F.: Social robots for education: A review. Sci. Robot. **3**(21), eaat5954 (2018)
2. Cameron, J.: The Terminator. Orion Pictures (1984)
3. Chiorri, C.: Psicometria e teoria dei test. McGraw-Hill Education (2016)
4. Chu, L., Fung, H.H.: Age differences in state curiosity: Examining the role of personal relevance. Gerontology **68**(3), 321–329 (2022)
5. D'Amico, A., Guastella, D., Chella, A.: A playful experiential learning system with educational robotics. Front. Robot. AI 33 (2020)
6. Deeley, M., Ridley, S., Hampton, F., Peoples, D., Powell, I.: Vangelis, Dick. Blade runner. Ladd Company, P.K. (1982)
7. Ferrari, F., Paladino, M.P., Jetten, J.: Blurring human-machine distinctions: Anthropomorphic appearance in social robots as a threat to human distinctiveness. Int. J. Soc. Robot. **8**(2), 287–302 (2016)
8. Fiske, S.T., Cuddy, A.J., Glick, P.: Universal dimensions of social cognition: Warmth and competence. Trends Cogn. Sci. **11**(2), 77–83 (2007)
9. Fridin, M., Belokopytov, M.: Acceptance of socially assistive humanoid robot by preschool and elementary school teachers. Comput. Hum. Behav. **33**, 23–31 (2014)
10. Gilly, M.C., Celsi, M.W., Schau, H.J.: It don't come easy: Overcoming obstacles to technology use within a resistant consumer group. J. Consum. Aff. **46**(1), 62–89 (2012)
11. Gockley, R., et al.: Designing robots for long-term social interaction. In: 2005 IEEE/RSJ International Conference on Intelligent Robots and Systems, pp. 1338–1343. IEEE (2005)
12. Gray, H.M., Gray, K., Wegner, D.M.: Dimensions of mind perception. Science **315**(5812), 619–619 (2007)
13. Haring, K.S., Silvera-Tawil, D., Matsumoto, Y., Velonaki, M., Watanabe, K.: Perception of an android robot in japan and australia: a cross-cultural comparison. In: Beetz, M., Johnston, B., Williams, M.-A. (eds.) ICSR 2014. LNCS (LNAI), vol. 8755, pp. 166–175. Springer, Cham (2014). https://doi.org/10.1007/978-3-319-11973-1_17
14. Haring, K.S., Silvera-Tawil, D., Watanabe, K., Velonaki, M.: The Influence Of Robot Appearance and Interactive Ability in HRI: A Cross-cultural Study, pp. 392–401 (2016)
15. Houston-Price, C., Nakai, S.: Distinguishing novelty and familiarity effects in infant preference procedures. Infant Child Develop. Int. J. Res. Practice **13**(4), 341–348 (2004)
16. Kim, S.W., Lee, Y.: A survey on elementary school teachers' attitude toward robot. In: E-Learn: World Conference on E-Learning in Corporate, Government, Healthcare, and Higher Education, pp. 1802–1807. Association for the Advancement of Computing in Education (AACE) (2015)
17. Lee, E., Lee, Y., Kye, B., Ko, B.: Elementary and middle school teachers', students' and parents' perception of robot-aided education in korea. In: EdMedia+ Innovate Learning, pp. 175–183. Association for the Advancement of Computing in Education (AACE) (2008)
18. Ministero Dell'Istruzione, DGCASIS: Docenti a tempo indeterminato. scuola statale (2020), https://dati.istruzione.it/opendata/opendata/catalogo/elements1/leaf/?area=Personale%20Scuola&datasetId=DS0600DOCTIT

19. Moore, G.C., Benbasat, I.: Development of an instrument to measure the perceptions of adopting an information technology innovation. Inf. Syst. Res. **2**(3), 192–222 (1991)
20. Reich-Stiebert, N., Eyssel, F.: Robots in the classroom: what teachers think about teaching and learning with education robots. In: Agah, A., Cabibihan, J.-J., Howard, A.M., Salichs, M.A., He, H. (eds.) ICSR 2016. LNCS (LNAI), vol. 9979, pp. 671–680. Springer, Cham (2016). https://doi.org/10.1007/978-3-319-47437-3_66
21. Serholt, S., et al.: Teachers' views on the use of empathic robotic tutors in the classroom. In: The 23rd IEEE International Symposium on Robot and Human Interactive Communication, pp. 955–960. IEEE (2014)
22. Serholt, S., et al.: The case of classroom robots: teachers' deliberations on the ethical tensions. AI Soc. **32**(4), 613–631 (2017)
23. Spaccatini, F., Pacilli, M.G., Giovannelli, I., Roccato, M., Penone, G.: Sexualized victims of stranger harassment and victim blaming: The moderating role of right-wing authoritarianism. Sexuality Culture **23**(3), 811–825 (2019)
24. Vega, A., Ramírez-Benavidez, K., Guerrero, L.A.: Tool utaut Applied To Measure Interaction Experience With Nao Robot, pp. 501–512 (2019)
25. Westlund, J.K.: Breazeal, C.: Lessons From Teachers on Performing HRI Studies With Young Children in Schools pp. 383–390 (2016)

Moveable Älıpbi: The Montessori Method for Robot-Assisted Alphabet Learning

Aida Zhanatkyzy[1] , Zhansaule Telisheva[1] , Aida Amirova[2] ,
Nurziya Oralbayeva[2] , Arna Aimysheva[1] , and Anara Sandygulova[1]([⊠])

[1] Department of Robotics and Mechatronics, School of Engineering and Digital
Sciences, Nazarbayev University, Astana, Kazakhstan
{aida.zhanatkyzy,zhansaule.telisheva,arna.aimysheva,
anara.sandygulova}@nu.edu.kz
[2] Graduate School of Education, Nazarbayev University, Astana, Kazakhstan
{aida.amirova,nurziya.oralbayeva}@nu.edu.kz

Abstract. The Montessori method is well-known for its child-centered
and hands-on learning approach for early literacy development. This
study is the first to apply the Montessori method in robot-assisted language learning (RALL). We developed an alphabet learning system that
consists of a Moveable alphabet, a tablet, and a social robot. We conducted a between-subjects experiment with 89 Kazakh children aged
6–11 that learned the Kazakh Latin alphabet either with a Montessori-
human (MH) or a Montessori-robot (MR) teacher. We examined the
effects of the learning method on children's learning gains and emotional
outcomes across these two conditions. Our results suggest that in the
Montessori learning environment the MH teacher was significantly more
effective in providing early literacy support than the MR teacher. The
emotional states were mixed between grades, but the children in the MR
condition felt happier than those in the MH condition in Grades 1 (ages
6–7) and 4 (ages 10–11). This exploratory study suggests testing the
method's effectiveness in long-term child-robot interactions, with varied
learning tasks over time.

Keywords: Human-robot interaction · Montessori method ·
Educational robots · Robot-assisted language learning

1 Introduction

Robots have become assistants and mediators in language learning and teaching.
Their application gave rise to robot-assisted language learning (RALL), which
has seen a worldwide increase in human-robot interaction (HRI). Social robots
are being used to teach core language skills of speaking and listening [1], writing [2], and reading [3]. As distinct from other technologies, they play a social
role (e.g., a peer) and have physical embodiment to support learner engagement
[4]. Although there has been growing evidence in support of robots as language

companions, they mostly focused on vocabulary knowledge [5,6]. Complex productive language skills such as writing are rarely sought in HRI [2,7]. To some extent, we address this gap and propose a robotic system to enable alphabet learning. In the following ten years, Kazakhstan intends to revert to the Latin-based alphabet of the Kazakh language; the current Kazakh alphabet is Cyrillic-based. This transition may benefit from diverse language learning approaches to be applied in primary grades in which children currently study three languages (Kazakh, Russian, English) and thus use two different alphabets (Cyrillic and Latin) at the same time. This work responds to potential linguistic challenges such as lower motivation to acquire the new alphabet and hence aims to find out effective alphabet learning scenarios to smooth the transition.

In this study, we apply a widely-recognized learning approach - the Montessori method - for early literacy development. It has been long considered effective for young children to engage in self-directed and developmentally appropriate literacy acquisition. Central to this approach is the idea that children's potential "unfolds" in specially designed environments reinforced by developmental manipulatives and self-corrective learning materials [8]. Montessori approach is reportedly different from traditional education practices [9–11]. The difference reflects physical environment, instructional methodology, and classroom practices. Children learn at their preferred pace through manipulation of instructional materials. As such, autonomy, self-discipline, and collaboration are essential for learning. These core principles are echoed in current practices of student-centred learning at different educational levels. Current evidence have reported on social and cognitive benefits such as increased learner autonomy and decision-making [12,13], effective language development [14] and learning gains [15]. Some studies compared to what extent students' academic and social outcomes in Montessori and traditional education differed. For example, children at pre-school age achieved considerably high literacy skills such as letter-word recognition and phonological decoding, whereas those aged 12 or over improved writing and social skills [16]. Another study found mixed results and did not support the general hypothesis that Montessori children achieve superior academic gains over non-Montessori children [8]. Considering emotional advantages, one study findings demonstrated that the method positively affects social competency and behaviour of 4–5-years-old children [17]. Furthermore, parents and teachers stated that the method brought positive changes in emotion-regulation of children. While supporters of the Montessori approach highlight both social and academic advantages for learners, existing research has not adequately confirmed these benefits.

Our investigation will empirically evaluate the applicability of the social robot modelling Montessori-like learning system in aiding children to learn the new alphabet. This approach may provide motivation for students to practice the alphabet supported by physical Moveable alphabet and self-correcting flashcards. Its multi-modal environment maintains child interest and engagement. Another feature that we highlight is pair learning which aligns well with the collaborative nature of the Montessori method. To the best of our knowledge, there has not been any research on child-robot interaction (CRI) that directly applies the Montessori method in language learning with a social robot. The name of our approach, "Moveable Älıpbi" refers to the Kazakh word "älıpbi" meaning "alphabet" in English; together, they stand for Moveable Alphabet. It represents both the teaching strategy and the target language. We contribute to the use and validation of the Montessori method for RAAL with 89 children ages 6 to 11 in this pioneering study. By applying the Montessori method and its principles to alphabet acquisition, we compare the effects of the two social agents: Montessori robot (MR) and Montessori human (MH) teacher. This comparison helps us identify whether or not the robot can aid children similarly well as the human teacher in the Montessori environment. We also consider different predictors that may influence the children's learning and affective experiences. This knowledge would help a wider HRI community to learn about different social learning paradigms as embedded into the robotic system. These contributions are salient in two aspects. First and foremost, the learning methods are commonly tested in child-robot interactions, but they might not be adapted to fit this context. Our contribution is thus to provide socially-situated evidence for the use of the existing learning approach in RALL. By this study, we evaluate if the minimally social robot with less input but motivating aspect can enhance children's learning. Furthermore, we explore the effectiveness of the Montessori robot compared to the human teacher baseline condition. This allows us to test the viability of the method in RAAL as an engaging way for literacy development. The results from this study would inform further steps in the long-term use of the system.

2   The Moveable Älıpbi System

2.1   Humanoid Robot NAO

The humanoid robot NAO is a social robot with an autonomous and programmable architecture developed by SoftBank Robotics. It is the mostly used robot in CRI research in robot-assisted educational and healthcare applications [18]. The robot is small-sized (58 cm) and easy to transport. Children like its friendly and human-like appearance. It has 25 °C of freedom and seven tactile sensors on different body parts. We used a custom Kazakh Speech Synthesis of child voice on the robot.

2.2   The Moveable Alphabet and Learning Activity

The Moveable Alphabet is among the sensory alphabets of the Montessori Language Curriculum [19]. It is designed to prepare children for writing, reading, and spelling to help them develop literacy skills from basic to advanced levels.

Our learning activity consists of 12 practice words spelled using wooden letters from the Moveable alphabet. While performing the activity, a child sees and selects a written word in the Kazakh Latin letters from flashcards and then

Fig. 1. Experimental conditions: Montessori Human tutor (left), Montessori Robot tutor (right)

spells it with the wooden letters. The order of the words are decided by children during practice. The robot or teacher only guides children on the first try and then simply observes them by asking questions like "Which word would you pick next" and "Are you done?" when they finish spelling words one by one. Once the child finishes spelling the word, the robot/teacher pronounces it correctly and then asks the child to repeat. The activity was validated by a Montessori practitioner prior to the experiment.

3   Methods

A primary school with the mixed language of instruction in the capital of Kazakhstan, Astana, was a research site for the experiment. The participants were randomly assigned to Montessori Human (MH) or Montessori Robot (MR) condition in a between-subject design.

3.1   Hypotheses

Drawing on current evidence on the Montessori method described in Sect. 1, we investigate its application with the social robot compared to the human condition and evaluate children's learning and emotional outcomes. The main hypotheses are as follows:

- H1: There will be no differences in the number of learned letters between the Montessori robot and the Montessori human teacher conditions.
- H2: Children in the Montessori robot condition will achieve more positive affective gains than children in the Montessori teacher condition.

3.2   Recruitment

This research was approved by the Nazarbayev University Institutional Research Ethics Committee (NU-IREC), dated 20.04.2022. Written child assent and informed consent forms were handed out to all children in the classroom when their teacher was present. The researchers ensured the provision of a simple explanation about the aim and the procedures of the study. The children were asked to show the forms to their parents so that they can decide whether to approve or decline child participation. Afterwards, they returned the forms to a classroom teacher who collected them for us.

3.3   Participants

A total of 89 children (44.9% of males and 55.1% of females) aged 6–11 years old participated in the experiment. The children had various linguistic and academic backgrounds. As education in Kazakhstan promotes trilingual policy, these children can be considered early bi-/multilinguals with varying degrees of language proficiency in two or more languages. Their interaction lasted for about 30–40 min.

3.4   Procedures

The experiment procedures consisted of a pre-test, a demographic survey, a learning activity, and a post-test. First, a pair of children in each condition were taken out of a classroom and walked with the two researchers to the experiment room. Children were seated at separate tables and were asked to complete a pre-test to assess their knowledge of the Kazakh Latin alphabet that shares similar letters with the English alphabet they already know. Then, another researcher conducted a survey to record children's demographic information, including their age, gender, linguistic background, and academic standing. Then, children were instructed to switch tables and take a seat either facing the robot or the human teacher. The setup for both conditions is shown in Fig. 1. After the intervention, a post-test was administered to the children to evaluate their learning gains with regard to the number of learned letters in the Kazakh Latin alphabet. As soon as the children finished all the procedures, the researchers returned them to the classroom and invited other participants.

3.5   Measures

Data were collected both through cognitive (e.g., learning gains) and affective measures (e.g., self-reporting survey). Our dependent variables were the following:

– **Learning Gain (LG)** is computed from the pre-tests and post-tests that children filled in before and after the session with the robot/human. A child was given a piece of paper with a list in two columns: one filled in with the Kazakh Cyrillic letters, and the other column would be filled in with the Kazakh Latin letters by a child. LG is then determined by counting the number of new learned letters in the post-test as compared to the pre-test (e.g. wrong or skipped letters in the pre-test that were then correct letters in the post-test are regarded as LG).

- **Sorting task.** A child was asked to physically sort five small pictures (a book, a tablet, a NAO robot, a computer, and a human) in ascending order according to their 1) Effectiveness to teach, 2) Easy to learn from, 3) Interesting, and 4) Favourite. We then noted the order on a 5-point Likert scale.
- **Automatic Emotion Analysis.** A camera was placed in front of the child capturing facial expressions for real-time emotional analysis. Facial Expression Recognition uses different datasets such as Affectnet and FER+ [20] which enable identification of the emotional states from the videos. Five different expressions were analysed: neutrality, happiness, sadness, anger, and surprise. After that score from 0 to 1 was given for each state depending on the duration of the video and the frequency of that emotion for each participant.

Our independent variables were the following:

- **Condition:** Montessori human and Montessori robot (see Sect. 2.2).
- **Gender:** distribution of male and female children.
- **Grades:** this variable includes all primary school grades between 1–4.
- **Language status:** children were grouped into monolinguals and bilinguals. The survey options included Kazakh only, Russian only, both Kazakh and Russian languages or other language. We calculated the number of languages in each domain of use (at home/at school/etc.). The children using one language in all situations are grouped into monolinguals, while those using more than one language were labeled as bilinguals.
- **Preferred/dominant language:** this variable includes three languages - Kazakh, Russian, or both (Kazakh and Russian or other language); identified by the children's general language preference for communication.
- **Favourite subject:** Children were asked an open question on their favourite subject. The responses were grouped into four categories: STEM (Maths, Technology, Science), Arts (Artwork, Music, Physical Education), Social (Kazakh, Russian, English, Self Knowledge), Mixed (when two or three subjects of different areas were mentioned as favourite).

4   Results

A series of one-way and two-way ANOVA tests were conducted to examine to what extent the independent variables, such as grades, preferred language and subject, affect the children's learning gains, sorting task choices, and emotional states over the session.

4.1   Learning Gain Analysis

On average, the number of learned Kazakh Latin alphabet letters was amounted to 2.27 ± 2.02 (Max = 8, Min = 0). A one-way ANOVA revealed that the children in the MH condition (2.82 ± 2.04) had more learning gains than those in the MR condition (1.73 ± 1.88): $F(1, 87) = 6.833, p = 0.011$. Figure 2A presents this result.

4.2   Automatic Emotion Analysis

The number of children who participated in this analysis was 68 (76.4% of 89 children) due to the absence of some children's video data. Happiness was analysed from facial expressions using one-way and two-way ANOVA tests to understand if there were any individual differences.

Two-way ANOVA tests analysing the effect of both conditions and grade variables showed a statistically significant result in happiness expressions: $F(3, 60) = 2.950, p = 0.04$. As shown in Fig. 2B, youngest and oldest groups of children had significant differences between MR and MH conditions. The children of Grade 1 (0.236 ± 0.135) and Grade 4 (0.167 ± 0.0423) in the MR condition had higher happiness scores than their peers in the MH condition (Grade 1 - 0.146 ± 0.0753, Grade 4 - 0.06 ± 0.0076).

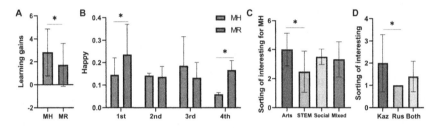

Fig. 2. A) Learning gains for two conditions; B) Happiness expression scores across conditions and grade levels; C) Sorting Task results for Interesting rating of the human by favourite subjects, and B) Sorting Task results for Interesting rating of the robot by grade levels.

4.3   Sorting Task Analysis

The analysis of the children's sorting task choices revealed some significant results. One-way ANOVA analysis by favourite subjects showed that the children reporting STEM subjects as their favourite rated (from 1 to 5) the human teacher to be more interesting (2.47 ± 1.41) than those children, who reported Arts subjects as their favourite (4 ± 1.13): $F(3, 40) = 3.951, p = 0.015$ (please refer to Fig. 2C).

5   Discussion

This study evaluated the effectiveness of the Montessori method for acquiring the Kazakh Latin alphabet with a social robot which was compared to a human teacher in the same learning environment. Overall, a between-subject experiment involving 89 children ages 6–11 in Grades 1–4 practiced the Kazakh Latin alphabet in the MR or the MH condition. We particularly measured learning gains and emotional states by the children's individual characteristics across the conditions.

Following the results from our previous studies on alphabet learning [7,21], we expected that children in either condition would perform similarly well in the MR and MT conditions. Both agents followed a scripted learning protocol and just guided children without significant teacher involvement, providing space for peer-supported learning. However, the results show children in the MH condition learned significantly more letters than their peers in the MR condition. Thus, our H1 is refuted. It appears that the presence of adult teacher may still influence children's learning experiences. For many reasons, robots cannot replace humans in any social interaction, but only a few research has examined how effective they can be in educational tasks compared to other learning agents [21–23]. Integrating robotic technologies into learning environments requires twofold objectives - addressing technical challenges and transforming educational practice [24]. This intersecting knowledge should be prioritized when bringing interdisciplinary solutions for social causes like technology-enhanced learning.

Our second hypothesis, declaring positive emotional states that were expressed by the children in the MR condition, revealed some interesting results. When we analysed "happiness" by grades, we found that children in general felt happier with the robot than those learning with the teacher. Especially, the children from Grade 1 (ages 6–7) and Grade 4 (ages 10–11) had significantly higher happy scores during the session. But those children in Grades 2–3 had no significant difference in happy states between the MR and MH conditions. We explain this result by developmental differences in children by their age. Previous studies [25,26] also found some positive emotional experiences in young children. For instance, the children aged 6–7 years old reported more happy states than older children aged 10-11 [27]. These results partly support our assumption claiming significantly positive emotions towards the robot. In light of that, our H2 is partially accepted. Additionally, we also explored if the children's preferred subjects predicted their responses to how interesting they found the robot and the human teacher. Interestingly, the children who preferred STEM subjects rated the human teacher more interesting than those who favored Arts subjects.

In sum, our results demonstrated that the Montessori robot could support alphabet learning, yet its effectiveness is not comparable to that of the human teacher. Children learning with the MH teacher outperformed those in the robot condition, with significant differences in learning gains. The emotional engagement with the robot revealed mixed analyses on the happiness continuum. Interestingly, children from Grades 1 and 4 were happier when interacting with the robot than their peers in the human teacher condition. Children's emotional engagement with the robot requires greater scholarly attention in future studies. The short-term nature of the study limits the conclusions we can derive from this study. However, we believe the results may encourage future research to adapt and validate child-centred educational approaches towards making robots socially responsive. To achieve this, a solid exploration of educational approaches in varied HRI contexts is needed.

Acknowledgment. The Nazarbayev University Collaborative Research Program grants 091019CRP2107 and OPCRP2022002 provided funding for this work.

References

1. Lee, S., Lee, S., et al.: On the effectiveness of robot-assisted language learning. ReCALL **23**, 25–58 (2011)
2. Hood, D., Lemaignan, S., Dillenbourg, P.: The cowriter project: Teaching a robot how to write. In: Proceedings of the Tenth Annual ACM/IEEE International Conference on Human-Robot Interaction Extended Abstracts, pp. 269–269, 2015
3. Gordon, G., Breazeal, C.: Bayesian active learning-based robot tutor for children's word-reading skills. In: Proceedings of the Twenty-Ninth AAAI Conference on Artificial Intelligence, AAAI 2015, pp. 1343–1349. AAAI Press (2015)
4. van den Berghe, R., Verhagen, J., Oudgenoeg-Paz, O., van der Ven, S.H.G., Leseman, P.P.M.: Social robots for language learning: A review. Rev. Educ. Res. **89**, 259–295 (2018)
5. Movellan, J.R., Eckhardt, M., Virnes, M., Rodriguez, A.: Sociable robot improves toddler vocabulary skills. In: 2009 4th ACM/IEEE International Conference on Human-Robot Interaction (HRI), pp. 307–308 (2009)
6. Alemi, M., Meghdari, A., Ghazisaedy, M.: Employing humanoid robots for teaching English language in Iranian junior high-schools. Int. J. Humanoid Robot. **11**, 1450022 (2014)
7. Sandygulova, A. ., et al.: Cowriting Kazakh: Learning a new script with a robot In: Proceedings of the 2020 ACM/IEEE International Conference on Human-Robot Interaction, pp. 113–120 (2020)
8. Lopata, C., Wallace, N., Finn, K.: Comparison of academic achievement between Montessori and traditional education programs. J. Res. Childhood Educ. **20**, 5–13 (2009)
9. Hertzberger, H.: Montessori primary school in delft, holland. Harv. Educ. Rev. **39**, 58–67 (1969)
10. Isaacs, B.: Understanding the Montessori Approach: Early Years Education in Practice (2018)
11. Marshall, C.R.: Montessori education: a review of the evidence base. NPJ Sci. Learn. **2** (2017)
12. Murray, A.K.: Public perceptions of Montessori education (2008)
13. Rathunde, K.: A comparison of Montessori and traditional middle schools: Motivation, quality of experience, and social context. Am. J. Educ. **111**, 341–371 (2005)
14. Soundy, C.: Portraits of exemplary Montessori practice for all literacy teachers. Early Childhood Educ. J. **31**, 127–131 (2003)
15. Dohrmann, K., Nishida, T., Gartner, A., Lipsky, D., Grimm, K.: High school outcomes for students in a public Montessori program. J. Res. Childhood Educ. **22**, 205–217 (2007)
16. Lillard, A., Else-Quest, N.: Evaluating Montessori education. Science (New York) **313**, 1893–4 (2006)
17. İman, E., Danişman, Demircan, Z., Yaya, D.: The effect of the montessori education method on pre-school children's social competence - behaviour and emotion regulation skills. Early Child Developm. Care **189**, 1–15 (2017)
18. Amirova, A., Rakhymbayeva, N., Yadollahi, E., Sandygulova, A., Johal, W.: 10 years of human-nao interaction research: A scoping review. Front. Robot. AI **8**, 744526 (2021)
19. M. Academy, Introducing the moveable alphabet. https://montessoriacademy.com.au/material-spotlight-moveable-alphabet.. (Accessed 09 March 2022)

20. Ali, M., Behzad, H., Mahoor, M.H.: Affectnet: A database for facial expression, valence, and arousal computing in the wild. IEEE Trans. Affect. Comput. **1**, 18–31 (2017)

21. Zhexenova, Z., et al.: A comparison of social robot to tablet and teacher in a new script learning context. Front. Robot. AI **7** (2020)

22. Westlund, J.K., Dickens, L.R., Jeong, S., Harris, P.L., DeSteno, D., Breazeal, C.: A comparison of children learning new words from robots, tablets, & people (2015)

23. Chen, H., Park, H.W., Breazeal, C.: Teaching and learning with children: Impact of reciprocal peer learning with a social robot on children's learning and emotive engagement. Comput. Educ. **150**, 1–22 (2020)

24. Belpaeme, T., Kennedy, J., Ramachandran, A., Scassellati, B., Tanaka, F.: Social robots for education: A review. Sci. Robot. **3**, eaat5954 (2018)

25. Sandygulova, A., O'Hare, G.M.P.: Age- and gender-based differences in children's interactions with a gender-matching robot. Int. J. Soc. Robot. **10**, 687–700 (2018)

26. Scheeff, M., Pinto, J., Rahardja, K., Snibbe, S.S., Tow, R.: Experiences with sparky, a social robot (2002)

27. Martínez-Miranda, J., Espinosa, H.P., Espinosa-Curiel, I.E., Avila-George, H., Rodríguez-Jacobo, J.: Age-based differences in preferences and affective reactions towards a robot's personality during interaction. Comput. Hum. Behav. **84**, 245–257 (2018)

Social Robots in Learning Scenarios: Useful Tools to Improve Students' Attention or Potential Sources of Distraction?

Samantha Charpentier[1], Mohamed Chetouani[2], Isis Truck[1],
David Cohen[2,3], and Salvatore M. Anzalone[1(✉)]

[1] Laboratoire de Cognitions Humaine et Artificielle, Université Paris 8, RNSR
200515259U, Saint Denis, France
anzalone.s@gmail.com
[2] Institut de Systemes Intelligents et de Robotique, Sorbonne Université, CNRS,
UMR7222, Paris, France
[3] Service de Psychiatrie de l'Enfant et de l'Adolescent, Hôpital de la
Pitié-Salpêtrière, Paris, France

Abstract. In this paper, we speculate about the use of social robots as convenient tools for improving learning in an educational scenario. We introduce an experimental setup in which students listen a story read by a storyteller while their attention levels are monitored through electrophysiological and behavioral measures: if the participants are judged inattentive by an electroencephalogram based measure or by the head's movements, a social robot will produce feedbacks to stimulate their attention to the shared task. We hypothesize that the participants will then realize their attention drop and will shift back their focus to the task, improving their learning. A comprehension questionnaire together with the score of a Narrative Transport Questionnaire, joined with the analysis of the collected electrophysiological data are explored to verify the effectiveness of this approach. First results with 16 adult students indicate how in learning scenarios social robots could act as a potential elements of distraction.

Keywords: Social robots in education · Sustained attention · Neurofeedback

1 Introduction

One of the main responsibilities of teachers is motivating students towards the learning activities of the classroom through a continuous stimulation of their engagement. According to Whitton and Moseley [33], the engagement of a person in a task is based on six notions: participation, captivation, passion, affiliation, incorporation and attention. The latter is a particularly important process: it can be defined as a state in which cognitive resources are focused on certain aspects of the environment rather than on others and the central nervous system is in a

© The Author(s), under exclusive license to Springer Nature Switzerland AG 2022
F. Cavallo et al. (Eds.): ICSR 2022, LNAI 13818, pp. 124–134, 2022.
https://doi.org/10.1007/978-3-031-24670-8_12

state of readiness to respond to stimuli [2]. As attention can be monitored by a lot of intuitive, visible cues [5,17], it becomes one of the main assets the teacher use to draw conclusions about students' actual engagement in learning activities. Such visible cues can "drive" the activities carried out by the classroom, with the goal of encouraging students' engagement. Goldberg et al. [17], tried to use machine learning to study such visual cues, highlighting "on-task" and "off-task" behaviors: the former, as asking questions, raising hand, taking notes, indicatives of attention; the latter, as shifting the gaze away, lying the head on the table, fooling around, connotative of inattention. Interestingly, despite the complexity on its estimation, the analysis of facial expressions resulted a better estimator of attention than head pose or gaze alone. This does not mean that the gaze and the head direction cannot provide a lot of information about attention. Blinks, time fixation, average eyes position, saccades, and pupil diameter contain information not only about the attentional phenomenon but also about the cognitive load [30]. Movements are also a good indicator of attention: if a person is, for instance, fidgeting, then he would be judged as inattentive. Furutani et al. [16] used a balance board and electroencephalography in an experiment where participants had to resolve different tasks: they noticed less the participant is attentive, more he tends to change his posture. It is important, however, to underline that the link between such visible"behavioural" cues and engagement is not straightforward: Nasir et al. [24] introduce the notion of productive engagement, stressing out that in an educational scenario, to maximize learning, engagement does not need to be maximized but optimized.

Together with behavioral cues, researchers showed how Electroencephalography (EEG) can also be used to monitor the attentional phenomenon in the brain. In particular, the literature shows that the theta/beta ratio can be exploited to evaluate the attention and the cognitive load [9,25]. Also the beta/alpha ratio is used as engagement index in sustained attention tasks [10]. The gamma band activity alone was also assessed [22] and could be also used as an indicator of sustained attention. Experiences involving the use of machine learning showed the potentials of this approach for the classification of mental state with raw EEG data [27] and for the detection of individuals with Attention Deficit/Hyperactivity Disorder (ADHD) in a population performing an attentional task [1].

Researchers focused also on ways to enhance people attention in educational environments as well as in working places [21,34]. In particular, the scientific literature shows that physical activities and meditation could improve attention [20,29]. At the same time, with a similar aim, the literature proposes also the technique of neurofeedback. This technique aims at the conscious control of the brain waves by presenting to the person a real-time feedback from her own brain activity [6]. Although its effectiveness is still debated [8,11], the neurofeedback remains interesting especially in the particular case of ADHD, with the specific goal of improving attention capabilities or working memory [12,14].

Scientific literature proposes also the use of social robots as tools for improving attention, in particular in educational scenarios. Social robots have the flexibility of acting as tutors or as proactive learning peers, with the effect of increasing cognitive and affective outcomes [7]. Maeda et al. [19] developed a robot with the ability of encouraging children to stay focused while resolving problems, showing the potential of the robot's presence at school. Similarly, Wang and Sugaya [31] adapted the neurofeedback technique to its use with a robot able to return appropriate feedback to a student in accord to his concentration level. Interestingly, participants reported the feeling to be concentrated because they heard the robot's voice. Donnermann et al. [13] conduced an experiment with young adults and the robot Pepper. The robot gave feedback after each answers of the participant: "That's right! Well done!"; "Unfortunately that's not correct " + [solution]. Participants reported to feel their motivation and attention increased.

In accord with this literature, in this paper we propose to explore the effects a social robot has on students' learning during an educational activity, the listening of a story. Similarly to Donnermann et al. [13] and to Anzalone et al. [3], thanks to the EEG analysis and the perception of head movements, the robot will be able to recognize attention breakdowns and, eventually, to execute appropriates feedback. We hypothesize that thanks to such feedbacks the participants will realize their attention drop and will shift back their focus to the learning task, improving the total amount of information retained during the whole activity.

2   Materials and Methods

The goal of this study is to assess the impact on learning of a social robot on students in an educational scenario. We chose, in particular, to focus on a listening task, as this is one of the main activities practiced in learning environments. We propose to employ an social robot capable of promoting attention towards the shared task: the robot will be able to recognize attention breakdowns using head movements and electroencephalography; in case of attention breakdown, the robot will give a feedback using gestures and speech. We compared the effect the robot has on attention in two randomized conditions for each participant: one in which the robot is not giving any feedback (Condition A) and a second one in which the robot acts as active companion (Condition B). Questionnaires are submitted to the participants to assess the information learnt, the involvement on narrative and their perception of the robot. A free interview has been conducted with each participant at the very end of the experiment.

2.1   Experimental Setup

The experience took place in an experimental room, as in Fig. 1. A small RGB-D camera, an Intel RealSense D435i[1] is placed in front of the participant that will wear a bluetooth EEG helmet with dry electrodes, an Enobio from NeuroElectrics[2] A Nao robot, from Softbank Robotics[3] will stand in front of the

---

[1] Intel RealSense D435i: https://www.intelrealsense.com/depth-camera-d435i/.

[2] Enobio from NeuroElectrics: https://www.neuroelectrics.com/solutions/enobio.

[3] Nao robot from Softbank Robotics: https://www.softbankrobotics.com/emea/en/nao.

student. The experience is recorded using a camescope. Behind a black curtain, two computers are used: one, using Microsoft Windows, for collection the EEG data; a second one, using ROS Kinetic[4] on Linux Ubuntu 16.04, for the control of the robot, for the head movements recognition and for the synchronous storage of the data. The two PC communicate between them and with the robot via Ethernet network. An hidden loudspeaker is used to spread the auditory stimulus, a story.

Fig. 1. The experimental setup.

Auditory Stimulus. The story employed as auditory stimulus is the chapter "Clochette" from the book "The Horla", by the french author Guy de Maupassant, written in 1887, available as royalty free audio book through the website Librivox[5] This story lasts approximately 9 min, and was cut in 2 distinct, non randomizable, parts: Part 1, an intro, of 4 min09 and Part 2, the core of the tale, of 4 min39. "Clochette" was chosen because of the length, the content of the story itself and the clarity of the lecture.

Robotic Platform. Nao is a small humanoid robot made by Softbank Robotics equipped with audio and video sensors, able to move and communicate with voice or gestures. Nao has an interesting track record of previous experiences with children with neurodevelopmental disorders [15,28]. A set of verbal and non-verbal, positive feedbacks made of gestures and speech were specifically developed for this experiment, such as "Interesting!" while nodding, or exclaiming "I like this!"

Head Movements. Participants' head movements were obtained by analysing in real-time the data from the camera. Participant's head was recognized using

---

[4] ROS, Robot Operating System: https://wiki.ros.org/kinetic.
[5] Clochette is the story of a seamstress who becomes lame because of a man: https:// librivox.org/short-story-collection-096-by-various/.

the library Mediapipe[6] extracting its pitch, its yaw and its position in 3D camera coordinates. Movements were inferred analysing the standard deviation of the pitch and of the yaw angles in a 0.5 s time window: a standard deviation value continuously over a threshold during the last 5 s was interpreted as head movement.

Electroencephalography. EEG analysis was performed using the Enobio-32 system through the software Neurosurfer v1.4, from NeuroElectrics[7]. In accord with the literature previously described, we focused on the use of the theta/beta ratio exploiting in real-time the data from the electrodes F3, F4, F7 and F8. A normalized attention score was calculated as average of the data from a 5 s window [23].

2.2 Neurofeedback Algorithm

The system can autonomously produce feedback through the robot, taking in account the head movements and the results from the EEG analysis [4]. In particular, while head movements could reveal shifts of the individual attention towards other elements of the environment, the theta/beta ratio can reflect mind wandering events, where the attention can drift to other thoughts. As a consequence, to take in account and capture both kind of events, a priority system has been put in place: drops of attention signalled by the theta/beta ratio have the precedence over the information from the head movements. Moreover, as a mechanism to avoid annoying closer reiterations of feedback, the system will wait 25 s between the last executed feedback and the next one.

2.3 Questionnaires

Three different questionnaires were given to each participant, two at the end of each narration, one at the end of the interaction with the robot.

- A 7 questions comprehension questionnaire, to evaluate the information learnt by the participant, submitted to them at the end of the narration of each part of the story;
- A standardized Transport Narrative Questionnaire (TNQ) [18], to assess the phenomenological experience of being absorbed in a story [26], submitted to the participants at the end of the narration of each part of the story;
- A standardized Godspeed test [32], after participants interacted with the robot, to evaluate their perceptions.

---

[6] Mediapipe library from Google: https://mediapipe.dev/.
[7] Neurosurfer from NeuroElectrics: https://www.neuroelectrics.com/wiki/index.php/ MediaWiki:Neurofeedback-url.

2.4   Experimental Protocol

The participant is welcomed and informed about the goals of the experience. Written consent is collected. Then he is invited to sit on the chair in front of the robot and, with the help of the experimenter, to wear a dry-electrodes EEG helmet. At the beginning of the experiment, for one minute, the signal is recorded to remove the artifacts caused by the eye blinks; then, for another minute, a baseline is built. Such baseline is produced during a short memory game, asking the participant to memorize 10 words written on a paper: the cognitive effort this task requires is not so different from listening a story and memorize information. The robot welcomes the participant and the experiment starts, following two randomized conditions: half of the participants will start with the condition A, half with the condition B. For each participant, each condition will be associated to one of the two possible chunks of the story.

Condition A, Without the Robot. The robot informs: "You are gonna listen a part of the story. " Then it is disabled, meaning not moving at all or saying anything. The participant listen a chunk of the story. Once done, he is invited to fill out the comprehension questionnaire and the TNQ.

Condition B, with the Robot. The robot informs: "We are going to listen something together. I'll provide feedbacks if you are inattentive. Try to be as attentive as you can !" The participant listens a chunk of the story. In case of attention breakdown captured, the robot can adopt 2 attentive postures, says: "I'm focusing", "It's interesting", "I like this story" or "It's cool, right ?" At the end of the Condition B, the participant is invited to fill out the comprehension questionnaire, the TNQ and the Godspeed.

2.5   Participants

One of the participants was excluded because of his long curly hair which made the EEG data analysis difficult. The remaining group was composed of 16 participants: 8 men and 8 women, aged between 23 years old and 42, mean 31. 7 of them had a master degree or a PhD. They reported no diagnosis of ADHD or epilepsy and had a good comprehension of the French language. Everybody gave his/her written consent.

3   Experimental Results

Collected data has been analysed via Python 3 using the SciPy library[8] Outliers were removed before any comparison. Shapiro-Wilk test has been employed to verify the normality of the data distributions.

---

[8] SciPy library: https://scipy.org/.

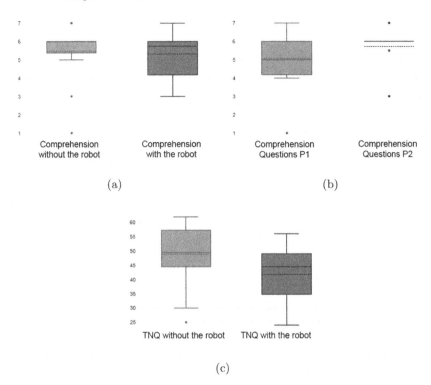

Fig. 2. Boxplot comparing the scores of the proposed questionnaires: 2a Comprehension questionnaire among the two experimental conditions; 2b Comprehension questionnaire among the two story chunks; 2c TNQ among the two experimental conditions.

The statistical analysis of the comprehension questionnaire Fig. 2a, was not able to reveal any difference on the information learnt between the two conditions (Mann-Whitney U test p-value = 0.318 > 0.05). As pointed out by several participants during the free interview at the end of the experiment, this result could originate from a difference on the two chunks of stories listened by the participants. A statistical analysis of the comprehension questionnaire comparing these two parts revealed, as in Fig. 2b, in fact, a difference between them: the first part of the story seems slightly more difficult to comprehend than the second part (Mann-Whitney U test p-value = 0.034 < 0.05).

At the same time, however, the statistical analysis of the TNQ comparing the two experimental conditions revealed, as in Fig. 2c, how students are more absorbed by the story when the robot is not active (Independent samples t-test p-value = 0.019 < 0.05). This difference could pinpoint the robot as potential source of distraction, at least for the specific scenario took in account on this experiment.

The results from the Godspeed questionnaire (78 ± 13.5) shows the robot can be perceived as credible by the participants. These results, together with the data from the free interviews clarify the point of view of the participants regarding the presence of the robot, reinforcing the interpretation of the robot as potential source of distraction: two of them reported they tried to ignore the robot's feedback in order to better focus to the story; one of them felt judged or scolded because of the robot in front of her; three of them did not like the design of the robot while other three did; one tried to challenge the system by being inattentive while three tried to stay focused to not trigger Nao; a last one reported a real sense of presence of the robot during the experience.

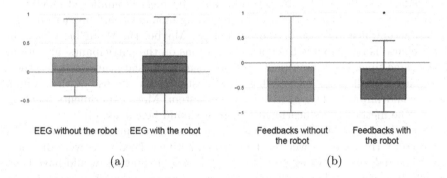

(a)   (b)

Fig. 3. Boxplot comparing the EEG scores: 3a between the two experimental conditions; 3b before against after the execution of a feedback.

Data analysis of the EEG average scores was not helpful: their comparison according to the two experimental conditions was not able to identify any difference (Independent samples t-test p-value = 0.856 >> 0.05). Similarly, a paired comparison of the EEG average score in a 5 s window before against another 5 s window after each feedback was also not able to identify any difference (Wilcoxon test p-value = 0.928 >> 0.05).

4   Conclusion and Future Work

Results highlight the potential of a social robot as source of distraction. In the particular scenario described in this paper, the robot seemed ignored, incapable of helping students to improve their attention level. Within the limits of the small sample size of the proposed work, the experiment revealed participants that were more absorbed by the story when the robot did not interfere with the narration. However, being transported by a story does not necessarily translated to a better comprehension of the described events. It is possible to question the role of the proposed story: the length of the narration, 4 min for each chunk, maybe be not enough to reveal changes in attention for selected population; at the same time, as the first chunk of the story was judged more complex than the second one, more time may be needed by the participants to get accustomed to the proposed narration. This can be particularly important especially for the ones having a bad auditory attention. At the same time, the age of the population chosen could be a decisive factor: the effects of the use of this system by children or by adolescents could be quite different because their investment may be diverse.

The statistical analysis was not able to signal any particular difference on the EEG data. As the results from the comprehension questionnaire remain high, it is possible to hypothesize that the story was too simple for the selected population. At the same time, as some users intentionally ignored the robot while some other did not seem to see the feedbacks at all, it is also possible to imagine that participants adopted strategies to protect themselves from the robot behaviors they judged as distracting. In addition, also the metrics employed should be revised: a robot that alerts the user in the wrong moment could impact on their overall acceptance and use of the technology. Maybe, the theta/beta ratio in this scenario is not capable to capture variations on the participants' attention; at the same time, head movements not necessarily translate the attention; their combination with other metrics based, as instance, on the use of the gamma band, could improve the sensitivity of the system. More experiments focusing just on the metrics for educational scenarios should be carried on.

From the pedagogical point of view, it is possible to question the feedbacks proposed by the robot as well as the learning activity. Feedbacks were distracting or ignored: maybe, using only non-verbal back-channelling would have been enough. In any case, a balance between quiet and more communicative feedbacks should be found. About the learning task, a more appropriate alternative to the listening can be found among classical pedagogical activity. In any case, while such results question the presence of the robot in an educational environment, they can push researchers towards a deeper reflection on the pedagogy methods in presence of social robots.

References

1. Alchalabi, A.E., Shirmohammadi, S., Eddin, A.N., Elsharnouby, M.: Focus: Detecting ADHD patients by an EEG-based serious game. IEEE Trans. Instrum. Measur. **67**(7), 1512–1520 (2018)
2. American Psychological Association: APA dictionary of psychology, 2nd edn. American Psychological Association, Washington, D.C (2015)
3. Anzalone, S., Tanet, A., Pallanca, O., Cohen, D., Chetouani, M.: A humanoid robot controlled by neurofeedback to reinforce attention in autism spectrum disorder. In: Proceedings of the 3rd Italian Workshop on Artificial Intelligence and Robotics (2016)
4. Anzalone, S., Tanet, A., Pallanca, O., Cohen, D., Chetouani, M.: A humanoid robot controlled by neurofeedback to reinforce attention in autism spectrum disorder. In: Proceedings of the 3rd Italian Workshop on Artificial Intelligence and Robotics. A workshop of the XV International Conference of the Italian Association for Artificial Intelligence (AI*IA 2016) (2016)
5. Anzalone, S.M., Boucenna, S., Ivaldi, S., Chetouani, M.: Evaluating the engagement with social robots. Int. J. Soc. Robot. **7**(4), 465–478 (2015)

6. Beatty, J., Legewie, H.: Biofeedback and Behavior: Introduction to the Proceedings, pp. 1–5. Springer, US, Boston, MA (1977), ISBN 978-1-4684-2526-0, https://doi.org/10.1007/978-1-4684-2526-0_1

7. Belpaeme, T., Kennedy, J., Ramachandran, A., Scassellati, B., Tanaka, F.: Social robots for education: a review. Sci. Robot. **3**(21), eaat5954 (2018)

8. Bussalb, A., et al.: Clinical and experimental factors influencing the efficacy of neurofeedback in ADHD: a meta-analysis. Front. Psychiatry **10**, 35 (2019)

9. Clarke, A.R., Barry, R.J., Karamacoska, D., Johnstone, S.J.: The EEG theta/beta ratio: a marker of arousal or cognitive processing capacity? Appl. Psychophysiol. Biofeedback **44**(2), 123–129 (2019). https://doi.org/10.1007/s10484-018-09428-6

10. Coelli, S., Sclocco, R., Barbieri, R., Reni, G., Zucca, C., Bianchi, A.M.: EEG-based index for engagement level monitoring during sustained attention. In: 2015 37th Annual International Conference of the IEEE Engineering in Medicine and Biology Society (EMBC), pp. 1512–1515 (2015)

11. Cortese, S., et al.: Neurofeedback for attention-deficit/hyperactivity disorder: meta-analysis of clinical and neuropsychological outcomes from randomized controlled trials. J. Am. Acad. Child Adolesc. Psychiatry **55**(6), 444–455 (2016)

12. Dobrakowski, P., Łebecka, G.: Individualized neurofeedback training may help achieve long-term improvement of working memory in children with adhd. Clin. EEG Neurosci. **51**(2), 94–101 (2020)

13. Donnermann, M., Schaper, P., Lugrin, B.: Integrating a social robot in higher education - a field study. In: 2020 29th IEEE International Conference on Robot and Human Interactive Communication (RO-MAN), pp. 573–579 (2020)

14. Enriquez Geppert, S., Smit, D., Garcia Pimenta, M., Arns, M.: Neurofeedback as a treatment intervention in ADHD: current evidence and practice, June 2019

15. Feng, H., Gutierrez, A., Zhang, J., Mahoor, M.H.: Can NAO robot improve eyegaze attention of children with high functioning autism? In: 2013 IEEE International Conference on Healthcare Informatics, pp. 484–484 (2013)

16. Furutani, R., Seino, Y., Tezuka, T., Satoh, T.: Monitoring the level of attention by posture measurement and EEG. In: Papafragou, A., Grodner, D., Mirman, D., Trueswell, J.C. (eds.) Proceedings of the 38th Annual Meeting of the Cognitive Science Society, Recogbizing and Representing Events, CogSci 2016, Philadelphia, PA, USA, 10–13 August 2016, cognitivesciencesociety.org (2016)

17. Goldberg, P., et al.: Attentive or Not? toward a machine learning approach to assessing students' visible engagement in classroom instruction. Educ. Psychol. Rev. **33**(1), 27–49 (2019). https://doi.org/10.1007/s10648-019-09514-z

18. Green, M., Brock, T.: Transport narrative questionnaire (2013)

19. Maeda, R., Even, J., Kanda, T.: Can a social robot encourage children's self-study? In: 2019 IEEE/RSJ International Conference on Intelligent Robots and Systems (IROS), pp. 1236–1242 (2019)

20. Manna, A., et al.: Neural correlates of focused attention and cognitive monitoring in meditation. Brain Res. Bull. **82**(1), 46–56 (2010). ISSN 0361-9230

21. Mijović, P., Ković, V., Vos, M.D., Mačužić, I., Todorović, P., Jeremić, B., Gligorijević, I.: Towards continuous and real-time attention monitoring at work: reaction time versus brain response. Ergonomics **60**(2), 241–254 (2017)

22. Müller, M., Gruber, T., Keil, A.: Modulation of induced gamma band activity in the human EEG by attention and visual information processing, January 2000

23. Nahaltahmasebi, P., Chetouani, M., Cohen, D., Anzalone, S.: Detecting attention breakdowns in robotic neurofeedback systems. In: Proceedings of the 4th Italian Workshop on Artificial Intelligence and Robotics. A workshop of the XVI International Conference of the Italian Association for Artificial Intelligence (AI*IA 2017) (2017)
24. Nasir, J., Bruno, B., Chetouani, M., Dillenbourg, P.: What if social robots look for productive engagement? Int. J. Soc. Robot. **14**(1), 55–71 (2022)
25. Ogrim, G., Kropotov, J., Hestad, K.: The quantitative EEG theta/beta ratio in attention deficit/hyperactivity disorder and normal controls: Sensitivity, specificity, and behavioral correlates. Psychiatry Res. **198**(3), 482–488 (2012). ISSN 0165–1781
26. Osanai, H., Kusumi, T.: Reliability and validity of the narrative transportation scale in Japanese. Japan. J. Pers. **25**(1), 50–61 (2016)
27. Phyo Wai, A.A., Dou, M., Guan, C.: Generalizability of EEG-based mental attention modeling with multiple cognitive tasks. In: 2020 42nd Annual International Conference of the IEEE Engineering in Medicine & Biology Society (EMBC), pp. 2959–2962 (2020)
28. Shamsuddin, S., Yussof, H., Ismail, L.I., Mohamed, S., Hanapiah, F.A., Zahari, N.I.: Initial response in HRI- a case study on evaluation of child with autism spectrum disorders interacting with a humanoid robot NAO. Procedia Engineering, vol. 41, pp. 1448–1455 (2012). ISSN 1877–7058, international Symposium on Robotics and Intelligent Sensors 2012 (IRIS 2012)
29. Slattery, E.J., O'Callaghan, E., Ryan, P., Fortune, D.G., McAvinue, L.P.: Popular interventions to enhance sustained attention in children and adolescents: a critical systematic review. Neurosci. Biobehav. Rev. **137**, 104633 (2022). ISSN 0149–7634
30. Szulewski, A., Roth, N., Howes, D.: The use of task-evoked pupillary response as an objective measure of cognitive load in novices and trained physicians: a new tool for the assessment of expertise. Acad. Med. J. the Assoc. Am. Med. Colleges **90**(7), 981–987 (2015)
31. Wang, K.J., Sugaya, M.: Focus and concentrate! exploring the use of conversational robot to improve self-learning performance during pandemic isolation by closed-loop brainwave neurofeedback. In: 2021 10th International IEEE/EMBS Conference on Neural Engineering (NER), pp. 928–932 (2021)
32. Weiss, A., Bartneck, C.: Meta analysis of the usage of the godspeed questionnaire series. In: 2015 24th IEEE International Symposium on Robot and Human Interactive Communication (RO-MAN), pp. 381–388 (2015)
33. Whitton, N., Moseley, A.: Deconstructing engagement: rethinking involvement in learning. Simul. Gaming **45**(4–5), 433–449 (2014)
34. Yi-Jung, L., Kang-Ming, C.: Improvement of attention in elementary school students through fixation focus training activity. Int. J. Environ. Res. Public Health **17**, 4780 (2020)

Are You Paying Attention? The Effect of Embodied Interaction with an Adaptive Robot Tutor on User Engagement and Learning Performance

Anita Vrins[(⊠)], Ethel Pruss, Jos Prinsen, Caterina Ceccato, and Maryam Alimardani [ⓘ]

Tilburg University, Warandelaan 2, 5037 AB Tilburg, The Netherlands
a.m.vrins@tilburguniversity.edu

Abstract. Robots are becoming increasingly popular as a teaching aid in language learning. For language learning, which relies on inter-personal interactions and references to the physical world, an agent's embodiment and ability to adapt to the student are both important factors. In this study, adaptive behavior and embodiment were combined in robot-assisted language learning. An online brain-computer interface (BCI) was used to monitor student's brain activity and prompt adaptive responses from the robot whenever a lapse of attention was detected. The response involved additional repetition of the latest word and an iconic gesture to illustrate its meaning. To isolate the effect of embodied interaction in such a system, participants completed learning tasks in two conditions: one where the adaptive robot was physically present, and another where videos of the robot appeared on a screen. Despite no changes in robot's behavior, participants reported higher engagement and more positive impressions of the robot, and also showed increased learning outcomes during the embodied interaction. This study confirms the importance of embodied interaction during adaptive learning and highlights the effectiveness of BCI systems in the design of future pedagogical robots.

Keywords: Adaptive learning · Embodied interaction · Robot-assisted language learning · Brain-computer interface (BCI) · EEG · Engagement

1 Introduction

Learning is a social process that involves interaction between teachers, students and peers. In recent years, technology has become more integrated with learning but as a result, the social aspects of learning are sometimes neglected when physically and socially interactive environments are replaced with screen applications. Social robots can attempt to fill this gap, particularly when it comes to language learning, by taking advantage of their embodiment to perform gestures and providing emotional support through social interaction [1]. A 2019 review of social robots in language learning [2] concluded that both adults and children generally found learning from robots enjoyable, resulting in increased motivation and engagement.

F. Cavallo et al. (Eds.): ICSR 2022, LNAI 13818, pp. 135–145, 2022.
https://doi.org/10.1007/978-3-031-24670-8_13

To effectively support students and keep them engaged in their learning task, a robot tutor must show sufficient social capabilities and intelligent adaptive behavior [3]. Most adaptive learning applications use subjective student feedback or the student's prior interactions with the system as a way to monitor engagement and progress levels, which in turn can be used to determine content and interventions from the system [4–6]. In human-robot interaction (HRI) studies, video analysis [7] and post-interaction surveys [8] have also been used, which can be useful for improving the behavior of the robot after an interaction. However, these methods rely on large amounts of data to make accurate predictions [5] and suffer from an inability to adapt to the user's needs in real time.

In recent years, an alternative approach has emerged in the form of brain computer interfaces (BCIs) that monitor the user's mental states and respond accordingly [9, 10]. Brain activity is often acquired using electroencephalogram (EEG) which is a wireless, portable and affordable neuroimaging technique [10]. Past studies have successfully used EEG to assess users' engagement and attention during HRI [11, 12]. For example, Alimardani et al. [11] used EEG to measure indicators of engagement in children during language learning and found that children were more engaged while learning from a robot tutor compared to a screen application. Szafir and Mutlu [12] reported a BCI-based story-telling robot that could improve information recall from the story by providing immediacy cues whenever an attention drop was detected. Similarly, using a VR learning environment, [13] demonstrated that the level of engagement measured by the EEG showed a significant positive relationship with student learning outcomes.

Research investigating BCI-based adaptive learning applications is still very limited, particularly when it comes to robot-assisted learning systems. Prior studies have primarily evaluated the possibility of BCI integration in virtual learning environments to enhance human-computer interaction [9, 13, 14]. Intelligent behavior is especially important when learning is facilitated by social robots as they mimic human behavior and appearance, creating an expectation of human-like responses [7]. This raises the question of whether the positive effects that have been found for adaptive virtual agents can be observed for a physically present robot that adapts to the needs of learners based on their brain activity. HRI studies that have investigated the effect of agent embodiment have found mixed results. In some instances, the physical presence of a robot tutor only seems to influence subjective preference, but not learning outcomes or motivation [15, 16]. On the other hand, [17] and [18] observed significant improvements in learning outcomes, motivation, and engagement as an effect of robot's physical presence.

The current study will add to this body of research by investigating whether a BCI-based adaptive learning system can improve students' engagement and learning outcomes during interaction with an embodied agent. A social robot was used as an embodied adaptive tutor in one condition, whereas in the other condition subjects experienced adaptive learning with a virtual robot tutor. The following research question was formulated:

RQ. *Does embodied interaction with an adaptive robot tutor improve users' learning outcomes, engagement, and impressions of the robot during second language learning?*

2 Methods

2.1 Participants

Twenty-seven participants (11 females, $M_{age} = 21$, $SD_{age} = 3$) were recruited. They were all proficient in English. All but 3 participants reported no prior experience with ROILA (Robot Interaction Language) and 15 had no prior experience with robots. The study was approved by the Research Ethics Committee of Tilburg School of Humanities and Digital Sciences. Prior to the experiment, participants read an information letter and signed an informed consent form.

2.2 Experimental Design and Material

Adaptive BCI System. The adaptive BCI system used in this study (Fig. 1) was developed and piloted by [19]. The Unicorn Hybrid Black EEG headset [20] was used to collect EEG signals from three frontal electrodes (Fz, F3, F4). The acquired signals were then processed using Simulink, MATLAB to extract the EEG Engagement Index (see details in [19]) The EEG Engagement Index (E) has been previously associated with attention level [21] and is calculated as in 1:

$$\text{EEG Engagement Index } = \frac{\beta}{(\alpha + \theta)} \tag{1}$$

where, α, β, and θ indicate the mean power in alpha (8–13 Hz), beta (13–30 Hz), and theta (4–8 Hz) frequency bands, respectively. The power in these bands was averaged over the three frontal channels.

The EEG Engagement Index was smoothed and normalized for each participant using their minimum and maximum EEG Engagement Index (E_{min} and E_{max}; see 2) that were obtained during a calibration phase at the beginning of the experiment (further explained in [19]), which involved a 60 s rest (E_{min}) and an n-back style memory game conducted by NAO (E_{max}), lasting 120 s.

$$E_{norm} = \frac{(E - E_{min})}{(E_{max} - E_{min})} \tag{2}$$

The resulting normalized EEG Engagement Index (E_{norm}) was used during the learning tasks to provide adaptive interventions. When the E_{norm} value fell below a specified threshold (0.55 as estimated during pilot studies [19]), it indicated low engagement or a lapse in attention from the participant. Subsequently, a signal was sent via the User Datagram Protocol (UDP) to the agent, which then triggered adaptive behavior in the learning task (i.e., an additional repetition of the last word and an iconic gesture to accompany the word).

Learning Task. Participants completed a second language learning task where they were introduced to ROILA words. ROILA (Robot Interaction Language) is an artificial language constructed with two goals in mind: making the vocabulary easily distinguishable for robots and simple for humans to learn (Designed Intelligence Group n.d.; Mubin

2011). Two sets of randomly selected ROILA words were prepared for each experimental condition (15 words per condition). Some of the words were adapted, where they remained in their original form, but their meanings in English were changed. This was done to include more words that have easily identifiable iconic gestures that can be performed by the robot as an adaptive learning aid. During the condition, each word was repeated two times with an additional third repetition and relevant gesture if the EEG Engagement Index dropped below the threshold. ROILA was chosen for the second language learning task due to the very low chance of participants having any familiarity with the language. As such, we can assume that any knowledge demonstrated by the participants at the end of the experiment will be as a result of the interventions.

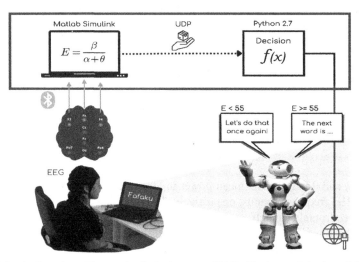

Fig. 1. Adaptive learning with an embodied robot tutor (NAO). The learner's brain activity is monitored using an EEG-based brain-computer interface during a language learning task; whenever a drop in engagement is detected the robot provides additional tutoring.

Conditions. The NAO 6 robot running NAOqi 2.8.7 was used as the tutor in two conditions; 1) Embodied condition and 2) Screen condition. In the Embodied condition, NAO was placed in front of the participant on a table next to a laptop on which the ROILA words were presented. A combination of the Python API (Python 2.7.18) and Choreographer software was used to program the robot's behavior. The robot vocalized the ROILA words, stated their meanings and performed iconic gestures whenever an extra repetition of the word was triggered.

In the Screen condition, full body recordings of the robot were displayed on the lap-top to represent a video-recorded tutor. An application was developed using Python 3.19, where videos of the robot were combined with subtitles of the ROILA words. The application was connected to the EEG Engagement measures and orchestrated the video queue. When E < 55 over the previous 10 s window, a video of the corresponding gesture was inserted into the queue before cutting to the next word video.

2.3 Experiment Procedure

All participants completed both conditions with a separate but comparable set of words (within-subject design; see Fig. 2). After receiving information and signing the consent form, participants d filled in a background questionnaire and were introduced to the robot. Meanwhile, the EEG headset was placed on the participant's head and the quality of signals were confirmed. Next participants executed two calibration tasks to obtain E_{min} and E_{max} for the adaptive BCI system.

With the BCI system calibrated, the participants then completed the learning task in both conditions in a random order. Each condition ended with a post-test vocabulary test and questionnaires (assessing engagement, robot impressions and system usability). Once both conditions were completed, the EEG headset was removed, the subject was debriefed, and the experiment was ended.

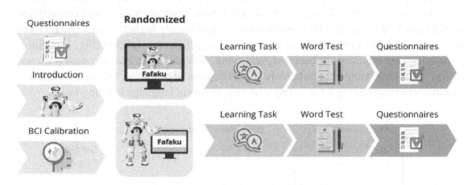

Fig. 2. Schematic overview of the experiment procedure.

2.4 Evaluation

Questionnaires. After each condition, participants filled two standardized questionnaires on a 5-point Likert scale:

1. The Godspeed Robot Impressions questionnaire [22]: This questionnaire is used to assess impressions of the robot and is divided into five scales: anthro-pomorphism (6 items), animacy (6 items), likeability (5 items), perceived intelligence (5 items), perceived safety (3 items).
2. The short-form User Engagement Scale [23]: this scale assesses subjective engagement levels using 12 items divided equally between 4 sub-scales: focused attention, perceived usability (reverse coded), aesthetic appeal and reward. The sub-scales can be combined into an overall engagement score by taking a mean of all items.

Vocabulary Test. A digital vocabulary test with a graphical user interface was developed to test learning outcomes in both conditions. The vocabulary test included a feature to play an audio recording of the ROILA word exactly as it was heard during the learning task in the robot's synthesized voice. This was meant to improve the participant's ability to recognize the word.

3 Results

Minor comments: Please include for all the statistical tests the results of the Shapiro-Wilk test for normally check.

3.1 Subjective Engagement

The obtained scores from the User Engagement Scale were compared between the Embodied and Screen conditions using paired samples t-tests. The scores were compared per sub-scale (focused attention, perceived usability, aesthetic appeal, and reward) and as the overall engagement. The results showed significantly higher overall Engagement scores for the Embodied condition as opposed to the Screen condition (Fig. 3A). Similar results were obtained for each sub-scale (Fig. 3B) indicating that physical presence of the robot tutor yielded significantly higher reports of attention, perceived usability, visual appeal and having a rewarding experience during language learning tasks.

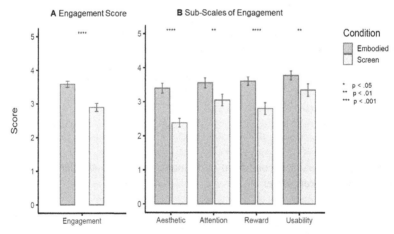

Fig. 3. A comparison of the short form User Engagement Scale [23] results from the Embodied and Screen conditions (N = 27). (A) The overall engagement score is computed by averaging the scores from four sub-scales. (B) The sub-scales include Aesthetic appeal, Focused attention, Reward, and Perceived usability which were compared across conditions separately.

3.2 Robot Impressions

The outcome of the Godspeed Robot Impressions Questionnaire is summarized in Fig. 4. Paired-samples t-tests confirmed a significantly higher score in the Embodied condition

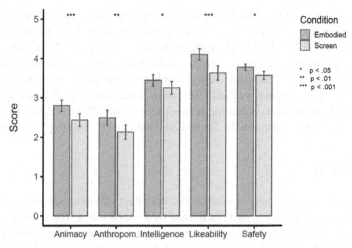

Fig. 4. A comparison of the Godspeed Robot Impressions Questionnaire between Embodied and Screen conditions. More positive impressions were reported for all sub-scales when the robot was physically present.

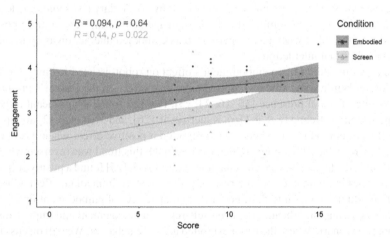

Fig. 5. The relationship between subjective engagement rating and vocabulary test scores in both Embodied and Screen conditions.

than Screen condition for all sub-scales Animacy, Anthropomorphism, Intelligence, Likeability and Safety, indicating that the embodied interaction with an adaptive robot tutor physically present in the room could lead to more favorable impressions compared to the virtual robot on a screen.

3.3 Vocabulary Test Scores

The post-interaction vocabulary tests had a possible score range of 0 to 15. A Shapiro-Wilk test confirmed that the test scores were normally distributed ($p = 0.08$) in both conditions. Consequently, a paired samples t-test was used to compare the two conditions. The test showed a significantly higher score in the Embodied (M = 10.56, SE = 0.55) than Screen (M = 8.78, SE = 0.60) condition (t(26) = 2.86, p = 0.004), supporting the hypothesis that interaction with the physical robot tutor increased learning outcomes.

Subsequently, the relationship between subjects' reported engagement and their vocabulary test performance was analyzed using Spearman's correlation (Fig. 5). The results showed a significant correlation between the two variables in the Screen condition (R = 0.44, p = 0.02), but not in the Embodied condition (R = 0.09, p = 0.64).

4   Discussion

The goal of the current study was to assess the effect of embodied interaction in an adaptive language learning system facilitated by a social robot. The system's adaptive behavior was generated based on the learner's neural indicators of attention extracted from EEG signals [19]. The effectiveness of the interaction was evaluated from 27 participants through a vocabulary test and subjectively reported questionnaires in two conditions; with a physically present robot (Embodied condition) and a virtual robot (Screen condition). The findings showed a significant positive effect of the robot's physical presence on the learning outcomes (measured by vocabulary test scores). Additionally, participants reported significantly higher engagement ratings and a more positive impression of the robot when they experienced an embodied interaction as opposed to a screen-based virtual interaction.

The previous literature on embodiment's effect on robot-assisted learning has been inconclusive. While some studies reported a positive effect on the learner's preference or perception of social presence [15, 16, 24, 25], few had found a significant effect on learning outcomes. Kennedy et al. [16], Kanero et al. [26], and Vogt et al. [2] all reported no effect from embodiment, whereas [18] reported a positive effect when a robot was added to a screen-based learning application (although this trend was reversed when the robot presented adaptive and social behavior). Konijn et al. [25] found a positive effect on long term learning outcomes but interestingly, there was no immediate effect. Contrary to previous studies, our study did find an immediate effect of embodiment on learning outcomes as well as significant effects on self-reported engagement and impressions of the robot in a scenario where the robot exhibited adaptive behavior. We will discuss three potential explanations for this contradiction: 1) the importance of learning tasks fully taking advantage of physical presence when testing for the effect of embodiment and 2) the possibility of a combined effect from adaptive behavior 3) possible confound effects emerging from the condition design.

The majority of tasks used in previous studies of embodied robot tutors either used a tablet to facilitate the task and communication with the robot [2, 16, 18 26] or were purely conversational [25]. Embodied gestures were rarely used to explain concepts, although they could be an integral part of why physical presence is beneficial [7]. In our study, iconic gestures were used when the adaptive system detected disengagement from the student. Similar approaches have been confirmed to support language learning [7]; furthermore, [27] showed that if non-verbal behavior was not used by a robot, learners preferred to communicate with a video-recorded tutor, which further indicates that the capacity for embodied behavior by itself is not enough to confer a benefit - it has to be put to use.

In addition to the use of gestures in learning tasks, the benefits of embodied tutoring interactions on students' learning outcomes also seem to depend on the social and adaptive behavior of the robot. [18] found that a positive effect from embodiment could turn negative when adaptive social interactions are added - possibly due to excessive or poorly timed interruptions that distract from the learning task. However, we hypothesized that when adaptive interactions are used only when the student needs them, they can instead be beneficial. The promise of BCI-based adaptations had previously been indicated by [12, 28] and this aspect of our system combined with embodied presence could explain why our study found immediate improvement in learning outcomes when others did not.

What should be critically reevaluated in future designs using this adaptive learning system is the experimental setup and by extension, the comparability of conditions. In our onscreen application, the robot was much smaller than in the 'embodied' condition and the laptop screen provided both the video and subtitles simultaneously. In addition, in this study we did not control for confound factors such as 'Zoom fatigue'. This effect is tied to exhaustion participants may feel as a consequence of video conferencing.

Truly adaptive robot behavior has not been explored thoroughly due to the difficulty of assessing the student's mental state in real time. When it comes to detecting boredom or disengagement, robots lack the perceptive abilities of human teachers. To compensate for this shortcoming, a novel passive BCI system was developed to keep track of the learner's level of engagement. What we have developed shows the possibility of integrating BCI into the world of HRI and robot-assisted teaching as a new way to personalize interactions between robot tutors and students. This study can be used as a guide for future HRI studies in designing adaptive learning experiences, both in terms of applications of BCI and the importance of embodiment.

5 Conclusion

Previous research in robot-assisted language learning has indicated that embodiment could be an important factor in language learning and that adapting to the student's mental state can improve the learning experience. However, the combination of adaptive behavior and embodiment had not been explored previously. In this study, an embodied adaptive robot tutor was compared to an identical video-recorded tutor. A novel adaptive learning system with a passive BCI component was developed to make the robot tutor react in real time when low engagement was detected. The results confirmed that the physical embodiment of the robot had a positive effect on learning in an adaptive setting: it led to an increase in learning outcomes, engagement, and more positive impressions of the robot. These findings further support the role of embodiment in learning as well as showing the potential of BCI systems to augment the capabilities of social robots.

References

1. Belpaeme, T., Kennedy, J., Ramachandran, A., Scassellati, B., Tanaka, F.: Social robots for education: a review. Sci. Rob. 3(8) (2018)

2. Vogt, P., et al.: Second language tutoring using social robots: a large-scale study. In: 2019 14th ACM/IEEE International Conference on Human-Robot Interaction (HRI). pp. 497–505. IEEE (2019)
3. Ahmad, M.I., Mubin, O., Shahid, S., Orlando, J.: Robot's adaptive emotional feed-back sustains children's social engagement and promotes their vocabulary learning: a long-term child–robot interaction study. Adapt. Behav. **27**(4), 243–266 (2019)
4. Martin, F., Chen, Y., Moore, R.L., Westine, C.D.: Systematic review of adaptive learning research designs, context, strategies, and technologies from 2009 to 2018. Educ. Technol. Res. Dev. **68**, 1903–1929 (2020)
5. Wang, S., Christensen, C., Cui, W., Tong, R., Yarnall, L., Shear, L., Feng, M.: When adaptive learning is effective learning: comparison of an adaptive learning system to teacher-led instruction. Interact. Learn. Environ. (2020)
6. Schodde, T., Hoffmann, L., Stange, S., Kopp, S.: Adapt, explain, engage—a study on how social robots can scaffold second-language learning of children. ACM Trans. Hum. Robot Inter. **9**, 1–27 (2020)
7. Wit, J.D., et al.: The effect of Arobot's gestures and adaptive tutoring on children's acquisition of second language vocabularies. In: The 2018 ACM/IEEE International Conference (2018)
8. Donnermann, M., Schaper, P., Lugrin, B.: Towards adaptive robotic tutors in universities: a field study. In: Ali, R., Lugrin, B., Charles, F. (eds.) PERSUASIVE 2021. LNCS, vol. 12684, pp. 33–46. Springer, Cham (2021). https://doi.org/10.1007/978-3-030-79460-6_3
9. Zander, T.O., Krol, L.R.: Team phypa: brain-computer interfacing for everyday human-computer interaction. Period Polytech. Electr. Eng. Comput. Sci. **61**, 209 (2017)
10. Alimardani, M., Hiraki, K.: Passive brain-computer interfaces for enhanced human-robot interaction. Front. Rob. AI July (2020)
11. Alimardani, M., van den Braak, S., Jouen, A.-L., Matsunaka, R., Hiraki, K.: Assessment of engagement and learning during child-robot interaction using EEG signals. In: Li, H., Ge, S.S., Wu, Y., Wykowska, A., He, H. (eds.) ICSR 2021. LNCS (LNAI), vol. 13086, pp. 671–682. Springer, Cham (2021). https://doi.org/10.1007/978-3-030-90525-5_59
12. Szafir, D., Mutlu, B.: Pay attention! Designing adaptive agents that monitor and improve user engagement. In: Conference on Human Factors in Computing Systems Proceedings, pp. 11–20 (2012)
13. Khedher, A.B., Jraidi, I., Frasson, C.: Tracking students' mental engagement using EEG signals during an interaction with a virtual learning environment. J. Intell. Learn. Syst. Appl. **11**, 1–14 (2019)
14. Rohani, D.A., Puthusserypady, S.: BCI inside a virtual reality classroom: a potential training tool for attention. EPJ Nonlinear Biomed. Phys. **3** (2015)
15. Looije, R., van der Zalm, A., Neerincx, M.A., Beun, R.J.: Help, I need somebody the effect of embodiment on playful learning. In: 2012 IEEE RO-MAN: The 21st IEEE International Symposium on Robot and Human Interactive Communication, pp. 718–724 (2012)
16. Kennedy, J., Baxter, P., Belpaeme, T.: Comparing robot embodiments in a guided discovery learning interaction with children. Int. J. Soc. Rob. **7** (2015)
17. Köse, H., Uluer, P., Akalın, N., Yorgancı, R., Özkul, A., Ince, G.: The effect of embodiment in sign language tutoring with assistive humanoid robots. Int. J. Soc. Robot. **7**, 537–548 (2015)
18. Kennedy, J., Baxter, P., Belpaeme, T.: The robot who tried too hard: Social behaviour of a robot tutor can negatively affect child learning. In: ACM/IEEE Inter-national Conference on Human-Robot Interaction 2015-March, pp. 67–74, March 2015
19. Prinsen, J., Pruss, E., Vrins, A., Ceccato, C.: A passive brain-computer interface for monitoring engagement during robot-assisted language learning. In: Proceedings of 2022 IEEE International Conference on Systems, Man and Cybernetics (2022)
20. g.tec Medical Engineering GmbH Austria: User Manual for Unicorn Brain Interface Hybrid Black, 1.18.00 ed (2019). https://www.unicorn-bi.com/

21. Pope, A.T., Bogart, E.H., Bartolome, D.S.: Biocybernetic system evaluates indices of operator engagement in automated task. Biol. Psychol. **40**(1–2), 187–195 (1995)
22. Bartneck, C., Kulić, D., Croft, E., Zoghbi, S.: Measurement instruments for the anthropomorphism, animacy, likeability, perceived intelligence, and perceived safety robots. Int. J. Soc. Robot. **1**(1), 71–81 (2009)
23. O'Brien, H.L., Cairns, P., Hall, M.: A practical approach to measuring user engagement with the refined user engagement scale (UES) and new UES short form. Int. J. Hum. Comput. Stud. **112**, 28–39 (2018)
24. Kim, Y., Tscholl, M.: Young children's embodied interactions with a social robot. Educ. Technol. Res. Dev. **69**, 2059–2081 (2021)
25. Konijn, E.A., Jansen, B., Bustos, V.M., Hobbelink, V.L.N.F., Daniel, V.P.: Social robots for (second) language learning in (migrant) primary school children. Int. J. Soc. Robot. **14**, 827–843 (2022)
26. Kanero, J., Tunalı, E.T., Oranç, C., Göksun, T., Küntay, A.C.: When even a robot tutor zooms: a study of embodiment, attitudes, and impressions. Front. Rob. AI **8**, 169 (2021)
27. Pütten, A., Straßmann, C., Krämer, N.: Language learning with artificial entities: effects of an artificial tutor's embodiment and behavior on users' alignment and evaluation. In: International Conference on Social Robotics, pp. 96–107 (2020)
28. Sauro, J., Lewis, J.R.: Quantifying the User Experience: Practical Statistics for User Research, Morgan Kaufmann (2016)

User Evaluation of Social Robots as a Tool in One-to-One Instructional Settings for Students with Learning Disabilities

Negin Azizi[1(✉)], Shruti Chandra[1], Mike Gray[2], Jennifer Fane[2], Melissa Sager[2], and Kerstin Dautenhahn[1]

[1] Electrical and Computer Engineering Department, University of Waterloo, 200 University Avenue, N2L3G1 Waterloo, ON, Canada
{n2azizi,shruti.chandra,kdautenh}@uwaterloo.ca
[2] Learning Disabilities Society, Vancouver, BC V5M 1Z8, Canada
{at,jennf,msager}@ldsociety.ca

Abstract. Learning is more challenging for students with learning disabilities. They often require supplementary learning support such as one-to-one instruction to address academic skill gaps. In this research, we explore the impact of using assistive technology- a social robot, as an educational tool for instructors to support students with learning disabilities. The purpose of the study was to a) to evaluate the acceptance of the social robot by the users, i.e., instructors and students in a real-world educational setting; b) understand the impact of the robot's intervention on student's engagement during learning tasks over multiple learning sessions. We conducted a multi-session between-subjects study with 16 students within two conditions, control and intervention condition with the QT robot. Our qualitative analysis suggests that instructors and students showed positive attitudes towards the social robot in their one-to-one sessions. In addition, the students were more engaged with their task in the presence of the robot, and displayed fewer off-task behaviours in the intervention condition, compared to the control condition. These results suggest that a social robot can be used as an effective educational tool for instructors in boosting engagement and mitigating off-task behaviours for students with learning disabilities.

Keywords: Learning disabilities · Socially assistive robots · Assistive technology · Robot-mediated instruction

1 Introduction

Learning disabilities (LD) is a heterogeneous life-long condition that includes a range of disorders that may affect the acquisition, retention or understanding of verbal or non-verbal information. Students with learning disabilities struggle with specific academic skills such as reading, writing or math, but otherwise demonstrate normal intellectual functioning [5,13]. Students with LD require

F. Cavallo et al. (Eds.): ICSR 2022, LNAI 13818, pp. 146–159, 2022.
https://doi.org/10.1007/978-3-031-24670-8_14

personalized instruction that consider their learning differences and targets their unique challenges [17]. Students with LD frequently struggle to stay focused on a task, and exhibit off-task behaviours such as work refusal, fidgeting, and off-topic conversations. Redirection strategies aid in mitigating off-task behaviours and help students stay on-task and make sustained academic progress[3]. Examples of these strategies include movement breaks, positive self-talk, and breathing exercises. [22].

In recent years, educators have explored the use of social robots to support learning for students with or without disabilities [15,21]. However, most of the research in the therapeutic context is focused on children with Autism Spectrum Disorder (ASD) [15]. Despite the pervasive use of assistive technology (AT) tools in educational settings, such as smartphones and tablet-based applications for students with LD [14], socially assistive robots (SAR) have not been explored for these students, especially in long-term interventions in real-world settings. Additionally, despite the possible advantages of AT, educators are infrequently trained or supported in using AT, yet are expected to become experts in their usage [1]. In this study, we developed an instructional protocol for the use of a social robot during one-to-one instruction for students with LD. The protocol can be used for students with a range of learning difficulties and can be employed into individualised student learning interventions without any alteration of their program.

The current work is an extension of an in-situ pilot study, conducted in May 2021 during the COVID-19 pandemic. The aim of the study was to explore the integration of a social robot as an assistive tool for instructors, providing redirection strategies in a one-to-one instruction setting with children with LD [2] This pilot study on robot-mediated instruction (RMI) was done in two phases, instruction as usual, and robot mediated instructions, both following the same procedure, except that in the robot-mediated sessions, the robot delivered the redirection strategies. The robot was operated by the instructor using an application interface, and employed via the study's instructional protocol. The results of the pilot study indicated that the intervention supported students in staying on-task, however there were limitations related to study design, such as technological complexity of the instructional protocol, and the absence of a control group.

Building from this work, the current study had an expanded scope that aimed to investigate how students with LD are impacted by a social robot as an instructional tool, and assessed the acceptance of the robot in one-to-one lessons as part of an in-situ study. Different from the pilot study, students were assigned to either a control or intervention condition.

The study poses the following research questions: RQ1: What is the level of technology acceptance the robot achieves with both students and instructors; RQ2: How does the use of a robot influence the engagement and off-task behaviours over the multiple sessions?

2   Background

With advances in technology, assistive tools have provided further learning opportunities for students with LD [4]. One-on-One interventions can benefit students with LD by targeting their needs in the delivery of instructions [23]. Socially assistive robotics (SAR) is a field that targets helping caregivers, clinicians, and educators with personalized interventions using robot [7]. SAR focuses on using a social robot to aid humans in the areas such as education and healthcare [6,20] mainly through social interaction, without any physical human-robot contact. SAR has been widely used in the treatment of children with ASD, e.g. for teaching social, emotional, and cognitive skills in a play-based scenario. For example, [27] conducted a study with the Nao robot teaching social rules through games to both typically developing children and children with ASD. Little research has been done using SAR for people with LD, specifically, in the context of academic instruction [15]. The few studies in this area include[18] who explored a model estimating the engagement of children with LD interacting with a robot and [16] who investigated the use of a social robot to improve visual motor skills in children with LD. A more recent study, [15] was conducted to assist children with LD in their reading tasks through human-robot interaction. Research has shown that social robots can be effective for students with disabilities, albeit limited research has been done on the instructors' attitude toward using robots in special education [10]. Thus, there is still a great need for more research on the acceptance of social robots from both the student and educator perspective. Technology acceptance, in particular in in-situ/field studies, are important steps towards illuminating how social robots could be used in a real-world applications for children with disabilities, cf. [19].

SAR can offer more engaging learning experiences and provide personalized support to help students' engagement [15]. Investigation of the technological acceptance of SAR is crucial, specifically, when it is used in real-world settings.

This study investigates student engagement in the presence of a social robot, exploring perceptions of instructors and students during robot-mediated sessions. The contributions of this study are as follows: 1) the integration of a social robot into an already existing program without changing the learning goals or curriculum[1]; 2) user evaluation using the technology acceptance model for the application of SAR in a real-world educational setting as part of a long-term study; 3) development of the robotic system to accommodate a range of scenarios and situations that instructors and students with LD may face in a typical session.

3   Study Method

The study was conducted at the premises of the Learning Disabilities Society (LDS), located in Vancouver, Canada. LDS provides one-to-one instruction for

---

[1] The existing program develops students' independence, confidence, and academic achievements through one-to-one instructions with certified instructors.

students with LD. During the intervention condition, the robot was placed on a table roughly 65 cm away from the student and instructor during their sessions (shown in Fig. 1. This study was approved by the Community Research Ethics Office[2] and the University of Waterloo Human Research Ethics Board (approval #43223).

Fig. 1. Study setting, showing the child with LD and the instructor on the left and the robot on the right.

Participants: Sixteen students between 7 and 12-years old (mean = 9.6, std = 1.25) with a suspected or diagnosed LD participated in the study. Five certified instructors (holding either a bachelors, master's degree or a teaching certificate) participated in this study (mean = 27.4, std = 1.74). Participants were existing LDS students who received one-to-one instruction with the participating instructor. The students struggled with reading tasks and it was hoped that they could benefit from an assistive robot. The students were randomly assigned to one of the two conditions. Eight students participated in the *control condition*, where seven students had five sessions, and one student had six sessions. Eight students were assigned to the *intervention condition* (robot-mediated instruction); two of those students had six sessions, and five had seven sessions. One student was withdrawn after the first session in the intervention condition, since they were uncomfortable having the robot in their lesson. The variance in the number of sessions by the students was due to missed sessions. While some students attended LDS twice a week and could make up missed sessions, some students were unable to do so as they only attended once a week. All instructors participated in both conditions, and none had used social robots previously. Three instructors had two students participating in the study, and two instructors had one student participating.

---

[2] The Community Research Ethics Office is located in Ontario, Canada, whose mandate is to strengthen and support community based research in Canada and internationally, http://www.communityresearchethics.com.

Material: We used the QT robot[3], a small humanoid, specifically designed for children with ASD. It can perform gestures using its head and hands, accompanied by speech and facial expressions, and seems very suitable to use with children with LD. To interact with the robot, we developed a web application interface for instructors to operate the robot during the intervention sessions. The app consisted of the protocol instructors followed during session, displayed as buttons. Examples of elements of the protocol are warm-up activities, games, and breathing exercises. The application was loaded onto a tablet, which the instructor used to control the robot to lead an activity or play a game with the student (as a part of the session).

In addition, we developed a reflection worksheet for instructors and students to reflect on the academic goal of the session, including its difficulty level, and to state if the goal was reached during the session or not. Instructors also reported students off-task behaviours, engagement and the redirection strategies used on the worksheet. Additionally, students were asked to take part in a paper-based visual survey about their experience with the robot three times during the study, to gauge whether and how their opinions of the QT robot changed over the duration of the intervention period. This survey included questions regarding the robot's friendliness, intelligence, and the student's enjoyment. In order to evaluate the instructors' acceptance of the robot in their lessons, we created an online survey, on Qualtrics using the Technology Acceptance Model (TAM) [9,12,24,25] consisting of the following categories: a) Perceived usefulness; b) Ease of use; c) Intention to use the robot (their willingness toward using it); d) Attitude toward using the robot (if they see any value in using it), e) Enjoyment, and f) Process of using the robot, on a 5 point Likert scale. In addition, we asked questions to rate instructors' interest in 'Affinity for Technology Interaction' (ATI) [11] on a 6-point Likert scale. Note, the TAM model was chosen since, while not as complex as other user acceptance models that are reported in the literature (e.g. UTAUT, [8]), was deemed most suitable for this in-situ study in order to answer our research questions without putting too much effort onto our participants. TAM has also been used successfully in a recently published in-situ study with children with ASD [19].

Procedure: This study was conducted after the pilot study, mentioned above, in which we investigated how the QT robot can influence the off-task behaviours of students with learning disabilities while working on a task. In this follow-up study, using a between-participant design involving a control and an intervention condition, we focused on designing a more structured session based on the lessons learned from the pilot study. Besides, we were interested in instructor's perception toward using the robot, in addition to students perception, and performance of the students in the lessons.

Students were randomly assigned to one of the two conditions. In order to provide an opportunity to interact with the robot to all the students, the control group later participated in the intervention condition after this study. In the intervention condition, the student only interacted with the instructor during a

---

[3] https://luxai.com/.

one-to-one instructional session, and in the intervention condition, the student interacted with the instructor and the QT Robot. During the intervention condition, the QT robot (controlled by the instructor) took over the instructor role and led the student through the session introduction and goal setting process and provided self-regulation strategies if necessary. Students took part in the study once a week as part of their regular sessions with their instructor. Some students had more lessons in a week at LDS, but all participated weekly in our study. The instructor and the student worked on a reading task that was challenging but achievable for the student. Both conditions employed the following phases:

1- Introduction Phase

Control Condition: The instructor introduced the session, and completed a warm-up activity with the student. Next, the student and instructor set a goal for the session and the student reflected on their mood and energy level on the reflection worksheet.

Intervention Condition: The phase began with the QT robot introducing itself, and introducing the session. Then, the robot and the student did a warm-up activity together and the robot asked the student to set a goal. Note, while QT performed some activities and behaviours autonomously, they were controlled by the instructor through the application. Thus ensured that the instructor was in full control of the session.

2- Working on goal

Control Condition: During the session, the instructor redirected the student back on task as needed. If the student remained off-task, the instructor used a redirection strategy (RS). If the student stayed on task, the instructor praised the student.

Intervention Condition: Intervention sessions followed the similar procedure as the control condition, except that QT delivered the RS or praise.

3- Goodbye

Control Condition: At the end of the session, the student reflected on their goal. Sessions finished with a game, regardless of goal completion. Once the session was completed, the instructor answered a few questions about how the session went and the student's engagement

Intervention Condition: Intervention sessions followed the similar procedure as the control condition, except that QT delivered and played a game with the student.

Students also responded to questions regarding their interaction with the QT robot three times during the study. The three *data collection points* occurred after the first, fourth, and last session. Instructors completed a technology acceptance questionnaire twice during the study, after the first and last session.

4   Study Results

The results of this study are presented in order of the research questions. First, we discuss the technology acceptance results of the users. Next, we present results regarding the impact of a robot as a tool on students' engagement level and off-task behaviours by comparing the control and intervention conditions.

Table 1. Instructors' perceptions after the last session

Instructor	Experience	Benefits for instructors	Benefits for students
I1	QT is effective as a reward system and my student enjoyed the interactive portions	Helpful for getting the students to stay on track/focus and help take pressure off me to do this	Helps give them a goal to work towards and be involved in fun and engaging activities
I2	Good, I like it	More usable with younger students	Motivation in younger students
I3	QT is a fun addition to the classroom. Most students enjoy QT's presence. A distraction at times, but the more they meet it the less distracting it is	Ability to set goals with the students in a fun, interactive way. Less pressure on the student. Praise on-task behaviours or take breaks with QT	More motivated and less pressured by QT's presence. It changes student's moods positively
I4	I enjoyed using QT	The strategies led by QT are helpful. Students respond better when QT leads them than when I do	The robot's novelty made students more engaged and allowed them to enjoy the session more. My student asked lots of questions about QT it was not in our sessions. QT seemed to make them more excited
I5	Good! Helpful for maintaining engagement	Diversity in lessons, engagement, motivation tool	Diverse breaks, motivation, engagement, discussion topic

Table 2. Open-ended questions

1. *How was your experience in using the QT robot?
2. Did you perceive any benefits for yourself in using the robot as an educational tool?
3. Do you see any benefits for students in using the robot?
4. Do you have any worries and concerns in using the robot as an educational tool?
5. *Did you face any difficulties in using the robot?
6. *Did you encounter any technical problems during the session with the robot?
7. *Do you have any suggestions to improve the interaction of the robot during the session?

* *These questions were asked after the last session*

4.1   Instructors' Perceptions

Open-Ended Questions: After the first and last session, we asked open-ended questions to the instructors regarding the usage of a robot and its potential benefits to students (see Table 2). Table 1 summarizes the experience of the instructors and the benefits of using a robot for them and the students.

Only two instructors responded to questions 5, 6, and 7. Regarding difficulties, one of them did not encounter any issues in any of the sessions. However, two instructors mentioned issues with one of the games (Tic-tac-toe) in which the robot did not respond appropriately; one of them was able to address this issue by restarting the game. The other instructor mentioned that the app was sometimes slow and had to be refreshed. Related to their suggestions to improve the interaction, one of them mentioned that the students really enjoyed the gestures of the robot, however, if it had shown more gestures, the students would have been more engaged. The other instructor suggested increasing the speaking and game playing pace. The word 'goal' spoken by the robot had a strange pronunciation, which was also noticed by the students. Regarding worries and concerns, after the first session, 3 instructors had concerns related to the distraction due to the novelty effect of the robot. Additionally, sometimes the robot glitched during a game, and adjustments to the robot's program were made to reduce these issues. However, after the last interaction, only one instructor had concerns. The instructor described the concern as follows, "Sometimes the students are more concerned with QT than with the lesson. However, this has appeared to diminish over time as they become familiar with the robot."

Affinity for Technology Interaction: Instructors reflected on their willingness to interact with technical systems on a six-point Likert scale, (1: Completely disagree, 6: Completely agree). The average score for this section was 3.97 after the first and 3.7 after the last interaction, which shows medium affinity for technology interaction. The scores of the third instructor dropped after the last interaction due to some glitchy behaviours of the robot in some sessions. However, the scores of other instructors did not change significantly.

Technology Acceptance Model (TAM): Table 3 shows the result of the TAM questionnaire completed by instructors on a five-point Likert scale(1: Strongly disagree, 5: Strongly agree).

As shown in Table 3, regarding the 'Perceived usefulness' and 'Ease of use', when comparing the first and the last session, only the first instructor, gave lower scores to the robot's usefulness and ease of use while others perceived the robot to be more useful and easier to use after the last interaction. Similarly, concerning the 'Intention to use', the instructors reflected on their wish to use the robot in their current and future lessons. Except for one instructor, the others gave higher scores in using the robot. For 'Attitude toward using the robot', instructors' opinion had little change concerning the value of the robot in lessons, and the scores show general positive attitudes. Regarding enjoyment, three instructors enjoyed using the robot more after the first session compared to the last session, for the others, the scores did not change. In addition, we asked a question 'Process of using the robot (scale 1–5 (unpleasant to pleasant))', all the instructors provided the score 4 and there was no change in the scores between the first and the last session.

4.2 Students' Perceptions

We asked students in the intervention condition (seven students) to reflect on their perception of the robot three times during the study with regards to the following aspects:

Enjoyment: We asked students to reflect on how much they enjoyed having the robot in class, on a 5 point scale (from "Awful" to "Fantastic"). At all three data collection points (the first, fourth, and last session), four students selected "Really good-Fantastic" and three students chose "Okay". None of them selected "Awful" or "Not very good" anytime.

Friendliness: At all three data collection points, all seven students gave 4–5 stars (1 to 5 stars; the more stars, the friendlier) for the robot's friendliness on a scale from 1 to 5 stars.

Intelligence: After the first session, 1 student gave "1–2", 2 students gave "3" and 4 students gave "4" stars for the robot intelligence on a scale from 1 to 5. After the fourth session, 4 students gave "3–4" and three "4–5" stars. However, after the last session, most of the students had a very positive attitude; 6 students gave "4–5" stars, and only 1 gave "3" stars.

Robot's Help: Students were asked if the robot helped them. After the first session, 2 students said "I don't know", 1 said "Maybe" and 4 said "Yes". After the fourth session, these changed to 3 students selecting "Maybe" and 4 students "Yes". After the last session, we got 1 "No", 2 "maybe"'s and 4 "yes"s from the students.

Use of a Robot in the Future and How Often: Next, we asked students how often they wanted the robot in the class, in the first session, 1 student said "Never-Rarely", and 1 "Sometimes", and 3 "Often-Always". After the fourth sessions, 6 students said "Sometimes", and 1 "Often-Always". After the last session, from those students who had not said "No" to having the robot in class, 1 student said "Sometimes" and 5 students said "Often-Always".

Perceived Role of the Robot: Students' opinion about the role of the robot, is shown in Fig. 2. After the first session, most students perceived the robot as a Friend, the next choice was a Helper, while fewer students reported Classmate, Stranger, Teacher as the role of the robot. After the fourth session, more students tended to see the robot as the Helper and fewer students chose Friend. Interestingly, after the last session, a more equal distribution of the roles "Classmate", "Teacher", "Helper" and "None" emerged. The choice of the robot's role as a "Friend" decreased strongly during the study.

Table 3. The average score of each instructors for the different categories in the TAM questionnaire, (FI: First Interaction, LI: Last Interaction, I: Instructor ID)

I	Perceived usefulness		Ease of use		Intention to use		Attitude toward using		Enjoyment	
	FI	LI	FI	LI	FI	LI	FI	LI	FI	LI
I1	3.83	3.33	3.83	3.33	4	4.33	4	3.5	4	4
I2	3.5	4	3.5	4	4.66	4	4	4	4.6	4
I3	3.33	3.66	3.33	3.66	4.33	4.33	4.5	3.5	4.6	4.6
I4	3.5	4.17	3.5	4.16	3.33	4.33	3	3.5	5	4.4
I5	4	4.33	4	4.33	5	5	5	4.5	5	4

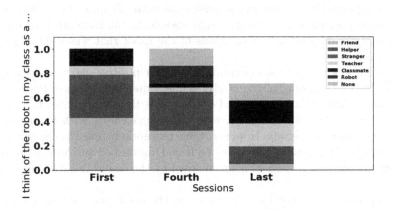

Fig. 2. The role of the robot shown at the three data collection points

4.3   Control vs. Intervention Conditions

We compared the students' reflections (completed at the beginning and at the end of every session) during the study. We measured the ratings for the sessions that the worksheets were completed (blank answers were removed from the analysis).

While we could not find any statistically significant differences between the control and intervention conditions, we observed the following tendencies:

Students were more engaged and completed their goal with a higher rate in the intervention sessions (Control: 83.8%, Intervention: 91%). Students in the intervention condition displayed fewer off-task behaviours than the control condition (Control: 51%, Intervention: 35%). The RS delivered by the robot was more successful than delivered by instructors in the control condition (Control: 86%, Intervention: 95%). Students were more engaged in the intervention condition ((Control : engaged: 50%, neutral: 29%, not engaged: 21% ; Intervention: engaged: 58%, neutral: 34%, not engaged: 7%))

5   Discussion and Conclusion

This study explored the use of a social robot in an already existing educational program, for students with LD, during one-to-one sessions with an instructor. Students were assigned to either a control or an intervention condition, and participated in multiple sessions. Conducting an in-situ study during the COVID-19 pandemic posed severe restrictions on recruitment and data collection. For example, many families preferred having online lessons during that period, and some cancelled their lessons due to sickness or moved to online after the study began in-person. Although we have video recordings of the sessions, wearing masks during lessons made behavioural analysis challenging. The duration of the study was also impacted by breaks in the school calendar. Despite the limitations of this in-situ experiment, the study design allowed for an in-depth investigation of instructors' and students' perceptions of the robot that was used as part of their program.

Students in the intervention condition held a positive attitude toward the robot from the beginning of the study. While some students gave fewer 'stars' to the robot's friendliness at the end of the study, they still wanted to have the robot in their future lessons. Moreover, their engagement with the robot did not change during the study. However, their perceptions towards the role of the robot changed. Interestingly, the role of a friend diminished and four major roles, a classmate, teacher, helper, or none emerged by the end of the study.(see Fig. 2 (RQ1).

Considering the instructor's responses to the open-ended questions, all the instructors enjoyed or found the intervention effective (See Table 1). The scores in the five dimensions of the TAM questionnaire during the study lied between 3.3 to 5, showing medium to good acceptance towards the tool. With a closer look, for the first, second, and fourth dimensions of TAM, the scores given by the first instructor lowered a bit after the last session. We believe that, this instructor had one student (who was mature) in the intervention group did not find the interaction with QT interesting. This experience likely negatively affected the instructor's opinion of the robot intervention. However, despite these lower scores, they mentioned that the robot was helpful for students to stay focused and more engaged. Overall, we did not see any significant difference in the enthusiasm of instructors to try technological devices between the beginning and end of the study (RQ1).

Comparing the results of the control and intervention conditions, the findings imply that the robot has a positive effect on students. Due to the nature of the in-situ study, and the low number of participants, statistical tests failed to show significant differences between the two conditions. While we could not find any pattern in students' engagement and goal completion over the sessions in the intervention condition, the results indicate that students were generally more engaged with their task and could complete their task with a higher rate compared to the control condition (RQ2).

The above-mentioned results helped us answer our two research questions. Concerning RQ1, the responses of the instructors through open-ended questions and questionnaires suggest that they had accepted the robot as a tool in their lessons to a great extent. Similarly, the students perceived the robot as intelligent, friendly and enjoyable, while simultaneously, showed willingness to use the robot in the future. To explore RQ2, we compared the intervention and control conditions. The results indicated that the robot helped students displaying fewer off-task behaviours and boosted their engagement during the intervention.

Robot-mediated instruction provides many challenges. Due to the wide range of needs of students with LD, it is challenging to find an intervention that suits all students. There are more complex assistive tools that can support students better, but they usually require some level of technical knowledge, which is not desirable [26]. Despite all the shortcomings, the results of the study suggest two major findings: 1) the social robot can assist student engagement and reduce off-task behaviours for students with learning disabilities, 2) Instructors can integrate the robot into the existing program with minimal technical background and training, and they generally hold a positive attitude towards the use of the robot, and its impact on students. In future work, it is recommended to 1) conduct a study with a larger group of both instructors and students during a longer-term study. 2) improve the application and the robot's skills, to be further adaptable to the needs of diverse students.

References

1. Atanga, C., Jones, B.A., Krueger, L.E., Lu, S.: Teachers of students with learning disabilities: assistive technology knowledge, perceptions, interests, and barriers. J. Spec. Educ. Technol. **35**(4), 236–248 (2020)
2. Azizi, N., Chandra, S., Gray, M., Sager, M., Fane, J., Dautenhahn, K.: An initial investigation into the use of social robots within an existing educational program for students with learning disabilities. In: 2022 31st IEEE International Conference on Robot and Human Interactive Communication (RO-MAN), pp. 1490–1497 (2022). https://doi.org/10.1109/RO-MAN53752.2022.9900735
3. Barga, N.K.: Students with learning disabilities in education: managing a disability. J. Learn. Disabil. **29**(4), 413–421 (1996)

4. Benmarrakchi, F., Ouherrou, N., Elhammoumi, O., El Kafi, J.: An innovative approach to involve students with learning disabilities in intelligent learning systems. In: Ezziyyani, M. (ed.) AI2SD 2018. AISC, vol. 914, pp. 39–50. Springer, Cham (2019). https://doi.org/10.1007/978-3-030-11884-6_4
5. Büttner, G., Hasselhorn, M.: Learning disabilities: debates on definitions, causes, subtypes, and responses. Int. J. Disabil. Dev. Educ. **58**(1), 75–87 (2011)
6. Chandra, S., Dillenbourg, P., Paiva, A.: Children teach handwriting to a social robot with different learning competencies. Int. J. Soc. Robot. **12**(3), 721–748 (2020)
7. Clabaugh, C., Matarić, M.: Escaping OZ: autonomy in socially assistive robotics. Ann. Rev. Control Robot. Autonom. Syst. **2**, 33–61 (2019)
8. Conti, D., Di Nuovo, S., Buono, S., Di Nuovo, A.: Robots in education and care of children with developmental disabilities: a study on acceptance by experienced and future professionals. Int. J. Soc. Robot. **9**(1), 51–62 (2017)
9. Davis, F.D., Bagozzi, R.P., Warshaw, P.R.: User acceptance of computer technology: a comparison of two theoretical models. Manag. Sci. **35**(8), 982–1003 (1989)
10. Di Battista, S., Pivetti, M., Moro, M., Menegatti, E.: Teachers' opinions towards educational robotics for special needs students: an exploratory Italian study. Robotics **9**(3), 72 (2020)
11. Franke, T., Attig, C., Wessel, D.: A personal resource for technology interaction: development and validation of the affinity for technology interaction (ati) scale. Int. J. Hum.-Comput. Interac. **35**(6), 456–467 (2019)
12. Ghazali, A.S., Ham, J., Barakova, E., Markopoulos, P.: Persuasive robots acceptance model (pram): roles of social responses within the acceptance model of persuasive robots. Int. J. Soc. Robot. **12**(5), 1075–1092 (2020)
13. Hassan, A.E.H.: Emotional and behavioral problems of children with learning disabilities. J. Educ. Policy Entrepreneurial Res. (JEPER) **2**(10), 66–74 (2015)
14. Ismaili, J., Ibrahimi, E.H.O.: Mobile learning as alternative to assistive technology devices for special needs students. Educ. Inf. Technol. **22**(3), 883–899 (2017)
15. Karageorgiou, E., et al.: Development of educational scenarios for child-robot interaction: the case of learning disabilities. In: Merdan, M., Lepuschitz, W., Koppensteiner, G., Balogh, R., Obdržálek, D. (eds.) RiE 2021. AISC, vol. 1359, pp. 26–33. Springer, Cham (2022). https://doi.org/10.1007/978-3-030-82544-7_3
16. Krishnaswamy, S., Shriber, L., Srimathveeravalli, G.: The design and efficacy of a robot-mediated visual motor program for children learning disabilities. J. Comput. Assist. Learn. **30**(2), 121–131 (2014)
17. Lyon, G.R., et al.: Rethinking learning disabilities. Rethinking Spec. Educ. New Century, 259–287 (2001)
18. Papakostas, G.A., et al.: Estimating children engagement interacting with robots in special education using machine learning. Math. Prob. Eng. (2021)
19. Syrdal, D.S., Dautenhahn, K., Robins, B., Karakosta, E., Jones, N.C.: Kaspar in the wild: experiences from deploying a small humanoid robot in a nursery school for children with autism. Paladyn, J. Behav. Robot. **11**(1), 301–326 (2020)
20. Tapus, A., Mataric, M.J., Scassellati, B.: Socially assistive robotics [grand challenges of robotics]. IEEE Robot. Autom. Mag. **14**(1), 35–42 (2007)
21. Tlili, A., Lin, V., Chen, N.S., Huang, R.: A systematic review on robot-assisted special education from the activity theory perspective. Educ. Technol. Soc. **23**(3), 95–109 (2020)
22. Turba, B.: The use of movement integration in a fifth grade classroom to reduce off-task behaviors at the beginning of the math period. Ph.D. thesis, Caldwell University (2019)

23. Vaughn, S., Linan-Thompson, S.: What is special about special education for students with learning disabilities? J. Spec. Educ. **37**(3), 140–147 (2003)
24. Venkatesh, V., Bala, H.: Technology acceptance model 3 and a research agenda on interventions. Decis. Sci. **39**(2), 273–315 (2008)
25. Venkatesh, V., Morris, M.G., Davis, G.B., Davis, F.D.: User acceptance of information technology: toward a unified view. MIS Q., 425–478 (2003)
26. Winter, E., Costello, A., O'Brien, M., Hickey, G.: Teachers' use of technology and the impact of covid-19. Irish Educ. Stud. **40**(2), 235–246 (2021)
27. Zhang, Y., et al.: Could social robots facilitate children with autism spectrum disorders in learning distrust and deception? Comput. Hum. Behav. **98**, 140–149 (2019)

Kinesthetic Teaching of a Robot over Multiple Sessions: Impacts on Speed and Success

Pourya Aliasghari[✉], Moojan Ghafurian, Chrystopher L. Nehaniv, and Kerstin Dautenhahn

Social and Intelligent Robotics Research Laboratory, Faculty of Engineering, University of Waterloo, Waterloo, Canada
{paliasghari,moojan,chrystopher.nehaniv,kerstin.dautenhahn}@uwaterloo.ca

Abstract. Social robots are expected to assist us soon in our everyday lives, but they may not be able to meet individuals' needs without the ability of learning new skills from humans. In a realistic setting such as a home environment, users may not be familiar with how to teach new tasks to a robot. Here, we ask whether it is possible for people without the experience of teaching a robot to become more proficient in doing so through repeated interaction. We show results of a study, where twenty-eight participants, who had never interacted with human-like robots, experienced teaching a set of physical cleaning tasks to a humanoid robot over five sessions. We report significant improvements in the success of kinesthetic teaching over time for some tasks. We also show improvements in the teaching speed over time. The results suggest that by gaining experience in kinesthetic teaching of domestic tasks to a robot over time, without any formal training or external intervention and feedback, non-experts can become more effective robot teachers.

Keywords: Kinesthetic teaching · Teaching by demonstration · Domestic robots

1 Introduction and Background

As technology continues to advance, social robots are likely to become a part of our daily lives. In an office or in a house, a robot can accomplish a variety of tasks, such as vacuum cleaning [8] and organizing cluttered spaces by sorting objects [15], which save us time and energy. Because of the complexity and dynamic characteristics of real-world settings such as home environments, robots cannot be programmed by their designers to know everything 'out of the box'. In fact, it is now widely acknowledged that robots need to learn new skills from users in order to succeed in helping people in the society [2]. Currently,

This research was undertaken, in part, thanks to funding from the Canada 150 Research Chairs Program. The authors wish to thank Delara Forghani for providing assistance with data encoding.

F. Cavallo et al. (Eds.): ICSR 2022, LNAI 13818, pp. 160–170, 2022.
https://doi.org/10.1007/978-3-031-24670-8_15

various robot learning methods are available, including imitation learning [3,14] and learning from demonstration [2], as well as techniques such as *kinesthetic teaching* that involve a human physically guiding the robot through a task, e.g., by grabbing onto and moving its arms. These approaches do not require coding of those tasks in advance, thereby providing an opportunity even for non-experts to teach robots and thus employ them more effectively in real-life environments [12].

In realistic settings, users who are not familiar with how to teach tasks to a robot may face some challenges while teaching the robot for the first time [13]. These challenges include the likelihood of unsuccessful demonstrations [2,10] and the occurrence of unnecessary moves that do not contribute to achieving the task's goal when showing a robot how to do physical tasks [11]. Moreover, the demonstrated trajectories might not be safe for the robot, e.g., if self-collisions occur or too much pressure is applied [9]. Various strategies have therefore been proposed and tested to improve how humans teach robots. Among these approaches is real-time generation of teaching guidance with the help of algorithms [7], offering human teachers instructional materials such as tutorials and videos before teaching commences [6], and letting humans watch or physically feel a well-defined trajectory in kinesthetic teaching scenarios [13].

In this work, we explore whether people who had never taught a task to a robot can improve in their kinesthetic teaching of a robot through gaining experience by themselves, as the existing literature implies that it might be too difficult for novice teachers to become more efficient teachers without any external help. In our study, unlike in the previous work, participants are not formally instructed on how to perform their demonstrations. Rather, they experience robot teaching through an unsupervised interaction with a robot over multiple sessions, i.e., without the presence of an experimenter. The robot itself only provides a few brief, verbal instructions on the teaching tasks. Specifically, our research question is: *How do participants' success at teaching a humanoid robot, as well as the time it takes them to teach a task, change over multiple sessions of unsupervised kinesthetic teaching of cleaning tasks to the robot?*

In kinesthetic teaching of robots, participants' demonstrations could be quantified by different metrics, such as (a) the success of guiding the robot through the task [6], (b) time spent on providing the demonstrations [6,7,13], (c) the accuracy of learning in case the system was capable of learning/improving based on participants' demonstrations [7], (d) total length of end-effector trajectory and smoothness of the demonstrations [13], and (e) the occurrences of help requests by the participants/human teachers [6,7]. In this article, demonstrations are evaluated based on their speed and success. We found a significant increase in the speed of performing teaching as well as significant improvements in the success of the demonstrations, i.e., task space covered by participants' demonstrations, as participants gained more experience. The success of the demonstrations has been estimated computationally using robot joint position data and validated against subjective evaluations of visual data. The proposed computational approach has the advantage of not requiring any vision system, which helps the robot track human teachers' performance in real-world situations.

To the best of our knowledge, no previous study has examined potential changes in success and timing of human participants' demonstrations of a physical task to a robot over time. Such an investigation helps to explore whether or not inexperienced and unsupervised human teachers can gradually become more experienced robot teachers through repeated teaching interactions with humanoid robots, as well as the manner in which this could occur. The overall approach of our experiment is comparable to the discovery method used in [13] with regards to allowing for trial-and-error to improve humans' teaching of robots; however, we have more trials, longer interaction times, and a naturalistic unsupervised setup without external intervention into how teaching occurs.

2 Methodology

Participants visited our lab for five in-person sessions each. Each session involved teaching a Pepper humanoid robot four cleaning tasks. In the first two tasks the participants were asked to teach the robot how to clear different pieces/particles, with a sponge, from two cutting boards fixed on a table. In the next two tasks, the participants were asked to teach the robot how to clear different patterns from specific areas on a whiteboard with the sponge. Participants were free to move the robot's hands and teach using any approach they wished to follow, with no hint directly given to them about the trajectories and how to provide the demonstrations, and without any time constraints to account for individual differences. For the second task of each kind (i.e., second and fourth task in each session), the areas to be cleaned were enlarged, introducing additional challenges.

As the purpose of the study was to understand how people's teaching strategies and demonstrations change over time, no real learning mechanism was included: the robot was observing the demonstrations and 'giving the appearance of learning'. Material and patterns to be cleaned varied across the five sessions of each participant (counterbalanced with a Latin square design), to give the participants the impression that each teaching session was about teaching something new. We used pieces of paper, paper clips, safety pins, binder clips, and buttons distributed on the cutting boards on the table, as well as a set of horizontal or vertical lines, cross hatching pattern, small circles, and random handwritten letters drawn on the whiteboard with whiteboard markers. To convey a more realistic human-robot teaching experience, i.e., to give participants the impression that the robot had learned during the session, the robot showed how it could perform a similar task, by cleaning the same particles on another table before the end of each session. This was done by executing one of the pre-recorded motions, decided in real-time based on participants' success of teaching.

A Pepper robot with a rectangular sponge attached to its left hand was used in this experiment. With Choregraphe, we programmed a block-based behaviour for running the sessions. To send additional commands to the robot in real-time, we developed another program using Python. During each session, the robot's behaviour was mainly autonomous. The experimenter was in another room watching the session through one-way mirrors (participants could not see

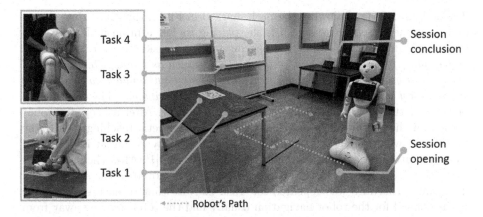

Fig. 1. Layout and sequence of the experimental setup (right) and two examples of participants teaching the robot how to perform the cleaning tasks (left). The robot followed the path marked on the picture to interact with participants and receive demonstrations of the tasks in four different locations.

the experimenter), and when necessary, remotely issued some commands. For example, the experimenter adjusted the position of the robot via arrow keys, to manually correct the robot's autonomous navigation errors.

2.1 Procedure

Prior to the first session, participants completed an online module to give consent, confirm they have no experience interacting with humanoid robots, and answer a few demographic questions. Upon arrival for a session and after wearing gaze tracker glasses with the experimenter's assistance (not discussed in this article due to page limits), participants entered the experimental room together with the experimenter. The experimenter then left the room and observed the study from an adjacent room, which had one-way mirrors. As shown in Fig. 1, the experiment included the following steps:

Session Opening: Each experimental session started with the robot greeting the participant and stating a few remarks defining the participant's role as a robot teacher. The robot also made participants aware of two common issues that could come up in demonstrations, by asking them to avoid stretching its arm too much and to be careful that its arm does not collide with any part of its body. The robot said: *"I need you to teach me how to perform some cleaning tasks by grabbing my arm and showing movements that I need to do. ... Before we move on, I want to remind you a few important things. Although I have multiple degrees of freedom in my arm, I have certain limitations. I may not be able to reach for objects that are too far or too close. Therefore, to provide useful instructions for me, please avoid stretching my arm too much. Also, be careful to perform actions in such a way that my arm doesn't collide with any part of my body."* In the first session, the robot also let the participants move its elbow and the whole arm afterwards to experience the feeling of such physical interaction.

Tasks 1 and 2: By following the path marked in Fig. 1, the robot then moved and positioned itself in front of a table, placing its left arm on it. It then gave some more information about the specific teaching task: "*I want to clear the [safety pins] from this blue area of this table, as much as I can. After the beep, I will let you grab and move my left arm to show me how should I do this. Please try your best not to shift my position in the entire experiment.*" The descriptions became shorter after the third session to avoid fatigue. After a beep, the robot turned off the motors in its left hand to allow kinesthetic teaching. While the participant was teaching the robot, Pepper was actively gazing at its left hand to appear attentive to the instructions, as suggested in [1]. After the participant said "done", the robot started its motors again and moved to the second task. The same procedure was repeated for Task 2. Note that to ensure safety, the paths defined for the robot navigation usually had the robot moving away from the participant and the participant needed to follow the robot.

Tasks 3 and 4: The robot proceeded to the whiteboard for Tasks 3 and 4, and placed its left hand on the tray. It then asked the participant to come closer and teach it how to clear the area of the whiteboard in front of it.

Session Conclusion: Next, the robot moved to the other table, placed its hand on it, and said: "*I will show you how I can now clear the [safety pins] from the table!*" Then, the experimenter chose and played a pre-defined cleaning behaviour of the robot from {no cleaning at all, partially cleaning, full cleaning}, whichever was the closest to the maximum success of the participant in teaching Tasks 1 and 2, in order to give participants a personalized impression of robot learning. Upon finishing, the robot asked the participants to complete a questionnaire about their workload (not discussed in this article due to page limits). Finally, the experimenter entered the room and helped the participant take off the eye tracker glasses. At the end of the fifth session, the experimenter debriefed the participants about the real purpose of the study. Note, to prevent making participants self-conscious of their behaviour, there was no indication that the study was to understand the behaviour of human teachers until this point.

2.2 Data Collection and Analysis

We report the time spent on providing each demonstration, as well as the amount of task space cleaned in the participants' demonstrations, i.e., how successful the cleaning demonstrations were. For each task, the time started when the beep was played and ended when the participants verbally indicated the task was complete. The success is estimated using the computational approach described below, which was also verified with an independent subjective approach.

Computational Approach: During teaching, the robot saved positions of all the joints in its left arm at a frequency 10 Hz. The data was then converted to a set of positions (trajectory) of the end-effector, i.e., the left-hand of the robot. This trajectory was obtained using the NAOqi Cartesian control API to compute forward kinematics relative to a frame attached between robot's wheels. An automatic post-processing procedure was performed on the obtained end-effector

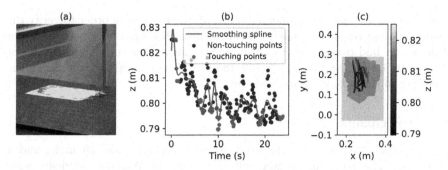

Fig. 2. Illustration of computational approach for estimating the success of demonstrations. An example for Task 2 is shown. (a) Picture of the partially cleaned task space, i.e., the yellow board on the table, (b) The vertical z-component of the robot's end-effector positions versus demonstration time along with the fit spline used to determine touching points, (c) The trajectory from the top view (projected on the x-y plane) and the board on the table. The green area, covering 47.0% of the task space, has been estimated as having been cleaned. (Color figure online)

trajectories to estimate how much the provided demonstrations could cover the task workspace. The first step was to determine the points at which contact happened between the robot's sponge and the surfaces being cleaned during each trajectory. For this, trajectories were examined along the axes orthogonal to the surfaces, which indicated how close the robot's hand was to them, i.e., the z-axis when clearing the table and the x-axis when cleaning the whiteboard. A 5th-degree spline with smoothing factor s was fit on the orthogonal component versus time. Touching points were determined based on two conditions: (a) the second derivative of the spline at those points was larger than a threshold $h \geq 0$, and (b) points were closer to the surface than the starting point plus a small tolerance $t > 0$ due to sponge compression during contact. This step is visualized for one example demonstration in Fig. 2(b). As can be seen, here the sponge appears to be periodically in contact with the table at the trajectory points marked as 'Touching points', to push the particles. In the next step, the orientation of the sponge at each touching point was found by approximating the first derivative of the trajectory projected on the cleaning surfaces, via its two adjacent neighbouring points. Finally, points covered by the sponge at the touching points inside a grid representing cleaning areas were marked as clean. Figure 2(c) illustrates the trajectory and the estimated cleaned area of the same example provided in Fig. 2(b). Parameters used in the computational method are $s = 0.003$, $h = 0.01$, and $t = 5\,\text{mm}$ for Tasks 1 and 2, and $s = 0.002$, $h = 0$, and $t = 5\,\text{mm}$ for Tasks 3 and 4.

Subjective Approach: We also assessed the pictures showing the task spaces after the sessions to subjectively rate the success of each demonstration. To minimize biases, cropped images containing only the teaching workspaces were displayed to the coder in a random order. Percentage of success was entered with a precision of 5%. The experimenter coded all the images. In order to verify the results, another researcher coded 25% of the data. Ratings of the random subset of data that had been coded twice showed an intra-class correlation coefficient of 0.95 (95% CI: 0.88 to 0.97, $F(139, 18.6) = 45.4, p < .0014$), confirming the reliability of the subjective method [16].

2.3 Participants

A total of 28 participants completed our study (12 female, 15 male, and 1 unknown). The participants were all University of Waterloo students aged between 18 and 31 (M = 21.54, SD = 2.55). Seven participants had programmed a robot before, but none of them had ever interacted with a human-like robot. Except for one participant, all were right-handed. The study received full ethics clearance from the University of Waterloo Human Research Ethics Committee.

3   Results

The average time spent on demonstrations of each task across the sessions is presented in Fig. 3(a). Tasks 1 and 2 demonstration times show a decreasing trend over the five sessions. A similar decrease is also noticeable for Tasks 3 and 4, but primarily between Session 1 and the other sessions. To assess the effect of the session number, one-way ANOVA tests were performed. We found statistically significant differences between at least two sessions in Tasks 1, 2, and 3 (Task 1: $F(4, 134) = 2.469, p < .05$, Task 2: $F(4, 134) = 4.347, p < .01$, Task 3: $F(4, 134) = 4.334, p < .01$, Task 4: $F(4, 134) = 1.430, p = .228$). Pair-wise comparisons adjusted with the Holm-Bonferroni method between Session 1 (as the baseline) and other sessions were then performed. According to one-sided Welch's t-tests (used due to unequal variances), demonstrations of Task 1 in Session 5 took significantly shorter time than in Session 1 ($t(37.03) = 2.749, p < .05$). In Task 2, demonstration times in Session 1 were significantly higher than in both Sessions 4 and 5 ($t(30.88) = 2.534, p < .05$ and $t(29.52) = 2.838, p < .05$, respectively). Student's t-tests (after having equal variances was confirmed) on Task 3 demonstration times showed statistically significant reductions in Session 2 ($t(54) = 2.893, p < .05$), Session 4 ($t(53) = 2.915, p < .05$), and Session 5 ($t(54) = 4.225, p < .001$) compared to Session 1.

The percentage of covered areas in the demonstrations was estimated using two methods described in Sect. 2.2: subjective and computational. Computational estimates had high positive correlations with the subjective estimates in all the tasks according to Pearson correlation analyses: $r(136) = .744, p < .001$ in Task 1, $r(137) = .837, p < .001$ in Task 2, $r(136) = .861, p < .001$ in Task 3, and $r(136) = .907, p < .001$ in Task 4. As these correlations support the validity of the computational method, we use results obtained with this method for reporting the success of demonstrations in the remainder of this paper.

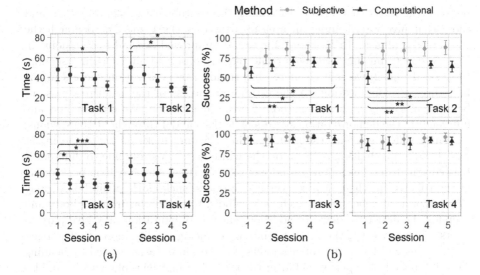

Fig. 3. (a) Time spent on the demonstrations and (b) Success of the demonstrations of the tasks, estimated using the subjective and computational approach, over all five sessions. 95% confidence intervals are shown. $* = p < .05$; $** = p < .01$; $*** = p < .001$.

According to one-way ANOVA tests performed on the success of the demonstrations over five sessions calculated using the computational method, the main effects of Session was statistically significant in Tasks 1 and 2 ($F(4, 133) = 3.250, p < .05$ and $F(4, 134) = 3.827, p < .001$, respectively). Success of the demonstrations in Tasks 3 and 4 was not found to be affected by the Session number ($F(4, 134) = 0.444, p = .777$ and $F(4, 134) = 0.627, p = .644$, respectively). It can be noticed from Fig. 3(b) that success rates of Tasks 1 and 2 show an increasing trend in the first three sessions and remain high thereafter, according to both methods. In Tasks 3 and 4, however, all success levels are constantly high from the first session onwards. In Task 1, according to Bonferroni-corrected one-sided Student's t-tests, demonstrations provided in Session 3 ($t(53) = -3.169, p < .01$), Session 4 ($t(52) = -2.774, p < .05$), and Session 5 ($t(53) = -2.602, p < .05$) were significantly more successful than those in Session 1. Another set of t-tests showed that demonstrations of Task 2 in Session 3 ($t(54) = -2.945, p < .01$), Session 4 ($t(41.10) = -3.649, p < .01$), and Session 5 ($t(54) = -2.717, p < .05$) were more successful compared to Session 1.

4   Discussion, Limitations, and Future Work

We studied how the time spent on providing demonstrations of a set of cleaning tasks as well as the success of demonstrations (measured based on the area cleaned during the demonstrations) changed over five sessions of teaching a humanoid robot in an unsupervised setting. We found general differences between the tasks that involved cleaning the whiteboard (tasks 3 and 4), and those that involved cleaning an area of a table (tasks 1 and 2). Although the speed of teaching in Tasks 1 and 2 gradually improved over all five sessions, in Task 3, significant improvements could only be observed after the first session. In Tasks 1 and 2, we saw an increasing trend in demonstration success in the first three sessions, leading to the estimated success of the last three sessions being significantly higher than those for the first session. We did not find any difference in the demonstration success of Tasks 3 and 4 throughout the sessions.

These differences suggest that teaching cleaning tasks on the table might have been more challenging than on the whiteboard, possibly due to differences between the same tasks done on horizontal or vertical surfaces. The positioning of the robot arm when cleaning vertical surfaces, such as the whiteboard, may allow important robot joints, such as its elbow, to remain far from its body and therefore be easier to move. In addition, such a configuration may give participants a better view of the robot's joints by reducing the likelihood that participants' arms will block the robot's joints. Furthermore, tasks related to cleaning the whiteboard were performed after those on cleaning the table, which can also affect participants' performance. A deeper analysis of participants' actions and their gaze behaviour is required to identify the sources of differences between these types of tasks. Future analysis will address those issues.

Although teaching the robot was done in an unsupervised setting and participants did not receive any feedback on their performance, learning effects were observed in the speed and success of the demonstrations [4]. In Tasks 1 and 2, participants could improve their teaching success up to a certain level over multiple sessions and increase their teaching speed thereafter. These effects imply that non-experienced users could adapt to the robot and improve their success in providing physical demonstrations of tasks when they became involved in teaching multiple sessions, without formal training on how to teach robots and without prior exposure to robot teaching. When no challenges were faced and demonstrations were successful from the beginning, e.g., in Task 3, non-experts could still improve their speed in providing those instructions. Aside from between-session learning effects described above, there might be within-session learning effects as well in our experiment. This means, participants' performance might have been improved from Task 1 to 4 throughout each experimental session. It is possible that this is why no significant improvement in speed was observed in Task 4: by teaching the robot three times before tackling Task 4 in every session, participants might have been already become used to teaching.

In this paper, findings related to the success of demonstrations were reported based on the proposed computational estimation method, which was verified through observation, i.e., a subjective approach. As seen in Fig. 3(b), computational evaluations of success were noticeably lower than subjective evaluations in Tasks 1 and 2. This is potentially because the computational estimates did not account for particle interactions and the 3D nature of the tasks, therefore only affecting tasks 1 and 2 that involved different particles. This means, e.g., a few pieces of paper could be pushed aside easily at once when they were close enough to each other in a particular area. When cleaning the whiteboard, since no particles were involved, the sponge could only clean the areas of contact with the whiteboard when enough force was applied. Still, despite the possibility of underestimating the success of demonstrations, the automatic computational method was found to be highly correlated with a validated human judgment-based subjective method. Using the computational method in future experiments, applications, and/or field studies, teachers' progress can be tracked automatically and reliably by the robot itself since no manual data coding is required. In realistic settings, such as in a house where no accurate vision system is available, this method can be especially helpful. Note that the differences between the subjective and computational method did not affect our study results, as our goal was to investigate possible improvements in robot teaching demonstrations over multiple sessions, which was observed similarly using both methods.

This work had several limitations. First, the study could benefit from the participation of the general public, and not only recruit university students who might have a positive bias towards using robots in the future. Furthermore, we avoided including an actual learning mechanism in our experiment. Lastly, although we considered both vertical and horizontal surfaces and varied the difficulty of the tasks in our experiment, the nature of the teaching tasks was the same. The results may change if a different type of teaching task is used.

For the purpose of our study, incorporating a real learning system would not affect participants' experience while demonstrating tasks to the robot. However, it could give participants a more realistic experience of how their instructions might be useful once a robot tries to learn from them and therefore, as a future work, might improve the study. In that case, some aspects of the interaction may need to be reconsidered. For example, the Pepper robot might not be a suitable choice for learning fine motor skills including forces, due to the lack of precision in its sensing and actuation. Future work can also focus on improving how humans teach robots by utilizing other strategies, e.g., by means of the robot providing social feedback to the teachers, to enable social learning through the communication of cues that reveal the robot's learning process or internal states [5].

5 Conclusion

We studied how repeated human-robot interactions when physically teaching a robot can affect success and speed of human teachers. Our study was aimed at human teachers who did not have prior experience of teaching a robot. As participants gained experience, we observed general improvements in success of demonstrations and speed of teaching. These results suggest that it was not too difficult for our participants to learn how to teach humanoid robot effectively other than by experiencing teaching the robot on their own over a few rounds of unsupervised teaching. Thus, while we know from the literature that it is possible to train human teachers explicitly in order to improve robot teaching [6,13], the key contribution to our study is to demonstrate that by allowing participants to explore robot teaching, and adapting to a robot over multiple sessions can be employed as an implicit, unsupervised strategy of training teachers. This option might be favourable in certain settings and applications, in particular when safety risks are minimal.

References

1. Aliasghari, P., Ghafurian, M., Nehaniv, C.L., Dautenhahn, K.: Impact of nonverbal robot behaviour on human teachers' perceptions of a learner robot. Interact. Stud. **22**(2), 141–176 (2021)
2. Argall, B.D., Chernova, S., Veloso, M., Browning, B.: A survey of robot learning from demonstration. Robot. Autonom. Syst. **57**(5), 469–483 (2009)
3. Billard, A., Calinon, S., Dillmann, R., Schaal, S.: Robot programming by demonstration. In: Siciliano, B., Khatib, O. (eds.) Springer Handbook of Robotics, pp. 1371–1394. Springer, Berlin (2008). https://doi.org/10.1007/978-3-540-30301-5_60
4. Bills, A.G.: General experimental psychology. Longmans, Green and Co (1934)
5. Breazeal, C.: Role of expressive behaviour for robots that learn from people. Philos. Trans. R. Soc. Biol. Sci. **364**, 3527–3538 (2009)
6. Cakmak, M., Takayama, L.: Teaching people how to teach robots: the effect of instructional materials and dialog design. In: Proceedings of the 2014 ACM/IEEE International Conference on Human-Robot Interaction, pp. 431–438 (2014)
7. Cakmak, M., Thomaz, A.L.: Eliciting good teaching from humans for machine learners. Artif. Intell. **217**, 198–215 (2014)
8. Fink, J., Bauwens, V., Kaplan, F., Dillenbourg, P.: Living with a vacuum cleaning robot. Int. J. Soc. Robot. **5**, 389–408 (2013)
9. Fischer, K., et al.: A comparison of types of robot control for programming by demonstration. In: 2016 11th ACM/IEEE International Conference on Human-Robot Interaction (HRI), pp. 213–220 (2016)
10. Grollman, D.H., Billard, A.: Donut as I do: learning from failed demonstrations. In: 2011 IEEE International Conference on Robotics and Automation, pp. 3804–3809 (2011)
11. Kaiser, M., Friedrich, H., Dillmann, U.: Obtaining good performance from a bad teacher. In: Programming by Demonstration vs. Learning from Examples Workshop at ML 1995 (1995)
12. Ravichandar, H., Polydoros, A.S., Chernova, S., Billard, A.: Recent advances in robot learning from demonstration. Ann. Rev. Control Robot. Autonom. Syst. **3**(1), 297–330 (2020)
13. Sakr, M., Freeman, M., Van der Loos, H.F.M., Croft, E.: Training human teacher to improve robot learning from demonstration: a pilot study on kinesthetic teaching. In: 2020 29th IEEE International Conference on Robot and Human Interactive Communication (RO-MAN), pp. 800–806 (2020)
14. Saunders, J., Nehaniv, C.L., Dautenhahn, K., Alissandrakis, A.: Self-imitation and environmental scaffolding for robot teaching. Int. J. Adv. Robot. Syst. **4**(1), 109–124 (2007)
15. Tanwani, A.K., Mor, N., Kubiatowicz, J., Gonzalez, J.E., Goldberg, K.: A fog robotics approach to deep robot learning: application to object recognition and grasp planning in surface decluttering. In: 2019 International Conference on Robotics and Automation (ICRA), pp. 4559–4566 (2019)
16. Weir, J.P.: Quantifying test-retest reliability using the intraclass correlation coefficient and the SEM. J. Strength Conditioning Res. **19**(1), 231–240 (2005)

Expanding the Use of Robotics in ASD Programs in a Real Educational Setting

Selene Caro-Via[✉][iD], Marc Espuña[iD], and Raquel Ros[iD]

La Salle - Ramon Llull University, 08022 Barcelona, Spain
`selene.caro@salle.url.edu`

Abstract. This work presents a first experience at a Spanish school, which approached us to expand the use of robots in their special needs programme. Based on the school requirements, we opted for instantiating an existing approach that fosters coordination and collaboration between players, adapting it to the school's requirements. Our main approach is that the performed activity must be accepted by both the children and the caregivers, as they will be the ones to use it in the future. The goal is to design different activities proposed by the school to be used in their everyday sessions and to constantly improve it until getting a final activity that can be used not only in this school, but also in other centers. We describe the developed robot-based interactive activity, as well as our findings, which involve a qualitative exploration. The main conclusion is that different degrees of personalisation must be integrated to the interaction performed by the robot.

Keywords: ASD · Collaboration · Interactive game · Robotics

1 Introduction

Nowadays, there are more than 450.000 people in Spain with Autistic Spectrum Disorder (ASD) [14]. A social robotics application area that has been largely explored is that of support to the autism community. In this field, a well known project is AuRoRA [6], which studies the use of robots as tools that might serve an educational or therapeutic role for children with autism to promote the didactic aspect and triadic relationships. One of the first experiments carried out was with Robota [3], and later on, with Kaspar [18], providing evidences that robots could help people with Autistic Spectrum Disorder (ASD) in different everyday tasks. Based on these successful experiences, different projects have emerged focusing on the support of social skills acquisition and knowledge gain through technology ranging from human-like robots to wearable robots [1].

In Spain, Experts in pediatrics, biomedical engineering, robotics and neurorehabilitation focus on using robotics (Pepper, from Softbank, and Milo, from Robokind) to support children on their learning of expressions and emotions [8]. Other robots, such as NAO from Softbank, have also been used in this

Supported by La Salle-Ramon Llull University.

domain application. Alabdulkareem et al. [1] reviews 38 articles, from which 8 (21.05%) use NAO. The robot is used for cognitive development (proactivity and self-initiation [2]), social and emotional development (imitation [12]; joint attention and turn-taking [15]; triadic and dyadic interactions [11]; to measure engagement [7,12,13]; and social communication skills [10,11,15]), and clinical and educational studies (eye contact [5]).

This study aims at giving an answer to a school in Spain, La Salle-La Seu d'Urgell school, which approached us to expand the use of robots in their special education programme, tailored to children with ASD. The school had a first experience with robots in the past, where a PLEO robot was used to support anxiety through animal care. In a previous study, Boladeras et al. [4] evidenced that integrating robots in the everyday life of children in a paediatric hospital, alleviates feelings of anxiety, loneliness and stress during long-term inpatient settings. The reason behind trying a pet robot at the school was because some children with ASD were afraid of real animals, and thus, the use of a pet robot was considered an intermediate step towards achieving such goal. Based on the positive outcomes that children displayed with PLEO, the school decided to explore alternative robotics platforms to further investigate the use of robotics for social skills acquisition.

Based on the school requirements and the existing literature, we opted for instantiating the approach proposed by Wainer et al. [17]. In their work, they propose "an experimental setup involving an autonomous, humanoid robot playing a dyadic cooperative video game to have children with autism become engaged in both the cooperative form of play as well as their social interactions with the other player". Thus, in this paper, we present our version of the interactive cooperative game, where we reproduce some of the features of Wainer's work, while introducing some differences required by the specific use case at the school.

The paper is structured as follows. Section 2 describes the interactive activity design and development based on [17], highlighting the design variations. Section 3 introduces the use case trials, followed by the outcome obtained in a pilot study carried out at the school during 3 d. Finally, Sect. 4 concludes the work along with describing future lines of research.

2   The Interactive Activity

The interactive activity consists of a video game that fosters coordination and collaboration between the players, where one player is the child and the other, either a typically developed human or a robot. The game consists of 3D shapes on the screen which have to be removed as the game develops. Each player controls a line on the screen, a horizontal and a vertical one (Fig. 1a), where the horizontal one moves up and down, and the vertical one, sideways. Each player has a remote control device to move the lines. The intersection point of both lines is depicted in yellow. To remove a figure, both players have to cooperate with each other: first agreeing on which figure to remove; second, moving their corresponding lines so that the intersection (yellow square) is placed over the

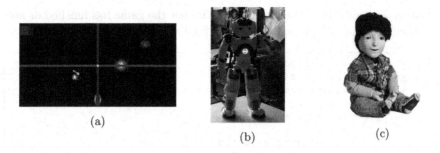

Fig. 1. (a) Game interface. (b) NAO robot used in this work. (c) Kaspar robot used in [17].

figure to be erased, and indicating so by pressing the select button, 'S', in their corresponding remote controls; and third, pressing the erase button, 'E', at the same time to finally remove the figure. By forcing such cooperative behaviours, children are expected to practice their collaborative social skills. Once all the objects are erased, new figures appear, ensuring that none of the objects are placed in the same row or column (to favour a simpler coordination activity).

2.1 The Robot

In this study we have used the NAO robot (Fig. 1b) instead of the Kaspar robot (Fig. 1c) used in the original study. The reason for such a choice is because the school already had a NAO, and thus, it was part of the requirements. In comparison to Kaspar, NAO is less human-like, i.e. the face has no realistic human traits.

The robot is programmed in Python with using the Naoqi library[1]. The pseudo code of the robot behaviour is presented in Algorithm 1. First, the robot waits for the child to select a figure. Every 30 s (instead of 5 s as done in [17]), the robot reminds the child to select a figure. If after three reminders, the child fails to select a figure, the robot does it (by moving its own line over the desired figure) and explicitly indicates so to the child through speech (lines 7–12). Next, the robot checks whether the child has reached the selected figure. If not, it waits one minute until prompting the child to move towards the figure. Once both players are on the selected figure, the robot stands up, raises its left arm and triggers a countdown through speech ("3, 2, 1, now!", line 20) to indicate the user to erase the figure and thus display a clear coordination signal. It then verifies that the figure has been properly removed, which will only take place if both players press the erase button 'E' at the same time. If the figure has not been erased, the robot verbally reminds the child that s/he can proceed whenever s/he wants (line 22). Once the figure has been erased, the robot gives positive feedback to the child and waits for the selection of the next figure (line

---

[1] http://doc.aldebaran.com/2-5/dev/python/install_guide.html.

25). At each round, the robot also checks whether the game has finished or not. If so, then it says goodbye and the session finalises.

```
while not game_finished:
    get_data_from_game ()
    if is_game_finished ():
        say_goodbye ()
        game_finished = True
    else:
        if not is_figure_selected ():
            if 30s_has_passed ():
                if 3_times_remembered ():
                    robot_selects_figure ()
                else:
                    reminder_to_select_figure ()
        else:
            #Only said once for each selection
            say_figure_to_erase ()
            if is_game_finished ():
                say_goodbye ()
                game_finished = True
            else if child_on_figure ():
                indicate_when_to_press ()
                if not figure_erased ():
                    wait_child_to_press ()
                #Indicate figure erased, number of figures
                #remaining, or motivate
                give_feedback ()
            else if child_more_1min_not_doing_anything ():
                motivate_child ()
```

Algorithm 1. Behaviour of the robot.

2.2   System Architecture

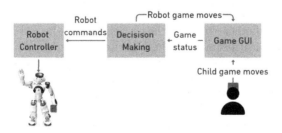

Fig. 2. Architecture and communication between the main modules of the system.

The system is composed of three main components: the decision making module, the graphical interface of the game and the robot itself (Fig. 2). The game application has been enhanced with respect to the one developed in [17] as follows:

1. Displaying not only 3D figures, but also textures. This allows to use other types of images in the game (for instance, animal images), which can be more meaningful to the children. This way, not only personalisation of the game can be achieved, but also vocabulary consolidation on different topics.
2. Ability to change the lighting of the scene, figure size and rotation speed. Depending on the user needs, these features may have an impact on the child perception and performance of the game.
3. When selecting figures, the game displays a green square that surrounds the selected object in order to help player cooperation.
4. Game levels, where in the lowest level, figures are static, while in the higher one, they are dynamic. This feature was not used in this work, since it would increase the variability of the set-up, which is not the aim at this point.
5. The game dynamically tries to place all the figures in random positions while avoiding to place more than one on the same row or column.
6. Customisable background and figure colours, as well as adding names to the figures.

All these parameters can be configured in the main configuration panel before starting the game. The game is developed using C++ with OpenGL API [9] using GLFW and GLEW extensions (all files available here).

The Wii consoles used in [17] have been replaced with 3D printed consoles containing a Raspberry Pico board. One of the consoles is blue (Fig. 3a), representing the vertical blue line in the screen. The control buttons placed at the right side of the console can only move the line right and left. The other console is red (Fig. 3b), representing the horizontal red line. In this case, the buttons on the console can only move the line up and down. Both consoles include two additional buttons: the 'S' and 'E' buttons, to respectively select or erase a given figure during the game. They are placed at the left side of the consoles. Since the robot cannot physically press buttons, we have built a stick (see Fig. 1b, left hand of the robot) to represent a console. It does not have any functionality: it only indicates the colour of the bar that the robot controls.

3 Use Case Trials

In order to carry out a first exploration on the applicability of the activity at the school, we ran a set of sessions with end-users. This section outlines the followed procedure, as well as the insights gathered through this first experience.

(a)   (b)

Fig. 3. Consoles used by human players. On the left side, the 'E' (Erase) and 'S' (Select) buttons. On the right side, the arrows to control each line.

3.1 Participants

Four children with level 1 ASD[2] have been selected for this study based on the caregivers[3] criteria. Childrens' names are coded using a 'U' (User) and a number to ensure anonymity. They are all male with the following ages: U1 aged 5, U2 aged 6, U3 aged 12, and U4 aged 14.

The use case trials were part of the robotic-based activities carried out at the school, and thus, did not require an additional ethical review and approval according to the institution procedures. A consent form describing this specific activity has been requested to all parents or legal tutors of the children who participated in the sessions.

3.2 Procedure

Two days before the 3-days trials, the NAO robot was introduced to the children at the school. The caregivers were in charge to do so, while the experimenter was remote. The experimenter was introduced to the children first and then the caregivers asked them to say something to the robot, such as say hello or to dance or sing. The game was described to the participant in the first session by the caregiver (except for one case, where the experimenter did so). Next, a short familiarisation phase (5 min) took place to verify that the child understood it.

We have conducted a total of four sessions for each child, where a human and a robot have been alternated as the partner player. This method is the same one as conducted in [17]. Therefore, the phase of playing with a typically developed human player is referred as H, while the phase where the child plays with NAO is referred to as R. The partner ordering is H1, R1, H2, and R2. We use the

---

[2] Without on-site help, deficiencies in social communication cause major issues. Difficulties initiating social interactions, displaying atypical or unsatisfactory responses to social openness from others. Behavioural inflexibility causes significant interference with functioning in one or more contexts. Difficulties alternating activities. Organisational and planning problems hinder autonomy.

[3] Caregivers have a degree in childhood and primary education. They are part of the Intensive Support for Inclusive Schooling (SIEI) of the school.

suffix 1 or 2 to distinguish between first or second round, either with human or robot. In our setup, the caregiver with whom the child is already familiar plays with the child, instead of a stranger (as in [17]). Our aim is to study the viability of robot-based interventions with the current practices at the school, and therefore, it is essential that the educators play an active role during the validation process as well.

The sessions spanned three days, with no child having more than two sessions on one single day. The time of the session was allocated with respect to each child availability according to the school schedule. In contrast to [17], the sessions have a duration of 15 to 20 min, instead of 25. This limit was set because of the camera recording limitations, which could only record 20 min. Once the user has played for 15 min, the game is stopped by the experimenter as soon as all the remaining figures in the screen are erased. For this reason, the duration of some sessions is longer than 15 min. If at any point of a session the child is not comfortable with the experience, the session is immediately stopped.

Table 1. For each user, we describe his partner per session, the robot control mode (A=Autonomous, F=Failure, T=Teleoperated) along with the minutes in such mode, people in class (U=user, C=carer, E=experimenter, O=other people), number of interruptions in each session and total duration of the session (in blue, sessions where the child is not comfortable; in orange, sessions where the robot has overheated).

	Session	1 (H1)	2 (R1)	3 (H2)	4 (R2)
U1	Player 2	C1	R	C1	R
	Robot control (min)	-	A (8) - F (6) - T (6)	-	T (16)
	People in class	U1, C1, E, 1 O	U1, C1, E	U1, C1, C2, C3, E, 4 O	U1, U4, C2, C3, E
	Interruptions	4	1	1	0
	Duration (min)	17	20	15	16
U2	Player 2	C3	R	C3	R
	Robot control (min)	-	A (6) - T (7)	-	A (14)
	People in class	U2, C3, E	U2, C3, E, 1 O	U2, C2, C3, E	U2, C3, E
	Interruptions	1	0	2	0
	Duration (min)	13	13	14	14
U3	Player 2	C2	R	C2	R
	Robot control (min)	-	T (13)	-	A (13) - T (5)
	People in class	U3, C1, C2, E, 1 O	U3, C2, C3, E, 2 O	U3, C2, C3, E	U2, C3, E
	Interruptions	2	2	5	2
	Duration (min)	12	13	15	18
U4	Player 2	C2	R	C2	R
	Robot control (min)	-	T (15)	-	A (11) - T (1)
	People in class	U4, C2, C5, E, 1 O	U4, C1, C2, E, 1 O	U4, C1, C2, C3, E, 4 O	U4, C2, C3, E
	Interruptions	2	0	2	1
	Duration (min)	20	15	15	12

The sessions took place at a classroom dedicated to the special needs program. Thus, during the execution of the game, other students or caregivers could also be present in the shared room, entering and leaving at any point. While these interruptions are not ideal, on the one hand we wanted to ensure that the interventions took place in a well-known space for them, to favour the children self-confidence when exposed to new people and artefacts (i.e. the experimenter, the robot and the game). On the other hand, we also wanted to set-up the sessions in the same conditions as it would normally take place. It is worth mentioning that children are used to see people going in and out of the room, so in this sense, such situations are already part of their routine. Thus, during the sessions, at least three people were present: the participant, the caregiver and the experimenter. Table 1 summarises the sessions details.

3.3   Qualitative Analysis

Next, we provide a qualitative description of the sessions, based on observations and annotations taken from the video recorded sessions, grouped by different themes, where C stands for caregiver, and U, for user.

Attention and Suggestions Consideration. In general, children do take into account their partner's suggestion (caregiver or robot) throughout the sessions. Nonetheless, when playing with the robot, U1 does not really pay attention to the robot's suggestions, unless the carer repeats them. In other occasions, U4 does not listen to the robot when he is concentrated talking to the carer or experimenter, and U3 only agrees with the robot if the suggestion is optimal for him. Saying the children's names helps them to pay attention to the robot.

Motivation. Most children were motivated to take part in the sessions (14 out of 16 sessions in total). They happily entered the room, smiling or even laughing. Even when they had difficulties erasing a figure (i.e. when more than one attempt was necessary to successfully erase a figure), all participants have smiled or laughed.

Only in two occasions participants manifested a certain rejection. In the first case, U1 indicated in his last session that he did not want to continue playing. However, with little encouragement, he finished the session. In fact, in previous sessions, this very same child was drawing the other player's attention (either C1 or the robot) when they were not cooperating in the activity, demonstrating his motivation into playing the game. In the second case, in U3's first session C2 detected that he was not comfortable playing the game (he had one hand on his head while playing with the other). He commented that the game was not that bad and that he liked the figures, but that constantly moving the bar to erase the figures bored him, impacting on his motivation towards playing the game (his first session lasted less than 15 min). However, in the following sessions he did not comment on this fact anymore, and actually, the time spent in the game gradually increased until reaching 18 min long.

Feedback. The main method used to motivate and provide feedback to the children is through verbal feedback, performed by all the carers and the robot.

Performing a high five in the H sessions when they managed to erase all figures was a spontaneously additional method put in place in the first caregiver's session, mainly to foster the engagement of the children in the game. Such encouragement was reduced in the next caregiver session, since the child was already engaged and no additional support was necessary. For instance, in U1's first session, the gesture occurred 8 times, while only 3 times in session 3.

All children agreed that the robot talked too much when it was working autonomously. They preferred the sentences and questions performed when the robot was teleoperated (see Section *Technical problems*) as it used their names and was more personal. Note that they were not aware of the control mode of the robot.

Curiosity. Children expressed curiosity towards the robot in different ways: asking about how it worked (U1 and U4), touching it (U1 and U3), or looking at it (U1, U2, and U3) with interest. In one occasion, U1 also clapped his hands in order to draw the robot's attention. It is also worth mentioning that U4 was specially interested in the robot and the game, constantly asking questions about its technical capabilities and programming.

Coordination. Initially all the participants opted for counting to synchronise their action on pressing the 'E' button. However, half of carers and children changed this agreement method throughout the game, to adapt it to different children characteristics. For instance, C2 suggested U3 to look at each other's eyes to know when to press the button. However, it did not work well, so they decided to add a nod gesture instead. Another example is U4, who changed the method different times, trying (i) counting with his fingers, (ii) nodding three times and, finally, (iii) looking to each other's eyes and nodding once (i.e. they look at each other and, when they see the other is looking back, they nod once).

The caregivers were interested in delegating the coordination responsibility to the child. Thus, while at the beginning of the first session the carer initiates the agreement method, in the following occasions they motivate the child to do so instead.

All the children, at least in one occasion during their first session, had started the erasing process before the object has been actually selected by both players, evidencing low coordination with their partner. Moreover, caregivers found that children do not indicate which figure to erase, neither verbally nor by pointing regardless of the carers having asked to do so.

Regarding to the sessions with the robot, the agreement method applied is always counting, with the robot being in charge of triggering it. We could observe that in contrast to the carer sessions, the children did not assume such responsibility at any point. This was clearly evident when, in a few occasions where the robot became inactive (see Section *Technical problems* for details), the children would continue playing without requiring or prompting any coordination sign from/to the robot. In fact, only U2 respects the robot and waits for its indications. In contrast, U1 for instance, only counted in one occasion.

Technical Problems. The robot was disconnected from the WiFi network from time to time (more specifically, 7 occasions with a maximum duration of 30 s), and thus, not receiving the controller's commands anymore. To avoid having to stop the session, we opted for teleoperating the robot as soon as the connection was automatically re-established. The remaining of the session was thus guided by the experimenter, who replicated the behaviour of the robot described in Sect. 2. However, since the utterances to be spoken by the robot had to be manually introduced at the very last minute, their frequency was reduced.

We took advantage of such technical inconvenient to further explore the potential of the interaction with the robot. Hence, in a few occasions, based on how the sessions were evolving and after observing the caregivers' behaviour when interacting with the children, a few general utterances spoken by the robot were added, such as, using their name, asking whether they enjoyed the game, with whom they preferred to play with or which was their favourite figure. We also introduced suggestions in regards to the game itself, such as asking the child to specify the figure to be erased, proposing alternative ones or asking the child to coordinate the erasing process. The children preferred this mode commenting that the robot felt closer and more enjoyable due to the decrease in number of utterances spoken by the robot.

The children also realised that once a figure is selected to erase it, it is not mandatory to wait for the agreement method to proceed erasing it, i.e. they can press the 'E' button without waiting for the countdown and the figure would be eliminated anyway since it was already selected. The problem with such lack of coordination is that the robot would sometimes refer to figures that had been just erased, leading to incoherent feedback until properly updating the game state.

Finally, a well-know problem with the NAO robot is its overheating, forcing 2 sessions to be reduced to less than 15 min, as indicated in Table 1. Regarding usability problems, children confuse the 'S' button with the 'E'. Luckily this only happened in their first session.

4   Conclusions

In this paper a new version of the interactive cooperative game proposed by Wainer et al. [17] is described. In our study, besides providing the caregivers general guidelines on the activity, we let them work with the children with no specific rules to observe alternative strategies. By detecting such real-time adjustments of the interactions, we have obtained different outcomes to further personalise the interaction with the children. Similar to other findings in the literature [16], personalisation is a key component to foster engagement by increasing the sense of closeness to the other. Some lessons learnt from our exploration study that point us on this direction are:

- Using the child's name motivates them to pay more attention to their partner, listening and considering their suggestions.

- Deciding with the child the coordination method that better suits them, not only ensures its appropriateness, but positively impacts the child involvement. Then, additional feedback is necessary for coordination, specially in the first sessions.
- Asking questions to make sure the child is enjoying and is not overwhelmed.
- Making suggestions during the game and offering space for dialogue when both players do not agree.
- Including additional motivational feedback modes, such as high five gestures.
- Using other activity personalisation features, such as thematic figures, colours, rotation speed, etc. according to each child's preferences.
- Discussing with the caregivers the skills to reinforce through the activity, such as assertiveness, role exchange (coordination responsibility) or eye contact.

The study presented in this paper not only seeks to explore the reactions of the children regarding the robot and the activity, but also that of the caregivers. The 3 day sessions carried out at the school gave us all an opportunity to explore what works and what does not. We want to emphasise that the aim of this work is not to define a strict protocol which cannot be changed, but rather to experience how the educators could use it in their everyday tasks. Thanks to their feedback, we can further develop activities that are truly useful for them, being the NAO robot a new companion to work with.

References

1. Alabdulkareem, A., Alhakbani, N., Al-Nafjan, A.: A systematic review of research on robot-assisted therapy for children with autism. Sensors **22**(3), 944 (2022)
2. van den Berk-Smeekens, I., et al.: Adherence and acceptability of a robot-assisted pivotal response treatment protocol for children with autism spectrum disorder. Sci. Rep. **10**, 8110 (2020)
3. Billard, A., Robins, B., Nadel, J., Dautenhahn, K.: Building robota, a mini-humanoid robot for the rehabilitation of children with autism. Assistive Technol. Official J. RESNA **19**, 37–49 (2007)
4. Díaz-Boladeras, M., et al.: Assessing pediatrics patients' psychological states from biomedical signals in a cloud of social robots. In: Kyriacou, E., Christofides, S., Pattichis, C.S. (eds.) XIV Mediterranean Conference on Medical and Biological Engineering and Computing 2016. IP, vol. 57, pp. 1179–1184. Springer, Cham (2016). https://doi.org/10.1007/978-3-319-32703-7_229
5. Conti, D., Trubia, G., Buono, S., Di Nuovo, S., Di Nuovo, A.: Social robots to support practitioners in the education and clinical care of children: The carer-aid project. Life Span Disabil. **23**, 17–30 (2020)
6. Dautenhahn, K., Robins, B.: Official web page of aurora project. https://aurora.herts.ac.uk/
7. Di Nuovo, A., Conti, D., Trubia, G., Buono, S., Di Nuovo, S.: Deep learning systems for estimating visual attention in robot-assisted therapy of children with autism and intellectual disability. Robotics **7**(2), 25 (2018)
8. Español, E.: La universidad de elche investiga el uso de robots para mejorar la respuesta de niños con tea. https://www.elespanol.com/alicante/vivir/salud/20220317/universidad-elche-investiga-robots-mejorar-respuesta-tea/657934624_0.html, March 2022

9. Group, K.: Official web page. https://www.opengl.org/
10. Kim, S., Hirokawa, M., Matsuda, S., Funahashi, A., Suzuki, K.: Smiles as a signal of prosocial behaviors toward the robot in the therapeutic setting for children with autism spectrum disorder. Front. Robot. AI **8**, 59975 (2021)
11. Marino, F., et al.: Outcomes of a robot-assisted social-emotional understanding intervention for young children with autism spectrum disorders. J. Autism Dev. Disord. **50**, 1973–1987 (2020)
12. Rakhymbayeva, N., Amirova, A., Sandygulova, A.: A long-term engagement with a social robot for autism therapy. Front. Robot. AI **8**, 180 (2021)
13. Rudovic, O., Lee, J., Mascarell-Maricic, L., Schuller, B.W., Picard, R.W.: Measuring engagement in robot-assisted autism therapy: a cross-cultural study. Front. Robot. AI **4**, 36 (2017)
14. Ministerio de Sanidad, S.S.E.I.: Estrategia española en trastornos del espectro del autismo. https://www.mdsocialesa2030.gob.es/derechos-sociales/discapacidad/docs/Estrategia_Espanola_en_TEA.pdf
15. Taheri, A., Meghdari, A., Alemi, M., Pouretemad, H.: Human-robot interaction in autism treatment: a case study on three pairs of autistic children as twins, siblings, and classmates. Int. J. Soc. Robot. **10**, 93–113 (2018)
16. Tsiakas, K., Abujelala, M., Makedon, F.: Task engagement as personalization feedback for socially-assistive robots and cognitive training. Technologies **6**, 49 (2018)
17. Wainer, J., Dautenhahn, K., Robins, B., Amirabdollahian, F.: A pilot study with a novel setup for collaborative play of the humanoid robot kaspar with children with autism. Int. J. Soc. Robot. **6**, 45–65 (2014)
18. Wood, L.J., Zaraki, A., Robins, B., Dautenhahn, K.: Developing kaspar: a humanoid robot for children with autism. Int. J. Soc. Robot. **13**(3), 491–508 (2019). https://doi.org/10.1007/s12369-019-00563-6

An Overview of Socially Assistive Robotics for Special Education

Shyamli Suneesh[1]($\boxtimes$) and Virginia Ruiz Garate[2]

[1] Faculty of Engineering, University of Bristol, Bristol, UK
hb21985@bristol.ac.uk
[2] Faculty of Environment and Technology, Bristol Robotics Laboratory,
University of the West of England, Bristol, UK
virginia.Ruizgarate@uwe.ac.uk

Abstract. Social Robots have been used in applications such as health-care, education, services, and entertainment. Among all these, Socially Assistive Robots (SARs) have proved to have significant impact in the assistance to people with learning disabilities or difficulties. This paper aims to provide an overview of the studies on SARs for people with Special Education Needs. We analyzed the role of SARs as a buddy, therapeutic assistant, and coach in various educational settings, with emphasis on children. We extracted data on aim, methods, challenges, outcomes, and the role of robots for a set of featured studies. The majority of presented experiments showed improvements in the participants' performance or abilities, their engagement, and interaction with peers during robotics sessions. Current trends in the development and design of Socially Assistive Robots such as the NAO and Pepper Robot show how they can be used to aid people with Special Education Needs. However, these robots still face major challenges such as the limited assessment on long-term effect and the few variations of use-cases analysed.

Keywords: Socially assistive robots · Special education needs ·
Rehabilitation · Serious games · Learning difficulties · Developmental
disability · Intellectual disability · Learning disability · Review

1 Introduction

According to the UK government, around 1.5 million pupils in England have special educational needs[1]. Across the years, these medical conditions that affect learning have been referred to with interchangeable terminology. Learning disabilities[2] are classified as a neurodevelopmental disorder originating before 18 years of age and setting limitations on intellectual functioning and social behaviour during everyday life [31]. Examples of learning disabilities include

---

[1] https://explore-education-statistics.service.gov.uk/find-statistics/special-educational-needs-in-england.

[2] Mental retardation, now referred to as intellectual disability in the US and learning disability in the UK [31].

© The Author(s), under exclusive license to Springer Nature Switzerland AG 2022
F. Cavallo et al. (Eds.): ICSR 2022, LNAI 13818, pp. 183–193, 2022.
https://doi.org/10.1007/978-3-031-24670-8_17

Autism, Down's syndrome, and Cerebral Palsy. Moreover, according to [5], "1 out of 4 autistic children are accompanied with a learning disability." The British Nomenclature[3] of naming learning conditions has been used to address these developmental disabilities [9], an umbrella term for a broad range of chronic conditions, throughout this review under two categories of "learning disabilities" and "learning difficulties" [1]. Learning difficulties, unlike learning disabilities, do not affect the IQ level of a person and they can perform social actions just like their neuro-typical peers. However, they face learning difficulties in terms of reading, writing, word formation etc. [10].

According to the Equality Act 2010 [6], children that suffer from any kind of learning impairments be it learning difficulties or disability of any form are entitled to receive support of Special Education for their holistic development. In recent years, there have been examples of several robots that helped children mitigate their life problems through robot assisted therapy [18], child play [26], child robot interaction [22] and more. By engaging in meaningful activities, the child users have shown significant improvement in their behaviour, individually and in social groups, motivating them to do a little better with each day forward and showcasing improvements in psychological well-being, happiness, and rates of learning [33].

The World Health Organization states that 10% of the world population has a disability of any kind. About 14% of the population in the USA and at-least 18% of the population in Europe would have disabilities [24]. On the one hand, some common examples of learning difficulties include dyslexia, dyscalculia, dysgraphia, and ADHD (attention deficit). Dyslexia is caused by limitations in the development of the brain and it is characterised by difficulty in reading, word and memory formation, which can lead to low self-confidence, depression and anxiety. 1 in 10 people in the UK suffer from dyslexia [14]. Dyscalculia is a persistent difficulty to understand numbers and infer mathematical operations; thus this can affect the child in varying degrees [17] suffered by 3% to 6% of the population in the UK and USA respectively. [3]. Dysgraphia is a developmental coordination disorder (DCD) appearing in early stages of human life and exhibits deficit [34] in the production of written language. 5% to 20% of all child population globally have some form of writing deficit such as dysgraphia [2]. This causes deterioration in social, personal, professional, and academic activities. ADHD is a combination of genetic, phenotypic and environmental factors. Globally, in children with ASD, 70% are reported to have a combination of around 40% anxiety and 30% ADHD [14]. Children with ADHD face difficulty in maintaining consistent attention and can be very hyperactive.

On the other hand, examples of learning disabilities include Autism Spectrum Disorder, Cerebral Palsy, and Down's Syndrome. In developed countries, around 2% of the population has been reported to be on the autistic spectrum [14]. Although the exact neural mechanisms behind ASD are unknown, Autism

---

[3] The current British nomenclature establishes learning disabilities (USA) as "learning difficulties" and call intellectual disabilities (USA) as "learning disabilities" [11].

Spectrum Disorder (ASD) displays autism across a range of conditions. ASD is generally characterised by speech delay, social interaction challenges, repetitive behaviours, and struggle in coping with the surrounding environment. Cerebral Palsy [18] refers to a group of permanent disorders that affects the development of movement, posture and language. Being the most common of physical disabilities that can occur in childhood, nearly 17 million people worldwide suffer from cerebral palsy [8]. Treatment given to such children include occupational and language therapy mainly focusing on improving functional movement and cognitive skills that can improve their quality of life. Down's syndrome is a learning disability caused by a genetic disorder which implies having an extra chromosome. According to the UN, around 3000 and 5000 children are born with DS every year [4]. DS causes delay in physical growth, diverse facial features [26], and are at higher risk of acquiring other life-long diseases.

Social robots are emerging as a novel and effective solution to aid caring and development of children with these diverse learning difficulties and disabilities. In general, social robots are becoming more and more commonly used in society [33], being deployed in multiple applications such as healthcare, education, entertainment, and service. This is motivated by the users' perceptions, who usually regard these robots as friendly supportive co-workers, hence stimulating their adoption. These social robots have the potential to assist children with chronic illness such as learning disabilities making them comfortable to manage their emotions as well as to develop healthy behaviours and mannerisms over time [21]. For example, AIBO [25] is a social robot dog produced by Sony in 1999 which displays unique features using Artificial Intelligence to express emotions. This robot intended to help people increase emotional bonding by petting the dog similar to a real one. Similarly, Paro is an artificial harp seal from Japan, produced in 2009 which was aimed to help with older adult care and therapy in hospitals and care homes. It has proved to show positive effects on older adults as it responds to petting sounds, body motion and blinking of eyes [25]. There are also humanoids such as the NAO robot, developed by Aldebaran Robotics, which has a childlike humanoid figure which makes it appealing for children to consider as a playmate. Moreover, it mimics human behaviour and is inbuilt with several features such as voice recognition and object detection. NAO is used in therapies for autistic children across the globe [25].

Ample areas that require human robot interaction use these social robots with the aim to enhance the life of a user. Among the many mentioned applications, Assistive Robots that are social in nature are used for educational purposes for people from different age groups, ranging from primary to tertiary education and more. Within the group of using Socially Assistive Robots (SARs) for education in general, this study focuses on the specific group of children with special needs (CSN) [29] by providing a comprehensive analysis on the use of SARs for special education. This study focuses on aim, methods, outcomes, and the role of robots within the studied research. We also put special attention to the specific challenges derived by the use of SARs with people with special needs.

2   Methodology

The aim of this review is to provide a broad summary of state-of-the-art research on use of SARs in Special Education. The major focus of this work was to explore each of the included studies to extract relevant features such as purpose of the study, number of participants involved, data analysis, intervention of social robot, outcomes of the study, and future scope for improvement. We based our search methodology on the PRISMA checklist for data extraction [27]. This summary can serve as a foundation for future work on specific applications of SARs for a learning condition.

To obtain a significant collection of papers for our review, a search of the databases Google Scholar and PubMed was perfomed between the time period of May 14, 2022 to May 20, 2022 with the set of keywords defined below, along with 8 websites that provide relevant definitions and information on child law. The bibliographic search was carried out using the following terminologies: (1) "social robot" AND "special education", (2) "social robots" AND ("dyslexia" OR "dysgraphia" OR "dyscalculia" OR "ADHD"), (3) "social robots" AND "healthcare", (4) "social robot" AND "learning disability", (5) "social robot" AND "intellectual disabilities", (6) "social robot" AND ("autism" OR "cerebral palsy" OR "down's syndrome"). These keywords were chosen to broaden the categories of medical conditions of children who require a support of special education. Including Socially Assistive Robots on the search, an intersection of social robotics and assistive robotics, gave rise to various subsets such as "care robot" [16], which could refer to robots for the elderly. Amongst these, there could be works relating only to regular education or other disease conditions, and not ones that are categorised under learning disability or difficulty. Thus, these had to be filtered out as they are out of the scope of this review.

First a fast screening of the most relevant results of the search engines was performed (~100 top papers per engine) focusing on the titles and abstract. These papers were filtered against the inclusion/exclusion criteria described in Subsects. 2.1 and 2.2. Then, a search for duplicates was done, after which the remaining papers were revised in depth through methods, age group, and roles such as coach, therapy assistant, buddy, again using the inclusion and exclusion criteria. The Search flow chart inspired by the PRISMA 2009 [21] is shown in Fig. 1.

2.1   Inclusion Criteria

The inclusion criteria were as the follows: 1) studies must be focused on the use of SARs with people who have a diagnosis of learning difficulties or learning disabilities; 2) studies must lay out the methodology of interactions with SARs such as through games or therapies; 3) studies must include at least one case or a group of participants and must involve them in engaging activities; 4) studies must report data collected among children and/or their parents and/or their

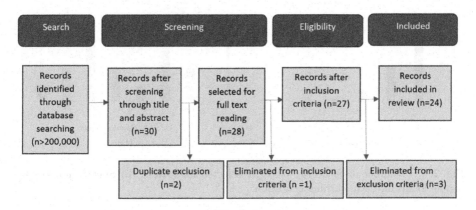

Fig. 1. Search Flowchart based on PRISMA 2009 [27]

teachers and/or therapists; 5) studies must be published and available in full-text in peer-reviewed journals or conference proceedings or meta-analysis that are available through the commonly used scientific databases (i.e. PubMed, and Google Scholar); 6) the studies must be published in the English language; 7) the timeline of studies taken are from 2010 to 2022.

2.2 Exclusion Criteria

The exclusion criteria were as the follows: 1) studies should not include robots meant to be used only for general education purpose such as in primary, secondary and tertiary schools; 2) studies testing social robots for syndromes such as Dementia, Alzheimer's, Parkinson's are excluded because they are not categorised under learning disability or difficulty and are classified as progressive disorders caused by neuro-degeneration [7]; 3) studies that use assistive technologies that are only non-robotic (e.g., computers, tablets, video games, virtual reality, etc.) are excluded; 4) studies that do not provide exhaustive information about the results obtained or that only have insufficient preliminary results are also excluded; 5) unpublished material is excluded; 6) articles dealing with narrative reviews, meta-analysis, and other types of literature review are excluded if no outcome measures are reported; 7) studies published before 2010 are excluded; 8) Studies that are not in the English language are excluded.

3 Results

An initial large amount of papers were obtained (>200,000), which were categorized after multiple steps. The initial fast screening filter against the inclusion/exclusion criteria described in Subsects. 2.1 and 2.2 lead to a first selection of 30 works, 26 from Google Scholar and 4 from PubMed (see Fig. 1). After removing 2 duplicates, the remaining 28 papers were revised in depth. 1 and

188   S. Suneesh and V. Ruiz Garate

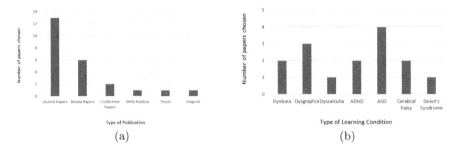

Fig. 2. (a) Number of each type of paper selected for review. (b) Specific number of papers found for each learning condition

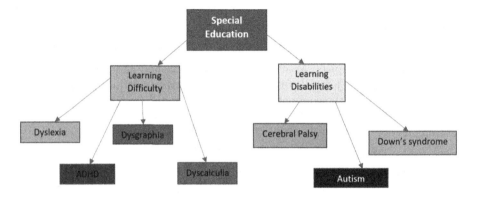

Fig. 3. Special Education conditions chosen for the Review

2 papers were eliminated respectively following the inclusion/exclusion criteria respectively. This led to a final sub-selection of 24 papers.

Amongst the 24 papers, 15 papers were specific to the particular learning conditions and 9 were of general nature which included reviews, mental health context, data analysis, and legal aspects. Additionally, 8 websites were of generic nature which included statistics, terminology, and child law information. The number of papers chosen under each type of publication has been shown in Fig. 2a.

While there is a wide range of learning disabilities and difficulties, for the purpose of this study, the most commonly occurring learning conditions have been chosen to observe the application of social robots in various contexts [1]. Figure 3 indicates the areas of research chosen to be reviewed in this paper and the specific distribution of papers under each learning condition has been shown in Fig. 2b.

Table 1 summarizes the research works found on the application of SARs to support the selected learning conditions.

Table 1. Table with features extracted from literature review under each learning condition. Dysl. stands for Dyslexia, Dysgr. for Dysgraphia, Dysc. for Dyscalculia, C. Palsy for Cerebral Palsy and D. Synd. for Down's Syndrome. Ther stands for Therapy.

Learn. cond.	Refs.	Robot used	Role	N. of participants	Action taken	Limitations
Dysl.	Khaled 2017 [24], Massimo 2015 [28]	NAO	Coach	School Children	English learning through play	Non-specific growth
Dysgr.	Thomas 2021 [22], Soukaina 2022 [23], Jianling 2021 [34]	NAO, QT Robot	Buddy	1(a 10 year old boy subjected to 20 weekly sessions), Children aged between 6 and 15	Learning by teaching method using the 'Co-Writer' Setup with a game 'Dynamico'	Single case study, More feedback required
Dysc.	Lavonda 2014 [17]	Darwin	Coach	44 students	SIRT with tablet-based math quiz	Increased boredom in activity monotony, Implement RBE
ADHD	Federica 2021 [12]	Pepper	Ther.	5 Children	Therapeutic session through games, Feedback through UTAUT questionnaire, Built personalised emotion response using AI	More participants required for increased validation and acceptance
ASD	Noreen 2020 [13], Sandra 2021 [19], Seong-Jin 2016 [20], David 2018 [22]	NAO, PARO, Lego Mindstorms	Buddy and Coach	8 children and 6 special education teachers, Reviews - ASD, 28 children - 24-month time period	Questionnaires and activities	Limited to emotional regualtion
C. Palsy	Madeline 2020 [15], Jaime 2020 [18]	NAO	Ther.	24 participants, One 8 year old - 16 sessions of physical therapy	Goal Directed Therapy (GDT) through Rehabilitation process	Limited details in terms of proposed methodology
D. Synd	Sheila 2018 [26]	MARIA T-21	Buddy	Children and teenagers of 2 groups; with and without DS aged between 5 and 15 years old	Specialised games	More participants required for validation

The array of selected reviewed papers provides an overall insight to the application of Socially Assistive Robots in different contexts, specifically under the categories of a coach, therapy assistant, and buddy. Out of the papers chosen for review, 38% constitute of SARs for therapy applications followed by 33% showcasing SARs as a coach, finally followed by 27% comprising papers describing SARs in the role of a buddy. It has been observed that social robots with anthropomorphic child-like design are generally used for interaction with children of age groups between 5 to 15 years old [29]. In terms of a robot coach, similarities have been found in different studies regarding the methodology of 'learning by teaching' where the child feels responsible and aware to correct the robot when it answers incorrectly [17,24,28,32]. In terms of buddy, the pattern observed is that the robot and child play games together and work as a team. In this way, the child gets a sense of belonging due to the recurrent child robot interaction and improves social skills [15,20,23,26]. In terms of therapy, the social robot can serve as an assistant to the therapist where activities are charted by the therapist for the robot to perform in duo with the child. Robot assisted therapy has shown significant improvement in persons who need therapy [12,18]. The experiments are formulated in a way that appeal and improve the human robot interaction so that participants have a relatable and realistic experience.

4   Discussion

Socially Assistive Robots play significant roles in helping people with learning conditions by playing the roles of a buddy, therapy assistant and coach. Table 1 suggests that robots used in social interaction experiments are highly dependent on the skills that are targeted to be developed in the participants, their age group, and purpose of the study conducted. For example, PARO has been used for improving social skills through pet-like interaction [19,20] and Lego Mindstorms for games to increase the intervention of play [13,32]. However, the NAO robot, having an anthropomorphically childlike figure and featuring a light toned voice, is the most commonly used robot for special education of children [33]. The NAO robot, QT robot, and Darwin robot have been used for dyslexia, dysgraphia and dyscalculia use cases respectively, using pedagogical methodologies of 'Learning through Play' and 'Learning by teaching', and resulting in improvement of child's learning curve and motivation to progress [17,23,24]. For therapeutic purposes, the NAO and Pepper have been respectively used in the Cerebral Palsy and ADHD use cases. In studies such as [12,15], these robots demonstrated to be suitable for conducting physical therapy sessions and emotional response sessions due to the versatility and motion features displayed by the humanoid robots. As a buddy, the MARIA T-21 and PARO have been successfully deployed with Down's Syndrome and ASD use cases where children were directed to play personalised games. These selected social robots displayed features suitable for expression of emotion which allowed the improvement of social interaction [19,26].

SARs show two main advantages for their use in special education: (i) as users are better able to manage their learning tasks and social relationships through the use of SARs, a significant improvement in their skills is observable, and (ii) SARs also serve as a valuable assistant to work with teaching professionals who constantly strive to improve the lives of the people with special needs [30]. The limitations however cover a wide range of aspects, such as the robot not being able to be completely independent, and thus still requiring the active presence of a therapist for robot assisted therapy [26] or of a teacher for a classroom activity. In most studies, the number of participants tested were either a group of few in short term or a single case in a long-term basis [34]. This poses a limitation to extrapolate the results to a larger range of participants. Also, in some occasions, the experiments designed are only feasible for short term activities [34], but not for continually prolonged ones. Moreover, there are new intrinsic challenges faced by the trainers due to the use of a new technology, as they must tailor new methods and approaches for their therapy/classroom activity.

Though the outcomes of this research are broad and cast a large net on challenges and opportunities of SARs in special education, this summary can serve as a guide for a narrower review on a specific learning condition, age group, or robot type. This review can also serve as foundation for future research on social robot designs and the development of Human Robot Interaction frameworks for a particular learning condition. For example, drawing inspiration from previous research studies, different personalized robot-child games/therapies can be developed for children with diverse types of dyslexia. Future works also point to addressing the multiple challenges and addressing improvisation, for example by promoting user-centric strategies which includes continuous feedback from inputs of teachers, parents, and concerned authorities along the design of the experiments and therapies/classes [22]. Similarly, novel research is starting to focus more on conducting experiments on large scale [34] to understand the wider capacity of robot performance.

5   Conclusion

This review has provided an overall picture of how socially assistive robots can assist children with special needs in improving their learning curve. Depending on the need, social robots can play the roles of therapy assistant, buddy, and coach in different scenarios. Apart from the multiple technical challenges such as the need to improve emotional response and to use more AI to improve personalised attention, SARs also face difficulties coming from their specific applications, such as lack of acceptance and economic barriers for their implementation. Despite these, the social robots have made a significant impact in the lives of many children by giving them the confidence to dwell independently. Thus, there is a good preliminary evidence to suggest social robots have a place in modern educational structures.

References

1. Types of learning disabilities, carehome.co.uk. https://www.carehome.co.uk/advice/types-of-learning-disabilities, Accessed 23 Oct 2022

2. What teachers need to know about dysgraphia, we are teachers (2018). https://www.weareteachers.com/dysgraphia/, Accessed 19 Aug 2022
3. What is dyscalculia?, the dyslexia association (2019). https://www.dyslexia.uk.net/specific-learning-difficulties/dyscalculia, Accessed 19 Aug 2022
4. World down syndrome's day, united nations (2019). https://www.un.org/en/observances/down-syndrome-day, Accessed 19 Aug 2022
5. Learning disability and autism, autistica (2020). https://www.autistica.org.uk/what-is-autism/signs-and-symptoms/learning-disability-and-autism, Accessed 19 Aug 2022
6. Special education needs, child law advice (2020). https://childlawadvice.org.uk/information-pages/special-educational-needs, Accessed 19 Aug 2022
7. . Alzheimer's and parkinson's disease: What's the connection? (2021). https://www.verywellhealth.com/parkinsons-and-alzheimers, Accessed 23 Oct 2022
8. millions of reasons campaign, world cp day (2022). https://worldcpday.org/, Accessed 19 Aug 2022
9. Developmental disabilities, centers for disease control and prevention (2022). https://www.cdc.gov/ncbddd/developmentaldisabilities/conditions.html, Accessed 23 Oct 2022
10. Learning disabilities, mental health foundation (2022). https://www.mentalhealth.org.uk/node/learningdisabilities, Accessed 19 Aug 2022
11. What's the difference between learning disabilities and intellectual disabilities, understood (2022). https://www.understood.org/en/articles/whats-the-difference-between-learning-disabilities-and-intellectual-disabilities, Accessed 19 Aug 2022
12. Amato, F., Di Gregorio, M., Monaco, C., Sebillo, M., Tortora, G., Vitiello, G.: Socially assistive robotics combined with artificial intelligence for adhd. In: 2021 IEEE 18th Annual Consumer Communications & Networking Conference (CCNC), pp. 1–6. IEEE (2021)
13. Arshad, N.I., Hashim, A.S., Ariffin, M.M., Aszemi, N.M., Low, H.M., Norman, A.A.: Robots as assistive technology tools to enhance cognitive abilities and foster valuable learning experiences among young children with autism spectrum disorder. IEEE Access 8, 116279–116291 (2020)
14. Barua, P.D., et al.: Artificial intelligence enabled personalised assistive tools to enhance education of children with neurodevelopmental disorders-a review. Int. J. Environ. Res, Public Health 19(3), 1192 (2022)
15. Blankenship, M.M., Bodine, C.: Socially assistive robots for children with cerebral palsy: a meta-analysis. IEEE Trans. Med. Rob. Bionics 3(1), 21–30 (2020)
16. Boada, J.P., Maestre, B.R., Genís, C.T.: The ethical issues of social assistive robotics: a critical literature review. Technol. Soc. 67, 101726 (2021)
17. Brown, L.N., Howard, A.M.: The positive effects of verbal encouragement in mathematics education using a social robot. In: 2014 IEEE Integrated STEM Education Conference, pp. 1–5. IEEE (2014)
18. Buitrago, J.A., Bolaños, A.M., Caicedo Bravo, E.: A motor learning therapeutic intervention for a child with cerebral palsy through a social assistive robot. Disabil. Rehabil. Assist. Technol. 15(3), 357–362 (2020)
19. Cano, S., González, C.S., Gil-Iranzo, R.M., Albiol-Pérez, S.: Affective communication for socially assistive robots (sars) for children with autism spectrum disorder: a systematic review. Sensors 21(15), 5166 (2021)
20. Cho, S.J., Ahn, D.H.: Socially assistive robotics in autism spectrum disorder. Hanyang Med. Rev. 36(1), 17–26 (2016)

21. Dawe, J., Sutherland, C., Barco, A., Broadbent, E.: Can social robots help children in healthcare contexts? a scoping review. BMJ Paediatrics Open **3**(1) (2019)
22. Gargot, T., et al.: "it is not the robot who learns, it is me." Treating severe dysgraphia using child-robot interaction. Front. Psychiat., 5 (2021)
23. Gouraguine, S., Qbadou, M., Mansouri, K.: Handwriting treatment and acquisition in dysgraphic children using a humanoid robot-assistant. In: 2022 IEEE Global Engineering Education Conference (EDUCON), pp. 1658–1663. IEEE (2022)
24. Hamdan, K., Amorri, A., Hamdan, F.: Robot technology impact on dyslexic students' English learning. Int. J. Educ. Pedagogical Sci. **11**(7), 1949–1954 (2017)
25. Korn, O.: Social robots-a new perspective in healthcare. Res. Outreach **114**, 78–81 (2020)
26. da Luz Schreider, S., et al.: Proposal of games for children and teenagers with down syndrome applied to a socially assistive robot. Balance **7**, 8 (2022)
27. Moher, D., Liberati, A., Tetzlaff, J., Altman, D.G., Group*, P.: Preferred reporting items for systematic reviews and meta-analyses: the prisma statement. Ann. Internal Med. **151**(4), 264–269 (2009)
28. Pistoia, M., Pinnelli, S., Borrelli, G.: Use of a robotic platform in dyslexiaaffected pupils: the robin project experience. Int. J. Educ. Inf. Technol. **9**, 46–47 (2015)
29. Pivetti, M., Di Battista, S., Agatolio, F., Simaku, B., Moro, M., Menegatti, E.: Educational robotics for children with neurodevelopmental disorders: a systematic review. Heliyon **6**(10), e05160 (2020)
30. Rabbitt, S.M., Kazdin, A.E., Scassellati, B.: Integrating socially assistive robotics into mental healthcare interventions: applications and recommendations for expanded use. Clin. Psychol. Rev. **35**, 35–46 (2015)
31. Schalock, R.L., Luckasson, R.A., Shogren, K.A.: The renaming of mental retardation: understanding the change to the term intellectual disability. Intell. Dev. Disabil. **45**(2), 116–124 (2007)
32. Silvera-Tawil, D., Roberts-Yates, C.: Socially-assistive robots to enhance learning for secondary students with intellectual disabilities and autism. In: 2018 27th IEEE International Symposium on Robot and Human Interactive Communication (RO-MAN), pp. 838–843. IEEE (2018)
33. Westra, L.: Evaluating research on social robots for individuals with intellectual disability (2020). bSc thesis https://essay.utwente.nl/82151/
34. Zou, J., Gauthier, S., APHP, P.S., Archambault, D., Anzalone, S.M., Cohen, D.: The irecheck project-asocial robot helping (2021). https://robot4learning.github.io/publication/HRI2021/R4L-HRI2021_Zou.pdf

Preliminary Investigation of the Acceptance of a Teleoperated Interactive Robot Participating in a Classroom by 5th Grade Students

Megumi Kawata[1]([✉]), Masashi Maeda[2], Yuichiro Yoshikawa[1],
Hirokazu Kumazaki[3], Hiroko Kamide[4], Jun Baba[5], Naomi Matsuura[2],
and Hiroshi Ishiguro[1]

[1] Graduate School of Engineering Science, Osaka University, Osaka, Japan
{kawata,yoshikawa,ishiguro}@irl.sys.es.osaka-u.ac.jp
[2] Elementary School Attached to Faculty of Education, Mie University,
Tsu, Mie, Japan
mmaeda@fuzoku.edu.mie-u.ac.jp, m5naomi@edu.mie-u.ac.jp
[3] Nagasaki University Graduate School of Biomedical Sciences, Nagasaki, Japan
kumazaki@tiara.ocn.ne.jp
[4] Activities of the Institute of Innovation for Future Society of Nagoya University
Nagoya, Aichi, Japan
kamide@coi.nagoya-u.ac.jp
[5] AI Lab CyberAgent, Inc., Tokyo, Japan
baba_jun@cyberagent.co.jp

Abstract. Efforts are being made to utilize interactive robots in schools. However, autonomous robots exhibit limitations pertaining to their behaviors and communication abilities. Therefore, a teleoperated interactive robot was considered, and its close communications with children in a classroom was analyzed. This robot can establish personal and long-term communication with the children. Additionally, multiple operators are expected to operate the robot. Therefore, the children's comfort with the robot, their decreased communication with their friends, and the potential negative effects on the development of their social skills if they become attached to the robots should be considered. To this end, we investigated how children behave with the robot and their impressions of the robot in their classroom. We installed a teleoperated interactive in a 5th grade classroom at an elementary school attached to Mie University of Education, and we conducted a survey using questionnaires and moral classes. The results obtained demonstrated that the children experienced peace of mind and were less stressed, suggesting that they had no rejection to a robot that is operated by multiple operators. In addition, the moral class helped conclude that the children accepted the robot as a class member; further, They showed concern for improving their friendships and class time. The robot's presence in the classroom could help make the class interactive and increase communication among the children.

Keywords: Human-robot interaction · Teleoperated interactive robot · Education support · Filed trial

© The Author(s), under exclusive license to Springer Nature Switzerland AG 2022
F. Cavallo et al. (Eds.): ICSR 2022, LNAI 13818, pp. 194–203, 2022.
https://doi.org/10.1007/978-3-031-24670-8_18

1   Introduction

School life, not only in terms of education, but also in terms of classroom activities and interactions, have a considerable influence on the development of children [2]. Instead of learning from teachers, children need to teach each other [9]. One teacher is assigned to several children. Therefore, for a teacher to practically provide individual support to the children with regard to education, classroom activities [3,9], and their level of adaptation to school life is difficult. Therefore, children need to build relationships among themselves [11].

Interactive Robots have been used in schools in various manners to support education, such as robots as classroom teachers, robots as companions and peers, and telepresence robots as teachers [10]. Kanda et al. installed an autonomous robot, "Robovie," in an elementary school [7]. The robot interacted with the children for two months. Then, Robovie established a friendly relationship with the children. Hashimoto et al. demonstrated that a teacher-type android robot motivated class students [4]. Matsuzoe et al. developed humanoid robots that exhibited different excellence levels [8]. The robot that exhibited a low excellence level was more effective than the robot that exhibited a high excellence level in motivating participants during learning activities. These pioneering studies suggest that robots can help support teachers' classroom management and assist children's learning and elevate their school life. Robots can understand children's abilities and their satisfaction with their school life individually; further, they can have personal, attentive, and long-lasting interactions with the children. However, autonomous robots exhibit limitations. Therefore, we proposed the use of teleoperated interactive robots [1]. Introducing such teleoperated robots into classrooms makes it possible for children to achieve close and long-term communication with teachers and children. However, such a communication style is expected to involve more than multi-person operators, which raises several problems. Moreover, thus, can cause concerns with regard to privacy issues. Further, the children's decreased interactions with their friends and the potential negative effects on the development of their social skills because of their relationship with the robots should be investigated [10]. We should also investigate how children behave with the robots and their impressions of the robots in their classrooms.

In this study, a teleoperated interactive robot "Sota" was installed in a 5th-grade classroom at an elementary school attached to the Faculty of Education, Mie University. Sota interacted with the students for three days on April 22, May 17, and May 24, 2022. On April 22, 2022, the first day the robot was installed in the classroom, a moral class was held on "how to interact with the robot." On the second and third days of the experiment, multiple operators who were not involved with education remotely controlled the robot and observed its interactions with the students during classroom activities, group work, and recess. To investigate how the children's impression of the robot changed and how the robot affected their school life, we conducted survey research using questionnaires on the first and last days. For a deep and qualitative investigation of their thoughts regarding how they should interact with the robot in class, we observed their discussions during the moral class.

2   Teleoperated Interactive Robot

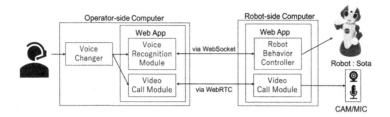

Fig. 1. System structure of teleoperated interactive robot, based on Baba, Jun, et al. "Teleoperated robot acting autonomous for better customer satisfaction."2020 [1].

2.1   Hardware

The system configuration of the teleoperated robot is shown in Fig. 1. The robot is Sota, manufactured by Vinston Corporation. The operator controls the robot remotely using WebRTC, a web application that enables video communication. In addition, the operator can view images from a wide-angle web camera installed on the back of the robot, listen to sounds in the classroom using an externally connected microphone, and talk with children in the classroom using the speakerphone on the front side of a box at the bottom of the robot. Moreover, a mini-PC is installed in the box to enable video communication of the web application program and control the robot. The mini-PC is wired to the Mie University elementary school network using a LAN cable.

2.2   Interactive Behavior

The operators operated the robot from an area far from the elementary school. The teleoperators can control the direction of the robot's gaze, and the robot can look at the speaker. In this study, the robot was set to be a character interested in school and said, "I want to attend the elementary school again." Further, the teleoperators were advised not to give their personal information to the children. When multiple remote operators were presented, they interacted with the children in the first and the second half of the operation time. To ensure that the robot's voice was consistent irrespective of the remote operator, we used "Morphvox," a voice changer software developed by Screaming Bee. The robot commended the students who participated in the class by looking at them and nodding and praising. They actively called out students' names and encouraged their opinions during group work. During recess, the robot interacted freely with the children. We did not disclose to the children that human operators remotely operated the robots.

3   Experiment

In this experiment, Sota was installed in a 5th-grade classroom C in an elementary school. The robot interacted with the students during recess and in class on April 22, May 17, and May 24, 2022. On April 22, 2022, the first day the robot was installed in the classroom, a moral class was held on "how to interact with robots." In addition, a questionnaire was used to investigate how the children's impression of the robot changed before and after the introduction of the robot, and how the robot affected them during class and recess. The questionnaire was used to compare the children's views in classrooms with and without the robot.

3.1   Participants

Ninety-six students in a 5th-grade classroom of an elementary school attached to the Faculty of Education, Mie University were the subjects of this study. Three 5th-grade classrooms are present, and we installed Sota in one of the classes.

3.2   Apparatus

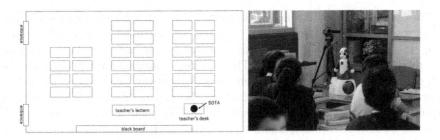

Fig. 2. Environment of class room

We set up Sota and a microphone (YAMAHA YVC-1000) in the classroom. The robot and the microphone were placed on the teacher's desk (Fig. 2). The remote operator used a laptop (Lenovo ideaPad Core-i7 SSID512 GB), a headset (Jabra 75 Evolve), and a voice conversion software, Morphvox. The remote operators accessed the remote control interface using Google chrome. The voice effect used by the remote operator was "child".

3.3   Measurements

The questionnaire included the following: (1) evaluation of the impression of the robot, (2) evaluation of the comfort during recess, and (3) evaluation of the children's comfort to present in class. Each item is listed in Table 1. In (1), to investigate the robot's impression, we measure the sense of comfort toward the robot and the degree to which the person attributed their mind to the robot. Therefore, we created items related to the peace of mind, stress, high performance, and controllability of the robot, based on Kamide et al. [5]. In addition, we created items measuring the degree of anthropomorphism of the robot, "Human Nature Positive" and "Human Nature Negative," and "Uniquely Human Positive" and "Uniquely Human Negative," based on the study by Kamide et al. [6]. Each rating consists of two questions, and the total number of items is 16. As for (3), the questionnaire consists of two items, "I feel comfortable during recess" and "It is easy to talk to my classmates during recess". (3) consists of four items: "It is easy to present a problem and obtain a clear answer," "It is easy to present a problem and obtain an unclear answer," 'It is easy to present to a group of people," and "It is easy to present in front of the whole class." We used the seven-choice method for (1)–(3), with the answers ranging from 1 "not at all agree" to 7 "agree very much." To analyze these questionnaires before the installation of the robot (hereon referred to as "pretest") and after the communication with the robot (hereon referred to as "posttest"), we enquired about their names and attendance numbers. In addition, we asked the subjects of the study to freely express their impressions regarding spending time with the robot.

3.4   Procedure

We installed the robot in one of the three 5th -grade classrooms present. The robot was installed in C class, and no robot was installed in A and B classes. The class with the robot is the experimental group, and the classes without the robot are the control groups. The children communicated freely with the robot during class and recess and were unaware that the robot was controlled by operators. As a pretest, a questionnaire was administered to all 5th graders on April 21, 2022. We created the questionnaire by Google form, and the teacher sent the URL of the questionnaire to the class children. The children answered the questionnaire using their iPads. The robots participated in the classes of the experimental group on April 22, 2022, May 17, 2022, and May 24, 2022. On April 22, 2022, during a moral class, the children has a session on "how to interact with the robot." We recorded the class. On April 22, 2022, one remote operator operated the robot, and on May 17, 2022, and May 24, 2022, two remote operators operated the robot-one during the first half and the other during the second half of the class. As a posttest, all 5th graders answered a questionnaire on May 24, 2022.

4   Results

The responses of 27 participants in the experimental group and 50 participants in the control group—who could respond during both survey periods, i.e., before and after the installation of the robots—among the 96 participants in the 5th-grade classrooms were analyzed. The classroom with or without the robot was a between-subject factor, and the survey period was a within-subject factor. We used a two-way ANOVA to analyze the data. Moreover, a simple main effect test

Table 1. Questionnaire

Peace of mind	1. I feel peace of mind with the robot
	2. I feel relieved
Stress	3. When I am with this robot, I feel restless
	4. This robot makes me feel stress
Performance	5. This robot seems to respond to my questions
	6. I think this robot recognizes its surroundings
Controllability	7. This robot is unlikely to harm human body
	8. The robot is unlikely to become uncontrollable
Human Nature Positive(HN+)	9. I think this robot is a fun-loving robot
	10. I think it is a sociable robot
Human Nature Negative(HN-)	11. I think this robot is impatient
	12. I think this robot is aggressive
Uniquely Human Positive(UH+)	13. I think this robot is polite
	14. I think this robot is nutty.
Uniquely Human Negative(UH-)	15. I think this robot has poor thoughts
	16. I think this robot is rude
Recess	1. I feel comfortable during recess
	2. It is easy to talk to classmates during recess
To present	1. It is easy to present a problem and obtain a clear answer
	2. It is easy to present a problem and obtain an unclear answer
	3. It is easy to present to a group of several people
	4. It is easy to present in front of the whole class

was conducted when the interaction effect was significant. The results for the main effects and interactions for each measure are summarized in Table 2.

4.1 Evaluation of the Impression of the Robot

We used significance levels adjusted by the Bonferroni method ($\alpha = .006 = .05/8$) to conduct a two-factor repeated-measures ANOVA.

Peace of Mind. The result demonstrated a significant difference in the robot factor ($F(1,75) = 12.7$, $p < 0.006$, $\eta2 = 0.093$), survey period factor ($F(1, 75) = 47.7$, $p < 0.006$, $\eta2 = 0.39$, $1-\beta = 1.0$), and interaction effects ($F(1, 75) = 8.82$, $p < 0.006$, $\eta2 = 0.11$, $1-\beta = 1.0$). The simple main effects exhibited significant differences in the with-robot condition ($F(1, 75) = 24.9$, $p < 0.006$, $\eta2 = 0.25$), and in the survey period condition (with-robot >without-robot, $p < 0.006$).

Stress. The result showed a significant difference in the survey period factor ($F(1, 75) = 7.5$, $p < 0.01$, $\eta2 = 0.09$, $1-\beta = 1.0$) and the interaction effects $F(1, 75) = 8.4$, $p < 0.01$, $\eta2 = 0.1$, $1-\beta = 1.0$). We did not observe any significant differences in the robot factor ($F(1, 75) = 3.6$, $p = 0.06$, $\eta2 = 0.05$, $1-\beta = 1.0$). The simple main effect of the robot factor was significant in the posttest ($F(1, 75) = 8.8$, $p < 0.006$ $\eta2 = 0.11$), and the simple main effect of the posttest factor was significant in the with-robot condition ($F(1, 26) = 21.9$, $p < 0.006$, $\eta2 = 0.13$).

Table 2. Main effects and interactions for each measure (a) Bold text indicates significant at the significance level adjusted by Bonferroni method ($p < 0.006$)

	Experimental group		Control group		Main effect		
	Pretest	Posttest	Pretest	Posttest	Robot	Survey period	Interaction
Peace of mind	5.25(1.12)	6.81(0.31)	4.8(1.47)	5.42(1.42)	**0.000**	**0.000**	**0.004**
Stress	1.94(1.05)	1.25(0.74)	2.05(1.15)	2.07(1.31)	0.062	**0.007**	**0.004**
Performance	5.46(1.47)	6.35(1.08)	5.18(1.43)	5.69(1.2)	0.089	**0.000**	0.218
Controllability	5.35(1.7)	6.22(1.37)	5.86(1.48)	6.14(1.38)	0.458	0.006	0.154
HN+	5.46(1.23)	6.22(0.95)	5.32(1.2)	5.65(1.35)	0.170	**0.000**	0.150
HN-	1.83(1.15)	1.4(0.74)	1.98(1.23)	1.76(1.14)	0.299	0.088	0.394
UH+	4.77(1.55)	5.85(1.29)	4.77(1.4)	5.04(1.32)	0.136	**0.000**	0.037
UH-	2.07(1.5)	1.38(0.97)	2.29(1.4)	2.15(1.35)	0.084	0.011	0.088
Break time	5.9(1.14)	6.48(0.84)	6.02(1.19)	6.27(1.07)	0.703	0.005	0.340
To present	5.0(1.3)	5.4(1.5)	4.9(1.5)	5.1(1.6)	0.834	0.554	0.420

Performance. The results showed a significant difference in the survey period factor ($F(1, 75) = 21.0$, $p < 0.006$, $\eta 2 = 0.06$). We did not observe any significant differences in the robot factor ($F(1, 75) = 3.0$, $p = 0.0089$, $\eta 2 = 0.03$), and the interaction effects ($F(1, 75) = 1.5$, $p = 0.22$, $\eta 2 = 0.004$).

Controllability. We did not observe any significant differences in the robot factor ($F(1, 75) = 0.6$, $p = 0.46$, $\eta 2 = 0.005$), the survey period factor ($F(1, 75) = 7.9$, $p = 0.0064$, $\eta 2 = 0.03$, $1 - \beta = 1.0$), and the interaction effects ($F(1, 75) = 2.1$, $p = 0.15$, $\eta 2 = 0.009$).

Human Nature Positive. The result showed a significant difference in the survey period factor ($F(1, 75) = 16.3$, $p < 0.006$, $\eta 2 = 0.04$). We did not observe any significant difference in the robot factor ($F(1, 75) = 1.9$, $p = 0.17$, $\eta 2 = 0.019$) and the interaction effects ($F(1, 75) = 2.5$, $p = 0.12$, $\eta 2 = 0.007$).

Human Nature Negative. We did not observe any significant differences in the robot factor ($F(1, 75) = 1.1$, $p = 0.3$, $\eta 2 = 0.01$), the survey period factor ($F(1, 75) = 7.2$, $p = 0.0089$, $\eta 2 = 0.018$), and the interaction effects ($F(1, 75) = 0.7$, $p = 0.4$, $\eta 2 = 0.002$).

Uniquely Human Positive. The result demonstrated a significant difference in the survey period factor ($F(1, 75) = 12.6$, $p < 0.006$, $\eta 2 = 0.05$). We did not observe any significant differences in the robot factor ($F(1, 75) = 2.3$, $p = 0.14$, $\eta 2 = 0.019$) and the interaction effects ($F(1, 75) = 4.5$, $p = 0.04$, $\eta 2 = 0.018$).

Uniquely Human Negative. We did not observe any significant differences in the robot factor ($F(1, 75) = 3.1$, $p = 0.081$, $\eta 2 = 0.03$), the survey period factor ($F(1, 75) = 6.8$, $p = 0.011$, $\eta 2 = 0.021$), and the interaction effects ($F(1, 75) = 3.0$, $p = 0.088$, $\eta 2 = 0.002$).

4.2   Evaluation of the Comfort During Recess

The result demonstrated a significant difference in the survey period factor ($F(1, 75) = 8.2$, $p < 0.01$, $\eta2 = 0.03$). We did not observe any significant differences in the robot factor ($F(1, 75) = 0.15$, $p = 0.7$, $\eta2 = 0.001$) and the interaction effects ($F(1, 75) = 0.9$, $p = 0.34$, $\eta2 = 0.003$).

4.3   Evaluation of the Children's Comfort to Present in Class

We did not observe any significant differences in the robot factor ($F(1, 75) = 0.3$, $p = 0.59$, $\eta2 = 0.003$), the survey period factor ($F(1, 75) = 3.6$, $p = 0.06$, $\eta2 = 0.007$), and the interaction effects ($F(1, 75) = 0.2$, $p = 0.65$, $\eta2 = 0.0004$).

4.4   Free Comments

The children commented about the robot being remotely operated by multiple people, such as "It was cute that the robot's voice changed," "I was surprised that the robot's voice increased," and "It was exciting but strange that the robot's voice changed."

4.5   Moral Class

During the moral class, the students had a 45-minute discussion about "how to interact with robots." After we analyzed the videos, the children suggested that the following behaviors are necessary to interact with the robot:

- Treating the robot as if they were friends
- Introducing ourselves to the robot
- Greeting the robot
- Not saying hurtful words to the robot
- Not discriminating the robot
- Not asking about the robot's private information
- Deciding the order for talking with the robot
- Not specially but equally treating the robot as a classmate (they should not decrease the respect they have for their classmates)
- Inviting friends to interact with the robot
- Not paying too much attention to the robot during the classes
- Reflecting on their own behavior by learning from the robot's large and clear reactions

5   Discussion

We investigated how children behave with the robot and their impressions of the robot in their classroom. The children interacted with the robots operated by multiple remote operators during classroom activities such as classes and recess; the children were unaware that human operators operated the robots.

After communicating with the robot, the children in the experimental group felt more peace of mind and relieved with the robot than the children in the control group. In addition, the children in the experimental group did not feel restless and stress with the robot than children in the control group. These results suggest that robots with multiple remote operators can communicate with children without inducing stress and ensuring peace of mine. The results did not show any interaction effects among the items of performance, controllability, and anthropomorphism toward the robot. We believe this is owing to the short communication period with the children. In this experiment, the robot participated in the class for only three days during the two-month period. Therefore, we believe that the children do not sufficiently understand the robot's functions and behaviors. In the future, the interactions between the robot and the students should be long-term and continuous. Then, the children's opinions regarding the degree of anthropomorphism of the robot should be obtained again.

A few children also felt uncomfortable with the voice change observed when the operator changed. However, when the first author monitored the classroom, the children did not seem to notice that the robot was operated by humans and that the operator changed; they assumed that the program had been changed. This suggests that the children did not have a strong negative impression of the change in the robot's voice due to a change in the operator. The children's opinions shared during the moral class indicate that when they talk with the robot, they interact like friends and do not say hurtful things. Based on these opinions, we believe children have accepted the robot as a class friend. Interestingly, there were a few their opinions that the children should consider the robot's privacy. Another opinion was that the children should treat the robot just as they would their classmates and not as a special friend.

The results did not show any interaction effects among the items of comfort during recess and comfort to present in class. However, in the moral class, the students shared the following: "They want to create a good class by having big reactions", and "They want to invite their friends to interact with the robot". This suggests that the robot's presence in the classroom could potentially improve human-human relationships, which is considered to be a positive impact on the development of social skills and increase interactions among classmates.

6   Conclusion

This study investigated how children accept a teleoperated interactive robot in a classroom and their impression of the robot. We installed Sota, a teleoperated interactive robot operated by multiple operators, in a 5th-grade classroom at an elementary school attached to the Faculty of Education, Mie University. We conducted a questionnaire survey before and after the installation of the robot, observed a moral class on "how to interact with robots," and analyzed the students' impressions of the robot and how they accepted the robot. The children in the classroom with the robot felt more peace of mind and less stress toward the robot compared to the children in the classroom without the robot. This observation indicates that children may not have strong negative reactions to a robot operated by multiple remote operators during the current experimental period. In addition, based on the moral class, many of the children commented that the robot should be accepted as a class member and their friend. In addition, the opinion that students need to care about their classmates and the class through interaction with the robot suggests that the robot's presence in the classroom could make classes active and increase interactions among classmates. In the future, we need to install the teleoperated interactive robot in the classroom for a long-term period and confirm how children's impressions change of the robot.

Acknowledgement. This research was partially supported by JST, Moonshot R&D Grant Number JPMJMS2011.

References

1. Baba, J., et al.: Teleoperated robot acting autonomous for better customer satisfaction. In: Extended Abstracts of the 2020 CHI Conference on Human Factors in Computing Systems, pp. 1–8 (2020)
2. Denault, A.S., Déry, M.: Participation in organized activities and conduct problems in elementary school: the mediating effect of social skills. J. Emot. Behav. Disord. **23**(3), 167–179 (2015)
3. Felder, R.M., Brent, R.: Understanding student differences. J. Eng. Educ. **94**(1), 57–72 (2005)
4. Hashimoto, T., Kato, N., Kobayashi, H.: Development of educational system with the android robot saya and evaluation. Int. J. Adv. Rob. Syst. **8**(3), 28 (2011)
5. Kamide, H., et al.: Anshin as a concept of subjective well-being between humans and robots in Japan. Adv. Rob. **29**(24), 1624–1636 (2015)
6. Kamide, H., et al.: Creation of a Japanese version of the anthropomorphic scale (Japanese). Pers. Res. **25**(3), 218–225 (2016)
7. Kanda, T., Sato, R., Saiwaki, N., Ishiguro, H.: A two-month field trial in an elementary school for long-term human-robot interaction. IEEE Trans. Rob. **23**(5), 962–971 (2007)
8. Matsuzoe, S., et al.: The difference of excellence in educational-support robots affects children's learning English vocabularies (Japanese). Trans. Jpn. Soc. Artif. Intell.: AI **28**(2), 170–178 (2013)
9. Reeve, J.: Teachers as facilitators: what autonomy-supportive teachers do and why their students benefit. Elem. School J. **106**(3), 225–236 (2006)
10. Sharkey, A.J.C.: Should we welcome robot teachers? Ethics Inf. Technol. **18**(4), 283–297 (2016). https://doi.org/10.1007/s10676-016-9387-z
11. Shigeo, K., et al.: A study on installing active learning style in the elementary school - in comparison with the current class structure - (japanese). Jpn. J. Educ. Counselin **7**(1), 1–9 (2016)

The Effects of Dyadic vs Triadic Interaction on Children's Cognitive and Affective Gains in Robot-Assisted Alphabet Learning

Zhansaule Telisheva[1] , Aida Zhanatkyzy[1] , Nurziya Oralbayeva[2] ,
Aida Amirova[2] , Arna Aimysheva[1] , and Anara Sandygulova[1]([envelope])

[1] Department of Robotics and Mechatronics, School of Engineering and Digital
Sciences, Nazarbayev University, Astana, Kazakhstan
{zhansaule.telisheva,aida.zhanatkyzy,arna.aimysheva,
anara.sandygulova}@nu.edu.kz
[2] Graduate School of Education, Nazarbayev University, Astana, Kazakhstan
{nurziya.oralbayeva,aida.amirova}@nu.edu.kz

Abstract. Robot-assisted language learning (RALL) is an emerging
field of human-robot interaction to support language acquisition and literacy development with a social robot in multi-modal ways. As learning is
an inherently social activity, the effectiveness of dyadic and triadic types
of social interaction in RALL and child-robot interaction (CRI) needs
to be investigated. In early literacy education, the Montessori method is
a remarkable child-centered and collaborative learning approach. Bridging these two spaces, our work attempts to examine if the nature of
social interaction, dyadic and triadic, affects children's outcomes in an
environment that adheres to the Montessori principles. To this end, we
conducted a between-subject design experiment with 33 Kazakh children
aged 6–8 to compare the effectiveness of learning Kazakh Latin in the
dyadic and triadic conditions in a Moveable Alphabet learning scenario
with a social robot. The analyses revealed mixed results for dyadic and
triadic conditions in terms of cognitive gains, while emotional engagement was better in the triadic condition. We discuss these results in the
perspective of key insights from the current study and implications for
future research.

Keywords: Child-robot interaction · Robot-assisted alphabet
learning · Montessori method · dyadic · triadic · One-to-one
interaction · Multi-party interaction

1 Introduction

Kazakhstan is officially a bilingual country where Kazakh-Russian bilingualism
is a common practice for the majority population. The country also strives to
become a trilingual/multilingual country introducing English as a foreign language for global integration through Trilingual language policy to its population [11]. In 2017, Kazakhstan officially announced its decision to transition the

© The Author(s), under exclusive license to Springer Nature Switzerland AG 2022
F. Cavallo et al. (Eds.): ICSR 2022, LNAI 13818, pp. 204–213, 2022.
https://doi.org/10.1007/978-3-031-24670-8_19

Kazakh alphabet from Cyrillic to Latin. This transition may bring critical challenges to literacy acquisition among first graders who learn to write in the two alphabets (Cyrillic and Latin) at the same time. Our work reflects these linguistic challenges and aims to find the best possible learning scenario for children in primary grades to acquire the Kazakh Latin alphabet.

Robot-assisted language learning (RALL) is a rapidly growing area in human-robot interaction (HRI). Here, social robots are used to teach individuals core language skills related to speaking, writing, reading, and/or listening. A recent survey [21] has highlighted that robots are advantageous in aiding language learning. Unlike other technologies, robots play a social role (e.g., a peer) and have a physical embodiment which is particularly beneficial for language learning [7]. There is growing evidence that robots help learners improve language skills, but mostly, vocabulary retention [2,19]. Current evidence focusing on productive language skills such as writing is rare [13,23]. Against this backdrop, we situate *robot-assisted alphabet learning (RAAL)* that provides children alphabet-training with a robot in an engaging learning environment following the Montessori method to early literacy development.

One of the notable educational practices is learning together with other people. Learning is a highly social activity when individuals work as teammates and peers. There is evidence in education-focused studies where students who worked in pairs gained better outcomes in academic tasks, such as vocabulary learning, than those who learned individually [26]. Nevertheless, the underlying benefits of pair work have little empirical backing, despite the broadly-defined pedagogical and theoretical grounding in support of collaborative work [14,25]. In this study, we define individual and pair work as dyadic and triadic interaction, respectively. According to the cognitive learning literature, dyadic context involves two people interacting with one another, whereas triadic relations include an object or another person into the interaction of the two [10]. The recent HRI survey [4] has found that most studies adopted the dyadic interaction with one robot and one human, and a few studies maintained triadic interaction with two humans and one robot. Predominantly dyadic CRI research in educational contexts investigated a child's perceptions of and relationship with the robot [16,17]. Meanwhile, triadic instances typical of HRI research often approached the triadic learning context through a child-robot-object paradigm [8]. However, the effects of multi-party child-child-robot interactions have not yet been empirically grounded. Thus, the questions arise, central to our study, as how two or more individuals engage with a robot and if the triadic learning context applies to HRI. To the best of our knowledge, this question has not yet been explored in language-focused HRI.

The Montessori method has been considered effective for young children to experience self-directed and engaging early literacy development. With a century-long history, it has proven itself viable, and its core principles are being widely adopted in current educational frameworks characterized by student-centred learning. Montessori classrooms are considerably different from what we anticipate in traditional schools [12,15,18]. In Montessori classes, children learn about the world through their senses. Visual aids and materials are very common to support hands-on learning, for instance, specially designed sensory manipulatives (e.g. wooden alphabet). The children enjoy the freedom of choice of learning and engaging with the environment. Most studies reported on social and cognitive benefits such as increased learner autonomy and effective decision-making [20,22], better language development [24] and high academic gains [9], among many others.

Thus far, there has been no child-robot interaction investigation reporting on the dyadic and triadic learning within the letter-learning context governed by the principles of the Montessori method for learning from a social robot. Our system entitled "Moveable Älıpbi[1]" symbolizes both the learning method and linguistic attachment to the Kazakh language. In this pioneering study, we contribute to the evaluation of the one-to-one and multi-party interaction within the RAAL following the Montessori method with 33 children aged 6–8. We apply the Montessori method in learning Kazakh Latin and identify whether it helps children learn the alphabet by comparing the effects of social interaction types: *dyadic/individual* (one child to one robot) vs. *triadic/pair* (two children to one robot).

Drawing on current evidence on the social interaction types and the Montessori method described above, we investigate the effectiveness of these applications with a robot and evaluate children's learning and affective outcomes in dyadic and triadic conditions. Thus, we test the following hypotheses:

- H1: Children will learn more during the triadic condition compared to the dyadic condition.
- H2: Children in the triadic condition will gain more positive affective outcomes compared to those in the dyadic condition.

The contributions of this work are novel in three aspects to: (1) exploring what kind of social learning groups, i.e., dyadic vs. triadic, is effective for a child learning a new alphabet; (2) applying the Montessori method in child-robot interaction; (3) identifying emotional states children communicate to a robot capable of displaying multimodal social cues (enhanced by child-like TTS and social gestures).

2   The Moveable Älıpbi System

The humanoid robot NAO is a social robot with an autonomous and programmable architecture developed by SoftBank Robotics. It is the widely used humanoid robot in CRI research for robot-assisted educational and healthcare applications [4]. The robot is small-sized (58 cm) and easy to transport. Child users like its non-threatening and human-like appearance. It has 25 degrees of freedom and seven tactile sensors on different parts of its body. We used a custom-designed Kazakh speech synthesis of the child voice on the robot.

---

[1] Here, the Kazakh word "älıpbi" means "alphabet" in English; together, they stand for Moveable Alphabet.

The Moveable Alphabet is among the sensory alphabets of the Montessori Language Curriculum [1]. It aims to prepare children for writing, reading, and spelling to help them develop literacy skills from basic to advanced levels. Our learning activity consists of 12 practice words spelled using wooden letters from the Moveable alphabet, adapted to represent the Kazakh Latin letters. While performing the activity, a child sees and selects a written word in the Kazakh Latin letters from flashcards and then spells it with the wooden letters. Children have a choice of order in what to practice the words. The robot only guides children during the first try and then observes them. The activity was validated by a Montessori practitioner.

3 Experiment

The experiment was conducted at a primary school with mixed language of instruction in the capital of Kazakhstan. It involved one meeting with the robot in either dyadic or triadic condition. All participants were assigned to a condition in a between-subject design and interacted with the robot for 30–40 min.

3.1 Participants

There were 33 children (19 males, 14 females) aged 6–8 years old. The children had diverse linguistic backgrounds. At the time of the experiment, children in the first grade with Kazakh or Russian language of instruction had spent approximately nine months writing in Cyrillic. They had also spent approximately the same amount of time learning and writing the English alphabet.

3.2 Recruitment

This research was approved by the Nazarbayev University Institutional Research Ethics Committee (NU-IREC) on April 20, 2022. Supporting information included an assent form for children and an informed consent form for parents or guardians. The researchers briefly explained the purpose of the study and the procedures involved in data collection. Assent and consent forms were distributed to children in their classrooms in the presence of their teachers. Children were asked to show the forms to their parents at home and return them to their teachers, who then collected the forms for us.

3.3 Conditions

The participants were assigned to either of the two conditions:

- **Dyadic condition** (N = 13): one child interacts with the robot teacher in a letter-learning activity, including the wooden letters of the Montessori Moveable alphabet and flashcards of written words.

- **Triadic condition** (N = 20): two children interact with the robot teacher in the same learning activity and using the same materials (Fig. 1).

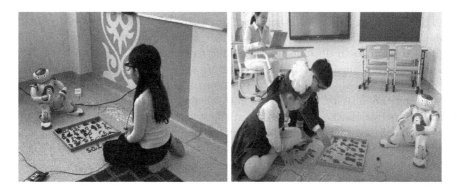

Fig. 1. Experimental conditions: Dyadic condition (left), Triadic condition (right)

3.4   Procedures

The experiment procedures consisted of a pre-test, demographic survey, a single learning activity session, a post-test, and a semi-structured interview. First, children were withdrawn from class and walked with the researchers to the experiment room. While walking with the children, the researchers started with an icebreaker warm-up talk to relax and engage the youngster. Upon entering the room with the setup, children were invited to take a seat individually at the table and were given a piece of paper for pre-test with two columns - one column already filled in with the Cyrillic Kazakh letters and the other column to be filled in by children with the Latin Kazakh letters - to record their prior knowledge of the Kazakh Latin alphabet. Then, the researchers conducted a demographics survey from each child to collect data about their age, gender, and linguistic background and preferences. After the tests were filled in and demographics taken, children were invited to change tables and take a seat facing the robot one by one. After the interaction, another researcher conducted a survey questionnaire with each child, asking the child to rate the agent's performance comparing it against other agents (e.g., human teacher, tablet, smartphone) on several criteria (see Sect. 3.5). Finally, each child was given a post-test as an evaluation metric for their learning gains in terms of memorizing the Kazakh Latin alphabet. As the children finished, the researchers brought them back to class and called for the next participants.

3.5   Measurements

Cognitive (e.g., learning gains) and affective (e.g., self-reporting survey) measures were used in data collection. Those were:

– **Learning Gain (LG)** is determined by counting the number of new learned letters in the post-test as compared to the pre-test (e.g. wrong or skipped letters in the pre-test and correct letters in the post-test are regarded as LG). LG would still be incremented if there is a new correct letter written in a post-test despite the fact that some of the correctly written letters in the pre-test were omitted in the post-test (i.e. some children forgot to copy previously known letters from the pre-test to the post-test). This metric was carefully analyzed for each case.

- **Sorting task.** A child was asked to physically sort five small pictures (a book, a tablet, a NAO robot, a computer, and a human) in ascending order according to their 1) Effectiveness, 2) Easy to learn from, 3) Interesting, and 4) Favourite. We then noted the order (as a 5-point Likert scale) they placed the interaction method in.
- **Robot role.** A child was asked to compare the robot to a friend, a sibling, a classmate, a teacher, a stranger.
- **Automatic Emotion Analysis.** A camera was placed in front of the child capturing facial expressions for real-time emotional analysis. Facial Expression Recognition uses different datasets such as Affectnet and FER+ [3] which enable identification of the emotional states from the videos. Five different expressions were analysed: neutrality, happiness, sadness, anger, and surprise. After that score from 0 to 1 was given for each state depending on the duration of the video and the frequency of that emotion for each participant.

4   Results

A series of one-way and two-way ANOVA tests was conducted to analyse the effect of the independent variables on the children's learning gains, facial expressions, and their survey data.

4.1   Learned Letters

Overall, during our experiment, the children were able to expand their knowledge of the Kazakh Latin alphabet. On average, the learning gain was amounted to 1.848 ± 2.28 (Max = 9, Min = 0).

A one-way ANOVA test showed a significant difference between children in dyadic and triadic groups: $F(1, 31) = 8.383, p = 0.007$. The children, who took part in the dyadic session, learned more letters (2.77 ± 3.03) than the children in the triadic (0.65 ± 1.04) session (see Fig. 2A).

4.2   Sorting Task

A one-way ANOVA test on the children's sorting task answers showed a statistically significant difference in terms of the effectiveness of the robot: $F(1, 21) = 5.987, p = 0.02$. The children in the triadic form rated the effectiveness of the robot higher (2.08 ± 0.996) than the children who participated in the dyadic form (3 ± 0.775). This result is shown in Fig. 2B.

Additionally, we conducted a chi-square test to see if there is a relationship between categorical variables such as the interaction types (dyadic/triadic) and the children's survey answers on what and who (robot's role) the robot is like. The chi-square test on the relationship of the interaction types and robot's role revealed a significant result: $\chi(5) = 11.578$, p = 0.041. Even though the rating

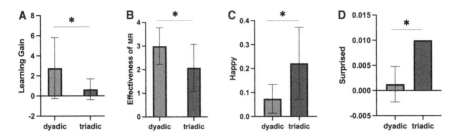

Fig. 2. A) Average number of learned letters, B) the rating of effectiveness of the robot, C) Happiness expression score, D) Surprise expression score split by the interaction types. Error bars show 95% Confidence Interval, * indicates significance at the 0.05 level.

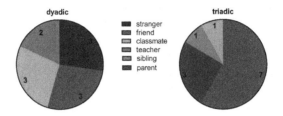

Fig. 3. Survey answer results on robot's role factor

of the robot among the children of the dyadic form of interaction was spread equally, most of the children (7 out of 12) rated the robot as a friend in the triadic interaction types (refer to Fig. 3).

4.3 Facial Expression Analysis

The analysis of facial expressions included only the data of 16 children, and five emotions such as neutral, happy, sad, angry, and surprise. One-way ANOVA revealed some significant results for happy ($F(1,14) = 6.826, p = 0.02$) and surprise ($F(1,14) = 49, p < 0.001$) scores when testing the effect of the interaction types. The children in the triadic form felt happier (0.222 ± 0.150) and more surprised (0.01 ± 0) compared to those in the dyadic sessions (happy - 0.0738 ± 0.0597, surprise - 0.00125 ± 0.00354). The results are presented in Fig. 2C and Fig. 2D respectively.

5 Discussion and Conclusion

This exploratory study aimed to evaluate the effectiveness of two social learning paradigms – dyadic and triadic – within the RAAL environment guided by the Montessori principles. We found that the dyadic (individual/one child per robot) type of interaction resulted in significantly higher learning gains as opposed to the triadic (pairs/two children per robot) interaction. Hence, our H1 is refuted.

This finding contradicts the previous studies which suggested pair learning to lead to much more gains in cognitively demanding tasks [26]. In fact, working in pairs may not always reflect a collaborative problem-solving effort and lead to effective performance [27]. For example, based on qualitative observations, children's low cognitive gains in the triadic condition can be attributed to the nature of the pair learning as children tended to split words during the activity, which, however, is not the case for the dyadic condition. Specifically, one-to-one child-robot interaction resulted in more learning gains as the child attended to all twelve words by himself/herself without disruption and was more focused throughout the entire session. Another explanation relates to the developmental stages predicted by the age of children who were first-graders (6–8 years old) in the current study. We observed that some tend to lack social skills vital for collaborative learning. Thus, the benefits of pair work are not yet entirely evident [14], and its effects on language learning still need to be measured across different social learning contexts and age groups. Yet, a triadic multi-party child-child-robot interaction might appear as a promising new area of investigation within the context of HRI.

Emotions analyses showed that children in the triadic condition were happier and more surprised in comparison with those in the dyadic condition. Our hypothesis that children who engaged in the triadic interaction type would have higher affective outcomes is thus accepted. Qualitative observations suggest that children felt more relaxed being around another child, hence more interactive and expressive in their emotions. Conversely, the majority of children who participated in one-to-one interaction were observed to be reserved and reticent to a new environment and stimulus, negatively affecting their emotional expressiveness. Another explanation of the better affective outcomes of the triadic group may relate to children's overall tendency to adjust their emotional states and behaviors depending on their peer's emotional reactions, which underlies the social and collaborative learning [5,12].

Interestingly, the rating of the robot's effectiveness was higher in the triadic group as compared to the dyadic group. This finding suggests that children interpreted the nature of their child-child-robot learning environment more effective than those children in child-robot interaction. This interpretation reflects an active involvement, collaborative effort, and social cognitive aspects of the interaction [10]. Additionally, our analysis of the relationship between the interaction type and the robot's role, reporting statistical significance, revealed that the robot was perceived more as a friend in the triadic condition. It may relate to the nature of the triadic condition in connecting the children and then transferring this child-child connection onto the robot. On the contrary, in the dyadic condition, children perceived the robot's role equally as a stranger, a friend, a classmate, and a teacher. This result reflects the existing HRI research findings on robot's role in the dyadic interaction [6].

All in all, our results showed that children gained higher learning gains in one-to-one interaction with the robot. As for the affective outcomes, our facial expression analyses revealed significance between triadic and dyadic forms of interactions in two emotional states, namely happy and surprise. These findings suggest that, when learning in pairs of two with one social robot, children are more expressive and relaxed due to being around another child, which (sub)consciously resulted in lower cognitive but higher affective outcomes. Our conclusions are limited due to the short-term nature of the study. However, we believe that the results could be foundational for the future research inquiries with regard to social interaction context and children's emotional engagement with the robot during a task and over longer period of time.

Acknowledgment. The Nazarbayev University Collaborative Research Program grants 091019CRP2107 and OPCRP2022002 provided funding for this work.

References

1. Academy, M.: Introducing the moveable alphabet. https://montessoriacademy.com.au/material-spotlight-moveable-alphabet, Accessed 09 Mar 2022
2. Alemi, M., Meghdari, A., Ghazisaedy, M.: Employing humanoid robots for teaching English language in Iranian junior high-schools. Int. J. Human. Rob. **11**, 1450022–1 (2014). https://doi.org/10.1142/S0219843614500224
3. Ali, M., Behzad, H., Mahoor, M.H.: Affectnet: a database for facial expression, valence, and arousal computing in the wild. IEEE Trans. Affect. Comput. **1**, 18–31 (2017)
4. Amirova, A., Rakhymbayeva, N., Yadollahi, E., Sandygulova, A., Johal, W.: 10 years of human-nao interaction research: a scoping review. Front. Rob. AI **8**, 744526 (2021). https://doi.org/10.3389/frobt.2021.744526
5. Bandura, A.: Social cognitive theory: an agentic perspective. Ann. Rev. Psychol. **52**(1), 1–26 (2001)
6. Belpaeme, T., Kennedy, J., Ramachandran, A., Scassellati, B., Tanaka, F.: Social robots for education: a review. Sci. Rob. **3**, eaat5954 (2018). https://doi.org/10.1126/scirobotics.aat5954
7. van den Berghe, R., Verhagen, J., Oudgenoeg-Paz, O., van der Ven, S.H.G., Leseman, P.P.M.: Social robots for language learning: a review. Rev. Educ. Res. **89**, 259–295 (2018)
8. Davison, D.: Child, robot and educational material: a triadic interaction. In: 2016 11th ACM/IEEE International Conference on Human-Robot Interaction (HRI), pp. 607–608. IEEE (2016)
9. Dohrmann, K., Nishida, T., Gartner, A., Lipsky, D., Grimm, K.: High school outcomes for students in a public Montessori program. J. Res. Childhood Educ. **22**, 205–217 (2007). https://doi.org/10.1080/02568540709594622
10. Elias, J., Bockelman, P., Streater, J., Gallagher, S., Fiore, S.: Towards triadic interactions in autism and beyond: transitional objects, joint attention, and social robotics. Proc. Human Factors Ergon. Soc. Ann. Meet. **55**, 1486–1490 (2011). https://doi.org/10.1177/1071181311551309
11. Goodman, B., Karabassova, L.: Bottom-up and top down: comparing language-in-education policy in Ukraine and Kazakhstan. In: Silova, I., Chankseliani, M. (eds.) Comparing Post-Socialist Transformations: Purposes, Policies, and Practices in Education, pp. 147–166. Symposium Books, Oxford (2018)
12. Hertzberger, H.: Montessori primary school in Delft, Holland. Harvard Educ. Rev. **39**, 58–67 (1969). https://doi.org/10.17763/haer.39.4.a0m374522202766g

13. Hood, D., Lemaignan, S., Dillenbourg, P.: The cowriter project: teaching a robot how to write. In: Proceedings of the Tenth Annual ACM/IEEE International Conference on Human-Robot Interaction Extended Abstracts, pp. 269–269 (2015)

14. Hyde, M.: Pair work-a blessing or a curse? an analysis of pair work from pedagogical, cultural, social and psychological perspectives. System **21**, 343–348 (1993). https://doi.org/10.1016/0346-251X(93)90024-B

15. Isaacs, B.: Understanding the montessori approach: early years education in practice (2018)

16. Kahn, P.H., Jr., et al.: "robovie, you'll have to go into the closet now": children's social and moral relationships with a humanoid robot. Dev. Psychol. **48**(2), 303 (2012)

17. Kanda, T., Shimada, M., Koizumi, S.: Children learning with a social robot. In: 2012 7th ACM/IEEE International Conference on Human-Robot Interaction (HRI), pp. 351–358. IEEE (2012)

18. Marshall, C.R.: Montessori education: a review of the evidence base. NPJ Sci. Learn. **2** (2017). https://doi.org/10.1038/s41539-017-0012-7

19. Movellan, J.R., Eckhardt, M., Virnes, M., Rodriguez, A.: Sociable robot improves toddler vocabulary skills. In: 2009 4th ACM/IEEE International Conference on Human-Robot Interaction (HRI), pp. 307–308 (2009). https://doi.org/10.1145/1514095.1514189

20. Murray, A.K.: Public perceptions of Montessori education (2008)

21. Randall, N.: A survey of robot-assisted language learning (rall). ACM Trans. Hum.-Robot Interact. (THRI) **9**(1), 1–36 (2019)

22. Rathunde, K.: A comparison of montessori and traditional middle schools: motivation, quality of experience, and social context. Am. J. Educ. **111**, 341–371 (2005). https://doi.org/10.1086/428885

23. Sandygulova, A., et al.: Cowriting kazakh: learning a new script with a robot. In: Proceedings of the 2020 ACM/IEEE International Conference on Human-Robot Interaction, pp. 113–120 (2020)

24. Soundy, C.: Portraits of exemplary Montessori practice for all literacy teachers. Early Childhood Educ. J. **31**, 127–131 (2003). https://doi.org/10.1023/B:ECEJ.0000005312.48974.0a

25. Storch, N.: Investigating the merits of pair work on a text editing task in esl classes. Lang. Teach. Res. **11**, 143–159 (2007)

26. Teng, M.F.: The effectiveness of group, pair and individual output tasks on learning phrasal verbs. Lang. Learn. J. **48**, 187–200 (2020)

27. Yelland, N.: Young children learning with logo: an analysis of strategies and interactions. J. Educ. Comput. Res. **9**(4), 465–486 (1993)

Social Robot Applications in Clinical and Assistive Scenarios

Deep Learning-Based Multi-modal COVID-19 Screening by Socially Assistive Robots Using Cough and Breathing Symptoms

Meysam Effati[1](✉) and Goldie Nejat[1,2,3]

[1] Autonomous Systems and Biomechatronics Laboratory (ASBLab), Department of Mechanical and Industrial Engineering, University of Toronto, Toronto, Canada
meysam.effati@utoronto.ca, nejat@mie.utotornto.ca
[2] Toronto Rehabilitation Institute, Toronto, Canada
[3] Rotman Research Institute, Baycrest Health Sciences, North York, Canada

Abstract. In this paper, we present the development of a novel autonomous social robot deep learning architecture capable of real-time COVID-19 screening during human-robot interactions. The architecture allows for autonomous preliminary multi-modal COVID-19 detection of cough and breathing symptoms using a VGG16 deep learning framework. We train and validate our VGG16 network using existing COVID datasets. We then perform real-time non-contact preliminary COVID-19 screening experiments with the Pepper robot. The results for our deep learning architecture demonstrate: 1) an average computation time of 4.57 s for detection, and 2) an accuracy of 84.4% with respect to self-reported COVID symptoms.

Keywords: Deep learning · Socially assistive robot · Real-time detection and classification · COVID-19 audio signals · Cough and breathing

1 Introduction

Social robots have been used to assist in the detection and screening of COVID-19 symptoms by performing tasks such as temperature screening [1], mask detection [2], and by asking COVID-19 screening questions [3, 4]. They have also been used to detect unimodal respiratory symptoms such as coughs [5].

In general, respiratory symptoms such as coughs and breathing are prevalent in COVID-19 [6]. Deep learning (DL) can be used to detect and classify these symptoms for positive or negative COVID-19 status [7]. A handful of DL methods have been used for the unimodal detection of COVID-19 using the aforementioned respiratory symptoms [8–12]. Only one multi-modal DL detection method for COVID-19 using cough and breathing symptoms exists thus far [7].

The use of social robots and DL together for the non-contact and autonomous detection of multi-modal COVID symptoms is a novel approach to aid with minimizing the spread of COVIID-19. In this paper, we present the development of an autonomous

F. Cavallo et al. (Eds.): ICSR 2022, LNAI 13818, pp. 217–227, 2022.
https://doi.org/10.1007/978-3-031-24670-8_20

social robot which is capable of real-time COVID-19 screening. The robot uniquely uses a novel DL multi-modal recognition and classification architecture for the non-contact detection of cough and breathing symptoms. We train our DL method using two COVID-19 symptom datasets. Then, we perform real-time multi-modal COVID-19 screening using the Pepper robot.

2 Related Work

In this section, we present the existing literature on: 1) DL approaches for the detection of COVID-19 incorporating various symptoms, and 2) robots used for COVID-19 screening.

2.1 Deep Learning Approaches to Detect COVID-19

Since COVID-19 infection can cause changes in the human respiratory system, people with COVID-19 produce distinct cough and breathing sounds [7]. These sounds have been mainly used for unimodal COVID-19 detection using different Convolutional Neural Network (CNN) structures [13].

Multi-modal COVID-19 detection can be used to enhance the accuracy (by approximately 15%) of the virus detection by incorporating the effects of different symptoms [14]. In general, there are two main approaches used for multi-modal detection: 1) concatenating different mode samples together as the multi-modal input to the CNN structure [7], or 2) performing unimodal detection first of each symptom individually and then combining the results with a weighting function [9, 15].

2.2 COVID-19 Screening Using Robots

Different types of robots such as ground mobile robots [16–18], drones [19, 20], and social robots [3–5, 21, 22] have been used for COVID-19 screening and monitoring. For example, in [16], infrared thermometers were integrated onto mobile robots for outdoor contactless temperature screening. The robots were designed to detect a car by using ultrasonic sensors and used the thermometers to measure temperature of the driver and passengers. The robots can also measure temperature of visitors to a hospital and use their 2 degrees-of-freedom manipulator to stop entry based on temperature levels. In [17], the quadruped Spot robot was teleoperated to monitor vital signs. Namely, IR and RGB cameras were used to measure skin temperature, heart rate, respiratory rate, and blood oxygen levels in a hospital setting. In [18], the 5G patrol robot was used for mask detection as well as temperature screening of individuals to help police officers in performing disease prevention inspections. The robot was equipped with 5 high resolution cameras and infrared thermometers to detect masks as well as scan the temperature of 10 people simultaneously in a 5m range from the robot. Drones have also been used for COVID-19 screening [19, 20].

Social robots such as AIMBOT and Cruzr from UBTECH were deployed for temperature and mask screening of patients and visitors at a hospital in Shenzhen [21]. These robots were equipped with both infrared and 2D cameras [22]. The Quori social robot was used to take the temperature of older adults and ask screening questions [3]. Users wore RFID tags for identification. A screening study with the robot at a care center showed that participants found the robot easy to use and friendly. In [4], the Misty II robot incorporated a Temp Screening Assistant that can be used for both temperature screening (via a thermal camera) as well as for asking health screening questions. In [5], a real-time auxiliary system was designed for COVID-19 screening. Speech recordings, temperature, and self-declared information were used as inputs. Coughs were detected from speech recordings using CNNs. Then, a Support Vector Machine (SVM) was used for the classification of the detected coughs to determine COVID status. It was mentioned in [5] that the auxiliary system had been embedded on a robot, however, no integration details or experiments were provided.

In general, robots have been able to detect unimodal symptoms (mainly temperature) [16–18, 20, 21] and/or ask screening questions [3–5]. The exceptions being in [17] and [5] where multiple vital signs/symptoms were monitored. However, to-date, to the authors' knowledge, no *multi-modal deep learning architecture* exists for autonomous real-time screening of multiple COVID-19 symptoms by a social robot.

3 Social Robot Deep Learning Architecture for Autonomous COVID-19 Symptom Detection

We have developed a deep learning architecture for autonomous multi-modal COVID-19 screening by a robot using both cough and breathing symptoms, Fig. 1. A microphone is used to record user's cough and breathing in audio WAV format. Each recording of the WAV format is converted to a spectrogram image in the *Conversion to Spectrograms Module*. We use the Visual Geometry Group (VGG) deep learning structure [23] for multi-modal classification. Namely, our *VGG16 Multi-modal Classification Module* takes the spectrograms as inputs and outputs a positive-COVID or negative-COVID result. The social robot interacts with the user to obtain cough and breathing inputs and reports the status of the screening using the *Robot Interaction Module*. Each module is discussed in detail below.

3.1 Spectrogram Conversion Module

The *Spectrogram Conversion Module* uses the audio WAV format of coughs and breaths obtained by the microphone as input. By taking the short-time Fourier transform (STFT) of the WAV files, the spectrograms that represent the visual form of the audio frequencies with respect to time for each of the WAV files are obtained. A log transformation is used to convert the amplitude of STFT outputs into decibels using the Librosa [24] python package. The FFT length and the sampling rate (kHz) which were used to obtain the spectrograms are 2,048 and 48,000, respectively.

3.2 VGG16 Multi-modal Classification Module

The *VGG16 Multi-modal Classification Module* uses the spectrograms to classify positive-COVID or negative-COVID status of the user. There are two DL classifiers which are trained separately for each of the cough and breathing symptoms, Fig. 2. Then, we apply our probability-based weighting function (f_w) for final multi-modal COVID-19 classification.

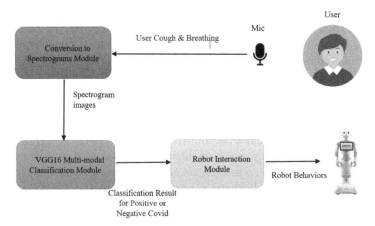

Fig. 1. Deep learning COVID-19 screening architecture for social robots.

Herein, we use the VGG16 structure [23] as it is a top 5 DL classifier and has achieved high accuracy with audio recordings for unimodal COVID-19 detection symptoms [25]. In fact, VGG16 outperformed all other CNN structures such as VGG13, VGG19, Densnet201, ResNet50, Inceptionv3, and InceptionResNetV2 by achieving higher accuracy when using breathing recordings for COVID-19 detection [25].

The VGG16 structure is composed of 13 convolutional layers for feature extraction, 5 max-pooling layers to reduce the dimensions of the feature maps, and 3 fully connected layers to compile the data extracted by previous layers [23]. Therefore, it has 16 layers with tunable parameters. As shown in Fig. 2, the inputs to the VGG16 classifiers are spectrograms with size of 224 × 224, and the outputs of the classifiers are binary numbers (1 for COVID-positive status and 0 for COVID-negative status).

VGG16 models have a block structure, and each block consists of a sequence of convolutions with 3 × 3 kernels with 1 × 1 padding and 2 × 2 maximum pooling with stride of 2 [23]. The number of filters for the first block of VGG16 is 64. Then this number is doubled for the blocks until it reaches 512 for the last block. VGG16 is completed by two fully connected layers (with 4096 neurons for each layer) and one output layer (with 1000 neurons) [23].

The outputs of the unimodal cough and breathing classifiers are provided as inputs to our multi-modal weighting function (f_w). In [15], we introduced a weighting function to incorporate different symptoms (S_i, $i \in \{1, ..., n\}$) for multi-modal COVID-19 detection:

$$f_w = \sum_{i=1}^{n} I_{S_i} w_{s_i}, \tag{1}$$

where I_{S_i} ($i \in \{1, ..., n\}$) is the output of each classifier for the unimodal detection of COVID-19 using each symptom and is defined as:

$$I_{S_i} = \begin{cases} 1, classified \ COVID - positive \\ 0, classified \ COVID - negative \end{cases} \quad (2)$$

The weights in Eq. (1) are defined as follows:

$$w_{S_i} = \frac{p_i}{\sum_{j=1}^{n} p_j}, \quad (3)$$

where $j \in \{1, ..., n\}$. p_i and p_j are the prevalence of each symptom. These values (p_i and p_j) represent the probability that a person who tested positive for COVID-19 has the considered symptom. To obtain p_i and p_j for each symptom, the clinical MIT dataset [6] was utilized. This statistical dataset contains symptoms prevalence (in percentages) of different people. The symptoms include both cough and shortness of breath. By using Eq. (1) and the MIT dataset [6] to obtain the weights (w_{S_i}), the following relationship is obtained for our weighting function:

$$f_w = 0.67I_G + 0.33I_B, \quad (4)$$

where I_C and I_B are the outputs of the classifiers for cough and breathing recordings, respectively. The output of f_w provides the probability of COVID-positivity.

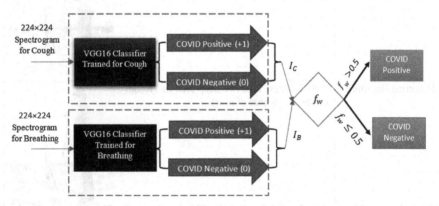

Fig. 2. Symptom classification and probability-based weighting function architecture for multi-modal COVID-19 detection using cough and breathing.

3.3 Robot Interaction Module

The *Robot Interaction Module* determines the robot's behaviors using a Finite State Machine during non-contact screening. The interaction procedure is shown in Table 1. An omnidirectional ReSpeaker USB Microphone Array is used to obtain both the cough and breathing audio signals.

Table 1. COVID-19 screening procedure by the pepper robot

Screening Stage	Robot Behaviors	
Greeting	Robot: Hello, my name is Pepper. I am a COVID-19 screening robot. (Robot waves)	
Hand Sanitization	Robot: Can you please sanitize your hands using the hand sanitizer located here. (Robot points to the hand sanitizer)	
Detecting Coughs	Robot: I am checking for COVID-19 symptoms. This will only take a few seconds. Please cough two times. (Robot gazes at user)	
Detecting Breathing	Robot: Please take two deep breaths. (Robot continues to gaze at user)	
COVID Assessment	Robot: *(For Negative-COVID):* Thank you, you have completed the screening process. According to my assessment, you have no symptoms of COVID and can proceed. Robot: *(For Positive-COVID):* Thank you, please proceed to the front desk for further assessment. Robot: Please stay safe and have a nice day! (Robot waves with both arms)	

3.4 Datasets

We used the Cambridge [26] and EPFL (COUGHVID) [27] datasets for training and validation of our classifiers. The ASBLab dataset was used for testing the trained models.

Cambridge Dataset [26]: The Cambridge dataset includes 459 crowdsourced labeled cough and breathing audio recordings from 355 participants in WebM format [18]. The samples are recorded using a microphone through Android and web applications. Sixty-two of the participants had tested positive for COVID-19 based on COVID-19 tests such as PCR.

EPFL (COUGHVID) Dataset [27]: The EPFL (COUGHVID) dataset includes 20,000 crowdsourced recordings for cough only. A wide range of participant ages, genders, geographic locations were included. The participants self-declared their COVID status (positive or negative) which were used to label the data. The recordings were gathered through microphones using a Web application deployed on a server [27].

ASBLab Dataset: WE have created the ASBLab dataset which includes 44 breathing and cough recordings of people in a public place over the course of a week. All individuals were wearing masks as required for entering buildings during COVID-19. Based on recent investigations [28], face masks muffle high frequency audio sounds. Therefore, we have created the ASBLab dataset to investigate varying audio signals for symptoms for our trained classification model when a person is wearing a mask. The participants' self-declared screening was used to label the data.

4 Training and Testing

We trained and validated our VGG16 cough and breathing networks on the Cambridge and EPFL datasets. We used a 70%–30% split for training and validation. The trained models were also tested as a proof-of-concept for COVID-19 screening of individuals in public places using the cough and breathing recordings of the ASBLab dataset to evaluate their performance. The weights of the CNN models were updated through training on the EPFL and Cambridge datasets. The number of epochs, batch size, and learning rate were 100, 5, and $1e^{-4}$, respectively. The number of training and validation recordings used from the Cambridge dataset were 321 and 137, respectively. Whereas the number of training and validation recordings utilized from the larger EPFL dataset were 8,347 and 2,627, respectively.

We compared our trained VGG16 multi-modal classification approach to CIdeR [7]. CIdeR has been designed for multi-modal classification of COVID-19 using cough and breathing recordings, however, without a weighting function. Therefore, the prevalence of cough and breathing symptoms is not considered and both symptoms are given equal importance in the multi-modal classification process. CIdeR uses a ResNet-50 structure with 1 input layer, 9 residual blocks (each consisting of a convolutional layer followed by a batch normalization layer) and 1 output layer. We also trained and tested CIdeR on the same datasets. The obtained classification accuracies for both methods are summarized in Table 2. As can be seen from the table, our multi-modal VGG16 had better test accuracy for the detection of COVID-19 using cough and breathing recordings.

Table 2. Comparison of Classification Test Accuracy of our Trained CNN model (VGG16 + Weighting Function) and CIdeR for cough and breathing symptoms. Cambridge Dataset (CD), EPFL Dataset (ED), and ASBLab Dataset (AD) are used as the Test Datasets.

	Cough			Breathing		Cough and breathing		
Dataset	CD	ED	AD	CD	AD	CD	AD	Average
Structure								
VGG16 + Weighting Function (our method)	86%	91%	96%	86%	90%	74%	95%	85%
CIdeR	81%	83%	78%	84%	87%	82%	81%	81%

5   Experiments with the Social Robot

The objective of our experiments was to test our DL-based architecture for real-time multi-modal COVID-19 screening using the Pepper robot from Softbank Robotics. We used test accuracy, precision, recall, F1-score and computation time to evaluate the automated screening process with participants.

The experiment took place in our lab with individuals entering our lab being screened by Pepper over a period of a month. The setup is shown in Fig. 3. The omnidirectional ReSpeaker USB Microphone Array was placed on the tripod on the left of the user at 0.5m to obtain both breathing and coughing audio signals. The hand sanitizer was located on the right side of the robot. Our deep learning COVID-19 screening architecture was run on a Dell laptop with Intel(R) Core (TM) i5-5300U CPU @ 2.30 GHz CPU and 8 GB RAM.

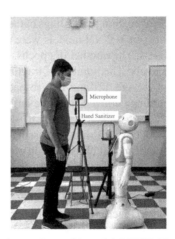

Fig. 3. Experimental setup for multi-modal COVID-19 screening by Pepper.

In total 45 anonymous people participated in the screening process. Namely, no identifiable information of the participants was stored by Pepper. Based on the participants' self-declared information, 40 people declared they were COVID-negative and 5 people declared they may be COVID-positive. To perform the screening process, each anonymous user approached the robot and stood 1m in front of Pepper, at which time Pepper would greet them. They then followed the instructions provided by the robot in Table 1. All the participants wore masks during the screening process due to COVID-19 building rules. A video of the interaction is presented on our YouTube channel here[1]. Based on the screening assessment conducted by Pepper, eight individuals were instructed by the robot to go to the front desk for further screening. Based on the self-declared COVID status, five people were from the labeled COVID-negative group and three people were from the labeled COVID-positive group. Hence, we obtained an accuracy of 84.4% (38/45). The accuracy, precision, recall, and F1-score measures are presented in Table 3. Table 4 provides the computation time for the main modules of our multi-modal deep learning COVID-19 screening architecture. The average total computation time was 4.57 s, where the generation of the log spectrograms had the longest computation time.

Table 3. Classification measures.

Measure	Value
Accuracy	84.4%
Precision	94.6%
Recall	87.5%
F1-score	90.4%

Table 4. Computation time for the main modules of our multi-modal COVID-19 screening architecture.

Architecture module	Average computation time (s)
Conversion to spectrograms (for both cough and breathing)	2.82
VGG16 classifier for cough	0.89
VGG16 classifier for breathing	0.86
Multi-modal classification (using weighting function)	0.0001
Total average computation time	**4.57**

6 Conclusions

In this paper, we developed a novel real-time multi-modal COVID-19 screening architecture for social robots using the VGG16 deep learning structure and a probability-based

---

[1] https://youtu.be/EFb6rHAmvRU.

weighting function. We trained and validated our architecture using the crowdsourced EPFL and Cambridge datasets for both cough and breathing as well as tested our architecture on the ASBLab dataset with people wearing masks. Our architecture was integrated on the Pepper robot for autonomous COVID-19 screening. The preliminary experiments show an accuracy of 84.4% for multi-modal symptom detection with a real-time computation time of 4.57 s.

References

1. Avgousti, S., Christoforou, E.G., Masouras, P., Panayides, A.S., Tsekos, N.V.: Robotic systems on the frontline against the pandemic. In: Ahram, T., Taiar, R. (eds.) IHIET 2021. LNNS, vol. 319, pp. 1105–1112. Springer, Cham (2022). https://doi.org/10.1007/978-3-030-85540-6_142
2. Li, Y., Yan, J., Hu, B.: Mask detection based on efficient-YOLO. In: 2021 40th Chinese Control Conference (CCC), IEEE, pp. 4056–4061 (2021)
3. Mucchiani, C., Cacchione, P., Johnson, M., Mead, R., Yim, M.: Deployment of a socially assistive robot for assessment of COVID-19 symptoms and exposure at an elder care setting. In: 2021 30th IEEE International Conference on Robot & Human Interactive Communication (RO-MAN), IEEE, pp. 1189–1195 (2021)
4. Shen, Y., et al.: Robots under COVID-19 pandemic: a comprehensive survey. IEEE Access 9, 1590–1615 (2020)
5. Wei, W., Wang, J., Ma, J., Cheng, N., Xiao, J.: A real-time robot-based auxiliary system for risk evaluation of COVID-19 infection. arXiv preprint arXiv:2008.07695 (2020)
6. Bertsimas, D., et al.: An aggregated dataset of clinical outcomes for COVID-19 patients (2020). http://www.covidanalytics.io/datasetdocumentation (2020)
7. Coppock, H., Gaskell, A., Tzirakis, P., Baird, A., Jones, L., Schuller, B.: End-to-end convolutional neural network enables COVID-19 detection from breath and cough audio: a pilot study. BMJ Innov. 7(2), 356–362 (2021)
8. Fakhry, A., Jiang, X., Xiao, J., Chaudhari, G., Han, A., Khanzada, A.: Virufy: a multi-branch deep learning network for automated detection of COVID-19, arXiv preprint arXiv:2103.01806 (2021)
9. Banerjee, A., Nilhani, A.: A residual network based deep learning model for detection of COVID-19 from Cough Sounds. arXiv preprint arXiv:2106.02348 (2021)
10. Laguarta, J., Hueto, F., Subirana, B.: COVID-19 artificial intelligence diagnosis using only cough recordings. IEEE Open J. Eng. Med. Biol. 1, 275–281 (2020)
11. Rao, S., Narayanaswamy, V., Esposito, M., Thiagarajan, J.I., Spanias, A.: COVID-19 detection using cough sound analysis and deep learning algorithms. Intell. Decis.Technol. 15, 1–11 (2021)
12. Rao, S., Narayanaswamy, V., Esposito, M., Thiagarajan, I., Spanias, A.: Deep learning with hyper-parameter tuning for COVID-19 cough detection. In: 2021 12th International Conference on Information, Intelligence, Systems & Applications (IISA), IEEE, pp. 1–5 (2021)
13. Imran, A., et al.: AI4COVID-19: AI enabled preliminary diagnosis for COVID-19 from cough samples via an app. Informat. Med. Unlock. 20, 100378 (2020)
14. Chetupalli, S.R., et al.: Multi-modal point-of-care diagnostics for COVID-19 based on acoustics and symptoms, arXiv preprint arXiv:2106.00639 (2021)
15. Effati, M., Sun, Y.-C., Naguib, H.E., Nejat, G.: Multimodal detection of COVID-19 symptoms using deep learning & probability-based weighting of modes. In: 2021 17th International Conference on Wireless and Mobile Computing, Networking and Communications (WiMob), IEEE, pp. 151–156 (2021)

16. Gong, Z., et al.: SHUYU robot: an automatic rapid temperature screening system. Chin. J. Mech. Eng. **33**(1), 1–4 (2020)
17. Huang, H.-W., *et al.*: Agile mobile robotic platform for contactless vital signs monitoring (2020)
18. Happich, J.: 5G edge patrol robots deployed in China to detect Covid-19 cases. eeNews Europe, March 2020
19. Elsayed, E.K., Alsayed, A.M., Salama, O.M., Alnour, A.M., Mohammed, H.A.: Deep learning for covid-19 facemask detection using autonomous drone based on IoT, In: 2020 International Conference on Computer, Control, Electrical, and Electronics Engineering (ICCCEEE), IEEE, pp. 1–5 (2021)
20. Mohammed, M., Hazairin, N.A., Al-Zubaidi, S., AK, S., Mustapha, S., Yusuf, E.: Toward a novel design for coronavirus detection and diagnosis system using IoT based drone technology, Int. J. Psychosoc. Rehabil. **24**(7), 2287–2295 (2020)
21. Ackerman, E.E., Shi, F.: Video Friday: robots help keep medical staff safe at COVID-19 Hospital–IEEE Spectrum. Accessed Nov 2020
22. Robotics, U.: Aimbot: Ubtech's Anti-Epidemic Solution (2020)
23. Simonyan, K., Zisserman, A,: Very deep convolutional networks for large-scale image recognition. *arXiv preprint* arXiv:1409.1556 (2014)
24. McFee, B., *et al.:* Librosa: Audio and music signal analysis in python. In: Proceedings of the 14th Python in Science Conference, vol. 8: Citeseer, pp. 18–25 (2015)
25. Nassif, A.B., Shahin, I., Bader, M., Hassan, A., Werghi, N.: COVID-19 detection systems using deep-learning algorithms based on speech and image data. Mathematics **10**(4), 564 (2022)
26. Brown, C., et al.: Exploring automatic diagnosis of covid-19 from crowdsourced respiratory sound data (2020). *arXiv preprint* arXiv:2006.05919
27. Orlandic, L., Teijeiro, T., Atienza, D.: The COUGHVID crowdsourcing dataset, a corpus for the study of large-scale cough analysis algorithms. Sci. Data **8**(1), 1–10 (2021)
28. Corey, R.M., Jones, U., Singer, A.C.: Acoustic effects of medical, cloth, and transparent face masks on speech signals. J. Acoust. Soc. Am. **148**(4), 2371–2375 (2020)

Social Robots to Support Assisted Living for Persons with Alzheimer's and Related Dementias

Tyler Morris[1]([✉]), Hiroko Dodge[2,3], Sylvia Cerel-Suhl[4], and Xiaopeng Zhao[1]

[1] University of Tennessee, Knoxville, TN 37996, USA
tmorri35@vols.utk.edu, xzhao9@utk.edu
[2] Oregon Health and Science University, Portland, OR 97239, USA
[3] Massachusetts General Hospital, Harvard Medical School, Boston, MA, USA
hdodge@mgh.harvard.edu
[4] Veterans Affairs Lexington Health Care, Lexington, KY 40502, USA
Sylvia.Cerel-Suhl@va.gov

Abstract. The demand for nursing staff, ancillary staff, and other forms of ancillary care for older adults with Alzheimer's and other dementias has been steadily increasing over the past few years. To augment this high demand for caregivers, socially assistive robots have been developed to provide cognitive, physical, and social stimuli as well as perform other necessary tasks to alleviate the burden on existing caregivers. This literature review, which includes 62 articles, provides an insight into the current capabilities and limitations of these social robots, as well as how users perceived the robots and what aspects of their design were either pleasing or displeasing. The challenges of future research and design were identified within these articles as well. Using these three key points, two major goals for the future direction of research into these social robots were suggested, which can be used to outline further development in this field.

Keywords: Socially assistive robots · Social robots · Assistive robots · Alzheimer's · Dementia · Healthcare

1 Introduction

Over the past few years, the demand for nursing staff, ancillary staff and assisted living facilities for older adults with Alzheimer's Disease (AD) and other related dementias (such as Parkinson's Disease and Huntington's Disease) have been on the rise [4]. However, the number of caregivers that can assist these patients has not grown to meet the current needs and will not be able to meet future needs . As a result, many organizations have done research into the development and feasibility of socially assistive robots (SARs) to help caregivers in caring for and potentially slowing the cognitive decline of patients with such mental conditions. These SARs are typically programmed to provide physical, cognitive, and social stimuli to further improve the overall well-being of the users [14]. Such capabilities not only assist in improving the overall quality of life for the

F. Cavallo et al. (Eds.): ICSR 2022, LNAI 13818, pp. 228–237, 2022.
https://doi.org/10.1007/978-3-031-24670-8_21

patients but also alleviate some of the burdens on the already overburdened caregivers [3]. As such, understanding the current state of these social robots, their capabilities, and their future progression is an important step in helping those older adults who are in such cognitive decline.

The terms "social robot" and "SAR" can be used interchangeably and refer to any system with some degree of autonomy designed to interact and communicate with humans, specifically with the goal to improve the cognitive, physical, and/or social wellbeing of a patient [32, 62]. More specifically, the term "SAR" or "socially assistive robot" can refer to a social robot that is able or is designed to interact with the environment directly. Many of the current uses of these robots include but are not limited to, interacting with groups of older adults, facilitating cognitive and physical exercise for older adults with AD and other dementias, facilitating social interactions between older adults with and without cognitive impairments, and providing a comfortable environment for older adults to participate in activities that might improve their overall wellbeing [7, 14, 15, 34]. Current issues, however, fall primarily with user acceptance, as some designs and applications of this technology have been rejected by older adults due to their unfamiliarity with emerging technologies and apprehensiveness about their overall appearance [7, 11, 41]. There are also, of course, limitations to the current capabilities of these social robots and challenges to overcome in future designs [4, 8, 10, 47, 59]. This review serves the purpose of analyzing these three key points – 1) current applications/ scenarios, 2) user acceptance, and 3) challenges and limitations – and providing a comprehensive review of the current state of SAR technology and pointing out future directions for further research. To do this, scholarly articles were gathered from the Google Scholar database using the keywords ("Socially Assistive Robot" OR "Social Robot") AND Dementia AND "assisted living", as well as limiting the search to review articles published since 2020 (apart from two articles from 2016 [14] and 2017 [7], which were chosen as they were the predecessors to another key article [15] and a key overview of user acceptance, respectively). From this, a total of 62 articles, conference proceedings, and these were put together to review applications, user acceptance, and challenges of social robots used for the care of older adults with AD and other related dementias.

2 Results

2.1 Applications/Scenarios

As previously mentioned, SARs have been designed to provide physical, cognitive, and social stimuli to patients with cognitive impairment [15, 16, 34]. Through a variety of games and activities (such as tic-tac-toe, matching games, conversations, and dancing sessions), social robots are designed to interact with participants so that they may use their minds and bodies in fun and engaging activities that they would normally not participate in. Through these activities, which can include cooperative sorting games to foster cognitive and social development [15, 16] or dances to encourage physical activity [15], patients work different parts of their mind and body so that each area receives constant stimulation and none deteriorate over time [50]. Most interactions can be split into one of two categories: human-robot interaction (HRI) or human-human interaction (HHI). HRIs tend to focus on the physical or cognitive stimulation of a single patient through games or activities, whereas HHIs involve the social robot interacting with a group of patients while helping them play a cooperative game to foster social interactions [7, 34]. SARs have also been programmed to set and give reminders for patients and help them through their daily tasks, such as taking their medication [59]. Furthermore, since these activities are administered by the SAR, it is possible to have them done in a patient's home so that they may feel more comfortable in a familiar environment. However, current studies have all been done in a laboratory setting and therefore future directions should investigate at-home studies. Regardless, these social robots can be designed with a variety of activities to improve the health and wellbeing of older adults with AD and dementia while also relieving some of the burdens from the currently overwhelmed caregivers and nursing staff.

These robots have already been proven effective in the realm of treating depressive symptoms in older adults [13] as well as effectively helping overwhelmed nursing staff and caregivers [25]. More experimental studies have shown that systems developed to interact with older adults with AD and related dementias increase mental and physical capabilities as well as foster social interaction between patients that would normally be nonexistent [15, 16]. As such, the applications described are fruitful and should be explored to better the well-being of older adults.

2.2 User Acceptance

While ensuring that the social robots are effective at providing meaningful physical, cognitive, and social stimulation is vitally important, it is also imperative that user acceptance is high for the individual designs as well. To answer the question of how users of the SARs perceive and accept the robots, virtually every study in which interactions were facilitated by researchers had some kind of pre-post experimental survey. User perception is typically evaluated by a point-based survey [14–16], group conversations and participant comments [11, 40], or a combination of both [7]. Furthermore, virtually all user acceptance surveys and data have come from participants with mild or no cognitive impairments, as collecting such data from those with more severe impairments is difficult due to their inability to use higher order language and reasoning [7, 11]. Most found that user acceptance increased with continuous use of the social robot, particularly after a few sessions [14–16]. Other studies have found that having groups of participants interact with the social robot rather than one-on-one HRI resulted in users having a more positive perception of the robot [34]. Lastly, some studies suggested that certain activities increase positive user perception of the robots, particularly when the activities match the interests of the participant [11]. All these results show that one way to increase the patient's perception of the social robot that they are interacting with is to: 1. Have them repeatedly interact with the robot to overcome previously held trepidations, and 2. Modify the activities hosted by the social robot to better align with the interests and desires of the participant.

General studies have also been done to evaluate how the design of the robot, specifically its outward appearance and its user interface, affect user perception. Older adults tend to prefer simpler interfaces with large buttons and text that are easier to read and understand [40]. Voice activation is also a positive for most users, but some with certain accents or those whose first language was not English often have trouble with the type of control [11]. Overall, however, participants preferred a tablet control when interacting with the robot due to its ease of use and how easy it was to read and understand [7].

Another important factor to consider when determining user acceptance of any given social robot is its outward appearance. Most social robots in development have a human-like appearance to mimic the form of caregivers, such as the PEPPER robot shown in Fig. 1 [59].

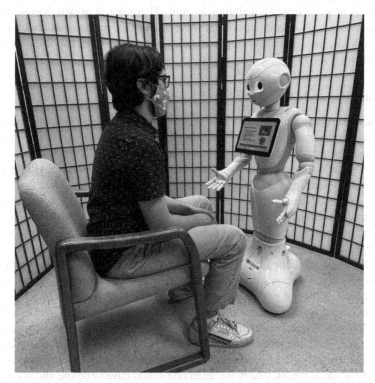

Fig. 1. A user testing cognitive rehab exercises using the humanoid robot, Pepper.

Social robots have this human-like design for a multitude of purposes, such as being more familiar with the patient or being able to interact with their environment more efficiently. These designs, however, are not received well by all patients; some studies find that older adults with cognitive disabilities find the human-like appearance of the social robots to be unsettling or disturbing, particularly because they do not blink or more too robotically [7]. Other designs for social robots have also been developed, such as the ENRICHME system, which are not humanoid and instead are simple designs [11]. Systems like this are also limited, however, by their inability to properly interact with the environment. Their inability to properly participate in the activities that they are presenting often leads to lower user perception of the system [7, 11], even though their appearance and user interface are more widely accepted. As such, a more interactive design with a less human-like appearance seems to be the best option for future SAR designs, preferably with either a tablet or voice control that can be used by anyone regardless of age, accent, etc.

Overall, studies have shown that multiple factors affect the user perception of a social robot. Experiments have shown that repeated interactions with any SAR will improve the overall user perception, as well as tailoring the activities to fit the interests and desires of the user. Further surveys have shown that more human-like appearances are less appealing to some users, but less human-like social robots cannot interact with the environment or participate in activities as well. Therefore, a middle-ground must be found such that initial interactions are positive and further interactions are encouraged so that the SARs can effectively improve the cognitive, physical, and social wellbeing of the patients.

2.3   Challenges and Limitations

While the most recent SAR designs have been proven effective at providing meaningful physical, cognitive, and social stimuli, there are still challenges that must be overcome so that they may be introduced to a wider range of patients and have a greater impact. These challenges include the adaptability of the systems, the ability of the SARs to interact with the environment and therefore perform more tasks and combining functionality with favorable designs. There will, of course, always be other challenges when developing such a complex technology, but these three stand out as major roadblocks to the proper implementation and success of social robots designed to care for older adults with AD and other related dementias.

The first major challenge and limitation of the current SARs is their ability to adapt to certain patients in certain scenarios. There are systems in development that can take physiological readings of participants to determine their physical and cognitive states [14–16], but these systems are not able to adapt the social robot to respond to any major changes. This would be difficult since it would require a higher-level artificial intelligence (AI) that can process information in real-time and make small changes to the activities to better suit the patient in that interaction. This challenge must be overcome to mass produce these social robots, otherwise, each one would have to be specifically designed for each patient and modified constantly as their cognitive state declines. The technology already exists for adaptive AI that can control multiple systems, but its integration into this specific field of technology is a key step in progressing the capabilities of SARs in healthcare.

Another major limitation of current SAR design is their ability to interact with the environment. Most social robots that are being used in research can move and gesture but are unable to properly interact with their surrounding environment [4]. However, most caregivers are required to physically interact with objects within the patients' homes to accomplish certain tasks such as organizing medication and cleaning [10]. Some social robots do have hands that can grip and pick up light objects, such as the PEPPER robot [59], but this interaction is limited by its dexterity and overall motor control. If social robots are to be the future of healthcare for those with AD and other related dementias, then they must be able properly to perform all required tasks given to them that would normally be done by human caregivers. This is challenging, however, as such complex robots are either highly expensive to produce or cannot perform a wide range of functions. Altogether, the current design limitations must be overcome to improve the overall functionality of the social robots to provide genuine healthcare to those in need.

The final challenge to overcome in the future development of SARs is the balance between functionality and user acceptance. As discussed earlier, many users feel uncomfortable with the human-like designs of some SARs at first and are therefore apprehensive about utilizing them [7]. However, these designs provide the most functionality since they can generally move around and interact with objects and people more efficiently than other designs [28]. Users do, however, respond better to non-human robots, such as robotic pets, with a higher user acceptance rate [19]. These social robots, however, are unable to interact with their environment and therefore are limited in their functionality as they cannot be updated to perform more physical tasks [27]. Therefore, a design that is both functional and appealing to users must be developed so that effective robots will be accepted by a wider community and benefit the well-being of those in need of their services.

3 Future Directions

3.1 At-Home Capabilities

Future research into social robots and their abilities to care for patients with AD and other related dementias should investigate how an at-home environment affects HRIs. Most research in the modern day takes place in a laboratory setting, which is often unfamiliar to the participants which in turn causes them to be more reserved and unresponsive [62]. However, elderly patients have reported feeling more comfortable participating in these experiments at home where they are in a familiar environment that they are more comfortable with [1]. Therefore, it stands to reason that participants might react differently to the social robots in the comfort of their own homes rather than in a laboratory setting. However, there are no studies that have compared participants' reactions to the SARs in different environments, thus leaving a gap in a key area of research into this new emerging technology. Some studies have investigated how effective home-based social robots are at caring for and improving the cognitive and physical states of participants [56], as well as how caregivers respond to the robots in an at-home environment [3]. These studies have found that, like in a laboratory setting, the robots effectively improved the cognitive and physical conditions of the participants as well as successfully gained the approval of caregivers in helping take care of the older adults [3, 56]. However, these studies do fail to determine if the environment played a role in affecting the responsiveness of the patients and their perception of the SARs. As such, future research should include studies done in a participant's home to determine if the environment has a major impact on user perception and acceptance of the social robot. The results of such studies could help in the future design of social robots as they might become more tailored to a patient's environment rather than a standard one, thus improving their functionality and effectiveness in healthcare.

3.2 Increasing User Perception and Acceptance

As mentioned earlier, the next crucial step in the development of social robots for the care of older adults with AD and other related dementias is to improve user acceptance and perceptions of the systems. Studies have shown that increased acceptance of the system helps encourage users to continue to interact with the robots [7], thus increasing their effectiveness. Therefore, to promote more interactions and thus improve the effectiveness of the SARs, future designs should consider how users would prefer the robots to look and be controlled. As mentioned earlier, older adults tend to prefer non-human-like appearances, since more human-like robots appear unsettling [7]. Thus, future designs should be less human-like; this could mean that future SAR designs might look like pets, since older adults have been shown to enjoy the presence of an animal, both real and robotic, and are encouraged to interact with them repeatedly, thus improving their effectiveness [19, 27, 52]. Additionally, user interfaces should be tailored to the preferences of the patients. Since most older adults prefer either voice controlled (given that they can understand them correctly) or large easy-to-read tablets [7, 41], these should be considered for all future SAR designs. By implementing these design choices, user perception and acceptance of social robots designed for healthcare are sure to increase, which in turn will increase their effectiveness and favorability to the public.

4 Conclusion

Overall, social robots to care for older adults with AD and other related dementias is an ever-growing field that has been proven effective yet is still limited by certain challenges. Experimental studies have shown that SARs can provide meaningful cognitive, physical, and social stimulation while caring for older adults, which proves that these systems are a viable way to provide much-needed encouragement and support to patients; this, however, has only been done in a laboratory setting and not in a participant's home, which may skew the results regarding the amount of HRI. Furthermore, several studies have pointed out aspects of social robot design that participants do and do not like, such as a preference for tablet and voice-control systems but wariness for human-like designs during the first few interactions. Lastly, several limitations have been identified throughout the ongoing development of these social robots, including their ability to adapt in real-time to patient responses and conditions, being able to properly interact with the environment, and having a balance in their design between functionality and appeal. Through these key points, it is apparent that future research into SARs must focus on developing designs that are appealing to the users while also providing meaningful and efficient care to better alleviate the already overburdened caregivers in the homes of the patients. Altogether, the future of social robots to support the care of older adults living with Alzheimer's Disease and other related dementia is a promising one, but there are still many challenges that must be overcome should these robots be used to help all of those in need.

References

1. Abou Allaban, A., Wang, M., Padır, T.: A systematic review of robotics research in support of in-home care for older adults. Information. **11**(2), 1–24 (2020)
2. Alimoradi, S., Gao, X.: Intelligence Complements from the Built Environment: A Review of Cps-Enabled Smart Buildings for Cognitively Declined Occupants. Available at SSRN 4000359, pp. 1–52 (2020)

3. Arthanat, S., et al.: Caregiver perspectives on a smart home-based socially assistive robot for individuals with Alzheimer's disease and related dementia. Disabil. Rehabil. Assist. Technol. **15**(7), 789–798 (2020)

4. Badr, N.G., Dankar, M.: Assistive healthcare robotics–challenges in nursing service innovation: critical review. In: ITM Web of Conferences, pp. 1–17. EDP Sciences (2022)

5. Bastardo, R., et al.: Methodological quality of user-centered usability evaluation of ambient assisted living solutions: a systematic literature review. Int. J. Environ. Res. Public Health **18**(21), 1–18 (2021)

6. Behera, C.K., et al.: State-of-the-art sensors for remote care of people with dementia during a pandemic: a systematic review. Sensors **21**(14), 1–21 (2021)

7. Beuscher, L.M., et al.: Socially assistive robots: measuring older adults' perceptions. J. Gerontol. Nurs. **43**(12), 35–43 (2017)

8. Boch, A., Lucaj, L., Corrigan, C.: A Robotic New Hope: Opportunities, Challenges, and Ethical Considerations of Social Robots, pp. 1–12. Technical University of Munich (2020)

9. Budak, K.B., et al.: Can technology impact loneliness in dementia? a scoping review on the role of assistive technologies in delivering psychosocial interventions in long-term care. Disabil. Rehabil. Assist. Technol. 1–13 (2021). https://doi.org/10.1080/17483107.2021.198 4594

10. Christoforou, E.G., et al.: The upcoming role for nursing and assistive robotics: opportunities and challenges ahead. Front. Dig. Health **2**, 1–12 (2020)

11. Coşar, S., et al.: ENRICHME: perception and interaction of an assistive robot for the elderly at Home. Int. J. Soc. Robot. **12**(3), 779–805 (2020). https://doi.org/10.1007/s12369-019-006 14-y

12. David, L., et al.: Nursing procedures for advanced dementia: traditional techniques versus autonomous robotic applications. Exp. Ther. Med. **23**(2), 1–9 (2022)

13. de Araujo, B.S., et al.: Effects of social robots on depressive symptoms in older adults: a scoping review. Lib. Hi Tech. **40**(5), 1108–1126 (2021)

14. Fan, J., et al.: A robotic coach architecture for elder care (ROCARE) based on multi-user engagement models. IEEE Trans. Neural Syst. Rehabil. Eng. **25**(8), 1153–1163 (2016)

15. Fan, J., et al.: SAR-connect: a socially assistive robotic system to support activity and social engagement of older adults. IEEE Trans. Rob. **38**(2), 1250–1269 (2021)

16. Fan, J., et al.: Field testing of Ro-Tri, a Robot-mediated triadic interaction for older adults. Int. J. Soc. Robot. **13**(7), 1711–1727 (2021)

17. Getson, C., Nejat, G.: Socially assistive robots helping older adults through the pandemic and life after COVID-19. Robotics **10**(3), 1–23 (2021)

18. Grossi, G., et al.: Positive technology for elderly well-being: a review. Pattern Recogn. Lett. **137**, 61–70 (2021)

19. Guerra, S., et al.: The use of robotic pets by community-dwelling older adults: a scoping review. Int. J. Soc. Robot. 1–12 (2022)

20. Gurrutxaga-Lerma, O.: Interventions to Prevent Loneliness in Older Adults Living in Nursing Homes, pp. 1–24. Navarra University (2021)

21. Hayden, L., et al.: A scoping review: sensory interventions for older adults living with dementia. Dementia **21**(4), 1416–1448 (2022)

22. Hirt, J., Vetsch, J., Heinrich, S.: Facilitators and barriers to implement nurse-led physical activities for people with dementia in nursing homes: a protocol for a mixed-methods systematic review. BMJ Open **11**(12), 1–6 (2021)

23. Huisman, C., Huisman, E., Kort, H.: Technological applications contributing to relieve care burden or to sleep of caregivers and people with dementia: a scoping review from the perspective of social isolation. Front. Public Health **10**, 1–14 (2022)

24. Hung, L., et al.: Facilitators and barriers to using telepresence robots in aged care settings: a scoping review. J. Rehabilit. Assist. Technol. Eng. **9**, 1–19 (2022)

25. Huter, K., et al.: Effectiveness of digital technologies to support nursing care: results of a scoping review. J. Multidiscip. Healthc. **13**, 1905–1926 (2020)
26. Jones, C., et al.: Effects of non-facilitated meaningful activities for people with dementia in long-term care facilities: a systematic review. Geriatr. Nurs. **41**(6), 863–871 (2020)
27. Koh, W.Q., Ang, F.X.H., Casey, D.: Impacts of low-cost robotic pets for older adults and people with dementia: scoping review. JMIR Rehabilit. Assist. Technol. **8**(1), 1–14 (2021)
28. Koh, W.Q., et al.: Barriers and facilitators to the implementation of social robots for older adults and people with dementia: a scoping review. BMC Geriatr. **21**(1), 1–17 (2021)
29. Konstantinidis, T.: A systematic review of the literature examining the use and application of robots and artificial intelligence for assisted living for persons living with dementia. In: Health Sciences, p. 55. University of Ontario Institute of Technology, Oshawa, Ontario, Canada (2021)
30. Kruse, C.S., et al.: Evaluating the facilitators, barriers, and medical outcomes commensurate with the use of assistive technology to support people with dementia: a systematic review literature, In: Healthcare, pp. 1–44. MDPI (2020)
31. Kyrarini, M., et al.: A survey of robots in healthcare. Technologies **9**(1), 1–28 (2021)
32. Lambert, A., et al.: A systematic review of ten years of research on human interaction with social robots. Int. J. Hum. Comput. Interact. **36**(19), 1804–1817 (2020)
33. Latikka, R., et al.: Older adults' loneliness, social isolation, and physical information and communication technology in the era of ambient assisted living: a systematic literature review. J. Med. Internet Res. **23**(12), 1–16 (2021)
34. Lin, Y.-C., et al.: Use of robots to encourage social engagement between older adults. Geriatr. Nurs. **43**, 97–103 (2022)
35. Loveys, K., et al.: Artificial intelligence for older people receiving long-term care: a systematic review of acceptability and effectiveness studies. Lancet Healthy Longevit. **3**(4), 286–297 (2022)
36. Lu, S.-C., et al.: Informatics and artificial intelligence approaches that promote use of integrative health therapies in nursing practice: a scoping review. OBM Integrat. Comp. Med. **5**(1), 1–22 (2020)
37. Łukasik, S., et al.: Role of assistive robots in the care of older people: survey study among medical and nursing students. J. Med. Internet Res. **22**(8), 1–18 (2020)
38. Lukkien, D.R., et al.: Toward responsible artificial intelligence in long-term care: a scoping review on practical approaches. Gerontologist, 1–14 (2021). https://doi.org/10.1093/geront/gnab180
39. Martinez-Martin, E., Escalona, F., Cazorla, M.: Socially assistive robots for older adults and people with autism: an overview. Electronics **9**(2), 1–16 (2020)
40. Migovich, M., et al.: System architecture and user interface design for a human-machine interaction system for dementia intervention. In: International Conference on Human-Computer Interaction, pp. 277–292. Springer (2021)
41. Miguel Cruz, A., et al.: Acceptance, adoption, and usability of information and communication technologies for people living with dementia and their care partners: a systematic review. Disabil. Rehabil. Assist. Technol. 1–15 (2021)
42. Mois, G., Beer, J.M.: The role of healthcare robotics in providing support to older adults: a socio-ecological perspective. Curr. Geriatr. Rep. **9**(2), 82–89 (2020)
43. Ozdemir, D., et al.: Design and implementation framework of social assistive robotics for people with dementia-a scoping review. Heal. Technol. **11**(2), 367–378 (2021)
44. Papadopoulos, C., et al.: The CARESSES study protocol: testing and evaluating culturally competent socially assistive robots among older adults residing in long term care homes through a controlled experimental trial. Arch. Public Health **78**(1), 1–10 (2020)

45. Papadopoulos, I., et al.: Enablers and barriers to the implementation of socially assistive humanoid robots in health and social care: a systematic review. BMJ Open **10**(1), 1–13 (2020)
46. Park, H.G., Perumean-Chaney, S.E., Bartolucci, A.A.: Exploring factors associated with successful nonpharmacological interventions for people with dementia. Dement. Neurocogn. Disorders **21**(1), 1–16 (2022)
47. Pirhonen, J., et al.: Can robots tackle late-life loneliness? scanning of future opportunities and challenges in assisted living facilities. Futures **124**, 1–12 (2020)
48. Reis, L., Mercer, K., Boger, J.: Technologies for fostering intergenerational connectivity and relationships: scoping review and emergent concepts. Technol. Soc. **64**, 1–20 (2021)
49. Robinson, F., Nejat, G.: An analysis of design recommendations for socially assistive robot helpers for effective human-robot interactions in senior care. J. Rehabilit. Assist. Technol. Eng. **9**, 1–17 (2022)
50. Rogers, W.A., Kadylak, T., Bayles, M.A.: Maximizing the benefits of participatory design for human-robot interaction research with older adults. Hum. Fact. **64**(3), 441–450 (2021)
51. Santos, N.B., et al.: A systematic mapping study of robotics in human care. Robot. Auton. Syst. **144**, 1–24 (2021)
52. Sheikh, A.B., et al.: Pet-assisted therapy for delirium and agitation in hospitalized patients with neurocognitive impairment: a review of Literature. Geriatrics **6**(4), 1–17 (2021)
53. Shibata, T., et al.: PARO as a biofeedback medical device for mental health in the COVID-19 Era. Sustainability **13**(20), 1–17 (2021)
54. Sumner, J., et al.: Co-designing technology for aging in place: a systematic review. Gerontologist **61**(7), 395–409 (2021)
55. Thakur, N., Han, C.Y.: A review of assistive technologies for activities of daily living of elderly, pp. 61–84. arXiv preprint arXiv:2106.12183 (2021)
56. Van Patten, R., et al.: Home-based cognitively assistive robots: maximizing cognitive functioning and maintaining independence in older adults without dementia. Clin. Interv. Aging **15**, 1129–1139 (2020)
57. Wang, J., et al.: A systematic review of factors influencing attitudes towards and intention to use the long-distance caregiving technologies for older adults. Int. J. Med. Informat. **153**, 1–11 (2021)
58. Wang, X., Shen, J., Chen, Q.: How PARO can help older people in elderly care facilities: a systematic review of RCT. Int. J. Nurs. Knowl. **33**(1), 29–39 (2022)
59. Woods, D., et al.: Social robots for older adults with dementia: a narrative review on challenges & future directions. In: International Conference on Social Robotics, pp. 411–420. Springer (2021)
60. Xie, B., et al.: Artificial intelligence for caregivers of persons with Alzheimer's disease and related dementias: systematic literature review. JMIR Med. Inform. **8**(8), 1–10 (2020)
61. Yuan, F., et al.: Assessing the acceptability of a humanoid robot for alzheimer's disease and related dementia care using an online survey. Int. J. Soc. Robotics. 1–15 (2022). https://doi.org/10.1007/s12369-021-00862-x
62. Yuan, F., et al.: A systematic review of robotic rehabilitation for cognitive training. Front. Robotics AI **8**, 1–24 (2021)

Assistant Robots in German Hospitals: Measuring Value Drivers and Willingness to Pay

Marija Radic[1]([✉]) [iD], Dubravko Radic[1,2] [iD], and Agnes Vosen[1]

[1] Fraunhofer Center for International Management and Knowledge Economy IMW, Neumarkt 9-19, 04109 Leipzig, Germany
marija.radic@imw.fraunhofer.de
[2] Chair of Service Management, University of Leipzig, Leipzig, Germany

Abstract. In 2030, the worldwide skilled workers shortage in healthcare will reach 15 million. Innovative solutions that meet this immense challenge are required. Assistant robots have the potential to mitigate this challenge by relieving health professionals of heavy physical work, reducing time spent on repetitive tasks and leaving more time for patients in need of care. Despite the growing interest, the market growth for robotic solutions in the healthcare sector is picking up only slowly due to mainly two challenges: financing as well as the fit of the product to the needs of the institution. While many studies explore the patient acceptance of robotic solutions, there is hardly any quantitative evidence on the preferences and willingness to pay of hospitals. The objective of this study is to close this research gap by exploring value drivers and willingness to pay of hospital decision makers in Germany for a hospital robot guide using a choice-based conjoint analysis. We, first, find that price, an elevator function, and a service package are the most important value drivers. We further determine that the revenue-maximizing purchase price for the robot guide is between 25.000 Euro for the basic robotic solution without additional features and 50.000 Euro for the best profile with all features. Finally, in line with current trends in the robotics market, our qualitative results show that flexible offers such as e.g. renting are very attractive for the target group of hospitals thus providing valuable insights for the adaptation of robot manufacturers' business models.

Keywords: Assistant robot · Robot guide · Healthcare · Hospital · Willingness to pay · Pricing

1 Introduction

The world will need 80 million health workers to meet the demands of the global population by the end of the decade, but the supply of health workers is expected to reach 65 million only over the same period. Without intervention, this will result in a worldwide net shortage of 15 million health workers in 2030 and cause serious consequences for the health of billions of people around the globe. Driven by economic growth, population growth, and aging of the population, the demand will be highest in upper middle-income countries [1]. The considerable shortage of skilled workers shows that innovative and

F. Cavallo et al. (Eds.): ICSR 2022, LNAI 13818, pp. 238–247, 2022.
https://doi.org/10.1007/978-3-031-24670-8_22

technical ideas are needed to meet these challenges. For a long time, robotic solutions were viewed with some skepticism. In recent years, however, their use has increased significantly due to their demonstration of support in relieving skilled workers of heavy physical work, reducing time spent on repetitive tasks and leaving more time for patients in need of care.

Due to the increasing demand for robotic solutions, the question of financing is becoming ever more acute. A recent study for the German market shows that financing and the fit of the product to the needs of the institution are currently among the five biggest obstacles for market growth [2]. From a robot manufacturer's perspective, it is thus elementary to understand customer preferences and the willingness to pay of healthcare providers for robotic solutions.

Numerous studies deal with different aspects of the acceptance of assistance robots in the healthcare sector [2–7]. There is hardly any evidence, however, on end users' willingness to pay for robotic solutions. In 2012, aspects like needs and preferences regarding robotics in personal health care were investigated in interviews with seven robotic company leaders and in user focus groups [8]. The study focuses on robots like vacuum robots, emotional robots, and exoskeletons. In this context, a willingness to pay of USD 300 for a home care robot manufactured by OLogic was determined in a company study. In another study, Kramer investigates the willingness to pay of caregiving relatives in Germany for the activation robot Paro [9]. An average willingness to pay of 487 to 1807 Euro was determined (depending on the type of assistive robot) by asking the participants directly what the robot is worth for them. In addition to the purchase option, a leasing version is considered. Here the average monthly willingness to pay was 30–130 Euro (again depending on the type of robot from locating systems to overall monitoring systems). The willingness to pay for an assistive robot such as Paro was on average 405 Euro and the average leasing rate 90 Euro. Fischinger et al. [10] found out that older adults in Austria perceive a suggested price of 1400 Euro as rather expensive for Hobbit, a care robot supporting independent living at home. Only 4.1% of the participants would be willing to pay if Hobbit costed 14.000 Euro. Interestingly, the willingness to rent the robot is with 77.6% estimated to be significantly higher than the willingness to purchase it with 34.7% [10].

The presentation of the literature shows that there are only a few studies which deal with the willingness to pay for robotic solutions. It also shows that there is a willingness to pay for robotic solutions, and that this willingness depends on the specific technology used. An assessment of the literature, however, reveals that previous studies heavily focus on a specific target group. - mostly patients and family caregivers, and less frequently institutional target groups such as clinics. Furthermore, most of these studies used general interview questions as a predictor for willingness to pay as opposed to using sophisticated statistical methods. From a methodological point of view asking directly for willingness to pay leads to a upward biased predictor for the real willingness to pay [11]. The literature overview shows that currently no study exists which evaluates the preferences and willingness to pay of hospitals for robotic solutions. The objective of this study is to contribute to closing this research gap by determining the value drivers and willingness to pay of German hospitals with respect to a healthcare robot guide using a sophisticated statistical approach.

2 Method and Data

In this study, a choice-based conjoint analysis (CBCA) was conducted to determine the preferences of potential users for the hospital robot guide [12]. Conjoint analysis is one of the indirect customer survey methods. The instruments developed for estimating price-sales functions based on indirectly collected data on willingness to pay represent real purchase situations more authentically than is the case with direct surveys. For the respondent, the price is one of several criteria relevant for the purchase decision [13]. To achieve the highest possible degree of realism, the respondents are presented with combinations of different prices and product features. They then decide whether they would buy a product with the respective characteristic attributes or which products or services they prefer at the given prices [14, 15]. In CBCA, the respondent compares a set of different, complete product profiles in each case and selects his or her personal favorite. In addition, the user is free not to select any of the different profiles. This distinguishes CBCA from traditional conjoint models. Subjects reveal their preferences by making purchasing decisions, not based on ordinal preference judgments (rankings) or metric preference judgments (ratings) [16]. Different discrete choice methods can be used for econometric modeling. In our case, we choose a probit model in which a nonlinear relationship is assumed between the observed choice decision of the subjects and the characteristics of the different alternatives.

The target group for the interviews were decision makers in German hospitals: commercial directors, medical directors, and nursing directors. The interviews were conducted in person in the hospitals. As part of the study, after an introductory briefing on the features and characteristics of the robotic solution, the subjects were presented with two different product configurations of the robotic solution. They were then asked to choose one of the two profiles which generated the subjectively higher value or whether both profiles were unacceptable at the given price. Overall, each participant was presented with sixteen randomly selected pairs of profiles. Finally, further variables such as the hospital size (number of beds), type of hospital operator, the hospital's degree of digitization, the hospital's decision makers for investment decisions, the interviewee's gender and function in the hospital and their subjectively assessed affinity for technology were queried.

The product attributes included in the CBCA comprised the following features (each with different levels): "touchscreen and voice recognition", "recognition function" and "personalized communication", an "individual design of the color", "information provision through a dialog system", an "additional carrying function", an "additional elevator driving function", an "additional follow me-function", "service and maintenance", and "price" (see Table 1 for a complete presentation of all attributes and levels). The attributes and levels were identified based on qualitative focus groups with patients, professionals, and a workshop with experts in the field of assistive robotics.

The robot guide is based on the Care-O-bot® 4 assistance robot and guides a person safely and attentively through a public building to the relevant destination. An example scenario for the assistant robot as a pilot is described as follows: A patient enters the entrance area of a clinic. After she has had her card scanned, the receptionist calls the assistant robot and tells it that the patient, who is in the hospital for the first time, should be accompanied to the X-ray department. The robot then accompanies the patient to the destination and says goodbye before returning to the reception area. By accompanying patients to different wards in a clinic or facility, assistant robots can reduce corresponding demands on staff. The criteria considered in the interview as well as in the conjoint analysis were presented to the interviewees as shown in Table 1. Overall, 38 decision makers were surveyed in face-to-face interviews at hospitals throughout Germany in January and February 2020.

Table 1. Product attributes and levels

1. Touch Screen and Voice Control	
The robot can interact with people in two ways: Either via touch screen only or via touch screen and voice control / a dialogue system	• Operation only by means of touchscreen • Operation by voice control only • Operation by means of touch screen and voice control
2. Recognition Function and Personal Address	
The assistant robot recognizes the patient and can address him personally and by name e.g. "Good morning, Mrs. Miller!"	• Function available • Function not available
3. Individual Design of the Color	
The assistant robot can be customized in terms of color e.g. to match the logo or color scheme of the hospital	• Individual color design possible • Individual color design not possible (basic color white)
4. Information Provision through Dialogue System	
On the way to the patient's destination, the robot points out other central points such as e.g. toilets, water dispensers or the cafeteria	• Function available • Function not available
5. Additional Function: Carrying Function	
A carrying function can support patients on the way to their destination carrying their bags, aids or other objects by means e.g. of a hook attached to the assistant robot	• Function available • Function not available
6. Additional Function: Elevator Function	

(continued)

242 M. Radic et al.

Table 1. (*continued*)

The robot is able to ride an elevator with or without a patient, find its way around several floors, and return to its base station independently	• Function available i.e. the assistant robot can ride an elevator, find its way around on several floors and return to the base station independently • Function not available i.e. the assistant robot only moves around one floor
7. <u>Additional Function:</u> Follow Me Function	
The robot pays attention whether the person is following and adjusts its speed accordingly	• Function available • Function not available
8. Service and Maintenance	
The service and maintenance contract covers software maintenance and repair as well as the replacement of defective components (excluding wear parts). Also included is a 24/7 telephone hotline and technical support for troubleshooting via a remote support interface	• Without service and maintenance contract: orders are charged according to time and effort • Service and maintenance contract is available • Service and maintenance contract is not available
9. Purchase price	
The assistance robot can be purchased at various price points:	• 25.000 EUR; 50.000 EUR; 75.000 EUR; 100.000 EUR

3 Empirical Results

First descriptive statistics show that nearly two thirds of the respondents are nursing directors, 18% are commercial directors and 16% medical directors. Two thirds of the respondents are male. On average, the respondents indicate that their affinity for technology is high. Concerning the hospitals they represent, the respondents estimate the degree of digitization of their hospitals as average. Regarding the hospital size, the average bed capacity is 800, i.e. rather large hospitals. Half of the hospitals are in public ownership, the remaining two quarters are in private and non-profit ownership, respectively. Sixty percent of the participants are located in Eastern Germany. About 55% of the hospitals are located in urban areas with over one hundred thousand inhabitants. While approximating the hospital landscape in Germany quite well, the study does not meet the requirements of a representative study.

Table 2 shows the probit estimation results for the sample of potential end users. Probits model the decision of the respondents to choose a hypothetical robotics solution or not [17, 18]. The values in the "parameter" column show the effect of a specific attribute-level on the utility. The "MFX" column contains the changes in choice probability in percentage points due to changes in the respective attributes. The "relative importance" column contains the importance value of the respective characteristic. This results from the absolute parameter values of the attributes relative to the sum of all parameter differences, i.e. parameter values that are large in terms of amount lead to large relative importances for an attribute, since a change in the attribute's value causes a large increase or loss in utility. We find that price is the most important characteristic, with a relative importance of 21%. An increase in price by 1 euro lowers the probability of choosing the corresponding profile by 5% points as shown in the "MFX" column. Moreover, this marginal effect is highly significant with a p-value equal to zero. The elevator function is the second most important feature with a relative importance of 20%. The presence of this feature increases the marginal choice-probability by 4%-points. Service is third most important feature with 17%. The presence of this feature increases the marginal choice-probability by 4%-points.

Table 2. Results of the probit estimation

Purchase option

variable	parameter	p-value	MFX	relative		
					observations	608
touchscreen	0.27	0.49	0.01	4%		
language	0.52	0.08	0.02	9%	pseudo-R²	0.47
recognition	0.60	0.06	0.02	10%		
color	0.03	0.93	0.00	1%	hit-rate	94%
dialog	0.84	0.02	0.03	15%		
carry	0.25	0.47	0.01	4%		
elevator	**1.05**	**0.00**	**0.04**	**20%**		
follow	0.00	0.00	0.00	0%		
service	**0.95**	**0.00**	**0.04**	**17%**		
ln_price	**-1.35**	**0.00**	**-0.05**	**21%**		
_cons	10.25	0.00	0.01			

The hit rate is 94%, which means that the model correctly predicts 94% of all selection decisions made by the respondents. The pseudo-R^2 based on the likelihood value for the estimated model is 0.47, which is a good result for a cross-sectional data set.

The revenue-maximizing price, which was determined using the results of the probit model as the product of the price and the respective estimated choice probability, is 25.000 Euros for the robotic solution without additional features (Fig. 1) and 50.000 Euro for the complete solution with all features (Fig. 2). Figure 1 and 2 show the peaks of the price-sales curves for the best profile with all features and the base profile without additional features.

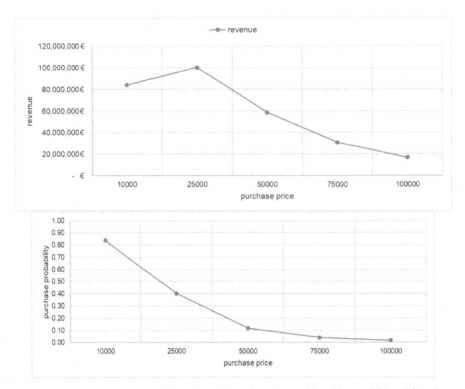

Fig. 1. Simulation tool for purchase prices of hospital robot guide without additional functions

The interviews provide further qualitative insights. The interviews specifically indicate that a rental option might be attractive as an additional financing model, which is why we included the question for each profile whether, first, both financing models are an option, and second, in case this question was affirmed, what the interviewee's preference between both options was. Figure 3 shows that a rental model is often more attractive than a purchase: 5% would probably or only buy, 53% are indifferent, 42% would probably or only rent. There is thus a strong preference for the rental model, which is to the best of our knowledge the first scientific evidence for this fact in the healthcare robotics literature.

The analysis shows that many respondents prefer to rent a robot to buying one. The main reason cited was the fast pace of technology development. New updates can thus be put into use more quickly. In addition, the robot can be tested for a limited time. As an argument against a rental model, respondents mention additional financing costs. These arguments are in line with changing business models emerging for robotic solutions which enable flexible short-term robot implementations without a long-term investment [19].

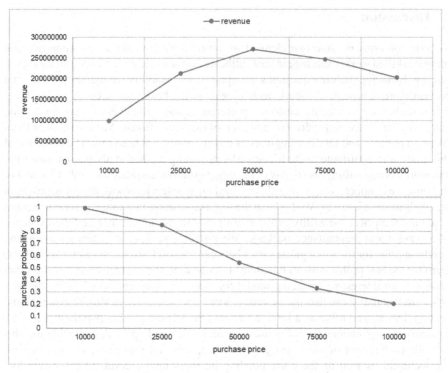

Fig. 2. Simulation tool for purchase prices of hospital robot guide with all functions

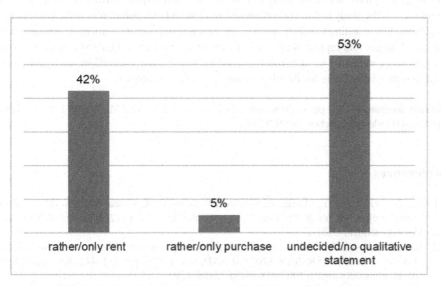

Fig. 3. Preference for purchase or rental option (n = 38 participants)

4 Discussion

Robotic solutions provide one element to improve patient care across countries and mitigate skilled worker shortage in the healthcare sector worldwide. Several studies show that e.g. financing, liability questions, acceptance and usability are major obstacles that prevent a breakthrough of robotic technologies in the healthcare sector [20–24]. Only a few studies try to identify customer preferences and willingness to pay for robotic solutions, which are major drivers, however, of market diffusion. Moreover, all of them focus on patients and family caregivers as target groups, not hospitals. The objective of this study is to contribute to the literature by providing the first study that measures the value drivers and willingness to pay of the target group of hospitals for a robot guide. For this aim, we conduct a conjoint analysis based on 38 interviews with decision makers in hospitals across Germany. We find that the three most important value drivers for a robot guide are the price, the ability of the robot guide to use an elevator and the existence of a service and maintenance package. We further find that the revenue maximizing purchase price for the robot guide varies between 25.000 Euro for the worst and 50.000 Euro for the best profile with all functions. Interestingly, the qualitative results show that renting is an interesting financing model for many respondents, which is in line with other studies that show that the business model landscape in robotics is changing and renting, leasing and robot as a service business models are gaining popularity [10, 25]. In terms of implications for robot manufacturers, the study provides valuable insights into the preferences of the target group of hospitals and thus provides guidance for the technical as well as the corresponding business model development. Several of the additional functions such as e.g. the elevator function, which is crucial specifically for large hospitals, are technically not yet mature and require further development. A limitation of the study is that cost information on the robotic solution is unfortunately not available thus resulting in information on the revenue maximizing, not profit maximizing prices. A larger and representative sample of interviewees would also be advantageous to gain more evidence on subgroups according to e.g. size, ownership, geography etc. and thus provide a basis for developing market access strategies.

Acknowledgments. The project is sponsored by the German Federal Ministry of Education and Research (Förderkennzeichen: 16SV7871K).

References

1. Liu, J.X., Goryakin, Y., Maeda, A., Bruckner, T., Scheffler, R.: Global health workforce labor market projections for 2030. Hum. Resour. Health **15**(1), 1–12 (2017). https://doi.org/10.1186/s12960-017-0187-2
2. Radic, M., Vosen, A., Graf, B.: Use of robotics in the German healthcare sector. In: Salichs, M.A., et al. (eds.) ICSR 2019. LNCS (LNAI), vol. 11876, pp. 434–442. Springer, Cham (2019). https://doi.org/10.1007/978-3-030-35888-4_40
3. Klein, G., Klein, B., Schlömer, F., Roßberg, H., Röhrich, K., Baumgarten, S.: Robotik in der Gesundheitswirtschaft. medhochzwei, Heidelberg (2017)
4. Meyer, S.: Mein Freund der Roboter: Servicerobotik für ältere Menschen. Eine Antwort auf den demografischen Wandel? VDE-Verlag, Berlin, Offenbach (2011)

5. Broadbent, E., Tamagawa, R., Kerse, N., Knock, B., Patience, A., MacDonald, B.: Retirement home staff and residents' preferences for healthcare robots. In: The 18th IEEE International Symposium on Robot and Human Interactive Communication Toyama, Japan (2009)
6. Broadbent, E., et al.: Attitudes towards health-care robots in a retirement village. Australas. J. Ageing 31(2), 115–120 (2012). https://doi.org/10.1111/j.1741-6612.2011.00551.x
7. Hebesberger, D., Koertner, T., Gisinger, C., Pripfl, J.: A long-term autonomous robot at a care hospital: a mixed methods study on social acceptance and experiences of staff and older adults. Int. J. Soc. Robot. 9(3), 417–429 (2017). https://doi.org/10.1007/s12369-016-0391-6
8. Bzura, C., Im, H., Malehorn, K., Liu, W.: The Emerging Role of Robotics in Personal Health Care: Bringing Smart Health Care Home (2012)
9. Kramer, B.: Die Akzeptanz neuer Technologien bei pflegenden Angehörigen von Menschen mit Demenz, Thesis (2016)
10. Fischinger, D., et al.: Hobbit, a care robot supporting independent living at home: First prototype and lessons learned. Robot. Auton. Syst. 75, 60–78 (2016). https://doi.org/10.1016/j.robot.2014.09.029
11. Breidert, C.: Estimation of Willingness-To-Pay: Theory, Measurement, Application. Springer, Berlin, Heidelberg (2007)
12. Green, P.E., Srinivasan, V.: Conjoint analysis in consumer research: issues and outlook. J. Consum. Res. 5, 103–122 (1978)
13. Meffert, H., Burmann, C., Kirchgeorg, M.: Marketing – Grundlagen marktorientierter Unternehmensführung, 11th edn. Gabler Verlag, Wiesbaden (2012)
14. Brown, T.C., Champ, P.A., Bishop, R.C., McCollum, D.W.: Which response format reveals the truth about donations to a public good? Land Econ. 72, 152–166 (1996). https://doi.org/10.2307/3146963
15. Damschroder, L.: An alternative approach for eliciting willingness-to-pay: A randomized internet trial. Judgm. Decis. Mak. 2(2), 96–106 (2007)
16. Balderjahn, I., Hedergott, D., Peyer, M.: Choice-Based Conjointanalyse. In: Baier D, Brusch M (ed) Conjointanalyse: Methoden, Anwendungen, Praxisbeispiele, pp. 129–146. Springer, Berlin, Heidelberg (2009)
17. Greene, W.H.: Econometric Analysis, 7th edn. Prentice Hall, Upper Saddle River (2012)
18. Bliss, C.I.: The method of probits. Science 79, 38–39 (1934). https://doi.org/10.1126/science.79.2037.38
19. Anandan, T. M.: Robotics-as-a-service benefits: Robotics-as-a-service helps with tighter global competition, allowing short-term robot without a long-term investment. One application reduced costs by 30%. Control Engi. 66(10), M1+ (2019)
20. Radic, M., Vosen, A.: Z. Gerontol. Geriatr. 53(7), 630–636 (2020). https://doi.org/10.1007/s00391-020-01791-6
21. Rebitschek, F.G., Wagner, G.G.: Z. Gerontol. Geriatr. 53(7), 637–643 (2020). https://doi.org/10.1007/s00391-020-01780-9
22. Łukasik, S., Tobis, S., Kropińska, S., Suwalska, A.: Role of assistive robots in the care of older people: survey study among medical and nursing students. J Med Internet Res 22(8), e18003 (2020). https://doi.org/10.2196/18003
23. Kuzmicheva, O., Martinez, S. F., Krebs, U., Spranger, M., Moosburner, S., Wagner, B., Gräser, A.: Overground robot based gait rehabilitation system MOPASS-overview and first results from usability testing. In: 2016 IEEE International Conference on Robotics and Automation (ICRA), pp. 3756–3763 (2016)
24. Fosch-Villaronga, E.: Robots, healthcare, and the law: Regulating automation in personal care. Routledge, London (2019)
25. Ivanov, S.: Ultimate transformation: How will automation technologies disrupt the travel, tourism and hospitality industries? Zeitschrift für Tourismuswissenschaft 11(1), 25–43 (2019). https://doi.org/10.1515/tw-2019-0003

Loneliness During COVID-19 Influences Mind and Likeability Ratings in the Uncanny Valley

Abdulaziz Abubshait[1]([✉]), Yicen Xie[2], Jung-Kuan Lin[2], Marissa Toma[2], and Eva Wiese[3]

[1] Italian Institute of Technology, Genova, Italy
abdulaziz.abubshait@iit.it
[2] George Mason University, Fairfax, VA, USA
[3] Technical University of Berlin, Berlin, Germany

Abstract. To combat the spread of the COVID-19 virus, countries enforced quarantines, physical and social restrictions on people. These restrictions left many feeling isolated and lonely due to prolonged quarantines and lockdowns. This raises questions about using robots as social support to alleviate these symptoms, while still complying with restrictions and regulations. Since acceptance of social robots as companions has traditionally been low, an event like COVID-19 could change acceptance of robots as social companions as loneliness can influence the likelihood of anthropomorphizing nonhuman agents. Here, we aimed to see if loneliness, due to COVID-19 restrictions, influence the Uncanny Valley pattern that prior work has shown. As such, participants saw robot images that varied in physical human-likeness and were asked to evaluate them regarding trustworthiness, mind perception and likability. The measurements were obtained once before COVID-19 (in 2016) and once at the peak of the pandemic in September 2020. Results show that ratings of mind perception and likability were significantly impacted by the pandemic, with less pronounced UV patterns for those who experienced the COVID-19 pandemic. However, no differences in the UV pattern was observed on trust. Post-hoc analyses also illustrated that people were more likely to judge machinelike robots negatively, which could be due to increased loneliness/anxiety. These data suggest that loneliness attenuates UV patterns that are observed in "Uncanny" robots and that people have more favorable attitudes towards humanlike robots when feeling lonely, which provides important considerations for the use of humanlike robots as social companions.

Keywords: Uncanny valley · Mind perception · Trust · Likability · Loneliness

1 Introduction

COVID-19 has been a global threat for people since the beginning of 2020. Despite the fact that pandemics are not novel, the specific economic, political, social and healthcare impacts of COVID-19 are unprecedented. As of September of 2021, the Center of Disease Control (CDC) showed that there have been more than 42 million confirmed cases of COVID-19 in the US and more than 214 million worldwide, with numbers still on the

F. Cavallo et al. (Eds.): ICSR 2022, LNAI 13818, pp. 248–262, 2022.
https://doi.org/10.1007/978-3-031-24670-8_23

rise. To combat the spread of the virus, countries have been recommending measures such as washing hands, wearing masks, social distancing and restricting unnecessary physical presence. Furthermore, many schools, businesses and public spaces moved their activities to online platforms [1]. Although social distancing measures can alleviate the spread of the virus, they have a significant impact on people's mental health. Specifically, loneliness during -or after- isolation caused by restrictive COVID-19 policies can cause negative effects, such as depression, helplessness and anxiety, which can lead to severe mental trauma in some people [1–5]. Saltzman and colleagues [6] investigated the potential impact of COVID-19 on loneliness and unhappiness, and showed that human social support is an effective coping strategy to alleviate loneliness and feelings of isolation. Thus, although people are protecting themselves and others from COVID-19 infections via social distancing, this intervention may have long-term negative consequences on people's mental health and wellbeing, which needs to be addressed.

Social robots could potentially address this issue given that they can serve as companions with complex social capabilities, while not posing risks of infection. Indeed, human-robot interaction (HRI) studies have found that companion robots can minimize feelings of loneliness by establishing different types of supportive relationships [7] and that certain degrees of social support can be established between robots and humans [8, 9]. These positive effects of social robots are particularly seen in older care homes, where the introduction of social robot companions leads to a general increase in well-being [10] and higher social engagement in dementia patients through interactions with the robot itself, as well as other patients as they engage with the robot together [11]. Interestingly, the introduction of social robots not only decreased stress levels in older patients but also in the care takers as a response to the increase in social engagement of their patients [12]. Social robots have also been successfully applied to other healthcare contexts: they can assist children and adults struggling with mental health issues to accomplish everyday tasks like going to a doctor's appointment [13, 14] or support stroke patients during their recovery process [15].

While positive effects of social robots on well-being have consistently been reported in the context of healthcare applications, the general population seems more reluctant to accept social robots as companions and do not easily engage in human-like interactions with them ([16] for a review). Neuroscience has shown that when we interact with other humans, areas in the brain that are specialized in processing social information are activated, which leads to an increased motivation to interact socially [17]. In order to fully activate these areas, our interaction partners need to be believed to have a mind - capable of having internal states like emotions, intentions and motivations (i.e., mind perception; [18]). Mind perception is not exclusive to agents who have a mind (e.g., humans), but it can also be ascribed to agents without actual minds, such as robots [18, 19]. The degree to which mind is perceived in nonhuman entities is modulated by their physical appearance [20–22], and robots that physically resemble humans are likely to be perceived to have sophisticated mental capacities, are evaluated more positively, make us feel socially more connected to them and lead to increased engagement in HRI [23].

Effects of physical human-likeness on social interactions are often examined with a spectrum of images that range from very machine-like to perfectly human-like [20, 24, 25]. Pak and colleagues [26], for instance, found increased trust in anthropomorphic compared to automated aids, and Lusk and Atkinson [27] reported that participants performed better when solving complex problems with an embodied human-like agent than with a disembodied machine-like agent. While these positive effects of physical human-likeness are observed when subjective ratings are used as outcome measures, the results are not nearly as straight forward when looking at cognitive performance in joint tasks ([28]; for review): For instance, Abubshait and colleagues [21] found that performance on a social attention task (i.e., identifying targets previously cued (or not) by the eye gaze of a social agent) was comparable across agents of all degrees of human-likeness, with the exception of a 60% human agent who showed a significantly stronger detrimental effect on performance than all the other agents. In line with this finding, Wiese and colleagues [29] showed that the presence of any kind of social agent had a facilitatory effect on performance during a sustained attention task (i.e., pressing a button when an agent of any kind of physical human-likeness is looking at a gun (but not a hairdryer), with the exception of a 70% human agent – which lead to a stronger vigilance decrement than very machinelike or perfectly human-like agents. Follow-up studies showed that processing the 70% human agent was associated with increased categorical uncertainty [30] and that pre-exposure to the agent images (which allowed participants to process them in more detail and resolve potential perceptual conflicts) [21, 29], suggesting that reduced performance on joint tasks with very human-like but not perfectly human agents may be due to uncertainty regarding the human nature of the agent.

The finding that agents with very human-like, but not perfectly human appearance have negative effects on HRI is in line with the Uncanny Valley (UV) theory [31]. It states that increasing the physical human-likeness of nonhuman entities initially increases ratings of warmth, familiarity, likability and/or eeriness, followed by a drop of these measures at around 70% of physical humanness, followed by a recovery and thus, an increase of agent ratings when physical humanlikeness reaches 100% human [32]. While the UV effect traditionally is related to feelings of eeriness and likability (or lack thereof), it can also extend to measures of trust [25] and mind perception [33, 34]. Since it was first proposed, the UV hypothesis has stimulated many controversial debates, due to scarce reliable and empirical supporting evidence ([32]; for review), and the majority of studies reporting a linear relationship between physical human-likeness and agent assessments instead [20, 24, 35]. Even to date, there is still a lot of inconsistency when comparing studies that look at the effect of varying levels of human-likeness on agent evaluations.

One explanation to these contradicting results could be due to the stimuli being used with evidence for a UV pattern when wild-type robot faces were used as stimuli [25], but no uniform evidence for an UV pattern with point-light figures [36] or morphed images [24]. In addition, individual differences in the observer [37] also seem to impact the evaluation of nonhuman agents: specifically, it was shown that – among other factors – higher compared to lower levels of anxiety and personal distress were associated with higher eeriness ratings for agents falling into the UV. It was also shown – although not in the context of the UV - that an increased need for social connection due to experimentally induced loneliness makes people perceive more human-likeness in nonhuman agents, and evaluate them more favorably (i.e., puppets: [38], robots: [39]). Specifically, people who reported feelings of loneliness were more likely to attribute human traits (e.g., free will) to inanimate objects (e.g., alarm clocks) in an attempt to fulfill their need for social connection [38]. Moreover, reminding people of their close relationships with humans reduced the extent to which nonhuman entities were anthropomorphized (e.g. [40]. People who were experimentally induced to feel lonely also attributed human traits to social robots [39]. Taken together, these studies suggest that negative emotional states, such as anxiety or loneliness, have an impact on how nonhuman agents are perceived. What has not been examined yet is how sustained aversive states induced by global disasters like the COVID-19 pandemic affect the non-rectilinear relationship between people's subjective assessments of nonhuman agents and the agents' human like physical appearance (i.e., the uncanny valley). However, in order to examine the potential of using companion robots to provide social support in times of crisis, it is absolutely essential to investigate how aversive emotional states associated with isolation and uncertainty affect people's perception of agents of varying levels of human-likeness.

To fill this gap and to build upon the unique circumstances caused by COVID-19, we explored whether and how people's evaluations of agents of varying degrees of human-likeness are changed during the pandemic compared it to pre-pandemic conditions. To do so, we compared data collected in September 2020 to the data of an identical experiment that was run before the COVID-19 pandemic in September 2016 [34]. In addition, we used the UCLA loneliness scale for the COVID-19 sample and assessed whether loneliness levels reported at the height of the pandemic influenced agent assessments.

2 Methods

2.1 Participants

Data from 69 students (46 females, M Age = 20.5) from George Mason University's student population were collected online in September 2020 and constitute the COVID-19 group. Five participants were excluded from data analysis for not completing the survey, which left the data of 64 participants for analysis. Participants received one course credit after completion via the university's participant pool (i.e., SONA system). The sample size was based the prior study [34] and kept equal to ensure sound comparisons. The PreCOVID-19 group consisted of 64 participants (33 females, M Age = 35), were participants collected online via MTurk and were not restricted to university students (see [34] for more details). Overall, data from 128 participants were included in the current study. Both studies were approved by GMU's Internal Review Board (IRB).

2.2 Agent Stimuli

The stimuli used in this experiment consisted of six images of agent faces that varied in physical humanlikeness from mechanistic robot to humanoid robot to human; see Fig. 1. The images were originally created by [25]. They were presented upright at a size of 274 × 338 pixels and were offset to the left; see Fig. 2. The trust, mind perception and likeability ratings were presented underneath the agent images.

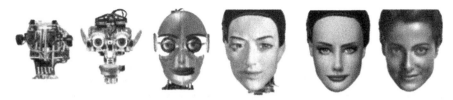

Fig. 1. We used six robot faces that participants assessed. The assessments were regarding whether the faces are trustworthy, whether they have a mind and weather they are likeable.

2.3 Procedure

All aspects of the experiment were programmed and presented in Qualtrics. Upon providing consent via Qualtrics, participants assessed different "robot faces" based on three measurements: trust, mind ratings and likability. The order of the measurements were assessed in separate blocks and were randomized between the participants. The order of the items within the measurements were counterbalanced and randomized for each face and the order of the faces was randomized; see Fig. 2. The rating scales were presented underneath the robot images. After completing the agent assessments, participants filled out the Revised UCLA loneliness scale (only the COVID-19 group). The PreCovid-19 group also completed individual difference questionnaires at the end of the task which were not included in the present study as the current research question is not concerned with individual differences in the UV, while the prior study was [34].

2.4 Trust

The trust measurement was based on [25] where participants were instructed that they have 100$ to share with each robot. Once they decided how much of the $100 to share with the robot, the money is given to the robot and tripled. Then, the robot will split the money how they see fit between itself and the participant. (For example, if the participant gives the robot $10, the robot will receive $30, and then split that $30 between the two of them). Any amount that the participant does not give to the robot is awarded to the participant. After deciding how much money goes to each robot, the imaginary money will be distributed according to the robots' decisions, and bonuses will be paid. Participants were not told how much money each robot gave to them to ensure that the sequence of presenting the robots did not influence their responses. As such, the amount of money that the participants gave to the robot was an index of how much they perceived it as trustworthy, with higher amounts correlating to more trust and lesser amounts meaning that participants did not trust the robot faces as much.

2.5 Mind Perception

The mind perception questionnaire was based on prior work that measured mind perception [41]. Here, participants were asked how much mind perception was perceived to each robot face (e.g., 'Rate how strongly you feel this robot has a mind', 'Do you think this robot likes to hang out with friends?'). The questions measured how much we perceived each robot to be able to experience internal states such as thoughts, emotion and feelings. The participants were asked to answer the questions on a scale of 1-to-7, with 1 being "Strongly disagree" and 7 being "Strongly Agree". Scoring was done by averaging all the items together. Higher mind perception ratings indicated more mind perception and vice-versa. There were a total of six robot images and six questions, putting the task at 30 questions total.

2.6 Likability

Here, participants were asked whether they thought each robot face was likable, which was based on Mathur and colleagues' work [25]. The question asked about each face's friendliness, enjoyableness and creepiness on a scale of −100-to- 100, with −100 being less friendly/more creepy, and 100 being more friendly/less creepy. Scoring was done by averaging all the items with higher likability scores suggesting higher likability. The likability section was used to ensure that we were replicating prior Uncanny Valley patterns with question that were traditionally used to measure the Uncanny Valley (e.g., creepiness and likability).

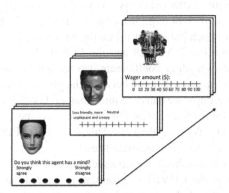

Fig. 2. Participants assessed the robot faces in a blocked manner with the order randomized within each block. The order of the blocks was also randomized between participants.

2.7 Loneliness Survey

Participants in the COVID-19 group completed a loneliness questionnaire after completing the agent assessment task. The survey assessed their level of loneliness and examine whether variations in the UV were due to loneliness scores. Specifically, we used the revised UCLA Loneliness scale [42, 43], which included statements such as 'I lack companionship' and 'There is no one I can turn to'. All items were answered with either 'Never', 'Rarely', 'Sometimes', or 'Often', which were scored with 0, 1, 2, or 3, respectively. Loneliness scores were created by summing the total of each participant's responses with higher scores indicating higher loneliness scoring for items 1, 4, 5, 6, 9, 10, 15, 16, 19 and 20 were reversed. This survey had a total of 20 items.

2.8 Analysis

The analysis of the data was borrowed from the method described in prior work [34, 36]. This method used a nested model comparison to test whether an nth level polynomial function fits the data better than a linear function using model difference statistics (e.g., Chi-Square difference test), and fit indices that penalize us for overfitting the data (e.g., BIC). Prior work suggests that if higher level polynomials fit better than a linear model, then it is considered evidence for the existence of a UV as the UV is characterized by a non-rectilinear pattern [36]. In addition to their method, we also included a dummy coded variable that indicated whether participants were in the PreCOVID-19 or COVID-19 group and an interaction between the dummy coded variable and the polynomial terms. As such, we compared a linear function to quadratic, cubic, quartic and quintic functions. All functions were fit using mixed linear models and contained a random intercept for each participant. This analysis was done to see if including an interaction term changes the model of best fit and to follow with the line of argumentation of prior work to ensure that we were observing an UV before directly comparing the two groups with one another.

After finding the function of best fit, we apply the function of best fit to each participant's individual data and extracted the polynomial derivative (i.e., coefficient) that is second to the leading coefficient (e.g., if the quintic function fits best, we extracted the 4th level coefficient for each participant). Finally, we compared the second-to-leading coefficients between the PreCOVID-19 and the COVID-19 groups using a t-test. By comparing the second-to-leading coefficients, we are able to determine whether the inflection point of each function differed between the groups. If the inflection point differed between the two groups, we can determine that the UV point differed significantly between the groups prior to rising again. This method was repeated for each of the three measurements separately. We used the False Discovery Rate (FDR) method to account for alpha inflation from conducting separate t-tests.

Finally, as a manipulation check, we ran a secondary nested model comparison to test if loneliness scores from the COVID-19 group, as measured via the UCLA loneliness questionnaire, interacted with the physical humanness to predict their assessments (i.e., trust, mind ratings and likability). If the interaction between the loneliness ratings and the physical humanness was meaningful in predicting agent assessments, then it would fit better than a model that does not contain the interaction. Thus, we are able to determine that modulations in the physical humanness-assessment relationship were due to group membership (i.e., PreCOVID-19 vs. COVID-19 group). To do so, we used an OLS regression with a single predictor (i.e., agent type) to predict the agent assessment. Next, we constructed a second OLS regression model that contained agent type, loneliness and their interaction as predictors of agent assessments. We used an OLS regression model as opposed to the polynomials for ease of interpretation of the analyses since we were not interested in characteristic shape of the relationship, but simply whether loneliness interacted with the physical humanness-agent assessment relationship. Finally, we compared the two models using an F-test to see if including loneliness scores and the interaction term predicted agent assessments significantly, above and beyond the single predictor model (i.e., with only agent type as a predictor). As such, we would predict that the model fit would be significantly better when we include the interaction between the loneliness scores and agent-type.

3 Results

3.1 Trust Results

Results of the model comparison for Trust showed that the quintic model fit significantly different than the linear model and was the best fit as it had the lowest BIC index (BIC $= 6883.1$, $\chi 2(2) = 19.68$, $p < 0.001$); See Table 1 and Fig. 3 for the results of the nested model comparison. Since the qui tic function fit the data best, we extracted the quartic coefficient separately for each participant and tested the between group differences using a t-test. The t-test showed no significant differences between the PreCovid-19 and the Covid-19 groups ($t(121.17) = -0.19$, $p = 0.84$, 95% CI $[-12.53, 10.31]$).

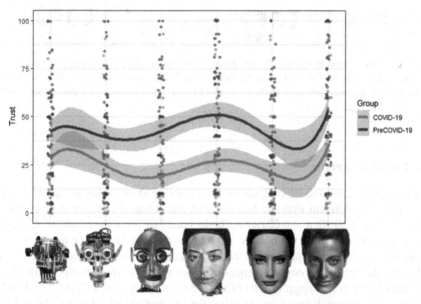

Fig. 3. The analysis showed that the quintic function fit the trust data best. Moreover, there were no detectable differences in polynomial derivatives (i.e., b coefficients) between the ProCOVID-19 and the COVID-19 groups. The shaded region represents the 95% confidence interval.

3.2 Mind Perception Results

Results of the nested model comparison for Mind Perception ratings showed that the quintic model fit significantly different than the linear model and it was the model of best as it had the lowest BIC value (BIC $= 2481.8$, $\chi 2(2) = 40.17$, $p < 0.001$); See Table 2 and Fig. 4 for the results of the nested model comparison. Since the quintic polynomial was the best fitting, we fit the function separately for each participant and extracted the quartic term to compare the UV point and tested the between group differences using a t-test. The t-test showed a significant difference between the ProCOVID-19 and the COVID-19 group (t(125.91) = 4.67, p < 0.001, 95% CI [0.80, 1.99], with lower polynomial derivative estimates for the PreCOVID-19 group (M = −1.73), compared to the COVID-19 group (M = −0.34).

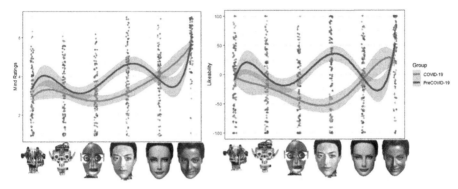

Fig. 4. Results showed that the quintic function fit the mind and likeability ratings best. Moreover, posthoc analyses showed significant differences in the UV point of the faces with a steeper UV for the PreCovid group compared to the COVID-19 group. The shaded region represents the 95% confidence interval.

3.3 Likability Results

Results of the nested model comparison for Likability showed that the quintic model fit significantly different than the linear model and it was the model of best (BIC = 8308.2, $\chi 2(2)$ = 30.90, p < 0.001); See Table 3 and Fig. 5 For the results of the nested model comparison. Since the quantic model was the best fitting, we fit the function separately for each participant and extracted the quartic term to compare the UV point and tested the between group differences using a t-test. The t-test showed a significant difference between the two groups (t(111.86) = 5.03, p < 0.001, 95% CI [51.77, 119.07]), with lower polynomial derivative estimates for the PreCOVID-19 group (M = 13.8), compared to the COVID-19 group (M = −71.6). P values of all the t-tests were corrected using the FDR method.

3.4 Loneliness Survey Results

Since we only find coefficient differences between the PreCOVID-19 and the COVID-19 groups in mind perception and likability ratings, we ran the manipulation check for only these two assessments. The results of the nested model comparison for the mind ratings showed that including the interaction between loneliness ratings and agent type predicted mind ratings above and beyond the single predictor model (F(2) = 3.86, SS = 14.34, p = .02) with the interaction model explaining 28% of the variance compared

Table 1. Model comparison of trust

	df	χ2	p	BIC
Linear				6895
Quadratic	2	20.81	<.001	6887.4
Cubic	2	2.52	<.001	6898.2
Quartic	2	21.98	<.001	6889.5
Quintic	2	19.68	<.001	6883.1

Table 2. Model comparison of MP

df	χ2	p	BIC
			2623.5
2	110.93	< 001	2525.8
2	15.61	< 001	2523.9
2	28.08	< 001	2508.7
2	40.17	< 001	2481.8

Table 3. Model comparison of likability

df	χ2	p	BIC
			8399.9
2	85.51	<.001	8327.7
2	4.85	.08	8336.1
2	23.61	<.001	8325.8
2	30.90	<.001	8308.2

to 26% of the variance for the single predictor model. The results of the nested model comparison for the likability ratings showed that including the interaction term between loneliness ratings and physical humanness predicted likability ratings above and beyond the single predictor model ($F(2) = 3.81$, $SS = 26914$, $p = .02$) with the interaction model explaining 4% of the variance compared to 2% of the variance for the single predictor model. Although these differences in the variance explained may seem negligible, it is not uncommon to see similar effects in social sciences. Since both models that contained the interaction between loneliness and physical humanness fit better than the model that predicted agent assessments from only physical humanness, we can conclude that the modulation that we observe in the UV pattern is due to participants' loneliness scores. As such, we can conclude that we passed the manipulation check.

3.5 Post-hoc Analysis

After fitting the models we descriptively observed that participants in the COVID-19 group judged the "machinelike" robots (i.e., robots that are considered to be low on physical human-likeness and do not traditionally evoke eerie/uncanny feelings) lower in mind and likability ratings overall compared to the PreCovid-19 group. To empirically test this observation, we averaged the scores of the first three robots for each of the two groups and compared them using a t-test. Results of the post-hoc t-test examining differences in mind ratings revealed that subjects in the COVID-19 group judged machinelike robots as having significantly less of a mind compared to the PreCOVID-19 group ($t(121.22)$ = -2.16, p = .04, 95% CI [-0.93, -0.04], M PreCOVID-19 = 3.40 vs. M COVID-19 = 2.91). Similarly, Participants in the COVID-19 group judged machinelike robots as significantly less likable compared to the PreCOVID-19 group ($t(125.79)$ = -2.03, p = .04, 95% CI [-31.74, -0.40], M PreCOVID-19 = -6.97 vs. M COVID-19 = -23.1). Both p values were corrected using the FDR method.

4   Discussion

Here, we aimed at investigating if perception of robots of varying degrees of human-likeness is changed during the COVID-19 pandemic. Specifically, we were interested in seeing whether the Uncanny Valley effect that has been shown in previous literature in ratings of trust, likability and mind ratings [25, 31, 34, 37] is changed due to feelings of loneliness. Thus, we asked all participants to judge robots of varying degrees of physical human-likeness on whether they trusted, perceived a mind to- and liked them. After completing these assessments, participants in the COVID-19 group rated their experience with loneliness during the COVID-19 pandemic via the UCLA loneliness questionnaire [42, 43]. The robot images that we used have previously shown a UV pattern on ratings of warmth, eeriness, likability and mind perception [25, 34]).

To examine whether UV was impacted by the COVID-19 pandemic, we compared data collected in September 2020 (during the pandemic) to data collected in September 2016 (before the pandemic); see Abubshait et al., 2017 [34] for the original dataset. Prior work has shown that people who experience loneliness are more likely to attribute human-like traits to nonhuman agents in an attempt to satisfy their need for social connection [39]. As such, we hypothesized that the Uncanny Valley effect should be attenuated for those who experienced loneliness during COVID-19 compared to those who did not. While our hypotheses were not supported for the trust task, we provide evidence for the assumption that loneliness during the COVID-19 pandemic influences the UV pattern for mind perception and likability ratings. Specifically, trust ratings showed that a UV shape was observed as the quintic function fit the data best, which also replicates prior work that shows that the UV pattern is shown when examining trust measures [25, 34]. However, there were no significant differences in the second-to-leading coefficient between the PreCOVID-19 and COVID-19 groups on measures of trust. This means that the inflection point of the UV effect was not different between those who experienced the COVID-19 pandemic and those who did not. With respect to the mind perception and likability ratings, the results showed that the UV shape existed as the quintic function was the best fitting model. Also, analyses for both these ratings showed that the inflection point

-as indicated by the second-to-leading coefficient- was significantly different between the PreCOVID-19 group and the COVID-19 group. The differences between the groups were such that very human-like (and traditionally uncanny) faces were perceived as more favorable for the COVID-19 group (i.e., less of an UV pattern) than the PreCOVID- 19 group. These differences are likely driven by the fact that participants in the COVID-19 group were experiencing loneliness as the manipulation check showed that loneliness ratings interacted with physical humanness and significantly explained more variance than physical humanness alone. This suggests that loneliness ratings were critical to understand the variations in ratings between the robot faces for those in the COVID-19 group, which is in line with our hypotheses (excluding the trust data).

The analyses of these data provide two major takeaways. First, the COVID-19 group perceived the uncanny faces as more favorable and having more mind. This effect can potentially be explained by prior work showing that loneliness increases sociality motivation (i.e., our need to have favorable social interaction with others [39]). Moreover, Eyssel and Reich [39] illustrated that these effects can extend to robots, where people who experience more loneliness are more likely to anthropomorphize and judge interactions with robots as more affectively pleasing. With regard to our data, it could be the case that increased feelings of loneliness that were brought on by lockdowns during the pandemic increased people's sociality motivation to interact with and seek social connection with others. As such, people were more likely to anthropomorphize human-like agents than mechanistic agents. Still, it is unclear why participants who experienced loneliness did not anthropomorphize all the robots to the same extent. The data observed here shows that these participants treated "mechanical" and "humanlike" robots categorically differently. One explanation could be that different agents of the categories would be influenced by loneliness differently, which is supported by prior work that suggests a categorical threshold that is observed between agents of varying physical humanness, which influences agent assessments [30]. However, this interpretation should be examined by future work.

Post-hoc analyses showed that the COVID-19 group judged "machine-like" robots more negatively with regard to likability (i.e., less likable/more eerie) and having less of a mind. This specific finding can be explained by prior work that showed that feelings of anxiety and uncertainty can increase people's likelihood to experience eeriness, which is negatively correlated with likability [44]. Since studies have shown that anxiety is correlated with feelings of loneliness [42], it is not surprising that people who experience loneliness could experience more adversity when facing uncertainty. This finding also fits with other studies that show that those influenced by the COVID-19 pandemic are more likely to engage in heuristic thinking [45]. In other words, heuristic thinking that is induced via loneliness could bias their responses to lower likability and mind ratings to resolve any eeriness feelings that could arise from uncertainty.

Together, our findings suggest that adversity during the COVID-19 pandemic biased people towards the extreme sides of the rating scales and away from the middle part of the scale. In other words people were more likely engage in heuristic thinking about these robots when rating them. As a result, machinelike robots were rated towards the left side of mind perception/likability scales (i.e., rated more negatively), while ratings for humanlike robots were biased towards the right (i.e., more positively). This specific finding has been shown in prior work that suggests that humans engage in categorical thinking when rating agents of varying degrees of humanness [24]. While their work did not focus on traits that cause people to be categorically biased in their subjective ratings towards robots (i.e., using only the extreme sides of a rating scale), it does invite questions for future work. For example, are robot/human traits that influence categorically biased responses towards robots? If so, do these translate to interaction with robots? Moreover, we invite future work to examine whether these effects translate to dynamic stimuli/real robots or are they solely observed in static images? Also, since we did not collect loneliness data in our PreCovid-19 group, it remains unclear to when extent this is correlated with our effects, which future work should address.

This experiment set out to examine the effects of loneliness that people experienced during the COVID-19 pandemic on the Uncanny Valley. Thus, we examined if the UV that prior work has shown is evident in people who were affected by the pandemic. The study showed that people were less likely to experience feelings of uncanniness when interacting with humanlike agents. However, they also perceived machinelike agents to be less likable and to have less of a mind. This has major implications for Human-Robot Interaction, as designers need to focus more on design implications that influence robots' appearance. For example, it seems that people are more willing to accept human-like robots as interaction partners. Another implication is that people are more critical of machine-like robots. This is an important consideration as people felt more positively towards, and were more likely to perceive minds to robots that are traditionally thought of as "Uncanny" robots. This specific finding marks a positive HRI finding as human acceptance of anthropomorphized and human-looking robots could be on the rise.

References

1. Ellis, K., Kao, K.-T., Pitman, T.: The pandemic preferred user. Fast Capital. **17**(2) (September 2020)
2. Bartoszek, A., Walkowiak, D., Bartoszek, A., Kardas, G.: Mental well-being (depression, loneliness, insomnia, daily life fatigue) during COVID-19 related home-confinement—a study from Poland. Int. J. Environ. Res. Public Health. **17**(20), 7417 (January 2020), Publisher: Multidisciplinary Digital Publishing Institute
3. Brooks, S.K., et al.: The psychological impact of quarantine and how to reduce it: rapid review of the evidence. Lancet **395**(10227), 912–920 (2020)
4. Groarke, J.M., Berry, E., Graham-Wisener, L., McKenna-Plumley, P.E., McGlinchey, E., Armour, C.: Loneliness in the UK during the COVID-19 pandemic: cross-sectional results from the COVID-19 psychological wellbeing study. PLoS One. **15**(9), e0239698 (September 2020). Publisher: Public Library of Science
5. Matias, T., Dominski, F.H., Marks, D.F.: Human needs in COVID-19 isolation. J. Health Psychol. **25**(7), 871–882 (June 2020). Publisher: SAGE Publications Ltd
6. Saltzman, L.Y., Hansel, T.C., Bordnick, P.S.: Loneliness, isolation, and social support factors in post-COVID-19 mental health. Psychol. Trauma Theor. Res. Pract. Policy. **12**(S1), S55–S57 (2020). Place: US Publisher: Educational Publishing Foundation
7. Odekerken-Schröder, G., Mele, C., Russo-Spena, T., Mahr, D., Ruggiero, A.: Mitigating loneliness with companion robots in the COVID-19 pandemic and beyond: an integrative framework and research agenda. J. Serv. Manage. **31**(6), 1149–1162 (January 2020). Publisher: Emerald Publishing Limited

8. Murphy, R.R., Gandudi, V.B.M., Adams, J.: Applications of robots for COVID-19 response. (August 2020)
9. Aymerich-Franch, L., Ferrer, I.: The implementation of social robots during the COVID-19 pandemic. arXiv:2007.03941 [cs] (January 2021)
10. Wada, K., Shibata, T.: Living with seal robots—its sociopsychological and physiological influences on the older at a care house. IEEE Trans. Robot. **23**(5), 972–980 (October 2007). Conference Name: IEEE Transactions on Robotics
11. Tamura, T., et al.: Is an entertainment robot useful in the care of older people with severe dementia? J. Gerontol. Ser. A **59**(1), M83–M85 (2004)
12. Wada, K., Shibata, T., Saito, T., Tanie, K.: Effects of robot-assisted activity for older people and nurses at a day service center. In: Proceedings of the IEEE, vol. 92(11), pp. 1780–1788 (November 2004). Conference Name: Proceedings of the IEEE
13. Alemi, M., Meghdari, A., Ghanbarzadeh, A., Moghadam, L.J., Ghanbarzadeh, A.: Impact of a social humanoid robot as a therapy assistant in children cancer treatment. In: Beetz, M., Johnston, B., Williams, M.-A. (eds.) Social Robotics, ser. Lecture Notes in Computer Science, pp. 11–22. Springer International Publishing, Cham (2014)
14. Libin, A., Libin, E.: Person-robot interactions from the robopsychologists' point of view: the robotic psychology and robotherapy approach. In: Proceedings of the IEEE, vol. 92(11), pp. 1789–1803 (November 2004). Conference Name: Proceedings of the IEEE
15. Tapus, A., Ţăpuş, C., Matarić, M.J.: User—robot personality matching and assistive robot behavior adaptation for post-stroke rehabilitation therapy. Intel. Serv. Robotics. **1**(2), 169 (February 2008)
16. Wiese, E., Metta, G., Wykowska, A.: Robots as intentional agents: using neuroscientific methods to make robots appear more social. Front. Psychol. **8** (October 2017)
17. Frith, C.D., Frith, U.: The neural basis of mentalizing. Neuron **50**(4), 531–534 (2006)
18. Gray, H.M., Gray, K., Wegner, D.M.: Dimensions of mind perception. Science. **315**(5812), 619 (February 2007). Publisher: American Association for the Advancement of Science
19. Wiese, E., Wykowska, A., Zwickel, J., Müller, H.J.: I see what you mean: how attentional selection is shaped by ascribing intentions to others. PLoS One. **7**(9), e45391 (September 2012)
20. Looser, C.E., Wheatley, T.: The tipping point of animacy: how, when, and where we perceive life in a face. Psychol. Sci. **21**(12), 1854–1862 (2010)
21. Abubshait, A., Momen, A., Wiese, E.: Pre-exposure to ambiguous faces modulates top-down control of attentional orienting to counterpredictive gaze cues. Front. Psychol. **11**(2234) (2020). https://doi.org/10.3389/fpsyg.2020.02234
22. Wiese, E., Buzzell, G.A., Abubshait, A., Beatty, P.J.: Seeing minds in others: mind perception modulates low-level social-cognitive performance and relates to ventromedial prefrontal structures. Cogn. Affect. Behav. Neurosci. **18**(5), 837–856 (2018). https://doi.org/10.3758/s13415-018-0608-2
23. Epley, N., Waytz, A., Cacioppo, J.T.: On seeing human: a three-factor theory of anthropomorphism. Psychol. Rev. **114**(4), 864–886 (2007)
24. Martini, M.C., Gonzalez, C.A., Wiese, E.: Seeing minds in others - can agents with robotic appearance have human-like preferences? PLoS ONE **11**(1), 1–23 (2016)
25. Mathur, M.B., Reichling, D.B.: Navigating a social world with robot partners: a quantitative cartography of the Uncanny Valley. Cognition. **146**, 22–32 (2016). Publisher: Elsevier B.V
26. Pak, R., Fink, N., Price, M., Bass, B., Sturre, L.: Decision support aids with anthropomorphic characteristics influence trust and performance in younger and older adults. Ergonomics **55**(9), 1059–1072 (2012)
27. Lusk, M., Atkinson, R.: Animated pedagogical agents: does their degree of embodiment impact learning from static or animated worked examples?. Appl. Cogn. Psychol. **21**(December 2006), 747–764 (2007)

28. Roesler, E., Manzey, D., Onnasch, L.: A meta-analysis on the effectiveness of anthropomorphism in human-robot interaction. Sci. Robot. **6**(58), eabj5425 (September 2021). Publisher: American Association for the Advancement of Science
29. Wiese, E., Mandell, A., Shaw, T., Smith, M.: Implicit mind perception alters vigilance performance because of cognitive conflict processing. J. Exp. Psychol. Appl. **25**(1), 25–40 (2019)
30. Weis, P., Wiese, E.: Cognitive Conflict as Possible Origin of the Uncanny Valley. (October 2017)
31. Mori, M.: The uncanny valley: The original essay by masahiro mori, pp. 33–35 (1970)
32. Kätsyri, J., Förger, K., Mäkäräinen, M., Takala, T.: A review of empirical evidence on different uncanny valley hypotheses: support for perceptual mismatch as one road to the valley of eeriness. Front. Psychol. **6**(MAR), 1–16 (2015)
33. Gray, K., Wegner, D.M.: Feeling robots and human zombies: mind perception and the uncanny valley. Cognition **125**(1), 125–130 (2012)
34. Abubshait, A., Momen, A., Wiese, E.: Seeing human: do individual differences modulate the Uncanny Valley? Proc. Hum. Fact. Ergon. Soc. Ann. Meet. **61**(1), 870–874 (2017)
35. Cheetham, M., Suter, P., Jancke, L.: Perceptual discrimination difficulty and familiarity in the Uncanny Valley: more like a 'Happy Valley'. Front. Psychol. **5**(OCT), 1–15 (2014)
36. Thompson, J.C., Trafton, J.G., McKnight, P.: The perception of humanness from the movements of synthetic agents. Perception **40**(6), 695–704 (2011)
37. MacDorman, K.F., Entezari, S.O.: Individual differences predict sensitivity to the uncanny valley. Interact. Stud. **16**(2), 141–172 (2015)
38. Epley, N., Waytz, A., Akalis, S., Cacioppo, J.T.: When we need a human: motivational determinants of anthropomorphism. Soc. Cogn. **26**(2), 143–155 (2008)
39. Eyssel, F., Reich, N.: Loneliness makes the heart grow fonder (of robots) — on the effects of loneliness on psychological anthropomorphism. In: 2013 8th ACM/IEEE International Conference on Human-Robot Interaction (HRI), pp. 121–122 (March 2013)
40. Bartz, J.A., Tchalova, K., Fenerci, C.: Reminders of social connection can attenuate anthropomorphism: a replication and extension of Epley, Akalis, Waytz, and Cacioppo (2008). Psychol. Sci. **27**(12), 1644–1650 (December 2016). Publisher: SAGE Publications Inc
41. Hackel, L.M., Looser, C.E., Van Bavel, J.J.: Group membership alters the threshold for mind perception: the role of social identity, collective identification, and intergroup threat. J. Exp. Soc. Psychol. **52**, 15–23 (2015)
42. Russell, D., Peplau, L.A., Cutrona, C.E.: The revised UCLA loneliness scale: concurrent and discriminant validity evidence. J. Personal. Soc. Psychol. **39**(3), 472–480 (1980). Place: US Publisher: American Psychological Association
43. Russell, D.W.: UCLA loneliness scale (version 3): reliability, validity, and factor structure. J. Personal. Assess. **66**(1), 20–40 (February 1996). Publisher: Routledgr
44. MacDorman, K.F., Entezari, S.O.: Individual differences predict sensitivity to the uncanny valley. Interact. Stud. **16**(2), 141–172 (January 2015). Publisher: John Benjamins
45. de Melo, C.M., Gratch, J., Krueger, F.: Heuristic thinking and altruism toward machines in people impacted by COVID-19. iScience **24**(3), 102228 (March 2021)

Telepresence Robot for Isolated Patients in the COVID-19 Pandemic: Effects of Socio-relationship and Telecommunication Device Types on Patients' Acceptance of Robots

Soyeon Shin⬤, Dahyun Kang⬤, and Sonya S. Kwak$^{(⊠)}$ ⬤

Center for Intelligent and Interactive Robotics, Korea Institute of Science and Technology, Seoul 02792, Korea
{soyeonshin,dahyun,sonakwak}@kist.re.kr

Abstract. Telecommunication devices can help mitigate the spread of the COVID-19 virus among the patients quarantined in hospitals. In contrast to the conventional telecommunication devices, a telepresence robot can deliver tangible communication cues from a remote sender to a receiver that vary according to level of interaction modalities. In the context of the COVID-19 pandemic, telecommunication interactants can be divided into two categories based on their socio-relationships. The types include those engaged in social-oriented relationships such as that between patients and families or acquaintances, and task-oriented relationships such as those between patients and doctors or nurses. We hypothesize that the types of telecommunication device used and socio-relationship would be factors affecting the COVID-19 patients' telecommunication experiences and acceptance of telepresence robots. We conducted a user study comparing three types of telecommunication devices namely floor-based robot versus desk-based robot versus tablet with the aforementioned two types of socio-relationships. The results indicated that the participants preferred telecommunication service in a social-oriented relationship to a task-oriented relationship. A mediation analysis revealed that social presence, competency, and familiarity mediates the effects of socio-relationship type on the satisfaction of the telecommunication service. Based on the socio-relationship type, different tendencies on the effect of telecommunication device types on service evaluation were observed.

Keywords: Telepresence robot · Socio-relationship type · Social presence

1 Introduction

To reduce the amount of face-to-face contact and prevent the spread of COVID-19, various attempts are being made to apply telepresence robots to hospital environments [1–7].

This work was supported by the Korea Institute of Science and Technology (KIST) Institutional Program under Grant (2E31581) and the Government-wide R&D Fund for Infections Disease Research (GFID), funded by the Ministry of the Interior and Safety, Republic of Korea (20014463). S. Shin and D. Kang—Equally contributed to this work.

F. Cavallo et al. (Eds.): ICSR 2022, LNAI 13818, pp. 263–276, 2022.
https://doi.org/10.1007/978-3-031-24670-8_24

Telepresence robots provide telemedicine [8] and virtual visiting services to patients who are isolated without the ability to see their families [1–3]. For example, a telepresence robot can support end-of-life conversation in palliative care [4, 5]. The telepresence robot "UBBO" has been used in the hospitals providing the virtual visits between families and patients in isolated rooms [7]. A virtual visit through a telepresence robot can help with the mental health of the patients. COVID-19 patients in an intensive care unit (ICU) with family visitation, either face-to-face or virtually, have shown a 30% lower risk of delirium compared to patients with limited family visits [9]. In terms of telemedicine, the social robot "Pudu" used in Chilean hospitals provides telecommunication service between COVID-19 patients and clinicians, particularly neurologists and psychologists [6]. In this way, a telepresence robot widens the opportunity for emotional exchanges between patients and family members, as well as safe treatment by medical staff, and it can be expected that the demand for telepresence robots will increase during this pandemic. Accordingly, the need for research on telepresence robot designs to effectively mediate remote senders and receivers is emerging.

Despite various attempts to apply telepresence robots to virtual visits and telemedicine for isolated COVID-19 patients [10], there is a lack of research on effective methods of human-robot interaction. In a previous study by Rae et al., the authors explored how the height of a floor-based telepresence robot affects the dominance and impressions of the remote sender during a negotiation and found that there was a significant difference in users' evaluations based on robot height [11]. In addition, Sirkin and Ju explored how the synchronized on-screen and in-space gestures of a desk-based telepresence robot affect the viewers' interpretation of the sender during a telepresence meeting and found a positive impact of the synchronization of a telepresence robot [12]. Although these studies investigated the impact of the attributes of a telepresence robot, such as the height and synchronized movement on users' acceptance of the robot, they were limited to a specific type of telepresence robot, either a floor- or a desk-based robot within a situation in which the users are remote but not in compulsory isolation. As in the COVID-19 pandemic, patients who are isolated from others can expect different modalities from a robot, and the impact of the type of telepresence robot on patients' acceptance needs to be explored. In addition, because a telepresence robot provides telecommunication services between the sender and receiver, the socio-relationship between telecommunication parties can affect the user's adoption of a telepresence robot [13]. Under the COVID-19 pandemic, the socio-relationship of the patients and their families during virtual visitations, and that of the patients and medical staff during medical consultations, differ in terms of intimacy level. Thus, it is necessary to explore a patient's adoption of a telepresence robot based on the socio-relationship type.

In this paper, we investigate how people perceive telecommunication differently according to the socio-relationship type between the patient and the interaction partner as well as the type of telepresence robot. We consider two modes of conversations according to socio-relationship types in which telepresence robots are mainly used in hospitals, i.e., virtual family visits, in which a social-oriented conversation with an intimate person takes place; and remote medical consultations, where a task-oriented conversation with a non-intimate person occurs. In addition, we compare these experiences according to the type of telepresence robot, i.e., desk- or floor-based. As a baseline, we added a tablet, which people most commonly use when they have a remotely sharing experience [14].

2 Related Works

2.1 Socio-relationship Type Between Telecommunication Parties in COVID-19 Pandemic

The types of socio-relationships can be divided into two, i.e., a professional relationship and a personal relationship [15]. A professional relationship is formed based on a task-oriented relationship in which the goals of the interaction parties' activities and attentions are external to their relationship [15, 16]. A personal relationship is constructed based on a social-oriented relationship in which the relationship itself and the people involved in the relationship is a matter of concern [15, 16].

Virtual visits and medical consultations are representative cases in which a telepresence robot can be used for COVID-19 patients in a hospital [17]. In a virtual family/friend visit, a conversation takes place between people in a social-oriented relationship. The conversation is characterized by casual and informal dialog in the exchange of socioemotional information [12, 18]. In a social-oriented conversation, to achieve socioemotional goals, interactants communicate by using socioemotional behaviors including positive expression, emotional support, and so on [12, 19]. By contrast, a medical consultation is a conversation which occurs between people in a task-oriented relationship. The conversation involves formal dialog in exchanging a patient's medical information. In a task-oriented conversation, to achieve functional goals, medical staff communicate by using task-focused behaviors, such as asking biomedical questions, giving biomedical information and counseling [12, 19].

The isolated COVID-19 patients have communications with their families, friends and medical staff. Families and friends, the subjects of sharing social-oriented conversation through virtual visits, have an intimate socio-relationship with the patient, whereas medical staff having task-oriented conversation through medical consultations have a non-intimate relationship with the patient. Kang's study demonstrated that participants who have a conversation remotely using a telepresence robot with an intimate person have a willingness to continue the interaction for a longer period of time and were more satisfied with the robot than with a non-intimate person [20]. Thus, it is expected that service of a telepresence robot will be evaluated more positively when the COVID-19 patient has a social-oriented conversation with an intimate person than when having a task-oriented conversation with a non-intimate person in a hospital.

Based on these backgrounds, we formulated the following hypotheses.

H1: Depending on the socio-relationship type, the telecommunication service will be evaluated differently.

The socio-relationship between the receiver and the sender can affect the social presence of the remote sender. Kang determined that participants perceived a greater social presence of the remote sender when telecommunicating with an intimate person than with a non-intimate person [20]. Verhagen et al. also revealed that the friendliness of an agent has a positive effect on the social presence of the agent [21]. In addition, Lee et al. found that social presence was a significant positive predictor of evaluation toward the agent [22]. Thus, during the COVID-19 pandemic in which the patients should be isolation from intimate friends and family members, it is likely that social presence, which could be affected by the socio-relationship type between interactants, can also have a positive effect on the service evaluation of a telepresence robot.

This analysis led to the following hypothesis.

H1-1: During the COVID-19 pandemic, the effect of the socio-relationship type on the evaluation of the telecommunication service will be mediated by the perceived social presence of the sender.

Verhagen et al. found that the characteristics of an agent, such as expertise and friendliness, can affect the social presence of an agent, which again has a positive effect on the level of service satisfaction regarding the agent [21]. It is expected that the perceived degree of competency might be associated with a task-oriented conversation such as a medical consultation, whereas the perceived familiarity is related to a social-oriented conversation such as a virtual visit. Thus, we expect that the perceived impressions of the remote sender including competency and familiarity can mediate the effect of the socio-relationship type between interactants on the telecommunication service.

This analysis led to the following hypothesis.

H1-2: During the COVID-19 pandemic, the effect of the socio-relationship type on the evaluation of the telecommunication service will be mediated by the perceived competency of the sender.

H1-3: During the COVID-19 pandemic, the effect of the socio-relationship type on the evaluation of the telecommunication service will be mediated by the perceived familiarity of the sender.

2.2   Telecommunication Device Type

Unlike traditional telecommunication devices, such as smartphones or tablet PCs, which support telecommunication through audio and visual cues, telepresence robots provide telecommunication services through not only audio and visual cues but also tangible communication cues using a physical embodiment and movements [23]. Because a telepresence robot delivers tangible communication cues in addition to audiovisual cues that can be delivered by other telecommunication devices, it can make a receiver feel more social presence of the remote sender. According to James et al.'s study, people feel a higher social presence of a remote sender when using a telepresence robot than when using an interface such as Skype [24].

According to the level of interaction modalities provided, telepresence robots can be classified into two types i.e., desk- and floor-based telepresence robots [25]. A desk-based robot provides head movement and audiovisual modality, whereas a floor-based robot offers mobility in addition to the modalities provided by a desk-based robot [26, 27]. A floor-based robot is able to move close to or far away from the patient through autonomous driving using wheels. With such mobility, a floor-based robot can deliver the desired movement of a remote sender more clearly by providing richer tangible communication cues than a desk-based robot. The social presence was affected by tangible communication cues of telecommunication devices [24], and it positively affected the evaluation toward the robot [22]. Thus, it is expected that the evaluation of the telecommunication service as well as social presence of an interactant would be different by telecommunication device type.

Based on these backgrounds, we formulated the following hypotheses.

H2: Depending on the telecommunication device type, the telecommunication service will be evaluated differently.

H2-1: During the COVID-19 pandemic, the effect of the telecommunication device type on the evaluation of the telecommunication service will be mediated by the perceived social presence of the sender.

2.3 Socio-relationship Type and Telecommunication Device Type in COVID-19 Pandemic

During pre-COVID-19 pandemic era in which patients were able to have face-to face visits and medical consultations, telecommunication was one of the options for interacting with the family members or medical staff. Contrarily, for COVID-19 patients, face-to-face contact is strongly limited because they are forcibly isolated to prevent the spread of the virus. For them, telecommunication is not an option they can choose, but the only way to see other individuals. In this vein, we expect that COVID-19 patients may have a greater desire to have communication opportunities that are similar to face-to-face communication than patients in pre-COVID-19.

We expected that the participants would be more satisfied with a telecommunication device providing richer tangible communication cues during the COVID-19 pandemic in H2. This is because the previous studies figured out that the interaction modalities of a telecommunication device can be an important factor enhancing the telecommunication quality by making the patients feel as if they are together with others [22, 28]. However, the degree of tangible communication cues that the patients want to use may differ depending on the interactant with which the patient communicates using a telecommunication device. According to Kang's study, the satisfaction of the telepresence robot differs depending on the socio-relationship type [20]. Moreover, James, Wise, and Langenhoves' study found that when people do social networking in a conference, they were more satisfied when using a floor-based robot compared to a tablet [24]. Therefore, it is expected that in a social-oriented conversation, in which COVID-19 patient who wants more social presence of their family and acquaintances, a device with greater degree of tangible communication cues could be welcomed. By contrast, in conversation with a person who is in a task-oriented relationship, such as medical staff, tangible communication cues might not be as powerful as in conversation with a person who is in a social-oriented relationship. Thus, we expected the differences in service evaluation by types of telecommunication device will be different according to the socio-relationship type.

This analysis led to the following hypothesis.

H3: In a social-oriented relationship, the telecommunication service will be evaluated differently depending on the telecommunication device type.

H4: In a task-oriented relationship, the telecommunication service will not be evaluated differently depending on the telecommunication device type.

3 Method

The experiment was a 2 (between-subjects: socio-relationship type between telecommunication parties, social-oriented relationship versus task-oriented relationship) × 3 (within-subjects: telecommunication device type, tablet versus desk-based robot versus floor-based robot) mixed-subjects design.

3.1 Participants

A total of 96 participants (64 females and 32 males) were recruited. The mean age of the participants was 30.07 years ($SD = 5.81$), ranging in age from 21 to 47 years. Among 96 participants, 77 of the participants had the experience of a quarantine, and none of the participants had been infected by the COVID-19 before. Since we recruited a sufficient number of participants, we could eliminate individual difference of each participant and ensure generalization of the results.

3.2 Stimuli

We made video stimuli to conduct online experiment. The floor-based robot used in the experiment was Temi. Temi can make a video call through a tablet placed on the head. It can move to a pre-designated location through autonomous driving. The remote sender can use a Temi mobile or web application to move the robot's location or control the head movement during a video call. The desk-based robot used in the experiment was Kubi, which can be used by inserting a tablet on the top, and can pan, nod, and tilt allowing the remote user to rotate the tablet in a desired direction. The tablet used in the experiment was an iPad. Under this scenario, a video call was made using Facetime on an iPad.

The experiment scenarios were created based on a situation in which telecommunication devices are applied in a hospital, i.e., virtual family visits and medical consultations. Under the conditions of a social-oriented relationship, a patient in a ward uses a telecommunication device during a virtual family visit with her sister, and under the condition of a task-oriented relationship, she uses a telepresence robot for a medical consultation with a doctor as shown in Table 1. Each of the two scripts consists of five turn-takes with similar lengths of speech, and the number of words in each script was set to be the same as 109. Under each scenario, the robot moves its head up and down or turns its head or body left and right. The tablet does neither turn its head to look around nor move. When using the floor-based robot, Temi, the robot enters alone remotely through the remote user's manipulation and stops in front of the patient. When using the desk-based robot, Kubi, or a tablet, a nurse in a protective suite enters and sets the devices on the table above the bed and then leaves.

Table 1. Experimental material

Socio-relation ship Type	Telepresence Robot Type		
	Floor-based robot	*Desk-based robot*	*Tablet*
Social-oriented			
Task-oriented			

Under the condition of a social-oriented relationship, the patient makes a video call with her sister for the first time after being hospitalized. The sister looks at the patient and around the room through the telepresence robot, or the robot turns its head in the direction where the patient is pointing during the video call. Under the condition of a task-oriented relationship, the doctor looks at the red spots on the patient's arm, verifies the patient's information and discusses the medication and symptoms. The detailed scenario of each condition is in Table 2.

3.3 Procedures

As it was prohibited to conduct face to face experiments due to the COVID-19, the experiment had to be conducted online. The participants were recruited through email connected to the given link. After receiving a brief guideline regarding the experiment and writing a consent form, a participant watched the video clips in order according to the experimental condition. After watching each video, the participant answered the questionnaire online. The participants were divided into two groups according to the socio-relationship type i.e., family visit or medical consultation. The participants were randomly assigned to either a family visit or a medical consultation condition. Each participant watched three types of videos: a video using a floor-based robot, a desk-based robot, and a tablet. The order of the telepresence robot type shown was counterbalanced to avoid the influence of a repeated experiment sequence. For a more immersive focus on a given video, the participants were encouraged to wear headsets or earphones while watching the video clips.

Table 2.   Detail scenario of each conditions

Socio-relationship Type					
Social-oriented relationship (virtual family visit)			*Task-oriented relationship (medical consultation)*		
Temi: *(Temi comes in remotely)*	Kubi: *(a nurse comes in and sets Kubi on the desk)*		Tablet: *(a nurse comes in and sets the tablet on the desk)*		
(When the video call screen is on display, the patient receives the call)					
Family member: How are you? Are you feeling well?			Doctor: How are you today? Did you sleep well?		
Temi: *(the robot head moves up and down)*	Kubi: *(the robot head moves up and down)*	Tablet: *(no movement)*	Patient: Yes, I slept well. But, I think I have red hives on my arms.		
Patient: I'm okay. I slept well too. But it's so boring here. I can't go out and there's nobody to talk to.			Doctor: Can you show me your arm?		
Family member: I know. It would be too hard to stay in the room for more than a week. How's the ward? Is there a restroom inside the room, too?			Patient: Okay. *(the patient rolls up the sleeve and brings the arm closer to the screen)*		
Patient: Yes. It's right next to my bed. *(pointing to the side where the toilet is)*			Temi: *(the robot head moves up and down)*	Kubi: *(the robot head moves up and down)*	Tablet: *(no movement)*
Temi: *(the robot turns and moves in the direction where the finger is pointing)*	Kubi: *(the tablet on the top rotates in the direction where the finger is pointing)*	Tablet: *(no movement)*	Doctor: This seems to be a temporary phenomenon due to the high fever. For now, there is no need to worry, and if this condition persists, please tell me again.		
Family member: I see. Are you alone in the room?			Patient: Okay, I will.		
Temi: *(the robot turns and moves from side to side)*	Kubi: *(the tablet on the top rotates from side to side)*	Tablet: *(no movement)*	Doctor: Then, I'll let you know the results.		
Family member: You might be depressed without seeing the sunlight.			Temi: *(the robot turns and moves to see the patient's name plate)*	Kubi: *(the tablet on the top rotates to see the patient's name plate)*	Tablet: *(no movement)*
Patient: Yes. That's true. But it makes me feel better when I talk to you and friends on video call.			Doctor: The inflammation in your lungs seems to be disappearing compared with last week. However, the oxygen saturation is still low, so we should keep an eye on it.		
Family member: We've felt so lonely and empty since you're been gone. Mom and Dad are worrying a lot too. I hope you get well soon and come home.			Patient: Okay. I also feel a bit nauseous after taking the new medicine from yesterday.		
Patient: I want to go home soon, too.			Doctor: Because of the antibiotics, you may feel a little nauseous.		
Family member: Okay, then take a rest. I have to go to work now, so I'll call you later			Temi: *(the robot turns and moves to see the patient's name plate)*	Kubi: *(the tablet on the top rotates to see the patient's name plate)*	Tablet: *(no movement)*
Patient: Okay. Call me when you get back home after work since I'm alone here.			Doctor: Then, I will reduce the dose of medicine or prescribe a stomach medicine together.		
			Patient: Okay. Thank you.		

3.4 Measures

During this experiment, the feeling of social presence was measured based on six items drawn from Nowak and Biocca's study [27]. The measurements included items such as "To what extent did you feel like you were inside the environment you saw/heard?" and "To what extent did you feel able to assess the remote sender's reactions to what you said?". The measurements were evaluated on a 7-point Likert scale.

The competency of the remote sender through the telepresence robot was measured based on five items from Andrist et al.'s study. The questionnaire was modified according to our scenario since the original text evaluated the competency of the robot that introduces landmarks worth visiting [28]. The measure included items such as "The remote sender provided by the telepresence robot was informative", "The remote sender provided by the telepresence robot handled the work like an expert", "The remote sender provided by the telepresence robot was knowledgeable", "The remote sender provided by the telepresence robot had significant expertise", and "The remote sender provided by the telepresence robot seemed to have a deep knowledge." The measurements were evaluated on a 7-point Likert scale.

The familiarity of the remote sender through the telepresence robot was measured based on 11 items from Kanda et al.'s study [29]. The participants answered a question to rate 11 adjective pairs on a 7-point scale, such as "friendly/unfriendly" and "kind/cruel."

The level of satisfaction regarding the telecommunication service was measured based on three items, drawn from Lee et al.'s study [30]. We asked the participants to rate whether the robot provided a good or poor service (1 = "very poor" and 7 = "very good"), how likely the participants believed the patient would use the service again (1 = "would avoid using the service" and 7 = "would want very much to use the service") and how satisfied the patient would be while using this service (1 = "completely dissatisfied" and 7 = "completely satisfied").

4 Results

4.1 Effects of Socio-relationship Type

An analysis of the evaluation of the telecommunication service with respect to the socio-relationship type was carried out using an independent t-test. As predicted by H1, there was a significant effect of socio-relationship type on service evaluation ($t(286) = 2.67$, $p = 0.008$). Participants who had a social-oriented conversation ($M = 5.58, SD = 1.16$) evaluated the telecommunication service more positively than participants who had a task-oriented conversation ($M = 5.20, SD = 1.27$) as shown in Fig. 1.

To evaluate the mediation effects, we employed the SPSS PROCESS macro, a computational tool for testing mediation and moderation as well as their combination [31]. We used PROCESS model 4 to test the hypotheses about the mediating effects. The results indicated that the intimacy level of socio-relationship was a significant positive predictor of social presence ($b = 0.78, SE = 0.16, p < 0.001$), a significant negative predictor of competency ($b = -0.50, SE = 0.13, p = 0.0001$), and a significant positive predictor of familiarity ($b = 1.02, SE = 0.10, p < 0.001$). Moreover, social presence was a significant positive predictor of service evaluation ($b = 0.37, SE = 0.05, p < 0.001$), as were competency ($b = 0.23$, $SE = 0.06$, $p = 0.0005$) and familiarity ($b = 0.29$, $SE = 0.08$, $p = 0.0004$). These results support the mediation hypothesis, H1–1, H1–2, and H1–3. The level of intimacy in socio-relationship was no longer a significant predictor of service evaluation after controlling for the mediator ($b = -0.10$, $SE = 0.14$, $p = 0.5051$), consistent with the full mediation (see Fig. 1).

4.2 Effects of Telecommunication Device Type

An analysis of the evaluation of the telecommunication service with respect to the telecommunication device type was carried out using a one-way ANOVA. According to our data, H2 was not supported. There was no significant effect of telecommunication device type on service evaluation ($F(2,285) = 2.520$, $p = 0.082$). This result showed that there is no difference on participant's satisfaction depending on telecommunication device type. Since the main effect of telecommunication device type in H2 was not supported, the mediating effect cannot be seen. Thus, H2–1 was also rejected. (see Fig. 2).

4.3 Effects of Telecommunication Device Type Per Socio-relationship Type

Service evaluation by socio-relationship type and (b) Mediation analysis results A one-way ANOVA was conducted to analyze the effect of telecommunication device types in social-oriented relationship, and that in task-oriented relationship, respectively followed by post hoc analysis. As predicted by H3, there was a significant effect of telecommunication device type on service evaluation in a social-oriented relationship ($F(2,141) = 3.325$, $p = 0.039$). Moreover, participants evaluated telecommunication service more positively when using a floor-based robot ($M = 5.85$, $SD = 1.17$) than when using a tablet ($M = 5.26$, $SD = 1.06$; $p = 0.043$). However, there was no significant difference in service evaluation between a desk-based robot and a tablet ($p > 0.05$), and between a desk-based robot and a floor-based robot ($p > 0.05$). As predicted in H4, there was no significant effect on service evaluation by the telecommunication device type in task-oriented relationship ($F(2,141) = 0.279$, $p = 0.757$) (see Fig. 2).

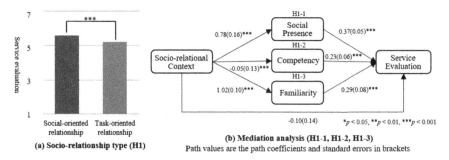

Fig. 1. Service evaluation by socio-relationship type and (b) Mediation analysis results

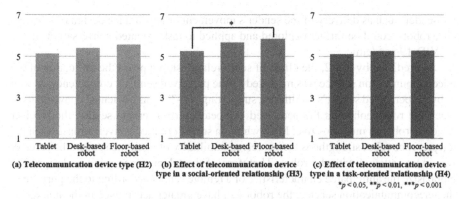

(a) Telecommunication device type (H2)
(b) Effect of telecommunication device type in a social-oriented relationship (H3)
(c) Effect of telecommunication device type in a task-oriented relationship (H4)

$*p < 0.05, **p < 0.01, ***p < 0.001$

Fig. 2. Service evaluation by telecommunication device type

5 Discussion

5.1 Summary and Interpretation of Results

The goal of this study was to examine the effects of socio-relationship type and telecommunication device type on the service evaluation.

As expected by H1, depending on the social-relationship type, participants under the social-oriented conversation were more satisfied with the telecommunication service than under the task-oriented conversation. The reason for this result might be due to the difference in the possibility of in-person visits. Although in medical consultation, there is a possibility that medical staff may contact the patient for medical treatment, in a virtual visit, it is impossible for a family member to meet the patient in the ward. Most likely, remote collaborations by telepresence robots still have difficulties in understanding the body language of a sender [32] and fail to convey the meaning of the sender's message because of the instability of video calls compared to in-person communication [33, 34]. Whereas the risk of miscommunication is relatively small in a social-oriented conversation, errors from miscommunication can be fatal in a task-oriented conversation such as medical consultation. Thus, the telepresence robots in task-oriented conversations where errors in telecommunication are critical might have a lower level of acceptance than that of telepresence robots in social-oriented conversations during the COVID-19 pandemic.

As predicted by H1–1, the effect of socio-relationship type on the evaluation of the telecommunication service was mediated by the perceived social presence of the sender. This indicates that the social presence is increased when the socio-relationship type is a social-oriented relationship, and it positively affects the evaluation of the telecommunication service as a medium. In particular, the use of the telepresence robots in hospitals during the COVID-19 pandemic has been mostly focused on telemedicine, which connects patients and medical staff. In contrast, our study results showed that, in this pandemic, telepresence robots could be more effectively applied to the social-oriented conversations, such as virtual visits, where the social presence of an intimate person was perceived as higher, than to task-oriented conversations, such as medical consultations. In future work, various factors that could improve the social presence of the sender, such as delivery of the sender's movement or appearance design of telepresence robots, could be further explored and applied to task-oriented conversations in the COVID-19 pandemic.

As predicted by H1–2, the effect of socio-relationship type on the evaluation of the telecommunication service was mediated by the perceived sender's competency, as well as by the perceived sender's familiarity, supporting H1–3. In task-oriented conversations, when the robot enhances the perceived competency of a remote sender, the receiver rated the robot as more positive. Meanwhile, in social-oriented conversations, when the telepresence robot strengthens the perceived familiarity of a remote sender, the receiver was more satisfied with the robot. Therefore, if the telepresence robot is designed to emphasize the anticipated characteristics of a remote sender according to the purpose of the telecommunication service, the robot will have greater acceptance in the market.

As predicted by H3, the telecommunication service was evaluated differently according to the telecommunication device type in a social-oriented relationship. In the virtual family visit, the participants evaluated telecommunication service with a floor-based robot more positively than with a tablet. This means that a telecommunication device with tangible communication cues can be more accepted while having social-oriented conversations. By contrast, no significant difference in service evaluation was found according to telecommunication device type in task-oriented conversations, such as medical consultations, supporting H4. This implies that people tend to regard that it is not necessary for the robot to deliver the tangible communication cues in task-oriented conversation unlike social-oriented conversation.

Our findings suggest that telepresence robots can be used more effectively in intimate relationships with social-oriented conversations than in non-intimate relationships with task-oriented conversations. Telepresence robots can be applied to support emotional exchanges not only for hospital patients, but also for overseas dispatch soldiers who live away from their families for a long time and for the elderly living alone in an isolated environment away from their families.

5.2 Limitation and Future Work

The participants did not use the telepresence robots as a patient in a hospital, but indirectly experimented with them by watching video stimuli. It is possible that the participants' immersion in the situation might be limited, as they evaluated the situation as a third party. Field trials with COVID-19 patients in hospitals should be conducted in the future.

According to the robot's appearance, the physical distance between a telepresence robot and a patient can be varied, and the different physical distance may have an effect on the patient's impression toward the robot; however, this was not considered in this study. In further studies, we will investigate the effect of physical distance caused by the appearance of the telepresence robot. In addition, the telemedicine situation in this study used in the experiment was a medical consultation service based on simple medical-related questions. Thus, the results of this study may be limited to a single application of telemedicine. Various telemedicine situations, including collaborative medicine, counseling, and psychotherapy should be further explored.

References

1. Rios, I.C., et al.: Virtual visits to inpatients by their loved ones during COVID-19 (2020)
2. Sasangohar, F., Dhala, A., Zheng, F., Ahmadi, N., Kash, B., Masud, F.: Use of telecritical care for family visitation to ICU during the COVID-19 pandemic: an interview study and sentiment analysis. BMJ Qual. Saf. **30**, 715–721 (2021)
3. Traverso, G., et al.: Assessment of the acceptability and feasibility of using mobile robotic systems for patient evaluation. JAMA Netw. Open **4**, 210667 (2021)
4. Wallace, C.L., Wladkowski, S.P., Gibson, A., White, P.: Grief during the COVID-19 pandemic: considerations for palliative care providers. J. Pain Symptom Manage. **60**, e70–e76 (2020)
5. Frydman, J.L., Choi, E.W., Lindenberger, E.C.: Families of COVID-19 patients say goodbye on video: a structured approach to virtual end-of-life conversations. J. Palliat. Med. **23**, 1564–1565 (2020)
6. Ruiz-Del-Solar, J., et al.: Mental and emotional health care for COVID-19 patients: employing Pudu, a telepresence robot. IEEE Robot. Autom. Mag. **28**, 82–89 (2021)
7. Lociciro, A., Guillon, A., Bodet-Contentin, L.: A telepresence robot in the room of a COVID-19 patient can provide virtual family presence. Canadian Journal of Anesthesia/Journal canadien d'anesthésie **68**(11), 1705–1706 (2021). https://doi.org/10.1007/s12630-021-02039-6
8. Mills, E.C., Savage, E., Lieder, J., Chiu, E.S.: Telemedicine and the COVID-19 pandemic: are we ready to go live? Adv. Skin Wound Care **33**, 410–417 (2020)
9. Pun, B.T., et al.: Prevalence and risk factors for delirium in critically ill patients with COVID-19 (COVID-D): a multicentre cohort study. Lancet Respir. Med. **9**, 239–250 (2021)
10. Murphy, R.R., Babu, V., Gandudi, M., Adams, J.: Applications of Robots for COVID-19 Response (2020)
11. Rae, I., Takayama, L., Mutlu, B.: The influence of height in robot-mediated communication. In: ACM/IEEE International Conference on Human-Robot Interaction, pp. 1–8 (2013)
12. Sirkin, D., Ju, W.: Consistency in physical and on-screen action improves perceptions of telepresence robots. In: Proceedings of the seventh annual ACM/IEEE international conference on Human-Robot Interaction - HRI 2012 (2012)
13. Kristoffersson, A., Coradeschi, S., Loutfi, A.: A review of mobile robotic telepresence. Adv. Hum.-Comput. Interact. **2013**, 17 (2013)
14. Jones, B., Witcraft, A., Bateman, S., Neustaedter, C., Tang, A.: Mechanics of camera work in mobile video collaboration. In: Conference on Human Factors in Computing Systems - Proceedings, pp. 957–966, Apr 2015
15. Lewicki, R.: Trust, trust development, and trust repair Negotiation pedagogy View project. The handbook of conflict resolution: Theory and practice. **1**, 86–107 (2000)
16. Pretty, G.M.H., Mccarthy, M.: Exploring psychological sense of community among women and men of the corporation. J. Community Psychol. **19** (1991)
17. Neustaedter, C., Venolia, G., Procyk, J., Hawkins, D.: To Beam or Not to Beam: A Study of Remote Telepresence Attendance at an Academic Conference (2016)
18. Adalgeirsson, S.O., Breazeal, C.: MeBot: A robotic platform for socially embodied telepresence, pp. 15–22 (2010)
19. Yang, L., Jones, B., Neustaedter, C., Singhal, S.: Shopping over distance through a telepresence robot. In: Proceedings of the ACM on Human-Computer Interaction, vol. 2, p. 18 (2018)
20. Kang, D.: The effect of tactility and socio-relational context on social presence and user satisfaction. In: ACM/IEEE International Conference on Human-Robot Interaction, pp. 718–720, Mar 2019

21. Verhagen, T., van Nes, J., Feldberg, F., van Dolen, W.: Virtual customer service agents: using social presence and personalization to shape online service encounters. J. Comput.-Mediat. Commun. **19**, 529–545 (2014)
22. Lee, K.M., Jung, Y., Kim, J., Kim, S.R.: Are physically embodied social agents better than disembodied social agents?: The effects of physical embodiment, tactile interaction, and people's loneliness in human–robot interaction. Int. J. Hum Comput Stud. **64**, 962–973 (2006)
23. Breazeal, C.: Toward sociable robots. Robot. Auton. Syst. **42**, 167–175 (2003)
24. James, M., Wise, D., Langenhove, L. van: Virtual strategic positioning to create social presence: reporting on the use of a telepresence robot. In: Papers on Social Representations, vol. 28, pp. 2.1–2.30 (2019)
25. Choi, J.J., Kwak, S.S.: Which is Your Favorite?: The Impact of Robot's Height on Consumer's Acceptance of a Telepresence Robot TT - Which is Your Favorite?: The Impact of Robot's Height on Consumer's Acceptance of a Telepresence Robot. Design Convergence Study. **15**, 59–70 (2016)
26. Lee, M.K., Takayama, L.: "Now, I Have a Body": Uses and Social Norms for Mobile Remote Presence in the Workplace. Proceedings of the SIGCHI Conference on Human Factors in Computing Systems. (2011)
27. Nowak, K.L., Biocca, F.: The effect of the agency and anthropomorphism on users' sense of telepresence, copresence, and social presence in virtual environments. In: Presence: Teleoperators and Virtual Environments, vol. 12, pp. 481–494 (2003)
28. Andrist, S., Spannan, E., Mutlu, B.: Rhetorical robots: Making robots more effective speakers using linguistic cues of expertise. In: ACM/IEEE International Conference on Human-Robot Interaction, pp. 341–348 (2013)
29. Kanda, T., Ishiguro, H., Ishida, T.: Psychological analysis on human-robot interaction. In: Proceedings - IEEE International Conference on Robotics and Automation, vol. 4, pp. 4166–4173 (2001)
30. Lee, M.K., Kiesler, S., Forlizzi, J., Srinivasa, S., Rybski, P.: Gracefully mitigating breakdowns in robotic services, pp. 203–210 (2010)
31. Hayes, A.F.: PROCESS: A versatile computational tool for observed variable mediation, moderation, and conditional process modeling (2012)
32. Zinina, A., Zaidelman, L., Arinkin, N., Kotov, A.: Non-verbal behavior of the robot companion: A contribution to the likeability. In: Procedia Computer Science. pp. 800–806. Elsevier B.V. (2020)
33. Tsui, K.M., Desai, M., Yanco, H.A., Uhlik, C.: Exploring use cases for telepresence robots. In: HRI 2011 - Proceedings of the 6th ACM/IEEE International Conference on Human-Robot Interaction, pp. 11–18 (2011)
34. Christie, B., Holloway, S.: Factors affecting the use of telecommunications by management. J. Occup. Psychol. **48**, 3–9 (1975)

Towards the Deployment of a Social Robot at an Elderly Day Care Facility

Sara Cooper[(✉)] and Raquel Ros

PAL Robotics, Carrer de Pujades 77, Barcelona, Spain
{sara.cooper,raquel.ros}@pal-robotics.com

Abstract. Life expectancy is increasing with time, and with it, more support is needed to provide care for the elderly. Social robots may in this context support with therapy, monitoring or entertainment activities. This paper describes current work on deploying our social robot ARI at an elderly day care centre focused on promoting engagement in the routines carried out at the centre. By using a user-centred design approach, the paper presents the prototype development process of three activities and their initial validation in a 2-day pilot study. The preliminary results highlight an increasing responsive behaviour of the elderly towards the robot on day 2 compared to day 1 in one of the activities. In contrast, in a second activity, the robot was mostly ignored, suggesting that further work must be done in terms of attracting the attention of the user, and not giving for granted that the mere presence of a robot will suffice to trigger curiosity towards initiating interactions.

Keywords: Elderly care · Social robot · Fostering engagement

1 Introduction

Life expectancy is increasing with time, and with it, more support is needed to live independently. In this context, social robots may offer cognitive support in healthcare sector by providing social interaction, by providing multi-modal behaviour to interact with clinical personnel and patients. Their use ranges from offering physical and cognitive stimulation, delivering reminders, monitoring temperature or falls, to providing entertainment [4,7,18]. The needs, desires, and concerns vary greatly from one person to another, and even more, from one care home to another. Thus, the solution needs to be flexible enough to adapt to the needs of each type of care center and end user.

In this paper, the PAL Robotics ARI robot [6,7] is used to increase awareness of the daily routines at an elderly day care center. Through a joint collaboration, the AMIBA project aimed at adapting the activities the social robot ARI could perform to fit their needs. To this end, an iterative process of discussions with the caregivers and prototyping took place, where the robot was slowly introduced to evaluate its potential in the near future. The following goals were defined:

© The Author(s), under exclusive license to Springer Nature Switzerland AG 2022
F. Cavallo et al. (Eds.): ICSR 2022, LNAI 13818, pp. 277–287, 2022.
https://doi.org/10.1007/978-3-031-24670-8_25

- To foster the involvement of the elderly in the day care routines
- To provide support to the staff when carrying out activities with the elderly
- To increase the accessibility of advanced robotic interventions to elderly users in a day care environment.

2 Related Work

In the past years, social robots have been gaining attention as supporting tools in human environments, with special interest the in the elderly care sector, through research projects, such as Hobbit [11], EnrichMe [10], GrowMeUp [1], SHAPES [6]). The role that such robots could play in elderly care has been reviewed in [2] identifying five key areas: affective therapy, cognitive training, social facilitator, companionship, and physiological therapy.

As a social facilitator, related studies showed that social robots can improve sociability and engagement among older adults [5,15]. When it comes to cognitive training, robots have indeed been found to positively impact on engagement and motivation towards different activities, offering personalised care and proving therapy effectiveness [17]. This is further enhanced by use of expressive robots [8], which adapt their behaviour based on the culture, cognitive decline and language requirements of each end-user.

Most of the cases however, focused on one-to-one interactions, personalising robot behaviour to each user. Interactions targeted at multiple users or groups have been less common. In [15], for example, social robots are described as mediators in group activities to increase social interactions and engagement in everyday activities. In addition, one of the advantages of sharing a social robot by multiple individuals in care settings is to reduce costs and share the burden of care givers [1,6,10,13]. Despite the advances made so far, there are still limitations when it comes to adopting such robots within healthcare [3], such as the fear of robots taking over caregivers jobs or the need of adaptation to different cultures and languages [8]. In this work, we aim at working hand-by-hand with the caregivers through an iterative co-design process to develop a prototype of an assistive robot that supports their everyday tasks in elderly group activities.

3 Understanding Users' Needs

Fundación AMIBA[1] is a non-profit organization in Barcelona (Spain) offering different services for elderly care, including a day care centre. It currently hosts 16 older adults, which cannot live fully independently.

One of the main barriers when talking to end-users is understanding what a social robot, such as ARI, is capable of. Thus, a first session was run (1) to better understand their daily routines (through interviews to the staff and observation of their activities), and (2) to show an interactive demo with ARI itself.

---

[1] https://sid-inico.usal.es/centros_servicios/fundacion-privada-amiba/.

3.1   A Day at the Day Care

The elderly arrive between 9:00 and 10:00 am. They are received by a caregiver at the entrance and are accompanied to the main room area. As they arrive, some have breakfast, and then start performing leisure activities (i.e., drawing, painting reading, playing puzzles, etc.). During this period, they individually perform short sessions of specific physiotherapy exercises tailored to their own needs, together with the psychotherapist. At 12:00 the whole group is gathered in the gym area for a 45 min group session of physical gross-motor exercises. Next, lunch takes place at 13:00, followed by free afternoon time where they usually gather on the sofas around the TV until 16:00, for tea time. People leave the day care at different times throughout the afternoon. At 18:00, the final user leaves and the day care closes.

When it comes to the user profile, it is worth noting that older adults attend the centre because their families do not wish for them to stay alone during the day. In other words, they do not come on their own free will. Some have slight dementia, others have had an ictus. In general, they do not easily engage neither with the activities carried out at the centre, nor with other adults or staff. This poses a great challenge for a social robot, as it requires an extra effort to attract the older adults' attention.

3.2   Interactive Demo

At the end of the observation session an interactive demo was presented to caregivers and older adults to showcase a set of activities carried by ARI in another similar project [6]: establishing video calls, monitoring body temperature, sending alerts to designated caregivers, providing the agenda of the day with events and reminders, filling in the weekly menu, and offering entertainment games (e.g., puzzles, memory games). A short presentation on how to use the robot followed the demo before allowing caregivers to play with it by themselves.

The existing activities were not considered to fit the needs of the caregivers and older adults. The games were too focused on entertainment, and they preferred more cognitive focused tasks. One-to-one personalised activities such as videocalls, daily menu, alerts or reminders, were not considered useful within the AMIBA context either. In contrast, more general tasks targeting the group as a whole, rather than individually, were preferred.

4   Iterative Development of Prototypes

Based on the feedback received from the caregivers and after the observation session at the centre, the following activities to be performed by the robot were identified:

- To greet the users upon arrival at the day care centre. The aim is to start the day with a welcoming message for the users, to empower them by feeling that they are central characters and the robot's attention is focused on them.

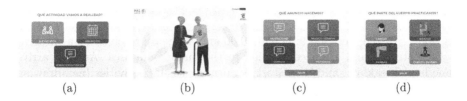

(a)   (b)   (c)   (d)

Fig. 1. Example screens displayed on ARI's touch-screen for adapted demo: a) "Which activity do you want to do? Welcoming, Announcements, Physical Exercises". b) Welcoming activity. c) "Which announcement do you want to provide?" Motricity, Music therapy, Lunch time, Tea time" d) "Which body part do you want to exercise? Head, Arms, Legs, Whole body". ©PAL Robotics

- To give announcements of the events taken place throughout the day. The announcements to be made were intended towards group activities (physiotherapy and music-therapy) and meals (lunch and tea time).
- To provide encouragement during the group physical exercises activity to keep them motivated while performing the exercises [9].

These features were gradually developed and tested at the care centre throughout the following 8 weeks.

In order to trigger the activities, a QR detection process was proposed to show the main menu view listing the available activities (Fig. 1a). The purpose was to only allow the caregivers to activate the robot to start any of the tasks.

Regarding the greeting activity, once it was set, the robot would detect the presence of a person through face detection. Unfortunately, at the time where these tests took place, users had to always use masks. Thus, chances of accurately detecting someone were low. For this reason, the detection mechanism was switched to a "manual mode", where every time an older adult came to the centre in the morning, the carer had to touch the screen to trigger the robot's greetings (Fig. 1b).

With respect to the events announcements, the carer could choose from the main menu the event to announce whenever needed (Fig. 1c). Variations on the schedule could take place on a daily basis. Thus, setting a fixed time where the robot could automatically trigger the announcement was discarded. Once the staff indicated the announcement, the robot would show an image on the screen related to the announcement and verbally call everyone to perform the new activity. Examples of the sentences used were: *"It is lunch time!"*, *"Let's go for lunch now!"*, *"It is already lunch time, let's go to eat!"*. Finally, regarding the physical exercises activity, a menu with the different main body parts was shown on the screen. The physiotherapist selects the main body part to work next (Fig. 1d) and the robot would then trigger encouraging messages regarding the body part to exercise. For example, "Let's move the head now", *"Come on everyone, moving the arms"*, *"Those legs need to be moving!"*. Variations on the robot's speech were always produced to avoid repetitive speech. No specific body motion description was provided since the carer indicated that she would

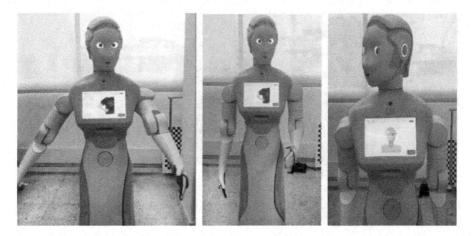

Fig. 2. Samples of the motions generated for the and arms to support the physical exercises activities. ©PAL Robotics

decide on the exercises to be performed spontaneously, based on how the elderly were all performing, rather than methodologically planning each day exercises. Thus, a set of general physical motions were developed to accompany the verbal encouragements (Fig. 2), including head, arm and body movements.

The robot behaviour was implement through state machines wrapped as Python ROS (Robotics Operating System) nodes to transition between the different behaviours and activities. A technical difficulty observed was the lack of WiFi connectivity at the centre, which prevented the use of Google's speech recogniser. Thus, the voice-bot had to be deactivated, greatly limiting potential automatic responses to user's speech. The first prototype was deployed at the day care so the caregivers could try it during the following days. We then interviewed the caregivers to gather feedback on the experience:

- QR code was not efficient to trigger welcoming messages, as most caregivers did not have a phone at hand and light conditions or brightness of phones affected scanning accuracy. It was then decided to trigger the main menu through the touchscreen instead. While this reduced the autonomous behaviour of the robot, caregivers preferred this approach.
- When providing announcements for events, care givers suggested to play music at the same time, to further attract the attention of older adults. Linking a melody to each type of event could increase awareness of the activities carried out, specially for those with cognitive decline.
- In terms of the robot's voice, the lack of expressivity in the voice was highlighted, being this one too plain. Thus, it was suggested to adjust the speed, pitch and volume according to the context.
- When providing greetings, carers requested the possibility to alternate between Catalan and Spanish languages, to adapt to the users' culture.

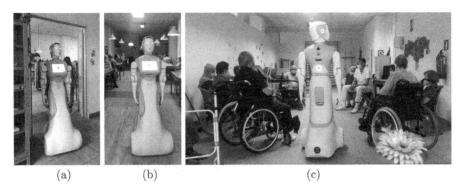

Fig. 3. Set-up for the robot of the three cases: (a) Greetings, (b) Announcements and (c) Physical exercises. ©PAL Robotics

- The use of verbal interaction is crucial for this target population, since it is the main channel of communication. Older adults attempted to talk to the robot about trivial conversations, and were disappointed when no response could be provided.
- Finally, staff members are really busy and it was difficult for them to spend time triggering the different activities. Thus, despite requiring a very simple process (pressing a sequence of two buttons maximum to set the activity), using the robot everyday was not a priority.

5   Use Case Study

Based on this new feedback, we evolved the prototype that was validated throughout two full morning sessions. During these sessions, the robot behaviours were triggered by a technical staff through the Wizard-of-Oz methodology. The aim was to reduce the caregivers workload (i.e. they did not have to spend time launching the different activities), while allowing the technical staff to also observe and take notes of the robot's interactive performance on-site. We next describe the observations made.

5.1   Greetings

The robot was placed at the entrance of the main room between 9 and 10 o'clock (Fig. 3a). Whenever older adults came in, the technical staff would trigger the robot to greet. Some adults came alone, others accompanied by caregivers. When evaluating the interaction, we annotated the number of adults that replied to the robot's greeting either on their own or when prompted by caregivers. Table 1 summarises the annotated interactions on day 1. Table 2 shows the results based on both days. A clear increase on the users' responses to the robot can be observed from day 1 to day 2 (increasing from %42.85 to %85.33). More people initiated the interaction, raising from 2 to 6, reducing the number of users that entirely ignored the robot. The number of those replies prompted by caregivers

Table 1. First day 'Greetings' interaction results: initiated by users ('Own'), 'Prompted by career' or ignored (-). U=user, C=carer and R=robot.

User	Context	Interaction	Own	Prompted by carer
1	U walks on his own (with a stick) and fast	U: replies good morning to the R	x	
2	U walks very slowly, holds C's arm	U: doesn't look at R. C: "Look, it said hi". U: nods		
3	U walks at normal speed holding C's arm	U pays attention to the R. Stops. C: "Listen what the robot tells you. It's looking at you" R greets again. U seems pleased recalling that she had to greet everyday at her work as well		x
4	U walks with a 'walker' on its own	U: doesn't even look at R	-	-
5	U walks at normal speed, holding C	C: "Look!" U looks at R, raises his hand (copying R's hand movement) C: "It's greeting you" R: greets again. U: looks at R for a while. Then enters the room. C2: "Did R say hi?" U: "yes"		x
6	U walks on its own (with a stick) and fast	U greeted tech staff. R greets. U doesn't even look at robot	-	-
7	U walks slow, with C's support	R greeted 4 times. Eventually U moved his head, noticing R		x
8	U in wheelchair	R greeted 3 times. C insisted U to greet back	-	x
9	U enters walking fast on her own	U ignored R	-	-
10	U walking slowly with C's support	U doesn't reply back to R	-	-
11	U in wheelchair	R greets, no reply back from U	-	-
12	U enters walking fast	U looks at R but doesn't reply back to R		
13	U in wheelchair with informal carer	They walked through without even noticing R (informal carer went straight into the next room, so no opportunity to slow down in front of R)	-	-
14	U wheelchair with C's support	C slowed down, U replied on its own	x	-

remained the same. It should be noted that quite a number of users needed help to walk (be it a walker, wheelchair or caregiver support), interfering their attention towards the robot. In contrast, users 1, 3 and 5, who walked without much difficulties, were more prone to pay attention to the robot.

5.2 Announcements

At 11:45, on both days, the robot was moved to the main room (Fig. 3b) to carry out the "physical exercise activity" announcement. Low interest on the robot from the elderly was observed, hardly glancing at the it. Similarly, at lunch time, right after the physical activity took place, the robot announced the meal time. However, most of them were already on their way to the dinning area, so little attention was paid to the robot.

5.3 Physical Exercises

Lastly, around 12 o'clock, older adults were moved to the physio room and sat in a circle (Fig. 3c). The robot was placed between them and, as the therapist

Table 2. 'Greetings' interaction summary

	Day 1	Day 2
Started interaction on their own	2	6
Started interaction when prompted by caregiver	4	4
Ignored the robot	8	2
Total number of participants	14	12
Percentage of responsive users	%42.85	%83.33

indicated the body part to work on, the technician would trigger the encouraging support, which involved speech and motion.

At the beginning the robot was constantly cheering users to do the exercises, and the participants would indicate that the robot was "talking too much". The verbal encouragements were therefore reduced to avoid disturbing the group. There were positive comments about the robot, where the adults would look at the robot and question its gender, or noticing that the robot was doing the exercises in the wrong way –as often new exercises that the robot was not programmed to do were proposed by the therapist. Remotely controlling the movements to better simulate the exercises worked well –for example, in a game where they had to pass a ball between them, the robot was teleoperated to track the ball by moving its head, demonstrating integration in the group activity. Older adults kept looking at the therapist for guidance, rather than the robot, which was considered as one more participant in the group.

6   Discussion

The AMIBA project was regarded as a difficult scenario due to the overall low engagement older adults presented in their everyday [19] and the short timeline that was given to prepare a working solution. Nevertheless, through the observation study and the deployment of the use case, several lessons have been learned.

6.1   On the Activities

The welcoming scenario has had a rather positive outcome, notably increasing a responsive behaviour of the adults towards the robot on the second day compared to the first day. A potential reason could be that the elderly felt more familiar with the robot, and thus, knew what to expect from the robot. However, depending on the older adult's walking abilities, their attention to the robot differed: the higher the walking difficulties, the lower the attention they could pay to the robot or the environment. Thus, based on context and the user's capabilities, the robot should adapt its engaging strategies to properly attract their attention more efficiently. In the announcements activity, proactively approaching older adults, inviting them to join the events and adjusting the prosody of the messages spoken by the robot could potentially promote higher engagement.

Finally, regarding the physical exercises, remotely controlling the robot movements allowed us to quickly adapt to the last minute instructions of the therapist, which were not previously programmed in the robot. Thus, future efforts should be placed to allow the robot to replicate, at least to some extend, the proposed movements at execution time. Additionally, a seamless mechanism to switch between exercises should be designed for the therapist, such as detecting keywords from speech (e.g. "arm exercises up", "head sides"), instead of having to press buttons on the screen every time. In any case, we believe that assisting the group sessions is an interesting role that the robot could play to improve interactions in group activities [16].

6.2   On the Technical Design

Several technical design decisions were identified and improved as follows:

- The use of QR codes to trigger the activities: though this approach made sense in terms of limiting the access to authorised personnel initially, it also involved an additional burden for the caregivers. Using NFC tags or adding lights from the robot side to point to QR area could increase robustness in the future.
- Adapting the solution to the spoken languages of the users may impact on the acceptability and willingness to engage with it[2];
- Providing music to both attract the attention of older adults and as an aid for event awareness, specially necessary for those with cognitive decline.

Moreover, the following technical difficulties have been detected throughout the development of the project, which should be addressed in future work:

- User privacy and internet reliability problems when using an online speech recognizer. As next steps an offline speech recognition system will be integrated on the robot, such as Vosk[3];
- Lack of expressivity in the robot's voice. Finding speech solutions that allow modifying the pitch, volume and overall rhythm of the voice in an easy an intuitive way is essential for further improvements.
- A faster and smoother robot body controller to generate motions (through use of Whole Body Control[4]), and gesture recognition systems to allow gesture imitation to adapt and recreate to the therapist's movements;
- To improve face detection while using face masks, combining approaches proposed in [12,14].

---

[2] Citizens in Catalonia are used to switch between Catalan and Spanish. However, they usually have a preferred language which should be used in this case.

[3] https://alphacephei.com/vosk/.

[4] https://github.com/pal-robotics/pal_wbc_utils.

Overall, the robot's awareness of the context should be included to both, increase the robot autonomy as well as its proactiveness when initiating interaction with older adults [15]. Nevertheless, the Wizard-of-Oz methodology to trigger robot behaviours proves to be a powerful approach at initial stages to allow end-users to gain a better understanding of the system's capabilities and to gather feedback on the design to improve acceptability and ease of use of the system.

7   Conclusions

The AMIBA project at a day care facility has been presented in this paper. It emphasises the need of a co-design process both with older adults and caregivers and to adapt the solutions to the needs of each site, but also highlights some common challenges and future works, such as improvement in the prosody of the robot speech, adaptability to languages and voice interactions, and in general, increase awareness in the surrounding environment. Future work will take these technical considerations into account and will carry out a longer pilot study with several cycles of co-design process in order to facilitate adoption of robots at such facilities.

Acknowledgments. This work was supported by the AMIBA project, funded by "Solicituds d'ajusts de la segona convocatória de cupons a la competitivitat empresarial 2021 - Indústria 4.0".

References

1. https://cordis.europa.eu/project/id/643647
2. Abdi, J., Al-Hindawi, A., Ng, T., Vizcaychipi, M.P.: Scoping review on the use of socially assistive robot technology in elderly care. BMJ Open **8**(2) (2018)
3. Broadbent, E., et al.: Attitudes towards health-care robots in a retirement village. Aust. J. Ageing **31**(2), 115–20 (2012)
4. Casas, J., Cespedes, N., Múnera, M., Cifuentes, C.A.: Human-robot interaction for rehabilitation scenarios. In: Control Systems Design of Bio-Robotics and Bio-Mechatronics with Advanced Applications, pp. 1–31 (2020)
5. Chu, M., Khosla, R., Khaksar, S., Nguyen, K.: Service innovation through social robot engagement to improve dementia care quality. Assist. Technol. **29**(1), 8–18 (2017)
6. Cooper, S., et al.: Social robotic application to support active and healthy ageing. In: 2021 30th IEEE International Conference on Robot & Human Interactive Communication (RO-MAN), pp. 1074–1080 (2021)
7. Cooper, S., Di Fava, A., Vivas, C., Marchionni, L., Ferro, F.: Ari: the social assistive robot and companion. In: 2020 29th IEEE International Conference on Robot and Human Interactive Communication (RO-MAN), pp. 745–751 (2020)
8. Cortellessa, G., Benedictis, R.D., Fracasso, F., Orlandini, A., Umbrico, A., Cesta, A.: Ai and robotics to help older adults: Revisiting projects in search of lessons learned. Paladyn J. Behav. Rob. **12**(1), 356–378 (2021)

9. Cruz-Sandoval, D., Penaloza, C.I., Favela, J., Castro-Coronel, A.P.: Towards social robots that support exercise therapies for persons with dementia. In: Proceedings of the 2018 ACM International Joint Conference and 2018 International Symposium on Pervasive and Ubiquitous Computing and Wearable Computers, pp. 1729–1734. Association for Computing Machinery (2018)

10. Fernandez-Carmona, M., et al.: Int. J. Social Rob. **12**(3) (2020)

11. Fischinger, D., et al.: Hobbit, a care robot supporting independent living at home: first prototype and lessons learned. Rob. Auton. Syst. **75**, 60–78 (2016)

12. Gonzalez, J., Belgiovine, G., Sciutti, A., Sandini, G., Francesco, R.: Towards a cognitive framework for multimodal person recognition in multiparty hri, pp. 412–416. Association for Computing Machinery (2021)

13. Hung, L., et al.: The benefits of and barriers to using a social robot paro in care settings: a scoping review. BMC Geriat. **19**(1) (2019)

14. Irfan, B., Ortiz, M.G., Lyubova, N., Belpaeme, T.: Multi-modal open world user identification. J. Human-Robot Interact. **11**(1) (2021)

15. Jøranson, N., Pedersen, I., Rokstad, A.M.M., Aamodt, G., Olsen, C., Ihlebæk, C.: Group activity with paro in nursing homes: systematic investigation of behaviors in participants. Int. Psychogeriat. **28**(8), 1345–54 (2016)

16. Melkas, H., Hennala, L., Pekkarinen, S., Kyrki, V.: Impacts of robot implementation on care personnel and clients in elderly-care institutions. Int. J. Med. Inf. **134**, 104041 (2020)

17. Salichs, E., Fernández-Rodicio, E., Castillo, J.C., Castro-González, Á., Malfaz, M., Salichs, M.Á.: A social robot assisting in cognitive stimulation therapy. In: Demazeau, Y., An, B., Bajo, J., Fernández-Caballero, A. (eds.) PAAMS 2018. LNCS (LNAI), vol. 10978, pp. 344–347. Springer, Cham (2018). https://doi.org/10.1007/978-3-319-94580-4_35

18. Tapus, A., Mataric, M.J., Scassellati, B.: Socially assistive robotics [grand challenges of robotics]. IEEE Rob. Autom. Maga. **14**(1), 35–42 (2007)

19. Thunberg, S., Ziemke, T.: Pandemic effects on social companion robot use in care homes. In: 2021 30th IEEE International Conference on Robot & Human Interactive Communication (RO-MAN), pp. 983–988 (2021)

Towards a Framework for the Whole-Body Teleoperation of a Humanoid Robot in Healthcare Settings

Francesco Porta[ID], Carmine Tommaso Recchiuto[✉][ID], Maura Casadio[ID], and Antonio Sgorbissa[ID]

Università degli Studi di Genova, Genoa, Italy
carmine.recchiuto@dibris.unige.it

Abstract. The use of robotic systems for doctor-patient interaction during Covid-19 and in post-pandemic phases has been proven useful. On the other hand, in current implementations, teleoperating a robot in critical contexts such as the medical scenario may induce a high mental workload on the operator, mainly due to the need to adapt to the remote control of a complex robot, and the reduced environmental awareness. Furthermore, robotic platforms for telemedicine do not usually offer the possibility of establishing physical contact with the patient, which may indeed be useful to show how to assume a certain posture, or to guide a specific movement.

The aim of this work is to overcome these limitations, by creating a framework in which the arms, the head, and the base of a humanoid robot can be easily teleoperated with a rapid learning curve and a low mental workload for the operator. The proposed approach is based on the real-time human pose estimation of the operator, which is calculated in real-time and transformed into correspondent skeleton joint angles, used as input to control the upper body joints of the Softbank Robotics robot Pepper. Experiments with users have been performed to check the effectiveness of the imitation system, by verifying the similarity between the human and robot pose and measuring its usability and perceived workload.

Keywords: Human pose estimation · Robot teleoperation · Humanoid robotics

1 Introduction

During the Covid-19 pandemics, healthcare personnel has been the most actively involved in fighting the virus, often being in strict contact with infected patients. This caused important consequences: emotional overload, physical fatigue, relentless work shifts, and obviously high risk of contagion [13]. In this context, providing easy-to-use technological tools that can reduce the need for physical interaction between doctors and patients is of the utmost importance. In particular, artificial intelligence (AI) and robotic technologies can play an important role in the use and delivery of telemedicine [2]. However, robot teleoperation typically induces a high mental workload on the operator due to the need to adapt to the remote control of a complex robot [22] and the reduced environmental awareness [17]. Moreover, physical contact with the patients

© The Author(s), under exclusive license to Springer Nature Switzerland AG 2022
F. Cavallo et al. (Eds.): ICSR 2022, LNAI 13818, pp. 288–298, 2022.
https://doi.org/10.1007/978-3-031-24670-8_26

has been proven to be fundamental in this kind of situation, but rarely robotic platforms for telemedicine have taken this into consideration [16]. Indeed, direct contact is essential from an emotional point of view: for example, for showing empathy, encouraging the patient to perform a certain action, or giving a reward for something the patient has achieved. Even if a telepresence robot cannot offer the same experience as an operator being physically present, remotely controlling a humanoid robot may allow the operator to guide the patient on how to assume a certain posture or show them how to perform a specific movement. This aspect would require having control of a human-like shaped robot: however, this would further increase the complexity of the system and the users' mental workload, unless the human body of the operator is used to control the robot, by directly mapping the operator's motion to the humanoid robot. Indeed, natural interfaces have been proven more effective in teleoperating a humanoid robot than classical interfaces (e.g., joysticks) [8].

About this, the use of human body poses to control a humanoid robot is a complex problem that can be split into two main sub-problems: (i) real-time single-person 3D human pose estimation, and (ii) extraction of suitable control commands for the robot from the estimated keypoints that compose the human skeleton model.

Concerning (i), several possible approaches based on different camera equipment, functioning principles, and performances, have been recently put forward. Among the others, researchers have set new state-of-the-art results for monocular view [23] or using multiple synchronized cameras [11], but inference times for real-time applications have not been taken into consideration in these works. About this, among all possible approaches, OpenPose [4] provides 2D real-time multi-person keypoint detection and its inference times outperform all previous state-of-the-art methods while maintaining high-quality results. In [19], OpenPose has been used along with an RGB-D sensor to obtain the 3D keypoints, fusing the optimal inference times of 2D pose estimation with the depth information from the camera.

Concerning (ii), researchers have developed various methods that comprehend the use of inverse kinematics [18,21] or analytical methods and geometry [7,20]. A novel analytical approach has been presented in [24], based on the geometrical calculation of the joint angles of a human skeleton model constructed with 3D keypoints using link vectors and virtual joints, subsequently mapped on a humanoid robot model. This approach shows a much lower average computational time with respect to the average inverse kinematics ones, while maintaining a low average posture mapping error and a good joint angle consistency between the robot and the human skeleton model.

On the basis of this analysis, this paper describes the design, implementation, and preliminary experimental evaluation of a framework for the immersive teleoperation of a humanoid robot, to be possibly used in healthcare settings. The framework gives the possibility to the operator to intuitively control the movements of the robot's head, arms, hip, and mobile base while visualizing through a monitor the video taken by cameras installed on the robot. The posture and movements of the operator will be directly replicated on the robot: thus, the remote operator will be able to pilot the robot in a simple and intuitive way, using their body and voice as controllers.

While a few attempts to teleoperate humanoids by adopting whole-body teleoperation approaches have been recently proposed [6], this is the first attempt, to the authors' knowledge, to develop a comprehensive framework to teleoperate robots that can be seamlessly deployed into a medical scenario, easy to install, and accessible to people without programming knowledge. Differently from existing teleoperation and visual feedback software, the specific context of application needs some specific functionalities: an audio communication interface, allowing the operator to verbally communicate with the patient through the robot; different control modalities of the robot's head, allowing the healthcare operator to focus on different aspects; hybrid approaches to control the robot's base, to leverage the autonomous capabilities of the robotic platform. All these aspects have been integrated into the overall system, and preliminarily tested, to assess the system's usability in this particular scope rather than focusing on the performance and precision of the robot's teleoperation, which have already been evaluated in previous works [6].

2   Software Architecture

Based on the aforementioned considerations, the architecture of the system has been designed considering some key aspects. First of all, the operator and the patient could possibly be in different places: hence, an audio communication interface has been implemented, which allows the healthcare operator to communicate verbally with the patient through the robot. Concerning the visual feedback, two cameras have been added to the robot. The cameras have been placed on the top of the head and on the right wrist: while the camera placed on the head of the robot offers general information about the position of the teleoperated robot in the environment and the position of the patient with respect to the robot, the cameras on the right wrist may be crucial to offer a focused view on some details of the patients (e.g., check if sores or wounds are healing).

Finally, the robot's whole-body control has been implemented so as to give the operator different possibilities, such as directly controlling the wheeled robot base through voice commands or allowing the robot to identify and autonomously track a person (i.e., the patient) in the room, and directly controlling the robot's head or allowing the robot to autonomously move the head, relying on the head camera to follow the wrist of the robot or a person's face.

Overall, a Graphical User Interface that embeds all these functionalities has been developed. The interface can also be controlled through voice commands, implemented using speech recognition Python libraries (Google Cloud), allowing the operator to switch between the aforementioned modalities, or to communicate with the patient through the robot's or their own voice. The application also embeds methodologies for 3D human pose estimation and posture mapping to the robot's joints, which are detailed in the following.

3D Human Pose Estimation. The extraction of the 3D keypoints from the human operator is performed fusing the 2D keypoints, obtained applying the OpenPose algorithm [4] to images acquired with a monocular camera, with the 3D data acquired from a depth sensor. The OpenPose standard output consists of a set of 25 keypoints, which are used to construct a complete skeleton model of the human body. A subset of the 25 keypoints has been used in the system, corresponding to the 9 keypoints needed to

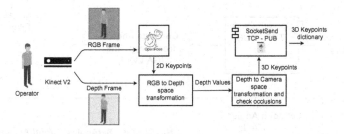

Fig. 1. Human pose estimation architecture

directly teleoperate the upper body of the robot using human posture mapping (Fig. 1). Please consider that in the current implementation, the RGB and the depth frame are considered aligned, given that both data are acquired with the same device. However, this does not affect the generality of the system.

Every time an RGB frame is available, it is passed as input to the OpenPose algorithm that elaborates it and outputs a list of 25 2D keypoints superimposed to the original image, so as to outline the skeleton of the recognized person. Relying on depth information, the keypoints are later transformed in the depth space, so that they can be directly used to calculate control commands for the robot. Finally, an occlusion checking algorithm has been specifically developed for this application.

The presented architecture has been implemented using the Microsoft Kinect V2 [5] RGB camera and depth sensor for the extraction of the 3D keypoints.

Posture Mapping to the Robot. The 3D keypoints computed with the proposed approach are directly used to calculate joint angles. In the current implementation, the geometrical analysis approach based on link vectors and virtual joints (GA-LVVJ) [24] has been adopted, which includes the following steps:

- Construct the link vectors of the human skeleton using the captured 3D keypoints;
- Construct the human virtual joints taking into consideration the human skeleton link vectors and robot joints;
- Establish the local link frames for the skeleton model;
- Calculate the joint angles of the human skeleton model using the local link frames and link vectors;
- Apply the calculated joint angles of the human skeleton model to the robot model.

Indeed, 3d keypoints cannot be directly converted into joint angles to pilot the robot, because the mechanical limits of the robot may sharply differ from the ones of the human body; therefore, the computed angles can exceed the physical limits of the robot joints. Moreover, the human body's skeleton joints may not correspond exactly to the joints of the robot. For these reasons, at each iteration, the computed angles need to be saturated to the maximum and minimum value physically reachable by each joint angle. The described system has been applied to the Softbank Robotics humanoid robot Pepper [14]. As visible in Fig. 2, the NaoQi APIs[1] have been used to send the computed joint angles to the robot.

---

[1] Reference site for NaoQi APIs: http://doc.aldebaran.com/2-5/naoqi/index.html.

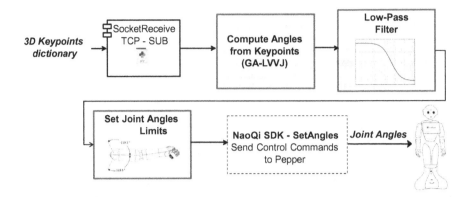

Fig. 2. Pepper teleoperation architecture

The code is open source and it is freely available on GitHub[2].

3   Experiments

Before testing the system in a medical setting, a pilot test to evaluate the feasibility, functionality and usability of the framework has been performed. The objective of the experiment was to evaluate the developed architecture from a subjective point of view, by estimating the usability of the system and the mental and physical workload on the operator through validated questionnaires, and from an objective point of view, by using quantitative data collected during the experiments.

To this aim, inexperienced subjects have been asked to teleoperate Pepper with the goal of finding five different markers placed in specific spots on a structure composed of cardboard boxes. More in detail, a structure composed of 4 boxes has been placed in the middle of the room, and 5 markers have been placed within the structure. The experiment has been repeated three times for each person, in the same session, changing the position of the markers. Indeed, markers were possibly placed in three fixed configurations, that have been presented to the participants in random order. At the beginning of the experiment, the robot Pepper has been placed in front of the structure, at a distance of around 80 cm. In the opposite part of the room, there was the computer running the program, equipped with a 27" display for visualizing all the necessary information for the operator: the GUI, the stream from the cameras installed on the robot, the output video of OpenPose and the video feedback for the experiment, that notified the detection of the markers. The CPU used for the experiment was an Intel Core i9-10900K (CPU @ 3.70 GHz) with 32 GB RAM, equipped with a Geforce GTX 1080. The Kinect v2 was placed at the height of around 1.5 m from the floor and the user was standing in

---

[2] The Github repository can be found here: https://github.com/FraPorta/pepper_openpose_teleoperation.

front of it during the whole duration of the experiment, at a distance of around 1.5 m. A picture of the experimental setup is visible in Fig. 3[3].

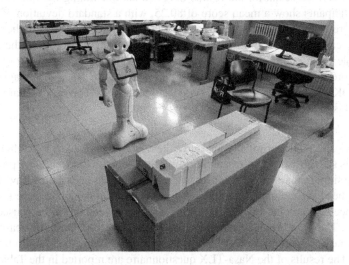

Fig. 3. Initial setup, with the robot ready in front of the structure with the Aruco markers. The two additional cameras on board the robot, as well as some of the markers hidden in the structure, can be seen in the picture. The operator is on the opposite side of the room, with the robot not on their line of sight.

Each trial has been considered as finished when all 5 markers have been detected and, at the end of the three trials, the participants have been asked to compile two questionnaires, the System Usability Scale (SUS) [3] and the Nasa - Task Load Index (TLX) [9]. The System Usability Scale is a ten-item scale that gives a view of the subjective evaluation of the usability of a system. Items are evaluated using a 5-points Likert scale. Nasa-TLX is a multi-dimensional questionnaire that consists of six sub-scales, representing independent variables: Mental, Physical and Temporal demands, Frustration, Effort, and Performance. A weighted combination of these dimensions is likely to represent the workload experienced by most people that perform a task [9].

4   Results and Discussion

Experiments have been conducted with ten participants, four females and six males. The age ranges from 23 to 27, with an average of 24.4 and a standard deviation of 1.265.

System Usability Scale. The System Usability Scale score ranges from 0 to 100, where 0 is the worst score and 100 is the best [3]. Based on previous works that have analyzed SUS scores data collected on different products [1], a system can be defined as at least

---

[3] For a practical demonstration of an experiment, see the video here: https://www.youtube.com/watch?v=4PLiOFP3QtI.

acceptable with a score above 70. Better systems usually get a score in the range from the upper 70s to the upper 80s, and only truly excellent products score over 90.

In the described scenario, the results obtained administrating the questionnaire to the ten participants show a mean score of 80.25, with a standard deviation of 9.3. The average score obtained belongs to the range of products that are a level higher than just acceptable, called "better products" in the acceptability scale. Moreover, the adjective ratings scale is an additional scale that provides a qualitative evaluation of a single average score and divides the 0–100 scale into six ranges: (i) Worst imaginable (ii) Poor (iii) OK (iv) Good (v) Excellent (vi) Best imaginable. The result obtained in this experiment is in the range between Good and Excellent.

Nasa-TLX. Nasa-TLX originally measures the overall workload as a weighted combination of its six subscales, but researchers usually eliminate the weighting process and analyze the single subscales or their average: this version has been called Raw TLX, and several studies have compared it to the original version, showing that there is basically no difference between the two [9]. For this reason, this version has been used for this experiment. The score for each subscale ranges from 0 to 100, but in this case, 0 is the best score, i.e., no workload, while 100 is the worst one, corresponding to the highest workload. The results of the Nasa-TLX questionnaire are reported in the Table 1.

Table 1. Results of the NASA-TLX scale questionnaire.

Subscale	Average score	Standard deviation
Mental demand	26.5	21.6
Physical demand	36.5	34.88
Temporal demand	23.5	18.71
Performance	16.5	10.01
Effort	37	24.85
Frustration	29	21.32
Overall workload	28.17	16.17

The average score of the perceived overall workload is 28.17, with a standard deviation of 16.17. Neither the original scale nor subsequent works have provided researchers with normalized data to understand what is an acceptable or unacceptable workload. Nevertheless, it is possible to find some benchmarks in the original studies for the validation of the scale. The mean of the overall workload across the 16 studies performed in [10] for the validation is 39. So it is possible to use this number and compare it to the result obtained in this study to evaluate it. The result obtained, lower than the aforementioned mean, should only be seen as an indicative evaluation since the benchmark is based on a small sample.

Finally, two subscales with the worst average scores are the Physical Demand and the Effort, with respectively 36.5 and 37, highlighting the aspects that the users have found more demanding during the tests.

Completion Times. The time needed to complete the tasks is a direct measure of the performances obtained by participants using the system. The average time spent for concluding each trial is respectively 431.68 s for the first trial, 355.72 s for the second trial, and 284.04 for the third one. The standard deviation of the results of the various participants for each trial is 170.91 for the first, 77.63 for the second, and 110.67 for the third. The full list of times is visible in Table 2.

Table 2. Time to complete the three trials of the experiment in seconds for the 10 participants.

Participant	First	Second	Third
1	581.27	364.43	424.58
2	222.85	355.46	262.92
3	181.57	376.16	192.56
4	279.59	375.24	246.81
5	624.82	382.23	373,12
6	439.12	489.36	482.37
7	339.69	249.56	165.64
8	669.30	407.80	148,71
9	455.45	345.17	257.96
10	523.17	211.81	285.69
Average	431.68	355.72	284.04
Standard deviation	170.91	77.63	110.67

The results obtained show that the average time improves over the three attempts: indeed, the paired t-test performed on the resulting times indicates that differences between the first and the third attempt are statistically significant at the 95% probability level ($p = 0.025$). This means that the users get better over time and they manage to adapt to the system and master the available tools to find the markers. Moreover, the standard deviation over the ten participants is higher for the first attempt with respect to the other two. This means that for the first attempt the obtained results are more spread out with respect to the average, probably because some people manage to adapt to the commands very quickly, while others need more time. Higher differences in the first trial may also be due to the background of the participants, some of which may have already used a Kinect for gaming purposes or may have had previous experience with robots.

Joint Angles Trajectories. The angles trajectories of the joints of the right arm (shoulder roll and shoulder pitch, elbow yaw and elbow roll) during two tries of the same participant are depicted in Fig. 4a and 4b. Both figures highlight how the trajectories of the human skeleton model and of the robot have good consistency, although there are some small deviations due to the self-collision avoidance system. Most of these deviations are almost negligible. Another borderline situation that determines difference in the trajectories can be observed in Fig. 4a: toward the end of the experiment, the elbow roll of the human skeleton has a leaping deviation, possibly given by a pose estimation error, where an angle moves from the minimum to the maximum value in a short time frame. The robot does not track this movement too fast for the motors, resulting in a safer and more natural behavior.

The similarity between the human pose and the robot has been further assessed by comparing the joint angles of the robot to the human skeleton model. The mean squared errors (MSE) between the calculated joint angle and the measured angle on the robot, computed during each iteration and averaged over the whole trial are all between 10^{-1} and 10^{-2} radiants, confirming that the robot pose on average is similar to the human skeleton model, and hence, since benchmarks performed on the OpenPose algorithm have shown a very high precision on the estimation of the upper body keypoints [4], to the human pose.

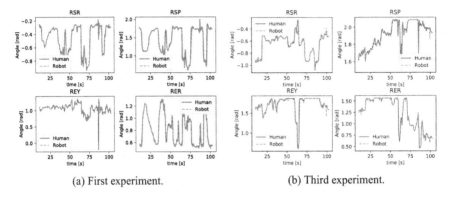

(a) First experiment.   (b) Third experiment.

Fig. 4. Trajectories of the joints of the right arm (Right Shoulder Roll, Right Shoulder Pitch, Right Elbow Yaw, and Right Elbow Roll) in radians during the first and third experiment of a participant.

Voice Commands and Visual Feedback. Voice commands are essential to the completion of the tasks assigned to the users because they are used to move the robot base around the environment and find the markers. Hence, the evaluation of the experiment's results is also affected by the language skills of the users and by the ambient noise level. Moreover, the Kinect's microphone did not have great quality and it had to be at least at a 1.5 m distance from the person. This affects the performance of the system, making the base movements and other voice commands less reliable and slower.

Based on the qualitative feedback from participants, the quality and time delay of the visual feedback, composed of the video stream of the two mini IP cameras installed on Pepper, were satisfying (around 100 ms) and did not cause any problems during the experiments. However, the video captured by the camera on the head of the robot, and the voice commands to control it were underused. In fact, most of the participants did not use this function and only relied on the camera on the arm, which was easier and more intuitive to control.

Computational Time. Finally, the computational time of the system has also been estimated, computing it starting from the human model extraction until the commands are sent to the robot. The average computational cost for calculating the joint angles with the GA-LVVJ method has been calculated in 0.59 ms. Moreover, the measured average computational time of a complete iteration of the architecture is 202 ms, with a minimum of 194 ms and a maximum of 212 ms. Hence, the robot is controlled with a frequency of 5 Hz and the maximum delay is around 0.2 s. Based on the qualitative feedback from the participants, this frequency allows the operator to confidently control the robot's movements most of the time without a noticeable delay.

5   Conclusions

This research paper describes the implementation and preliminary testing of an intuitive and immersive teleoperation framework, aimed at easily controlling a humanoid robot in a healthcare setting by directly piloting its upper limbs, head, and torso with body movements. Questionnaires results confirm that the system is valuable in terms of usability and workload perceived by the operators, while the collected data prove that the system is able to correctly reproduce human movements. All participants in the experiments were able to complete the task, suggesting that the visual feedback allows the operator to have a good understanding of the situation in front of the robot while giving them the possibility to explore more in detail certain areas using the secondary camera installed on the arm.

Future work can include the implementation of a different human pose estimation method that does not rely on depth cameras, the analysis of the correlation between user's and robot's joints trajectories, and the evaluation of the system in a real healthcare scenario. This scenario may include embedding the robots with partial autonomy. For example, when not remotely controlled, the robot can interact autonomously with people, e.g., to reduce isolation through conversation [15], until a doctor or a relative decides to embody themselves in the robot for direct interaction. As another example, we will explore shared autonomy scenarios in which some functionalities are under the direct control of the operator, whereas other functionalities are prerogative of the robot (e.g., obstacle avoidance during motion [12]).

References

1. Bangor, A., Kortum, P.T., Miller, J.T.: An empirical evaluation of the system usability scale. International Journal of Human-Computer Interaction **24**(6), 574–594 (2008)
2. Bhaskar, S., et al.: Designing futuristic telemedicine using artificial intelligence and robotics in the covid-19 era. Front. Public Health **8** (2020)
3. Brooke, J.: SUS: a quick and dirty usability scale. Usability Eval. Ind. **189** (1995)
4. Cao, Z., Hidalgo, G., Simon, T., Wei, S.E., Sheikh, Y.: OpenPose: realtime multi-person 2D pose estimation using part affinity fields. IEEE Trans. Pattern Anal. Mach. Intell. **43**(1), 172–186 (2019)
5. Caruso, L., Russo, R., Savino, S.: Microsoft Kinect V2 vision system in a manufacturing application. Rob. Comput. Integr. Manuf. **48**, 174–181 (2017)
6. Dalin, E., Bergonzani, I., Anne, T., Ivaldi, S., Mouret, J.B.: Whole-body teleoperation of the TALOS humanoid robot: preliminary results. In: ICRA 2021–5th Workshop on Teleoperation of Dynamic Legged Robots in Real Scenarios (2021)

7. Filiatrault, S., Crétu, A.: Human arm motion imitation by a humanoid robot. In: 2014 IEEE International Symposium on Robotic and Sensors Environments (ROSE) Proceedings, pp. 31–36 (2014)

8. Grabowski, A., Jankowski, J., Wodzyński, M.: Teleoperated mobile robot with two arms: the influence of a human-machine interface, VR training and operator age. Int. J. Hum. Comput. Stud. **156**, 102707 (2021)

9. Hart, S.: Nasa-task load index (NASA-TLX); 20 years later. In: Proceedings of the Human Factors and Ergonomics Society Annual Meeting, vol. 50 (2006)

10. Hart, S.G., Staveland, L.E.: Development of NASA-TLX (task load index): results of empirical and theoretical research. In: Hancock, P.A., Meshkati, N. (eds.) Human Mental Workload, Advances in Psychology, vol. 52, pp. 139–183. North-Holland (1988)

11. Iskakov, K., Burkov, E., Lempitsky, V., Malkov, Y.: Learnable triangulation of human pose. In: International Conference on Computer Vision (ICCV) (2019)

12. Mastrogiovanni, F., Sgorbissa, A., Zaccaria, R.: Robust navigation in an unknown environment with minimal sensing and representation. IEEE Trans. Syst. Man Cybern. B Cybern. **39**(1), 212–229 (2009). https://doi.org/10.1109/TSMCB.2008.2004505

13. Mei, B.D., Lega, I., Sampaolo, L., Valli, M.: Covid-19: stress management among healthcare workers (2020). https://www.epicentro.iss.it/en/coronavirus/sars-cov-2-stress-management-healthcare-workers

14. Pandey, A.K., Gelin, R.: A mass-produced sociable humanoid robot: pepper: the first machine of its kind. IEEE Rob. Autom. Mag. **25**(3), 40–48 (2018)

15. Papadopoulos, C., et al..: The caresses randomised controlled trial: exploring the health-related impact of culturally competent artificial intelligence embedded into socially assistive robots and tested in older adult care homes. Int. J. Soc. al Robotics **14**(1), 245–256 (2022). https://doi.org/10.1007/s12369-021-00781-x

16. Parviainen, J., Turja, T., Van Aerschot, L.: Social robots and human touch in care: the perceived usefulness of robot assistance among healthcare professionals. In: Korn, O. (ed.) Social Robots: Technological, Societal and Ethical Aspects of Human-Robot Interaction. HIS, pp. 187–204. Springer, Cham (2019). https://doi.org/10.1007/978-3-030-17107-0_10

17. Recchiuto, C., Sgorbissa, A., Zaccaria, R.: Visual feedback with multiple cameras in a UAVs human-swarm interface. Robot. Auton. Syst. **80**(C), 43–54 (2016)

18. Riley, M., Ude, A., Wade, K., Atkeson, C.: Enabling real-time full-body imitation: a natural way of transferring human movement to humanoids. In: 2003 IEEE International Conference on Robotics and Automation (Cat. No.03CH37422), vol. 2, pp. 2368–2374 (2003)

19. Rolley-Parnell, E., et al.: Bi-manual articulated robot teleoperation using an external rgb-d range sensor. In: 2018 15th International Conference on Control, Automation, Robotics and Vision (ICARCV), pp. 298–304 (2018)

20. Tomić, M., Chevallereau, C., Jovanović, K., Potkonjak, V., Rodić, A.: Human to humanoid motion conversion for dual-arm manipulation tasks. Robotica **36**(8), 1167–1187 (2018)

21. Wang, Z., Liang, R., Chen, Z., Liang, B.: Fast and intuitive kinematics mapping for human-robot motion imitating: a virtual-joint-based approach. IFAC-PapersOnLine **53**(2), 10011–10018 (2020). 21st IFAC World Congress

22. Whitney, D., Rosen, E., Phillips, E., Konidaris, G., Tellex, S.: Comparing robot grasping teleoperation across desktop and virtual reality with ROS reality. In: Amato, N.M., Hager, G., Thomas, S., Torres-Torriti, M. (eds.) Robotics Research. SPAR, vol. 10, pp. 335–350. Springer, Cham (2020). https://doi.org/10.1007/978-3-030-28619-4_28

23. Wu, H., Xiao, B.: 3D human pose estimation via explicit compositional depth maps. Proc. AAAI Conf. Artif. Intell. **34**(07), 12378–12385 (2020)

24. Zhang, Z., Niu, Y., Yan, Z., Lin, S.: Real-time whole-body imitation by humanoid robots and task-oriented teleoperation using an analytical mapping method and quantitative evaluation. Appl. Sci. **8**(10) (2018)

Social Robots in the Stuttering Clinic: A Human-Centred Exploration with Speech Language Pathologists

Shruti Chandra[1]([✉]) [ID], Torrey Loucks[2,3], Gerardo Chavez Castaneda[1], and Kerstin Dautenhahn[1,4] [ID]

[1] Social and Intelligent Robotics Research Laboratory (SIRRL), Department of Electrical and Computer Engineering, University of Waterloo, Waterloo, ON, Canada
{shruti.chandra,kdautenh}@uwaterloo.ca, gerardo@chavezcastaneda.com
[2] Department of Communication Sciences and Disorders, Institute of Stuttering Treatment and Research (ISTAR), Faculty of Rehabilitation Medicine, University of Alberta, Edmonton, Canada
loucks@ualberta.ca
[3] Department of Communication Sciences and Disorders, Jacksonville University, Jacksonville, FL, USA
tloucks@ju.edu
[4] System Design Engineering Department, University of Waterloo, 200 University Ave, N2L3G1 Waterloo, ON, Canada

Abstract. This research aims to explore the feasibility of integrating social robots as a tool for speech-language pathologists in stuttering intervention. This research followed an exploratory, human-centred approach leveraging the Double Diamond Design Process Model. In this study, we employed co-design tools, including a survey, one-to-one semi-structured expert interviews and a focus group to understand challenges frequently reported by speech-language pathologists and discuss opportunities for social robots to face some of these challenges. The qualitative results of our study revealed five major themes, pointing towards several avenues for social robots to aid speech-language pathologists and their clients over the course of a stuttering intervention program.

Keywords: Stuttering · Stammering · Socially assistive robots · Assistive technology · Speech language pathologists · Human-centred exploration · Co-design

1 Introduction

Social robots (SRs) are being employed across a wide range of healthcare and rehabilitation settings, with a range of populations, to support healthcare workers and facilitate more effective intervention [9,16]. Social robots have been

---

Notes: https://designthinking.ideo.com/faq/whats-the-difference-between-human-centered-design-and-design-thinking.

F. Cavallo et al. (Eds.): ICSR 2022, LNAI 13818, pp. 299–313, 2022.
https://doi.org/10.1007/978-3-031-24670-8_27

extensively employed for children with autism spectrum disorder, a neurodevelopmental disorder, compared to children with other developmental disorders such as learning disabilities or children with specific educational needs [13,18]. Despite the demonstrated therapeutic benefits of robot-assisted healthcare for people with special needs, little to no empirical research has been conducted on people with developmental stuttering, which onsets at childhood. Due to the absence of prior research in this application area, it was crucial to first investigate if social robots are suitable for stuttering intervention. A human-centred design project begins by empathizing with the different stakeholders and ends with proposing context-appropriate solutions to suit their needs. Following this approach, in this research we evaluated opportunities for SRs to support speech-language pathologists (SLPs) and their clients[1] in clinic-based stuttering intervention.

Stuttering is prevalent worldwide. It is a neurodevelopmental disorder that impedes an individual's ability to speak fluently. People who stutter know exactly what they intend to say, but the flow of speech production is interrupted by involuntary repetitions, prolongations, or cessation of sounds [20]. Along with its disruptive effects on speech communication, stuttering also significantly impacts the quality of life by negatively affecting social, emotional and psychological domains. Developmental stuttering is the most common type of stuttering [22], beginning in early childhood, typically between the ages of 2 to 5 years [11]. The speech disruptions in childhood are accompanied by negative socioemotional impacts as the children transition into adolescence and adulthood. Speech-language pathologists (SLPs) are the primary professionals responsible for identifying and treating speech and language disorders, including stuttering. The therapeutic framework typically includes three phases: *Establishment*, in which clients learn skills to meet their fluency goals; *Transfer*, where they apply the learned skills inside and outside the clinic; and *Maintenance*, in which clients develop a plan to maintain fluency skills over the long term [19]. SLPs work most closely with clients who stutter in the first two phases.

In the current study, we employed a series of co-design tools, including a survey, semi-structured one-to-one expert interviews and a focus group with four SLPs from the Institute of Stuttering Treatment and Research (ISTAR) in Canada, to document some challenges SLPs and their clients encounter during the treatment and explore the possibilities for social robots to mitigate some of these challenges.

2 Background

Technological-based interventions have previously been incorporated into stuttering treatment. The following is a non-exhaustive list: altered auditory feedback devices, metronomes for controlling speech rate, EMG biofeedback, and virtual reality [2,8]. Human-robot interactions (HRI) have not yet been introduced

---

[1] The clients, in the context of this paper, are people who stutter and who receive speech therapy from SLPs.

in stuttering intervention, despite expanding literature indicating the potential for SRs to aid clinicians. Introducing HRI into this field requires preliminary exploration to assess its viability. In the past decade, many studies suggest that social robots can support activities involving verbal-articulatory tasks, communication games and turn-taking activities [3,7,12,23]. Studies focused on language disorders, and logopedic interventions suggest that SRs are beneficial for increasing motivation, learning readiness and improving children's attention span, yet further research is required to determine how robots can best be applied in speech therapy with SLPs [13,14]. Moreover, social robots' physical presence can result in more children engagement than on-screen virtual robots [5].

We took a human-centred design approach to conceptualize suitable social robot applications in stuttering intervention. We followed the Double Diamond Design Process Model, which consists of four stages: Discovery, Definition, Development and Delivery [4] (see Fig. 1). The first two phases define the problem space, and the second two phases define possible solutions. The present study addresses the first diamond. Having conducted a prior literature review on stuttering treatment approaches [17] and use of SRs as supplements in the stuttering clinic [6], our next step was to investigate the needs of the various stakeholders (e.g., SLPs, children with stuttering, and parents of children with stuttering) through a structured survey, one-to-one semi-structured expert interviews and a focus group with four SLPs from ISTAR (Institute for Stuttering Treatment and Research), who are highly experienced in stuttering intervention. The current study aims to 1) identify the challenges that SLPs and their clients face during remote and in-person stuttering therapy sessions; 2) explore opportunities for social robots to mitigate some of their challenges. The study was conducted in an online format using the Zoom platform.

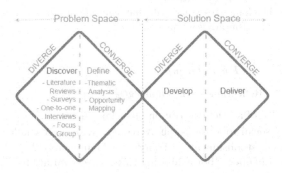

Fig. 1. Double diamond design process model. Based on [4]

3   Methods

Participants: Our participants included four SLPs; all were females, between 29 and 52 years old (mean = 38.5, SD = 10.08), located in Edmonton, Canada.

All were registered at the Alberta College of Speech-Language Pathologists and Audiologists in the province of Alberta. The participants' professional clinical experience with stuttering ranged from 4 to 28 years. The number of participants is a convenience sample based on the availability of SLPs with extensive experience treating stuttering. None of them has interacted with robots before. This study was approved by the Community Research Ethics Office and the University of Waterloo Human Research Ethics Board (application # 43821).

Procedure: We developed the survey on Qualtrics[2] and collected all data online. The survey questions are related to demographics, prior experience with social robots and experience using technology. To measure the participants' experience with technology, we asked them about their tendency towards engagement or avoidance of intensive technology using the 'Affinity for Technology Interaction' on a 6-point Likert scale [15]. After completing the survey, we conducted semi-structured one-to-one expert interviews of approximately one hour with each SLP, where the interviewer was an HRI researcher (the first author). The one-to-one interviews focused on exploring the challenges of the clinicians and their clients. We started the interview by gathering brief information about their profession. Following that, we asked four questions related to challenges, one by one (see the set of questions below). The questions asked to SLPs were in the context of preschool and school-age children.

One-to-one Interviews

1. What are the most common challenges that you face with your clients?

2. What do you think are the major challenges that might prevent young clients (preschool & school-age children) from making progress during a therapy session?

3. What are the major challenges you face in keeping your clients engaged during a therapy session?

4. What are the challenges you think that your clients face in engaging in a therapy session?

Focus Group

[Reflection on the challenges]

[Video of a brief description of social robots]]

1. How could a social robot help you overcome any of these challenges in online therapy [Establishment — Transfer — Maintenance]?
[Video of pepper robot exhibiting three speech variations]

2. Are there speech related therapy techniques that a social robot could help with?

3. Can you think of other ways that a robot could help you during a remote treatment session beyond what we have discussed ?
[Reflection on the above questions]

4. What would be your concerns if you were to use SRs in therapy sessions?

---

[2] https://www.qualtrics.com/.

Since the interview had a semi-structured format, the researcher also asked other related questions depending on the clinicians' responses; however, all four questions were covered by the end. Moreover, all the questions were intended to relate to both in-person and remote therapy settings. After the interviews, we conducted a single hour-long focus group with all four participants. Two researchers conducted the focus group, one from the field of HRI (first author) and one who is a stuttering researcher (second author). Video and audio recordings were obtained for qualitative analyses. We initiated the focus group by showing participants a list of challenges from previous interviews (see the questions above). We asked each participant to reflect on the challenges and share their experience with others. Afterwards, we showed them a 4-min video that included the definition of social robotics, displayed characteristics of various robots (such as their sensors and actuators) and finally provided a summary of fields where social robots have been useful adjuncts to treatment and education. Afterwards, we asked the focus group how social robots could overcome some reported challenges. Following this discussion, we showed a 30-sec video of the humanoid Pepper robot [21] exhibiting three variations of speech; slow speech, high pitch speech and speech with pauses between the words. The purpose of this video was to illustrate how a robot could vary speech as one potential application to related speech treatment activities. We ended the focus group by asking participants to reflect on the concerns around social robots.

Analysis: We collected the survey results and audio/video recordings. The audio data was transcribed to text data using the Python offline open source speech recognition toolkit, 'Vosk'[3]. The accuracy of the transcription varied from 70–80% accuracy. To ensure the transcriptions were correct, a researcher cross-checked the transcriptions by watching each recorded video. A second researcher checked 20% of the transcriptions to ensure accuracy. Then, the two researchers analysed the transcribed data from the interviews and focus group using thematic analysis. This inductive "bottom-up" approach uses a six-phase method [10] to identify the themes. We began with familiarising ourselves with the transcript, then organising it systematically to generate codes. The next step was to group the codes into themes. Afterwards, the two researchers discussed and iteratively resolved any disagreements until all the themes were defined.

4 Results

4.1 Affinity for Technology Interaction

Before the interviews, we collected SLPs' responses to assess their tendency towards intensive technology interaction on a six-point Likert scale, (1: Largely disagree, 6: Completely agree). The average score was 3.5 and the range was between 3.2 and 3.8. These results show that SLPs had medium affinity for technology interaction.

---

[3] https://pypi.org/project/vosk/.

4.2   Challenges Identified by Speech-Language Pathologists

Identifying challenges that SLPs face in a clinical setting is an essential step towards proposing beneficial roles and functionalities for social robots. As shown in Table 1, the thematic analysis results revealed a list of themes for each interview question and the subsequent reflections from the focus group session. For the first question related to the common challenges, seven themes emerged. Eight themes emerged for the question related to the challenges that prevent their clients from making progress. For the following two questions that explored the engagement aspect, 5 and 3 themes emerged, respectively. In total, we identified 23 themes emerging out of the SLPs' responses.

Pain Points, i.e. Persistent or Recurring Problems that SLPs Face: Among the challenges mentioned above, we also inquired about the challenges that are most frustrating to SLPs. These challenges include the following themes: 1) lack of behavioural control (e.g., managing behaviours of clients with attention issues); 2) lack of commitment from clients and their families (e.g., clients forget to do their homework or being informal in remote therapy); 3) Extensive and time-demanding preparation for therapy material; and 4) constant adaptation to clients' needs during therapy sessions.

4.3   Opportunities for Social Robots to Help Overcome the Challenges

During the focus group, we asked four questions to investigate participants' perceptions of social robots in overcoming any challenges they identified in the previous step (see the questions in the Procedure section). Before asking these questions, we showed a list of the challenges to the SLPs to prompt reflection on the pre-identified challenges during the one-to-one interview. We again applied the thematic analysis to the SLPs' responses and found five themes that revealed opportunities for social robots to address some of these challenges. The themes are presented as follows:

Social Robots Have 'X Factors': The SLPs considered that social robots appear to have several unique or noteworthy qualities, such as the potential to be programmed for fun, humorous, engaging, and motivating additions to a clinical setting. The SLPs perceived social robots as a novel, intriguing, unique and different. The SLPs frequently commented that a social robot could also help provide reinforcement and reminders to clients. During the focus group, the SLPs provided several examples of leveraging SRs in therapy to boost their clients' involvement, attention and mood during a therapy session.

Social Robots in Different Roles: SLPs envisaged SRs as adjuncts, similar to other technological tools. They imagined the role of the SRs as a partner for structured activities, but never directed any aspect of treatment. SRs could be homework or interactive practice partners for younger clients for speech tasks. To promote success in transfers, SRs could be incorporated into a play scenario as a transition partners (to practise tasks in easy ways to increase the comfort

Table 1. List of the themes that emerged under each interview question. 'Match' column indicates possible opportunities of leveraging social robots for the respective themes representing challenges. R: Remote session format, I: In-person session format

	Themes of identified challenges	Match
	Most common challenges that are faced with clients	
1	Stuttering does not bother children (R‖I)	
2	Completing homework (R‖I)	*
3	Therapy is not enjoyable due to high dysfluency in early stage of practice (R‖I)	
4	Reinforcement not having an effect on children (R‖I)	*
5	Low parental engagement into quality practice time (R‖I)	
6	Clients not finding time to practice (R‖I)	
7	Apparent lack of progress (R‖I)	*
	Challenges that prevent that younger clients from making progress	
1	Parents lack of openness and willingness (R‖I)	
2	Aversion to video call sessions (R)	
3	Difficulty acquiring new speech skills (R‖I)	
4	Multi-language (R‖I)	
5	Co-existing disorders (R‖I)	*
6	Unsettling factors (R‖I)	
7	Transferring can be a challenge (R‖I)	*
8	Communication more through texting (R‖I)	
	Major challenges in keeping clients engaged in a therapy session	
1	Unwillingness to do practices (R‖I)	*
2	Tiredness (R‖I)	
3	Scared of speaking situation (R‖I)	
4	Limited interest from children (R‖I)	*
5	Learning speech skills is hard (R‖I)	
	Major challenges that clients face in engaging in a therapy session	
1	Finding enough material to keep the clients engaged for longer (R‖I)	*
2	Lack of eye contact on video call (R)	
3	Finding a soft spot to balance clients' excitement and engagement (R‖I)	

of a client and to help prepare for more challenging tasks that they would eventually do in the real-world scenario). For adolescents and adults, SRs could be conversation partners that provide feedback or cues for a specific fluency skill. The themes presented below are specific to therapy components:

Social Robots as Consistent Speech Models: SLPs envisioned SRs could be programmed with a consistent model of slow speech or prolonged speech technique [17] (e.g., stretching a syllable in a word for some time) in a structured speech practice session based on previously reaching a treatment goal under direct treatment by an SLP. Here, SRs would provide an extension for practising and stabilizing fluency skills.

Social Robots for Establishment, Transfer and Maintenance: For each of the three phases, SLPs imagined social robots could participate at different levels. In the establishment phase, SRs could promote children's engagement by being novel and entertaining partners. This could keep a child engaged with the clinician during a session and establish specific speech goals by playing supervised games with the SR. During the maintenance phase, SRs could be an engaging and motivating incentive for children to practice skills. For instance, a warm-up for therapy with the SR could add elements of fun and uniqueness. For the transfer phase, SRs could be transition partners. Across the three phases, SRs could reduce the workload of an SLP. For example, a clinician mentioned: *"I am working with one of them while the other group is being led through with the warm-up with a social robot, I could see that being something that they might enjoy doing, and it's not harmful to their progress because they're already at a point where they can accurately self-evaluate themselves anyway. So, it might be a way to reduce some load on us as clinicians to always be with that client in that kind of group format, which can be helpful."*

Social Robots to Reinforce Social and Speech Skills: In structured conversation activities, a social robot could remind a child to pause before initiating a response. For instance, *'if the client responds within one to two seconds, the SR could ask, 'did you think of your answer first? and promoting actually a pause time that addresses a clinical goal'*. SRs could be a source of reinforcement for young children by delivering praise after a child responds. In addition, the SLPs suggested the SR could motivate the practice of clear speech[4]. *"I think it could be reinforcing for kids who are working on clear speech. I think it would be really good because I have already heard lots of clients will say they talked to Siri or Google Home, and they find it's super motivating that when they actually say like hey SIRI, play me my song or whatever the song is, they kind of validating and wanna practice more. So, a robot could be in that way, or it could just gently say, oh 'I don't understand'."* In addition, they envisioned SRs could be advantageous for repetitive practice activities in their therapy routine when active direction by the SLP is not required.

In each of the above themes, SLPs also emphasized the potential application of SRs for clients' independent or home-based practice and activities in the presence of an SLP. There was consensus among the clinicians that motivation and reinforcement provided by SRs could particularly benefit stuttering clients with co-existing disorders.

4.4   Questions, Uncertainties and Concerns Around Social Robots

The following themes reveal concerns of the SLPs related to the flexibility and feasibility of SRs.

---

[4] Clear speech is a form of overt production that is more understandable to unfamiliar and familiar listeners and is expected to involve distinct articulatory movements.

Need for Human-Human Connection: Stuttering therapy is meant to support social skills and establish connections between people through social interactions. Rapport building between clinicians and clients is a crucial element of speech therapy. For younger clients, therapy also aims to support parental involvement in the therapeutic process. An SR must not hinder rapport building between any stakeholders.

Extra Load on SLPs: SLPs are often overloaded by the need to plan and prepare therapy materials that are frequently customised to a client. If incorporating SRs into therapy increases their workload, then the short-term benefits of an SR might not be realised. For example, preparing activities with the robot might need several iterations and be perceived as time-consuming. Moreover, teaching strategies are challenging as they require a great amount of multi-sensing and adaptation. Using a robot would add one more thing to oversee and may slow down therapy progress.

Robot-Centric: SLPs also raised concerns regarding the feasibility of using social robots in terms of programming and adaptation. Other concerns include SR applications' quality and appropriateness to a specific population. For teenage clients, SRs might be perceived as too juvenile. For younger children, could the SR understand their speech accurately? Similarly, SLPs also mentioned that an SR might provide generic feedback, e.g., 'good job' or 'not a good job', that is not specific enough for the therapy goal.

Accessibility of SR Outside the Clinical Setting: Even if SLPs found social robots could be helpful, they wondered if an effective SR could be accessible outside the clinic.

Is the SR Just an Expensive Toy: SLPs mentioned a concern about maintenance cost for SRs. SRs are expensive, and if the clients manipulate and play with them during therapy, there is a possibility of damage.

Areas Where SR are not being Useful: SRs might not be helpful when parents and children perform activities together, such as reading a book or playing on the floor. Some SLPs also stated that SRs are more useful for in-person therapy sessions than remote sessions. Using robots "in person" was essential to efficacy.

Perceptions of the Stuttering Community: Some fluency skills have been criticised as leading to speech that sounds 'robotic'. Using a robot might create an incorrect perception that the treatment aims to develop robotic speech. Moreover, using a robot as a conversational partner instead of other people was also identified as a practice that could be criticised within the community of people who stutter.

4.5 Intersection of the Identified Challenges and Opportunities for Social Robots in Stuttering Therapy

In the previous sections, we identified a list of themes of challenges faced by SLPs and their clients and several themes revealing opportunities for SRs. We mapped the challenges with the opportunities and found 8 points of intersection where SRs could be beneficial (see Table 1).

Completing Homework: There are several reasons for not completing homework, such as parents forgetting to do homework with the children, not having adequate practice material at home, or lacking effective strategies to motivate their practice. SLPs suggested SRs could be homework partners. *"I could see possibly if it actually can be available outside our therapy time, so it could be where they could be linked into the robot and to practice with their mom or dad.... and they could practice that way, it is like a homework practice partner"*

Reinforcement not Having an Effect on Children: Behavioural-based stuttering treatment approaches include verbal contingencies on children's speech, where parents provide comments after a child's clear or stuttered speech. These comments act as reinforcers or prompt to reattempt the utterance. For some children, reinforcement from a parent is not always effective. SRs could be useful to supplement such verbal reinforcement. *"I could see it potentially with the younger ones and being a source of like reinforcement but even when I am thinking about how to maybe trade (use) a robot if that's possible to provide praise or something like that personal speech"*

Apparent Lack of Progress: This theme contains several factors that could impede a client's progress, particularly related to the maintenance phase. *"Maintenance is always a challenge about how to keep the practice going on, which kind of brings it to social robots.... In maintenance, I think it could be something that would be motivating for people to do their practice if there was maybe some kind of incentivized reason for doing social robot work, it might actually be more engaging for that child to have somebody lead through this cycle so could be used in maintenance for a warm-up with a social robot, and they do their social robot warm up with that person..., maybe more often because it is kind of fun and different and unique"*

Transfer can be a Challenge: In the transfer phase, clients apply techniques from the establishment phase in outside environments. SRs could aid in overcoming some transition challenges. *"In transfer, it could be used as a transition partner, that is not to say that we need that because we generally find ways to be able to transition without the use of a social robot right now, and it is effective and efficient. The social robot might just be a fun add-on"*

Unwillingness to do Practises: SRs could motivate and encourage certain clients who either do not want to do therapy or do it just because of their parents. *"Usually 9 to 11-year-olds, that tends to be the age category, 'I don't want to be here'. They can be just quite stubborn"* *"If they were more engaged [with SR] that might help with being able to manage behaviour because that might be motivating for them to be sitting and engaging in the session work...so I could see how you know it's something unique, a novel which might initially be interesting to them."*

Limited Interest from Children: Some children have limited interest and motivation, either because they might find practices boring or only like certain activities. As suggested by the SLPs, the SR could be helpful if it prompts and helps to sustain interest in treatment. *"It [SR] can help with the intrigue, and an engagement... because of it can provide some intrigue for clients that cannot support the problem of engagements also possibly of motivation."*

Finding Enough Material to Keep the Clients Engaged Over Multiple Sessions: The factors under this theme include the need for activities that engage young clients for longer periods. Clinicians mentioned that if the SR engages the younger clients, it could be programmed with a repertoire of activities that could be readily retrieved and implemented. *"If they [clients] feel like that they do not know what anything to do at home then maybe link into this [SR] and there is a bank of activities with different language levels that the parent can choose, and they could practice that way, it is like a homework practice partner"*

4.6 Material/Activities Used in Stuttering Therapy

SLPs deliver child-centred play-based speech therapy to younger clients, focusing on their speech goals around play (e.g., games, toys). Play is considered a principal medium of teaching fundamental skills critical for children's social and cognitive development (e.g., turn-taking, listening skills, practising waiting, and thinking before speaking). Play-based therapies bring fun and enjoyment to providing and receiving therapy and are designed to be functional and meaningful to each client. Besides, they are crucial during the maintenance phase, where clients work independently. The choice of play-based activities depends on several factors, such as the interest, needs, and ages of clients and the goals of therapy sessions. As motor practice is essential for progress, the initial therapy stage would include activities that provide abundant trials. These activities are primarily structured, showing predictability or pattern, embedded with reinforcers (e.g., verbal praise) and incentives; for instance, structured games include board games and scripted play routines. As clients progress, semi-structured and spontaneous activities are slowly incorporated during therapy. Moreover, both digital (e.g., online chess game, virtual book reading etc.) and physical materials (e.g., I spy game[5]) can be used to provide therapy.

5 Discussion

This study provides context for the application of social robots for stuttering intervention. We applied co-design tools, including a survey, one-to-one expert interviews and a focus group with four highly experienced speech pathologists.

Challenges and Opportunities. The thematic analysis of the interview data revealed 23 themes, demonstrating a wide diversity of the challenges experienced by SLPs and their clients. The thematic analysis of the focus group data revealed

---

[5] A guessing game where a player (an SLP) chooses an object within sight and announces to another player (a client) naming the first letter of the object. The client attempt to guess this object.

five significant themes overlaying several opportunities for social robots in therapy. The possibilities and opportunities for employing social robots in therapy interventions emerging from the themes are tremendous and hold the potential to aid SLPs and people with stuttering. Some examples include the possibility of integrating SRs in all three phases of stuttering programs, providing a consistent model of speech for speech practices (independently or with SLPs), promoting social and speech skills for people with stuttering and other comorbidities.

Intersection of Challenges and Opportunities: By mapping the themes of the challenges with the themes of opportunities, we could match 8 themes of challenges where SRs could be viable to aid SLPs and their clients. As HRI researchers, we believe that the possibilities to implement SRs could also extend to other themes; however, those were not identified by the small group of SLPs, and we could not include them in this study. Thus, we only matched those themes with the opportunities that the SLPs explicitly mentioned to avoid our subjective biasing in the proposed application of SRs in the stuttering clinic. Out of 23 themes of challenges, 21 themes reside in both remote and in-person settings. Therefore, the challenges experienced by SLPs and their clients are similar to the virtual and in-person contexts. The specific application of social robots could differ depending on the context but could still support similar therapy goals. Since the study was done during the pandemic, most of the questions regarding social robots were designed to explore the potential of using SRs in virtual care. Interestingly, the emerging themes associated with social robots were not distinguished in physical or virtual settings and covered independent and speech practices with SLPs.

Concerns: Providing efficacious and engaging speech therapy is challenging and complex. The emerging themes related to the concerns of SLPs indicate the complexity of speech therapy- it involves constant multi-sensing, adaptation and personalisation from SLPs. Not only does it require substantial planning of material individualised to each client, but it also necessitates active shaping of the interaction and embedding appropriate instructions and feedback into it, taking into account the abilities and needs of the client at the moment. Considering this complexity, the concerns of SLPs extend to the feasibility and adaptability of social robots in a therapy session and the preparation required to develop social robot applications and the usage of SRs during the therapy. SRs can be applied for some therapy components, considering their impact on human-human connection as it is a core of therapy treatments. It should be noted that these SLPs (and most SLPs) have not interacted with social robots and had a medium affinity towards technological supplements to therapy. The concerns associated with the perceptions of the stuttering community can be addressed by providing clarifications through publications or other academic presentations. Concerns such as maintenance cost and accessibility of SRs outside the lab are an important open problems in the social robotics field and are not specific to the stuttering clinic. This concern can only be addressed by future development of versatile but inexpensive, robust, easy to use and easy to maintain SRs [1].

The Relevance of a Human-Centred Approach: Conducting exploratory user research at this early stage unveiled two inaccurate presumptions of the research team: 1) Due to the ongoing pandemic at the time of the study, we believed that SLPs would be transitioning from in-person to virtual care; however, during the interviews, we realised that they have been providing hybrid therapy (virtual and in-person care) for several years. Hence, they were already proficient in conducting therapy remotely; 2) we assumed that engaging younger clients are inherently challenging; thus, we focused two of our research questions on the aspect of 'engagement'. Though SLPs confirmed that engagement is essential for speech therapy, they already employ multiple strategies to address it. In contrast, they reported that *sustaining* engagement for a longer duration, especially with younger clients, can often be a more significant challenge. Although both of these presumptions did not affect our data collection and results, they highlight that we might have embarked on developing unfruitful solutions without getting feedback from potential users very early on.

Problem Space Definition: The discovery and exploration of the challenges mentioned above, opportunities and concerns will help define the boundaries of the design space for the following stages. Thanks to the valuable insights from field experts, we identified several traits and constraints to guide us in developing appropriate solutions to apply SRs in stuttering interventions.

Limitations: This study has a few limitations. Due to the articles' length limit, we could not describe all the themes we reported under challenges; we described only eight themes that could be matched with the themes of opportunities for SRs. Due to the COVID-19 pandemic, we conducted the study remotely, limiting direct interaction between SLPs, the research team, and social robots. Considering the nature of this specific population of stakeholders, we could recruit only four speech-language pathologists who were interested and accessible for participating in the study. Another limitation is that we recruited only SLPs as stakeholders. The involvement of other stakeholders, such as children and adolescents with stuttering and parents/carers, could influence the identified challenges and opportunities for social robots.

6   Conclusion and Future Work

Following a human-centred approach, we investigated the challenges of SLPs and their clients and opportunities to employ social robots in therapeutic stuttering interventions. The thematic analysis of the qualitative data revealed five major themes showing the opportunities for social robots. Mapping the challenges and the opportunities identified by the SLPs, the results present several future avenues for social robots to help overcome some of the challenges. Having defined the problem space (first diamond [4]) in the current study, our next step is to address the solution space (second diamond). We plan to continue running co-design sessions to create prototypes of SR applications and evaluate them with other stakeholders to identify the most feasible solutions.

Acknowledgments. This research was undertaken, in part, thanks to funding from the Canada 150 Research Chairs Program.

References

1. Mahdi, H., Akgun, S.A., Saleh, S., Dautenhahn, K.: A survey on the design and evolution of social robots - past, present and future. Rob. Auton. Syst., 104193 (2022). https://doi.org/10.1016/j.robot.2022.104193
2. Almudhi, A.: Evolution in technology and changes in the perspective of stuttering therapy: a review study. Saudi J. Biol. Sci. **28**(1), 623–627 (2021)
3. Amanatiadis, A., Kaburlasos, V.G., Dardani, C., Chatzichristofis, S.A., Mitropoulos, A.: Social robots in special education: creating dynamic interactions for optimal experience. IEEE Consum. Electron. Mag. **9**(3), 39–45 (2020)
4. Ball, J.: The double diamond: a universally accepted depiction of the design process (2019). https://www.designcouncil.org.uk/our-work/news-opinion/double-diamond-universally-accepted-depiction-design-process/
5. Belpaeme, T., et al.: Multimodal child-robot interaction: building social bonds. J. Hum. Rob. Interact. **1**(2) (2012)
6. Chandra, S., Gupta, G., Loucks, T., Dautenhahn, K.: Opportunities for social robots in the stuttering clinic: a review and proposed scenarios. Paladyn J. Behav. Rob. **13**(1), 23–44 (2022). https://doi.org/10.1515/pjbr-2022-0001
7. Charron, N., Kim Lindley-Soucy, E.D., Lewis, L., Craig, M., et al.: Robot therapy. New Hampshire J. Educ. **21**(Fall), 10983 (2019)
8. Chaudhary, C., John, S., Kumaran, S., Guddattu, V., Krishnan, G.: Technological interventions in stuttering: a systematic review. Technol. Disabil. (Preprint), 1–22 (2022)
9. Cifuentes, C.A., Pinto, M.J., Céspedes, N., Múnera, M.: Social robots in therapy and care. Current Rob. Rep. **1**(3), 59–74 (2020)
10. Clarke, V., Braun, V., Hayfield, N.: Thematic analysis. Qual. Psychol. Pract. Guide Res. Methods **222**, 248 (2015)
11. Dalton, P., Hardcastle, W.J.: Disorders of Fluency. Wiley-Blackwell (1989)
12. David, D.O., Costescu, C.A., Matu, S., Szentagotai, A., Dobrean, A.: Effects of a robot-enhanced intervention for children with ASD on teaching turn-taking skills. J. Educ. Comput. Res. **58**(1), 29–62 (2020)
13. Egido-García, V., Estévez, D., Corrales-Paredes, A., Terrón-López, M.J., Velasco-Quintana, P.J.: Integration of a social robot in a pedagogical and logopedic intervention with children: a case study. Sensors **20**(22), 6483 (2020)
14. Estévez, D., Terrón-López, M.J., Velasco-Quintana, P.J., Rodríguez-Jiménez, R.M., Álvarez-Manzano, V.: A case study of a robot-assisted speech therapy for children with language disorders. Sustainability **13**(5), 2771 (2021)
15. Franke, T., Attig, C., Wessel, D.: A personal resource for technology interaction: development and validation of the affinity for technology interaction (ATI) scale. Int. J. Hum. Comput. Interact. **35**(6), 456–467 (2019)
16. González-González, C.S., Violant-Holz, V., Gil-Iranzo, R.M.: Social robots in hospitals: a systematic review. Appl. Sci. **11**(13), 5976 (2021)
17. Gupta, G., Chandra, S., Dautenhahn, K., Loucks, T.: Stuttering treatment approaches from the past two decades: comprehensive survey and review. J. Stud. Res. **11**(2) (2022)

18. Karageorgiou, E., et al.: Development of educational scenarios for child-robot inter-action: the case of learning disabilities. In: Merdan, M., Lepuschitz, W., Koppen-steiner, G., Balogh, R., Obdržálek, D. (eds.) RiE 2021. AISC, vol. 1359, pp. 26–33. Springer, Cham (2022). https://doi.org/10.1007/978-3-030-82544-7_3

19. Kully, D.A., Langevin, M., Lomheim, H.: Intensive treatment of stuttering in ado-lescents and adults. In: Stuttering and Related Disorders of Fluency, pp. 213–232 (2007)

20. World Health Organization: Manual of the international statistical classification of diseases, injuries, and causes of death, vol. 1. Geneva (Switzerland) WHO (1977)

21. Pandey, A.K., Gelin, R.: A mass-produced sociable humanoid robot: pepper: the first machine of its kind. IEEE Rob. Autom. Mag. 25(3), 40–48 (2018)

22. Prasse, J.E., Kikano, G.E.: Stuttering: an overview. Am. Fam. Physician 77(9), 1271–1276 (2008)

23. Silvera-Tawil, D., Bradford, D., Roberts-Yates, C.: Talk to me: the role of human-robot interaction in improving verbal communication skills in students with autism or intellectual disability. In: 2018 27th IEEE International Symposium on Robot and Human Interactive Communication (RO-MAN), pp. 1–6. IEEE (2018)

Evaluating Human-in-the-Loop Assistive Feeding Robots Under Different Levels of Autonomy with VR Simulation and Physiological Sensors

Tong Xu[1]([✉]), Tianlin Zhao[2], Jesus G. Cruz-Garza[1,3],
Tapomayukh Bhattacharjee[2], and Saleh Kalantari[1]

[1] Department of Human Centered Design, Cornell University, Ithaca,
NY 14850, USA
{tx66,jgc243,sk3268}@cornell.edu
[2] Department of Computer Science, Cornell University, Ithaca, NY 14850, USA
{tz68,tapomayukh}@cornell.edu
[3] Department of Neurosurgery, Houston Methodist Research Institute, Houston, USA

Abstract. Feeding assistance is one of the most fundamental and time-consuming activities of daily living. In this study, we designed, implemented, and tested a system for virtual response testing of a human-in-the-loop assistive feeding robot with physiological measurements. The study focused on how different levels of autonomy (fully autonomous vs. partial autonomous) in feeding robots affected user experience. In a within-subject experiment with randomized order, we found statistically significant differences in Duration, Usability, Workload, and Success rate between Autonomy Modes. The results from EEG measures were consistent with the self-reported results in evaluating the Usability and Workload. Our findings support the potential of VR simulation and biometric sensors as an effective way to evaluate user interactions with an assistive robot, and suggest users' preference to collaborate with the robot.

Keywords: Human-robot interaction · Human-robot collaboration · Virtual reality · Robot autonomy · Electroencephalogram (EEG)

1 Introduction

According to a 2014 survey, nearly 24 million people in the United States aged 18 years or older needed assistance with activities of daily living (ADLs) such as feeding, dressing, and bathing [9]. While caregivers can provide assistance for these tasks, they create a significant social burden and care-recipients may feel a loss of independence [16,22]. One alternative that may help care recipients to feel more in control of their lives is the use of assistive robots [6–8,13,18,20]. In the current project we focused on feeding assistance because it is one of the most fundamental ADLs that care-recipients need help with, and also because it is one of the most time-consuming activities for caregivers [6,7,14,18,20].

F. Cavallo et al. (Eds.): ICSR 2022, LNAI 13818, pp. 314–327, 2022.
https://doi.org/10.1007/978-3-031-24670-8_28

Fig. 1. Virtual Environment. a) The overall setup of the virtual environment. b) The participant's view of robot under full autonomous condition. c) The participant's view of robot under partially autonomous condition.

An assortment of robot-assisted feeding systems have been developed to help people who have mobility impairments [6, 7, 18, 20, 36, 38, 41]. These robots incorporate various degrees of user autonomy-some allow users to have more direct control over the movements of the robot, while others only have one fixed motion to which the users must adjust [3]. Previous studies have found that users do not always favor higher levels of control over feeding robots; there seems to be a "sweet spot" beyond which further adjustability is perceived as more of a hassle than a benefit [7, 21]. It also seems likely that different users may prefer different levels of control for different types of feeding assistance [11].

Researchers in this area have generally relied on self-reported surveys and qualitative interviews to measure the usefulness of different feeding-robot designs. While these methods provide important feedback and insights, they suffer from mono-method bias, in which the correlation between outcomes in various studies may be caused by the sources of measurement error that they share in common. This can increase the risk of false-positive results [34]. Adding physiological measurements can help to reduce this problem, and can sometimes reveal unconscious mechanisms and responses of which the users themselves were not aware [5]. Electroencephalogram (EEG) data is one of the most commonly used measurements for this purpose. Previous research has established that users' cognitive workload can be measured by deceases in alpha power (8–12 Hz) in the "Pz" (Parietal mid-line) EEG channel, increases in theta power (4–7 Hz) in the "Fz" (Frontal mid-line) channel, and increases in the theta-Fz to alpha-Pz ratio. Similarly, users' fatigue can be measured by increases in alpha-Pz, increases in theta-Fz, and increases in the theta-Fz to alpha-Pz ratio [25, 39].

One important challenge in studies of feeding tasks is the need to maintain consistency between multiple trials while adding more participants to improve the overall validity of the findings, due to the impossibility to prepare food samples with exactly the same size, proportion, and texture for the whole span of studies. A solution to this problem is to use virtual reality (VR), where researchers are able to fully isolate and adjust experimental variables such as the participant position and the size of the food item. Today's VR systems with head-mounted displays (HMD) provide a very high level of realism and immersion [40], and has been used for evaluation of HRI systems [29]. Recent study found few measurable difference in behavioral and in physiological measures when tasks were conducted in VR vs. real-world environments, and generally suggested using VR as an alternative for validation and evaluation of HRI systems [17,28,42]. The VR technology will offers a tremendous advantage in allowing researchers to isolate and adjust environmental variables in a way that would not be possible in the real world [27]. In the current study we made use of a VR environment in order to have better control over experimental variables, to more easily scale up the number of participants, and to minimize the preparation time and cost.

The study focused on how different levels of autonomy in feeding robots affects user experience. We proposed two main hypotheses: (H1) Feeding tasks with fully autonomous robots will have lower success rate and a shorter duration compared to partially autonomous robots; and (H2) users will report lower workload and higher usability for fully autonomous robots compared to partially autonomous robots. While we selected one specific task, the findings should also be able to provide some insights for the more general ADL task category.

Our study has two main contributions: First, we designed, implemented, and tested a system for the virtual simulation of a human-in-the-loop assistive feeding robot, with physiological and neuroscientific measurements. Second, while related factors have been evaluated in prior studies, our current work took the novel approach of using EEG indicators of workload and fatigue in triangulation with self-reported feedback, as well as the novel VR approach for simulating a human-in-the-loop assistive feeding robot.

2   System Design

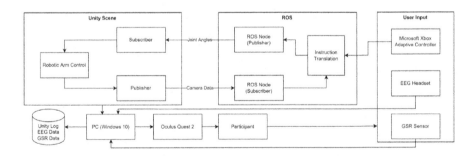

Fig. 2. System Architecture: the Unity Scene runs on the PC, with its subscriber listening to the robot instructions sent from ROS nodes. The PC then projects the scene to the VR Headset and forwards users' input to the ROS for interaction. The physiological data and log files are stored locally in the PC.

We developed our VR system based on the Unity game engine 2020.3.19f and imported the 6-DoF JACO 2 robotic arm as used in [7] from Unified Robot Description Format (URDF) files with the Unity URDF importer package.

We established bi-directional publisher-subscriber communication between the robotic arm and control system with ROS-TCP-Connector package. This allowed us to simultaneously send instructions to the robot and read data such as joint positions and camera data for decision-making.

Figure 2 shows our overall system architecture. We installed the Robot Operating System (ROS Melodic Morenia) on the Windows Subsystem for Linux (Ubuntu 18.04) to set up the work space. We used the Microsoft Xbox Adaptive Controller, designed specifically for users with disabilities, as an input device. Participants were able to provide inputs by pressing the two large buttons on the controller's top surface. For outputs, we used an Oculus Quest 2 HMD, with 183×1920 resolution per eye, about $90°$ field of view, and 120 Hz refresh rate. We designed a fork in Blender as our feeding utensil that the robot arm uses to feed. We also purchased and modified a commercial "suburban home" environment setup and food models to create realistic home environment (Fig. 1).

3   Methodology

3.1   Experimental Setup

EEG data was collected using the mBrainTrain Smarting Pro headset with 32 channels and up to 1000 Hz sampling rate. We used Oculus Quest 2 headset for displaying the virtual environments (Fig. 3).

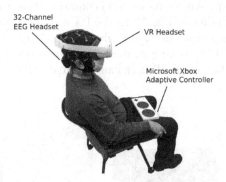

Fig. 3. Experiment Setup: One of the participants wearing 32-channel EEG headset, VR headset, and interacting with the Xbox Adaptive Controller

3.2   Experiment Procedure

The study protocol was reviewed and approved by the Institutional Review Board at Cornell University (Protocol #IRB0008538). All participants provided written informed consent to participate in the study. All experiments were performed in accordance with relevant guidelines and regulations. As illustrated in

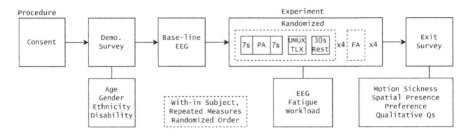

Fig. 4. Experiment Procedure: The experiment started from consent, followed by demographic survey, base-line EEG data collection, experiment with 4 PA and 4 FA blocks with randomized order, and exit survey about preference and other measures.

Fig. 4, each participant was provided with an introduction to the study, followed by consent and pre-experiment survey, then fitted with the EEG headset. We then introduced the adaptive controller, and collected baseline EEG data.

During the experiment, the participants were asked to use the virtual robotic arm to "feed" themselves three types of food (grapes, carrots, and bananas), using a variety of pick-up and movement strategies. All animations were pre-defined based on possible robot joint positions, applying linear interpolation between key positions to guarantee the smoothness of the animations.

The experiment consisted of eight blocks with randomized order, each of the block contained three trials, or three bites of the food on the plate. Four of the blocks were in Partially Autonomous (PA) condition, the other four were in Full Autonomous (FA) condition (Fig. 5). In the PA condition, the participants were asked to make the decisions on: food selection; pick-up strategy: tilted-angle, vertical, or tilted-vertical; feeding strategy: tilted or vertical; time to feed. In the FA condition, the robot made all decisions automatically.

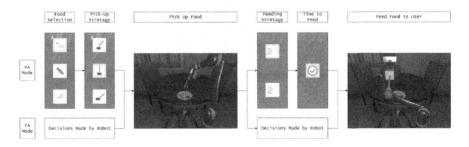

Fig. 5. Phases in each task. In PA condition, users made decisions on: food selection, pick-up strategy, feeding strategy, and time to feed. In FA condition, all the decisions were made by the robot.

As found in our previous study, users were able to make decisions intuitively, helping the robots at critical decision-making points where they could fail in the real world due to uncertainty [7]. We also assigned success rate for each pick-up strategy with respect to the type of the food based on results from [18]. A failed attempt would lead to an immediate additional attempt, up to three consecutive failures which would result in giving up the current trial and labeling it as failed.

Seven-second windows were added before and after each block for comparison. Additionally, participants were asked to answer questions regarding Workload and Usability verbally after each block, followed by a 30 s break. Physiological data was collected during the whole experiment.

After the experiment, participants were asked to finish the post-experiment survey with Simulator Sickness, Spacial Presence, Preference, feedback on the system.

3.3 Participant

Participants (n = 20) were healthy adults recruited from university's participant pool. They were given credits as compensation. The average age was 22.25 (SD = 4.62); with 45% (n = 9) male, 55% (n = 11) female; 5 (25%) White, 1 (5%) Black or African American, 13 (65%) Asian, and 1 (5%) of other ethnicity. No participant reported to have disabilities.

3.4 Measures

Two performance measures were based on users' interaction with the system:

Success was defined as number of successful trials per block, which can range from 0 to 3.

Duration was defined as average time spent on the 3 trials per block in seconds, including additional time caused by giving commands and failures.

The two main dependent variables were measured after each block:

Usability was measured with the Usability Metric for User Experience (UMUX) [19], a four-item 7-point Likert scale. The scale highly correlates with System Usability Scale, $r = .96$, $p < .001$, and has good internal consistency with a Cronbach's alpha of .94. We rescaled the results to a theoretical range of 0–100 according to the authors' instruction.

Workload was measured with the NASA-TLX scale [23,24]. We used 7-point Likert questions to be consistent with UMUX presented at the same time, and weighted all the subscales equally, resulting in possible score from 6 to 42.

In addition to self-reported measures, we also calculated three indicators from brain activity: alpha power at Pz, theta power at Fz, and theta Fz to alpha Pz ratio. More details regarding signal processing are provided in Sect. 3.5.

We also measured the following variables after the experiment:

Simulator Sickness was measured with the Simulator Sickness Questionnaire [30]. The total score was calculated accordingly.

Spacial Presence was measured with the MEC Spatial Presence Questionnaire [43]. We used the 4-item 5-point version of the Self Location and Possible Actions subscale, both of them are reported to have good internal validity, Cronbach's alpha = .92 and .81, respectively.

Preference was measured with a single 7-point Likert question, with two modes (PA and FA) on each end.

3.5   EEG Data Processing

The EEG data were analyzed using the EEGLAB [15] software package for MAT-LAB. Data were imported at their original sampling rate 250 Hz, low-pass filtered 100 Hz, high-pass filtered 1 Hz, and then ran through the Cleanline algorithm, which selectively filtered out 60 Hz power-line noise using an adaptive frequency-domain (multi-taper) regression technique. Noisy channels were rejected, the identified artifactual channels were interpolated from neighboring channels using spherical spline. Artifactual bursts in continuous data was corrected using Artifact Subspace Reconstruction [12,35], followed by common average referencing. Independent Component Analysis (ICA) [4,33] with the ICLabel function [37] was used to identify and remove those components with a large probability (P>0.50) of being non-brain ICs from the data. A final visual inspection was conducted by the team to identify remaining artifactual ICs.

EEG features analyzed in this study were frequency-band power, associated to the tasks performed [32], with the Multitaper power spectral density estimate function in Matlab. This measurement indicates how strongly a particular frequency range contributes to an EEG time-series signal, over the selected time window. Frequency band-power features were computed using the windows for the blocks. The log-transformed (dB) EEG power was analyzed for all statistical comparisons. The band power features were calculated for three typical EEG frequency bands related to workload : Theta (4–8 Hz), Alpha (8–12 Hz), Beta (12–30 Hz) [25,39]. The band powers were then averaged per block.

4   Results

Data were analyzed with the R language, an open source environment for statistical computing. We first fitted linear mixed models to examine the effects of Mode on dependent measures while controlling for the random effects of Participant with library "lme4", and then estimated the differences between FA and PA modes with library "emmeans", and reported t-test results, effect sizes (cohen's d), and 95% confidential intervals (CIs).

4.1   Descriptive Results

The average reported simulator sickness was 45.07 (SD = 36.53) out of a theoretical maximum of 235.62, indicating an acceptable experience. The Self Location

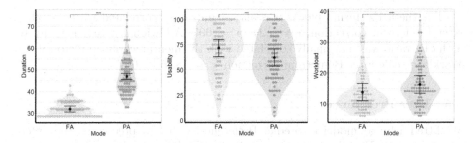

Fig. 6. Duration (left), Usability (middle), and Workload (right) in PA and FA conditions. Violins and points are from unadjusted descriptive results. The black dots and bar represent model estimated mean values and 95% CIs. *:p<.05, **:p<.01, ***:p<.001,****:p<.0001,

score of Spacial Presence was 11.90 (SD = 4.19) out of 20, and the Possible Action score was 10.90 (SD = 3.40) out of 20, indicating a medium level of presence and immersion. This was expected as the participants were not able to move around freely as they are in the real world to mimic the experience of users with disability. The participants also reported to be neutral when asked which mode they prefer, with a mean of 4.00 (SD = 2.20) on the 7-point scale.

4.2   Mode on Task Performance

There was a marginal effect of Mode on Success, $t(139) = 3.55, p = .089, d = .27$. FA condition may have higher Success, compared to the PA condition, by .14, 95% CI: [–.02,0.30]; and a main effect of Mode on Duration, $t(139) = 15.17, p < .001, d = 2.40$. FA condition has shorter Duration, compared to the PA condition, by 14.98s, 95% CI: [13.03,16.94] (Fig. 6, left).

While between condition difference in Duration was as expected, the difference in Success was not. Therefore, H1 was not fully supported.

4.3   Mode on Workload and Usability

There was a main effect of Mode on Usability, $t(139) = 3.55, p < .001, d = .56$. FA condition has higher Usability, compared to the PA condition, by 9.58, 95% CI: [4.25,14.90] (Fig. 6, middle); and a main effect of Mode on Workload, $t(139) = 4.25, p < .001, d = .67$. FA condition has lower Workload, compared to the PA condition, by 2.45, 95% CI: [1.31,3.59] (Fig. 6, right).

Between condition differences in both Usability and Workload were as expected. Therefore, H2 was supported.

4.4   EEG Indicators of Mental Workload

There was a very marginal main effect of Mode on theta Fz during blocks, $t(139) = 1.65, p = .102, d = 0.26$. FA condition tended to have lower theta Fz, compared to the PA condition, by 0.15, 95% CI: [–0.03,0.33].

The theta Fz during blocks was also significantly correlated with Usability after Bonferroni correction, $r = -.24$, $p = .007$. Additionally, the theta Fz to alpha Pz ratio was marginally correlated with the mental workload factor of the Workload scale after Bonferroni correction, $r = .18$, $p = .061$.

4.5   User Preference

We fitted a linear model to predict Preference with four predictors: the difference in average Usability between conditions (FA-PA), the difference in average Workload between conditions (FA-PA), Ethnicity, and Handedness.

The model regression was significant and explains 84.24% of the variance in Preference, $R^2=.84$, adjusted $R^2=.79$, $F(4,13)=17.37$, $p < .001$. All predictors are significant, Difference in Usability (unstandardized coefficient $\beta=.21$, $p<.001$) and Workload ($\beta=.53$, $p<.001$), White Ethnicity ($\beta=1.30$, $p=.040$), and Right Handedness ($\beta=2.46$, $p=.013$) lead to preference of FA over PA.

5   Discussion

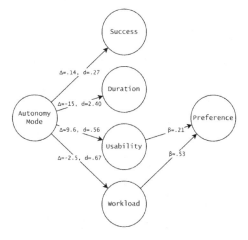

Fig. 7. Summary of findings. Autonomy Mode: FA compared to PA. Preference: FA compared to PA. All links are significant or marginally significant. Links from Autonomy Mode are at Block level, all the links towards Preference are at Participant level.

In this study, we examined the effects of Autonomous Mode (Partial Autonomous, PA vs. Fully Autonomous, FA) on Success Rate, Duration, Workload, and Usability. All the effects were significant or marginally significant. The effect on Duration was very large (d=2.40), effects to on Usability and Workload were medium-large (d=.56 and .67), and the effect on Success was small-medium (d=.27). However, while we hypothesized a higher success rate in PA condition, we actually found it to be lower, compared to the FA condition.

The findings from EEG data was consistent with the self-reported results, and also supported our H2. We found a very marginal difference between Autonomous Modes in the Theta power at Fz channel, one indicator that is believed to be an indicator of both Workload and Fatigue [25], plus correlations between EEG indicators and self-reported Workload and Usability.

As summarized in Fig. 7, the effect of Autonomy Mode on Preference was through two different routes with opposite directions: Compared to PA mode, FA mode gained preference by improving usability, but also lost preference by decreasing user workload. This implied that people prefer to have higher level of control over the task that's being performed, or to collaborate with the robot instead of asking it to do all the jobs. Together, these two routes resulted in a neutral opinion on preference among our participants, consistent with previous studies evaluating assistive robots for ADL and IADL tasks [7,31].

The difference between PA and FA conditions in number of successful trials (.14) was very small below even 5% of the 3 trials per block. Similarly, the difference in Duration, despite its very large effect size, was just 15s. Our participants may not care much about them, especially given the relatively short time span of the experiment. This could potentially explain the lack of relationship between these two variables and the user preference.

While the hypothesis was partially supported, the lower success rate found in PA condition was not consistent with previous studies where human were believed to have the expertise and to be able to choose the best pick-up strategy [7]. There are at least three possible explanations: First, since our participants are exclusively healthy adults, they have no experience with assistive robots, and hence unable to choose the best pick-up strategy. Second, picking up food with the robot is very different from picking up food with hand holding forks. This fact, coupled with some lost details in the VR environment, made the task in the experiment very different from its equivalent task in daily life. Transferring skills to a different scenario is known as far transfer, and are generally less likely to happen [2]. Last, daily activities such as riding bikes and in our case, eating with forks, are believed to be linked to tacit knowledge, or know-how, that cannot be easily transmitted, in our case, to the robot [26].

We have found difference between conditions in only one of three EEG indicators suggested in [39]. The difference was marginally significant but consistent with the self-reported result. The EEG signal is susceptible noises introduced by participants movement as well as interference from other devices, in our case, the PC, VR headset, and even the Bluetooth connection used by the headset itself. These noises will increase the variance within conditions and result in a lower effect size, which requires a large sample size to determine a clear difference. Also, most of the existing indicators are based on studies conducted under highly controlled lab environments. The feeding task we implemented and tested requires different mental processes to happen, and thus brain areas to work coordinately at the same time. This limited the external validity, or generalizability [10] of the indicators found in previous studies to our scenario. In addition to between-condition difference, the connection was also suggested by the correlation between EEG indicators and self-reported measures.

The regression model explained about 85% of the variance in user preference, and also revealed some interesting relationships. Higher Workload led to higher level of preference, suggesting that users may prefer to be more control during this specific task, rather than letting the robot make all the decisions. The model recommended an interaction that is both high in workload and usability, and possibly also control over the robot, to maximize user preference. This finding is consistent with studies about human-robot collaboration in other tasks where human's cognitive abilities were combined with the physical capabilities of robots for better performance [1].

Another interesting finding is the effect of handedness on user preference, since many robotic arms, including ours, are placed on the right side of the wheelchair regardless of the participant's handedness. This could be unnatural and strange for left-handed users, resulting in increased effort and workload. In our study, we found them to prefer the PA mode more than right-handed participants, switching the side of arm may result in an opposite effect.

Virtual Reality has the potential to immersively mimic physical environments and interactions, accurately manipulate active variables, and easily control confounding variables [27]. In this study, we were able to find the differences in our dependent measures between different autonomous modes. While not conclusive, our findings supported the potential of VR simulation in evaluation of interactions with assistive robot, and more importantly, study of the users during such interactions. This potential is further extended by the ability to collect other physiological and behavioral data simultaneously without affecting immersion.

While we designed the interaction to simulate limited mobility, participants with disabilities should be included in future studies to ensure generalizability of the findings. Moreover, all the results we have are based on the short-term interaction with the assistive robot. Over long periods of time, situations may change, and users may get more accustomed to, and comfortable with the robot. Including long-term interaction with the robots in the study may lead to different results and other useful outcomes. Additionally, while the a priori estimated power assuming medium effect sizes was .77, an effective sample size above 500 will help us to achieve better powers in comparisons of brain activities which were found to be of relatively small effect sizes in this study.

Future studies might also consider including other independent variables, such as handedness. We could also define more autonomous levels outside the range of the FA and PA modes used in the study, such as the teleoperation and assisted teleoperation modes described in [3]. Other data sources, such as Galvanic Skin Response (GSR), or eye movement, may also help us better understand our participants, and provide more insights for design of assistive robots.

To sum, in this study, we used VR simulation to examine the differences between assistive feeding robots with full or partially autonomous level, and found full autonomous mode to have marginally higher success rate, shorter duration, higher usability, and lower workload. We also found usability and workload, together with demographic variables, could explain a majority of the variance in user preference. The findings supported the potential of VR simulation, together with physiological sensors, in evaluation of assistive robot and its users in the more general ADL task category.

Acknowledgment. This work was funded by the National Science Foundation IIS (#2132846).

References

1. Ajoudani, A., Zanchettin, A.M., Ivaldi, S., Albu-Schäffer, A., Kosuge, K., Khatib, O.: Progress and prospects of the human–robot collaboration. Auton. Robot. **42**(5), 957–975 (2017). https://doi.org/10.1007/s10514-017-9677-2
2. Barnett, S.M., Ceci, S.J.: When and where do we apply what we learn? A taxonomy for far transfer. Psychol. Bull. **128**(4), 612–637 (2002). https://doi.org/10.1037/0033-2909.128.4.612
3. Beer, J.M., Fisk, A.D., Rogers, W.A.: Toward a framework for levels of robot autonomy in human-robot interaction. J. Hum.-Robot Interact. **3**(2), 74–99 (2014). https://doi.org/10.5898/JHRI.3.2.Beer
4. Bell, A.J., Sejnowski, T.J.: An information-maximization approach to blind separation and blind deconvolution. Neural Comput. **7**(6), 1129–1159 (1995). https://doi.org/10.1162/neco.1995.7.6.1129
5. Bell, L., Vogt, J., Willemse, C., Routledge, T., Butler, L.T., Sakaki, M.: Beyond self-report: a review of physiological and neuroscientific methods to investigate consumer behavior. Front. Psychol. **9**, 1655 (2018). https://doi.org/10.3389/fpsyg.2018.01655
6. Bhattacharjee, T., Cabrera, M.E., Caspi, A., Cakmak, M., Srinivasa, S.S.: A community-centered design framework for robot-assisted feeding systems. In: The 21st International ACM SIGACCESS Conference on Computers and Accessibility, ASSETS 2019, pp. 482–494. Association for Computing Machinery, New York (October 2019). https://doi.org/10/gm8cqd
7. Bhattacharjee, T., et al.: Is More autonomy always better? exploring preferences of users with mobility impairments in robot-assisted feeding. In: Proceedings of the 2020 ACM/IEEE International Conference on Human-Robot Interaction, HRI 2020, pp. 181–190. Association for Computing Machinery, New York (March 2020). https://doi.org/10/ggpw2d
8. Brose, S.W., et al.: The role of assistive robotics in the lives of persons with disability. Am. J. Phys. Med. Rehabilit. **89**(6), 509–521 (2010). https://doi.org/10.1097/PHM.0b013e3181cf569b
9. U.S. Census Bureau: Americans with disabilities: 2014 (2014)
10. Calder, B.J., Phillips, L.W., Tybout, A.M.: The concept of external validity. J. Consumer Res. **9**(3), 240–244 (1982). https://doi.org/10.1086/208920
11. Carlson, T., Demiris, Y.: Collaborative control for a robotic wheelchair: evaluation of performance, attention, and workload. IEEE Trans. Syst. Man Cybern. Part B (Cybern.) **42**(3), 876–888 (2012). https://doi.org/10.1109/TSMCB.2011.2181833
12. Chang, C.Y., Hsu, S.H., Pion-Tonachini, L., Jung, T.P.: Evaluation of artifact subspace reconstruction for automatic artifact components removal in multi-channel eeg recordings. IEEE Trans. Biomed. Eng. **67**(4), 1114–1121 (2019). https://doi.org/10.1109/TBME.2019.2930186

13. Chen, T.L., et al.: Older adults' acceptance of a robot for partner dance-based exercise. PLoS ONE **12**(10), e0182736 (2017). https://doi.org/10.1371/journal.pone.0182736

14. Chio, A., et al.: Caregiver time use in ALS. Neurology **67**(5), 902–904 (2006). https://doi.org/10.1212/01.wnl.0000233840.41688.df

15. Delorme, A., Makeig, S.: EEGLAB: An open source toolbox for analysis of single-trial EEG dynamics including independent component analysis. J. Neurosci. Methods **134**(1), 9–21 (2004). https://doi.org/10/bqr2f2

16. Dreer, L.E., Elliott, T.R., Shewchuk, R., Berry, J.W., Rivera, P.: Family caregivers of persons with spinal cord injury: Predicting caregivers at risk for probable depression. Rehabil. Psychol. **52**(3), 351 (2007). https://doi.org/10.1037/0090-5550.52.3.351

17. Duguleana, M., Barbuceanu, F.G., Mogan, G.: Evaluating human-robot interaction during a manipulation experiment conducted in immersive virtual reality. In: Shumaker, R. (ed.) VMR 2011. LNCS, vol. 6773, pp. 164–173. Springer, Heidelberg (2011). https://doi.org/10.1007/978-3-642-22021-0_19

18. Feng, R., et al.: Robot-assisted feeding: Generalizing skewering strategies across food items on a realistic plate. In: International Symposium on Robotics Research (ISRR 2019) (2019). https://doi.org/10.1007/978-3-030-95459-8_26

19. Finstad, K.: The Usability Metric for User Experience. Interact. Comput. **22**(5), 323–327 (2010). https://doi.org/10/ctr6r4

20. Gallenberger, D., Bhattacharjee, T., Kim, Y., Srinivasa, S.S.: Transfer depends on acquisition: Analyzing manipulation strategies for robotic feeding. In: ACM/IEEE International Conference on Human-Robot Interaction (HRI), Best Paper Award for Technical Advances in HRI (2019). https://doi.org/10.1109/HRI.2019.8673309

21. Gopinath, D., Jain, S., Argall, B.D.: Human-in-the-loop optimization of shared autonomy in assistive robotics. IEEE Robot. Autom. Lett. **2**(1), 247–254 (2017). https://doi.org/10.1109/LRA.2016.2593928

22. Graça, Á., Nascimento, M.A.d., Lavado, E.L., Garanhani, M.R.: Quality of life of primary caregivers of spinal cord injury survivors. Revista brasileira de enfermagem **66**, 79–84 (2013).https://doi.org/10.1590/S0034-71672013000100012

23. Hart, S.G., Staveland, L.E.: Development of NASA-TLX (task load index): results of empirical and theoretical research. In: Advances in Psychology, vol. 52, pp. 139–183. Elsevier (1988). https://doi.org/10.1016/S0166-4115(08)62386-9

24. Hart, S.G., Staveland, L.E.: NASA TLX Paper and Pencil Version (August 2019). https://humansystems.arc.nasa.gov/groups/tlx/tlxpaperpencil.php

25. Holm, A., Lukander, K., Korpela, J., Sallinen, M., Müller, K.M.I.: Estimating brain load from the EEG. Scient. World J. **9**, 639–651 (2009). https://doi.org/10.1100/tsw.2009.83

26. Howells, J.: Tacit knowledge. Technol. Anal. Strategic Manag. **8**(2), 91–106 (1996). https://doi.org/10.1080/09537329608524237

27. Kalantari, S., Neo, J.R.J.: Virtual environments for design research: lessons learned from use of fully immersive virtual reality in interior design research. J. Inter. Des. **45**(3), 27–42 (2020). https://doi.org/10.1111/joid.12171

28. Kalantari, S., Rounds, J.D., Kan, J., Tripathi, V., Cruz-Garza, J.G.: Comparing physiological responses during cognitive tests in virtual environments vs. in identical real-world environments. Scient. Reports **11**(1), 10227 (2021). https://doi.org/10/gj47cr

29. Kaufeld, M., Nickel, P.: Level of robot autonomy and information aids in human-robot interaction affect human mental workload – an investigation in virtual reality.

In: Duffy, V.G. (ed.) HCII 2019. LNCS, vol. 11581, pp. 278–291. Springer, Cham (2019). https://doi.org/10.1007/978-3-030-22216-1_21
30. Kennedy, R.S., Lane, N.E., Berbaum, K.S., Lilienthal, M.G.: Simulator sickness questionnaire: an enhanced method for quantifying simulator sickness. Int. J. Aviation Psychol. 3(3), 203–220 (1993). https://doi.org/10/bbh54v
31. Kim, D., et al.: How autonomy impacts performance and satisfaction: results from a study with spinal cord injured subjects using an assistive robot. IEEE Trans. Syst. Man Cybern. - Part A: Syst. Hum. 42(1), 2–14 (2012). https://doi.org/10.1109/TSMCA.2011.2159589
32. Lotte, F., et al.: A review of classification algorithms for eeg-based brain-computer interfaces: a 10 year update. J. Neural Eng. 15(3), 031005 (2018). https://doi.org/10.1088/1741-2552/aab2f2
33. Makeig, S., Bell, A., Jung, T.P., Sejnowski, T.J.: Independent component analysis of electroencephalographic data. In: Advances in Neural Information Processing Systems 8 (1995)
34. Matthay, E.C., Glymour, M.M.: A graphical catalog of threats to validity. Epidemiology (Cambridge, Mass.) 31(3), 376–384 (2020). https://doi.org/10/ggjn2f
35. Mullen, T.R., et al.: Real-time neuroimaging and cognitive monitoring using wearable dry eeg. IEEE Trans. Biomed. Eng. 62(11), 2553–2567 (2015). https://doi.org/10.1109/TBME.2015.2481482
36. Park, D., et al.: Active robot-assisted feeding with a general-purpose mobile manipulator: Design, evaluation, and lessons learned. Robot. Auton. Syst. 124, 103344 (2020). https://doi.org/10.1016/j.robot.2019.103344
37. Pion-Tonachini, L., Kreutz-Delgado, K., Makeig, S.: Iclabel: An automated electroencephalographic independent component classifier, dataset, and website. Neuroimage 198, 181–197 (2019). https://doi.org/10.1016/j.neuroimage.2019.05.026
38. Rhodes, T., Veloso, M.: Robot-driven trajectory improvement for feeding tasks. In: 2018 IEEE/RSJ International Conference on Intelligent Robots and Systems (IROS), pp. 2991–2996 (October 2018). https://doi.org/10.1109/IROS.2018.8593525
39. Roy, R.N., Drougard, N., Gateau, T., Dehais, F., Chanel, C.P.C.: How can physiological computing benefit human-robot interaction? Robotics 9(4), 100 (2020). https://doi.org/10.3390/robotics9040100
40. Slater, M.: Immersion and the illusion of presence in virtual reality. Br. J. Psychol. 109(3), 431–433 (2018). https://doi.org/10.1111/bjop.12305
41. Song, W.K., Song, W.J., Kim, Y., Kim, J.: Usability test of KNRC self-feeding robot. In: IEEE International Conference on Rehabilitation Robotics: [proceedings] 2013, p. 6650501 (June 2013). https://doi.org/10.1109/ICORR.2013.6650501
42. Villani, V., Capelli, B., Sabattini, L.: Use of virtual reality for the evaluation of human-robot interaction systems in complex scenarios. In: 2018 27th IEEE International Symposium on Robot and Human Interactive Communication (RO-MAN). pp. 422–427 (August 2018). https://doi.org/10.1109/ROMAN.2018.8525738
43. Vorderer, P., et al.: MEC Spatial Presence Questionnaire (MEC-SPQ) (2004)

On the Way to the Future—Assistant Robots in Hospitals and Care Facilities

Marija Radic(✉) 🆔, Agnes Vosen, and Caroline Michler

Fraunhofer Center for International Management and Knowledge Economy IMW,
Neumarkt 9-19, 04109 Leipzig, Germany
`marija.radic@imw.fraunhofer.de`

Abstract. Assistance robots in the healthcare sector represent an innovative solution to support and relieve the workload of nursing staff but have rarely been used to date. The aim of the study is to identify the added value, experiences, relevant drivers and barriers for the use of assistance robots in healthcare. From May to June 2021, an online survey was carried out with 279 participants from German clinics, inpatient and outpatient care. The target group addressed by the survey was commercial, medical or nursing management, since it can be assumed that they make the investment decisions for assistance robots. In general, the greatest advantages are seen in the relief of the nursing staff and in greater efficiency in the processes. The participants see the greatest added value in cleaning and surgical robots. They also have the most experience with these robotics scenarios so far. Liability, financing and the legal framework can be identified as the greatest obstacles. Compared to clinics and inpatient care, the majority of outpatient care has a more pessimistic perception of the use of assistance robots in healthcare. Overall, the results show that the participants have a positive attitude towards assistance robots and see their added value for use in the healthcare system. At the same time, however, many obstacles still prevent a wide diffusion. It is thus necessary that hurdles, especially in financing, liability issues and other regulations, are removed so that assistant robots can develop their full potential for the German healthcare system.

Keywords: Assistant robots · Healthcare · Hospital · Care · Financing · Time savings

1 Introduction

Ensuring adequate and high-quality healthcare is one of the cornerstones of our society. On the one hand, it faces considerable current and future challenges. On the other hand, these are reflected in the growing proportion of older people. The United Nations predicts that the proportion of people over 65 in Germany will rise to 26% in 2030, compared with 23% in Europe and 12% worldwide. These figures put Germany above both the projected European and global levels [1]. This future increase in demand will be offset by a short supply of skilled workers. In a study, Scheffler et al. [2] predict the demand and supply of healthcare workers on a global level for the year 2030. It is found that

F. Cavallo et al. (Eds.): ICSR 2022, LNAI 13818, pp. 328–337, 2022.
https://doi.org/10.1007/978-3-031-24670-8_29

imbalances in the healthcare labor market are expected in high, middle as well as low-income countries [2]. Flake et al. [3] assume a 44 and 38% increase in German demand for nurses by 2035 due to an aging society. The analysis assumes that the current staffing ratio will remain unchanged. Since the supply of skilled nursing staff already does not meet demand, the shortage of skilled workers is expected to worsen further [3].

Innovative solutions are needed to overcome these major challenges. One potential approach to relieve and support nursing staff is the use of assistance robots in healthcare. Hebesberger et al. [4] are investigating which functions robots can assume in elderly care. Particularly desirable are "fetch and bring" tasks, entertainment and information as well as support in physically demanding tasks. Despite the great potential of assistance robots, their actual use in healthcare is still low [5]. This raises the question of drivers and barriers for the use of assistive robots in healthcare. Numerous studies address the acceptance of robots from the perspective of caregivers and patients or residents of care facilities. In a comprehensive literature review, Papadopoulos et al. [6] identify twelve studies that examine drivers and barriers to the implementation of socially assistive humanoid robots in health and care settings. Most drivers identified are pleasure, ease of use, personalization, and an establishment of trust between the robot and the user. Prevalent barriers can be summarized under the categories of technical problems, a limited functionality of the robot as well as an individual negative attitude towards robotic systems, for example driven by concerns about a dehumanization of care. When looking at the study design of the selected studies, it becomes apparent that primarily the perspective of the cared-for person is investigated. Only four of the twelve studies look at the perspective of the caregivers. Not a single study looks at the perspective of the decision-makers in the organizations who make the actual investment decision. In addition, the studies focus on the home environment or use in care facilities, but not on use in a hospital context. Six studies are from European countries, 2 from Japan, 2 from Israel, and 2 from Australia. One each was conducted in Canada and the USA. Studies from Germany are not included [6]. Only recently, Fracasso et al. published their study on social robots' acceptance and marketability in Germany and Italy [7].

There are already few studies investigating the financing of robotic solutions [5, 8, 9]. In a 2018 study, Radic et al. [5] already identify financing as a relevant obstacle. Fischinger et al. [8] as well as Kramer [9] query the willingness to pay regarding robotic technologies and include the option of purchase by means of rent or leasing rate. While in Kramer [9] the preference for a purchase via leasing rate is rather low, Fischinger et al. [8] show that the willingness to purchase a robot increases significantly as soon as the option of leasing is available. The surveys are aimed at users of the robot, i.e., participants over 70 years of age [8] or family caregivers [9]. A survey with decision makers from the health care sector does not take place.

The aim of this study is to contribute to the research gaps in the literature outlined above by collecting a comprehensive perspective of clinics and care facilities on the use of assistive robots in Germany. In addition to nursing facilities, clinics throughout Germany are also addressed. Furthermore, the study addresses the rarely considered management personnel in the medical, commercial, and nursing sectors, who make the actual investment decisions in the facilities. Regarding nursing facilities, the survey is aimed at both the inpatient and outpatient sectors. This not only enables a broader coverage of the opinion, but also allows a comparison and differentiation along these three subgroups. The survey also takes a closer look at additional issues such as financing, including leasing and robot-as-a-service, as well as the potential time savings for selected robot types.

2 Methods

By means of a nationwide online survey conducted between May and July 2021, assessments of the added value of and experiences with various robotics scenarios, drivers and barriers to the use of robotics solutions in healthcare, as well as questions of financing and time savings were investigated. Together with robotics experts, 19 robotic scenarios were selected that cover the range of available assistive robots. The survey was conducted on a voluntary basis and without compensation. The target group of the online survey were decision-makers in the healthcare sector, i.e. commercial or medical managers or nursing service managers in hospitals, inpatient and outpatient care facilities, who usually make decisions about investments in the organizations. In addition to the content-related questions, descriptive information on the position, type of facility, size and location of the facility was also requested.

Table 1 describes the participants by type of facility. A total of 279 people participated in the survey. The participants were recruited by email based on almost 5,500 addresses that were identified nationwide through company databases. This approach was flanked by a cooperation with different healthcare associations which distributed the survey information through newsletters to their member institutions. More than 46% of respondents work in inpatient care. More than 30% and 20% are assigned to outpatient care and clinics, respectively. If these proportions are compared with the actual number of facilities in Germany in 2019, it becomes apparent that clinics are significantly overrepresented [10], whereas outpatient care is significantly underrepresented. The proportion of inpatient care in the sample is relatively representative of the actual number of inpatient care facilities [11].

Table 1. Study participants by type of facility

Type of facility	Number of participants	Relative proportion in %
Clinics	63	22,6
Inpatient nursing facilities	129	46,2
Outpatient nursing facilities	87	31,2
Total	279	100,0

Regarding the size of the facilities, the complete range from less than 10 to more than 500 employees is covered (cf. Table 2). Only around two percent of small companies with fewer than ten employees took part in the study. At about 65%, small and medium-sized facilities with 10 to 250 employees make up the largest share. Almost one-third are large facilities with more than 250 employees. Since only just over 60% of respondents provided information on the size of their facility, it is not possible to make a statement on the size-related representativeness.

Table 2. Study participants by size of facility

Size of facility	Number of facilities	Relative proportion in %
less than 10 employees	2	1,2
10–50 employees	47	27,2
50–100 employees	38	21,9
100–250 employees	29	16,7
250–500 employees	14	8,1
More than 500 employees	43	24,9
Total	173	100,0

Geographically, study participants from all 16 German states are represented in the sample. However, various German states are over- or under-represented, so that overall geographic representativeness is not given.

3   Results

In the following, the results are presented on the focus areas of added value and experiences, drivers and barriers, and financing options and time savings.

3.1   Added Value of Different Robotics Scenarios

The survey asked about the added value of nineteen different robotics scenarios (see Fig. 1). These scenarios cover the current range of interesting assistance robots that are already on the market or in development. The participants were asked to assess whether the added value of the robotics scenario was low, medium or high.

Figure 1 shows that robots for physical relief are attributed a high added value. Overall, 59% of the participants attribute a high added value to cleaning robots. For disinfection robots, the value is 53%. Operating room robots achieve a similarly positive result with 52%, whereby this result is strongly driven by the responses of the clinics. Among the participants from hospitals, the OR robot takes first place by far with 75%. Driverless transport systems (AGVs) also have a high added value for clinics with 59%. This clearly shows that clinics have somewhat different needs than care facilities. Often, clinics are also larger facilities, as can also be seen from our survey. AGVs are particularly suitable for large clinics in order to be able to transport materials, such as laundry, over long distances. For outpatient and inpatient care facilities, cleaning robots are in first place. These are attributed a high added value by 64% and 57% respectively, followed by disinfection robots (55% and 52%). Cleaning robots are in third place among hospitals with 54%.

A look at the lower end of the spectrum is also worthwhile: The added value of robots for guiding people, handling and eating aids, and robots for supporting personal hygiene are rated lowest. For all individual subgroups, robots for personal hygiene support are in last place. They are followed at a considerable distance by the other two robotics solutions - except for ambulatory care. There, AGVs are not seen as very promising and are in third last place.

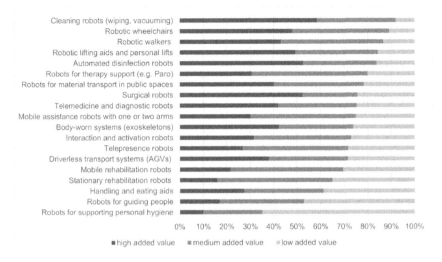

Fig. 1. Added value of different robotic scenarios

3.2 Experience with Robotic Solutions

In addition to the expected added value, previous experience was also queried for the same scenarios (see Fig. 2). The question as to the extent to which the participants had gained experience with assistance robots could be answered with "have experience" or "have no experience".

It is evident that, overall, only a small proportion of facilities still have prior experience with assistance robots. Almost 28% of respondents state that they have experience with cleaning robots. More than 16% have prior experience with surgical robots, and nearly 14% with robotic lifting aids and personal lifts. Only one in ten facilities has had experience with all other robotic scenarios.

In addition to cleaning robots (25%) and lifting aids (12%), facilities for inpatient care also have some experience with interaction and activation robots (13%) as well as with robots for therapy support such as Paro (13%). In ambulatory care, there is also some experience with cleaning robots (30%) as well as lifting aids (18%). Less than 10% of facilities in outpatient care have experience with all other scenarios. Among hospitals, more than half now have experience with surgical robots. 30% of the participating clinics have experience with cleaning robots, and 23% with AGVs. Similarly, clinics have some experience with telemedicine and diagnostic robots (18%), with robots for material transport in public spaces (16%), and with exoskeletons (15%). Clinics also have experience with interaction and activation robots (12%) and lifting aids (12%). Less than 10% of clinic participants have experience with all other robot types. In summary, clinics have the most experience with assistive robots to date. This is particularly due to the high prevalence of surgical robots. In addition, large clinics are well suited for the use of AGVs or even disinfection robots.

Comparing Fig. 2 with Fig. 1 above, a correlation can be seen between the assessment of added value and experience with assistance robots which is, however, not significant for all scenarios This suggests that the more experience there is with a robot, the higher the added value is assessed, which is an important finding with regard to the further diffusion of assistance robots in healthcare.

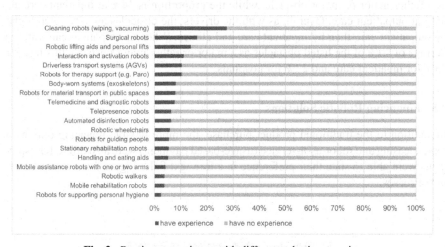

Fig. 2. Previous experience with different robotic scenarios

3.3   Drivers for the Use of Assistance Robots

Asked about the main motives for using assistance robots, more than half of the respondents state that the most important driver is the relief of personnel, closely followed by higher efficiency in processes. At the same time, the majority of respondents see rather no or only minor advantages in the alleviation of the shortage of skilled workers of lower costs for hospital and nursing home operators.

Looking at the results differentiated by hospitals, inpatient and outpatient care facilities, we find that the answers regarding the drivers are similar but differ quantitatively in that hospitals and inpatient care show higher approval ratings and thus assess the drivers significantly more optimistically than outpatient care.

3.4   Barriers to the Use of Assistance Robots

More than half of the respondents identify liability, financing, legal framework conditions, the willingness of employees to change, and the fear of a reduction in human contact as major or rather major obstacles. Fear of job loss among caregivers and a lack of trust in manufacturers are seen as the least significant barriers in a relative comparison. More than half of the respondents see these as no or rather minor obstacles.

A differentiated look at the three subgroups reveals differences. Inpatient care primarily rates financing and the legal framework as major obstacles. While 58% of outpatient care and 56% of inpatient care rate financing as a major or rather major obstacle, this assessment is 48% for clinics. Respondents from clinics and outpatient care, on the other hand, rate the reduction of human contact through the use of assistance robots as a relatively large obstacle. For clinics, liability issues also represent a significant obstacle, whereas outpatient care weights the willingness of employees to change as the strongest obstacle. It is also interesting to note that data protection is perceived as a much greater obstacle at hospitals than at care facilities: 56% of respondents from hospitals rate this as a rather major or major obstacle, while the proportion is 44% at inpatient care and 36% at outpatient care. Overall, as with the drivers, the obstacles are also rated higher by outpatient care than by inpatient care and clinics. Whereas outpatient care rates an average of 40% of the listed obstacles as a major or rather major obstacle, this figure is 33% for inpatient care and 22% for hospitals.

3.5   Financing Robotic Solutions

In addition to the traditional product purchase, the more flexible financing options of rental, leasing and robot-as-a-service (usage-based payment) were also offered. Respondents were able to state their preference in a free-text field. Figure 3 shows the results of the survey.

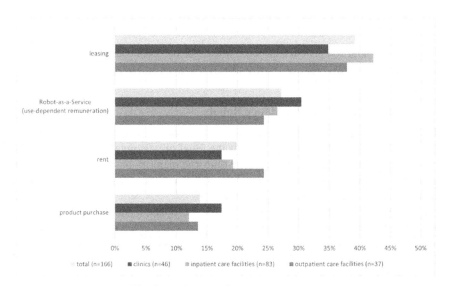

Fig. 3. Preferences for financing options

A clear preference can be derived from the results: The classic product purchase is in last place with 14%. All flexible solutions receive higher approval. Leasing is by far the preferred financing option with 39%, followed by robot-as-a-service, which is desired by 27% of respondents, and rent, which is preferred by 20% of respondents. The analysis also shows that the results are consistent across all subgroups. At the same time, the participants were given the opportunity to justify their assessment in a free text field. The short innovation cycles of technologies were most frequently cited as an argument against purchasing a product. However, tax reasons were also cited, such as the possibility of depreciation, which in turn make a purchase more attractive.

3.6 Time Savings Through the Use of Assistance Robots

For the survey of potential time savings, 5 heterogeneous robotic solutions were considered: Assistant robots as pilots, lifting robots, activation and communication robots, autonomous transport robots for ward / laundry trolleys and disinfection robots. The participants were asked to estimate how many hours of work they could save per robot, station and day in their facility by using the respective solution.

Overall, half of the participants expect a relief of two hours or more through the use of activation and communication robots as well as autonomous transport robots for ward / laundry trolleys and disinfection robots. For assistance robots as pilots, the value is about one hour and for lifting robots 1.5 h. A quarter of the participants even expect a relief of three or more hours when using assistance robots as pilots, lifting robots and autonomous transport robots for storage / laundry trolleys. For activation and communication robots and disinfection robots, a quarter of the participants even expect a relief of four hours or more.

In general, clinics see a higher relief potential. Half of the participants expect a reduction in workload of at least four hours for disinfection robots, at least three hours for autonomous transport robots for ward/laundry trolleys, and at least two hours for the other three scenarios. A quarter of the participants from the hospital sector even expect at least twice as much relief. Inpatient care expects similar values for relief as those already outlined for the overall sample. Only in the case of assistance robots as pilots do half of the participants expect a relief of one hour or less, which is understandable in view of the longer lengths of stay of residents. Outpatient care is much more reserved in its assessment. Half of the participants expect the robots to save between less than one hour and a maximum of one hour. However, it is striking that a quarter of the participants see the savings through activation and communication robots at at least four hours.

4 Discussion

The data collected provide a wide-ranging view of the current perspective of the German hospital and care landscape on the topic of assistance robotics. Regarding the assessment of the added value of various robotic solutions, the results show that robots that physically relieve staff are of particular interest to the participants. It is also noticeable that care facilities are particularly interested in cleaning and disinfection robots. Hospitals, on the other hand, favor surgical robots and automated guided vehicles (AGVs).

The biggest drivers for the spread of assistance robots in both clinics and care facilities are the relief of staff, greater efficiency, and increased work attractiveness. The biggest obstacle is clearly the question of liability. There is an urgent need for action here, as the legal situation, which has apparently not been sufficiently clarified to date, is holding back the widespread use of robots. The same applies to the general legal framework that governs the use of robots. For more than 50% of the participants, the fear of a reduction in human contact and the willingness of employees to change also represent a major or rather major obstacle. In the case of clinics, the fear of a reduction in human contact represents the greatest obstacle, along with liability. Data protection is also a major issue for clinics, whereas the legal framework is seen as less limiting. For both types of care facilities, immature technology is still a major obstacle, whereas the fear of reducing human contact is less pronounced. Outpatient care facilities see the greatest problem in the willingness of staff to change.

A key barrier to the diffusion of assistive robots is financing. This study sheds light for the first time on the preferences of healthcare institutions for different financing models. Flexible financing models such as renting, leasing or robot-as-a-service are increasingly outpacing the classic alternative of product purchase. This is due to ever shorter technology cycles and the associated obsolescence of robotics solutions.

The surveyed assessment of time savings generally shows a clear added value for the various scenarios. For clinics in particular, robots can offer a great deal of relief. For outpatient care, activation and communication robots seem to be particularly attractive.

5 Conclusion

The study offers many new insights into the perspective of decision-makers in hospitals and care facilities on the use of assistive robots in Germany. There is a clear acceptance and openness to the topic, which is most pronounced in hospitals, followed by inpatient care. Outpatient care is somewhat more reserved. Added value is seen for many robotic scenarios, although the assessment of added value is probably also related to the technological maturity of the solutions and the possibility of gaining experience with them.

Robots are seen by the facilities surveyed as a tool for reducing workload and increasing efficiency and employer attractiveness, but not as a substitute for a lack of skilled workers. The results on time savings are also to be seen here in terms of relieving the burden on personnel. However, the study also reveals many obstacles: Liability, financing and legal framework, as well as fear of reducing human contact and employees' willingness to change. These issues need to be addressed. Regarding the first three points, the legislator in particular is called upon. As far as financing is concerned, in addition to subsidies, manufacturers are primarily called upon to offer flexible financing models, which, according to our findings, are particularly attractive to potential buyers. The two points of fear of a reduction in human contact and the willingness of employees to change should be addressed through communication, information events and testing opportunities.

References

1. United Nations: Department of Economic and Social Affairs, Population Division, World Population Ageing 2019. Highlights, New York (2019)
2. Scheffler, R.M., et al.: Forecasting imbalances in the global health labor market and devising policy respons-es. Hum Resour Health **16**(5), 1 (2018). https://doi.org/10.1186/s12960-017-0264-6
3. Flake, R., Kochskämper, S., Risius, P., Seyda, S.: Fachkräfteengpass in der Altenpflege: Status quo und Perspektiven, IW-Trends-Vierteljahresschrift zur empirischen Wirtschaftsforschung **45**(3), 21–39 (2018). https://doi.org/10.2373/1864-810X.18-03-02
4. Hebesberger, D., Körtner, T., Pripfl, J., Gisinger, C., Hanheide, M.: What do staff in eldercare want a robot for? An assessment of potential tasks and user requirements for a long-term deployment, In: IROS Workshop on "Bridging User Needs to Deployed Applications of Service Robots" (2015)
5. Radic, M., Vosen, A., Graf, B.: Use of Robotics in the German Healthcare Sector. In: Salichs, M.A., et al. (eds.) ICSR 2019. LNCS (LNAI), vol. 11876, pp. 434–442. Springer, Cham (2019). https://doi.org/10.1007/978-3-030-35888-4_40
6. Papadopoulos, I., Koulouglioti, C., Lazzarino, R., Ali, S.: Enablers and barriers to the implementation of socially assistive humanoid robots in health and social care: a systematic review. BMJ Open **10**(1), e033096 (2020). https://doi.org/10.1136/bmjopen-2019-033096
7. Fracasso, F., Buchweitz, L., Theil, A., et al.: social robots acceptance and marketability in italy and germany: a cross-national study focusing on assisted living for older adults. Int. J. Soc. Rob. **14**, 1463–1480 (2022). https://doi.org/10.1007/s12369-022-00884-z
8. Fischinger, D., et al.: Hobbit, a care robot supporting independent living at home: First prototype and lessons learned. Rob. Auton. Syst. **75**, 60–78 (2016). https://doi.org/10.1016/j.robot.2014.09.029
9. Kramer, B.: Die Akzeptanz neuer Technologien bei pflegenden Angehörigen von Menschen mit Demenz, Dissertation (2016). https://doi.org/10.11588/heidok.00020856
10. Statista, Anzahl der Krankenhäuser in Deutschland in den Jahren 2000 bis 2019. Quelle: Statistisches Bundesamt. https://de.statista.com/statistik/daten/studie/2617/umfrage/anzahl-der-krankenhaeuser-in-deutschland-seit-2000/
11. Statista, Anzahl von Pflegeheimen und ambulanten Pflegediensten in Deutschland in den Jahren 1999 bis 2019. Quelle: Statistisches Bundesamt (Destatis Pflegestatistik 2019). https://de.statista.com/statistik/daten/studie/2729/umfrage/anzahl-der-pflegeheime-und-ambulanten-pflegedienste-seit-1999/

Development of Robotic Care for Older Adults with Dementia: Focus Group and Survey Study

Fengpei Yuan[1]([✉])(iD), Marie Boltz[2](iD), Betsy Kemeny[3](iD), Sharon Bowland[1](iD), Kristina Wick[4](iD), and Xiaopeng Zhao[1](iD)

[1] University of Tennessee, Knoxville, TN 37996, USA
fyuan6@vols.utk.edu, {sbowland,xzhao9}@utk.edu
[2] Penn State University, University Park, PA 16802, USA
mpb40@psu.edu
[3] Slippery Rock University, Slippery Rock, PA 16057, USA
martha.kemeny@sru.edu
[4] University of Tennessee, Chattanooga, TN 37403, USA
Kristina-Wick@utc.edu

Abstract. The number of people with dementia has been growing worldwide. The cognitive deficits in people with dementia usually lead to lower independence and quality of life. Socially assistive robots (SARs) have demonstrated potential to assist dementia care and reduce workload in caregivers. To successfully and effectively develop robotic care for dementia, end-users are needed to continuously participate in the robot development lifecycle. In this paper, we discussed a focus group and survey study conducted with a group of nine older adults, including seven dementia caregivers, to investigate the acceptance of using SAR for dementia care and to identify potential concerns from the end-users' perspective. Ongoing research ideas, designs and experiments related to SARs for dementia care were presented to the focus group along with demonstrations of various functions of a humanoid social robot Pepper. The results suggest overall positive attitudes and perceptions of older adults towards using SARs to assist dementia care. The group also made recommendations for future research in this field, such as addressing user interaction design challenges for people with dementia, pet-robot interaction, and potential decision-making issues by SARs.

Keywords: Focus groups · Participatory design · Dementia care

1 Introduction

Worldwide, the number of people with dementia has grown over the past few decades. In the USA, approximately 6.5 million older adults (aged ≥ 65) are living with Alzheimer's disease or other related dementias (ADRD), which progressively destroy memory, thinking, and other cognitive capabilities, leading to

Supported by National Institute of Health under the grant number R01AG077003.

F. Cavallo et al. (Eds.): ICSR 2022, LNAI 13818, pp. 338–347, 2022.
https://doi.org/10.1007/978-3-031-24670-8_30

lower independence and quality of life [1]. In 2021, more than 11 million Americans cared for persons living with dementia (PLWDs) as informal caregivers, e.g., family, friend, or other unpaid caregivers. Dementia caregiving is exhausting and time-intensive which contributes to an increased risk for poor mental and physical health [2]. Moreover, excessive demands on caregivers are compounded by a shortage of formal caregivers in the workforce [3].

Artificial intelligence (AI) and AI-empowered socially assistive robots (SARs) have the potential to supplement caregiver support, reduce workload in caregivers, and improve quality of life for both persons with ADRD and their caregivers [4]. To successfully integrate use of SAR as a tool for dementia care, development must include continuous user evaluation to ensure user friendliness, understand user needs, and refine the design and functions of the SAR [5,6].

The primary objective of this study was to collaborate with end-users of dementia care tools, such as caregivers of PLWDs, and obtain continuous feedback over the course of SAR development. A focus group and survey study with a group of older adults (including caregivers) interested in creative learning was conducted. This study aimed to answer the following research questions: 1) How do older adults and caregivers perceive use of the SAR as a caregiving tool for PLWDs? 2) What are the challenges or concerns in using SARs for dementia care from end-user perspective after direct interaction with the SAR? 3) What can a SAR do to support dementia caregivers, especially informal caregivers?

2   Method

The study was conducted with nine older adults from Seniors for Creative Learning and was held at John O'Connor Senior Center at Knoxville, TN, USA. The study protocol was approved by the Institutional Review Board (IRB) (IRB number is UTK IRB-21-06631-XM). A total of nine older adults (6F/3M) provided consent to participate in the study. Demographic information of the participants is listed in Table 1. Seven participants reported having cared for PLWDs.

2.1   Procedures

The researchers, including one facilitator and one note taker, first conducted a focus group, which began with a 20-min overview of AI and robotics for people with dementia, using examples of research projects conducted at the University of Tennessee. For each research project, the facilitator explained the study goal (e.g., using SAR to supplement diagnosis of Alzheimer's, deliver reminiscence, and assist PLWD to complete activities of daily living), research approach, and showed relevant illustrative images and/or videos of PLWD-robot interaction. Two examples of the slides used during the presentation are shown in Fig. 1. After the presentation, participants had the opportunity to ask questions for approximately 15 min while written notes of their questions, comments, and suggestions were taken by the note taker. Next, the functions of the humanoid Pepper robot were demonstrated for approximately 20 min including singing, dancing, presentation, and a Tic-Tac-Toe game. Participants then had one-to-one

Table 1. Descriptive statistics of participants ($n = 9$).

Demographic variables	Statistic
Gender	n (%)
Female	6 (66.67%)
Male	3 (33.33%)
Age (years)	n (%)
50–65	1 (11.11%)
65–75	2 (22.22%)
75–85	6 (66.67%)
Highest level of education	n (%)
Some college	4 (55.55%)
College graduate	2 (22.22%)
Post-graduate	3 (33.33%)
Familiarity with technology	Mean ± SD
Smartphones	2.89 ± 1.27
Tablets	2.56 ± 1.13
Computers	3.33 ± 1.01
Robots	1.56 ± 0.77

For the items associated with familiarity with technology (i.e., Rows *Smartphones*, *Tablets*, *Computers*, and *Robots*), 1 = Not at all familiar, 2 = Slightly familiar, 3 = Moderately familiar, 4 = Very familiar.

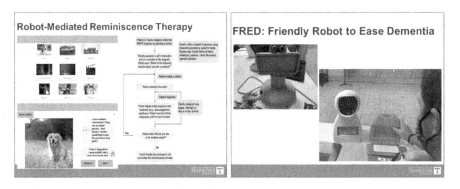

Fig. 1. Examples of slides used to present potential robot functions for dementia care. The left image exhibited reminiscence therapy developed in a robot Pepper [7]. The right image introduced a low-cost social robot designed for dementia care using Information and Communications Technology (ICT) and 3D printing technology [8].

interactions with the robot, as illustrated in Fig. 2. Following the demonstration, a written survey was distributed to participants to capture their opinions about using SAR technology to assist with the dementia care and their needs and requirements experienced in the dementia caregiving journey. See Sect. 2.2 for details of the survey.

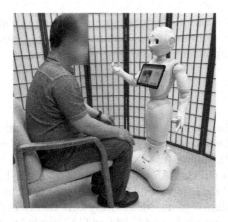

Fig. 2. One-to-one interaction between a user and the robot during a demonstration.

2.2 Data Collection

A mixed-method approach was adopted to collect data from participants to identify broad themes, perceptions, and potential concerns of older adults related to using SAR to assist with dementia care. This technique allowed participants to have exploratory, in-depth discussions on robotic care for dementia, which guides the future development of SAR for dementia care. In focus group, the note taker took written notes on the question-and answer session with the participants.

The post-test survey consisted of two parts (Part I and II). Each part included both quantitative and open-ended questions. Part I included general questions on the robot's usability for dementia care. The first five questions collected demographic information including age, gender, highest level of education, and familiarity with technologies. The remaining Part I questions were designed to ascertain participants' perceptions of utilizing Pepper robot to care for PLWD, including the user interface (UI) design and usefulness of a list of robot functions. In addition, an open-ended question was included at the end of Part I to capture any additional comments, suggestions, or concerns from the participants regarding developing a SAR to provide dementia care. Part II of the survey targeted at people with experience caring for PLWDs. Beginning questions were designed to learn caregivers' relationship to PLWDs, the intensity and duration of dementia care they provide per week, and their access to tools and resources to help them plan and/or access care for the PLWD. We additionally added two open-ended questions to capture what caregivers report they need the most.

2.3 Data Analysis

Descriptive statistics including mean (M) and standard deviation (SD) were used to analyze the quantitative data collected through survey. Considering the small sample size, all the comments from the focus group session and from open-ended questions in the survey were manually analyzed by one coder using content analysis. The transcript from the focus group session and open-ended questions on the survey were content analyzed to summarize, and determine which themes emerged from the respondents' answers

3   Results

After participating in the focus group, all the nine participants finished Part I of the survey and the seven caregivers finished Part II. Caregivers reported as child (CA1 and CA2), spouse (CA4), friend (CA3), respite caregiver (CA7), and other family (not specified, CA5 and CA6) of a PLWD. Two caregivers (CA2 and CA7) mentioned that they cared for PLWDs for 6–12 months and two (CA4 and CA6) for more than 5 years. Meanwhile, CA2 mentioned that she needed to provide 1–4 h of care per week, and CA6 and CA7 needed to provide 10–19 hours of care per week. Four caregivers indicated they had access to tools/resources (e.g., The 36-h Day Book) to help them plan and/or access care for PLWDs, while two indicated they had no such access. The quantitative and qualitative response are summarized in the sections below.

3.1   Quantitative Data

The mean (SD) of responses to the questions in Part I related to use of a robot Pepper with current appearance, sounding voice, and height are 4.50 (0.53), 3.67 (1.37), and 4.86 (0.38), respectively. The extent of usefulness of the listed robot functions rated by participants for people with Alzheimer's is listed in Table 2.

Table 2. Participants' responses, M and SD, to the usefulness of robot functions for PLWDs (1= *Not useful at all*, 5 = *Very useful*).

Robot function	M ± SD
F1: Monitor people's movement at home to reduce risks of fall	4.78 ± 0.44
F2: Help people with walking and stand-up	4.67 ± 0.50
F3: Monitor people's medication use to avoid errors in drug use	4.67 ± 0.50
F4: Monitor ambient environmental conditions to improve people's safety and wellness	4.78 ± 0.44
F5: Regulate heating, humidity, lighting, and TV channel	4.78 ± 0.44
F6: Undertake comprehensive geriatric assessment for people	4.33 ± 0.87
F7: Link to care planning for people	4.38 ± 0.52
F8: Monitor people's physiological deterioration	4.78 ± 0.44
F9: Monitor people's cognitive deterioration	4.78 ± 0.44
F10: Provide advice and support for people when their caregivers are out of house	4.33 ± 1.00

3.2   Qualitative Data

In the focus group, participants provided their perspectives regarding using SAR to assist with dementia care. Five topics, including robot acceptance, robot function, user interface, implementation setting, and cost, were identified themes based on their questions and comments, as recorded in Table 3. Four participants responded to the open-ended question in Part I of the survey, as recorded in Table 4. Four caregivers provided responses to the open-ended questions in Part II are listed in Table 5.

Table 3. Themes that emerged from focus group.

Theme	Examples of questions or comments from participants
Robot acceptance	*Do all people with dementia accept the robot?*
Robot function	*Can the robot shake hands?*
	Can the robot sing the song 'Rocky Top'?
	Can the robot detect emergency falls?
	Is the robot recording everything, like the conversation?
	How's the robot's performance going, compared to professional clinicians?
User interface	*The tablet on the robot might be too small for people with dementia to see it clearly*
Implementation setting	*Pets, such as dogs and cats, might be aggressive to the robot.*
	Did you expect the robot to be used at home or hospital?
Cost	*Do you expect the cost of the robot will be reduced in the future?*

Table 4. Participants' responses to the open-ended question ("Do you have any additional comments, suggestions, or concerns you would like to share, in order to develop a robot to provide Alzheimer's care?") of Survey Part I.

ID	Response
P1	*None at this time. But great idea!*
P4	*It is wonderful that you are doing this research. I wish I had had a "Pepper" or "FRED" when I was helping care for my mom and dad who both had dementia. BRAVO!*
P7	*The robot must be presented as a companion, not a machine*
P9	*The current voice seems to have some distortion, and it would be helpful if it could speak slower. The UT model (FRED) appeals to me more than the full size model. I think robots are great to assist human activities (I've worked around them in manufacturing for example) but personally find the efforts to make them appear more like real people to be a bit unsettling. I would also hope that humans would monitor the AI to make sure it was getting accurate information and conclusions*

Table 5. Caregivers' responses to the open-ended questions in Part II.

ID	Response to "If I could change one thing to improve my experience as a caregiver caring for an aging person with dementia, it would be"	Response to question "What is the biggest barrier as a family caregiver?"
CA1		*The ongoing never ending stress and watching the person decline*
CA2	*I wish I had made use of respite care facility so I or my dad could take a break from caring for my mom*	*Burn out*
CA6	*More patience for me*	*Lack of power to make person follow suggestions*
CA7	*It takes a lot of patience in some cases. It's easier for a non-family member to interact with them*	*Time. Often spouses are too close to understanding. Children have to work and care for their own families*

4   Discussions and Conclusion

In this study, we conducted a focus group ($n = 9$) and survey study with older adults from Seniors for Creative Learning regarding the design and development of robotic care for PLWDs. The mixed-method approach allowed us to gain significant insights about participants' perceptions, needs, requirements, and concerns. Generally, participants showed positive acceptance and attitudes towards using SARs for dementia care and agreed that there is potential usefulness for this technology (as indicated in Table 2 and Table 4). Moreover, we identified specific concerns from these stakeholders' perspective in terms of using SARs for dementia care. Discussions on these concerns are provided as follows.

4.1   Challenges in User Interface Design for Dementia

One participant pointed out that the tablet (246-175-14.5-mm) on the robot Pepper might be too small for people with dementia to clearly see the screen. We found a similar issue in our previous usability study of robot-assisted reminiscence therapy program [7], where we noticed that some persons with ADRD sat too close to the robot impeding their ability to clearly see the content on the tablet. As discussed in our previous study [7], sitting close to the robot interfered with the robot's body movements and possibly reduced the effectiveness of the robot's body movements in communication. The development of the technologies such as flexible display [9] and virtual and augmented Reality [4] might allow us to address this design issue (i.e., integration of a robot-based system with a large enough touchscreen) and enable large screens while improving portability.

Compared to the current appearance (*Mean* = 4.50, *SD* = 0.53) and height (*Mean* = 4.86, *SD* = 0.38), participants provided a low rating score (*Mean* = 3.67, *SD* = 1.37) to the voice in Pepper robot, which might be explained by

P9's comment that Pepper's voice seemed to have some distortion and that Pepper should speak slower (Table 4). Our previous usability study of the robot-mediated reminiscence therapy with persons with MCI and ADRD found similar result, i.e., a comparatively low rating to the robot's voice by users [7]. Hearing loss and slower cognitive processing speed occur gradually in the aging population and people with ADRD [10], which may have contributed to difficulty of our end-users had capturing and understanding the robot's verbal communication. In addition, the robot developers, usually young adults, may have not recognized these communication barriers which ultimately impair both communication and social interaction between the user and the robot. Thus, it is imperative that the robot's design include voice characteristics which account for the speed and volume needed to maximize communication with the end-user. Developing a process that allows the user to choose the most optimal setting for themselves at the very beginning of the user-robot interaction may mitigate known communication barriers in the older adults population.

4.2   Pet-Robot Interaction

One interesting topic raised by the participants is how pets, such as dogs and cats, would respond and interact with a SAR. Compared to human-robot interaction, there is only limited number of preliminary studies on pet-robot interaction [11,12]. In a recent study using a 58cm-tall humanoid robot NAO, Qin et al. [11] investigated whether dogs would respond to the robot after the robot called their names and whether dogs would follow 'sit' commands by the robot. Their preliminary results showed that dogs showed positive behaviors to social robots and that social robots could influence dog's behaviors. However, many factors may influence the relationship and interaction between pets and SARs, for example, the type of pet (dog vs cat), size and appearance of the SAR, with/without the presence of pet owners, and short vs. long-term interaction. For end-users to successfully accept and use the SAR at home, robot developers should further study the pet-robot interaction.

4.3   Decision-Making by SARs for Dementia Care

Interestingly, participants rated robot functions F6, F7, and F10 relatively low compared to other robot functions, as reported in Table 2. The rating difference may related to the fact that functions F6, F7, and F10 involve decision-making of dementia care, for example, diagnosis of dementia in F6, while the other seven functions focus on monitoring. This suggests that older adults and people with ADRD do not trust a robot to make decisions, which is consistent with previous findings [7]. Yet, user trust is a critical factor influencing user's intention to use of a robot. We therefore suggest implementing strategies to improve user trust, such as improving the robots' performance, providing user training, and offering opportunities for the user to interact with SARs for a longer period of time.

4.4   Caregivers Needs in Dementia

Despite only 4 dementia caregivers responding to the open-ended questions in Part II of the questionnaire, their comments reflect significant physical and psychological stress and burden on dementia caregivers due to caregiving demands. For example, the caregivers (CA6 and CA7 in Table 5) described problems in communication between themselves and the person with dementia. Moreover, they also discussed issue with caregiver-life balance and struggles in finding time and a balance between care assistance duties and their own needs.

Additional comments from our caregivers provided insight related to using SARs and other technologies for dementia care to reduce caregivers' burden. On one hand, technology-assisted interventions can be developed directly for PLWDs, such as the respite care (CA2 and CA7), cognitive exercise, and companionship [7,8]). Conversely, technology-assisted interventions can also be designed to target caregivers by providing accessible and personalized information to improve CAs' knowledge, along with developing coping abilities, care skills, and strategies aimed at promoting a balance between dementia caregiving and their own needs [13,14].

4.5   Other Considerations or Concerns

Feedback from participants also indicates other factors or concerns which might influence their use of SARs in dementia care, such as robot functions, appearance, and the size of a SAR, and cost. The robot functions (e.g., shaking hands, singing preferable songs, and detecting falls), and usefulness of the robot, received the most attention from the focus group, as shown in Table 3. In summary, to successfully utilize the SAR, the utility and benefits of the SAR end-users during dementia care should be clarified [15]. Further, the focus group identified potential areas for future research such as affordability of SARs [4,5,16].

In this paper, we discussed the results of a focus group and survey study using a group of older adults (including dementia caregivers) to evaluate their perceptions, attitudes, and concerns for using SARs to supplement dementia care. Despite the small sample size, the group reported a positive perception of the robotic care and agreed with the potential usefulness of SARs. Comments from participants suggested a list of factors, such UI design principles specifically for PLWDs, pet-robot interaction, decision-making issues by SARs, and personalized design of the robot's appearance and size. Which may need to be taken into consideration in future studies. To make the findings more representative and generalizable, we need to access to a larger number of end-users and keep closely collaborating with them in future work. Further research opportunities include identifying additional collaborators to evaluate the robots functions and appearance.

References

1. Alzheimer's Association: 2022 Alzheimer's disease facts and figures. Alzheimer's & Association, 18 (2022)

2. Brodaty, H., Donkin, M.: Family caregivers of people with dementia. Dialogues Clin. Neurosci. **11**(2), 217 (2009)
3. Osterman, P.: Who will Care for Us?: Long-Term Care and the Long-Term Workforce. Russell Sage Foundation (2022)
4. Yuan, F., Klavon, E., Liu, Z., Lopez, R.P., Zhao, X.: A systematic review of robotic rehabilitation for cognitive training. Front. Rob. AI **8**, 605715 (2021)
5. Yuan, F., et al.: Assessing the acceptability of a humanoid robot for Alzheimer's disease and related dementia care using an online survey. Int. J. Soc. Rob., 1–15 (2022)
6. Hartson, R., Pyla, P.S.: The UX Book: Process and Guidelines for Ensuring a Quality User Experience. Elsevier (2012)
7. Yuan, F., et al.: Cognitive exercise for persons with Alzheimer's disease and related dementia Using a social robot (2022). Submitted to IEEE Transactions on Robotics on April 29, 2022
8. Mitchell, K., Zhao, X.: Testing for acceptance of an assistive social robot for dementia and caregiving. In: Alzheimer's Association International Conference, San Diego, USA, 31 July–4 August 2022
9. Park, J., et al.: Research on flexible display at ULSAN national institute of science and technology. NPJ Flexible Electron. **1**(1), 1–13 (2017)
10. Ford, A.H., Hankey, G.J., Yeap, B.B., Golledge, J., Flicker, L., Almeida, O.P.: Hearing loss and the risk of dementia in later life. Maturitas **112**, 1–11 (2018)
11. Qin, M., Huang, Y., Stumph, E., Santos, L., Scassellati, B.: Dog sit! Domestic dogs (canis familiaris) follow a robot's sit commands. In: Companion of the 2020 ACM/IEEE International Conference on Human-Robot Interaction, pp. 16–24 (2020)
12. Kasuga, H., Ikeda, Y.: Pet dogs' and their owners' reactions toward four differently shaped speaking agents: a report on qualitative results in a pilot test. In: Degen, H., Ntoa, S. (eds.) HCII 2021. LNCS (LNAI), vol. 12797, pp. 359–376. Springer, Cham (2021). https://doi.org/10.1007/978-3-030-77772-2_24
13. Bressan, V., Visintini, C., Palese, A.: What do family caregivers of people with dementia need? A mixed-method systematic review. Health Soc. Care Community **28**(6), 1942–1960 (2020)
14. Yuan, F., Blackburn, J., Condon, C., Bowland, S., Lopez, R.P., Zhao, X.: A social robot-based psycho-educational program to enhance Alzheimer's caregiver health. In: 2021 IEEE/ACM Conference on Connected Health: Applications, Systems and Engineering Technologies (CHASE), pp. 124–125. IEEE (2021)
15. de Graaf, M.M., Allouch, S.B., van Dijk, J.A.: Long-term evaluation of a social robot in real homes. Interact. Stud. **17**(3), 462–491 (2016)
16. Koh, W.Q., Felding, S.A., Toomey, E., Casey, D.: Barriers and facilitators to the implementation of social robots for older adults and people with dementia: a scoping review protocol. Systems Control Found. Appl. **10**(1), 1–6 (2021)

A Mobile Social Hand Disinfection Robot for Use in Hospitals

Oskar Palinko$^{(\boxtimes)}$ ⓘ, Rasmus P. Junge ⓘ, Daniel G. Holm ⓘ,
and Leon Bodenhagen ⓘ

University of Southern Denmark, Campusvej 55, 5230 Odense, Denmark
ospa@mmmi.sdu.dk

Abstract. Prevention of infectious diseases as the Covid-19 is of essential importance for the well-being of humanity. This is especially so at hospitals, where many vulnerable individuals frequent. Hand disinfection is one of the methods for preventing communicable diseases. In this paper we introduce a new modular mobile service robot designed for hand disinfection in hospitals and other public spaces. It consists of two separable parts: the driving base and the disinfection stand. The base was made in a horseshoe shape which allows it to lift its payload (the stand) near its center of gravity and distribute the weight evenly on its four wheels. The stand is able to function both in conjunction with the base and also autonomously. The whole robot was designed with social interaction in mind to achieve better hand sanitization compliance, which is of essential importance in hospitals for preventing infectious diseases. We conducted a test of how well the robot is able to find and approach people in its vicinity who face different directions. Even though the robot does not achieve its goal position ideally, it always ends up facing the user, which is even more important for starting an interaction than reaching its goal position very precisely.

Keywords: Social robotics · Human-robot interaction · Hand disinfection · Healthcare robotics

1 Introduction

Robots are making their ways from factory floors to our everyday living environments. They are becoming more present in a number of different fields of applications: logistics, product advertisement, meal preparation, home companionship, etc. One of these fields is healthcare robotics. Since 2020, robots have been started to be utilized for combating the Covid pandemic, e.g. for facilitating hand disinfection. Our team has designed such a hand disinfection robot as a modular system, see Fig. 1. Its two main elements are the mobile base and the smart disinfection stand. One base is intended to service multiple stand units. There are several reasons why a disinfection stand should be mobile and self-relocatable: 1) to bring disinfection closer to people to convince them to sanitize

F. Cavallo et al. (Eds.): ICSR 2022, LNAI 13818, pp. 348–358, 2022.
https://doi.org/10.1007/978-3-031-24670-8_31

Fig. 1. The mobile base and the stand separated (left) and the unified hand disinfection robot in interaction with a person (right).

their hands, 2) to drive to a logistic center for disinfectant refill, 3) to recharge its battery, 4) to relocate based on daily pedestrian traffic needs and 5) to respond to changes in the hospital environment.

In this paper we will focus only on the functionality of the mobile base and not the disinfection stand, which will be covered separately.

Even though robots are becoming more ubiquitous in our environment, their capabilities for interacting with people still leave much room for improvement. Verbal interaction for agents and robots have achieved a very high level of sophistication, as exemplified in products like smart speakers, home assistants and recently even personal companion robots. However, in contrast with verbal communication, robots are less proficient in using non-verbal communication cues, like eye gaze, lights, gestures, etc. which our robot is designed to utilize in the future. To initiate a successful interaction, it is very important for the robot to position itself in front of the human. We conducted a test of this ability and we report on it in later sections.

2   Related Work

Service robots are autonomous systems which perform useful tasks in people's everyday environments and outside of industrial and outdoor applications [19]. These robots are usually mobile and navigate autonomously. Service robots are becoming more ubiquitous with the widespread use of advancements like AI, cloud computing, big data and biometrics [23]. They have become even more relevant during the Covid-19 pandemic as social distancing between people became a necessity. Example fields of use include hospitality [17,20], health care [7,15], as well as other fields [14,21]. As contact with delivery personnel seemed a possible way of spreading the virus, mobile delivery robots and drones saw an increased demand [3].

The emergence of the Covid-19 pandemic created an additional impetus for the development and use of robots in the human environment [10,21]. A number of authors have explored creating robots for automatic throat swabbing for Covid diagnosis [11,22]. Hygienically, it makes perfect sense to use robots in this situation to prevent any healthcare professionals from being infected while applying the swabs. However, from the human-robot interaction perspective, a robotic swabbing arm might be seen somewhat invasive. Screening is another clear application area, as it is easy to equip robots with thermal sensors which would allow easy detection of fever in public spaces [4,8]. In many situations however there is no need for a robot to do this, as thermal cameras can have a large field of view, so there might not be a need to move the sensor around. Telehealth systems were available even before the pandemic to reduce contact with infectious patients, but they were under-utilized until the emergence of Covid [24]. However, telepresence robots have proven to be effective in reducing potential infection points between patients and robots [12]. On the other hand, telepresence robots need to be used with great attention to ethical questions, as what is appropriate to communicate using such a robot and what is not.

A subcategory of Covid-19 related robots are the ones designed for disinfection in public spaces with high human frequency like hospitals, malls, airports, etc. One of the prominent class of these robots use ultraviolet light to sanitize high contact areas when humans are not present [1]. Another class sprays disinfectant liquid in aerosol form [13]. Finally, hand disinfection has also been found to contribute to combating Covid-19 [2]. Robotic hand disinfection interfaces can help nudge people to use the hand sanitizer more regularly than a customary, non-interactive sanitizer dispenser, as in [16]. In that paper the authors detail how an interactive agent displayed on a screen on top of a hand sanitizer unit is able to increase hand disinfection compliance significantly. The authors also found that people rub their hands longer when the robot asks them to do so, which improves the efficiency of the disinfectant. Our current research aims at building upon this static disinfection robot and make it mobile with additional interaction and logistic capabilities. These properties should lead to even higher compliance with hand disinfection requirements. The proposed design is modular, featuring a small footprint, and making use of widely available and rather inexpensive components such that the combined solution can be feasible for the healthcare domain.

3 Approach

In the following, the modular design of both hardware and software is outlined as well as an experiment for verifying the design on the scenario where a person is approached by the robot.

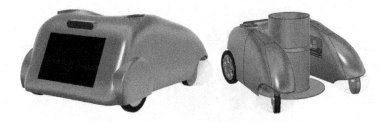

Fig. 2. A rendered view of a) the front of the mobile base and b) the back of it with a lower part of the disinfection stand attached.

3.1   Robot Design

Robot Shape. The modular robot is composed of two components: a mobile base unit and one or multiple disinfection stands that can be coupled with the robot. This base unit, which is the focus of this paper, was designed in a U or horseshoe shape, see Fig. 2. This allows it to drive up to the hand sanitizer unit and lift it near the robot's vertical projection of its center of gravity, which leads to even distribution of the stand's weight on the robot's four wheels. It also makes sure that the whole system is not easily tipped over. The mobile base's chassis has been built out of 20×20 mm aluminum profiles interconnected with right angled corner pieces, see Fig. 3. The shell of the robot was designed to look "organic" with smoothly flowing curvatures, resembling shapes found in nature. It was 3D printed in pieces using fused deposition modeling and joined using epoxy adhesive.

The two end parts of the robot's horseshoe design have a diverging angle, which allows for the robot to couple with the stand even if the guiding to the stand is not perfectly accurate. Because of the shape of these "legs" and the cylindrical cross section of the stand at this height, the robot will passively auto-correct its trajectory if the stand makes contact with the legs before the bottom of the horseshoe. It is a type of passively compliant behavior.

The mobile base could pose a tripping hazard only if it drives around without a stand connected to it. For this reason a light superstructure needs to be added to it, e.g. a flag on a tall pole or a light 3D printed bridge connecting to the tallest point of the shell. An emergency stop button is installed just above the robot's screen and camera.

Drive Train and Lifting Mechanism. The robot supports a differential drive train using the two front wheels (the ones close to the screen). The wheels in the back are heavy duty casters with ball bearing support (see Fig. 3). The drive wheels are directly connected to the output shaft of two high torque servo motors (Dynamixel XM540-W270) capable of delivering 10 Nm each. The radial load of these motors is 40 N, which, assuming even distribution of the stand's weight would allow a total weight of around 16 kg. Lifting of the stand is performed with two linear actuators on the two sides of the horseshoe brace, which lifts

Fig. 3. Robot chassis.

by pushing up a lip on the stand at 20 cm height from the ground. The lifted stand's bottom plate pushes against the bottom of the mobile unit's chassis on three sides, thus ensuring a wobble-free coupling. The bottom of the stand is lifted off the ground by only 2 cm.

Sensors and Interaction Capabilities. Two LIDARs (RPLIDAR A1, with the possibility of upgrade) are located on the "shoulders" of the mobile base, see Fig. 2. Their location is chosen such, that most of the field around the robot is covered by at least one of them, except a narrow area just behind the coupled stand, if present. When a stand is carried, the robot would not move backwards, so this lack of field coverage would not pose a problem.

An **inertial measurement unit (IMU)**, consisting of a 3-axis accelerometer and a 3-axis gyroscope is located on the robot's controller board. It is used for improving localization.

A **camera** (RealSense D455) is placed at the front of the robot's shell just above the screen. It is employed for detecting people and potentially low lying obstacles in front of the robot.

As part of the robot's interaction system, a 10-inch **touchscreen** is mounted in the front of the shell. It is used in our current study for displaying a set of simulated robotic eyes. As both the stand and mobile base contain a screen, it was decided that when the two units are coupled, the stand's screen takes over the interaction role, as it is near the eye-level of a human user. While the mobile base is operating by itself, the aforementioned screen will be employed for interaction. The eyes allow for one-way communication from the robot to the user. Smooth movement of the face clearly indicates the direction of the interest of the robot, while fast, saccade movement of the pupils display the simulated gaze. The eyes can also show emotions, such as happiness, confusion, anger and neutral. This is done by changing the shape of their outline. A **speaker system** and a **microphone** are installed in the stand just under the screen which improve the robot's interaction potential.

Fig. 4. Experimental layout. The test subject is being approached by the mobile robot.

Software Architecture. The robot's software is based on the Robot Operating System (ROS). It relies on part of the standard ROS navigation package, with added support for Google Cartographer [6] and a tuned TEB local planner [18] for significantly improved mapping and trajectory planning respectively. An important enabler for social interaction of the robot is the people detector and tracking package developed for mobile robots [9], that enables projection of people and objects and their pose to the navigation map. With the use of the CenterNet object detector [25] for detecting a person's keypoints, orientation and center in the image, the algorithm can then further determine the location of the person by using the depth component of the RGB-D camera to get the distance to the center point of the person. Location and orientation detection and tracking are extremely important for the robot to be able to approach and interact with people. An accurate approach could mean the difference between a successful interaction resulting in hand sanitization compliance and a failed opportunity. For this reason, in the next section we will investigate how well the robot is able to approach a person and locate itself properly for social interaction, relying on the above mentioned people detector and tracker.

3.2 Experimental Design

The study focuses on testing the accuracy and reliability of the robot approaching people, which is an essential first step in starting a successful social interaction between the system and the user. The optical motion tracking system OptiTrack was used to get accurate measurements of both the trajectory and orientation of the robot and human subject. The experiment was conducted at one of the robotics labs at our university, due to the fixed location of the motion tracking system. This meant consistent light conditions and a controlled environment with the testing area shielded off to avoid misleading detection of other

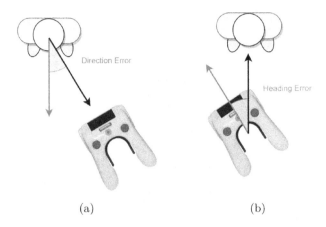

(a)   (b)

Fig. 5. Definition of the a) direction error and b) heading error.

users of the lab. Throughout the test the robot started its approach from the same position and orientation in its local map. The target person kept static between repetitions, see Fig. 4.

We decided to test 8 different orientations of a person. We stared at 0° angle between the person and robot and moved in 45° increments to complete a full circle (0, 45, 90, 135, 180, 225, 270 and 315°). An interactive robot usually approaches a person from the front, but we considered all angles to test the technical capabilities of our system. To eliminate inter-human variance, only one person was used as the target of detection (one of the experimenters), with 5 tracking markers positioned in the same position on the chest of the subject. There were 10 repetitions of approaches for each angle, for a total of 80 approaches. The robot continuously detected and tracked the target person's location and orientation during the approach, and sent an updated goal to the navigation stack with a frequency of 2 Hz. This continued up to about 2 m away from the detected person, where the field of view of the camera became too small for reliable person detection (as only parts of the body are seen at distances <2 m, due to the position and pitch of the camera). The robot's navigation was set up to reach a destination position 1m away from the person, with an orientation of 180° compared to the person's pose, making the robot face the subject directly. The 1m distance was chosen on the border between the social and personal spaces [5], where robots could come close enough to offer hand sanitization but not too close to invade one's privacy. It should be noted that the navigation planner had a goal tolerance of 0.1 m for the position, and 0.05 rad margin for the robot's heading. Data was collected throughout the experiments from the motion capture system, followed by calculation of the directional and heading error for the final position. Directional error is the difference between the person's orientation and the robot's location, while heading error is the difference between the robot's orientation and the person's location, see Fig. 5.

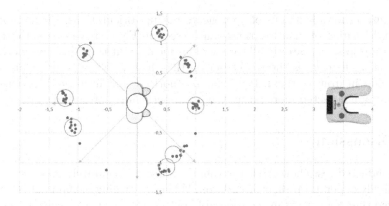

Fig. 6. Visualization of the results depicting the static person and the eight different approach directions (green arrows) as well as the final locations of the robot (blue dots). Red circles indicate the average placement of the robot for the individual approach directions. (Color figure online)

4   Results

As described in the previous section, the robot completed 80 approaches of the target person under 8 different angles. The final positions of the approaches of the robot compared to the person are shown in Fig. 6. The robot's icon represents the starting position. Blue dots show the final positions in each approach. The center of the red circles represents the average position of the 10 repetitions for each angle. It can be noticed that head on angles (0, 180°) are detected accurately, while perpendicular orientations (90, 270°) are mostly inaccurate and gravitate towards the initial position of the robot. Diagonal orientations have less precision and accuracy than head on locations.

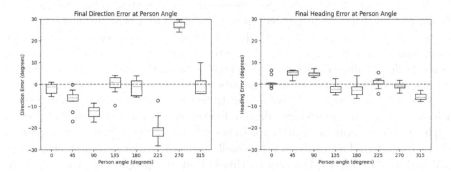

Fig. 7. Observed a) direction error and b) heading error for final pose of the robot after approaching a person from various starting configurations.

Figure 6 shows locations of approaches but not orientations. Errors in direction and heading of final locations can be seen in Fig. 7. It can be noticed that direction is less accurate than heading. This means that the robot was more able to orient itself towards the target person than how well it was able to position itself right in front of them. It can be also noticed that head on directions and headings are detected more accurately than perpendicular and diagonal ones.

5 Discussion

The conducted test shows that the robot's ability to accurately approach a person, highly depends on their orientation. When no turning or minimal turning is required the robot performs considerably better, likely due to localization of the robot in its map is easier as it can highly rely on its odometry. We have unfortunately experienced that the localization gets partly skewed when turning while driving forwards, which also might be the cause for the unsuccessful approaches in the 90 and 270° tests. This issues does however not occur in the same manner for the 180° test, as the final orientation adjustment in the approach happened while turning on its place, compared to an otherwise more natural car-like turning approach. In this case the localization skewing isn't as prominent.

Another possible explanation for the suboptimal results in the 90 and 270° configurations is that the clearance for the person is not identical at all sides, especially in the vertical direction in Fig. 6, where it might have affected the autonomous navigation such that car-like trajectories, which the TEB local planner otherwise aims for, were harder to achieve. Instead the robot approached with a sharp angle, which combined with a slight skewing of the localization in its local map and the goal tolerance, resulted in the final position with limited accuracy.

6 Conclusion and Future Work

In the first part of the paper, we presented a new mobile robot designed for lifting a hand disinfection payload from the ground and near the center of mass of the robot. This warrants a U shaped chassis. It also features a passively compliant design, which allows picking up the stand even if the robot's heading is not perfectly aligned with it. This is facilitated by the fact that the two caster wheels are located in the back of the robot at the tips of the U shape.

Once the robot was built, we set out to test how well it can approach people, which is crucial in establishing effective interaction. It was observed that certain angles result in more accurate approaches while other end further away from a desired location. This problem is especially pronounced for perpendicular angles (90 and 270°). One explanation to this is that the people detector is able to determine the person's angle less accurately like this, as it relies on detecting the two shoulders of a person. However, we mitigate this issue by continuously estimating the person's pose while the robot is approaching. In this case, the subject does not stay perpendicular towards the robot at all times, which enables better detection.

Finally we observed that heading error is smaller than direction error for the robot, which means that the robot is better at orienting itself towards the person than locating itself right in front of them. High accuracy with heading will be useful in real-world interaction with people as it is very important that the robot displays a good understanding of the person's whereabouts.

After the approach of people has been solved in a satisfactory manner, future work will include higher level interaction capabilities using speech, gaze, sound, movement, etc. with the goal of improving hand disinfection compliance using a most efficient combination of these modalities and signals.

Acknowledgement. This study was funded by the European Regional Development Fund under the HanDiRob project.

References

1. Ackerman, E.: Autonomous robots are helping kill coronavirus in hospitals. IEEE Spectr. **11** (2020)
2. Bana, P.R., Tsai, Y.L., Knight, H.: SanitizerBot: a hand sanitizer service robot. In: Companion of the 2021 ACM/IEEE International Conference on Human-Robot Interaction, pp. 661–661 (2021)
3. Bogue, R.: Robots in a contagious world. Ind. Rob Int. J. Rob. Res. Appl. (2020)
4. Gong, Z., et al.: Shuyu robot: an automatic rapid temperature screening system. Chin. J. Mech. Eng. **33**(1), 1–4 (2020)
5. Hall, E.T.: Proxemics [and comments and replies]. Curr. Anthropol. **9**(2/3), 83–108 (1968)
6. Hess, W., Kohler, D., Rapp, H., Andor, D.: Real-time loop closure in 2D LIDAR SLAM. In: 2016 IEEE International Conference on Robotics and Automation (ICRA) (2016). https://doi.org/10.1109/ICRA.2016.7487258
7. Holland, J.: Service robots in the healthcare sector. Robotics **10**(1), 47 (2021)
8. Huang, H.W., et al.: Agile mobile robotic platform for contactless vital signs monitoring (2020)
9. Juel, W.K., Haarslev, F., Krüger, N., Bodenhagen, L.: An integrated object detection and tracking framework for mobile robots. In: 17th International Conference on Informatics in Control, Automation and Robotics, pp. 513–520 (2020). https://doi.org/10.5220/0009888405130520
10. Kaiser, M.S., Al Mamun, S., Mahmud, M., Tania, M.H.: Healthcare robots to combat COVID-19. In: Santosh, K.C., Joshi, A. (eds.) COVID-19: Prediction, Decision-Making, and its Impacts. LNDECT, vol. 60, pp. 83–97. Springer, Singapore (2021). https://doi.org/10.1007/978-981-15-9682-7_10
11. Li, S.Q., et al.: Clinical application of an intelligent oropharyngeal swab robot: implication for the Covid-19 pandemic. Eur. Respir. J. **56**(2), 2001912 (2020)
12. Lociciro, A., Guillon, A., Bodet-Contentin, L.: A telepresence robot in the room of a covid-19 patient can provide virtual family presence. Can. J. Anesth./Journal canadien d'anesthésie **68**(11), 1705–1706 (2021)
13. Mohammed, M., et al.: Design and development of spray disinfection system to combat coronavirus (covid-19) using IoT based robotics technology. Revista Argentina de Clínica Psicológica **29**(5), 228 (2020)

14. Murphy, R.R., Gandudi, V.B.M., Adams, J.: Applications of robots for COVID-19 response. arXiv preprint arXiv:2008.06976 (2020)
15. Ozturkcan, S., Merdin-Uygur, E.: Humanoid service robots: the future of healthcare? J. Inf. Technol. Teach. Cases **12**, 63–169 (2021)
16. Palinko, O., et al.: A robotic interface for motivating and educating proper hand sanitization using speech and gaze interaction. In: 2021 30th IEEE International Conference on Robot & Human Interactive Communication (RO-MAN), pp. 763–769. IEEE (2021)
17. Romero, J., Lado, N.: Service robots and COVID-19: exploring perceptions of prevention efficacy at hotels in generation Z. Int. J. Contemp. Hospitality Manag. **33**(11), 4057–4078 (2021)
18. Rösmann, C., Hoffmann, F., Bertram, T.: Integrated online trajectory planning and optimization in distinctive topologies. Robot. Auton. Syst. **88**, 142–153 (2017). https://doi.org/10.1016/j.robot.2016.11.007
19. Schraft, R.D., Schmierer, G.: Service Robots. CRC Press (2000)
20. Seyitoğlu, F., Ivanov, S.: Service robots as a tool for physical distancing in tourism. Curr. Issue Tour. **24**(12), 1631–1634 (2021)
21. Shen, Y., et al.: Robots under COVID-19 pandemic: a comprehensive survey. IEEE Access **9**, 1590–1615 (2020)
22. Wang, S., Wang, K., Tang, R., Qiao, J., Liu, H., Hou, Z.G.: Design of a low-cost miniature robot to assist the covid-19 nasopharyngeal swab sampling. IEEE Trans. Med. Rob. Bionics **3**(1), 289–293 (2020)
23. Wirtz, J., et al.: Brave new world: service robots in the frontline. J. Serv. Manag. (2018)
24. Wosik, J., et al.: Telehealth transformation: Covid-19 and the rise of virtual care. J. Am. Med. Inform. Assoc. **27**(6), 957–962 (2020)
25. Zhou, X., Wang, D., Krähenbühl, P.: Objects as points. arXiv preprint arXiv:1904.07850 (2019)

Iterative Development of a Service Robot for Laundry Transport in Nursing Homes

Jonas Frei[1(✉)], Andreas Ziltener[2], Markus Wüst[1], Anina Havelka[2], and Katrin Lohan[1,3]

[1] Eastern Switzerland University of Applied Sciences, 9471 Buchs SG, Switzerland
`jonas.frei@ost.ch`
[2] University of Applied Sciences of the Grisons, 7000 Chur, Switzerland
[3] Heriot-Watt University, Edinburgh EH14 4AS, Scotland, UK

Abstract. In the Agebots project, a multidisciplinary team investigated and tested the use of service robots in elderly care. Applications such as material transport, entertainment, companionship, reminder, information, and fitness exercises were studied. The project is being conducted in collaboration with a nursing home and a robotics manufacturer. In this paper, the task "laundry transport" is presented. With the goal of reducing nurses' walking distances and workload, four variants of a laundry transporter were designed and tested in a replicated and a real environment using a human-centered design approach. In addition, three possible human-robot communication interface designs were investigated with respect to the behavior of the transport robot.

Keywords: Human-centered robotics · Service robotics · Social human robot interaction

1 Introduction

Service robotics could be the solution to several challenges nursing homes are facing [18,30]. By 2050, over 27% of the Swiss population will be 65 and older. This will pose major challenges for nursing homes in particular [5,6]. A shortage of skilled workers is already evident. This situation will be exacerbated by the rising demand for nurses, which is expected to increase by 36% in Switzerland by 2030 [21,24].

The work presented here is part of the Agebots project. In general, the development of robot prototypes is driven by technology. Four different dimensions need to be considered for a successful use of service robots in elderly care: human [3,23], technology [16,22,25], business [1,10], and law [7,26]. A detailed description of the method used in this three-year research project is published in [14]. Table 1 gives an overview of the project phases with reference to the technology readiness levels (TRL). Prior to the laboratory test, a comprehensive test concept was developed based on the methods presented by Bartneck et al. [2],

Supported by Innosuisse - Swiss Innovation Agency, 36691.1 IP-SBM.

Table 1. Agebots project phases

#	Project phase	Results	TRL
1	Understanding	144 challenges identified for nursing staff and the elderly	1
2	Ideation	Generated 15 application fields with 170 ideas for nursing staff and 10 application fields with 88 ideas for the elderly	2
3	Technology	Produced 7 robotic systems and conducted functional tests	3
4	Lab Test 1	Conducted feasibility testing with non-users and initial legal analysis. Reduction of the 25 applications fields to 12	4
5	Iteration 1	Development of applications and adaptation of the robotic systems based on the results of Lab Test I. Created a relational database for the analysis of the qualitative and quantitative data and populated it with insights	
6	Lab Test 2	Conducted usability and acceptance tests with the nursing staff and the elderly of the nursing home in a replicated environment. Developed a business plan to open up new markets for the robot manufacturer	5
7	Iteration 2	Development and adaptation of applications	
8	Field Test 1	Examined the desirable, feasible, and economical application in the nursing home environment	6
9	Iteration 3	Development and adaptation of applications	
10	Field Test 2	Examining of the legally compliant, desirable, feasible, and economical application in the nursing home environment	7
11	Marketing (planned)	Market launch and distribution of the service robot systems in German-speaking countries by the robot manufacturer	8

Heerink et al. [17], and Weiss et al. [31]. The concept describes the basic elements of the test setup: objectives, methods, cases, environment, infrastructure, organization, objects, types and plan. The challenges of stakeholders, such as nurses and the elderly, were identified through observations and interviews [9].

Parallel to the project, a quantitative survey was carried out in the German-speaking part of Europe with approximately 1500 nursing homes. 160 of the facilities surveyed completed the questionnaire in full. In the online survey, the applications identified in the project were visualized with short videos from laboratory tests. Subsequently, respondents had to answer various questions about these applications. Among other things, respondents were asked for each application whether they would find it beneficial if Lio were to take them over. Lio the service robot system mainly used in the Agebots project.

As can be seen from the survey results in Fig. 1, material transport is the most requested application. In this context, laundry transport was chosen because there is no interaction with elderly during the actual transport and there is a great potential for saving walking distances. The nursing staff supports the residents daily in their morning routine, changing the laundry in the bathroom on a regular basis. According to the nursing home management involved in the project, the nurses have to change the dirty laundry one room at a time. In

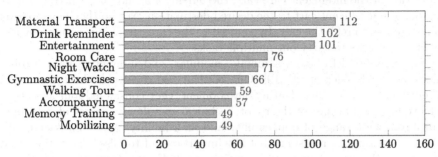

**In which tasks do you think it would be useful
for a robot like Lio to take over?**

Fig. 1. Top 10 survey results, n = 160, multiple answers

between, they have to discard the dirty laundry, disinfect the trolley and load fresh laundry again. This results in a very inefficient routine for the nurse: get new laundry, walk to the resident's room, change the laundry, walk to the laundry drop off, dispose the dirty laundry, disinfect the trolley, and then start all over again by getting fresh laundry. For safety reasons, it is forbidden to leave a trolley unattended in the hallway (e.g. an elderly person could trip over the trolley). Taking a trolley with dirty laundry into another resident's room is also forbidden for hygienic reasons. As a result, the nurses have to spend a considerable amount of their working time walking. Here a service robot could come to help by surveying it's immediate neighborhood and ensuring that contact with dirty laundry and accidents are prohibited.

2   Related Work

Past projects such as the STRANDS-project have focused on the feasibility and capability of mobile robots to endure usage for long periods of time without intervention [13,15]. With their goal of enabling a robot to achieve robust and intelligent behavior in human environments through adaptation to and exploitation of long-term experience, they have accomplished essential pioneering work in the field of healthcare robotics. Consistent with the findings of Hawes et al. [15] and Pineau et al. [28], the application studied must satisfy various requirements. I.e., Lio needs to position and orientate itself in space, map its environment, annotate locations and restricted areas, plan a path, navigate around temporary obstacles, communicate with caregivers and the elderly, and be easy to use. All these requirements are important prerequisites for the functionality of the presented task of laundry transport.

Together with Fraunhofer IPA, Graf et al. [12] developed an intelligent care cart based on MLR's CASERO 4 platform and tested it in two nursing homes in Mannheim. The intelligent care cart is operated by a nurse via a smartphone. Possible destinations are positions outside the resident's room, the storage (to replenish supplies) and the battery charging station. Thanks to the autonomous navigation of the intelligent care cart, the nursing staff no longer needs to walk to bring the intelligent cart to the desired destination. Nor do they have to walk to the storage to refill the cart. In contrast to the care cart, Lio is a multipurpose robot that allows to carry out multiple tasks.

The SMOOTH-Robot is a mobile, modular, and interactive service robot developed by Krüger et al. [19]. One of their use cases was the collection of laundry and garbage bins. During development, they considered four aspects to achieve high acceptance of the robot: technical complexity, degree of anthropomorphism, wide range of applicability and affordability. A key message of the study on anthropomorphism is that it is important not to raise expectations that the state of the art cannot meet. Therefore, a robotic appearance is preferable to a human-like appearance. Further it is emphasized that socially aware navigation is important when a robot is used in a space occupied by humans. Another issue is the safety and cognitive prerequisites needed for successful human-robot interaction (HRI). Human interaction is multimodal, incremental, and highly dynamic. Humans communicate through body orientation, speed, gaze, mimic, gesture and speech, often using multiple channels simultaneously. Consideration of these principles in HRI leads to extreme complexity. Therefore, according to the authors, it is unlikely that this problem can be solved within the next decade.

Langedijk et al. [20] identified various challenges in testing two service robots in the wild. Thereof, the technical challenges are of particular interest for our research questions. A realistic twin of the actual working environment should be replicated in the laboratory. Narrow aisles or grouped chairs are typical challenges for robots. Another technical challenge that may occur in the preparation phase is a poor network connection. In addition, the robot must have sufficient error handling capabilities to cope with unexpected changes in the environment.

3   Development, Experimentation and Tests

An agile product development approach [4,29] using rapid prototyping [11,27] and 3D printing was selected. This allowed for a flexible and human-centered design (see Fig. 3). An overview of the development process is shown in Fig. 2.

3.1   Verification of the Suitability for Reducing Walking Distances

As described in the introduction, nurses spend a substantial amount of their time walking during their shift. The number of steps taken by several nurses during a week was recorded with a pedometer. It was shown that a nurse covers an average of 9000–12000 steps during a shift (8 h). It was also measured that 100 steps take about 50 s. This results in a walking time of 80 to 100 min per shift.

To check the suitability of a laundry transporter to shorten walking distances, a simulation was conducted during the project phases 1 to 3 (see Table 1 and Fig. 2). A nurse was chosen to do his or her daily work during the early shift.

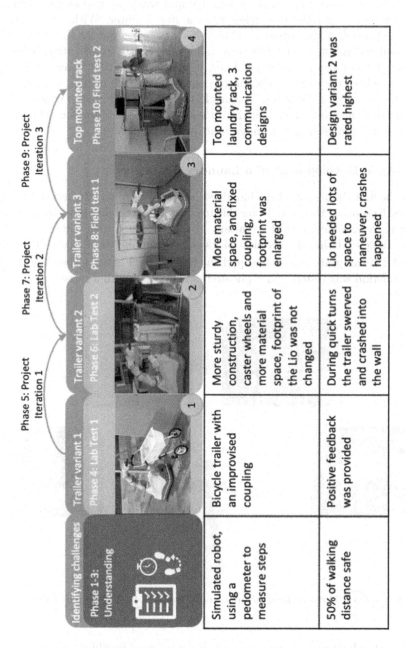

Fig. 2. Development process overview

A researcher then took on the role of the robot, manually pushing a material trolley around with bags for dirty laundry and trash, as well as fresh laundry. Both the nurse and the researcher wore a step counter. Without the human simulated robot, a step count of 1315 steps was registered for the nurse. With the simulated robot, the nurse's step count was reduced to 583 steps, while the simulated robot made 646 steps. Thus, having a robot that takes the laundry items to where they are needed on the command of the nursing staff can save over 50% of walking distances. This neglects human adaptability, which leads to nurses using the reduced walking distance for other tasks. Therefore, the walking distance will probably not decrease that much in reality.

3.2   Agile Development of a Laundry Transporter

After the first simulation of the laundry task, it was evaluated whether Lio could be used to support the task. To be able to check the feasibility quickly, easily, and inexpensively, a bicycle trailer (variant 1) was bought during the project phase 4 (see Table 1). Using the simplest of means, a coupling was fitted to the trailer so that Lio can grab, release and pull the trailer (see Fig. 2: (1) and Fig. 3: (1)). This function was tested in a replicated environment with a nurse.

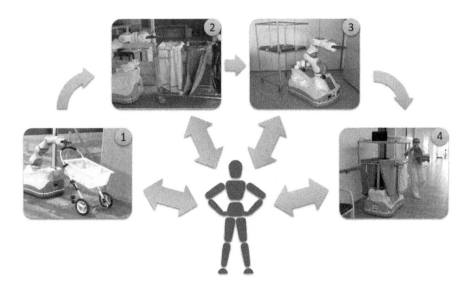

Fig. 3. (1)-(3): Three variants of the laundry trailer; (4): Top mounted laundry rack

Since the lab test 1 showed good results in terms of feasibility and the nursing staff gave positive feedback, an improved trailer (variant 2) was designed and built during the project phase 5 (see Table 1). This was done to incorporate more space and to sturdy the construction and coupling. For this purpose, a metal

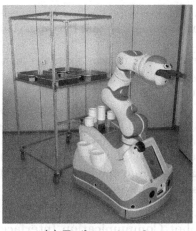
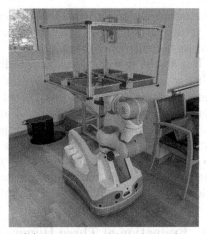

(a) Trailer variant 3   (b) Top mounted laundry rack

Fig. 4. Laundry transporters developed in project phases 7 and 9

frame with four caster wheels was developed, to which three different material bags can be attached (see Fig. 2: ② and Fig. 3: ②).

During the project phase 6 (see Table 1), the trailer variant 2 was tested in the replicated environment. Lio had enough power to pull this new, heavier trailer. Gripping and releasing the newly developed coupling also worked very well. However, only the footprint of Lio and not that of the attached trailer was considered when planning the path. During quick turns the trailer swerved and crashed into the walls. But even if Lio had known about the trailer, there would have been no way to prevent it from swerving due to the roller bearing coupling. After these tests, it was clear that a completely different design was needed.

In project phase 7 (see Table 1), a new trailer (variant 3) was designed with four squarely arranged bag hangers and a removable fresh laundry tray, offering even more space and featuring a fixed coupling to counteract swaying (see Fig. 2: ③, Fig. 3: ③ and Fig. 4a). To deal with the path planning issue, the footprint of the robot was increased in ROS by the additional area of the trailer to allow the path planner to account for the trailer and avoid collisions. Also the local cost map had to be enlarged, because otherwise the back end of the robot was almost at the edge of the local cost map and thus the path planner had only little time to react to obstacles.

During project phase 8 (see Table 1), a feasibility test was conducted for trailer variant 3. Lio can navigate between obstacles with the enlarged footprint and local cost map. However, the path planner occasionally provides poor solutions, especially when it has to reverse the direction of travel. Also, the trailer is very fast when turning, as Lio rotates around its front axis, and the target position and orientation are not always approached accurately. Even worse, Lio sometimes collides with the environment. This could be because the wheels of the trailer partially block the view of the laser scanners, so that Lio can no longer perceive the surroundings properly.

Due to the described navigation difficulties a shift away from the laundry trailer to a top mounted laundry rack (see Fig. 2: ④, Fig. 3: ④ and Fig. 4b) is made in project phase 9 (see Table 1). Other solutions like adapting Lio and rewriting the planner were discussed and deemed out of scope for this project. The top mounted laundry rack only slightly increases Lio's footprint, making it much easier to navigate than with the trailer. It can be used as an add-on for Lio or it can be further developed into a stand-alone solution. It is important to note that due to the radical design change, the prototype is at a TRL of 4–5, which is below the TRL targeted at this stage of the project.

3.3   Evaluation of Three Human-Robot Communication Interfaces

In addition to the aforementioned technical developments, the communication interface design was also discussed and improved during the project. For this purpose, the required communication between the robot and the nurse was clarified in several design meetings with the stakeholders. Three possible human-robot communication interface designs were evaluated for practicality and usefulness in project phase 10 (see Table 1) using the top mounted laundry rack:

- **Design 1 - Initially defined sequence of targets:** At the beginning of 1, the nurse defines a sequence with all the targets to be approached. The robot is then prompted with a command to move independently to the next target in the sequence.
- **Design 2 - Flexible sequence of targets:** The robot receives the target as a command, which it then moves to independently.
- **Design 3 - Follow Me:** The robot follows the nurse. A start and stop command activates or deactivates the Follow-Me behavior. The nurse must be in the robot's field of view.

The targets in the designs 1 and 2 correspond to the room numbers of the residents or the nursing wards. For each target, a stopping point is defined in the corridor where Lio can stay for a longer period of time. In design 3, the robot simply stops at the position where it received the stop command.

The three designs were tested in the nursing home involved in this project. Two scientists accompanied a nurse during laundry distribution on three consecutive days for three hours. Due to the immense time and financial effort, only one nurse was accompanied. The Wizard of Oz principle [8] was used in the experiment, with one scientist taking over the communication and navigation of the robot. The other scientist was responsible for observations and annotations.

At the beginning of each test, the laundry rack was filled with fresh laundry and the nurse was informed by the researchers about the particular design. During the test, the wizard interacted with the nurse according to the predefined flowchart of the design. He positioned himself behind the robot and spoke its parts of the dialogue. Over the course of the three days, the rooms and the nurse's path varied. The amount of laundry changed also varied. At the end of the laundry distribution, the transport robot accompanied the nurse to the laundry drop-off.

The nurse completed five questionnaires at different times. Before and after the overall experiment, one questionnaire was completed with specific questions about laundry distribution and another with questions based on the Technology Usage Inventory. After each experiment, a questionnaire with specific questions and a System Usability Scale was completed.

After each experiment, the nurse was interviewed by a scientist. The interview focused on the subject's personal feelings about working with the transport robot. A video of the interviews was recorded and a transcript was made.

The results of the tests showed that the nurse used and utilized the transport robot for laundry distribution. According to the questionnaires, the nurse was curious and open to working with the robot. The nurse also believed that there is potential for service and transport robots in the care sector, both before and after the experiments. During the interview, the nurse said that she appreciated the fact that the use of the transport robot reduced her walking distances. She also liked that the robot waited outside the room and did not drive in.

The nurse ranked the three designs in the following order: 1) design 2 - flexible sequence of targets, 2) design 1 - initially defined sequence of targets, 3) existing workflow with the trolley 4) design 3 - follow Me. This rating is further supported by the evaluation of the System Usability Scale. Designs 1 and 2 achieved a very good rating of 87.5 points, while design 3 only achieved 77.5 points.

In the interview, the nurse indicated that she preferred design 2 over the others because of its greater flexibility. On the other hand, however, she noted that the order of the rooms is usually known and therefore it might be easier to determine the order at the beginning of the nursing round.

When interviewed about the third application, the nurse mentioned that the robot moved too slowly and that, compared to the other applications, she had to concentrate more on the robot in order not to get out of its field of vision. To do this, she had to adjust her walking speed to match that of the robot. Another problem that both the researcher and the nurse observed was that the robot stopped and waited at critical points, such as near a door or in the middle of the hallway, creating a safety issue. These were the nurse's main reasons for rating the third design even lower than the current situation.

According to the nurse, the robot was easy to use and she rated it overall as a support in daily work. It does not need to be disinfected between rooms, nor does it need to be carried when performing another activity, e.g., accompanying an elderly.

4   Discussion, Conclusion and Outlook

According to the quantitative study conducted, material transport is the most common application requested by nursing homes. Over the course of ten project phases, three different variants of a laundry trailer as well as a top mounted laundry rack were iteratively developed, manufactured, and tested in a replicated and a real environment. In addition, three possible human-robot communication interface designs were investigated with respect to the behavior of the robot.

It is shown that the employment of service robots for laundry transport is suitable for reducing the walking distances of the nurses. Savings of over 50% of walking distances were recorded. These savings relieve the nurses and allow them to pursue more important tasks.

Lio's wide range of applicability, coupled with the technical complexity of the task, is a problem that is not easy to solve. In particular, many problems were found with the navigation of the robot, which increased with its size. These results are consistent with those of the SMOOTH robot project [19] and support their emphasis on implementing human aware navigation.

The replicated test environment as it was described by Langedijk et al. [20] proved extremely useful in the early phases of the project. It allowed for quick iterations, the involvement of all stakeholders, and simplified the identification of challenges. During the COVID-19 pandemic, the replicated environment was also of great value as it allowed to proceed with some tests at a time when they would not even have been conceivable in a nursing home.

Although a reduction in walking distances by using a service robot has be demonstrated, this use should also be questioned from an economic point of view. As described, hygienic and safety reasons prohibit the nurse from simply leaving the cart in the hallway or taking it to another room. Using a simple lock or a hermetically sealable bag could therefore be just as effective and cheaper than using a transport robot. However, adding additional functionality to the transport robot might again favor the robot over these simple approaches. But due to the described navigation problems, a dedicated robot, such as the intelligent care cart [12], could be superior to a multi-purpose robot, simply because a dedicated robot can usually be built smaller and is therefore more maneuverable.

During the investigation of the three possible human-robot communication interface designs, it appeared that the nurse focused on the wizard when communicating. An influence on the result cannot be excluded, and therefore the rating of the nurse should be taken with caution.

Although interface design 2 was considered the best solution due to its high flexibility and autonomous movement of the robot between positions, design 1 received a high rating as well. In particular, the simplicity of being able to define the targets in advance was appreciated in design 1. A hybrid solution with a predefined sequence of targets that can be changed as needed during runtime could therefore be an even better solution.

Due to the complexity of the laundry task, more time should be invested to understand the required human-robot interaction strategies. An important aspect of transportation in an environment as unstructured and active as a nursing home hallway is the fallibility and adaptability of a robot's path planning. This requires a small and easy to maneuver platform, which at the same time provides enough space to transport the laundry.

References

1. Aarikka-Stenroos, L., Lehtimäki, T.: Commercializing a radical innovation: probing the way to the market. Ind. Mark. Manage. **43**(8), 1372–1384 (2014)
2. Bartneck, C., Kulić, D., Croft, E., Zoghbi, S.: Measurement instruments for the anthropomorphism, animacy, likeability, perceived intelligence, and perceived safety of robots. Int. J. Soc. Robot. **1**(1), 71–81 (2009)
3. Beer, J.M., Prakash, A., Mitzner, T.L., Rogers, W.A.: Understanding Robot Acceptance. Tech. rep, Georgia Institute of Technology (2011)
4. Böhmer, A.I., Hostettler, R., Richter, C., Lindemann, U., Conradt, J., Knoll, A.: Towards agile product development-the role of prototyping. In: DS 87–4 Proceedings of the 21st International Conference on Engineering Design (ICED 17) Vol 4: Design Methods and Tools, Vancouver, Canada, 21–25.08. 2017 (2017)
5. Bundesamt für Statistik: Alters- und pflegeheime (2020). https://www.bfs.admin.ch/bfs/de/home/statistiken/gesundheit/gesundheitswesen/alters-pflegeheime.html
6. Christen, A., Hürzeler, F., Jucker, S., Roos, E.: Die Zukunft des Pflegeheimmarkts (2015). https://extranet.curaviva-bl.ch/files/AQLR6FF/pflegeheimmarkts_de.pdf
7. Confédération suisse: Swiss code of obligations. https://www.fedlex.admin.ch/eli/cc/27/317_321_377/de
8. Dahlbäck, N., Jönsson, A., Ahrenberg, L.: Wizard of oz studies—why and how. Knowl. Based Syst. **6**(4), 258–266 (1993)
9. Döring, N., Bortz, J.: Forschungsmethoden und Evaluation. Springerverlag, Wiesbaden (2016)
10. Frattini, F., De Massis, A., Chiesa, V., Cassia, L., Campopiano, G.: Bringing to market technological innovation:what distinguishes success from failure. Int. J. Eng. Business Manage. **4**(Godište 2012), 4–15 (2012)
11. Gordon, V.S., Bieman, J.M.: Rapid prototyping: lessons learned. IEEE Softw. **12**(1), 85–95 (1995)
12. Graf, B., King, R.S., Schiller, C., Roessner, A.: Development of an intelligent care cart and new supplies concepts for care homes and hospitals. In: Proceedings of ISR 2016: 47st International Symposium on Robotics, pp. 1–6. VDE (2016)
13. Hanheide, M., Hebesberger, D., Krajnik, T.: The When, Where, and How: An Adaptive Robotic Info-Terminal for Care Home Residents: A long-term Study. In: Proceeding of the ACM/IEEE International Conference on Human-Robot Interaction (HRI). ACM/IEEE, Vienna (2017). https://doi.org/10.1145/2909824.3020228
14. Havelka, A., et al: "hey robot, where is my drink?": Project agebots: multidisciplinary perspectives on service robotics in the field of elderly care. In: Connected Living: international and interdisciplinary conference (2021), Frankfurt am Main (2021)
15. Hawes, N., et al.: The strands project: long-term autonomy in everyday environments. IEEE Robot. Autom. Mag. **24**(3), 146–156 (2017)
16. Hebesberger, D., Körtner, T., Pripfl, J., Gisinger, C., Hanheide, M.: What do staff in eldercare want a robot for? an assessment of potential tasks and user requirements for a long-term deployment. In: IROS Workshop on "Bridging user needs to deployed applications of service robots" (2015)
17. Heerink, M., Kröse, B., Evers, V., Wielinga, B.: Assessing acceptance of assistive social agent technology by older adults: the almere model. Int. J. Soc. Robot. **2**(4), 361–375 (2010)

18. Klein, B., Graf, B., Schlömer, I.F., Roßberg, H., Röhricht, K., Baumgarten, S.: Robotik in der Gesundheitswirtschaft. Stiftung Münch, 1 edn. (2018)
19. Krüger, N., et al.: The smooth-robot: A modular, interactive service robot. Frontiers in Robotics and AI 8 (2021). https://doi.org/10.3389/frobt.2021. 645639,https://www.frontiersin.org/articles/10.3389/frobt.2021.645639
20. Langedijk, R.M., Odabasi, C., Fischer, K., Graf, B.: Studying drink-serving service robots in the real world. In: 2020 29th IEEE International Conference on Robot and Human Interactive Communication (RO-MAN), pp. 788–793. IEEE (2020)
21. Maalouf, N., Sidaoui, A., Elhajj, I.H., Asmar, D.: Robotics in nursing: a scoping review. J. Nurs. Scholarsh. **50**(6), 590–600 (2018)
22. Mankins, J.: Technology Readiness Levels. A White Paper, NASA, Washington, DC (1995)
23. Melkas, H., Hennala, L., Pekkarinen, S., Kyrki, V.: Impacts of robot implementation on care personnel and clients in elderly-care institutions. Int. J. Med. Inform. **134**, 104041 (2020)
24. Merçay, C., Grünig, A.: Gesundheitspersonal in der schweiz- zukünftiger bedarf bis 2030 und die folgen für den nachwuchsbedarf. Obsan Bulletin (2016)
25. Merda, M., Schmidt, K., Kähler, B.: Pflege 4.0 - einsatz moderner technologien aus der sicht professionell pflegender. Tech. rep., Berufsgenossenschaft für Gesundheitsdienst und Wohlfahrtspflege (BGW), Hamburg (2017)
26. Official Journal of the European Union: Eu general data protection regulation (gdpr). https://gdpr.eu/
27. Onuh, S.O., Yusuf, Y.Y.: Rapid prototyping technology: applications and benefits for rapid product development. J. Intell. Manuf. **10**(3), 301–311 (1999)
28. Pineau, J., Montemerlo, M., Pollack, M., Roy, N., Thrun, S.: Towards robotic assistants in nursing homes: challenges and results. Robot. Auton. Syst. **42**(3–4), 271–281 (2003)
29. Riesener, M., Doelle, C., Perau, S., Lossie, P., Schuh, G.: Methodology for iterative system modeling in agile product development. Procedia CIRP **100**, 439–444 (2021)
30. Seifert, A., Ackermann, T.: Digitalisierung und technikeinsatz in institutionen für menschen im alter. Studie im Auftrag von CURAVIVA Schweiz (2020)
31. Weiss, A., Bernhaupt, R., Lankes, M., Tscheligi, M.: The usus evaluation framework for human-robot interaction. In: AISB2009: Proceedings of the Symposium on New Frontiers in Human-Robot Interaction. vol. 4, pp. 11–26. Citeseer (2009)

Exploring the Potential of Light-Enhanced HRI to Promote Social Interactions in People with Dementia

Femke Knaapen[ID], Kynthia Chamilothori[ID], and Giulia Perugia[✉][ID]

Eindhoven University of Technology, Eindhoven, The Netherlands
f.h.j.knaapen@student.tue.nl, {k.chamilothori,g.perugia}@tue.nl

Abstract. Research has shown that a pet robot could constitute a leverage point to open a communication channel in a triadic relation between a person with dementia and others. Additionally, tangible light projections have been shown to capture the attention of people with dementia and contribute to social interaction. Following these findings, we designed a prototype of a light-enhanced Human-Robot Interaction (HRI) for people with dementia using the robot Pleo and tested its potential to foster social interaction with 19 experts in the field of dementia and care technology in a within-subjects online study. Experts were shown a video of the prototype, as well as two videos of comparable activities with only the light or only the robot. Results showed no significant differences in the activities' potential to stimulate social interaction and enjoyment, while they disclosed that the light-enhanced HRI could be more difficult to understand at a cognitive level. While experts considered the robot-only activity as more suited for individual interactions, they perceived the light-enhanced HRI as more suited for small sized groups. This latter result seems to suggest that adding a tangible light to an HRI for people with dementia could convert it from an individual to a group activity.

Keywords: Social robotics · Human-robot interaction · Dementia

1 Introduction

Dementia is an umbrella term describing multiple conditions (e.g., Alzheimer's disease) that cause cognitive and functional impairment, affect mood and behavior, and diminish people's ability to perform daily activities [26]. Studies have shown that individuals with dementia spend most of their time not engaged in meaningful activities [28]. This could be detrimental for their mental health, as it might magnify the boredom, apathy and loneliness that often accompany the progression of dementia [8]. Engaging persons with dementia in meaningful activities can yield beneficial effects such as increasing positive emotions, improving quality of life, and decreasing challenging behaviors [19]. When people with dementia are engaged in activities, most of these activities are carried out in groups [21]. Such co-activities are important in dementia, because social

F. Cavallo et al. (Eds.): ICSR 2022, LNAI 13818, pp. 371–380, 2022.
https://doi.org/10.1007/978-3-031-24670-8_33

interaction can largely influence engagement and give the person with dementia a sense of purpose [6].

Engaging in meaningful social interaction with others also plays a crucial role in positively influencing well-being and quality of life [14]. Most people with dementia really want to connect with others socially [23], develop and maintain social relations and ties, and communicate as best as they can with their residual capabilities [24]. However, as dementia progresses and cognition, physical function and communication decline, achieving social interactions becomes challenging [15]. Interactive technologies could have a pivotal role in supporting the interaction of people with dementia with others and keep their social life active. The aim of this research is to *explore whether light-enhanced Human-Robot Interaction (HRI)*—the augmentation of the interaction with a robot by means of light—*has the potential to stimulate social interaction in people with dementia.*

1.1   Pet Robots as Social Mediators

In recent years, a nascent interest in the use of interactive technologies to promote the engagement of people with dementia in meaningful activities has sprung and has yielded promising results [18]. Most of the technologies designed for people with dementia still adopt an assistive approach and mostly focus on promoting safety, self-independence, or providing services for persons with dementia [27]. However, a growing number of interactive technologies are now designed to pursue *eudaimonia* (i.e., the meaningful life), so as to say promoting enjoyment, social interaction, and relaxation [12]. Examples of technologies that have shown potential for successful psycho-social stimulation in the care of people with dementia are pet robots [13].

While social robotics showed promising evidence in using pet robots to engage people with dementia, many studies in the HRI literature focused on the interaction between pet robots and the user alone. Only a few studies addressed whether pet robots could be used as *social mediators* to promote the interaction of people with dementia with others [16,22]. In an exploratory research by Marti et al. [16], the seal robot Paro was used as a social mediator between the person with dementia and the therapist in a triadic relation (patient-therapist-robot). The authors noticed that the emotional relationship between the patient and the robot created a "leverage point" for the therapist to open a communication channel with the patient.

The current study follows this direction and tries to bring it one step forward. Since it has been observed that pet robots can mediate the interactions of people with dementia with others [16], but also take away the attention of the person with dementia from others [21], in this study, we use a tangible light design to *highlight* the social mediation role of the robot, and guide the attention of the person with dementia towards the robot but *also* towards others. Following Feng et al. [10], we consider this approach particularly promising to intercept the attention that pet robots receive as interactive stimuli and direct it towards other people, thus promoting meaningful social connections.

Fig. 1. The three conditions. Left: Light-only. Center: Light-enhanced HRI. Right: Robot-only.

1.2 The Role of Light in Social Interaction

Anderiesen et al. [1] found that the *sensation* produced by the experience of play is extremely suitable for people with dementia. Clinical studies show that both the sensory and emotional areas of the brain remain relatively untouched in people with dementia [4]. Sensory experiences can provide pleasure to the person with dementia, which can contribute to their overall well-being [5]. For this reason, sensory stimulation is a widely recommended non-pharmacological intervention for this target group [25]. In a co-design session for the development of a product that is now known as the *Tovertafel*, Anderiesen [1] found that light projections projected on a coffee table were a sensory stimulation in their own respect. Additionally, Anderiesen discovered that the light-based games increased the social engagement of the players. An example of light installation showing the potential of tangible light to promote social interaction is Lumafluid [17], in which colored spotlights highlighted the users and light connections were drawn between them to stimulate communication and interaction. The existence of light designs promoting social interactions between people, both with and without dementia, made us hypothesize that a 'simple' light could be used to stimulate social interaction in people with dementia, and highlight the social mediating role of a robot, thus enhancing the "sociability" of the interaction.

2   The Light-Enhanced HRI Prototype

This research focuses on assessing the potential of a light-enhanced HRI activity. To this end, we designed an activity inspired by a simple ball throwing game. In this activity, a person could pass a ball of light to a pet robot, or to other people. We chose this activity as it is a type of activity people with dementia are usually familiar with, it can be performed on a table, does not entail physical effort, and it has a social dimension attached to it (i.e., turn-taking activity). We chose to use the dinosaur robot Pleo[1] for this activity as it could easily fit on a table, could be easily re-programmed, and had a light sensor on its nose, hence it could detect light and interact with it. The light used in the game was projected on a table using an Acer H7532BD projector and a mirror. To enable Pleo to interact with the light, its behavior was re-programmed using the PleoRB Development

---

[1] https://www.pleoworld.com/.

Kit so that it could detect the ball of light projected on the table through the light sensor positioned on its nose, catch it, and pass it on to another person. Pleo was also programmed to avoid the ball of light or ask for it during the game.

Due to the preliminary nature of the prototype and the exploratory nature of this research, the light-enhanced HRI activity could not be tested with people with dementia. We created a video illustrating the activity and the different scenarios and asked experts in dementia care and/or technologies and the clinical staff of nursing homes to evaluate the potential of the activity in the video, as well as the potential of two similar activities with only the light and only the robot (see Fig. 1). Hence, we formulated the following research question: *How do experts evaluate the potential of the light-enhanced HRI activity to promote social interaction between people with dementia and others?*

3   Experimental Method

The study used a within-subjects design and was carried out online. Experts in dementia and care technology were asked to answer questions about videos of three different activities. In the *light-enhanced HRI* condition, they were shown a video of two healthy people playing the light ball throwing game with Pleo. In the *light-only* condition, they were shown a video of two healthy people playing the same game, this time without Pleo. Finally, in the *robot-only* condition, they were shown a video of two healthy people interacting with Pleo only, without the light ball throwing game. In this latter condition, the people in the video interacted with the robot in the setting that is commercially available and the robot's behaviors were not altered by any programming.

3.1   Participants

To recruit participants, we contacted research experts, as well as nursing home clinical staff. Participants had either a background in dementia and care technologies, or worked with people with dementia in care facilities. In total, 19 experts (17 women and 2 men) participated in our study. The experts had an age comprised between 22 and 64 years ($M = 43.84$, $SD = 13.26$) and different occupations ($N = 8$ nursing home staff, $N = 4$ welfare workers, $N = 7$ university staff). Since not all of the participants spoke English, we gave them the possibility to fill out the questionnaire in Dutch ($N = 15$) or English ($N = 4$).

3.2   Measures

Given the lack of tools aimed at assessing the *potential* of activities for people with dementia in their prototype phase, we developed a questionnaire inspired by [2,3,7,9,11,19]. The questionnaire consisted of three scales: *Cognitive Understanding*, *Attitude/enjoyment*, and *Social Interaction*, as well as three items rating *sensorial feel*, four items rating suitability for different *group sizes*, and one item rating the *inclusion of self in other*, i.e., how much the activity could help the people bond with each other. The scales and items in the questionnaire were measured on 7-point Likert scales and were phrased so that it was clear that the experts were supposed to evaluate the *potential* of the activity for people with dementia and not the interactions observed in the videos. In each condition, the experts were also asked *open questions*: (i) what they thought of the activity in general, (ii) whether they would use it in the daily care of people with dementia and why (or why not), (iii) what challenges they envisioned in the use of the activity in daily care, and (iv) whether they would want to change anything about the activity and why. While the order of presentation of questions did not change, the order of presentation of the items within each construct was randomized across conditions. The full questionnaire can be found on OSF.

3.3 Procedure

The study was conducted on LimeSurvey. On the first page of the questionnaire, participants were asked to provide their consent to participate. If they agreed to participate, they were asked demographic questions regarding their age, gender, educational background, and job. Then, they were told that they would watch videos of three different activities acted out by healthy persons and were explained they had to judge the potential of these activities for persons with mild to moderate dementia. Participants were asked to watch the videos in full screen. After watching the first video, they rated its potential using the questionnaire in Sect. 3.2, then they continued to the second and third videos. After each condition, participants could take a break before proceeding to the next condition. The order of presentation of the conditions was randomized across participants. The questionnaire took about 45 min to complete. Participants were thanked for their participation with a 10 € Amazon gift card. The study was approved by the Ethical Review Board of the Human-Technology Interaction Group of Eindhoven University of Technology (n. 1623).

4   Results

4.1   Factorial Analysis

To understand whether the items included under Cognitive understanding, Attitude/enjoyment, and Social Interaction could be reduced to three unique scales, we performed an exploratory factorial analysis on the three constructs (see Table 1). *Cognitive Understanding* obtained good to excellent reliability for all conditions (light-enhanced HRI: $\alpha = .919$, light only: $\alpha = .800$, robot only: $\alpha = .708$) and the items in it achieved high factor loadings for most activities. For the robot-only condition, however, two factor loadings were low. Since the Cronbach's alpha of this condition was good and did not increase upon removal of the items, we decided to leave the items in. For the construct *Attitude/enjoyment*, one item had low factor loadings in both the light-enhanced HRI and light-only condition ("I think this activity might be boring for the person with dementia"). When testing for the construct's reliability using Cronbach's alpha (light-enhanced HRI:

Table 1. Factor loadings on each scale item. The reverse-coded items are signalled with an asterisk. The items in Italics were removed from the final scale.

	Factor loading		
Cognitive understanding	Robot and light	Robot only	Light only
Item 1 - Understand	.756	.573	.857
Item 2 - Play without help	.886	.821	.739
Item 3 - Too abstract*	.724	.081	.560
Item 4 - Only play with help*	.924	.815	.392
Item 5 - Unnecessarily complex*	.728	.295	.607
Item 6 - Confusing	.930	.712	.820
Attitude/enjoyment	Robot and light	Robot only	Light only
Item 1 - Enjoy activity	.899	.894	.837
Item 2 - Improve mood	.668	.806	.755
Item 3 - Boring*	.297	.680	.456
Item 4 - Feel confident	.774	.820	.898
Social interaction	Robot and light	Robot only	Light only
Item 1 - Attention to others	.842	.609	.337
Item 2 - Speak with others	.706	.752	.452
Item 3 - Support interaction	.885	.907	.817
Item 4 - Social interaction easier	.831	.797	.826
Item 5 - Interaction more pleasant	.795	.820	.884
Item 6 - Communicate more	.767	.526	.569

$\alpha = .838$, light only: $\alpha = .878$, robot only: $\alpha = .873$), removing item 3 was found to increase the α for both the light-only and the light-enhanced HRI condition, hence the item was removed from the scale. Lastly, the construct *Social Interaction* achieved good to excellent reliability (light-enhanced HRI: $\alpha = .905$, light only: $\alpha = .764$, robot only: $\alpha = .878$). However, while the factor loadings were high for the robot-only and light-enhanced HRI conditions, they were moderate to high for the light-only condition. Since the Cronbach's α of the construct was good in this condition, we decided to keep the construct. As a result of the factorial analysis, we averaged the items within each construct.

4.2   Differences in the Potential of the Three Activities

We performed Shapiro-Wilk and Levene's tests to check whether our data met the assumptions of normality and homogeneity of variance. We ran repeated-measures ANOVAs for the dependent variables respecting the assumptions, and Friedman's tests for those which did not. Significant results were then analyzed with Bonferroni-corrected pairwise t-tests or Wilcoxon signed-rank tests.

The results showed no significant effect of the type of activity on sensorial feel (visibility, stimulation and overstimulation), attitude/enjoyment, social interaction and the inclusion of self in other (see Table 2). However, they showed a significant difference in cognitive understanding and group size (see Table 2).

Post-hoc analyses disclosed that the light-enhanced HRI was significantly *more difficult to understand* (i.e., lower in cognitive understanding) than the

Table 2. Descriptive statistics (M, SD) and results of the repeated measures ANOVAs or Friedman's tests. Significant results in bold signalled by an asterisk.

ITEM / SCALE	Robot & light		Robot only		Light only		Results	
	M	SD	M	SD	M	SD	Q or F-value	p
Sensorial feel - Visibility	4.21	1.32	5.05	1.03	4.26	1.73	$Q(2) = 2.067$	.356
Sensorial feel - Stimulation	4.58	1.47	4.74	1.52	4.05	1.75	$Q(2) = 2.000$	.368
Sensorial feel - Overstimul.	3.74	1.52	3.53	1.47	3.05	1.27	$Q(2) = 2.000$	.368
Cognitive Understanding	3.58	1.22	4.92	0.73	4.22	1.02	$F(2,36) = 18.65$	**<.001***
Attitude/enjoyment	4.70	0.93	4.91	1.12	4.81	0.94	$F(2,36) = 0.32$	.730
Social Interaction	4.61	1.13	4.49	0.93	4.93	0.71	$F(2,36) = 1.40$	.260
Inclusion of Self in Other	3.00	1.56	2.33	1.56	3.53	1.81	$Q(2) = 3.970$	.137
Group size - Individual	4.11	1.88	6.05	0.62	3.63	1.95	$Q(2) = 22.370$	**<.001***
Group size - 2–3 ppl	5.37	1.34	4.32	1.83	5.47	0.84	$Q(2) = 2.346$	.309
Group size - 4–5 ppl	3.53	2.12	2.89	1.63	4.26	1.56	$Q(2) = 4.484$	.106
Group size - >5 ppl	2.26	1.28	2.21	1.36	2.79	1.58	$Q(2) = 6.50$	**.039***

robot-only ($t(18) = -5.699, p < .001$) and light-only condition ($t(18) = -3.393, p = .003$) and the light-only condition was significantly more difficult to understand than the robot-only condition ($t(18) = 3.024, p = .007$). In terms of *group size*, the experts perceived the robot-only activity as more suited for an *individual activity* than the light-enhanced HRI ($z = -3.570, p < .001$), and light-only activities ($z = 3.572, p < .001$). However, the light-enhanced HRI and light-only condition did not differ in their perceived suitability for individual activities ($z = 1.136, p = .301$). Lastly, Wilcoxon signed-rank tests for *large group size* (> 5 people) did not show any significant differences in suitability for a large group activity between the light-enhanced HRI and the robot-only condition ($z = 0.834, p = .473$), nor between the robot-only and light-only condition ($z = -1.671, p = .099$). The difference between the light-enhanced HRI and light-only condition approached but did not reach significance ($z = -2.140, p = .056$).

4.3 Open Questions

The open questions provided us with interesting insights. Many experts were unsure as to whether the *choice of Pleo* as a pet robot was fitting for people with dementia. Some of them thought it was too *childish* or that people with dementia might not recognize it due to lack of familiarity with dinosaurs. In addition, experts often indicated that the light-enhanced HRI could be *too difficult* to understand for people with dementia. Here, a number of bottlenecks were identified due to the activity's reliance on abstract thinking. Experts noted that it might be difficult for a person with dementia to: (1) understand that the light projection represents a ball; (2) understand that this light ball can be grasped and thrown to another person; (3) understand that the light ball can be thrown to the robot and not just to other persons. To address (1) and (2), some experts suggested to modify the light projection so that it looked more like a *real ball*. When it comes to its potential use, experts thought that the light-enhanced HRI could be used to *stimulate social interaction* in a similar way as the other two activities but also to *stimulate movement*. This use was highlighted for the light-only activity as well, but not for the robot-only activity. Thirteen out of 19 experts (68%) indicated that they would use the light-enhanced HRI.

5   Discussion

This research examined how experts evaluated the potential of a light-enhanced HRI activity to promote social interaction in people with dementia. Our results did not disclose any statistically significant differences between the light-enhanced HRI we designed and the light-only and robot-only conditions in terms of social interaction. Interestingly though, results indicated that experts perceive the robot-only activity as an individual activity. Although no significant differences were found, descriptive statistics suggest that the light-enhanced HRI was perceived as the most suitable for a small group activity (2–3 people), and the light-only activity as suitable for both small and medium sized groups (2–5 people). While the results from group size show that the addition of light to the interaction with a pet robot could convert the HRI from individual to group-based, the light-only condition seems to be more scalable in size than the light-enhanced HRI, and hence more suited for a real-life context. Besides, it scores better on cognitive understanding than the light-enhanced HRI, and is perceived as less likely to overstimulate the senses of a person with dementia.

Given the study results, the light-only activity seems like a more promising activity to bring to institutionalized contexts than the light-enhanced HRI, especially as it is less expensive. While the light only activity shows potential to increase social interaction, it might not be able to bring to the social interaction the affective component that is needed for long-term engagement, which pet robots are known to bring [20]. The addition of a robot to a light-only activity could create a setting in which the interaction not only acts as a prompt for social engagement but also provides an emotional ground to encourage meaningful human connection. The current design could be improved by creating a context in which it is logical for people with dementia to see the robot as a player of the game; such as by changing the light design to resemble a tennis ball, and use a pet robot that justifies the throwing of a ball, such as a dog (e.g., AIBO).

Limitations. The current study has been limited by the recruitment of experts instead of people with dementia. While the approach we followed is useful to test the potential of a prototype in the early phases of development, it does not give insights into the actual perceptions and behavior of people with dementia. A second limitation of the study is its within-subject design. Although the order of presentation of the conditions was randomized, participants could compare the activities to each other, hence a carryover effect could have been at work.

6   Conclusion

This paper described a first exploration of the combination of social robotics and tangible light in an activity for people with dementia. Result show that the addition of light to the interaction with a pet robot can change the nature of the interaction from individual to social. However, they also show that an activity with light only achieves similar results in terms of social interaction, and better results in terms of ease of understanding. We pose that, compared to the light-only activity, the light-enhanced HRI brings an affective nuance that is crucial to sustain long-term engagement and suggest to further refine the current prototype and test it directly with people with dementia.

Acknowledgment. This work was funded by the National Science Foundation IIS (#2132846).

References

1. Anderiesen, H.: Playful Design for Activation: Co-designing serious games for people with moderate to severe dementia to reduce apathy. TU Delft (2017)
2. Aron, A., Aron, E.N., Smollan, D.: Inclusion of other in the self scale and the structure of interpersonal closeness. J. Pers. Soc. Psychol. **63**(4), 596–612 (1992)
3. Asghar, I., Cang, S., Yu, H.: Impact evaluation of assistive technology support for the people with dementia. Assist. Technol. **31**(4), 180–192 (2019)
4. Başar, E., Güntekin, B., Tülay, E., Yener, G.G.: Evoked and event related coherence of Alzheimer patients manifest differentiation of sensory-cognitive networks. Brain Res. **1357** 79–90 (2010)
5. Bowlby, C.: Therapeutic Activities with Persons Disabled by Alzheimer's Disease and Related Disorders. Aspen Publishers, Gaithersburg Md (1993)
6. Brandtzæg, P.B., Følstad, A., Heim, J.: Enjoyment: lessons from Karasek. In: Blythe, M., Monk, A. (eds.) Funology 2. HIS, pp. 331–341. Springer, Cham (2018). https://doi.org/10.1007/978-3-319-68213-6_21
7. Brooke, J.: SUS: A quick and dirty usability scale. Usability Eval. Ind., p. 189 (1995)
8. Cacioppo, J.T., Hughes, M.E., Waite, L.J., Hawkley, L.C., Thisted, R.A.: Loneliness as a specific risk factor for depressive symptoms: Cross-sectional and longitudinal analyses. Psychol. Aging **21**(1), 140–151 (2006)
9. Cohen-Mansfield, J., Dakheel-Ali, M., Marx, M.S.: Engagement in persons with dementia: the concept and its measurement. Am. J. Geriatric Psych. **17**(4), 299–307 (2009)
10. Feng, Y., Perugia, G., Yu, S., Barakova, E.I., Hu, J., Rauterberg, G.: Context-enhanced human-robot interaction: exploring the role of system interactivity and multimodal stimuli on the engagement of people with dementia. Int. J. Soc. Robot. **14**(3), 807–826 (2022)
11. Heerink, M., Kröse, B., Evers, V., Wielinga, B.: Assessing acceptance of assistive social agent technology by older adults: the almere model. Int. J. Soc. Robot. **2**(4), 361–375 (2010)
12. IJsselsteijn, W., Tummers-Heemels, A., Brankaert, R.: Warm technology: a novel perspective on design for and with people living with Dementia. In: Brankaert, R., Kenning, G. (eds.) HCI and Design in the Context of Dementia. HIS, pp. 33–47. Springer, Cham (2020). https://doi.org/10.1007/978-3-030-32835-1_3
13. Jøranson, N., Pedersen, I., Rokstad, A.M.M., Ihlebæk, C.: Effects on Symptoms of Agitation and Depression in Persons With Dementia Participating in Robot-Assisted Activity: a Cluster-Randomized Controlled Trial. J. Am. Med. Directors Assoc. **16**(10), 867–873 (2015)

14. Kitwood, T., Bredin, K.: Towards a theory of dementia care: personhood and well-being. Ageing Soc. **12**(3), 269–287 (1992)

15. Mabire, J.B., Gay, M.C., Vrignaud, P., Garitte, C., Vernooij-Dassen, M.: Social interactions between people with dementia: pilot evaluation of an observational instrument in a nursing home. Int. Psychogeriatrics **28**(6), 1005–1015 (2016)

16. Marti, P., Bacigalupo, M., Giusti, L., Mennecozzi, C., Shibata, T.: Socially Assistive Robotics in the treatment of behavioural and psychological symptoms of dementia. In: Proceedings of the First IEEE/RAS-EMBS International Conference on Biomedical Robotics and Biomechatronics, 2006, pp. 483–488 (2006)

17. Monaci, G., et al.: *LumaFluid*: A responsive environment to stimulate social interaction in public spaces. In: Paternò, F., de Ruyter, B., Markopoulos, P., Santoro, C., van Loenen, E., Luyten, K. (eds.) AmI 2012. LNCS, vol. 7683, pp. 391–396. Springer, Heidelberg (2012). https://doi.org/10.1007/978-3-642-34898-3_32

18. Neal, I., du Toit, S.H., Lovarini, M.: The use of technology to promote meaningful engagement for adults with dementia in residential aged care: a scoping review. Int. Psychogeriatr. **32**(8), 913–935 (2020)

19. Orsulic-Jeras, S., Judge, K.S., Camp, C.J.: Montessori-based activities for long-term care residents with advanced dementia: Effects on engagement and affect. Gerontologist **40**(1), 107–111 (2000)

20. Perugia, G.: ENGAGE-DEM: A Model of Engagement of People with Dementia. Ph.D. thesis, Industrial Design (2018), proefschrift

21. Perugia, G., Díaz-Boladeras, M., Català-Mallofré, A., Barakova, E.I., Rauterberg, M.: Engage-dem: a model of engagement of people with dementia. IEEE Trans. Affect. Comput. **13**(2), 926–943 (2022)

22. Perugia, G., Rodríguez-Martín, D., Boladeras, M.D., Mallofré, A.C., Barakova, E., Rauterberg, M.: Electrodermal activity: explorations in the psychophysiology of engagement with social robots in dementia. In: 2017 26th IEEE International Symposium on Robot and Human Interactive Communication (RO-MAN), pp. 1248–1254. IEEE (2017)

23. Rousseaux, M., Sève, A., Vallet, M., Pasquier, F., Mackowiak-Cordoliani, M.A.: An analysis of communication in conversation in patients with dementia. Neuropsychologia **48**(13), 3884–3890 (2010)

24. Saunders, P.A., de Medeiros, K., Doyle, P., Mosby, A.: The discourse of friendship: Mediators of communication among dementia residents in long-term care. Dementia **11**(3), 347–361 (2012)

25. Swaab, D.F., Dubelaar, E.J., Scherder, E.J., Van Someren, E.J., Verwer, R.W.: Therapeutic strategies for Alzheimer disease: Focus on neuronal reactivation of metabolically impaired neurons. In: Alzheimer Disease and Associated Disorders. vol. 17 Suppl. 4. Alzheimer Dis Assoc Disord (2003)

26. Thabtah, F., Peebles, D., Retzler, J., Hathurusingha, C.: A review of dementia screening tools based on mobile application. Heal. Technol. **10**(5), 1011–1022 (2020)

27. Topo, P.: Technology studies to meet the needs of people with dementia and their caregivers: A literature review (2009)

28. Von Kutzleben, M., Schmid, W., Halek, M., Holle, B., Bartholomeyczik, S.: Community-dwelling persons with dementia: What do they need? What do they demand? What do they do? A systematic review on the subjective experiences of persons with dementia. Aging Ment. Health **16**(3), 378–390 (2012)

Development and Assessment
of a Friendly Robot to Ease Dementia

Robert Bray$^{(\boxtimes)}$ ⓘ, Luke MacDougallⓘ, Cody Blankenshipⓘ,
Kimberly Mitchellⓘ, Fengpei Yuanⓘ, Sylvia Cerel-Suhl, and Xiaopeng Zhaoⓘ

University of Tennessee, Knoxville, TN 37996, USA
{rbray2,lmacdoug,cblank10,fyuan6}@vols.utk.edu,
{kmitch57,xzhao9}@utk.edu

Abstract. Worldwide, there are approximately 10 million new cases of
dementia reported each year. Societies are facing a growing shortage of
healthcare for dementia. In this paper, we built a low-cost, humanoid,
Friendly Robot to ease Dementia (FRED) aimed to provide a more
affordable and accessible socially-assistive robot to people with cognitive
decline. Two prototypes of FRED with different bodies were created.
Both prototypes were designed with five functions, including creating
a contact, making a phone call, providing reminders, answering questions, and playing games. A usability study was performed with college
students in order to assess users' attitudes, perceptions, and experiences
towards each prototype's user interface design and functions . The results
suggest that participants preferred the Version 2 prototype, although,
overall, perceptions were positive towards both.

Keywords: Socially assistive robot · Dementia care · Low-cost

1 Introduction

With a steady increase in life expectancy, the prevalence of dementia has been
constantly increasing worldwide. There are nearly 10 million new cases of dementia reported each year [1]. In the United States alone, approximately 6.5 million
people aged 65 or above live with Alzheimer's Disease and Alzheimer's Disease
related dementias (AD/ADRD) in 2022 [1]. It is predicted that the number of
people living with AD/ADRD (PLWDs) in the U.S. will grow to 7.1 million by
2025 and 12.7 million by 2050 [1]. Dementias are associated with an irreversible,
progressive decline of cognition, function, and behavior, which damages PLWD's
social relationships and sense of well-being and may lead to severe disability and
death [2]. As a result, society is facing growing shortages of workforce to care
for PLWDs. Meanwhile, the long-lasting, time-intensive, exhausting dementia
caregiving can lead to increased risk for poor mental health in caregivers [3].

Rapidly evolving information and communication technologies (ICTs), artificial intelligence (AI), and AI-empowered socially assistive robots (SARs) have
showed the potential to supplement dementia care, support the delivery of care,

© The Author(s), under exclusive license to Springer Nature Switzerland AG 2022
F. Cavallo et al. (Eds.): ICSR 2022, LNAI 13818, pp. 381–391, 2022.
https://doi.org/10.1007/978-3-031-24670-8_34

and promote physical and mental wellbeing of both PLWDs and caregivers [4–6]. For example, human-like SARs such as Pepper and NAO for PLWDs have been indicated to become an effective therapy as companions to help PLWDs with their cognitive function, motor skills, language, and communication skill [7]. Animal-like SARs such as PARO and AIBO appear to positively influence PLWDs' psychosocial domains such as reduced agitation, reduced loneliness, and improved quality of life [8]. However, the high costs of these robots have been a big barrier hindering PLWD access to and use of such robotic care. One of each of the following robots have the pricetags which follow: NAO, AIBO, and PARO approximately cost $10,000, $3000, and $6000, respectively.

Leveraging the advanced ICTs and 3D printing technologies, we developed an affordable robot as a companion and assistant for PLWDs, named Friendly Robot to Ease Dementia (FRED). The robot FRED is capable of providing entertainment (e.g., singing, playing brain games), delivering reminders, and initiating verbal and nonverbal communication with the user. We designed and developed two prototypes of FRED and evaluated their feasibility with young adults. The work here is our first step towards developing accessible, low-cost, but engaging and interactive SARs for dementia care.

2   Prototype Development

Two versions of FRED were developed in order to assess the perception and user experience of two different body designs. Both versions were developed with the same robot functions and verbal interaction. Version 1 (V1) was implemented with body movement (e.g., head movement) as the secondary feedback, and Version 2 (V2) with an LED face as its secondary feedback.

2.1   Mechanical Design

FRED's body is fully additive manufacturing using 3-D printing techniques, which is low-cost and resource efficient. Multiple FRED bodies could be produced without the creation of a specialized production line, and could also be made by anyone who has a 3D printer. In order to evaluate the perception of the two body designs, the same color and type of material was used for each body. The color chosen was a neutral gray color. Polylactic acid filament (PLA) was used for the FRED bodies, which is a low-cost, flexible filament that can be used for many different shapes. The appearance and size of FRED compared to humans is shown in Fig. 1.

FRED Version 1 (V1) was the prototype that focused on the aspect of movement within its design. This robot body is comprised of three parts: the hemispherical base, the cylindrical neck, and the rectangular phone face. The hemispherical base is hollow in order to hold the electrical components of FRED. This base will be the foundation of the robot and ensure the structure does not topple easily while storing all the bulky components that make up the facilities of the robot. The cylindrical neck houses the servo for movement, and the rectangular head houses the phone. FRED Version 2 (V2) was the prototype that specialized in an LED face. This model consists of two parts: the large curved body and the conical-shaped head. The large body is half hollow, where the hollow section holds the electrical components, and the other half of the body contains a space for the phone to be securely placed. The phone is kept in place by a sliding door that is easy to remove. The conical-shaped head features an LED board that represents FRED's face.

Fig. 1. Examples of participants interacting with the two FREDs.

2.2 Robot Operating System

FRED was created to be used on the Android platform through the user's phone, which would reduce cost by eliminating specialty hardware. Additionally, since the Android operating system has many features to handle input/output devices, such as the microphone, speakers, and camera, and a wide array of application programming interfaces (APIs), it is convenient to use an Android phone for development. Also, the automatic threading in Android makes it easy to achieve continuous speech recognition.

The phone is the central device in this system. An Arduino Uno, specifically the Wifi Rev2 model, was used to control the servo in Version 1 and the LED face in Version 2. We chose the Rev2 in this project because of its wifi and bluetooth capabilities, as well as its smaller form factor than a Raspberry Pi. The phone communicates with the Arduino through a Bluetooth Low Energy (BLE) connection, which allows the phone to communicate without a wire connection and create a more compact design. Users are able to control and interact with FRED through voice commands. Voice interaction eliminates problems with touch interface related to tremors or weakness in users. The voice interactions are powered by an automated speech system that uses the speech recognition and speech-to-text libraries built into Android.

2.3 Robot Functions

There are certain activities and functions that are desired in robots that assist people with ADRD and mild cognitive impairment (MCI). In a prior online survey to learn the acceptability of a humanoid SAR for dementia care and users' needs [9], Yuan *et al.* collected responses from people with MCI or ADRD, their caregivers, and the general public. The study found that the top three most required robot functions by PLWDs were reminding them to take their medicine, making emergency calls, and contacting medical professionals. Other additional requested functions included memory games, creating appointments, and asking for the time or date of that day. In another study performed by Zushnegg *et al.* [10], caregivers and dementia trainers suggested that SARs could offer potential support in dementia care in terms of communication/contact with others (e.g. telephone calls), reminders, recreational activities (e.g. providing music), and eating/drinking (e.g. helping cook). In another recent study [11], Shin *et al.* performed qualitative interviews with PLWDs, family, and clinicians about the current and potential functions of a telepresence robot. They found that the most desired function for a telepresence robot was reminders for medication and that the second-most desired robot function was access to emergency help and services.

Following these study results and using a user-centered design principle, we designed five robot functions to meet the needs and requirements by people with cognitive decline during their daily activities. The five functions included creating a contact, making a phone call, providing reminders for daily living tasks, asking for the date of an event, and playing a shape game for entertainment and brain stimulation. These robot functions were evaluated by users through pre-programmed voice commands, as seen in Table 1. It should be noted that these functions are not fully developed, since the focus of this study is to learn users' attitude toward and perception of the robot design and functions, which will be useful to refine the robot.

Table 1. Voice commands to start each task.

Task	Command
Start FRED	"Hey FRED"
Create a contact	"FRED, I'd like to create a contact."
Make a call	"Please call Tom."
Set a reminder	"FRED, remind me to drink water every 15 min"
Inquire football time	"FRED, when's the next UT football game?"
Play a game	"FRED, I'd like to play a shapes game."
Move head	"FRED, look left." or "FRED, look right."

2.4   User Interface Design in Phone

The graphical user interface (GUI) for the phone of the FRED robot was designed in order to be easily understood by older adults with MCI or ADRD. Figure 2 shows examples of the GUI in different robot functions. The first goal for the GUI was to have a simple, friendly font and simple icons. The font used throughout the FRED app is a Sans Serif. In order to create cohesion in the app, a color palette was created using shades of orange, grey, and white. The navigation system is designed to be as simple as possible. All activity screens originate from the home screen, and the user is able to start any of them with a voice command. The voice commands are aimed at being as close to conversational language as possible. For example, the user could say "FRED, I want to make a contact." or "FRED, can I create a contact, please?" The home screen displays FRED's face, which is animated while he talks. Humanoid features, like eyes and a mouth, may have positive impacts on human-robot interactions and increase the amount of secondary responses that help with learning [12].

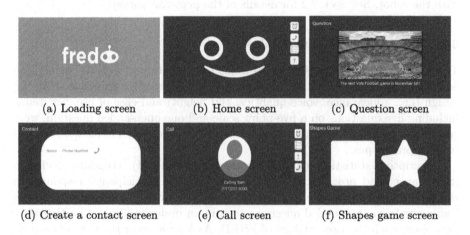

(a) Loading screen   (b) Home screen   (c) Question screen

(d) Create a contact screen   (e) Call screen   (f) Shapes game screen

Fig. 2. Examples of graphical user interface on the phone of FRED.

3   Usability Study

We conducted a pilot study to assess user acceptance, perception, and experience of the robot FRED through usability testing with young adults. Survey and observation approaches were used to learn users' perception of FRED's user interface (UI) design and functions. The study protocol was approved by the Institutional Review Board (IRB) of the University of Tennessee, Knoxville. IRB number is UTK IRB-21-06480-XM. We recruited potential participants via emails. The participants were students recruited from the University of Tennessee, Knoxville. Eligible participants included adults who met these criteria, 1) aged above 18, 2) able to understand and speak English fluently, and 3) no severe hearing or visual impairments that would interfere with interacting with the robot FRED.

3.1   Experimental Procedure

After obtaining consent using an appropriate consent form from the participant, a demographic survey was distributed to the participant to collect his/her demographic information (e.g., age, gender and education), experience with technologies (including tablets and robots), cognitive status, and experience with providing dementia care. The participant firstly interacted with FRED V1, then V2. Upon interacting with each version, there was a paper listing the tasks the participants needed to do, as shown in Fig. 1. During the experiment, the user-robot interaction was video recorded. After the experiment, a post-test questionnaire was distributed to learn participants' perception, acceptance, and experience with the robot. See Sect. 3.2 for details of the post-test survey.

3.2   Data Collection and Analysis

The post-test survey consisted of 19 items to evaluate participants' perception and user experience of FRED, for example, users' positive response to its UI design (i.e., appearance, voice qualities, and height) and ease of use. Six items, including five questions on a five-point scale and one open-ended question, were specifically targeted at V1 and V2 separately. The other seven items were applied to both prototypes.

Descriptive statistics including frequency, mean (M), standard deviation (SD), range, and proportions were used to analyze participants' responses to the survey. Considering the small sample size, we manually went through all the comments from open-ended questions to gain an understanding of participants' experience with the two versions of FRED. As for the recorded videos, we used Simple Video Coder [13], a free, open-source software for efficiently coding social video data, to code participants' interaction behaviors during the experiment, including the participants' emotions (such as laughter/giggling/joy, frowning, and confusion) and robot-related failures during the tasks.

4   Results

Sixteen young adults participated in our usability study. Their demographic information can be seen in Table 2. All participants were aged between 18–30 years old. The study contained a higher number of male participants (69%). The majority of participants identified with the "some college" category of education (56%), and few were college graduates. On average, participants were moderately familiar with robots, while they were very familiar with other technologies, such as tablets and smartphones. Two participants reported that they helped care for someone with moderate dementia due to Alzheimer's and other dementia. Three participants cared for someone with ADRD as an extended family member. One participant has been caring for their family member for 1–5 years.

According to the post-test survey results, the participants preferred the appearance of FRED V2 at 53.3%. Eighty percent of participants preferred to

Table 2. Demographics of participants (n=16). Participants were given the following options for the familiarity with technology questions: 1=Not at all familiar, 2=Slightly familiar, 3=Moderately familiar, 4=Very familiar, and 5=Extremely familiar.

Demographic variable	Statistic
Age	*n* (%)
18–30	16 (100%)
Gender	*n* (%)
Female	5 (31%)
Male	11 (69%)
Highest level of education	*n* (%)
7th–11th grade	2 (13%)
High school graduate	2 (13%)
Some college	9 (56%)
College graduate	2 (13%)
Post-graduate	1 (6%)
Familiarity with technology	M ± SD
Smartphones	4.06 ± 1.06
Tablets	3.88 ± 1.088
Computers	4.06 ± 1.063
Robots	2.93 ± 0.704

interact with FRED through both the tablet and speech. Additionally, 73.3% of participants would purchase FRED for a loved one. Looking at the desired tasks in Fig. 3, the tasks already created for FRED, like creating a contact, are desired by participants. The participants also want additional functionality of preventing falls (4.0%), ordering food (12.0%), shopping (7.0%), and contacting emergency services (13.0%).

Table 3 shows participants' responses to the post-test survey regarding each FRED version. Q1 shows that participants, on average, *probably* wanted to have a robot in their homes to assist them with daily activities. Q4 and Q5 are similar, showing that participants *probably* wanted FRED to be their friend and would follow advice provided by FRED. On average, users felt like they would be more likely to be able to use V2 without any help with a mean difference of 0.93. Users also felt more afraid that V1 was going to break during use. Q6-8 are specific questions about what users prefer. Users preferred the current appearance of V2. Although robot's voice was the same for both, users slightly preferred V2's voice. Users did not report any preference of one height over the other, with a minor difference of 0.07 in the mean rating to FRED's height (Q8 in Table 3).

In examining the coding results for experiment videos in Fig. 4, Version 1 had many more robot-related failures than Version 2 with 70.7% of the failures. V1 also had many more instances of user laughter during testing with 87.5%. It was found that all codes of confusion, frustration, and shock came from testing with V1, either from the head movements or speech recognition failures.

388   R. Bray et al.

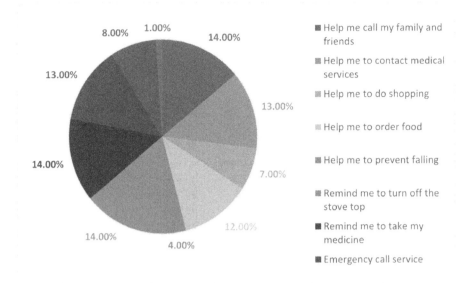

Fig. 3. Desired robot functions in FRED according to the survey question "What function(s) do you think the robot can have? You can choose multiple options."

Table 3. Post-test survey results

Question	Statistic ($M \pm SD$)
Q1: Do you think you would ever like to use a robot to assist your daily activities or to keep you company?	4.20 ± 1.08
Q2: Would you like FRED to be your friend?	4.07 ± 1.22
Q3: Would you be likely to follow the advice provided by FRED?	3.87 ± 0.99
Q4: Did you feel like you could use Version X FRED without any help?	V1: 3.40 ± 1.24 V2: 4.33 ± 1.05
Q5: When using the Version X FRED, were you afraid you would break something?	V1: 1.53 ± 0.52 V2: 1.00 ± 0.00
Q6: How likely do you think people would be to use a Version X with its current appearance?	V1: 3.07 ± 0.70 V2: 3.60 ± 0.99
Q7: How likely do you think people would be to use a robot which has the current sounding voice as Version X?	V1: 3.07 ± 1.16 V2: 3.40 ± 0.99
Q8: How likely do you think people would be to use a robot which has the current height as Version X?	V1: 3.80 ± 0.78 V2: 3.73 ± 0.88

Note: Q1-4: 1 = No, 2 = Probably not, 3 = Maybe, 4 = Probably, 5 = Yes.
Q5: 1 = No, 2 = A little bit, 3 = Yes.
Q6-8: 1 = Very unlikely, 2 = Unlikely, 3 = Neutral, 4 = Likely, 5 = Very likely.

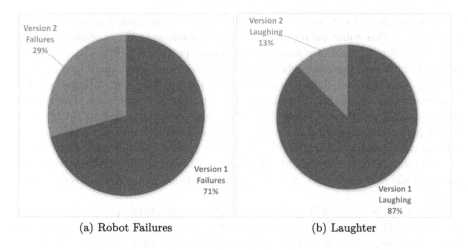

(a) Robot Failures   (b) Laughter

Fig. 4. Video coding results.

5   Discussion and Conclusion

We evaluated the functions of the two prototypes of FRED with college-aged students from a University. Overall, it seems that users would like to have FRED in the home to assist them and their loved ones in their daily lives. Most users would choose to purchase FRED for a loved one if money were not a problem, and their desired robot functions aligned with those assessed in the test. When examining the post-test survey results and the observations from video coding, it appears that users prefer V2 over V1. From version-specific questions, users thought V2 was less likely to break and preferred the appearance of it over V1.

During the experiments, the robot FRED cannot robustly respond in time and participants had to retry the functions (by repeating the verbal commands in Table 1). Students showed understanding of such robot malfunctions and did not often show obvious negative emotions such as frustration or anger. Some participants even laughed when FRED made errors, for example, when FRED thought the square shape was not on the left. Additionally, during the experiment, some participants provided affirmation for FRED's responses. This indicates that those participants were attributing some human-like qualities to FRED, which can contribute to better perceived enjoyment and higher intention to use the robot FRED [14].

One big issue in the current two prototypes of FRED is the unreliable speech services. FRED cannot always capture the user's verbal input (e.g., "Hey FRED"), which became worse if the participant had an accent. Therefore, in our next step, we will implement more reliable and stable speech service into FRED.

Currently, the market contains a few solutions for affordable robots for older adults and people with ADRD, such as the Joy for All (JfA) animals. These robots are affordable, furry companions that provide a pet-like experience without the complications of caring for a real pet. A qualitative analysis of internet reviews for the JfA cat was performed by Koh et al. to gather perceptions and outcomes of this robot as reported by family members and caretakers [15]. It was found that the robotic animal was mostly perceived positively, and many reported increased positive interactions and emotions from their loved one or patient. Although this data is not fit for comparison with the data gathered in this work, it is important to compare FRED to similar solutions. The reports of increased interactions due to the JfA robots is encouraging to future work with FRED. FRED could potentially provide deeper interactions for people with ADRD than a robotic animal due to its conversation abilities and brain games. Additionally, FRED can provide the utility of functions like creating contacts, making calls and reminders, and answering questions in addition to social interaction.

In this paper, we built a low-cost SAR for dementia care and conducted a usability study to evaluate its acceptability and usability. The testing results show that participants would like to have FRED assist their loved ones, and that they prefer V2 of the robot. Although the results seem convincing, more testing needs to be done to draw conclusions about the opinions of the population, since the number of participants is relatively small. Additionally, evaluation needs to be performed with the target population of older adults with ADRD. The opinions examined are of college students who are much more familiar with technology in general. Therefore, the results reported in this work do not lead to any conclusions about the perception of FRED among older adults or PLWDs, rather it shows the perceptions of young people who may interact with FRED for their loved one. Future work will seek to fix the issues identified in this paper and test with PLWDs to learn end-users' perception and experience with the FRED's UI design and functions.

References

1. Association, A.: 2022 Alzheimer's disease facts and figures. Alzheimers Dement. **18**(4), 700–789 (2022)
2. Duong, S., Patel, T., Chang, F.: Dementia: what pharmacists need to know. Canadian Pharm. J. Revue des Pharmaciens du Canada **150**(2), 118–129 (2017)
3. Hong, S.J., Ko, E., Choi, M., Sung, N.J., Han, M.I.: Depression, anxiety and associated factors in family caregivers of people with dementia. J. Korean Neuropsychiatr. Assoc. **61**(3), 162 (2022)
4. Yuan, F., Klavon, E., Liu, Z., Lopez, R.P., Zhao, X.: A systematic review of robotic rehabilitation for cognitive training. Front. Robot. AI **8**, 105 (2021)
5. Hirt, J., Ballhausen, N., Hering, A., Kliegel, M., Beer, T., Meyer, G.: Social robot interventions for people with dementia: a systematic review on effects and quality of reporting. J. Alzheimers Dis. **79**(2), 773–792 (2021)
6. Gerłowska, J., Furtak-Niczyporuk, M., Rejdak, K.: Robotic assistance for people with dementia: a viable option for the future? Expert Rev. Med. Devices **17**(6), 507–518 (2020)
7. Sather, R., Soufineyestani, M., Khan, A., Imtiaz, N.: Use of humanoid robot in dementia care: a literature review. J. Aging Sci. **9**, 249 (2021)

8. Pu, L., Moyle, W., Jones, C., Todorovic, M.: The effectiveness of social robots for older adults: a systematic review and meta-analysis of randomized controlled studies. Gerontologist **59**(1), e37–e51 (2019)
9. Yuan, F., et al.: Assessing the acceptability of a humanoid robot for Alzheimer's disease and related dementia care using an online survey (2022)
10. Zuschnegg, J., et al.: Humanoid socially assistive robots in dementia care: a qualitative study about expectations of caregivers and dementia trainers. Aging Mental Health **26**(6), 1270–1280 (2022)
11. Shin, M.H., McLaren, J., Ramsey, A., Sullivan, J.L., Moo, L.: Improving a mobile telepresence robot for people with Alzheimer disease and related dementias: semistructured interviews With stakeholders. JMIR Aging **5**(2), e32322 (2022)
12. Belpaeme, T., Kennedy, J., Ramachandran, A., Scassellati, B., Tanaka, F.: Social robots for education: A review. Sci. Robot. **3**(21), eaat5954 (2018). https://www.science.org/doi/abs/10.1126/scirobotics.aat5954
13. Barto, D., Bird, C.W., Hamilton, D.A., Fink, B.C.: The simple video coder: a free tool for efficiently coding social video data. Behav. Res. Methods **49**(4), 1563–1568 (2017)
14. Heerink, M., Kröse, B., Evers, V., Wielinga, B.: Assessing acceptance of assistive social agent technology by older adults: the almere model. Int. J. Soc. Robot. **2**(4), 361–375 (2010)
15. Koh, W.Q., Whelan, S., Heins, P., Casey, D., Toomey, E., Dröes, R.M.: The usability and impact of a low-cost pet robot for older adults and people with dementia: Qualitative content analysis of user experiences and perceptions on consumer websites. JMIR Aging **5**(1), e29224 (2022). https://aging.jmir.org/2022/1/e29224

A New Study of Integration Between Social Robotic Systems and the Metaverse for Dealing with Healthcare in the Post-COVID-19 Situations

Chutisant Kerdvibulvech[1]([✉]) and Chin-Chen Chang[2]

[1] Graduate School of Communication Arts and Management Innovation, National Institute
of Development Administration, 148 SeriThai Road, Klong-Chan, Bangkapi,
Bangkok 10240, Thailand
chutisant.ker@nida.ac.th

[2] Department of Information Engineering and Computer Science, Feng Chia University,
Xitun District, No. 100, Wenhua Road, Taichung City 40712, Taiwan

Abstract. With the popularity of the metaverse, researchers are turning to augmented reality and virtual reality to innovate their recent pain points, particularly healthcare issues during COVID-19. At the same time, social robots can be a great tool for alleviating many challenges during the pandemic. However, before the integrated technology's possibilities for the metaverse and social robots can be suitably harnessed, certain recent developments for integration during the pandemic should be addressed. For this reason, this paper proposes a new systematic summary of pioneering social robotic systems using the metaverse through immersive experiences from an interdisciplinary healthcare perspective during the COVID-19 outbreak. We also highlight social robots to deal with medical healthcare issues during the virus outbreak both elderly adults and younger people. Moreover, we compare recent metaverse-driven social robotic works for dealing with assisted living and healthcare issues through telepresence and remote interaction during COVID-19. Ultimately, we provide a recommendation and forecast a future scenario for the integration between socially interactive robots and metaverse technology to improve and help the quality of life both in the current COVID-19 situation and in the post-COVID-19 society.

Keywords: Social robots · Augmented reality · Virtual reality · Healthcare · COVID-19 · Telepresence

1 Introduction

Due to the rapid developments of artificial intelligence (AI), a social robot is currently a very practical area of artificial intelligence for interacting with humans and robots to help deal with some recently particular problems, including the COVID-19 pandemic. This is because it has proved to help healthcare people during the COVID-19 outbreak in

F. Cavallo et al. (Eds.): ICSR 2022, LNAI 13818, pp. 392–401, 2022.
https://doi.org/10.1007/978-3-031-24670-8_35

hospitals, particularly in dealing with some repeated functions, such as spraying disinfectants, checking for facial masks, controlling disease, implementing physical distancing rules, and maintenance of socioeconomic activities. At the same time, the metaverse has recently become a new technological buzzword that has drawn attention from government sectors and businesses of all sizes. The metaverse refers to a family of immersive technologies seamlessly like virtual reality, augmented reality, mixed reality, etc. With obvious support from a giant tech company like Facebook which majorly rebranded itself to "Meta | Social Metaverse Company" in October 2021, many people have high expectations toward metaverse, hoping that it will become another engine for opening up new and unlimited opportunities. Despite its popularity, the metaverse is still far from mature. Some people think about the future where people virtually live in a 3D world of the metaverse, introducing some opportunities for healthcare people during the COVID-19 outbreak. In recent years, the world has suffered from an outbreak of pandemic diseases, including COVID-19. This disease has disrupted the ways people communicate and interact with one another, either temporarily or permanently. Speaking of COVID-19 disease control, a basic guideline from World Health Organization includes mask-wearing, social distancing, and public gathering avoidance. These guidelines are proved to be effective in controlling the COVID-19 disease, as discussed by Khataee et al. [1] and Kim et al. [2]. Nevertheless, they are quite ineffective for mental health, as presented by Marroquín et al. [3], as well as some types of communication and interaction, such as facial masks hide facial expressions and make lip reading impossible for elderly people described by Brotto et al. [4], the frustration of work-related online meetings during COVID-19 explained by Karl et al. [5], students with inadequate resources for online learning during COVID-19 discussed by Parsons et al. [6], and the adaptation of virtual scientific and robotic conferences, such as The IEEE International Conference on Robotics and Automation supported by the IEEE Robotics and Automation Society, during the COVID-19 pandemic proposed by [7]. Even though the COVID-19 situation may not seem to end soon, there are some parts of the world like Europe and North America that have taken a path toward endemic COVID-19 during the past few months. Worldwide relaxation in COVID-19 disease control has also hinted that we may be close to entering a post-pandemic society. With the concern about spreading diseases or being infected by diseases still in mind, individuals, as well as organizations, need a new way of communication and interaction; a new way that can effectively compromise between disease control and human communication/interaction. At this point, the metaverse is a high-potential technological solution as it is always the extended reality's nature to cook up data in a virtual world, data in a physical world, and human-computer interaction, and eventually deliver the most compromising solution, as proposed by Kerdvibulvech and Dong [8]. Nevertheless, as each technology has unique strengths and weaknesses, the same as unique requirements regarding each individual and organization, it is necessary to think carefully before jumping into the premature world of the metaverse, especially at this uncertain time after COVID-19.

Therefore, in this paper, we explore recent social robotic systems applying the new technology of the metaverse, focusing on the issues of healthcare in the post-pandemic society. This can help people to understand the roles of extended reality-based social robotic systems for dealing with healthcare issues through telepresence and remote inter-action. In our methodology, we mainly select recent research works from the databases of IEEE, Scopus, and DBLP using the keywords of "Healthcare", "Social Robotic", "Vir-tual Reality", "Augmented Reality", and "COVID-19". The paper is divided into two major parts: social robotic systems for medical healthcare during COVID-19 (Sect. 2) and metaverse-based social robots helping healthcare issues during the outbreak (Sect. 3). The first major part is to examine broadly and generally how to utilize social robots to tackle medical healthcare issues during the pandemic. The second major part concen-trates on the potentiality of how to integrate the metaverse into social robotic systems to tackle the pandemic. Finally, in Sect. 4, we summarize the paper in an interdisciplinary metaverse-driven social robotic view and try to predict the next scene of this integrated field.

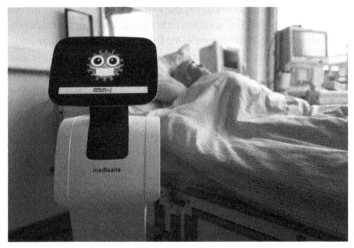

Fig. 1. The autonomously home care humanoid robot, called Temi, for establishing video tele-phony between patients and relatives via an online system during the virus outbreak, presented by Follmann et al. [9].

2 Social Robotic Systems for Healthcare During COVID-19

In this section, we describe recent examples of utilizing social robots to tackle medical healthcare issues during the pandemic. This section is divided into two subsections: 1. Social Robots to Assist the Elderly People for Healthcare and 2. Social Robotic Systems for Healthcare for Every Generation, as follows.

2.1 Social Robots to Assist the Elderly People for Healthcare

To begin with, there are several social robotic works for helping senior citizens during the virus outbreak for assisted living and healthcare, such as [9,10] and [11]. First,

Follmann et al. [9] proposed a research work in which the social media of nursing home inhabitants and patients who are senior citizens in hospitals are treated through virtual encounters and robots. Figure 1 shows the home care robot for giving patients possibly access to communicate with their nurses and doctors, even their families, as a personal robot for the home. It is important to note that even though this home care robot can be beneficial for virtual encounters through telepresence, it is not exactly a metaverse-based robotic system. Second, similarly, Getson et al. [10] surveyed how socially assistive robots have specifically helped people, particularly senior citizens, through the virus outbreak. In their survey, the acceptance of robots and the user experience of senior citizens with socially assistive robots during the COVID-19 outbreak are discussed for the future design of socially assistive robots. Third, Miller and McDaniel [11] gave a discussion about robotics for aging in place socially and brought awareness to the difficulties of identifying depression, quarantine, and non-physical health, particularly during the pandemic. They focus on raising awareness of the topic of depression among senior citizens in social robots.

2.2 Social Robotic Systems for Healthcare for Every Generation

More broadly, there are recent examples of applying social robots to deal with healthcare issues during the pandemic for not only senior citizens but also every citizen in different cases. For instance, Gao et al. [12] give a good survey of the basic requirements for infectious disease administration and robots, including the framework of how robots can be utilized in various cases, such as clinical care, inbound and outbound logistics, and laboratory automation in hospitals. However, they suggest looking carefully at the ethical utilization of robots for more sustainability in the future possible pandemics globally. In addition, Tang et al. [13] provide a useful overview of recyclable and end-effector designs for robot-assisted swab sampling to actively sense or passively regulate the force employed on COVID-19 patients. Moreover, Courtney and Royall [14] reviewed robotic systems in the analytical and clinical laboratories during the virus outbreak. According to their review, there are probably about 1,350 robots distributed per 1 million daily test capacity during the COVID-1 pandemic. Nevertheless, their use in laboratories has been unrevealed from view. Besides, Getson and Nejat [15] explained the opportunities to use socially assistive robots for adopting robots to screen and help healthcare workers in the COVID-19 era. They find that autonomous screening using socially assistive robots can be a possible system in long-term care homes. Also, Lallo et al. [16] give an interesting recommendation about medical robots in the context of infectious diseases, including opportunities, challenges, and lessons from the virus outbreak. They attempt to predict key research difficulties for possibly quick deployment to defeat the COVID-19 outbreak or similar diseases in the future.

However, although the mentioned works focus on social robots to deal with healthcare cases, they do not use the technology of the metaverse to make the systems more immersive for dealing with COVID-19 problems. The next section will explore the metaverse-driven social robotic works for medical healthcare during the COVID-19 era.

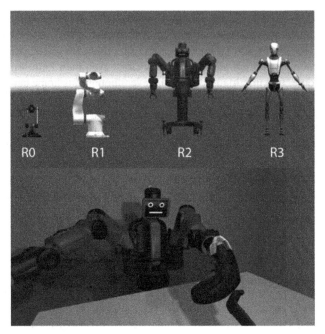

Fig. 2. The metaverse-collaboration scene with robots was presented by Badia et al. [17] for testing and developing collaboration in situations of severe risks, such as the COVID-19 era.

3   Metaverse-Based Social Robots Helping Healthcare Issues During the Outbreak

This section covers recent examples of how to integrate the metaverse into social robotic systems for tackling healthcare during the COVID-19 outbreak and future potential pandemics. For example, in 2022, Badia et al. [17] presented the utilization of the metaverse for safe testing and developing collaboration among robots, humans, and environments. As illustrated in Fig. 2, they design collaborative robots to help humans more safely in circumstances of extreme risks, such as a virus pandemic. Their research aim is to use the metaverse, particularly virtual reality, to simulate collaboration scenarios for assisted living, such as dangerous scenarios in real life or the COVID-19 outbreak for healthcare workers which can make the previous model of collaboration more difficult. They also attempt to utilize collaborative robot digital twins for many aspects, including healthcare. Moreover, Sobrepera [18] presented a social robot-augmented telehealth platform, called Lil'Flo, during the virus outbreak. Their socially assistive robot consists of arms, a body, and a face with a fisheye camera to play games with patients using a computer vision method. In their conclusion, they mention that virtual reality and augmented reality technologies could improve telerehabilitation and quality of life more interactively. In addition, Huang et al. [19] built a user-friendly robot teleoperation interface using the metaverse, particularly augmented reality, with multi-view mixing during manipulation tasks. Their robot teleoperation interface can allow users to view augmented scenes from cameras with depth information for manipulation so that the users can see some occluded parts. Similar research for muti-view mixing for robot teleoperation using the metaverse is also presented by Wei et al. [20]. Although they do not directly mention that their robot teleoperation interface was tested in a pandemic situation, we assume that it can apply to use in situations of severe risks, specifically in the COVID-19 era.

Furthermore, as a part of the utilization of robotics, artificial intelligence, and recent tools to defeat Covid-19 presented by Jain et al. [21], Sushma and Anamika [22] discussed the important role of the metaverse, particularly virtual reality, to fight the COVID-19 pandemic with an audio − video virtual environment, including the utilization of artificial intelligence and robotic tools to fight the outbreak. They suggest that artificial intelligence-assisted intelligent humanoid robots can be applied to decrease human contact and contain the propagation of the virus during COVID-19. Additionally, Alves et al. [23] presented the metaverse-based robot simulator for Aether™ during COVID-19. Their simulator is an assistive small robot built to socially support senior citizens and people living with developmental disabilities, a group of conditions due to an impairment in mental, physical, cognitive, learning, or behavior areas. It can help healthcare workers by relieving the burden of care by controlling the long-term care facilities for tripping endangerments in situations of severe risks, such as the COVID-19 era. By using virtual reality and simulation, their goal is to help their target groups, particularly persons with disabilities, to receive a greater degree of independence during the virus outbreak. Furthermore, Motaharifar et al. [24] explored how metaverse and artificial intelligence can support decreasing physical contact in medical training during the virus outbreak. They suggest augmented reality and virtual reality-driven robotic and telesurgery for surgical pieces of advice from doctors remotely during the COVID-19 era. They explain that two kinds of data are basically accessible in medically robotic-assisted surgery. The first one is kinematic data which can be available when a robotic device is used. One of the most general forms of capturing kinematic data is utilizing force sensors, encoders, and magnetic field locating sensors. The second one is video data which can basically be saved in all slightly invasive surgeries applying endoscopy approaches. Also similarly, Abdelaal et al. [25] developed an application for robot-assisted surgery for including a camera view added in traditional metaverse-based surgical training simulators to recognize the advantages of skill assessment and training. Even though they do not directly mention that their application of robot-assisted surgery using virtual reality was tested in a pandemic situation, we presume that it can be further applied in the COVID-19 situation.

We also give an overview of each recent mentioned research that combines the metaverse and social robots dealing with the COVID-19 outbreak directly and future potential pandemics, as illustrated in Table 1. It can be seen that all aforementioned research works [17, 18, 21, 23, 24] presented in/after 2021 are aimed to deal with the COVID-19 outbreak directly. Nevertheless, although other mentioned research works [19, 20, 25], as proposed around 2020–2021, apply the metaverse for social robotic systems, they focus more broadly on tackling general tasks or broadly pandemics. A possible reason is that the first known COVID-19 outbreak started in November 2019. Therefore, they were not sure if their systems can specifically deal with COVID-19. Nonetheless, at this moment, it is quite obvious that their systems for social robot teleoperation using virtual reality

Table. 1. Overview of each recent research that combines the metaverse and social robots dealing with a pandemic and healthcare

Integrating the metaverse into social robotic systems for tackling the COVID-19 outbreak directly		Integrating the metaverse into social robotic systems for tackling future potential pandemics	
Year	Research works	Year	Research works
2022	Badia et al. [17] for the utilization of the metaverse for safe testing and developing collaboration with robots	2020	Huang et al. [19] for a user-friendly robot teleoperation interface using virtual reality with multi-view mixing during manipulation tasks
2021	Sobrepera [18] for a social robot augmented telehealth platform, called Lil'Flo		
2021	Jain et al. [21] for the Use of AI, Robotics, and Modern Tools to Fight Covid-19	2021	Wei et al. [20] for muti-view mixing for robot teleoperation using the metaverse
2021	Alves et al. [23] for the metaverse-based robot simulator for Aether™	2020	Abdelaal et al. [25] for an application of robot-assisted surgery for including a camera view added in traditional metaverse-based surgical training simulators
2021	Motaharifar et al. [24] for supporting decreasing the physical contact in medical training		

with multi-view merging during manipulation tasks and socially robot-assisted surgery for including a camera view added in traditional metaverse-based surgical training simulators can apply to help tackle both the COVID-19 outbreak and any future potential pandemics.

4   Conclusions and Recommendations

Due to the increasing essential of social robotics in human daily living and society, this paper has presented a summary of recent social robotic systems applying the metaverse technology for the related issues of assisted living and healthcare during COVID-19 and in the post-COVID-19 society. We have encompassed two main sections in this work: 1) Social robotic systems for medical healthcare during COVID-19; 2) Metaverse-based social robots helping healthcare issues during the outbreak. In our method, we majorly choose related works of social robotic systems utilizing the metaverse for assisted living and healthcare during the pandemic from the databases of IEEE, Scopus, and DBLP using the related keywords. We begin to explore solely social robots to deal with assisted living and medical healthcare during the pandemic both elderly adults and younger people. Next, we discuss recent examples of how to integrate virtual reality and/or augmented reality into social robotic systems for tackling the virus outbreak and future potential pandemics. Later, we compare state-of-the-art metaverse-driven social robotic works for dealing with healthcare issues through telepresence, remote interaction, and teleoperation in the current pandemic situations and in the post-COVID-19 era.

In the future, due to the quickly growing advancement of computer vision, machine learning, and deep learning in the next decade [26], we believe that this advancement can increase the robustness of metaverse applications of social robotic systems for dealing with assisted living and medical healthcare to improve and help the quality of life in the post-pandemic situations cognitively, interactively, and effectively. According to de Freitas et al.'s review [27], the global metaverse market for virtual reality technology is forecasted to escalate from 6.30 billion USD to 84.09 billion USD between 2021 and 2028. In this way, we forecast that the market size of metaverse applications of socially interactive robots through telepresence and remote interaction among robots, humans, and environments will be globally and markedly increased in the next six years (or in 2028), particularly when the 6G beyond network is fully established in the future direction in the age of smartphone connectedness on the integration of social robots into our human society.

Acknowledgments. This research presented herein was partially supported by a research grant from the Research Center, NIDA (National Institute of Development Administration).

References

1. Khataee, H., Scheuring, I., Czirok, A., Neufeld, Z.: Effects of social distancing on the spreading of COVID-19 inferred from mobile phone data. Sci. Rep. **11**, 1661 (2021)
2. Kim, H., et al.: Social distancing and mask-wearing could avoid recurrent stay-at-home restrictions during COVID-19 respiratory pandemic in New York City. Sci. Rep. **12**, 10312 (2022)
3. Marroquína, B., Vine, V., Morgan, R.: Mental health during the COVID-19 pandemic: Effects of stay-at-home policies, social distancing behavior, and social resources. Psych. Res.**293**, 8555 (2020)
4. Brotto, D., et al.: How great is the negative impact of masking and social distancing and how can we enhance communication skills in the elderly people? Aging Clin. Exp. Res.**33**(5), 1157–1161 (2021). https://doi.org/10.1007/s40520-021-01830-1
5. Karl, K.A., Peluchette, J.V., Aghakhani, N.: Virtual Work Meetings During the COVID-19 Pandemic: The Good, Bad, and Ugly. SAGE Public Health Emergency Collection, Small Group Res. **53**, 3 (2022)
6. Parsons, D., Gander, T., Baker, K., Vo, D.: The Post-COVID-19 Impact on Distance Learning for New Zealand Teachers. Int. J. Online Pedagog. Course Des. **12**, 1 (2022)
7. Vogel, J., Ajoudani, A.: Virtual conferences in times of COVID-19: embracing the potential [Young Professionals]. IEEE Robotics Autom. Mag. **27**(3), 19 (2020)
8. Kerdvibulvech, C., Dong, Z.Y.: Roles of artificial intelligence and extended reality development in the Post-COVID-19 Era. In: Stephanidis, C., et al. (eds.) HCII 2021. LNCS, vol. 13095, pp. 445–454. Springer, Cham (2021). https://doi.org/10.1007/978-3-030-90963-5_34
9. Follmann, A., et al.: Reducing Loneliness in Stationary Geriatric Care with Robots and Virtual Encounters—A Contribution to the COVID-19 Pandemic Int. J. Environ. Res. Public Health **18**(9), 4846 (2021). https://doi.org/10.3390/ijerph18094846

10. Getson, C., Goldie N.: Socially assistive robots helping older adults through the pandemic and life after COVID-19. Robotics **10**(3), 106 (2021). https://doi.org/10.3390/robotics1003 0106
11. Tang, R., Zheng, J., Wang, S.: Design of novel end-effectors for robot-assisted swab sampling to combat respiratory infectious diseases. In: Annual International Conference on IEEE Engineering Medicine and Biology Society, vol. 2021, pp. 4757–4760 (2021). https://doi.org/10.1109/EMBC46164.2021.9630889. PMID: 34892274
12. Getson, C., Nejat, G.: The adoption of socially assistive robots for long-term care: During COVID-19 and in a post-pandemic society. Healthc Manage Forum **17**, 8404704221106406 (2022) doi: https://doi.org/10.1177/08404704221106406. Epub ahead of print. PMID: 35714374; PMCID: PMC9207582
13. Miller, J., McDaniel, T.: Social robotics to address isolation and depression among the aging during and after COVID-19. In: Stephanidis, C., Antona, M., Ntoa, S. (eds.) HCII 2021. CCIS, vol. 1420, pp. 164–171. Springer, Cham (2021). https://doi.org/10.1007/978-3-030-78642-7_22
14. Courtney, P., Royall, P.G.: Using robotics in laboratories during the COVID-19 outbreak: a review. IEEE Robot. Autom. Mag. **28**(1), 28–39 (2021). https://doi.org/10.1109/MRA.2020.3045067
15. Gao, A., et al.: Progress in robotics for combating infectious diseases. Sci Robot. **6**(52), eabf1462 (2021). doi: https://doi.org/10.1126/scirobotics.abf1462. PMID: 34043552
16. Di Lallo, A., Murphy, R., Krieger, A., Zhu, J., Taylor, R.H., Su, H.: Medical robots for infectious diseases: lessons and challenges from the COVID-19 pandemic. IEEE Robot. Autom. Mag. **28**(1), 18–27 (2021). https://doi.org/10.1109/MRA.2020.3045671
17. Badia, S.B., et al.: Virtual reality for safe testing and development in collaborative robotics: challenges and perspectives. Electronics **11**(11), 1726 (2022). https://doi.org/10.3390/electronics11111726
18. Sobrepera, M.J., Lee, V.G., Garg, S., Mendonca, R., Johnson, M.J.: Perceived usefulness of a social robot augmented telehealth platform by therapists in the United States. IEEE Robot Autom Lett. **6**(2), 2946–2953 (2021). Epub 2021 Feb 25. PMID: 33748417; PMCID: PMC7978113 doi: https://doi.org/10.1109/lra.2021.3062349
19. Huang, B., Timmons, N.G., Li.m Q.:. Augmented reality with multi-view merging for robot teleoperation. In: Companion of the 2020 ACM/IEEE International Conference on Human-Robot Interaction (HRI 2020). Association for Computing Machinery, New York, pp. 260–262 (2020). https://doi.org/10.1145/3371382.3378336
20. Jain, A., Sharma, A., Wang, J., Ram, M.: Use of AI, robotics, and modern tools to fight Covid-19. In: Use of AI, Robotics, and Modern Tools to Fight Covid-19. River Publishers (2021)
21. Sushma, M., Anamika, R.: 13 Virtual reality: solution to reduce the impact of COVID-19 on global economy. In: Use of AI, Robotics, and Modern Tools to Fight Covid-19, pp. 195–210. River Publishers, IEEE (2021)
22. Dos Reis Alves, S.F., Uribe-Quevedo, A., Chen, D., Morris, J., Radmard, S.: Leveraging simulation and virtual reality for a long term care facility service robot during COVID-19, SVR 2021: 187–191 (2021)
23. Motaharifar, M.: Applications of haptic technology, virtual reality, and artificial intelligence in medical training Dduring the COVID-19 pandemic. Front. Robot. AI **8**, 612949 (2021)
24. Abdelaal, A.E., Avinash, A., Kalia, M., Hager, G.D., Salcudean, S.E.: A multi-camera, multi-view system for training and skill assessment for robot-assisted surgery. Int. J. Comput. Assist. Radiol. Surg. **15**(8), 1369–1377 (2020). https://doi.org/10.1007/s11548-020-02176-1
25. Wei, D., Huang, B., Li, Q.: Multi-view merging for robot teleoperation with virtual reality. IEEE Robot. Autom. Lett **6**(4), 8537–8544 (2021). https://doi.org/10.1109/LRA.2021.3109348

26. Siriborvornratanakul, T.: Human behavior in image-based Road Health Inspection Systems despite the emerging AutoML. J. Big Data **9**, 96 (2022). https://doi.org/10.1186/s40537-022-00646-8
27. de Freitas,F.V., Gomes, M.V.M., Winkler, I.: Benefits and challenges of virtual-reality-Based industrial usability testing and design reviews: a patents landscape and literature review. Appli. Sci. **12**(3), 1755 (2022). https://doi.org/10.3390/app12031755

HapticPalm: A Wearable Robotic Device for Haptics and Rehabilitative Hand Treatments

Danilo Troisi[1,2], Mihai Dragusanu[1], Alberto Villani[1],
Domenico Prattichizzo[1,3], and Monica Malvezzi[1(✉)]

[1] Department of Information Engineering and Mathematics, University of Siena,
Siena, Italy
`monica.malvezzi@unisi.it`
[2] Information Engineering Department, University of Pisa, Pisa, Italy
[3] Department of Humanoids and Human Centered Mechatronics,
Istituto Italiano di Tecnologia, Genova, Italy

Abstract. In this paper we present HapticPalm, a wearable device based on a 3-DoF parallel robotic structure, that can be used in different applications, from rendering haptic perception to rehabilitation of specific hand pathologies. The paper focuses in particular on the design of the contact interfaces between the device end effector and the palm, that have to simulate the interaction with different surfaces.

Keywords: Rehabilitation robotics · Haptics · Wearable robots

1 Introduction

The use of robots or robotic devices in rehabilitation is rapidly increasing: as stated by *Mordor Intelligence*, rehabilitation robots market is expected to register a compounded annual growth rate of about 26% over the 2021–2026 period. The motivations of such an increasing trend are manifold. Medical rehabilitation required by people suffering from injuries are often complex, long-term, with psychological and physical dimensions, and outcomes are difficult to guarantee. Robot rehabilitation therapy can deliver high-intensity training, without the need of a continuous physical interaction with physiotherapists. However, one of the main concerns for the implementation of the rehabilitation is usually the cost and the technical complexity of the robotic devices. In this paper we focus on hand rehabilitation.

Our primary tactile interactions with the world around us are provided thanks to our hands. According to Klatzky and Lederman tactile feelings in the palm impact hand-closing interactions [1]. The biomechanical structure of palm bones, muscles and ligaments allows the radial abduction, ulnar adduction, palmar flexion/dorsiflexion, opposition/apposition of thumb and combined movements. During apposition the side part of thumb is in touch with other fingers, while the pulp side of thumb distal is in contact with fingertips of other digits during opposition [2].

F. Cavallo et al. (Eds.): ICSR 2022, LNAI 13818, pp. 402–411, 2022.
https://doi.org/10.1007/978-3-031-24670-8_36

Unfortunately, traumas, fractures, sprains, tissue pathologies, and illnesses that cause persistent pains or syndromes occurs frequently in the hand. Many of these painful hand problems are commonly treated using manual therapy (MT), which involves joint mobilizations, rhythmic stimulation, and force applications. The MT is also a typical alternative treatment for musculoskeletal illnesses as CRPS-I [3] a chronic painful syndrome that consists of several alterations of perceived sensation and many of hand problems as carpal tunnel syndrome, a common condition that affects the hands and forearms and causes tingling, numbness and pain, the stenosing tenosynovitis which develops when inflammation constricts the area inside the sheath that covers the finger's affected tendon and De Quervain's tenosynovitis, a painful condition that affects your wrist's thumb side tendons.

Usually, hand issues can be treated by following two main different paths: conservative clinical therapy or, in severe cases, surgical treatment. Conservative clinical therapy basically consists in patient education to pain control, desensitization therapy, gradual exercises to increase the strength and flexibility of the affected hand and manual therapy. According to [4,5], MT can reduce discomfort and enhance hand functionality while the preliminary studies presented by researchers in [6–8] assessed that MT has analgesic effects and can activates enzymatic anti-oxidative system, reducing the oxidative stress, which is responsible of an inflammatory event cascade, and alleviating the pain.

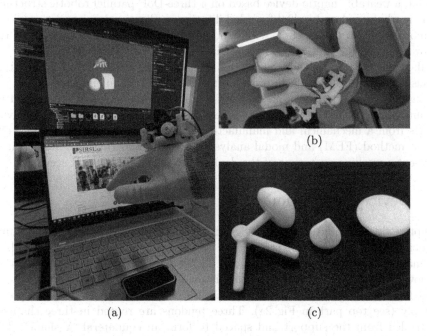

(a)   (b)   (c)

Fig. 1. New HapticPalm prototype for rehabilitation in virtual reality. In (a) the complete system. (b) Bottom view of the new prototype while in (c) the new new interchangeable modules.

1.1   Related Works and Contributions

The literature of haptic devices for hand palm is mainly based on localized and fixed contact points on the palm. There are two main types of haptic interaction: force/pressure and vibrotactile. The devices using the first one employ tight bands, tendons, and small rigid links to stimulate the palm, some examples are reported in [9–12] while the devices providing the second type of stimuli employ vibrotactile matrices in contact with the palm to reduce the number of actuators, however, often the similarity between the desired stimulus and the transmitted signal is in this case compromised [13,14]. Kovacs et al. in [15] show a combination of the two main types of interfaces, where a mobile mass encounters the palm in case of collision between a hand avatar and the surrounding environment in virtual reality, while in [16,17] pneumatic solutions are presented.

Nowadays different haptic technologies are combined with Virtual reality (VR) environments, games and robots for rehabilitation purposes [18–20]. Research in the haptic field for hand rehabilitation has produced practical tools and specific therapy for hand joint, ligament, skin issues and pain [21]. In [22] by using a multi-finger device, Ferre et al., created a haptic framework that collects and replicates manual therapy techniques while Bouri et al. in [23] presents an innovative haptic device able to activate hand joint reproducing the MT for hemiplegic children rehabilitation.

In this paper we present the improvements and the applicability of Haptic-Palm, a wearable haptic device based on a three-DoF parallel robotic structure, previously introduced in [24] for rehabilitation application in virtual scenario as a motivational tool for people with hand pain/impairments. The system and the new wearable haptic device is shown in Fig. 1. In particular in this paper we will: i) briefly describe the HapticPalm for hand palm stimulation based on tendons; ii) introduce the new improved version of HapticPalm end-effector and the design of new interchangeable modules able to provide compliant and vibrating stimulation on hand palm as it is suggested in [25,26] iii) detail the new device parts from a mechanical and manufacturing point of view, including finite element method (FEM) and modal analysis, hardware and control description; v) present a working prototype of the device with a preliminary VR scenario.

2   Device Description

HapticPalm is a haptic device designed for rendering forces on the hand palm, previously introduced and preliminary tested on a VR application in [24]. It is made up of two primary parts, one on the back of the hand and the other below the palm. The hand back part is made up of a mechanical support for the force actuation/transmission mechanism, a microcontroller, and a power supply (see top part in Fig. 2a). Three tendons are routed in three channels extruded from the support and spaced to form an equilateral "Y-shape". The tendons transfer the forces applied by the motors from the back of the hand to the device's end-effector (highlighted in the red circle in Fig. 2a). The pulleys design allow the regulation of initial tendon tension. This design ensures an easy

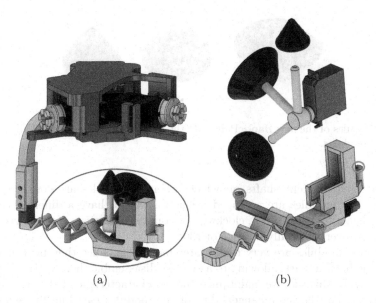

(a)   (b)

Fig. 2. CAD model of the new HapticPalm. (a) HapticPalm CAD model. (b) New interchangeable CAD modules and new end-effector compliant structure.

wearability and avoids the problems associated with parallel mechanisms based on rigid links, which have higher weight and lower flexibility/adaptability and necessitate appropriate procedures to be adapted to different users and needs, as well as the greater complexity to relocate the implementation to ergonomic points of the hand [27]. To ensure ergonomics for multiple users and enabling them to temporarily remove the end-effector from the palm without removing the device, the rigid link (red and yellow elements in Fig. 2a) connecting the two main parts is designed with an adjustable telescopic height and two revolute joints, connecting the link to the end-effector and to the top of the device.

2.1 Design of the End-Effector with Interchangeable Modules

The end-effector is composed of a "wave" shaped compliant link [28] supporting the contact modules, three elements for easy connection/disconnection of the tendons, and the new interchangeable modules mechanism (see Fig. 2b). The first is connected directly to the part on the back by means of a "C" shaped rigid link previously described while the remaining parts are connected to the actuation system through the tendons. With respect to the version presented in [24] the compliant mechanism allows the tip-palm disconnection when no contacts and forces have to be rendered on the palm. The connection points between tendons and the HapticPalm end-effector components have a triangular structure made up of three links with a *ad hoc* locking system for the cables (highlighted by the green circles in Fig. 2b). The new end-effector consists of a shaft, directly connected to a micro servo, which is able to rotate to change module, since

Fig. 3. Modules of the new HapticPalm. M1 the plane-shaped module, M2 and M3 the spherical modules.

it hosts three different shafts on which different modules are connected (see Fig. 2b). The modules are arranged in such a way to have a different contact shapes when a rotation of 65°, clockwise or counter-clockwise, of the micro-servo is applied, covering totally a range of 130°.

The new modules are very easily interchangeable, since they present just a hole in the bottom part, allowing to assemble/disassemble them without the use of any tool. In this way we maintained the old characteristic of the HapticPalm end-effector, i.e. the interchangeability of the modules (see Fig. 2b), while the mobile element allows to feel different stimuli on the palm without the need of manual intervention. Three contact modules were realized (Fig. 3): a plane-shaped one (M1) that slightly modified with respect to the previous version, to introduce special edge reproducing the contact with edges and flat shapes respectively; two spherical modules with different curvature radii (M2 and M3) reproducing curved surfaces/corners and providing to the user different kind of pressure cues on the palm. The literature reports that pressure associated with vibrations provides different benefits depending on the select frequency. In particular, in a range of frequencies between (50–400) Hz the following benefits can be observed: muscle relaxation occurs 50 Hz, spasticity is inhibited 100 Hz, pain is relieved 200 Hz, and muscles are trained up 300 Hz [26]. HapticPalm end-effector has been therefore designed to house a vibromotor, needed to provide vibrations to the palm corresponding to the above mentioned clinical requirements.

2.2 Structural Analyses

The wearability and manufacturing constraints that guided the design process lead to a structure that could undergo to relatively high stationary and dynamic solicitations. In order to evaluate the mechanical resistance and the vibration characteristic of the mechanical structure of the device a set of Finite Element Analyses were carried out. The software that we used for this purpose is AutoDesk Fusion 360. We started with a static structural analysis and then we evaluated the response of the device to the vibrations induced by the vibromotor when vibration cues are applied.

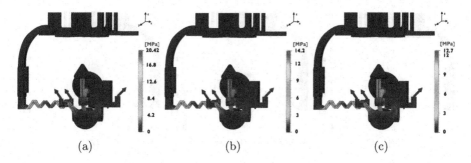

Fig. 4. Results of the FEM structural analysis. The blue arrows indicate the forces applied in the simulations, corresponding to tendons. Equivalent stress values obtained when (a) a pure normal force, aligned with z-axis, (b) a force with components along y and z, and (c) a force with components along x and z, are applied to the palm (Color figure online)

Stationary Structural Analysis. The aim of the FEM analysis is to evaluate the stress response of the end-effector when it is constrained and/or loaded in different ways, reproducing the application of a specific pressure on the hand palm. The considered materials for the static structural analysis is ABS. The forces are applied in the three areas where the tendons are connected, in order to simulate their tension when they act on the end-effector. The constrain is applied at the top of the connection site of the end-effector (lower-left part of see Fig. 4). The analyzed loading cases are:

- Case 1 - Three forces with the same magnitude F are applied along the z-axis (Fig. 4a).
- Case 2 - The tendon along the y-axis is exerting a force with magnitude F, while the other two with exert forces with magnitude $F/2$. This load configuration represent the case in which the device exerts a feedback force on the left/right part of the hand palm (Fig. 4b).
- Case 3 - The tendon along the x-axis pulls the end-effector with F force, while the tensions on the other two tendons are $F/2$. This time the configuration represents the case in which we want to move the end-effector on the upper/lower part of the hand (Fig. 4c).

Results relative to the numerical simulations in which $F = 1N$ are reported in Fig. 4. It is evident that the most stressed zone of the end-effector in each case is in correspondence of the compliant wave link.

Modal Analysis. Since in this version of the end-effector a vibromotor was installed, we carried out a modal analysis that is coherent with the vibration frequencies that can be reproduced with it by taking into account the frequencies useful for physical benefits already described. We searched 8 modes of vibration in the frequency range of (50–400) Hz. We brief report three results of them Fig. 5, interesting in particular the end-effector. It is evidenced that in that

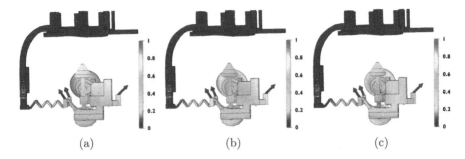

Fig. 5. Results of the modal analysis. (a) 110 Hz (b) 215 Hz (c) 375 Hz

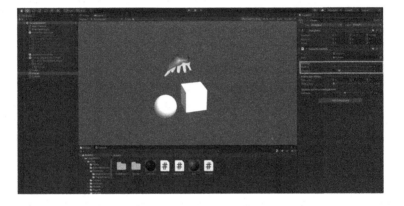

Fig. 6. The testing virtual scenario. It is composed by a avatar hand and two different objects. The cube allows to use M1 and M3 modules while the sphere allows to test M2 module.

cases Fig. 5a and Fig. 5b, i.e. 110 Hz 215 Hz, the vibration is transmitted to the palm in a good way, especially in the first case.

3   Prototype

The prototype of the HapticPalm device for rehabilitation propose in virtual scenario is shown in Fig. 1. All structural components are produced using an FDM (Fused Deposition Modeling) technique with ABS material. Three MG-90S microservos with a 5V battery are employed to transmit forces to the HapticPalm end-effector. They have a 0.20 Nm stall torque. The Elegoo Nano V3+ microcontroller (ELEGOO Inc.,CHN), is employed for the control and data processing part while serial communication was used for transmission with the virtual environment.

As stated before, a 3-DoF, tendon-based, parallel transmission is used to produce the force on the hand palm. The cables are attached to the "Y-arranged" links of the end-effector on one side and on the other to the pulleys of the motors, located on the platform worn of the back of the hand. The thread length required to link the end-effector to the platform on the back of the hand when it is under tension determines the minimum size of each tendon. The pulleys contain an external part that enables the extra tendon to be wrapped in order to modify the cables length to adapt the device to different user hand sizes.

Moreover, the device is embedded in a glove with a suitably designed hole in the center of the palm allowing the direct contact with the end-effector. The glove is employed to avoid uncertainty in orientation and to assist or guide the user's hand between the tendons when wearing the device. The end-effector houses a BMS-303 Micro-Servo and a Micro 612 coreless vibration-motor in order to change the module in contact with the hand palm and to allow the user to have vibrations on the palm according to the previously mentioned clinical requirements. Finally the end-effector is passively supported by the 3D-printed compliant "wave" shaped link, as previously introduced, that allows to detach the end-effector from the palm when no contact rendering is needed.

3.1   VR Application

To use the device exploiting the different types of contacts, we have developed a virtual reality scenario. The scenario was created in Unity, graphic engine, and each of the objects can interact with in the simulated environment. The two objects are made to test the end-effector modules (see Fig. 6). Specifically, the cube is for testing the M1 and M3 modules, while the sphere for M2 module. In particular, as soon as the user positions the avatar hand over one of the objects, with the HapticPalm worn, the appropriate module will be automatically selected. As soon as the avatar hand moves towards the object and virtually touches it, the user will start feeling the interaction through the device. It is also possible to activate the vibration during the interaction by selecting the check box highlighted in Fig. 6. In this way, the device can be used both for enriching the navigation is VR environment through haptic feedback on the palm, and for making the physiotherapy exercises more interactive and therefore enhancing the rehabilitation process.

4   Conclusion and Future Works

We presented an upgrade in the design of HapticPalm, a wearable robotic device for hand palm. The new end-effector design was improved taking into account the opinion of users that tested the previous device. The new interchangeable modules and the replacement of the spring with a wave-joint shaped link improved wearability and easy of use. In the future, we plan to carry out a comparison between the previous version of the device and the current one in terms of exertable force, usability and immersivity of VR experience. In fact, the introduced vibromotor, allows the user to have a more immersive experience in VR, distracting, in this way, the user from the pain on the hand in case of rehabilitation use. Future improvements will be focused on the optimization of the general structure of the device, to reduce its dimension and therefore to improve its usability and adaptability. A more immersive virtual environment will be created, with new objects and a more user friendly GUI, and a set of user studies will be realized.

References

1. Lederman, S.J., Klatzky, R.L.: Hand movements: a window into haptic object recognition. Cogn. Psychol. **19**(3), 342–368 (1987)
2. Van Nierop, O.A., van der Helm, A., Overbeeke, K.J., Djajadiningrat, T.J.: A natural human hand model. Vis. Comput. **24**(1), 31–44 (2008)
3. Moss, P., Sluka, K., Wright, A.: The initial effects of knee joint mobilization on osteoarthritic hyperalgesia. Man. Ther. **12**(2), 109–118 (2007)
4. Bialosky, J.E., Bishop, M.D., Price, D.D., Robinson, M.E., George, S.Z.: The mechanisms of manual therapy in the treatment of musculoskeletal pain: a comprehensive model. Man. Ther. **14**(5), 531–538 (2009)
5. Camarinos, J., Marinko, L.: Effectiveness of manual physical therapy for painful shoulder conditions: a systematic review. J. Manual Manip. Therapy **17**(4), 206–215 (2009)
6. Martins, D.F., et al.: Ankle joint mobilization decreases hypersensitivity by activation of peripheral opioid receptors in a mouse model of postoperative pain. Pain Med. **13**(8), 1049–1058 (2012)
7. Martins, D., Mazzardo-Martins, L., Cidral-Filho, F., Gadotti, V., Santos, A.: Peripheral and spinal activation of cannabinoid receptors by joint mobilization alleviates postoperative pain in mice. Neuroscience **255**, 110–121 (2013)
8. Salgado, A.S., et al.: Manual therapy reduces pain behavior and oxidative stress in a murine model of complex regional pain syndrome type i. Brain Sci. **9**(8), 197 (2019)
9. Minamizawa, K., Kamuro, S., Fukamachi, S., Kawakami, N., Tachi, S.: Ghostglove: Haptic existence of the virtual world. In: ACM SIGGRAPH 2008 new tech demos, p. 1 (2008)
10. Minamizawa, K., Kamuro, S., Kawakami, N., Tachi, S.: A palm-worn haptic display for bimanual operations in virtual environments. In: Ferre, M. (ed.) EuroHaptics 2008. LNCS, vol. 5024, pp. 458–463. Springer, Heidelberg (2008). https://doi.org/10.1007/978-3-540-69057-3_59
11. Son, B., Park, J.: Haptic feedback to the palm and fingers for improved tactile perception of large objects. In: Proceedings of the 31st Annual ACM Symposium on User Interface Software and Technology, pp. 757–763 (2018)
12. Son, B., Park, J.: Tactile sensitivity to distributed patterns in a palm. In: Proceedings of the 20th ACM International Conference on Multimodal Interaction, pp. 486–491 (2018)
13. Gollner, U., Bieling,T.,Joost, G.: Mobile lorm glove: introducing a communication device for deaf-blind people. In: Proceedings of the Sixth International Conference on Tangible, Embedded and Embodied Interaction, pp. 127–130 (2012)

14. Borja, E.F., Lara, D.A., Quevedo, W.X., Andaluz, V.H.: Haptic stimulation glove for fine motor rehabilitation in virtual reality eDnvironments. In: De Paolis, L.T., Bourdot, P. (eds.) AVR 2018. LNCS, vol. 10851, pp. 211–229. Springer, Cham (2018). https://doi.org/10.1007/978-3-319-95282-6_16
15. Kovacs, R., et al.: Haptic pivot: On-demand handhelds in vr. In: Proceedings of the 33rd Annual ACM Symposium on User Interface Software and Technology, pp. 1046–1059 (2020)
16. Kajimoto, H.: Design of cylindrical whole-hand haptic interface using electrocutaneous display. In: Isokoski, P., Springare, J. (eds.) EuroHaptics 2012. LNCS, vol. 7283, pp. 67–72. Springer, Heidelberg (2012). https://doi.org/10.1007/978-3-642-31404-9_12
17. Zubrycki, I., Granosik, G.: Novel haptic device using jamming principle for providing kinaesthetic feedback in glove-based control interface. J. Intell. Robot. Syst. **85**(3–4), 413–429 (2017)
18. Wu, H.-C., Liao, Y.-C., Cheng, Y.-H., Shih, P.-C., Tsai, C.-M., Lin, C.-Y.: The potential effect of a vibrotactile glove rehabilitation system on motor recovery in chronic post-stroke hemiparesis. Technol. Health Care **25**(6), 1183–1187 (2017)
19. Huang, X., Naghdy, F., Naghdy, G., Du, H.: Clinical effectiveness of combined virtual reality and robot assisted fine hand motion rehabilitation in subacute stroke patients. In: 2017 International Conference on Rehabilitation Robotics (ICORR). IEEE, pp. 511–515 (2017)
20. Maris, A., et al.: The impact of robot-mediated adaptive i-travle training on impaired upper limb function in chronic stroke and multiple sclerosis. Disabil. Rehabil. Assist. Technol. **13**(1), 1–9 (2018)
21. Dragusanu, M., Troisi, D., Villani, A., Prattichizzo, D., Malvezzi, M.: Happ: A haptic portable pad for hand disease manual treatment. In: 31st IEEE International Conference on Robot and Human Interactive Communication, RO-MAN (2022)
22. Ferre, M., Galiana, I., Wirz, R., Tuttle, N.: Haptic device for capturing and simulating hand manipulation rehabilitation. IEEE/ASME Trans. Mechatron. **16**(5), 808–815 (2011)
23. Bouri, M.,Baur, C., Clavel, R., Newman, C., Zedka, M.: Handreha: a new hand and wrist haptic device for hemiplegic children. In: *ACHI 2013, The Sixth International Conference on Advances in Computer-Human Interactions*, pp. 286–292 (2013)
24. Dragusanu, M., Villani, A., Prattichizzo, D., Malvezzi, M.: Design of a wearable haptic device for hand palm cutaneous feedback. Front. Robot. AI p. 254 (2021)
25. Cardinale, M., Wakeling, J.: Whole body vibration exercise: are vibrations good for you? Br. J. Sports Med. **39**(9), 585–589 (2005)
26. Saggini, R., Carmignano, S.M., Palermo, T., Bellomo, R.G.: Mechanical vibration in rehabilitation: state of the art (2016)
27. Malvezzi, M., Chinello, F., Prattichizzo, D., Pacchierotti, C.: Design of personalized wearable haptic interfaces to account for fingertip size and shape. IEEE Trans. Haptics **14**(2), 266–272 (2021)
28. Dragusanu, M., Achilli, G.M., Valigi, M.C., Prattichizzo, D., Malvezzi, M., Salvietti, G.: The wavejoints: A novel methodology to design soft-rigid grippers made by monolithic 3d printed fingers with adjustable joint stiffness. In: 2022 International Conference on Robotics and Automation (ICRA). IEEE, pp. 6173–6179 (2022)

Collaborative Social Robots Through Dynamic Game

Play Dynamics in a Collaborative Game with a Robot as a Play-Mediator

Negin Azizi[✉], Kevin Fan, Melanie Jouaiti, and Kerstin Dautenhahn

Electrical and Computer Engineering Department, University of Waterloo,
200 University Avenue, Waterloo, ON N2L3G1, Canada
{negin.azizi,k36fan,mjouaiti,kerstin.dautenhahn}@uwaterloo.ca

Abstract. While game-play is widely used in HRI, using a robot as a play-mediator, where two individuals interact with each other through a robot, has not been fully studied yet. However, understanding the play dynamics of this type of game is an important step towards designing an engaging experience. In this work, participants played two collaborative games which involved teleoperating a mobile robot. Each game consisted in achieving the same task but involved two different collaboration strategies: one where the players shared tasks and one where joint action was necessary. In this paper, we focus on how both players collaborated with each other in terms of coordination and communication using video and joystick data.

Keywords: Engagement · Cooperative game · Teleoperation · Coordination

1 Introduction

Play is a widely used element in Human-Robot Interaction (HRI) experiments [6, 10,12,13], as it provides an enjoyable and clearly structured context. Play is also paramount for child development [1], as well as for enjoyment, and has therefore been studied extensively in child-robot interaction [15], including robots as tutors or game partners for pairs of children, e.g. [3,22], or as a referee for pairs of adult participants [21]. However, only a few studies explored using a robot to mediate play between two participants [18], whereby the robot serves as a medium rather than an autonomous agent.

In order to facilitate play for children with upper limb impairments, we previously reported on the design of the MyJay robot as a play-mediator [14]. The main goal of MyJay is to enable children to play with their peers through the robot, to provide a fun, motivating and engaging experience for the children, despite the challenges they face. To do so, we need to better understand the play dynamics of how two people can play with MyJay. As a first step we investigate play dynamics of pairs of adult participants playing a game through MyJay.

© The Author(s), under exclusive license to Springer Nature Switzerland AG 2022
F. Cavallo et al. (Eds.): ICSR 2022, LNAI 13818, pp. 415–426, 2022.
https://doi.org/10.1007/978-3-031-24670-8_37

In particular, we study how different kinds of collaborative games influence how players collaborate and communicate with each other. In our experimental design, two participants controlled the same robot, each using a joystick. In the *Shared* condition, the participants were each responsible for different functionalities of the robot, facilitating turn-taking. In the *Fusion* condition, the robot answered to commands, if and only if both players agreed on the next course of action, i.e. gave the same command at the same time. Thus, in this condition coordination between the players is paramount.

This study will allow us to design a more enjoyable game, which can later be translated to a play or therapy setting for children with upper-limb challenges.

2   Related Work

Play is especially important in the context of therapy, as it maintains motivation and engagement. Social robots are still scarce in the literature related to upper limb rehabilitation. One study [23] used the Cozmo robot as a motivator in the therapy exercises, as the robot reacted positively when the children performed the required therapy, correctly. Another study [11], designed a Pacman-like game with small graspable mobile robots to encourage children to perform grasping and manipulation tasks.

Tasevski et al. designed a robot that was meant to increase the motivation of the children [20]. Their robot improved non-verbal communication, gestures, and verbal production. Fridin et al. observed that children with cerebral palsy were more involved in the therapy when using the Nao robot to carry out repetitive training [7]. The robot provided feedback and adapted the exercises based on performance. Another study considered if the Ursus robot could adapt the exercises to each participant, while monitoring and learning from the interaction, thanks to the proposed cognitive architecture [2]. They reported increased collaborative behaviours from the children interacting with the robot.

In previous works, the differences between collaborative versus competitive gameplay have been studied in educational [19] and therapeutic [16] settings. Novak et al. showed that participants preferred playing with a partner rather than playing alone. However, preferences in terms of competitive or collaborative gameplay differed across individuals, and most players liked one condition and disliked the other [16]. Sanchez et al. observed emerging competitive behaviours in a classroom setting and introduced an h-index like scoring policy to encourage cooperation amongst students. Arellano et al. compared physiological data in the case of solo, competitive and collaborative play. They reported that players experienced similar levels of arousal in individual and collaborative contexts [8].

Moreover, humans favour collaboration/cooperation and prefer to work together, even when it is not necessary and less effective [4].

Considering the benefits of robot-assisted play therapy and collaborative play, we designed a game with two collaborative scenarios. In each scenario, the two participants played with the MyJay robot to complete a task using different collaborative strategies.

3   Research Questions

The purpose of this experiment was to study play dynamics with the robot MyJay in a collaborative multi-player game with two different collaborative controls. We are interested in how participants adapt to each other. We also want to see how the two different conditions influence participants' enjoyment and engagement. In the Fusion condition, we particularly investigate coordination. In the Shared condition, we evaluate turn-taking. We hypothesize that the Fusion control mode might promote better collaboration and lead to better engagement and enjoyment. We aim to answer the following specific research questions:

RQ1: Which collaborative robot control condition best promotes collaboration among the participants?

RQ2: Which robot control condition provides the best game experience in terms of enjoyment?

RQ3: Which strategies do participants employ to achieve collaboration?

4   Material and Methods

4.1   Study Overview

In this study, pairs of participants played together through a robot play-mediator, the MyJay robot, which is able to pick up and throw balls. The dimensions of the robot were $570 \times 330 \times 525$ mm. The robot was placed in a 2.85×2.28 m playpen with 10 foam balls (with a diameter of 101.6 mm) scattered across the floor. The robot operated within the pen, participants stood outside the pen. The game consisted in cleaning up the play pen, i.e. collecting the balls by picking them up with the robot and throwing them into a box, as fast as possible in two different collaborative control conditions. This study was approved by the University of Waterloo Human Research Ethics Board.

4.2   Experiment Design

Upon arrival in the experiment room, participants were equipped with heart-rate sensors. First, they performed baseline tasks to acquire baseline heart-rate data: read a text for 3 min to acquire resting heart-rate data; play a speed game on a tablet to acquire excited heart-rate data. (The participants played the fruit Ninja game, where they had to slice fruits and avoid bombs[1].) Afterwards, participants played individually with the robot for 3 min to acquire baseline joystick and heart-rate data. They were free to navigate, pick up and throw balls via the joystick. The joystick functionalities, as well as the robot capabilities were explained to each participant beforehand. The analysis of the heart-rate data is out of the scope of this paper. Participants then played together in the following two conditions:

---

[1] https://www.halfbrick.com/games/fruit-ninja.

Shared Condition: One participant is in charge of navigation and the other one of handling the balls. Only the required functionalities are active on each joystick.

Fusion Condition: Both participants can control every functionality of the robot but the robot answers commands if and only if both participants give the same commands at the same time, by averaging the two control commands. This condition was inspired by [9].

Before each condition, the rules were explained to the participants, i.e. what they could do with their joystick. The conditions were randomised for each pair. For each condition, we recorded joystick and heart-rate data, as well as videos. After each condition, the participants completed a questionnaire to assess their engagement and enjoyment. Finally, participants were thanked for their participation and escorted out of the study room. The study lasted between 45 min to an hour.

4.3   Participants

Twenty-four pairs of adult participants were recruited from the University of Waterloo. Participants were instructed to come with a friend. We did not have any age constraints, but only fully Covid-19 vaccinated students (undergraduate and graduate level) could take part in our study, due to our University guidelines at the time of the study. Participants received the information letter regarding the study beforehand and provided consent. They each received a 10C\$ gift-card to thank them for their participation.

4.4   Materials

MyJay Robot. In this paper, our custom robot MyJay[2] (See Fig. 1) was tele-operated by two XBox controllers. This robot was designed as a play-mediator robot with a zoomorphic appearance, aiming at facilitating play for children with upper limb challenges [14]. It can navigate in any direction and also has an intake, an elevator and a flywheel mechanism that allows it to pick up balls and shoot them.

Questionnaire. Participants were asked to rate the following items with a 5-point Likert scale (ranging from 1 = strongly disagree to 5 = strongly agree), after each condition:

The questionnaire contained selected items from [5,17]. However, in this paper, we will report results only for the following items:

---

[2] https://github.com/hamzaMahdi/myjay-bot.

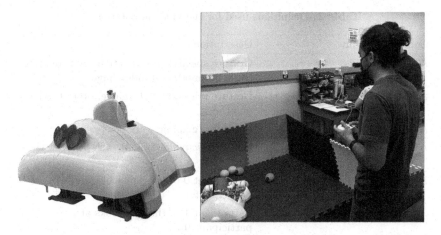

Fig. 1. Left: The MyJay robot; Right: the experimental setup with a pair of participants playing

- Q1: The activity was pleasurable to me.
- Q2: I felt connected with others during the activity.
- Q3: I liked interacting with others during the activity.
- Q4: The activity was fun.
- Q5: I am good at the activity.
- Q6: I cooperated with others during the activity.
- Q7: The activity made me feel good.
- Q8: I felt frustrated while using MyJay.
- Q9: I found MyJay confusing to use.
- Q10: Using MyJay was challenging.

4.5 Video Analysis

The videos were labelled with some behavioural events defined in Table 1, such as pointing, gesturing, giggling/laughing, both participants looking at each other, one participant looking at the other, looking at the experimenter, cheering, and talking. For each behavioural event, we counted the number of occurrences.

Table 1. Definitions used for the video annotations

Code	Behaviour	Description
A1	Pointing	Gesture specifying a direction, by extending the arm, hand, and index finger
A2	Gesturing	Gesture relevant to the game, other than pointing
A3	Laughing	Laughing/giggling
A4	Looking at each other	Both participants look at each other at the same time
A5	P0 looking at P1	Participant 0 of the pair looks at participant 1
A6	P1 looking at P0	Participant 1 of the pair looks at participant 0
A7	Looking at experimenters	Gaze directing towards the experimenters
A8	Cheering	Shouting for joy/excited behaviour like hugging/high fives
A9	Talking	Estimation of sentences uttered between participants

One of the authors of this paper defined definitions for each behavioural event and annotated all the videos. Another author was trained on those definitions and annotated 10% of the videos. The inter-rater agreement was 86%.

5 Results

5.1 Fusion Condition: Coordination

In the Fusion condition, we are interested in the coordination between participants. To see if the participants were coordinated, we checked the proportion of time when both players activated the same joystick axis at the same time. First we define *overall coordination* as: $\sum(J1 == J2)/T_n$ where J1 and J2 are the joystick of the first and second player respectively and T_n is the number of timesteps, (overall coordination values for Forward/Backward axis (FB): 0.64 ± 0.07, Left/Right axis (LR): 0.63 ± 0.07), this metric considers all the data and although it provides a good overview of how coordinated the participants were across the entire interaction, it can be biased if there was a lot of idle time. We therefore define *active coordination*, which only considers the data when at least one of the joysticks is active, as $\sum(J1 \text{ AND } J2)/\sum(J1 \text{ OR } J2)$ (FB:0.36 ± 0.06, LR: 0.32 ± 0.06). See Fig. 2 for results on overall and active coordination. We also calculated how often each joystick was active to detect play imbalance and if a player was just randomly giving commands (J1: 0.5 ± 0.08, J2: 0.39 ± 0.13) and the Pearson correlation coefficient (FB: 0.41 ± 0.13, LR: 0.27 ± 0.14). Figure 4 shows an example of windowed time lagged cross-correlation

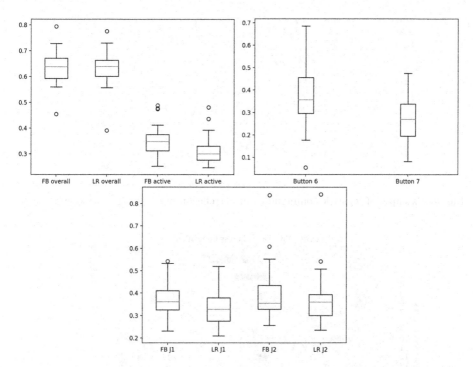

Fig. 2. Top Left: Overall and active coordination for the joystick (FB: forward/backward axis of the joystick; LR: left/right axis of the joystick). Top Right: Active coordination for the buttons. Bottom: Percentage of time where each joystick is active during the interaction

where the leader-follower relationship varies over time between both participants (Fig. 3).

5.2 Shared Condition: Turn-Taking

In the Shared condition, we evaluate turn-taking. Specifically, we measure whether the players respected their assigned roles and if they were waiting for their turn to give commands.

Overlap is defined as J_B AND $(J_{FB}$ OR $J_{LR})/J_B$ OR $(J_{FB}$ OR $J_{LR})$. Results show that participants did not always wait for their turn, as evidenced by $40 \pm 14\%$ of overlap on average, with a minimum of 13% and a maximum of 67%.

In 7 pairs, the person in charge of navigation was still pressing the button to try and shoot balls, even though it was made clear to them that the buttons were deactivated. In 19 pairs, the person in charge of the balls also tried to navigate the robot by moving the stick on the joystick.

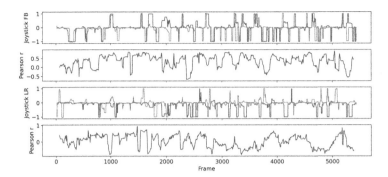

Fig. 3. Example of joystick commands and correlation over a sliding window for pair 10.

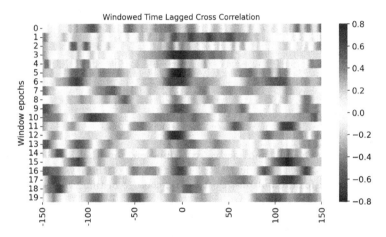

Fig. 4. Example of windowed time lagged cross-correlation for the forward/backward direction for pair 10.

5.3   Video Analysis

Overall, the participant pairs communicated more with each other in the Fusion condition than in the Shared one. The video analysis revealed the different collaboration strategies that the participants adopted in the Fusion condition: in most cases, a leader emerged and gave most of the commands, usually by pointing and talking. In some pairs, the "leader" also placed their joystick in front of their partner, so that they could see and replicate the commands. For the Shared condition, participants mostly played independently. The video annotations revealed that the participants performed more pointing gestures, giggled/laughed more, looked at each other more and talked a lot more in the Fusion condition (See Fig. 5).

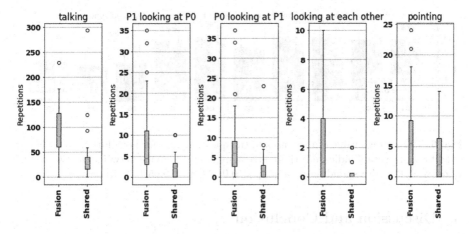

Fig. 5. Comparison of video features between the shared and fusion conditions

However, no correlation could be found between the video analysis (number of cooperative behaviours, amount of talking) and the coordination scores computed in Sect. 5.1.

We conducted a statistical test on the annotated video features (behavioural events) to investigate if there is a difference between the Shared and Fusion conditions. Since the features are independent, we applied the paired t-test for each feature, and found a significant difference – participants talked significantly more (p-value < 0.001), looked at each other more ('P1 looking at P0': p-value < 0.01, 'P0 looking at P1': p-value < 0.005, 'looking at each other': $p < 0.005$), and pointed more ($p < 0.01$) in the Fusion condition (see Fig. 5) compared to the Shared condition. This shows increased communication for this condition.

5.4 Questionnaire Results

All 48 participants responded to the questionnaire, three participants failed to answer one question each, and this question was excluded from the results for them in both conditions. The results reflect that participants enjoyed the Shared condition more and perceived they were better in it, while the Fusion condition was more challenging for them. Despite the fact that participants liked interacting with their peers equally in both conditions, they felt more connected in the Fusion condition and cooperated more. The level of frustration for both tasks is very similar, but the Shared condition was negligibly more confusing to participants. The average value of responses to each question is shown in Fig. 6.

The results were analyzed to find a difference between the two conditions. To test our hypothesis, we conducted the paired t-test, and it showed there are significant in mean Q5 and Q6 ($p < 0.05$) and Q1, Q7, and Q10 ($p < 0.01$) between the Shared and Fusion conditions. The participants answered the questions consistently in both conditions (Cronbachs's α measure: 0.83 with a confidence level of 0.01).

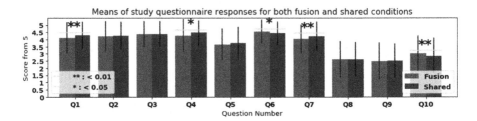

Fig. 6. The average value of responses to the questionnaire for both Fusion and Shared conditions, the stars indicate if there is a significant difference between the two conditions, with the corresponding p value, $p < 0.01$ **; $p < 0.05$ *

6   Discussion and Conclusion

In this paper, we presented a user study where pairs of participants played together through a robot play-mediator. The game involved collaborative navigation and ball handling in two conditions, which explored different types of collaboration: sharing tasks (Shared condition) or simultaneously performing a joint task (Fusion condition). Here, we focused on how both players collaborated with each other, in terms of coordination and communication, using video and joystick data.

Preliminary results confirmed our hypothesis that the Fusion condition promoted communication between the participants better than the Shared condition, probably because the latter condition was more challenging. Questionnaire results indicated that the participants enjoyed the activity more in the Shared condition (RQ2), but cooperated better and felt more connected in the Fusion condition, though they found the Fusion condition more challenging. This does not support our hypothesis that participants might enjoy the Fusion condition better, however, this result could be explained by the increased difficulty of the Fusion condition which also promoted better collaboration (RQ1).

Overall, joystick coordination was quite low, as most participants gave random commands about half of the time, hoping to match their partner's command. Moreover, in the Shared condition, participants did not always respect their assigned tasks. In terms of play dynamics (RQ3), the video analysis revealed that participants communicated more, through speech, gaze and gesture, in the Fusion condition. Moreover, an interaction leader would usually emerge and they would announce commands out loud or place their joystick in front of their partner, so that they could copy the commands.

Due to space constraints, the heart-rate data and some questionnaire items were out of the scope of this paper. In future publications, we will analyze these data and investigate how the conditions promoted engagement.

Acknowledgments. We thank all the participants who willingly participated. This research was undertaken, in part, thanks to funding from the Canada 150 Research Chairs Program.

References

1. Besio, S., Bulgarelli, D., Stancheva-Popkostadinova, V.: Play development in children with disabilties. De Gruyter Open Poland (2017)
2. Calderita, L.V., Manso, L.J., Bustos, P., Suárez-Mejías, C., Fernández, F., Bandera, A.: Therapist: towards an autonomous socially interactive robot for motor and neurorehabilitation therapies for children. JMIR Rehabil. Assistive Technol. 1(1), e3151 (2014)
3. Chandra, S., Dillenbourg, P., Paiva, A.: Classification of children's handwriting errors for the design of an educational co-writer robotic peer. In: Proceedings of the 2017 Conference on Interaction Design and Children, pp. 215–225 (2017)
4. Curioni, A., Voinov, P., Allritz, M., Wolf, T., Call, J., Knoblich, G.: Human adults prefer to cooperate even when it is costly. Proc. R. Soc. B **289**(1973), 20220128 (2022)
5. Davidson, S.: A Multi-dimensional model of enjoyment: development and validation of an enjoyment scale (ENJOY). Embry-Riddle Aeronautical University (2018)
6. Fridin, M.: Storytelling by a kindergarten social assistive robot: a tool for constructive learning in preschool education. Comput. Educ. **70**, 53–64 (2014)
7. Fridin, M., Belokopytov, M.: Robotics agent coacher for CP motor function (RAC CP Fun). Robotica **32**(8), 1265–1279 (2014)
8. Gábana Arellano, D., Tokarchuk, L., Gunes, H.: Measuring affective, physiological and behavioural differences in solo, competitive and collaborative games. In: Poppe, R., Meyer, J.-J., Veltkamp, R., Dastani, M. (eds.) INTETAIN 2016. LNICST, vol. 178, pp. 184–193. Springer, Cham (2017). https://doi.org/10.1007/978-3-319-49616-0_18
9. Goldberg, K., Chen, B.: Collaborative control of robot motion: 000000robustness to error. In: Proceedings 2001 IEEE/RSJ International Conference on Intelligent Robots and Systems. Expanding the Societal Role of Robotics in the Next Millennium (Cat. No. 01CH37180), vol. 2, pp. 655–660. IEEE (2001)
10. Gonzalez-Pacheco, V., Ramey, A., Alonso-Martín, F., Castro-Gonzalez, A., Salichs, M.A.: Maggie: a social robot as a gaming platform. Int. J. Soc. Robot. **3**(4), 371–381 (2011)
11. Guneysu Ozgur, A., et al.: Iterative design of an upper limb rehabilitation game with tangible robots. In: Proceedings of the 2018 ACM/IEEE International Conference on Human-Robot Interaction, pp. 241–250 (2018)
12. Häring, M., Kuchenbrandt, D., André, E.: Would you like to play with me? How robots' group membership and task features influence human-robot interaction. In: 2014 9th ACM/IEEE International Conference on Human-Robot Interaction (HRI), pp. 9–16. IEEE (2014)
13. Kose-Bagci, H., Ferrari, E., Dautenhahn, K., Syrdal, D.S., Nehaniv, C.L.: Effects of embodiment and gestures on social interaction in drumming games with a humanoid robot. Adv. Robot. **23**(14), 1951–1996 (2009)
14. Mahdi, H., Saleh, S., Shariff, O., Dautenhahn, K.: Creating MyJay: a new design for robot-assisted play for children with physical special needs. In: Wagner, A.R., et al. (eds.) ICSR 2020. LNCS (LNAI), vol. 12483, pp. 676–687. Springer, Cham (2020). https://doi.org/10.1007/978-3-030-62056-1_56
15. Muñoz, J.E., Dautenhahn, K.: Robo Ludens: a game design taxonomy for multiplayer games using socially interactive robots. ACM Trans. Hum. Rob. Interact. (THRI) **10**(4), 1–28 (2021)

16. Novak, D., Nagle, A., Keller, U., Riener, R.: Increasing motivation in robot-aided arm rehabilitation with competitive and cooperative gameplay. J. Neuroeng. Rehabil. **11**(1), 1–15 (2014)
17. O'Brien, H.L., Cairns, P., Hall, M.: A practical approach to measuring user engagement with the refined user engagement scale (UES) and new UES short form. Int. J. Hum. Comput. Stud. **112**, 28–39 (2018)
18. Papadopoulos, F., Dautenhahn, K., Ho, W.C.: Exploring the use of robots as social mediators in a remote human-human collaborative communication experiment. Paladyn **3**(1), 1–10 (2012)
19. Sánchez-Martín, J., Cañada-Cañada, F., Dávila-Acedo, M.A.: Just a game? Gamifying a general science class at university: collaborative and competitive work implications. Thinking Skills Creativity **26**, 51–59 (2017)
20. Tasevski, J., Gnjatović, M., Borovac, B.: Assessing the children's receptivity to the robot Marko. Acta Polytechnica Hungarica **15**(5), 47–66 (2018)
21. Vázquez, M., May, A., Steinfeld, A., Chen, W.H.: A deceptive robot referee in a multiplayer gaming environment. In: 2011 International Conference on Collaboration Technologies and Systems (CTS), pp. 204–211. IEEE (2011)
22. Wainer, J., Robins, B., Amirabdollahian, F., Dautenhahn, K.: Using the humanoid robot Kaspar to autonomously play triadic games and facilitate collaborative play among children with autism. IEEE Trans. Auton. Ment. Dev. **6**(3), 183–199 (2014)
23. Wood, K.C., Lathan, C.E., Kaufman, K.R.: Feasibility of gestural feedback treatment for upper extremity movement in children with cerebral palsy. IEEE Trans. Neural Syst. Rehabil. Eng. **21**(2), 300–305 (2012)

Imitating Human Strategy for Social Robot in Real-Time Two-Player Games

Chuanxiong Zheng[1], Hui Wang[1], Lei Zhang[1], Jiangshan Hao[1],
Randy Gomez[2], Keisuke Nakamura[2], and Guangliang Li[1(✉)]

[1] Ocean University of China, Qingdao, China
guangliangli@ouc.edu.cn
[2] Honda Research Institute Japan Co., Ltd., Wako, Japan
{r.gomez,keisuke}@jp.honda-ri.com

Abstract. In this paper, we build upon the latest advances in the field of gaming AI and social robots by developing a social robot Haru to learn and imitate human strategy in a real-time two player game. Results of our two preliminary user studies show that with our proposed framework, Haru is able to learn and imitate human strategies from different human players, and adapt strategies accordingly when the human player changes the game strategy. Moreover, our user study shows the preference of human players to our Haru which can adapt and imitate human strategy during game playing over Haru with fixed strategies. In addition, our results show that the level of fixed strategy seems to have an effect on the acceptance of social robot in game playing and the distraction of human player from playing the game will decrease Haru's performance.

Keywords: Social robot · Imitation learning · Human-robot interaction · Gaming AI

1 Introduction

In recent years, social robots have attracted lots of attention due to advances in artificial intelligence (AI). As social robots become more like companions or partners than just tools, there is a growing need for social robots to interact with people in an entertaining or anthropomorphic way [5]. Games have always played an important and indispensable role in the interaction between social robots and humans.

For example, since games play an important role in children's education in the early learning stages, many researchers have tried to develop social robots capable of playing games with children. Ali et al. [1] allows a social robot to demonstrate creative behaviors in playing Droodle creative games with children to forge their creative thinking. Park et al. [16] explored a novel paradigm to foster a growth mindset in young children by designing a peer-like social robot to play a puzzle solving game with them. However, in most of their work, the social robot's level and strategy in playing the game are fixed, and cannot adapt to or learn from its human partners.

© The Author(s), under exclusive license to Springer Nature Switzerland AG 2022
F. Cavallo et al. (Eds.): ICSR 2022, LNAI 13818, pp. 427–438, 2022.
https://doi.org/10.1007/978-3-031-24670-8_38

On the other hand, as ideal domains, there is a long history of using games as benchmark task domains for studying and testing machine learning algorithms. For example, recent advances in AI over the past few years have shown that powerful algorithms combined with large amounts of data can beat the human world champions in the game of Go [18]. Therefore, in this paper, we build upon the latest advances in the field of gaming AI and social robots by developing a social robot Haru to learn and imitate human strategy in a real-time two-player game. As shown in Fig. 1, with our proposed framework, Haru can learn how to play the game and imitate the human player's strategy during the game playing with him/her via a popular inverse reinforcement learning method—generative adversarial imitation learning (GAIL) [12]. Meanwhile, Haru will interact with the human player by expressing emotions and speech. For example, when Haru scores or loses points, it will make happy or sad expressions and speaks some words to express its emotion.

Fig. 1. A human player plays the Atari game with social robot Haru on the simulation platform.

We conducted two preliminary studies to test our method. In the first study, the first author and four novice human players were recruited to evaluate the ability of Haru to imitate strategies of human players. Our preliminary results show that Haru can imitate different strategies of the same human player and learn strategies from different users. In the second study with 21 participants, our results show the preference of human players to our developed Haru with adaptive game level, in comparison with Haru of fixed game levels. This paper is focused on developing the technology to support our studies for UNICEF's Artificial Intelligence for Children project[1].

2   Related Work

Social robots are progressively moving from labs to human's daily life, e.g., as educational and entertainment partners [8]. Ashktorab et al. [2] investigated

---

[1] https://www.unicef.org/globalinsight/media/2206/file.

human-AI collaboration in a collaborative AI-driven word association game and tested various dimensions of subjective social perceptions (such as rapport, intelligence, creativity and likeability) of participants towards their partners when participants believe they are playing with an AI or with a human. Scassellati et al. [17] studied home-based intervention for increasing social communication skills of children with autism spectrum disorder (ASD) using social robots. Based on a 'learning by playing' concept, Janssen et al. [13] tried to motivate children to learn arithmetic through interaction with social robot. Correia et al. [8] took social robots as entertainment partners and developed a social robotic game player that is able to successfully play a team card game—Sueca. The robot was shown to be able to balance its ability to play the card game with natural and social behaviours towards its partner and its opponents. In a pedagogical setting, Chen et al. [7] proposed a novel active role-switching (ARS) policy which adaptively switchs between tutor/tutee roles and studied how the three different child-agent interaction paradigms (tutee, tutor, and peer agents) impact children's learning and affective engagement. Mohammadi et al. [15] even studied how different personalities of humanoid robot NICO on acceptance within human-robot interaction scenario in a turn-taking jeopardy dice game.

Most of the above research focused on using social robots with fixed level in game playing to study problems in human-robot interaction. We claim that as educational and entertainment partners, human users might expect social robots to improve the performance during game playing with human users. In this paper, we proposed a framework that can facilitate social robot Haru to learn and imitate the human strategies in the game, and studied the preference of human users towards social robot Haru with adaptive game level in comparison with the one with fixed levels.

3   Methodology

In this section, we present the proposed framework allowing a social robot Haru to learn and imitate human strategy in a real-time two-player game via a inverse reinforcement learning method—generative adversarial imitation learning (GAIL) [12]. The proposed framework consists of two modules: a interaction module and a training module, as shown in Fig. 2. In the interaction module, a human player can play games with Haru and interact with it at the same time. The trajectory of game playing by the human player in the interaction module will be delivered to the training module, where the strategy of game playing for Haru will be trained. In the training module, Haru's game strategy is trained using trajectories of game playing by the human player via the imitating method—GAIL algorithm. Then the final trained strategy will be delivered to Haru in the interaction module. Haru will use the new learned strategy to play with the human player. The cycle will be repeated until the human user stops playing.

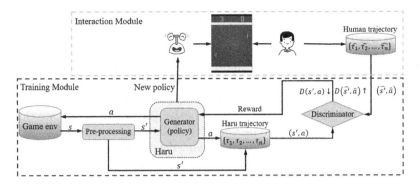

Fig. 2. Illustration of our proposed framework for Haru to learn and imitate human game strategy.

3.1 Interaction Module

In the interaction module, Haru is set to play an Atari game PONG with a human player. This setup can be extended to other games. The human player's trajectories consisting of state-action pairs in game playing will be stored and transferred to the training module by the end of each round. If new policy is transferred from the training module, Haru will update the policy with the new one to play with the human player. In other cases, Haru will keep the current policy and continue playing the game with the human player.

Previous research shows that slight changes in a robot's expression can influence how people perceive and interact with the robot [10]. Moreover, robots with rich expressions and interesting language are considered to be more human-like and more interesting than robots with fewer facial expressions, and are also more likely to attract human's attention [3,6]. Therefore, in the interaction module, Haru is allowed to interact with human player during the game playing with simple expressions and speech to maximize human player's engagement. For example, when Haru scores or loses points, it will make happy or sad expressions and speak some words to express its emotions.

3.2 Training Module

When the training module receives the trajectories of game playing by the human player from the interaction module, a policy will be trained for Haru to learn to imitate the human strategy of game playing with the GAIL algorithm [12]. To ensure that Haru has the same state and action space as the human player, the location coordinates of the game characters will be extracted to represent the state for both Haru and human player in pre-process.

Specifically, as shown in Fig. 2, in the training module, Haru will use a generator (i.e., policy) to interact with the game environment and obtain Haru trajectories consisting of state-action pairs. The obtained Haru trajectories and received human trajectory from the interaction module will be used to train a discriminator $D(s, a)$. The discriminator $D(s, a)$ will provide rewards to update the generator of Haru. A new updated policy will be used by Haru to interact with the game environment and then the discriminator $D(s, a)$ will be further updated. This cycle will be repeated until the discriminator $D(s, a)$ cannot discriminate state-action pairs in the Haru trajectory from those in the Human trajectory. By the end of training, a policy imitating the human strategy of game playing will be obtained. The new trained policy will be delivered to the interaction module for Haru to play with the human player. In another round of training, Haru will use the last trained policy to interact with game environment, instead of training from scratch. New delivered human trajectory will be used to train Haru to obtain a new policy imitating the strategy of the human user.

4   Experiments

4.1   Experimental Platform

We used the social robot Haru [11,21] as the experimental platform in our studies. Haru consists of two large square eyes and a body base. Each eye uses a TFT screen display with a size of 3 in., while the inner eye (the eye goggles) has a rectangular border consisting of an addressable LED strip. Inside the body, there is a matrix of addressable LEDs (the mouth). The robot is also equipped with built-in stereo speakers for vocalization. The LED matrix (the mouth) at the base of Haru's body, in conjunction with the LED matrix of the eyes, is capable of a range of emotional expressions (see Fig. 3(a)).

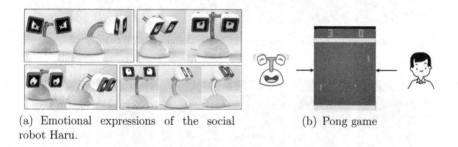

(a) Emotional expressions of the social robot Haru.

(b) Pong game

Fig. 3. (a) Examples of emotional expressions by Haru. (b) Screenshot of the Pong game, the numbers on the top of the game screen are scores of two players.

4.2   Game Task

In our study, we chose the Pong game from Atari games that is widely used as bench-marking tasks in deep reinforcement learning research [14]. In addition, the PettingZoo [19] framework was implemented to integrate with the game Pong to enable a human player to play together with Haru. In the game, Haru and the human player each control a racket to hit the ball (Haru with the left orange one, the human player with the right green one). Each player will move the racket up and down to hit the ball. If the ball crosses the opponent's racket, the player will score +1 and the opponent gets −1 point. The scores for both players are displayed on the player's own side of top part in the game screen. The player who gets 21 points first will win the game round (see Fig. 3(b)).

4.3   Experiment Setup

Study One. To verify whether Haru can successfully learn and imitate human strategy in game playing, we recruited five subjects to play with Haru. First, the first author tried to play with Haru using two different game strategies:

- Strategy 1: The human player controls the racket to move up and down while following the ball's movement, and tries to return to a fixed position each time she serves the ball (see Fig. 4(a)).
- Strategy 2: The human player does not move the racket with the ball until she judges the ball is approaching her side and decide to serve the ball, and the position of the racket will not return to the initial position but keeps at the point she serves the ball (see Fig. 4(b)).

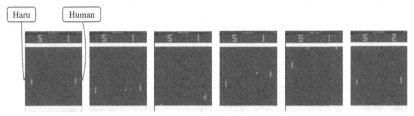

(a) Screenshots of the human player plays the game with Strategy 1

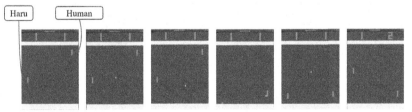

(b) Screenshots of the human player plays the game with Strategy 2

Fig. 4. Screenshots of the human player plays the game with the two strategies. Haru controls the left racket (orange one) and the human player controls the right racket (green one) to catch the ball (white) served by the opponent. (Color figure online)

In the study, the first author played with Haru for a total of five rounds, using Strategy 1 in the first and second round and Strategy 2 in the third and fourth round. Haru's performance will be evaluated and observed in the third and fifth round. Then four other subjects who are not familiar with the system and the Pong game were recruited to play a total of five game rounds with Haru. All four players were briefly informed of the game rules before playing. The first three players (P1, P2 and P3) played the game with Haru without distraction, while the fourth player (P4) was distracted by conversing with the author during game playing. The fourth player's distractions led to lapses in game behavior, and we will investigate the effect on Haru's learning performance when the player lapses in the game.

Study Two. In the second user study, we investigate the preference of human users towards social robot Haru with adaptive game level in comparison with the one with fixed levels. 21 participants (11 male, 10 female) ranging from 23 to 28 years old were recruited. All participants are students in the campus and have some experience in robotics. Three conditions were set in our within-subject study:

- Condition 1: Haru with adaptive game strategy by learning and imitating the human strategy
- Condition 2: Haru with a fixed strategy in the game well above the average human game
- Condition 3: Haru with a fixed strategy in the game well below the average human game.

The 21 participants was briefly introduced the rules of the game and then each participant played the game with Haru in all three conditions. The order in which each participant played with Haru in the three conditions was randomly assigned. In condition 2 and 3, participants were required to play the game for two game rounds and could choose whether to continue playing for up to three rounds. In Condition 1, participants were required to play for three game rounds and could choose whether to continue playing for a maximum of four rounds.

All participants filled out a questionnaire at the end of game playing in each condition, and the purpose of the study was revealed at the end of the experiment. We used the Godspeed [4] questionnaire to assess the concepts of anthropomorphism, animacy, likability, and perceived intelligence on Haru in the three conditions. In addition, a second questionnaire was created to test the playing experience and satisfaction of human players with Haru's game level in the three conditions. Four semantic variables were included in the playing experience part: fun, exciting, enjoyable, and likeable. Three semantic variables were included in the satisfaction of Haru's game level: appropriate, satisfying, and friendly. Finally, we set two questions to investigate whether participants perceived a change in Haru's game strategy during playing and whether they would like to continue playing the game if they were allowed to do so. All questions in the questionnaires were in 5-point scales.

5   Results and Discussion

5.1   Study One

Figure 5 shows the imitated strategies of Haru in game playing with the first author in Study One. Figure 5(a) shows Haru's strategy in the third game round

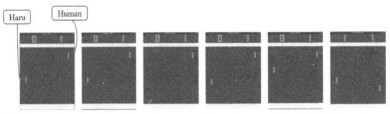

(a) Screenshots of Haru learned strategy from human player's Strategy 1

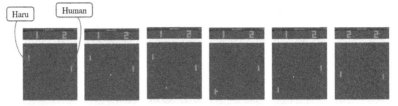

(b) Screenshots of Haru learned strategy from human player's Strategy 2

Fig. 5. The imitated strategies of Haru from human player's Strategy 1 (a) and Strategy 2 (b).

learned from human Strategy 1 in Fig. 4 (a). As we can see, Haru successfully learned the Strategy 1 of human player by controlling its racket to follow the ball whenever the ball moves up or down and return to a fixed initial position after serving the ball. Figure 5(b) shows Haru's strategy in the fifth game round learned from human Strategy 2 in Fig. 4 (b). As we can see, Haru also successfully imitated the Strategy 2 of human player by not moving the racket to follow the ball's movement until serving the ball and not returning to a fixed initial position after serving.

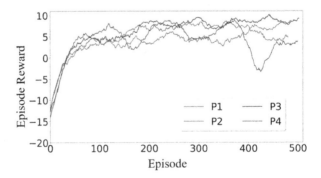

Fig. 6. Learning curves of Haru playing with the four participants in Study One.

We also evaluated the performance of Haru learning from playing with other four human players in Study One. Haru's learning curves were plotted in terms of obtained accumulated environmental rewards in the game, as shown in Fig. 6. As we can see from Fig. 6, Haru can learn and imitate game strategies from different human players (P1, P2 and P3). When the human player was distracted (P4), Haru's performance was getting worse.

In summary, our results in Study One show that with our framework, Haru can learn to imitate game strategies of human players and the distraction of human player from playing the game will decrease Haru's performance since Haru is trying to imitate the human player's game strategy in real-time.

5.2 Study Two

Table 1 shows the reported results from the two questionnaires in Study Two. Welch's t-test was used to evaluate the level of significance in the differences between Condition 1 with Haru of adaptive game strategy, Condition 2 with Haru of fixed high-level strategy and Condition 3 with Haru of fixed low-level strategy. As we can see from Table 1, human players showed preference to our Haru with adaptive game strategy in Condition 1 over the one with fixed high-level strategy in Condition 2 (likability, $p = 0.01$), while both Harus are perceived to be similar in terms of anthropomorphism, animacy and perceived intelligence. In contrast, Haru with adaptive game strategy in Condition 1 was shown to be significantly different from Haru of fixed low-level strategy in Condition 3 in all four aspects ($p < 0.01$): anthropomorphism, animacy, likability and perceived intelligence.

Table 1. Mean scores and standard deviations of questions in the two questionnaires in the three conditions. p_1 is the p-value of Condition 1 vs. Condition 2, and p_2 is the p-value of Condition 1 vs. Condition 3. Note that, Ant - anthropomorphism, Ani - animacy, Lik - likability, Int - intelligence, GES - game experience satisfaction, GLS - game level satisfaction. Significance level: $p < 0.05$.

Scale	Condition 1	Condition 2	Condition 3	p_1	p_2
Ant	3.95 ± 0.72	3.81 ± 0.53	2.97 ± 0.99	0.49	$p<0.01$
Ani	4.13 ± 0.59	3.91 ± 0.54	2.82 ± 0.91	0.12	$p<0.01$
Lik	4.31 ± 0.61	4.00 ± 0.66	3.55 ± 1.03	0.01	$p<0.01$
Int	3.94 ± 0.53	3.83 ± 0.53	2.71 ± 0.82	0.46	$p<0.01$
GES	4.26 ± 0.74	3.44 ± 0.96	3.13 ± 1.06	$p<0.01$	$p<0.01$
GLS	4.27 ± 0.61	3.48 ± 1.19	2.94 ± 0.97	$p<0.01$	$p<0.01$

We also reported the results from the filled second questionnaire we created to evaluate the playing experience and satisfaction of human players with Haru's game level in the three conditions in Table 1. We first used Cronbach's α [9] to check the internal consistency or reliability of composite rating scales in our second questionnaire, and the collected data is considered to be reliable when $\alpha > 0.6$ [20]. The α for data collected of questions in terms of playing experience are 0.80, 0.87 and 0.89, and 0.68, 0.92 and 0.80 in terms of satisfaction with the game level of Haru, in the three conditions respectively. This indicated that the collected data of our created questionnaire is reliable and of high-quality. The Welch's t-test showed that scores of playing experience and satisfaction with

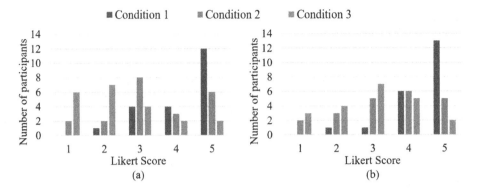

Fig. 7. (a) Distribution of participants' scores on perceiving changes in Haru's playing strategy in the three conditions. (b) Distribution of participants' scores on willingness to continue playing in the three conditions. Note that, Condition 1: Haru with adaptive strategy; Condition 2: Haru with fixed high-level strategy; Condition 3: Haru with fixed low-level strategy.

Haru of adaptive strategy in Condition 1 are significantly higher than those with Haru of fixed strategies (high and low).

Figure 7 shows the distribution of scores from participants to indicate whether they perceived a change in Haru's game strategy during the game (a) and whether they were willing to continue playing the game if they were allowed to do so (b). From Fig. 7 we can see that 12 participants observed the strategy changes of Haru in Condition 1 and 6 participants observed the strategy changes of Haru in Condition 2 (fixed high-level), while only 2 participants observed the changes in Condition 3 (fixed low-level). In addition, 13 participants were willing to continue playing with the adaptive strategy Haru, and only 5 participants were willing to continue playing the game when playing with the fixed high level Haru, while only 2 participants were willing to continue playing with the low level Haru.

Finally, we counted the number of game rounds played by participants in the three conditions. We found that, in Condition 1, 13 participants completed all four rounds of game playing, 5 players quit during the fourth round, and only 3 players quit during the third round. In contrast, in Condition 2 with fixed high-level strategy, only 5 participants completed all three rounds of game playing, 8 players dropped out during the third round, and 8 players dropped out during the second round, while in Condition 3 with fixed low-level strategy, only 2 participants completed all three rounds, 7 players dropped out during the third round, and 12 players dropped out during the second round.

In summary, our results in Study Two show the preference of human players to our Haru which can adapt and imitate human strategy during game playing over the one with fixed strategies. In addition, the level of fixed strategy seems to have an effect on the acceptance of social robot in game playing.

6   Conclusion

In this paper, we developed a social robot Haru which can learn and imitate human strategy in a real-time two-player game. Our results of our two user studies show that Haru can learn and imitate human strategies from different human players, and adapt strategies accordingly when the human player changes the game strategy. Our further results show the preference of human players to our Haru which can adapt and imitate human strategy during game playing over the one with fixed strategies. Finally, the level of fixed strategy seems to have an effect on the acceptance of social robot in game playing. Currently, we have finished developing an autonomous system that can play with humans. In the future, we will be deploying the robot in the field and perform user studies on the effectiveness of the system with children players.

References

1. Ali, S., Moroso, T., Breazeal, C.: Can children learn creativity from a social robot? In: Proceedings of the 2019 on Creativity and Cognition, pp. 359–368 (2019)
2. Ashktorab, Z., et al.: Human-AI collaboration in a cooperative game setting: measuring social perception and outcomes. Proc. ACM Hum. Comput. Interact. 4(CSCW2), 1–20 (2020)
3. Bartneck, C., Kanda, T., Mubin, O., Al Mahmud, A.: Does the design of a robot influence its animacy and perceived intelligence? Int. J. Soc. Robot. 1(2), 195–204 (2009)
4. Bartneck, C., Kulić, D., Croft, E., Zoghbi, S.: Measurement instruments for the anthropomorphism, animacy, likeability, perceived intelligence, and perceived safety of robots. Int. J. Soc. Robot. 1(1), 71–81 (2009)
5. Breazeal, C.: Toward sociable robots. Robot. Auton. Syst. 42(3–4), 167–175 (2003)
6. Bruce, A., Nourbakhsh, I., Simmons, R.: The role of expressiveness and attention in human-robot interaction. In: Proceedings 2002 IEEE International Conference on Robotics and Automation (Cat. No. 02CH37292), vol. 4, pp. 4138–4142. IEEE (2002)
7. Chen, H., Park, H.W., Breazeal, C.: Teaching and learning with children: impact of reciprocal peer learning with a social robot on children's learning and emotive engagement. Comput. Educ. 150, 103836 (2020)
8. Correia, F., Alves-Oliveira, P., Ribeiro, T., Melo, F.S., Paiva, A.: A social robot as a card game player. In: Proceedings of the 13th AAAI Conference on Artificial Intelligence and Interactive Digital Entertainment (AIIDE) (2017)
9. Cronbach, L.J.: Coefficient alpha and the internal structure of tests. Psychometrika 16(3), 297–334 (1951)
10. Gockley, R., Forlizzi, J., Simmons, R.: Interactions with a moody robot. In: Proceedings of the 1st ACM SIGCHI/SIGART Conference on Human-Robot Interaction (HRI), pp. 186–193 (2006)
11. Gomez, R., Szapiro, D., Galindo, K., Nakamura, K.: Haru: hardware design of an experimental tabletop robot assistant. In: Proceedings of the 2018 ACM/IEEE International Conference on Human-Robot Interaction (HRI), pp. 233–240. IEEE (2018)

12. Ho, J., Ermon, S.: Generative adversarial imitation learning. Adv. Neural Inf. Process. Syst. **29** (2016)
13. Janssen, J.B., van der Wal, C.C., Neerincx, M.A., Looije, R.: Motivating children to learn arithmetic with an adaptive robot game. In: Mutlu, B., Bartneck, C., Ham, J., Evers, V., Kanda, T. (eds.) ICSR 2011. LNCS (LNAI), vol. 7072, pp. 153–162. Springer, Heidelberg (2011). https://doi.org/10.1007/978-3-642-25504-5_16
14. Mnih, V., et al.: Playing Atari with deep reinforcement learning. ArXiv Preprint ArXiv:1312.5602 (2013)
15. Mohammadi, H.B., et al.: Designing a personality-driven robot for a human-robot interaction scenario. In: Proceedings of the 2019 International Conference on Robotics and Automation (ICRA), pp. 4317–4324. IEEE (2019)
16. Park, H.W., Rosenberg-Kima, R., Rosenberg, M., Gordon, G., Breazeal, C.: Growing growth mindset with a social robot peer. In: Proceedings of the 2017 ACM/IEEE International Conference on Human-Robot Interaction (HRI), pp. 137–145 (2017)
17. Scassellati, B., et al.: Improving social skills in children with ASD using a long-term, in-home social robot. Sci. Rob. **3**(21), eaat7544 (2018)
18. Silver, D., et al.: Mastering the game of go with deep neural networks and tree search. Nature **529**(7587), 484–489 (2016)
19. Terry, J., et al.: PettingZoo: gym for multi-agent reinforcement learning. Adv. Neural. Inf. Process. Syst. **34**, 15032–15043 (2021)
20. Tinakon, W., Nahathai, W.: A comparison of reliability and construct validity between the original and revised versions of the Rosenberg self-esteem scale. Psychiatry Investig. **9**(1), 54 (2012)
21. Vasylkiv, Y., et al.: Shaping affective robot Haru's reactive response. In: Proceedings of the 2021 30th IEEE International Conference on Robot & Human Interactive Communication (RO-MAN), pp. 989–996. IEEE (2021)

Personalized Storytelling with Social Robot Haru

Hui Wang[1] , Lei Zhang[1] , Chuanxiong Zheng[1] , Randy Gomez[2] ,
Keisuke Nakamura[2] , and Guangliang Li[1(✉)]

[1] Ocean University of China, Qingdao, China
guangliangli@ouc.edu.cn
[2] Honda Research Institute Japan Co., Ltd., Wako, Japan
{r.gomez,keisuke}@jp.honda-ri.com

Abstract. In previous studies of applying storytelling to robotics, the emotions and actions of robots are usually pre-determined, resulting in a homogeneous storytelling style for the robot. In this paper, we propose an empathic and adaptive framework for robot's storytelling that facilitates social robot Haru to learn from human teachers. In this framework, the robot Haru performs empathic storytelling based on the human teacher's voice, and then changes its narrative styles (e.g., featured by pitch, emotion, action, etc.) to capture the listener's attention. The whole experiment was conducted on social robot Haru. Haru's communicative modality involves face and body movements, sound voice and non-verbal sound, which have great potentials for storytelling. The affective robot for storytelling was compared to a neural one and human teachers. Preliminary results show the social robot for storytelling can make use of human teachers as integral to the design of the system and provide a personalized storytelling experience. Moreover, participants had positive attitudes toward storytelling by an affective robot compared to a neutral one.

Keywords: Storytelling · Social robot · Empathy · Human-robot interaction

1 Introduction

Over the past decades, media digitization has advanced the ways of storytelling, such as movies, television series, and computer games, which demonstrates the general increasing interest of human in stories [16]. Storytelling for children plays an important role in early education stages. Oral storytelling has been found to facilitate self-expression, empathic understanding and two-way communication, supporting children's speaking and listening practice.

Social robots, as autonomous or semi-autonomous robots that can interact and communicate with humans by following social norms, are engaging, encouraging imagination and innovation, and potentially increasing literacy and creativity, especially for children [5]. Moreover, social robots can bring a different experience to users through nonverbal and emotional capabilities [18]. Research on applying oral storytelling to social robotics in educational settings has attracted lots of interest [10]. For example, Striepe took the initiative to create a robot storyteller [18]. Compared with traditional media (such as books or audiobooks), social robots can narrate stories in a better way using their physical presence as well as multimodal interactive behavior. Meanwhile, robot's storytelling can bring a different experience using methods beyond human capabilities, such as adjusting the lighting etc. [16].

Social robots can adjust their styles of storytelling (e.g., gesture, voice tone, volume, etc.) during the task. Elliott et al. [7] showed that emotions are important for perceiving narratives by robot's storytelling. In past studies on robot's storytelling, the robot's emotions and actions are usually predetermined [6], resulting in relatively homogeneous style in storytelling. Zabala et al. tried to adapt the robot's personality featured via body language according to the sentiment of its speech [24]. In this paper, we explore the way to personalize the robot's storytelling by mimicking a storyteller. In this case, the storytelling by social robots can be natural, believable and realistic, maximizing the positive impact of robots on users and increasing their engagement.

Fig. 1. Haru imitates the storytelling style of a human teacher. (Image courtesy of HRI-JP/European Commission, JRC; artwork by Deborah Szapiro).

Specifically, we present a framework in which a social robot can adapt its style of storytelling (e.g., featured by gesture, emotion, and associated voice parameter settings) to achieve meaningful, sustained human-robot interaction by mimicking the storytelling style of a human teacher, as shown in Fig. 1. The whole experiment was performed on the social robot Haru, whose multimodal expressiveness brings the potential for human-robot emotional interaction and provides excellent technical support for Haru's storytelling. This paper is focused on developing the technology to support our studies for UNICEF's Artificial Intelligence for Children project[1].

The rest of this paper is organized as follows. We present the related work in Sect. 2 and in Sect. 3 we present the robotic platform and methodology. In Sect. 4, we describe the experimental conditions and setup, followed by results and discussion in Sect. 5. Finally, we conclude the paper in Sect. 6.

2   Related Work

When humans interact with robots, they tend to anthropomorphize them and treat them in the same way as they treat other humans [8]. Humanoid robots can potentially play the roles of human partners for learning and interaction. To achieve socially engaging interactions with humans, robots are expected to learn and produce human-like attributes [4]. Thus, storytelling in a personalized and engaging way is very important for robots. For example, Hubbard et al. [11] showed that a key aspect of a successful storytelling process is the degree to which the recipient feels integrated into the story. Good storytelling experience can improve the robot's receptivity. Using a robot and gendered voice as a medium for storytelling, Steinhaeusser et al. investigated the robot's perceived anthropomorphism and the influence of its voice (female, male, or neutral) on recipients' attitude towards the robotic storyteller concerning gender and cross-gender effects [17]. Costa et al. [6] explored the importance of facial expressions and vocal rhythm on the robot's storytelling. Their results show that effective facial expressions and voice settings lead to a good storytelling experience for users. Furthermore, facial expressions and vocal rhythms are important for creating interesting and effective storytellers, both in virtual and on real robot. Xu et al. [23] showed that appropriate emotional body language can improve the experience of robot's storytelling, and that the robot's physical expression increased the robot's credibility, reliability, and realism.

Recently, interests in designing a real-time adaptive emotional storytelling agent have increased. In the study of [24], the robot could adjust its body language, speech rhythm, gestures, and emotional cues based on extracted textual emotions, which in a way helps to adapt the robot's personality to the user. Striepe and Lugrin showed that the emotional robot is able to transport the user into the story equally well as the traditional audio book [18]. However, in their study, the emotions were pre-set and did not adjust to the responses of the human teacher or the audience. Park [14] used an affective reinforcement learning method to train a robot to select appropriate stories for children based on engagement and language skills, thus positively impacting students' academic performance. Gomez et al. maximized the specific communication capabilities of the robot Haru by leveraging Haru's various expressive capabilities to achieve meaningful human-robot interaction and maximum user acceptance during storytelling [10]. In addition, some studies also attempted to increase audience's

---

[1] https://www.unicef.org/globalinsight/media/2206/file.

engagement by changing the story content. For example, Azuar et al. [2] developed a storytelling program with emotion recognition, and the robot can modify the evolution of the story according to the audience's emotions. In Nichols's work [12,13], participants can create a unique story with an intelligent agent and they emphasized the importance of robot conveying the emotional content of stories.

Previous work mostly focused on regulating the emotion of robot based on the content of stories. However, the sentiment of text in the story is not obvious in many cases. Meanwhile, most of the existing used sentiment analyzers such as Flair, VADER and TextBlob did not consider the context in the story and only analyze the polarity of individual word. In this paper, we propose a framework to facilitate social robots to imitate the narrative of a human teacher for storytelling and adjust its style of storytelling according to the human teacher's emotions, making use of human teachers as integral to the design of the system and providing a personalized storytelling experience.

3   Robotic Platform and Methodology

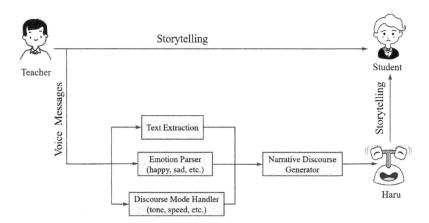

Fig. 2. The diagram that illustrates the mechanism of imitating the storyteller (teacher) by Haru.

Our goal is to develop a real-time adaptive emotional storytelling agent capable of building positive social relationships with users. The proposed framework is shown in Fig. 2. Imagine that a human teacher would like to tell stories to a number of students remotely. As a telepresent robot, Haru will tell stories to students physically. During storytelling, Haru can change its narratives (e.g., pitch, mood, etc.) to mirror the storyteller's style of telling the story to capture the listener's attention. Our approach focuses more on empathic storytelling using the storyteller's voice feedback.

"Anger"   "Curiosity"   "Shyness"   "Relaxed"   "Cool"   "Boredom"

Fig. 3. Examples of a few Haru's emotions expressed through the animated emotive routines.

3.1 Robotic Platform

Haru is a platform designed to support the study of social presence and emotion and empathetic engagement for long-term human-robot interaction in different contexts [21]. Haru has a series of "expressive routines" that are designed and curated by animators (as shown in Fig. 3). These routine files cover an open-loop combinations of movement, voice, eyes, mouth, etc. The multimodal combination can be used to express various subtle emotions, thus maximizing empathy [9]. All of these bring potentials for affective engagement during human-robot interaction and provide excellent technical support for Haru's storytelling.

3.2 Methodology

Our proposed framework consists of five modules: emotion detector, text extraction, emotion parser, discourse mode handler and narrative discourse generator. During storytelling, firstly, the text extraction module will record the audio of the human teacher (storyteller) and convert it into text. Then, the emotion detector module will analyse and detect the sentiment of human teacher from the recording, which will be used by Haru to mimic the emotions of the human teacher in the emotion parser module during storytelling. Meanwhile, the discourse mode handler module will modify Haru's voice and intonation according to the human teacher's style of storytelling to add emphasis to the speech using the sentiment detected via the emotion detector module. Finally, the narrative discourse generator module will integrate and synchronize the outputs of the text extraction module, emotion parser module and discourse mode handler module, to generate personalized storytelling for Haru based on the speech of human storyteller.

Emotion Detector. In the proposed framework, Haru's emotion is determined by the human teacher's sentiment extracted from the speech. The emotion detector module uses the librosa toolkit to extract features in human teacher's speech to represent the style of storytelling, including rhythmic features (pitch and tuning, intensity), voice quality features (spectral energy distribution), spectral features (Mel-frequency cepstral coefficients (MFCC)) etc. These features are widely used in speech recognition tasks [19]. A convolutional neural network (CNN) was used as speech emotion recognition model [15]. The ESD dataset was used for model training [25]. ESD is a multi-speaker emotional speech dataset that can be used for various speech synthesis and speech conversion tasks. We used a total of 17498 utterances from 10 English speakers (5 males and 5 females) in the dataset with 5 categories of labels (angry, happy, neutral, sad, and surprise). The average utterance duration is 2.76 s. The ratio of training set to test set was 4:1. The Adam optimizer was used to train the model for 30 epochs with a batch size of 256.

Text Extraction. In the text extraction module, the Pyaudio library is used to record the audio of the human teacher with a microphone. Then, a speech recognition model [22] is used to convert the real-time audio of the human teacher into text.

Emotion Parser. In the emotion parser module, Haru will mimic the sentiments of the human teacher during storytelling based on the detected emotions represented by a series of features in the emotion detector module. Haru can express different types of emotions using LCE screen eyes and the LED mouth, neck and eye movements, and a rotating base. These movements and expressions are synchronized with the voice stream, which can be complementary to the story content. This is expected to add interest to human user and support long-term human-robot communication.

Discourse Mode Handler. During storytelling, in the discourse model handler module, Haru's voice and intonation will be modified according to the detected human teacher's style of storytelling represented by a series of features in the emotion detector module, to add emphasis to the speech. In addition, the pitch is also modified according to emotions, as Bänziger [3] indicated that the speed and pitch of speech should be higher when expressing anger, happiness or fear than when expressing sadness or fear. Therefore, we allowed Haru to adjust speech parameters including emphasis, pitch, speed, volume, and emotion during storytelling to imitate the style of human teacher.

Narrative Discourse Generator. The narrative discourse generator module is mainly used to integrate and synchronize the outputs from the above "text extraction", "emotion parser" and "discourse mode handler" modules. In this way, Haru can adjust its emotional behavior according to the sentiments in the speech of human storyteller extracted by the emotion detector, and generate seamless and fluent storytelling narratives.

4 Experiment

Our goal is to allow Haru mimic a human teacher by altering her narratives to reflect the storyteller's style of storytelling, thereby optimizing the interactive service and capturing the audience's attention. To this end, we conducted a preliminary study to test the ability of Haru imitating the way of telling stories by a human teacher.

4.1   Experimental Conditions

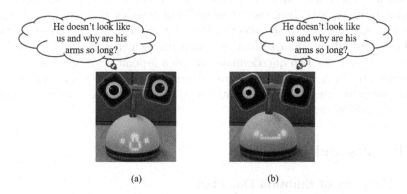

Fig. 4. (a) The affective robot Haru used in Condition 1 of our experiment (b) The neutral robot Haru used in Condition 2 of our experiment.

In our experiment, as shown in Fig. 4, we tested two conditions:

- Condition 1: An affective robot Haru developed with our proposed framework was used to mirror the human teacher's style of storytelling and change its narratives (e.g., pitch, mood, etc.) with emotional displays, nonverbal behaviors, and lip synchronization.
- Condition 2: A neural robot was used to tell stories with only lip synchronization, without displaying any emotional or nonverbal behaviors.

4.2   Experimental Setup

To avoid the effect of well-known stories on the experimental results due to the familiarity of different users, we chose the story "The Orangutan and the Chimpanzees" [20] (about 350 words) in our experiment. The story focuses on a chimpanzee family that adopts a orangutan. When the orangutan grows up, he decides to run away from home because he feels that he looks different from his brothers and sisters. However, when his family gets into trouble, only the orangutan can help them. The whole story is told from a third person's perspective and has a variety of shifts between emotions, which is a potentially ideal material for human teachers to show emotions for storytelling.

Due to COVID19, we only recruited 20 subjects in our study. 10 subjects were randomly selected and assigned the role of "teacher" for performing experiment with the affective Haru in the first condition. Another 10 subjects were assigned the role of "students" as listeners for performing experiments in both conditions. The "teacher" was informed of the story 20 min in advance in order to get familiar with the text in the story. After both the "teachers" and "students" finished experiments in the first condition, the "students" were asked to fill out a questionnaire which include 12 closed questions to evaluate the affective Haru's overall performance and compare the differences between affective Haru's storytelling and the human teacher's style, e.g., the experience of listening to the story. Then, the "students" will evaluate the neural Haru's performance and compare to the affective Haru after finishing experiments in both conditions by filling out a second questionnaire, which contains 10 questions. The questions in the two questionnaire are on a 5-point scale, and are from the questionnaires in [1,13,18], e.g., expressiveness, intelligence level, completeness of the narrative content (content integrity), etc. The whole experiment lasted approximately 25 min.

5   Results and Discussion

5.1   Accuracy of Emotion Detection

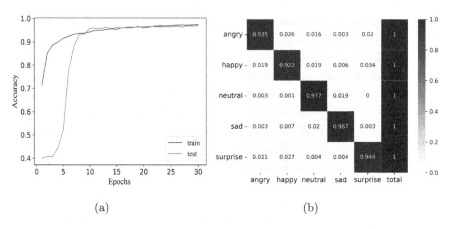

(a)   (b)

Fig. 5. Accuracy of emotion prediction on the training and test dataset during the training process (a) and the final prediction accuracy of five emotions shown in the confusion matrices (b).

Figure 5(a) shows the accuracy of emotion prediction during the training process in the emotion detector module of our framework. After 30 epochs' training, the prediction accuracy on both the training and test sets converges to a similar level and stabilizes at about 0.95. To further analyze the accuracy and misclassification of the emotion prediction model, we plotted the confusion matrix of the emotional prediction model (as shown in Fig. 5(b)). From Fig. 5(b) we can see that, the accuracy of recognizing "neutral" and "sad" can be above 0.95, while the accuracy of predicting "angry", "happy" and "surprise" is also greater than 0.9. The misclassification for all five emotions is very low.

Table 1. Average scores of four questions in the questionnaires evaluating both affective and neutral Haru, and significance levels of the difference between the two robots in the two conditions by performing a Student's t-test. Note that the means were averaged over data collected from 10 participants. Significance level: $p < 0.05$

	Question	Condition 1	Condition 2	T-Test
Q1	During storytelling, Do you feel a change in Haru's mood, tone of voice and expression?	4.70 ± 0.46	2.60 ± 1.56	$t = 3.87$, p <0.01
Q2	Do you think Haru's changing emotions have a positive impact on storytelling?	4.60 ± 0.66	2.50 ± 1.43	$t = 3.99$, p <0.01
Q3	Is there a big difference in the effectiveness of Haru's storytelling compared to human teachers?	1.90 ± 0.70	4.20 ± 0.75	$t = -6.73$, p <0.01
Q4	Is there a big difference in Haru's storytelling ability compared to human teachers?	1.90 ± 0.70	4.10 ± 0.70	$t = -6.67$, p <0.01

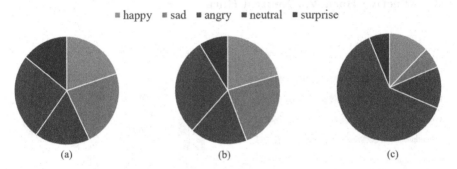

■ happy   ■ sad   ■ angry   ■ neutral   ■ surprise

(a)   (b)   (c)

Fig. 6. Distribution of emotions perceived by students during storytelling by affective Haru (a), human teacher (b), and neutral Haru (c). Note that each plot was averaged over data collected from 10 participants.

5.2 Affective and Neutral Haru Vs. Human Teacher

First, we compared the perceived storytelling experience by students in the two tested conditions to human teachers. Table 1 show the average scores of four questions in the questionnaires evaluating both affective and neutral Harus. In addition, a student t-test was performed to compare the affective and neutral Haru in the two conditions in terms of the scores of the four questions in Table 1. From Table 1 we can see that, students can perceive that the affective Haru had obvious emotion, tone and expression changes during storytelling, which improves the listener's sense of immersion and has a positive effect on storytelling (Q1 and Q2). In contrast, the neutral Haru in the second condition was reported to have unobvious emotional changes and ineffective storytelling. These differences between affective Haru and neutral Haru are significant ($p < 0.01$). More importantly, the effectiveness and ability of storytelling by the affective Haru was reported to be similar to human teachers, while those by the neutral Haru had big differences from human teachers (Q3 and Q4). These differences between affective Haru and neutral Haru are also tested to be significant ($p < 0.01$).

Figure 6 shows the distribution of emotions felt by students during storytelling of affective Haru, human teachers and neutral Haru respectively. As can be seen from Fig. 6, in the first condition, the emotions perceived by the students during affective Haru's storytelling were similar to those of the human teacher's storytelling. This indicates that in most cases, our affective Haru can imitate the human teacher's emotions for storytelling, with occasional errors caused by emotion recognition errors. In contrast, in the second condition, since the neutral Haru only has the function of lip synchronization without the change of emotions, the perceived emotions by students were mostly neutral, with occasional emotional changes. We speculate that this might be because that the students misjudged an emotional change when hearing some interrogative sentences or some intonation words (e.g., Hum, Wow).

5.3   Affective Haru Vs. Neutral Haru

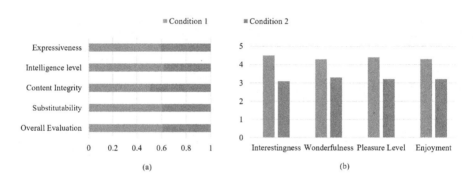

(a)   (b)

Fig. 7. Normalized average scores of performance (a) and average scores of experience (b) in storytelling for affective Haru in Condition 1 and neutral Haru in Condition 2. Note that each plot was averaged over data collected from 10 participants in each condition.

Table 2. Comparisons of performance and experience of storytelling between the affective and neutral robots in both conditions by performing t-test with data collected from filled questionnaires.

Storytelling performance		Storytelling experience	
Expressive	t = 3.87, p <0.01	Interestingness	t = 3.18, p <0.01
Intelligence Level	t = 3.99, p = 0.01	Wonderfulness	t = 2.23, p = 0.04
Content integrity	t = −0.29, p = 0.77	Pleasure level	t = 2.85, p = 0.01
Substitutability	t = 2.95, p <0.01	Enjoyment	t = 2.24, p = 0.04
Overall evaluation	t = 4.15, p <0.01		

We also compared the affective Haru and neutral Haru in terms of the performance and experience of storytelling felt by students. The performance of both Harus' storytelling was evaluated from five aspects: expressiveness, intelligence level, completeness of the narrative content (content integrity), whether it can replace human teachers in storytelling (substitutability), and overall evaluation. For comparison purposes, we have normalised the data as shown in Fig. 7 (a). The experience of storytelling by both affective and neutral Harus was evaluated from four perspectives: interestingness, wonderfulness, pleasure level and enjoyment, as shown in Fig. 7 (b). Table 2 shows the level of significance in terms of difference between the two robots in both conditions by performing t-test with data collected from filled questionnaires. From Fig. 7(a) we can see that both affective Haru and neutral Haru can give a complete elaboration of the story content, and there is no significant difference between them ($p = 0.77$). However, the performance of storytelling by affective Haru was found to be significantly higher than that of neutral Haru in terms of expressiveness, intelligence level, substitutability and overall evaluation. The average scores for experience of storytelling by affective Haru is also significantly higher than those of neutral Haru, shown in Table 2. These results suggest that the affective robot Haru received more positive evaluations in the storytelling task than the neutral Haru.

6 Conclusion

General interest on applying storytelling to robotics is increasing. In previous studies, the emotions and actions of robot's storytelling are predetermined, resulting in a homogeneous style. In this paper, we propose a method for social robot Haru to tell stories empathically by imitating the emotions of human teachers during storytelling. Our preliminary results show that social robot Haru for storytelling can make use of human teachers as integral to the design of the system and provide a personalized storytelling experience. Moreover, participants reported to have positive attitudes toward the storytelling by our designed affective Haru robot compared to a neutral one. Currently, we have finished developing and autonomous system that can mimic the storytelling of a human teacher, and in the future we will be deploying the robot in the field and perform user studies on the effectiveness of the system. Moreover, in future work, we would like to further improve the storytelling ability of the affective Haru robot by adding nonverbal behaviors such as gaze.

References

1. Appel, M., Lugrin, B., Kühle, M., Heindl, C.: The emotional robotic storyteller: on the influence of affect congruency on narrative transportation, robot perception, and persuasion. Comput. Hum. Behav. **120**, 106749 (2021)

2. Azuar, D., Gallud, G., Escalona, F., Gomez-Donoso, F., Cazorla, M.: A story-telling social robot with emotion recognition capabilities for the intellectually chal-lenged. In: Silva, M.F., Luís Lima, J., Reis, L.P., Sanfeliu, A., Tardioli, D. (eds.) ROBOT 2019. AISC, vol. 1093, pp. 599–609. Springer, Cham (2020). https://doi.org/10.1007/978-3-030-36150-1_49
3. Bänziger, T., Scherer, K.R.: The role of intonation in emotional expressions. Speech Commun. **46**(3–4), 252–267 (2005)
4. Cabibihan, J.J., So, W.C., Pramanik, S.: Human-recognizable robotic gestures. IEEE Trans. Auton. Ment. Dev. **4**(4), 305–314 (2012)
5. Chen, G.D., Wang, C.Y., et al.: A survey on storytelling with robots. In: Proceedings of International Conference on Technologies for E-Learning and Digital Entertainment, pp. 450–456. Springer, Heidelberg (2011). https://doi.org/10.1007/978-3-642-23456-9_81
6. Costa, S., Brunete, A., Bae, B.C., Mavridis, N.: Emotional storytelling using virtual and robotic agents. Int. J. Humanoid Rob. **15**(03), 1850006 (2018)
7. Elliott, C., Brzezinski, J., Sheth, S., Salvatoriello, R.: Story-morphing in the affective reasoning paradigm: generating stories semi-automatically for use with "emotionally intelligent" multimedia agents. In: Proceedings of the 2nd International Conference on Autonomous Agents (Agents), pp. 181–188 (1998)
8. Fink, J.: Anthropomorphism and human likeness in the design of robots and human-robot interaction. In: Ge, S.S., Khatib, O., Cabibihan, J.-J., Simmons, R., Williams, M.-A. (eds.) ICSR 2012. LNCS (LNAI), vol. 7621, pp. 199–208. Springer, Heidelberg (2012). https://doi.org/10.1007/978-3-642-34103-8_20
9. Gomez, R.: Meet Haru the unassuming big-eyed robot helping researchers study social robotics. IEEE Spectr. (2020)
10. Gomez, R., et al.: Exploring affective storytelling with an embodied agent. In: Proceedings of 2021 30th IEEE International Conference on Robot & Human Interactive Communication (RO-MAN), pp. 1249–1255. IEEE (2021)
11. Hubbard, L.J., Chen, Y., Colunga, E., Kim, P., Yeh, T.: Child-robot interaction to integrate reflective storytelling into creative play. In: Proceedings of Creativity and Cognition, pp. 1–8 (2021)
12. Nichols, E., Gao, L., Gomez, R.: Collaborative storytelling with large-scale neural language models. In: Motion, Interaction and Games, pp. 1–10 (2020)
13. Nichols, E., Gao, L., Vasylkiv, Y., Gomez, R.: Collaborative storytelling with social robots. In: Proceedings of 2021 IEEE/RSJ International Conference on Intelligent Robots and Systems (IROS), pp. 1903–1910. IEEE (2021)
14. Park, H.W., Grover, I., Spaulding, S., Gomez, L., Breazeal, C.: A model-free affective reinforcement learning approach to personalization of an autonomous social robot companion for early literacy education. In: Proceedings of the AAAI Conference on Artificial Intelligence, vol. 33, pp. 687–694 (2019)
15. de Pinto, M.G., Polignano, M., Lops, P., Semeraro, G.: Emotions understanding model from spoken language using deep neural networks and mel-frequency cepstral coefficients. In: Proceedings of 2020 IEEE Conference on Evolving and adaptive intelligent Systems (EAIS), pp. 1–5. IEEE (2020)
16. Shihab, K., Ramadhan, H.: Modeling and evaluating of emotional processes. Editorial Advisory Board, p. 128 (2008)
17. Steinhaeusser, S.C., Schaper, P., Bediako Akuffo, O., Friedrich, P., Ön, J., Lugrin, B.: Anthropomorphize me! Effects of robot gender on listeners' perception of the social robot NAO in a storytelling use case. In: Proceedings of Companion of the 2021 ACM/IEEE International Conference on Human-Robot Interaction (HRI), pp. 529–534 (2021)

18. Striepe, H., Lugrin, B.: There once was a robot storyteller: measuring the effects of emotion and non-verbal behaviour. In: Proceedings of International Conference on Social Robotics (ICSR), pp. 126–136. Springer, Cham (2017). https://doi.org/10.1007/978-3-319-70022-9_13

19. Swain, M., Routray, A., Kabisatpathy, P.: Databases, features and classifiers for speech emotion recognition: a review. Int. J. Speech Technol. **21**(1), 93–120 (2018). https://doi.org/10.1007/s10772-018-9491-z

20. https://www.imdb.com/title/tt9201722/

21. Wang, X., Xu, W., Liang, B., Li, C.: Design and development of teleoperation system for space robot. J. Harbin Inst. Technol. **42**(3), 337–342 (2010)

22. Xu, J., Matta, K., Islam, S., Nürnberger, A.: German speech recognition system using DeepSpeech. In: Proceedings of the 4th International Conference on Natural Language Processing and Information Retrieval (NLPIR), pp. 102–106 (2020)

23. Xu, J., Broekens, J., Hindriks, K., Neerincx, M.A.: Effects of a robotic storyteller's moody gestures on storytelling perception. In: 2015 International Conference on Affective Computing and Intelligent Interaction (ACII), pp. 449–455. IEEE (2015)

24. Zabala, U., Rodriguez, I., Martínez-Otzeta, J.M., Lazkano, E.: Expressing robot personality through talking body language. Appl. Sci. **11**(10), 4639 (2021)

25. Zhou, K., Sisman, B., Liu, R., Li, H.: Emotional voice conversion: theory, databases and ESD. Speech Commun. **137**, 1–18 (2022)

Enabling Learning Through Play: Inclusive Gaze-Controlled Human-Robot Interface for Joystick-Based Toys

Vinay Krishna Sharma[(⊠)], L. R. D. Murthy, and Pradipta Biswas

Indian Institute of Science Bangalore, Bengaluru, India
{vinaysharma,lrdmurthy,pradipta}@iisc.ac.in

Abstract. A significant proportion of the world population is living with some form of disability. The most isolated section of disability spectrum are persons with severe speech and motor impairment (SSMI). They face challenges not only in everyday activities but in accessing education and proper employment in later stages of life. Persons with SSMI must rely on manual gaze-based interactions for everyday communication. This research aims to enable and support the learning and education of persons with SSMI through engaging eye-gaze-controlled playful activities. This work proposes and evaluates gaze-based interaction to drive a toy car using augmented and mixed reality interfaces. The results show improvements in otherwise dull, gaze-based generic pointing and selection tasks after performing an unrelated yet more engaging and playful car driving activity.

Keywords: Eye-gaze tracking · Assistive toys · Augmented and mixed reality interfaces · User interaction design · Human-Robot Interaction

1 Introduction

A significant proportion of the world's population lives with some form of disability. Persons with disabilities have a different range of functional and cognitive capabilities based on their underlying medical condition. A congenital disorder or damage to the brain or the spinal cord caused by an accident, or a neurodevelopmental disease leads to involuntary muscle control referred to as spasticity. Persons with severe speech and motor impairment (SSMI) belong to an isolated part of the disability spectrum. The complexity of their physical conditions restricts them from having natural interactions with their environments even for activities of daily living (ADL). Advances in robotics and technology have provided opportunities to design systems to enable and support persons with disabilities in everyday activities, communication, education, and fun.

Most of the generic toys come with a physical remote controller (or gaming pad/console) which can have thumb-sticks and/or buttons to control the toy like a remote-controlled (RC) car. Persons with motor impairment face difficulties in grabbing and manipulating objects because of their limited range of physical movement. Though there are assistive toys specially designed for persons with special needs, their accessibility

F. Cavallo et al. (Eds.): ICSR 2022, LNAI 13818, pp. 452–461, 2022.
https://doi.org/10.1007/978-3-031-24670-8_40

and affordability become a major concern given the population and economic conditions of a developing country like India [14]. On the other hand, there are ample avenues and outlets accessible to buy any generic toy at an affordable price. This research work proposes an inclusive eye-gaze-controlled human-robot interface for generic joystick-based toys to be used by persons with SSMI. The proposed work is evaluated through user trials performed at Vidyasagar school for special children (formerly the Spastic Society of India), Chennai.

2 Related Work

Applications of eye tracking in the automotive, aviation, gaming, advertisement, and assistive technology have been extensively explored for more than two decades now [1]. Accurate and precise eye-tracking requires expensive hardware and setups. Researchers are working on developing non-invasive and inexpensive webcam-based eye-gaze tracking which does not require physical hardware and calibration [2, 6]. There are numerous benefits associated with play. The activity of playing promotes the development of intellectual, social, psychological, motor, and sensory-perceptual functions [3]. Researchers are focusing on developing various assistive toys and playful activities for supporting education and learning in kids with different range of abilities [8]. Playing with toys promote physical and mental wellbeing of kids [7]. Fun and playful interactions with toys help reducing stress and psychological symptoms associated to any medical disorders like agitation and aggression [8]. The more the children engage with activities of play the better their mental and physical development will be.

Researchers are also exploring the usefulness of extended reality interfaces in assistive and rehabilitative activities [5]. User centric design approach has always been the true driver of a successful system when it comes to designing solutions for persons with different range of abilities. Iromec [9] was one of the first play robot designed for children with limited mobility. It explores multiple play scenarios and roles for robot assisted play [12]. Inclusive Human-Robot Interaction can bridge the physical gap of disability and the cultural divide by providing collaborative and user centric solutions for persons belonging to the autism spectrum [10]. Persons with disabilities are more inclined towards using technology like tablets, smartphones, and laptops. This inclination can be exploited to design interactive and engaging solutions for supporting education and performance assessment [11]. The increasing potential of robotics as an enabler for the persons with different range of abilities has been reviewed in [13].

These solutions focused on users with specific medical conditions and are not affordable for a developing country like India. This research aims to propose an affordable, user-agnostic, gaze-controlled interaction with generic toys for persons with SSMI.

3 Multimodal Joystick Controller Design

The proposed joystick controller mechanism is a physical embodiment to operate on a joystick/thumb-stick and buttons of a gaming console, controller or hand-held remote controller for toys like cars, drones, trucks and robot arms. Using this mechanism, a user can play video games, drive a toy car, fly a drone, or operate a robotic arm with their functional natural modalities of interaction like eye-gaze, gesture speech. The proposed joystick controller provides an interface that can receive commands from these natural interfaces as input and generates a corresponding movement of the thumb-sticks linkage proportionally. Using natural modalities of interaction instead of manual operation provides a better connection and realization of the activity for the targeted users. The proposed joystick controller is generic and modular in its design to fit on any available gaming console/remote controller and can be customized based on the user experience and uses (Figs. 1 and 2). The present implementation of the joystick controller takes only the eye-gaze points of the users as input. In the present work, the mechanical embodiment is mounted on the physical remote controller of a digital RC car. And the interaction module comprises of a bespoke webcam-based eye tracking program [6] to track the user's eye-gaze point on the screen.

4   User Interface Design

This work explores eye-gaze pointing and selection functionality in two types of augmented reality (AR)-based interfaces, screen-based and headset-based. Two interactive games (tasks) were designed to perform pointing and selection on a screen-based live video see-through interface and headset-based mixed reality (MR) interface. The first task was adapted from ISO 9421–9 task with a single target sphere (green ball) of a size and a distance randomly selected from three predefined levels. The second task was to drive a toy car to reach a defined goal location using the live video-see through four-way control user interface. Both tasks are described below in detail.

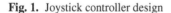

Fig. 1. Joystick controller design   **Fig. 2.** Final joystick controller System

The task comprised a fixed central sphere (ball) of red color and a target sphere of green color. The target ball appears on the periphery of an imaginary sphere randomly chosen from a set of concentric spheres centered at the center red ball. Once the center red sphere is interacted with, it vanishes, and the green target sphere of a random size selected from predefined set, appears on the interface at the periphery of the randomly selected imaginary sphere and at random angles (inclination and azimuth angle) from the center red ball. After the successful selection of a target ball, it vanishes, and the red central ball appears again marking the start of the next iteration. For each iteration the size of target balls and distance from the center ball are randomly selected from a predefined set of values giving nine Index of Difficulties (IDs).

The goal of the toy car driving task was to drive the car to reach a designated target location using the four-way control, i.e. forward, left, right, and backward on the interface. The proposed joystick controller mechanism was used to control the joystick of the toy car corresponding to the eye-gaze interactions made by the users on the interface. Both these above tasks were realized and evaluated on two types of AR-based graphical user interfaces, screen and headset based, as described below.

4.1 Screen-Based Video See-Through AR Interface

The screen-based AR interface was designed using Unity3D and Windows Forms Application in C#. A Logitech USB camera was used to render the real background in the AR interface. The live-view camera was used to keep the look and feel of the task environment uniform in both the tasks. The interface ran on an MSI Creator Z16 Laptop with a Core i7-11800H, a GeForce RTX 3060 GPU, and a 2560 x 1600 touch display. Over the live real-time video from the camera, the center red ball and the subsequent target green balls were rendered as Unity sphere game objects. The live video-stream from the USB camera was overlaid with four buttons for the four-way control of the toy car. The toy car and goal destination (red table) can be seen on the interface (Figs. 3 and 4). The users can drive the car to the destination by interacting with the four buttons based on live visual feedback from the camera. The selection of targets and buttons is done by pointing the mouse cursor at the target objects and clicking. The mouse cursor is controlled through the eye-gaze of the user and clicking is triggered by dwelling at the location for 500 ms.

4.1.1 Webcam-Based Eye-Gaze Tracking

The MAGE-Net model proposed in [6] was trained on both MPIIGaze [15] and PARKS-Gaze [16] datasets. This model was chosen due to its lower number of parameters and to obtain faster gaze predictions. In order to obtain gaze predictions from the model, the facial detection and facial landmark detection steps were performed on each camera frame using OpenFace 2.0 toolkit [17]. Using these landmarks, the normalized face and eye crops for both left and right eyes were obtained using the procedure reported in [6]. These normalized face and normalized eye crops act as the inputs to the MAGE-Net model and the network provides predictions in the form of normalized gaze angles in the face coordinate system. These normalized gaze angles are converted to screen coordinate system using head rotation, extrinsic camera calibration parameters and the display dimensions using the process described in [2]. These transformed gaze estimates in the screen coordinate system are mapped to the cursor position, thereby the cursor follows the user's eye movement. This eye-tracking implementation was used for the toy car driving task. However, a commercially available Tobii PC Eye Mini screen-mounted eye-tracker was used for the eye-gaze pointing and selection task.

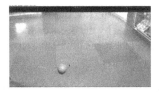

Fig. 3. Pointing and selection task: green target sphere (Color figure online)

Fig. 4. Toy car driving task with the red table as destination (Color figure online)

4.2 Eye-Gaze Controlled Headset Based Mixed Reality (MR) Interface

The MR interface was designed for the Hololens2 headset using Unity 3D and Microsoft Mixed Reality Toolkit (MRTK). The Hololens2 headset allows users to see the real world around them augmented with virtual objects spatially placed in their surroundings. The pointing and selection task was realized by using red and green spherical game objects as done for AR interface. The four-way control interface for car driving task comprised of four translucent interactable buttons tabbed in scene view of the user. The Hololens2 comes with inbuilt eye-gaze tracking functionality and the same has been used for performing both tasks. The eye-tracking for Hololens2 requires calibration for every new user. Figures 5, 6, and 7 show the MR interface for both the tasks.

Fig. 5. User wearing Hololens2 (Color figure online)

Fig. 6. Pointing and selection task: green target sphere (Color figure online)

Fig. 7. Toy Car Driving Task with red table as destination (Color figure online)

5   User Study

A total of 10 participants took part in the study, out of which two were completely new to the use and practice of eye-tracking. Six out of the total were quadriplegic and were confined to a wheelchair with minimum to no voluntary hand, head, or body movement control. The demography of individual users is described in the table below (Table 1):

The main objectives of this research are to quantify improvements in performance of individuals with SSMI on an eye-gaze based representative pointing and selection task induced by performing a more engaging and unrelated eye-gaze based toy car driving task. The metrics used to analyze the results for pointing task are target selection times based on the IDs. The engagement of the users is measured by the duration of their engagement with the task before getting distracted, as advised by the special educator or caregiver. The number of iterations of successful attempts given the total engagement time corresponds to better performance of the user. The user trials were performed after a preparatory pilot study with end users. A user-centric design approach has been taken

Table 1. Description of participants

Code	Sex	Age	Class	Remarks
ME	F	14	10th	Cerebral Palsy, Intellectual Disability, Uses a motorized wheelchair
NK	M	16	11th	Cerebral Palsy, Strabismus, Spasticity, Uses a motorized wheelchair
ND	F	17	11th	Speech and Learning Disability
SS	F	16	11th	Learning and Intellectual Disability
VW	F	11	8th	Cerebral Palsy, Athetoid movements, muscle stiffness, manual wheelchair
KA	F	18	Voc	Cerebral Palsy, non-verbal, muscle stiffness, manual wheelchair
KP	M	15	11th	Severe Cerebral Palsy, non-verbal, involuntary muscle movements
PD	M	10	9th	Mild Cerebral Palsy, non-verbal
SR	F	14	10th	Non-verbal, quadriplegic, involuntary muscle movements
DA	M	19	Voc	Non-verbal, quadriplegic, Uses manual wheelchair

while iterating over possible solutions based on face-to-face interaction with the end users, special educators, trainers, and parents of persons with SSMI. The following section covers the details and observations of the pilot study.

5.1 Pilot Study

The participants had to perform the eye-gaze pointing and selection task, followed by the eye-gaze car driving task and finally eye-gaze pointing and selection task again. The participants were given a trial session for each interface before the actual task. The experiment was repeated the next day.

All users could perform the eye-gaze Pointing Task and eye-gaze Car Driving Task. However, participants could select 3 targets of varying difficulty in around 2 min 20 secs of average engagement time. It was difficult for them to engage for longer durations with the pointing task even though a Tobii eye-tracker was used. The Four-Way RC Car task was loved by all the users equally which used the webcam-based eye-gaze tracking. The users found it more engaging and interacted with it for longer durations, about 12 min on average before getting tired or distracted. Surprisingly, rather than driving the car to the goal location, hitting a wall or any collision with an object elicited excitement in the end users. The users were able to drive the car to reach a 50 cm wide target at 2.75 m in front and 1.2 m on the side (from the axis of the scene camera) in about 2 min 12 s on average. On the other hand, only four users could perform both tasks in headset based MR interface. The main reasons could be non-familiarity with the MR headset, inability to perform eye calibration due to neck-muscle stiffness, and lack of understanding. The users took around 30 s per target selection for Pointing task and around 2 min for the Four-Way RC Car task in MR.

5.2 Confirmatory Study

The proposed experiments were updated and modified based on the observations and findings of the Pilot Study. The target sizes were increased by decreasing the ID. The pointer size and color were adapted to the user's behavior based on their trainer's feedback. There were more collisions and multiple retakes for the car driving task during the pilot study. The reason was the continuous dwell-based control of the toy car. The toy car keeps moving in the direction corresponding to the button the user dwelled at on the interface until the gaze is taken off that button. This continuous control was changed to a step-based control where any action is triggered only for a fixed duration of half a second, users must look away and dwell on the button again to trigger the next action. The eye-gaze-based interaction with the user interface for the car control was further aided by using nearest neighbors for triggering the four-way control. This allowed the users to interact with the four-way buttons by bringing their eye-gaze within a Euclidean distance threshold of 200 pixels of the four-way control buttons.

The user trials took over a consecutive period of three days. The users must perform the tasks in the order of Pointing Task-Driving Task-Pointing Task again. The task completion times, successful iterations, and task engagement times were recorded. The users were first given the pointing task till they get distracted. The average engagement time for the users in the pointing and selection task pilot study was 2 min 43 s. We kept a threshold of 5 min for the first pointing and selection task. Next, the participants drive the car to the goal location. The threshold for engaging with this activity was set to 15 min, ambitious to the average engagement time in the pilot study which was 10 min. Then the users performed the pointing and selection task again. The users performed the same set of tasks in both the type of interfaces subject to feasibility given their physical and medical conditions. All the trials were demonstrated and explained to the special educators, trainers, caregivers, and parents and were conducted in their presence after acquiring necessary ethical approvals and consents.

6 Results

6.1 Screen-Based AR Interface

The eye-gaze based pointing and selection task is used as a representative activity of interacting with object on a user-interface screen. This activity can be extrapolated to various actions and interactions that can be performed on a user interface. The users were taking more time for selecting the targets of same difficulty during their initial attempt with the pointing and selection task. The number of average successful iterations was 5 with an average engagement time of 2 min 55 s. The Fig. 8 below shows a comparison between the pointing task performance before and after the car driving task using the movement time (MT). The figure also shows the performance of the expert user as a baseline.

The users have taken almost half the time for pointing and selecting the targets of the same difficulty after the car driving task. The users found the car driving activity more engaging and fun, as compared to the dull pointing and selection task. This can be attributed to the playfulness associated with the toy car movements, the feeling of independence and control from driving the car, and the associated excitement. All ten participants could engage with the car driving task for at least 15 min, surpassing our threshold. The participants could drive the car to 7 goal locations on average successfully during their car driving task. The average task completion time for the driving task was 45 s. In their second attempt at the pointing and selection task after the car driving task, the users engaged for 3 min and 39 secs on average and could perform 8 successful iterations on average. The target selection time of the users reduced, and their engagement time increased. There is a significant improvement ($p < 0.05$) in selection times for the same ID between before and after conditions. All the users except one follow the same improvement trend. This exception can be attributed to the medical condition of strabismus (crossed eyes) where estimating the point of eye-gaze of the user becomes problematic using any vision-based technique. This situation may be improved with user-specific calibration, but the scope of this work is to come up with an affordable user agnostic calibration-free eye-gaze controlled interface.

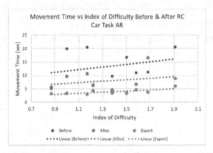

Fig. 8. MT vs ID Before and After Driving Task on screen-based AR Interface

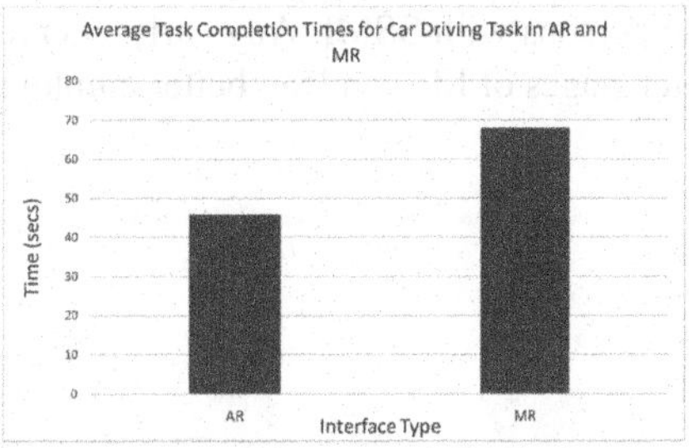

Fig. 9. Task completion times for the driving task in screen-based AR and MR interfaces

6.2 Headset-Based Mixed Reality Interface

Total of four users with severe speech impairment and learning disabilities could perform the task in the MR interface. The physical requirement of wearing a headset was a major limitation. However, the participants took lesser time for selecting the targets of the same ID after the car driving task. The difference between the before and after selection times was not significant ($p > 0.05$). The participants took on average 1 min 8 s for the car driving task. The Fig. 10 below shows a comparison of the selection times before and after the car driving task and that of an expert user as a baseline. The users took less time on average for car driving task in screen-based AR interface than headset-based MR interface (Fig. 9). However, users performed more iterations in headset-based MR pointing and selection task as compared to that of screen-based AR interface (Fig. 11). This can mainly be attributed to user calibrated state of the art near-eye eye-gaze tracking provided by Hololens2 headset as compared to user agnostic calibration free affordable webcam based eye-gaze tracking used with the screen based AR interface.

7 Discussion and Future Work

The results of this study show that type of activity can positively impact the performance of interaction. The representative pointing and selection task was seen as dull and boring by users with a different range of abilities. The users were getting distracted and frustrated quickly, given their short attention span. There are factors like aesthetics and audio-visual feedback that can affect the level of engagement with any interface to some extent, but that is not explored as part of this work. This work hypothesized that a more interesting, playful, and engaging activity can improve the user performance on a task and while keeping the modality of interaction and interfaces the same. The users could engage for longer durations with car driving task. Both tasks used eye-gaze con troll as a modality to interact with the user interface (AR and MR). Car driving task, being more playful and interesting for the users, trained or practiced the eye-gaze control as skill in an unintended manner for an unrelated task. This unintentional training of eye-gaze control skill helped the users to perform better in the representative pointing and selection task. This supports the possibility of using eye-gaze-based playful interactions as a skill building block for the persons with SSMI. Any early interventions during childhood, when continued till later stages of life can lead better employability by leveraging the skills learned.

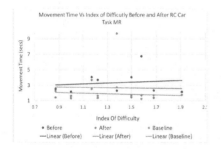
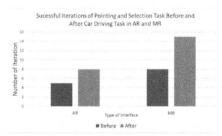

Fig. 10. MT vs ID Before and After Driving Task on headset-based MR Interface

Fig. 11. Comparison of Pointing and Selection Task in AR and MR

The results also show some promising solutions offered by AR and MR interfaces to persons with different ranges of abilities. There are many educational applications planned to be built on top of the interfaces proposed in this work. These applications can augment educational content with real-world play activities to support learning. This has the potential to support the special educators, trainers, and family members by reducing the dependence of our users on them. It can also provide tools for special educators to teach and train persons with different range of abilities more efficiently.

One of the foundational goals of this work is design an affordable and inclusive system that can be easily accessible to the masses. The proposed system runs on a laptop and uses a 3D printed components to control the toy car. The future work involves deploying the whole system into smartphones to expand the number of end users.

Acknowledgement. We thank Mr. Sunil Nahar for Nahar Center of Robotics and Prototyping Lab and the Director and staff of Vidyasagar School, Chennai for their inputs and cooperation.

References

1. Alsharif, S., Kuzmicheva, O., Gräser, A.: Gaze Gesture-Based Human Robot Interface, ZweitetransdisziplinäreKonferenz,TechnischeUnterstützungssysteme, die Menschen wirklichwollen (2016)
2. Murthy, L.R.D., Mukhopadhyay, A., Biswas, P.: Distraction detection in automotive environment using appearance-based gaze estimation. In: ACM International Conference on Intelligent User Interfaces (IUI 2022) (2022)
3. Hsieh, H.C.: Effects of ordinary and adaptive toys on pre-school children with developmental disabilities. Res. Dev. Disabil. **29**(5), 459–466 (2008)
4. Prabuwono, A.S., Allehaibi, K.H.S., Kurnianingsih, K.: Assistive robotic technology: a review. Comput. Eng. Appl. J. **6**(2), 71–78 (2017)
5. Petrie, H., Carmien, S., & Lewis, A.: Assistive technology abandonment: research realities and potentials. In: International Conference on Computers Helping People With Special Needs, pp. 532–540. Springer, Cham (2018)
6. Murthy, L.R.D., Biswas, P.: Appearance-based Gaze Estimation using Attention and Difference Mechanism. In: 2021 IEEE/CVF Conference on Computer Vision and Pattern Recognition Workshops (CVPRW), pp. 3137–3146. IEEE (2021)
7. Ray, D.C., Lee, K.R., Meany-Walen, K.K., Carlson, S.E., Carnes-Holt, K.L., Ware, J.N.: Use of toys in child-centered play therapy. Int. J. Play Ther. **22**(1), 43 (2013)
8. Sposito, A.M.P., et al.: Puppets as a strategy for communication with Brazilian children with cancer. Nurs. Health Sci. **18**(1), 30–37 (2016)
9. Patrizia, M., Claudio, M., Leonardo, G., Alessandro, P.: A robotic toy for children with special needs: From requirements to design. In: 2009 IEEE International Conference on Rehabilitation Robotics, pp. 918–923. IEEE (2009)
10. Kim, E., Paul, R., Shic, F., Scassellati, B.: Bridging the research gap: Making HRI useful to individuals with autism (2012)
11. Uncular, D., Artut, S.: Design of a robotic toy and user interfaces for autism spectrum disorder risk assessment. Uludağ Üniversitesi Fen-Edebiyat Fakültesi Sosyal Bilimler Dergisi **20**(36), 101–140 (2018)
12. Robins, B., et al.: Human-centred design methods: Developing scenarios for robot assisted play informed by user panels and field trials. Int. J. Hum Comput Stud. **68**(12), 873–898 (2010)
13. Gardeazabal, X., Abascal, J.: Use of robots for play by children with cerebral palsy. Multidiscip. Digit. Pub. Inst. Proc. **31**(1), 75 (2019)
14. Swaminathan, M., Pal, J.: Ludic design for accessibility in the global south. In: M. Stein and J. Lazar. Assistive Technology and the Developing World. Oxford University Press (2020). https://www.microsoft.com/en-us/research/publication/ludic-design-for-accessibility
15. Zhang, X., Sugano, Y., Fritz, M., Bulling, A.: It's written all over your face: Full-face appearance-based gaze estimation. In: Proceedings of the IEEE Conference on Computer Vision and Pattern Recognition Workshops, pp. 51–60 (2017)
16. Murthy, L.R.D., Mukhopadhyay, A., Anand, K., Aggarwal, S., Biswas, P.: PARKS-Gaze - a precision-focused gaze estimation dataset in the wild under extreme head poses. In: 27th International Conference on Intelligent User Interfaces (IUI 2022 Companion). Association for Computing Machinery, New York, NY, USA, pp. 81–84 (2022). https://doi.org/10.1145/3490100.3516467
17. Baltrusaitis, T., Zadeh, A., Lim, Y. C., Morency, L. P.: Openface 2.0: Facial behavior analysis toolkit. In: 2018 13th IEEE International Conference on Automatic Face and Gesture Recognition (FG 2018), pp. 59–66. IEEE (2018)

Introducing the Social Robot EBO: An Interactive and Socially Aware Storyteller Robot for Therapies with Older Adults

Gerardo Pérez, Trinidad Rodríguez, Pilar Bachiller[iD], Pablo Bustos[iD], and Pedro Núñez[✉][iD]

Escuela Politécnica, Universidad de Extremadura, Badajoz, Spain
pnuntru@unex.es
http://robolab.unex.es

Abstract. Storytelling has played a fundamental role throughout the ages in people's socialization and entertainment, regardless of age and gender. Research on storytelling with robots has been gaining enormous interest in the scientific community in recent years. In this paper, we present EBO, a social robot designed by the RoboLab Robotics and Computer Vision Laboratory of the University of Extremadura capable of engaging in conversations and interactive storytelling, accompanying the speech with the appropriate emotions, movements, and images. The robot has a screen in the center of its body, on which a wide range of images or facial expressions can be displayed in real-time. In addition, EBO is equipped with different range sensors along its perimeter, a microphone, loudspeakers, and an RGB camera, which allows it to be aware of its surroundings during operation. Thanks to this ability, EBO can interact socially with the people around it, from children to older adults, focusing its dialogues, narratives, and emotions according to the objectives set by the professionals. This article focuses on the robot architecture's main hardware and software components and different social experiments we have conducted in real contexts. We also present the tool: EboTalk, a user interface with which the generation of specific dialogs, narratives, and emotions can be defined quickly and without significant technical knowledge by professionals. The experiments validate the proposed solution in the context of elderly care.

Keywords: Human-robot interaction · Storytelling robot

1 Introduction

Since our origins, storytelling has been central to our ancestors' socialization and entertainment. Over the years, storytelling has been using different media that have evolved with technical developments. Initially, it was voice storytelling, then written storytelling, such as novels and plays, then cinema, radio or television, and more currently, role-playing games or video games. Many of these popular

F. Cavallo et al. (Eds.): ICSR 2022, LNAI 13818, pp. 462–472, 2022.
https://doi.org/10.1007/978-3-031-24670-8_41

types of storytelling represent passive experiences for the audience where, basically, they listen to a story without having the possibility of making changes to the storyline. There are also interactive experiences in written narratives (the 'Choose Your Own Adventure' book series), role-playing games ('Call of Cthulhu', 'Dungeon and dragons') or in the classic computer video games of the 80's, where without great technical boasts, there was a whole stream of interactive narrative games (*e.g.*, classic conversational (or text) adventures, such as the Spanish games 'The Original Adventure', 'Cozumel' or 'Jabato'). As technologies advance, new opportunities arise. This last is the case of social robots, understood as those robots that behave as humans would. A social robot usually can interact with people through different channels, including voice, and in addition, it can express emotions during a conversation. Robots can become a versatile storytelling tool for multiple purposes, from learning, companionship, or therapy with the elderly [6].

In this article, we present the EBO robot, a social robot equipped with multiple sensors for interaction with older people and the ability to display images and facial expressions that identify basic emotions. We also present the EboTalk application, a tool for interactive story generation in which a professional without technical knowledge builds the dialogues and stories and associates the robot's emotion and motion with the player's actions. In our approach, as the **main novelty**, a human player interacts with the robot to build a story. The narrative begins with the EBO robot describing an initial situation with different options to be chosen by the older adult, and it is the latter responds by adding a line to the story in the manner of a conversational adventure. Then, the robot and the person cooperate in the narration, which is further enriched with movements and facial expressions depending on the answers given by the player. This is also one of the **main contributions** of this work. The theme of the narrative and the main objectives to be achieved (cognitive stimulation, socio-emotional or simple entertainment) are defined at the beginning of the therapy. Therefore, the caregiver uses EboTalk to generate the skeleton of the narratives.

2   Related Works

As social robots become more widespread, they present a new avenue for storytelling with a higher level of interactivity. The scientific literature has made concrete contributions on issues related to how robots should connect with an audience [1–5], but so far, most of these works are based on the assumption that the content of these narratives is fixed and does not allow for alterations.

The use of social robots has been increasing in recent years. Social robots are a significant advantage in some areas, such as in the care and attention of the elderly. In general, they represent attractive and fun tools capable of capturing the attention of these groups while supporting caregivers in activities related to physical, cognitive, or socio-emotional stimulation. Along with the latter, the benefits of storytelling are well known, contributing to improving their listening and reflection skills, their social awareness, cognitive and emotional stimulation, and also to remember their emotional vocabulary and their own experiences. In educational settings, especially over the last years, several robotic storytellers have been proposed [1,3] to support students' learning process and analyze the effects on their learning. In [6], a narrative robot capable of collaborating with people to create original stories was created, although the freedom given in this interaction made it difficult to control the quality of the narration. Most of these works, moreover, did not include the accompaniment of gestures and facial expressions during the story, which undoubtedly enriches the narrative process by avoiding a trivial text reading. In [7], the authors include the latter in their narrator robot NarRob, although it lacks interactivity. Our EBO robot is designed to interact socially with older people. Unlike previous works, its main novelty is the possibility of accompanying interactive stories with emotions, facial expressions, and motions associated with that emotion. Dialogues and narration are easily generated with the tool we also present in this article.

The use of robots with the elderly is also a topic of interest in the last decade. Clearly, in developed countries, the population is very aged, and robots can help this group and professionals. These years, most of the work is focused on companion robots for socio-emotional stimulation [8]. In [9] they describe a robotic platform developed as a personal coach for older adults aiming to motivate them to participate in physical activities. In [10], the authors go even further and present a robot to support older adults with low vision. For mental healthcare of the elderly, the work presented in [11] summarizes the main contributions. Recently, the work presented in [12] uses a concept similar to the one presented in this article for cognitive therapies with promising results. Ebo is a user-friendly platform with capabilities that facilitate affective interaction with the elderly. Our article shows how, in addition, the emotions associated with the player's actions improve the acceptance of the game.

3   Overview of the Proposed Robotics System for Cognitive Therapies

Figure 1 describes the system proposed in our paper. First, the professional team builds a customized narrative game from the EboTalk tool. This tool is simple and can be easily used by personnel without robotics knowledge. The narrative game is composed of scenes, each with an associated story, an image, dialogues, keywords, and the emotions that the robot will have to depend on the actions. These emotions are shown on the robot in two complementary ways: through movements associated with the emotion and the facial expression on Ebo's screen. Next, Ebo uses this game for the therapy through a set of software components that work in a coordinated manner to achieve the goal. The current version performs supervised therapy using the well-known 'Wizard of Oz' [13] technique. The entire session during the game is stored for later analysis by the team of professionals.

The following subsections briefly describe both the Ebo storytelling robot and the EboTalk application.

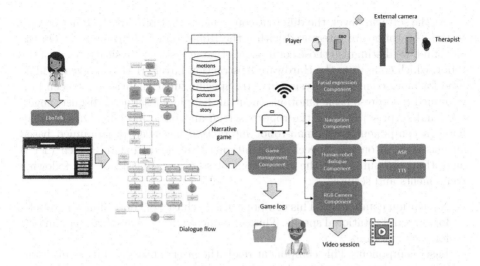

Fig. 1. Overview of the complete system for cognitive therapies with the elderly. Our proposal uses EboTalk for the professional to generate narratives that are then played back by the Ebo robot. All sessions are saved for later analysis.

3.1   EBO: An Interactive and Socially Aware Storyteller Robot

The Ebo storytelling robot of the RoboLab research group of the University of Extremadura was developed within the *Emorobotic* project: *emotional Management through Robot Programming in Primary Education*. Figure 2 shows a schematic and an image of the real Ebo robot. Ebo is a differential platform composed of a set of devices to acquire information from the environment and with the capabilities to express emotions and pictures on its screen. A prototyping system was followed for the external shape to maximize end-user acceptance, resulting in a plastic housing as shown in Fig. 2. The robot has a diameter of less than 15cm, and its weight is less than one kilogram. In its current version, adapted for therapies with older adults, the Table 1 summarizes its harware components:

Table 1. Ebo robot's Hardware components

Hardware component
Raspberry pi 3B+, which includes a CSI port and where the host system is executed to control the other hardware components
Camera with CSI connector: to capture visual information
Servomotor model SG90: provides movements to position the camera at a certain vertical angle
Resistive display (PiTFT 3.5"): for displaying images (e.g. emotions)
5 laser sensors (VL53L0X): to obtain distance information of objects around the robot
PWM pin extender (Adafruit 16-Channel PWM): to provide a stable output to the servo motor and configure the 5 lasers
Built-in microphone and speaker: to provide, on the one hand, audio to the system and output audio information to the outside
2 DC 298:1 (73 RPM) motors in differential configuration to move the base of the base robot
Motor controller (DRV8835)
Battery (7.4 V) responsible for supplying power to the robot. The DC-DC voltage regulator (D24V50F5) reduces the voltage from 7.4 V to 5 V

At the software level, the different components that provide the functionality to the Ebo robot are integrated within the RoboComp [14] framework. On the one hand, we distinguish those components that access the physical devices of the robot, which constitute the Hardware Abstraction Layer (HAL), and that will be used for more complex analysis software. Specific functionalities have been programmed to express basic emotions (neutral, happiness, sadness, disgust, anger, fear, and surprise) in both the robot's screen and basic motions. On the other hand, a component for human-robot interaction has been programmed based on classical Automatic Speech Recognition (ASR) and Text-to-Speech (TTS) algorithms. In summary, the robot control software consists of the following components and scripts:

- Navigation component. This component is in charge of controlling the robot's forward and rotational speeds. This component will receive specific commands for each emotion.
- Laser component. This component reads the laser sensors and uses this information to detect possible collisions during basic movements.
- RGB Camera component. This component controls the servomotor of the camera. Our idea is to follow the face and facial expression of the player during the game.
- Display Component. This component displays pictures in the screen during the narrative game.
- Facial expression component. This component is in charge of generating emotional expressions in Ebo's screen.
- HRI component. This component calls the ASR and TTS algorithms depending on the phase of the game in which it is located. The systems used in the current version employ Google's algorithms, which implies a stable internet connection during the game.

When the EBO robot starts, a WIFI network is created where the rest of the components interacting with the robot will be connected. EBO works autonomously, but a teleoperator can also control it through a friendly and straightforward interface. Communication should be as immediate as possible, so it is predefined through the EboTalk tool. In any case, modifying the dialog flow during game supervision must be possible. The interface, in turn, must allow the possibility of sending emotions and small movements to the robot to accompany the dialogue with some aspects of emotionality.

In addition to this essential control software, the EBO robot can be integrated with the CORTEX cognitive architecture [15], on which the RoboLab research group is collaborating intensively. Thanks to this more complex software, the social skills of the EBO robot are considerably increased by running new software in distributed teams.

3.2   EboTalk

The development of the narrative is done with the EboTalk tool (see Fig. 3). EboTalk is implemented in Python and provides the skills for the generation of

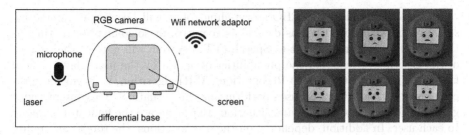

Fig. 2. The Ebo storytelling robot. Device schematic and some of the facial expressions associated to basic emotions.

dialog flow, descriptions, or keywords for use by the Ebo robot (or any other type of robot). EboTalk presents a friendly interface; thus, any user can use it without knowledge of robotics, chatbot, or programming language. The tool generates the flow of descriptions and actions in a .json format that is subsequently read by the code implemented in EBO. Along with the narrative flow, EboTalk adds specific motion and an emotional state to the robot from the set of basic emotions described above.

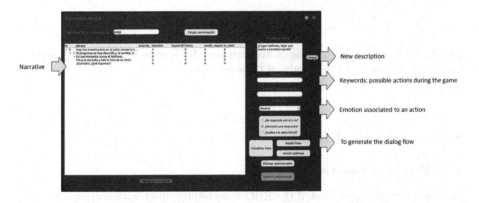

Fig. 3. The user interface of EboTalk, the interactive dialog and narration designer for the EBO robot (Spanish version).

The interactive narratives on which we base our current work in progress originate in the classic conversational (or text) adventures. This genre of videogames, prevalent in the golden age of the 8 bits, stood out because the description of the situation in which a player finds himself comes mainly from a text. All the possible actions the player could perform at any given moment had to be done equally through text and natural language. The result of each action generates a new narrative, and so on. In many of these games, some images offer complimentary help to the narration.

Based on this idea, our EBO storytelling robot will become an interactive social robot with objectives as diverse as cognitive or socio-emotional stimulation. On the one hand, a Text-to-Speech (TTS) system will narrate the content of the descriptive text and the possibilities of action by the user/player. Then, through an Automatic Speech Recognition (ASR) algorithm, it listens and processes the actions that the user performs in this situation. This interactivity gives rise to new descriptions and situations that generate the final story, unique to each user. In addition, depending on the user's actions, the robot can modify its facial expression and convey basic emotions. Figure 4 shows a typical tree of conversational adventures and their application in our case.

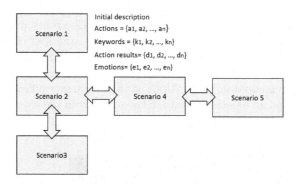

Fig. 4. Basic narrative consisting of five scenarios. Each scene is composed of actions, keywords, emotions and the results of these actions.

4 Experimental Results

4.1 Previous Experiences

Our research group has tested the EBO storytelling robot with a group of volunteer older adults, users of a daycare center in Cáceres. These volunteers receive interventions at the center, including occupational therapy, physiotherapy, and cognitive stimulation, among other services. Before evaluating the narrated stories, we validated the acceptance of the Ebo robot during human-robot interactions using the 'Wizard of Oz' technique. The procedure followed consisted of the following stages. The first contact with the EBO was performed in a group setting, in groups of three people, in which we could already observe the reactions and predisposition to talk to the EBO as if it were a person. The individual interactions consisted of a 12–15 min conversation. A total of four interactions were conducted for each participant. Figure 5 shows a snapshot of the experiment. After an evaluation through video viewing of the conversations and personal interviews, data were collected to assess the acceptability of the EBO. Some of the variables evaluated by professionals using questionnaires were i) the interest and relevance of the conversation; ii) the high fluency of the conversation; and iii) the perception that the EBO listened to each user. Other variables acquired by observations were i) visual contact with EBO; ii) ability to follow a conversation; iii) pauses during the interaction. The results obtained were very satisfactory and allowed, in addition, the improvement of specific aspects in the voice and social behavior of the EBO robot (e.g., tone, voice intensity, pause times, among others).

Fig. 5. Interaction tests between an elderly person and the EBO robot in a daycare center in Cáceres, Spain.

4.2   Interactive Narrative

In the development of the narrative game, the professionals defined specific objectives of cognitive and socioemotional stimulation and a direct narrative that reinforces basic concepts of the end user's daily life. The whole game has a high emotional component, trying to recreate real situations of the users. The Table 2 shows the description of a specific scene obtained from the EboTalk tool.

We conducted a set of experiments with the same volunteers at the daycare center three months after. Our study included a narrative play session led by the EBO storytelling robot, personalized for each user and supervised by a professional. To evaluate the preliminary results of the narrative game, we used questionnaires to the users (players) and direct observation of the professionals. The table below shows some of the questions we used in the evaluation. We used a questionnaire motivated in the work presented in [16] (see Table 2). As in the previous study, the professionals perceived results were very satisfactory. Volunteers showed more significant interest than other activities, and their attention during the game session was very close. The questionnaires were also very revealing, and all users responded positively to the above questions (Table 3).

Table 2. Example of basic narration for a given scene

Narrative description and objectives	Cognitive stimulation based on the monitoring of activities of daily living				
Scene 1	Today we are in the living room watching TV. The program is very dull, and you feel like doing something different to tell you the truth. Just then, the phone rings. You look at the screen, and your granddaughter's picture comes up. How nice!				
	You have the following options: Answer the phone or let the phone ring				
	You can always look, and I'll explain whatever you want				
	You can also go to the kitchen or go to the bedroom				
Actions	Answer the phone	Let the phone ring		Go	Look
Keywords	Living	Bedroom	Kitchen	Phone	Screen
Action results	Answer the phone: your granddaughter speaks to you in her sweet voice: 'Grandma, I'm coming home to eat with you today. Her favorite food is Spanish omelet.' Emotion: 'happy!' Motion: 'happiness'				
	Let it ring: the truth is that you don't feel like talking to her that much now. Emotion: 'sad'. Motion: 'sad'				
	Go + keyword: Ok, you go to + keyword (next scene). Emotion: 'surprise'. Motion: 'go to'				
	Look + keyword: Ok + description associated to the keyword. Emotion: normal. Motion: 'turn'				

Table 3. Question of function evaluation questionnaire for the Ebo storyteller robot

No	Evaluation questionnaire item
1	Which did you feel about the EBO robot feeling? Happiness, Sadness, Anger, Standard, Do not know
2	Do you want to use it again?
3	Could you hear the talk?
4	Is it easy to talk?
5	Is the flow of talk natural?
6	Did you feel that you were interested?
7	Was the feeling suggested?
8	Did you feel friendly?
9	Were you able to talk without getting tired?
10	Are you satisfied with EBO as a storyteller?

5 Conclusions

In this article, we have presented the EBO robot, a social robot with the ability to tell interactive stories and add emotional components that enrich the narrative. This robot has been used to interact with older adults, although what is presented in this article can easily be used with other groups. The EBOTalk tool allows the generation of narratives without much technical knowledge, adding the thread and the different options that can be carried out after the narration. In this way, in the form of a game, the user can engage in conversations that modify the course of the narrative interactively, always accompanied by facial expressions, images, and other aids. A preliminary study has been conducted in a day care center, where we evaluate the acceptability and other metrics in real interaction with our EBO robot.

Acknowledge. This work has been partially supported by FEDER funds and by the Government of Extremadura project GR21018, by the Spanish ministry of Science and Innovation TED2021-131739B-C22, and by the FEDER project 0770_EuroAGE2_4_E (Interreg V-A Portugal-Spain (POCTEP) Program).

References

1. Mutlu, B., Forlizzi, J., Hodgins, J.: A storytelling robot: modeling and evaluation of human-like gaze behavior. In: 2006 6th IEEE-RAS International Conference on Humanoid Robots, pp. 518–523, December 2006
2. Gelin, R., et al. Towards a storytelling humanoid robot. In: AAAI Fall Symposium Series (2010)
3. Kory, J., Breazeal, C.: Storytelling with robots: learning companions for preschool children's language development. In: The 23rd IEEE International Symposium on Robot and Human Interactive Communication, pp. 643–648, August 2014
4. Costa, S., Brunete, A., Bae, B.-C., Mavridis, N.: Emotional storytelling using virtual and robotic agents. Int. J. Humanoid Rob. **15** (2018)
5. Ligthart, M.E.U., Neerincx, M.A., Hindriks, K.V.: Design patterns for an interactive storytelling robot to support children's engagement and agency. In: ACM/IEEE International Conference on Human-Robot Interaction, pp. 409–418 (2020)
6. Nichols, E., Gao, L., Vasylkiv, Y., Gomez, R.: Design and analysis of a collaborative story generation game for social robots. Front. Comput. Sci. **3** (2021)
7. Augello, A., Infantino, I., Maniscalco, U., Pilato, G., Vella, F.: Introducing NarRob, a robotic storyteller. In: International Conference on Games and Learning Alliance, pp. 387–396 (2018)
8. Bradwell, H.L., Edwards, K.J., Winnington, R., et al.: Companion robots for older people: importance of user-centred design demonstrated through observations and focus groups comparing preferences of older people and roboticists in South West England (2019)
9. Avioz-Sarig, O., Olatunji, S., Sarne-Fleischmann, V., et al.: Robotic system for physical training of older adults. Int. J. Soc. Rob. **13**, 1109–1124 (2021)
10. Zhou, E., Shi, Z., Qiao, X., Matarić, M., Bittner, A.: Designing a socially assistive robot to support older adults with low vision. In: International Conference on Social Robotics, pp. 443–452 (2021)
11. Shibata, T., Wada, K.: Robot therapy: a new approach for mental healthcare of the elderly - a mini-review. Gerontology **57**(4), 378–386 (2010)
12. Tokunaga, S., Tamura, K., Otake-Matsuura, M.A.: Dialogue-based system with photo and storytelling for older adults: toward daily cognitive training. Front. Rob. AI J. **8** (2021)
13. Kelley, J.F.: Natural language and computers: six empirical steps for writing an easy-to-use computer application. Ph.D. dissertation, The Johns Hopkins University (1983)
14. Manso, L., Bachiller, P., Bustos, P., Núñez, P., Cintas, R., Calderita, L.: RoboComp: a tool-based robotics framework. In: Ando, N., Balakirsky, S., Hemker, T., Reggiani, M., von Stryk, O. (eds.) SIMPAR 2010. LNCS (LNAI), vol. 6472, pp. 251–262. Springer, Heidelberg (2010). https://doi.org/10.1007/978-3-642-17319-6_25

15. Bustos García, P., Manso Argüelles, L., Bandera, A.J., Bandera, J.P., García-Varea, I., Martínez-Gómez, J.: The cortex cognitive robotics architecture: use cases. Cogn. Syst. Res. **55**, 107–123 (2019)
16. Hiroko Matsumoto, H., Uchida, T., Bessyo, K.: Method of evaluating dialogue robots for visually impaired and elderly people. Memoirs of the Faculty of Engineering (2017)

Design and Evaluate User's Robot Perception and Acceptance

Self-perception of Interaction Errors Through Human Non-verbal Feedback and Robot Context

Fernando Loureiro[1]([✉]), João Avelino[1,2][iD], Plinio Moreno[1,2][iD], and Alexandre Bernardino[1,2][iD]

[1] Instituto Superior Técnico - University of Lisbon, Lisbon, Portugal
fernando.a.a.d.r.loureiro@tecnico.ulisboa.pt
[2] Institute for Systems and Robotics - Lisbon, Lisbon, Portugal
{javelino,plinio,alex}@isr.tecnico.ulisboa.pt

Abstract. During human-robot interactions, robots may exhibit inappropriate social behavior due to a lack of social awareness (Social Norm Violations) or hardware/software issues (Technical Failures). The ability to detect such errors would allow robots to take corrective actions immediately and learn how to avoid future misbehavior, which is especially relevant during first encounters with people. Monitoring the reaction of humans interacting with the robot is one way to detect the occurrence of social errors. While humans interact by displaying various social signals (e.g., gestures, facial expressions, speech) that reflect their inner state, they can be ambiguous or difficult to process in unstructured scenarios. Moreover, social robots in the wild need to detect signals without the aid of markers or microphones on humans. Thus, our research focuses on error detection and classification using nonverbal social signals captured through the robot's onboard RGB camera (Eye Gaze, Head Pose, Facial Expressions, and Emotions) and robot action logs for context. Our two-step pipeline uses a cascade of Random Forest classifiers and a proposed low-cost yet accurate emotion detector. To evaluate the proposed methodology, we have labeled an available dataset of videos taken from the robot's perspective that performs human-robot interactions during a block assembly game, where the robot causes Social Norm Violations and technical failures. Our results show that the proposed system can detect and classify the failures with about 80% balanced accuracy in the used dataset and is significantly more effective than the baseline and other combinations of the proposed features.

Keywords: Social robotics · Social signals · Interaction errors

This work was funded by Fundação para a Ciência e a Tecnologia (FCT) through Ph. D. grants SFRH/BD/133098/2017 and COVID/BD/152458/2022, the LARSyS - FCT Project UIDB/50009/2020, and the FCT project HAVATAR-PTDC/EEI-ROB/1155/2020.

1   Introduction

Neither humans nor robots can always comply with social scripts and expectations. Even though they are paramount interaction guidelines for interaction between social agents, they are susceptible to failures related to perception, judgment, behavioral errors, or in the robotics case, Technical Failure (TF). We argue that, during first encounters, interaction errors are even more likely to occur given the lack of information between parties. For instance, even though social scripts can guide a robot to open the interaction with a target person, two types of errors are bound to happen due to the considerable complexity of the set of exchanged social signals and culturally dependent gestures. First, the group of norms the robot follows may be inappropriate for people interacting with it, e.g., due to cultural differences or personality mismatches. Breaking people's expectations this way constitutes a Social Norm Violation (SNV). Second, due to sensors, hardware, and software issues, the robot's ongoing actions may fail to complete making it behave erratically. These failures are classified as TFs. Giuliani et al. [8] proposed this nomenclature. Since these events are bound to happen and may hinder or even invalidate interactions, it is of paramount importance that social robots can be aware of them and react accordingly. This information complements social norms and scripts, making the interaction more robust to failures.

In this paper, we worked towards creating the self-perception of robot interaction failures by developing automatic error detectors and classifiers. Mobile social robots need to interact with people in the wild, without personal information, relying only on their own sensors, and having resource constraints. Furthermore, noise and phenomena like the cocktail party effect [3] render audio signals useless in uncontrolled scenarios. Thus, we focused on non-verbal visual data that a robot can extract with its own RGB sensors and logs of its actions to design an algorithm that detects and classifies failures from users' reactions and the robot's actions. We built our proposed method upon known features as classifiers from Human–Robot Interaction (HRI) and machine learning that, as far as we know, have not been applied together for this problem. We focused on the user's head features (head pose, gaze direction, Facial Action Unit (FAU)s, and emotions) and the robot's speech and arm gestures. The algorithm uses a cascade of Random Forest algorithms that first detect when an error occurs and then classify it as SNV or TF on a frame-by-frame basis.

Our contributions are threefold:

- a dataset of human head features, robot action logs, and error labels collected during a HRI experiment,
- a pipeline for error detection and classification that relies on features extracted from egocentric RGB images (non-verbal behaviors) and logs of the robot's actions,
- ablation studies that evaluate the behavior of error detection and classification when using distinct sets of input features.

2   Related Work

Previous studies have addressed how people react to robot failures in the last decade [4,8–10,15,16,18], attempting to identify relevant features. They focused on joint task execution during cooking or building tasks [4,9,15], identifying gaze shifting, head movements, facial expressions, and speech as prominent features. In addition, people's emotions evolve with human-human and HRI experiences, which they express through their faces. While some studies noticed how people changed their mood/emotions according to what they were experiencing with the robots [4,9] along the experiments, as far as we know, people have not developed automatic error detection and classification algorithms using them. However, these social signals can be ambiguous, with the same expression having two possibly opposite meanings (e.g., laughter can be related to both positive and negative feedback [7]). Thus, we believe that context is relevant to disambiguating such cases. However, we do not know past studies that investigated this hypothesis.

Regarding automatic error detectors proposed in past works, Trung and colleagues [18] tested distinct combinations of classifiers fed with 3D coordinates of head, shoulders, and neck. They collected and described their data collection method in their previous work [15]. The goal was to use human reactions to detect robot failures and classify them as TFs or SNVs. They tested several classic classifiers (K-Nearest Neighbour (KNN), Naive Bayes, Random Forest), obtaining accuracy results higher than 90%. However, they noted that the test set contained the same people from the training set, claiming that the classifier could be used in real-life scenarios if the robot has seen those subjects before. Kontogiorgos et al.'s recent work [11] used lexical, visual, and acoustic features to detect conversational failures. They also classify them as 5 types related to their conversational task, but not as SNV or TF. Their visual features were gaze, FAU, and head pose.

Table 1 summarizes some characteristics of features used in related works with automatic failure detectors and classifiers, relating them to the scope of this paper.

Thus, the **baseline** of our study used a Random Forest algorithm with the non-verbal features previously used in automatic error detectors and classifiers [10,18] that the robot's onboard sensors can extract. Therefore, the baseline features are the 3D head pose (position and roll/pitch/yaw) and gaze features (one normalized direction vector per eye and the average x/y direction in radians). Although Kontogiorgos and colleagues [11] used FAUs in their recent study, we did not consider them part of the baseline since we intended to test them against emotions during the ablation studies.

Table 1. Summary of error detection and classification features and characteristics related to the scope of this work: automatic detection and classification of interaction errors and SNVs and TFs using non-verbal features through the robot's onboard sensors.

	Gaze	Head move-ments	Body move-ments	Speech	Emotions	FAU	Hand gesture	3D body pose	3D head pose	Robot's actions
Tested on automatic systems	Yes [10,11]	Yes [10]	No	Yes [10,11]	No	Yes [11]	No	Yes [18]	Yes [10]	No
Used to detect errors	Yes [10,11]	Yes [10]	No	Yes [10,11]	No	Yes [11]	No	Yes [18]	Yes [10,11]	No
Used to classify as SNV and TF	No	No	No	No	No	No	No	Yes [18]	Yes [10]	No
Non-verbal features	Yes	Yes	Yes	No	Yes	Yes	Yes	Yes	Yes	Yes
Easy to extract with onboard small sensors	Yes [2]	No ([10] used a hat with markers)	Yes [19]	No (subjects in [10,11] used a microphone)	Yes (Sect. 4)	Yes [2]	Yes [17]	No ([18] used an external Kinect)	Yes [2]	Yes

3   Dataset and Experimental Setup

3.1   Dataset Description

To have data with the robot's action logs, clean data, and spontaneous reactions, we created a dyadic interaction in which 24 participants played a board game in a human-robot team to win a bar of chocolate. We needed samples that represented three scenarios: (i) no reaction to the robot, (ii) negative feedback due to errors, and (iii) positive feedback due to a positive robot action. Even though our detector targets negative feedback (interaction errors), positive reactions to the robot's actions are relevant for training since we would risk having a trained model that only considers action features otherwise.

We collected this data using the procedure described in our previous work [1]. It consisted of a game where people had to collect blocks around a room and pile them up correctly on a board. The robot, shown in Fig. 1, helped participants by keeping track of time or warning them when they misplaced a block. To provoke spontaneous reactions from people, we manipulated the game's difficulty and the robot's personality. The "Grumpy robot" was responsible for losing a simple game, while the "Kind robot" was responsible for winning a seemingly impossible game. According to questionnaires, participants recognized both robots' critical role in the game's outcome. The reactions in the videos are distinct: smiles and neutral expressions for the "Kind robot" and laughter, confusion, or shock for the "Grumpy robot." We have acquired approximately 4 h of data. Data collected from the robot's RGB camera consisted of 10 452 frames with SNVs, 208 48 frames with TFs, and 169 107 frames without errors. We note that SNVs and TFs can occur simultaneously.

3.2 Experimental Setup

We split the experimental setup into two parts. First, we evaluated the complete error detection and classification pipeline, focusing on the additional new features and the median filter. Then, we separately assessed the performance of the error detector and error classifier modules and checked out which features make a difference in their performance. In this paper, we do not focus on classifier selection and assume that Random Forest is the best non-deep learning method for the task. Classifier selection was extensively studied in the past works [10] [18], in our workshop paper [13], and [12]. Random Forest was overall the most accurate, even when compared to outlier detection methods (Isolation Forest). Since this paper follows a more human-centric approach, we focus on which of the social signals that robots detect are more meaningful to understand that something went wrong.

For training and evaluation, we randomly split the dataset as 75 % for training and 25 % for testing. The splitting process ensures that samples from participants in the training set do not appear on the test set. Since our paper focuses on first encounters, we want the robot to "see" people in the test set for the first time. During the experiments, we evaluated each condition 30 in random dataset splits (except when we explicitly state otherwise). We call each of these individual evaluations a *run*.

4   Proposed Pipeline

We propose a system that detects and classifies robot interaction errors according to the taxonomy of Giuliani et al. [8], i.e., as SNVs or TFs. Since our goal is to use this algorithm in the real robot in future real-world scenarios, we followed an egocentric perspective, relying only on the robot's onboard sensors. We propose a two-step model that first detects errors and then classifies them on a frame-by-frame basis. Both detector and classifier are Random Forests that use visual head/face features composed of OpenFace's [2] extracted features and features related to the robot context.

The first set of features contains the baseline features used by previous automatic error detection: 3D head pose (position and roll/pitch/yaw) and gaze features (one normalized direction vector per eye and the average x/y direction in radians). Additionally, we introduced FAUs (a vector of 17 Action Unit intensities and 18 Action Unit presences [2]) and Emotions (the dominant emotion of Ekman's [5] set or neutral). For emotion detection, we propose our "AverageAU" method that uses the association between FAUs proposed in [6]. We can represent this method with Eq. 1:

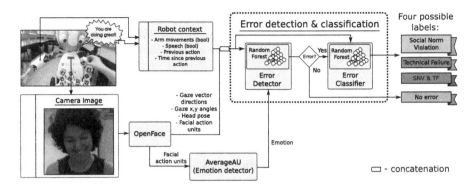

Fig. 1. Proposed frame-by-frame system for error detection and classification using the robot's onboard sensors. The two sources of information are the robot's camera and proprioception. We extracted visual features with OpenFace and concatenated them with the robot context features of arm movements and speech. In addition, we detect the current emotion from FAUs. The system performs error detection and classification in two steps. First, a Random Forest classifier fed with all features detects whether an error occurred. If it did not detect one, the system outputs the *No error* label. Otherwise, a second Random Forest classifier uses all features except the user's emotion to classify the error as *SNV*, *TF*, or both at the same time.

$$\hat{m} = \begin{cases} m^* = \arg\max_m f(m) = \frac{\sum_{n=1}^{N_m} \boldsymbol{I}(\mathrm{FAU}_m(n))}{N_m} & \text{for} \quad f(m^*) > \tau \\ \text{Neutral} & \text{Otherwise} \end{cases} \quad (1)$$

where $\hat{m}$ is the estimated emotion, $\boldsymbol{I}(j)$ is the intensity of FAU j, $\mathbf{FAU}_m$ is a vector of size N_m with the ids of action units associated to emotion m, and τ is a threshold. Table 2 lists the FAUs related to each emotion, according to Ekman [6]. For instance $f(m = \text{Hapiness}) = \frac{I(6)+I(12)}{2}$. Our previous experiments found an optimal value of 0.8 for τ. This method allows us to leverage data extracted with OpenPose without needing additional computationally intensive emotion detectors. Plus, it achieved 74.92 % accuracy in the CK+ dataset [14]. It also achieved 94.3 % and 75.42 % accuracy in two representative cases of our dataset. Further evaluation of emotion detectors is outside the scope of this paper. For more information please check the Master's thesis of Fernando Loureiro [12]. Since we compute the emotions from the FAUs, one could say that we are repeating features unnecessarily. However, by computing emotions, we added structural information that the machine learning algorithms do not need to learn, thus making the learning procedure potentially easier. We note that unlike Kontogiorgos et al. [10], we did not use the accumulated number of head movements over a time window since this information was prone to noise when using Open-Face. Unlike Kontogiorgos et al. [10] our goal was to have a system that could operate without external motion capture markers. Moreover, we also did not use their speech features (word count/response time/questions) since (i) we focus

Table 2. FAUs used to detect each basic emotion according to Ekman [6].

m	Anger	Disgust	Fear	Happiness	Sadness	Surprise
FAU$_m$	4, 5, 7 and 23	9, 15 and 16	1, 2, 4, 5, 20 and 26	6 and 12	1, 4 and 15	1, 2, 5 and 26

on non-verbal features and (ii) speech recognition is unreliable in non-controlled environments (like public places).

Our second set of features is related to the robot co ntext. In fact, Kontogiorgos et al. [10] highlight the role of contextual features to which their annotators had access, unlike the automatic system. And a subset of the overall context is composed of the robot's actions. Indeed, if we think about Human–Human Interaction (HHI), we usually reason about our actions when we receive negative feedback from someone. Thus, we introduced the following robot context features: (i) current action, (ii) previous action, and (iii) time since the previous action. We encode actions as two boolean vector entries that signal whether there was an arm movement, speech, or none. The current and previous actions can consist of speech and arm movements simultaneously.

As shown in Fig. 1, the first step is to extract and compute the complete set of visual and context features, which we concatenate. Then, a Random Forest error detector uses all features to classify them as *error* or *no error*. After the Random Forest error detector, we used a median filter on its results, with a window of 30 frames, which equates to 2 s in our system. This filter smooths the output by using past results to reject spurious miss-classifications. The algorithm outputs *no error* if that is the result of median filtering. Otherwise, it uses a second Random Forest to classify the error as SNV, TF, or both. Unlike the error detector in the first stage, the error classifier Random Forest does not use emotions as features (but uses all the remaining ones). We do not use emotions for error classification since they did not improve the algorithm's accuracy during our tests. Thus, the final output of our algorithm is either *SNV, TF, SNV & TF*, or *No error*.

4.1   Pipeline Results

The complete pipeline addresses a multilabel problem, with four possible labels (*SNV, TF, TF&SNV*, and *No error*). In addition, the dataset is unbalanced, having significantly more samples without errors. Thus, the two metrics used for evaluation are the hamming loss and balanced accuracy.

Our algorithm (Fig. 1) without the median filter achieved an average balanced accuracy of 79.63 % while the baseline (with only the functional features from the state-of-the-art) only achieved 57.29 %. A t-test showed a statistically significant difference ($t(14) = 22.74$, $p < 0.0001$) between conditions. We obtained a large effect size (Cohen's $d = 7.29$). The proposed method's hamming loss was also statistically significantly lower than the baseline ($t(14) = 26.53$, $p < 0.0001$, Cohen's $d = 7.903$). We illustrate the results on Fig. 2a.

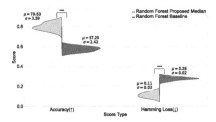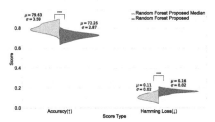

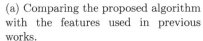

(a) Comparing the proposed algorithm with the features used in previous works.

(b) Comparing the proposed algorithm with and without median filter.

Fig. 2. Comparing the proposed algorithm with the features used in previous works. ↑ - higher scores are better; ↓ - lower scores are better

Adding the median filter as shown in Fig. 2b produced a significant improvement in the accuracy, as assessed through a paired-samples t-test ($t(14) = 9.64$, $p < 0.0001$). It increased from 72.26 % to 79.63 %, with a large effect size (Cohen's $d = 2.27$). Additionally, there was a significant decrease in the Hamming Loss ($t(14 = 10.19)$, $p < 0.0001$) with a large effect size (Cohen's $d = 2.6$).

5 Ablation Studies

In this section, we present ablation studies where we analyze the impact of distinct feature sets on the performance of error detection and error classification. The feature sets consisted of:

- Baseline (3D head pose and gaze features)
- Baseline + FAU (BF)
- Baseline + Emotions (BE)
- Baseline + FAU + current robot Actions (BFA)
- Baseline + FAU + current robot Actions + Emotion (BFAE)
- Baseline + FAU + current robot Actions + Emotion + Last action (BFAEL)
- Baseline + FAU + current robot Actions + Emotion + Last action + Time since last action (BFAELT)

5.1 Error Detector

We evaluated the performance of the Random Forest error detector (the pipeline's first module) with distinct sets of proposed features. First, we compared the performance using the baseline features against the baseline with action units. The results are depicted in Fig. 3 and Table 3. We used a paired-samples t-test when the result followed a normal distribution and a Wilcoxon signed rank test otherwise.

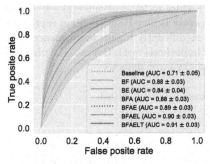

(a) Receiver operating characteristic curves for error detectors using distinct sets of features.

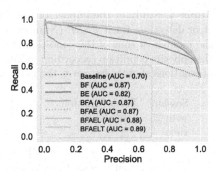

(b) Precision/recall curves for error detectors using distinct sets of features.

Fig. 3. ROC average (±1 standard deviation) and Precision/Recall curves of the error detector for distinct sets of features. The greatest the area under the curve (AUC) the better the performance.

Table 3. Descriptive statistics and statistical analysis of Accuracy and F1 score metrics for distinct sets of features for the Random Forest error detector.

(a) Error detector statistics for Accuracy and F1 score with distinct combinations of features.

Features sets	Accuracy		F1	
	μ	σ	μ	σ
Baseline	65.2%	3.28%	64.3%	3.59%
BF	79.1%	3.22%	78.9%	3.22%
BE	74.7%	3.69%	74.6%	3.81%
BFA	79.3%	3.27%	79.1%	3.38%
BFAE	79.6%	3.47%	79.5%	3.55%
BFAEL	81.4%	3.46%	81.3%	3.46%
BFAELT	82.0%	3.44%	81.9%	3.53%

(b) Hypothesis tests for error detection using Random Forest with multiple sets of features. **** means that $p < 0.0001$. For normal data we used Cohen's d to measure the effect size, while for non-normal data we used the rank-biserial correlation r.

Feature sets	Accuracy			F1 score		
	t-test			t-test		
	$t(29)$	p	d	$t(29)$	p	d
Baseline v.s. BF	24.17	****	4.33	23.22	****	4.30
Baseline v.s. BE	16.88	****	2.72	16.44	****	2.77
BE v.s. BF	12.40	****	1.28	12.15	****	1.25
BFA v.s. BF	13.23	****	1.29	12.86	****	1.27
BFAE v.s. BFA	2.86	0.008	0.10	2.82	0.009	0.10
BFAEL v.s. BFAE	7.72	****	0.51	7.76	****	0.51
	Wilcoxon			Wilcoxon		
	W	p	r	W	p	r
BFAEL v.s. BFAELT	121	0.022	0.48	126	0.03	0.46

As we can see, all features significantly improved the results over the baseline, and adding more features makes the algorithm more accurate. We can see that adding FAU was more enhancing than emotions. Additionally, the small effect size of the BFAE v.s. BFA test (Table 3b) suggests that Emotions may not yield a very positive overall contribution. Since the slightly positive result may have happened due to a lucky set of training/evaluation splits, one of our concerns was whether emotion features could actually degrade the results. To answer this question, we performed an additional study comparing the detector with all features against a version of it without emotions. This experiment was composed of 10 training/evaluation sessions with 25 *runs* each. Each *run* consists of (i) randomly sampling 75% of the videos for training and 25% for the test set; (ii) computing the accuracy of each condition on the test set; (iii) performing the McNemar's test between conditions; and (iv) testing the accuracy of each condition for statistically significant differences over all runs. The

Table 4. Study of the impact of the Emotion feature in 25 experimental sessions of error detection. Each *#SBR* (Number of Significantly Better Runs) column represents the number of runs of the condition that had a significantly higher performance than the opposite condition (according to McNemar's hypothesis test). Overall, the presence of emotions slightly improves the performance of the error detector.

Session with 25 runs	With Emotions (BFAELT)			No emotions (BFALT)			t-test		
	μ	σ	#SBR	μ	σ	#SBR	$t(24)$	p	d
1	78.9%	2.84%	13	78.6%	2.89%	5	2.91	0.008	0.14
2	80.3%	3.53%	12	79.9%	3.71%	4	2.01	0.056	0.09
3	79.0%	3.50%	9	78.82%	3.78%	4	1.58	0.128	0.06
4	80.3%	3.61%	10	80.1%	3.83%	10	0.84	0.408	0.04
5	80.5%	3.02%	15	80.1%	3.24%	4	2.40	0.025	0.11
6	80.7%	2.64%	13	80.5%	3.04%	7	1.04	0.307	0.06
7	79.1%	2.54%	12	78.9%	2.59%	6	1.85	0.076	0.111
8	81.0%	2.75%	14	80.8%	2.85%	3	2.62	0.015	0.088
9	80.8%	3.81%	10	80.6%	3.58%	3	1.48	0.152	0.057
							Wilcoxon test		
							W	p	r
10	80.2%	3.41%	12	80.2%	3.54%	3	129.0	0.38	0.21

McNemar hypothesis test tells us that one algorithm makes more mistakes than the other if the p-value is below 0.05. Otherwise, the algorithms fail similarly. As seen in Table 4, when the detector uses emotions, it generally performs significantly better (according to McNemar's test) in more runs than without emotions. Although the average accuracy was only significantly better with emotion features in 3 of the 10 runs, adding the emotion feature did never significantly degrade the average accuracy.

5.2 Error Classifier

Similar to the previous experiments, we also evaluated the performance of the Random Forest error classifier with distinct features. Since this classifier assumes that an error occurred, we only used data samples that contain them. Error classification is a multilabel problem since the output can be SNV, TF, or SNV&TF. To deal with this problem with a different number of samples per label, we used the hamming loss in addition to the balanced accuracy. We show the results in Tables 5. When FAUs were present, all features except emotions significantly improved the algorithm's performance.

Since the effect of adding emotion features is not clear, we performed a similar experiment as we did for the error detector. We performed 10 training/evaluation

Table 5. Descriptive statistics and statistical analysis of Accuracy and Hamming Loss
for distinct sets of features for the Random Forest error classifier.

(a) Error classifier statistics for Accuracy
and Hamming Loss with distinct
combinations of features.

Features sets	Accuracy		Hamming loss	
	μ	σ	μ	σ
Baseline	58.7%	10.3%	0.27	0.08
BF	62.9%	9.47%	0.24	0.07
BE	60.7%	9.88%	0.26	0.07
BFA	67.1%	9.57%	0.20	0.06
BFAE	67.3%	9.59%%	0.20	0.06
BFAEL	71.1%	8.83%	0.16	0.05
BFAELT	74.6%	8.60%	0.14	0.05

(b) Hypothesis tests for error classification using Random
Forest with multiple sets of features.

Feature sets	Accuracy			Hamming loss		
	Wilcoxon			Wilcoxon		
	W	p	r	W	p	r
BF v.s. Baseline	11.0	****	0.95	23.0	****	0.90
BE v.s. Baseline	13.0	****	0.94	25.0	****	0.89
BFA v.s. BE	0.0	****	1.0			
BFAE v.s. BFA				215	0.73	0.08
BFAEL v.s. BFAE				0.0	****	1.0
	t-test			t-test		
	$t(29)$	p	d	$t(29)$	p	d
BE v.s. BF	4.21	***	0.23	3.56	0.001	0.27
BFA v.s. BE				8.90	****	0.92
BFAE v.s. BFA	1.06	0.29	0.025			
BFAEL v.s. BFAE	8.87	****	0.40			
BFAELT v.s. BFAEL	11.84	****	0.40	11.78	****	0.52

Table 6. Study of the impact of the Emotion feature in 25 experimental sessions of
error classification. Overall, there is a tendency for the presence of emotions to degrade
the accuracy of error classification.

Session with 25 runs	With emotions (E)		No emotions (NE)		t-test		
	μ	σ	μ	σ	$t(24)$	p	d
1	72.4%	9.51%	72.8%	9.43%	1.83	0.09	0.04
2	74.5%	10.2%	74.9%	9.67%	1.32	0.20	0.03
3	75.3%	9.77%	75.6%	9.59%	1.13	0.27	0.03
4	75.0%	9.88%	75.2%	9.83%	1.11	0.28	0.02
5	74.7%	10.1%	74.8%	9.83%	0.66	0.51	0.01
6	75.1%	9.94%	75.6%	9.78%	1.64	0.11	0.05
7	76.3%	10.2%	76.5%	10.1%	0.95	0.35	0.02
8	73.9%	9.42%	74.25%	9.13%	1.32	0.20	0.03
					Wilcoxon		
					W	p	r
9	75.1%	7.66%	75.4%	7.63%	109.0	0.16	0.33
10	74.4%	8.16%	74.78%	8.19%	90.0	0.05	0.45

sessions with 25 *runs* each. Each *run* consists of (i) randomly sampling 75% of the
error samples for training and 25% for the test set; (ii) computing the accuracy of
each condition on the test set; and (iii) testing the accuracy of each condition for
statistically significant differences over all runs. As shown in Table 6, emotions
frequently degrade the results of error classification.

6   Conclusions and Future Work

In this paper, we put our efforts into making robots autonomously detect their failures during HRI. We proposed an algorithm that detects and classifies HRI errors during one-to-one interactions. Our goal was to build a system that only relied on non-verbal features that the robot could extract with its sensors (for possible in-the-wild non-invasive interactions). We used a baseline of features from previous automatic error detectors and classifiers that met these requirements and showed that the proposed set of features improved the results. Then, we broke down the system with ablation studies to study the contribution of the additional features.

Our results showed that FAUs and robot context features significantly improve error classification results. Although previous works show links between these social signals and interaction errors [4], as far as we know, this was the first attempt to create a working automatic error detector and classifier that uses them. Emotions, however, did not significantly enhance the results. First, they provided minor improvements to the Random Forest error detector. Nonetheless, since they are computationally fast to compute with the *AverageAU* method, we used them for error detection. However, for the Random Forest error classifier, emotions actually degraded the results. A possible reason for minor improvements is that the classifier intrinsically captures the structural knowledge that relates FAUs to emotions. Thus, it may not need emotion detection algorithms to have the necessary information. The deterioration of the results of the error classifier may also result from the accumulation of errors in FAU estimation that get amplified with a wrongly estimated emotion. This issue needs further clarification, possibly by labeling people's emotions and using the ground truth as a feature.

The next step for this work is to test whether the proposed system works in different scenarios, possibly in in-the-wild Human–Robot Interactions.

References

1. Avelino, J., Gonçalves, A., Ventura, R., Garcia-Marques, L., Bernardino, A.: Collecting social signals in constructive and destructive events during human-robot collaborative tasks. In: Companion of the 2020 ACM/IEEE International Conference on Human-Robot Interaction, HRI 2020, pp. 107–109. Association for Computing Machinery, New York (2020). https://doi.org/10.1145/3371382.3378259
2. Baltrusaitis, T., Zadeh, A., Lim, Y.C., Morency, L.P.: OpenFace 2.0: facial behavior analysis toolkit. In: IEEE International Conference on Automatic Face & Gesture Recognition. IEEE (2018). https://doi.org/10.1109/fg.2018.00019
3. Bronkhorst, A.W.: The cocktail party phenomenon: a review of research on speech intelligibility in multiple-talker conditions. Acta Acustica United Acustica **86**(1), 117–128 (2000)
4. Cahya, D.E., Ramakrishnan, R., Giuliani, M.: Static and temporal differences in social signals between error-free and erroneous situations in human-robot collaboration. In: Salichs, M.A., et al. (eds.) ICSR 2019. LNCS (LNAI), vol. 11876, pp. 189–199. Springer, Cham (2019). https://doi.org/10.1007/978-3-030-35888-4_18

5. Ekman, P.: An argument for basic emotions. Cogn. Emotion **6**(3–4), 169–200 (1992)
6. Ekman, P., Friesen, W.V.: Measuring facial movement. Environ. Psychol. Nonverbal Behav. **1**(1), 56–75 (1976)
7. Ethofer, T.: Are you laughing at me? neural correlates of social intent attribution to auditory and visual laughter. Human Brain Mapp. **41**(2), 353–361 (2020). https://doi.org/10.1002/hbm.24806
8. Giuliani, M., Mirnig, N., Stollnberger, G., Stadler, S., Buchner, R., Tscheligi, M.: Systematic analysis of video data from different human-robot interaction studies: a categorization of social signals during error situations. Front. Psychol. **6**, 931 (2015)
9. Hayes, C.J., Moosaei, M., Riek, L.D.: Exploring implicit human responses to robot mistakes in a learning from demonstration task. In: 2016 25th IEEE International Symposium on Robot and Human Interactive Communication (RO-MAN). IEEE (2016)
10. Kontogiorgos, D., Pereira, A., Sahindal, B., van Waveren, S., Gustafson, J.: Behavioural responses to robot conversational failures. In: Proceedings of the 2020 ACM/IEEE International Conference on Human-Robot Interaction. ACM (2020). https://doi.org/10.1145/3319502.3374782
11. Kontogiorgos, D., Tran, M., Gustafson, J., Soleymani, M.: A systematic cross-corpus analysis of human reactions to robot conversational failures. In: Proceedings of the 2021 International Conference on Multimodal Interaction, pp. 112–120 (2021)
12. Loureiro, F.: Detecting Interaction Failures through Emotional Feedback and Robot Context. Master's thesis, Instituto Superior Técnico, Universidade de Lisboa (2021)
13. Loureiro, F., Avelino, J., Moreno, P., Bernardino, A.: Detecting human-robot interaction failures through egocentric visual head-face analysis. In: EgoVIP - Egocentric vision for interactive perception, learning, and control, Workshop at IROS 2021 (2021)
14. Lucey, P., Cohn, J.F., Kanade, T., Saragih, J., Ambadar, Z., Matthews, I.: The extended cohn-kanade dataset (ck+): a complete dataset for action unit and emotion-specified expression. In: 2010 IEEE Computer Society Conference on Computer Vision and Pattern Recognition - Workshops. IEEE (2010). https://doi.org/10.1109/cvprw.2010.5543262
15. Mirnig, N., Stollnberger, G., Miksch, M., Stadler, S., Giuliani, M., Tscheligi, M.: To err is robot: how humans assess and act toward an erroneous social robot. Front. Rob. Artif. Intell. **4** (2017). https://doi.org/10.3389/frobt.2017.00021
16. Salem, M., Lakatos, G., Amirabdollahian, F., Dautenhahn, K.: Would you trust a (faulty) robot? In: Proceedings of the Tenth Annual ACM/IEEE International Conference on Human-Robot Interaction - HRI 2015. ACM Press (2015)
17. Simon, T., Joo, H., Matthews, I., Sheikh, Y.: Hand keypoint detection in single images using multiview bootstrapping. In: CVPR (2017)
18. Trung, P., et al.: Head and shoulders: automatic error detection in human-robot interaction. In: ACM International Conference on Multimodal Interaction. ACM Press (2017). https://doi.org/10.1145/3136755.3136785
19. Wei, S.E., Ramakrishna, V., Kanade, T., Sheikh, Y.: Convolutional pose machines. In: IEEE Conference on Computer Vision and Pattern Recognition (2016)

The Effect of Anthropomorphism on Diffusion or Responsibility in HRI

Erika Tuvo[1], Paola Ricciardelli[1,2] (iD), and Francesca Ciardo[3](✉) (iD)

[1] University of Milano-Bicocca, 20120 Milan, Italy
[2] NeuroMI: Milan Center for Neuroscience, Milan, Italy
[3] Italian Institute of Technology, 16163 Genoa, Italy
`francesca.ciardo@iit.it`

Abstract. Recent studies showed that in Human-Robot Interaction (HRI), humans perceive less agency over the negative outcomes of their actions, raising the Diffusion of responsibility (DOR) phenomenon. In the present study, we examined the effect of anthropomorphism on the reduction of agency when interacting with robots. To this end, young adults played a risk-taking task, in which they were asked to stop an inflating balloon before it reaches a pin and burst. However, every time they acted to stop the inflation of the balloon they were losing points from a starting score. Participants play the task alone, or together with a co-agent. Within-task, we manipulated the co-agent: a human, a robotic arm, and a humanoid robot. Results showed lower agency ratings reported when participants shared the task with the co-agent compared to when they performed the task alone. Interestingly, such a reduction was comparable across the three co-agents. This suggests that DOR in HRI occurs similarly to when interacting with a human being regardless of the level of anthropomorphism of the robotic partner.

Keywords: Anthropomorphism · Diffusion of responsibility · Human–Robot Interaction

1 Introduction

The diffusion of responsibility (DOR) is a socio-psychological phenomenon defined as the perception, in the presence of other people, of feeling less responsible for the consequences of one's actions, especially if these are negative [1, 2]. This phenomenon was studied in emergencies in which humans, when in the presence of other humans, tend to provide help with less probability than when they are alone. This is thought to occur because the responsibility for the negative consequences of our decision is perceived as divided among all those present [3, 4]. Therefore, as the number of people involved in social situations increases, the sense of personal responsibility decreases [1–3, 5]. It appears clear that the Sense of Agency (SoA), i.e. the feeling of being in control of one's actions and the consequences associated with them [6, 7], is crucially linked to the DOR phenomenon. Specifically, in a social context, the less control people perceive over their actions, the less they feel responsible for negative consequences. In two recent

F. Cavallo et al. (Eds.): ICSR 2022, LNAI 13818, pp. 488–497, 2022.
https://doi.org/10.1007/978-3-031-24670-8_43

studies, Beyer and colleagues (2017; 2018) showed that SoA is reduced when humans interact with the avatar of another human being, but not when they are interacting with a non-agentic avatar [i.e. a tool, 7, 8]. In Beyer and colleagues' work [7], the reduction in agency ratings was also mirrored at the electrophysiological level with a reduction of the feedback-related negativity amplitude associated with outcome monitoring. The reduction of SoA in social contexts has been explained as the consequence of the fact that in the presence of other potential agents, the representation of their actions interferes with action selection, increasing interference in our own action planning processes [7–9]. Increased interference (or action disfluency), in turn, has been shown to decrease SoA over action outcomes [10]. Interestingly, a recent study in Human-Robot Interaction (HRI) shows that a reduction in SoA and DOR occurs also when the co-player is a robot [11, 12]. In Ciardo and colleagues' study [11], participants played the Ballon Risk-Taking task (BART) proposed by Beyer and colleagues [7] in two different conditions (i.e., individual vs. joint). In the individual condition, participants played the task alone, whereas, in the Joint condition, they played either with the Cozmo robot, with a non-agentic air pump, or with another human being. The authors [11] showed that the reduction in SoA in Joint conditions occurred for the Cozmo robot and the human partner but not for the non-agentic air pump, suggesting that DOR of responsibility in HRI might be linked to the attribution of intentionality to the robotic agents. Hinz and colleagues [12] replicated the study focusing on how the presence of the Cozmo robot affected the neural correlates of action selection. The results showed that in HRI the amplitude of the Readiness Potential component was larger than when participants were acting with Cozmo, suggesting that during HRI the selection of the action is more engaging since the participants have to represent also the consequences of the robot's actions. Furthermore, the analysis of the monitoring of the outcomes showed that the presence of the robot influences the attention allocated to the number of points lost [12]. Specifically, less attention was allocated to the outcome for the Joint compared to the Individual condition.

Taken together, the evidence shows that DOR and reduced SoA occur in HRI similarly to what happens in human-human interactions. However, the reviewed studies did not take into account that robots can differ in the level of human likeness and anthropomorphism. Specifically, previous studies [11, 12] used as a co-agent the Cozmo robot, which is characterized by a high level of anthropomorphism in terms of facial expression and movement but it does not resemble humans in physical appearance. However, anthropomorphism plays a major role in HRI, as social cognitive phenomena such as joint attention seem to only occur when we can attribute a certain level of intentionality to the agent [13, see 14 for a review]. Anthropomorphism can be driven by the human-like physical appearance of an agent and has been shown to influence the ability to represent the actions of robotic agents [15].

2   Aim

The present study aims to test whether the human-likeness of the appearance of robotic agents affects the DOR over negative outcomes generated by human actions. To this end, we replicated Beyers and colleagues' studies [7, 8, 11, 12] but added two robotic co-agents that differed in the level of human-likeness in physical appearance. Specifically, we asked human participants to perform a task in which actions were followed by negative outcomes either alone, or together with three different co-agents: a human being, a humanoid robot, and a robotic arm. As robotic co-agents, we employed the iCub humanoid robot [16] and the Kuka robotic arm [17]. Based on previous studies, we predicted that SoA ratings should be higher for the Individual than for all the Joint conditions.

Regarding the effect of anthropomorphism, we predicted that, among the Joint conditions, anthropomorphism should modulate the SoA rating. Specifically, the SoA ratings were expected to decrease more as the co-agent resembles a human being.

3 Materials and Methods

3.1 Participants

Thirty young adults (8 males; 1 left-handed, mean age $= 24 \pm 3.02$, and 22 females, all right-handed, mean age $= 23.27 \pm 2.14$) took part in the study. The study was approved by the local ethical committee (Department of Psychology, University of Milano-Bicocca). The sample size was estimated a priori according to previous experiments (Beyer et al., 2017; 2018), and by a priori power analysis. According to it, 30 participants should have been tested to detect a large effect size [Cohen's F2 $= 0.35$, alpha (one-tailed) $= .05$ and power $= 0.85$].

Participants gave their written consent prior the participation. All had normal or corrected-to-normal vision. They received 0.2 CFU as compensation for their participation. All participants were naïve about the aim of the study, and they were debriefed at the end of the experiment.

3.2 Apparatus and Stimuli

The apparatus was constituted of a 21" inches screen (1280x800 pixels) connected to a laptop (4.00 GB Ram, processor: Intel® Core (TM) ^{2} Duo CPU 2.53GHz). The stimuli were the image of a pin (1000x1000 pixels), the image of a red balloon (113x135 pixels), and the image of the three co-agents: a human being, the humanoid robot iCub, and the robotic arm Kuka see Fig. 1. The image for the human co-agent was a girl aged 18–30 and it was selected from the Karolinska Directed Emotional Faces studio [18]. The human co-agent was named "Chiara", whereas the robot co-agents were named and introduced with their commercial names, i.e. iCub and Kuka, respectively. Responses were executed on a QWERTY keyboard and a standard mouse. Stimulus presentation and data collection were controlled by Opensesame software (v 3.3.10) [19].

3.3 Procedure

The experiment was run in a quiet and lit room where the participants were alone for the duration of the task. Participants were seated approximately at a distance of 60 cm from the screen, and they were requested to perform the diffusion of responsibility (DOR) task used in Beyer et al. [7, 8]. Participants were asked to stop the inflation of a balloon before it reached a pin and burst (see Fig. 1). However, every time they stopped the balloon they lost some points from the starting amount of 10,000. The number of points lost in each trial varied as a function of the size at which the balloon was stopped (Tab. 1) but they lost more points if the balloon had exploded. In this way, every time the participants chose to act, the action (i.e., stopping the balloon) resulted to be costly, but less costly than not acting.

Table 1. Payoff structure of the task. The table shows the payoff sections in which the inflating sequence is reported as a function of the corresponding balloon size and the number of points lost. Within each payoff section, the actual number of points varied randomly from trial to trial.

Payoff section	Stop Balloon size	Outcome
4	The balloon is stopped at over 50% of the maximum size	$-15/-1$
3	Participants stop the balloon at a size between 49% and 33% of the maximum size	$-29/-16$
2	The balloon stop size is between 33% and 17% of the maximum size	$-45/-31$
1	Participants stop the balloon at a size lower or equal to < 17% of the maximum size	$-60/-46$
0	The balloon burst	$-100/-80$

The task comprised two different types of trials: Individual and Joint trials. In the Individual trials, participants were the only ones who could stop the balloon. In the Joint trials, participants were told that one of the co-agents was also in charge to stop the inflation of the balloon. In the case in which the co-agent stopped the balloon, participants did not lose any points. Co-agents' behavior was programmed to stop the balloon only in 60% of the Joint trials, and only after the balloon had reached 90% of its size.

Each trial started with a 1000 ms frame indicating the condition of the trial (Individual or Joint). In the Joint trials, the frame also displayed the image of the player with whom the participants were playing. Then, a fixation point was presented for a random 800–1000 ms time. Next, the balloon inflation sequence began. The balloon was presented at its initial size (i.e., 0.05% of the image size) for 500 ms and then began to inflate. The speed at which the balloon inflated varied both from trial to trial and within each trial. In Joint trials, two gray circles were also presented in the lower right corner and the upper left corner of the screen, indicating the presence of two players. Furthermore, when one of the two players executed a response, the corresponding circle turned from grey to blue, to avoid ambiguity in the case of simultaneous responses. When the action was executed by the co-agent, a "beep" sound was played to signal that the co-agent acted.

In both Individual and Joint trials, if the balloon was not stopped before it reached the pin, the explosion was simulated through the presentation of an image with the word "pop". At the end of each trial, a fixation point was presented for 1000 ms followed by feedback for 2000 ms indicating how many points participants lost. Then, an 8-point Likert scale with the question 'How much control did you feel over the outcome?' (in

Italian) was presented. The endpoints of the scale labels were 1 = 'No control' and 8 = 'Full control' (in Italian).

The task consisted of 8 blocks of 20 trials each. Trails were divided into two conditions, 40 trials in the Individual condition and 120 trials in the Joint condition.

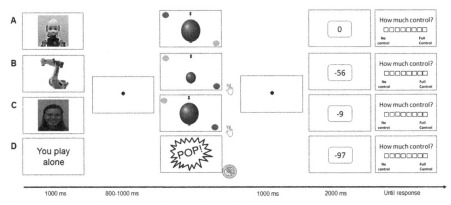

Fig. 1. DOR task. iCub action (A), low-risk valid trial (B), high-risk valid trial (C), Explosion (D).

After completing the task, participants were asked to rate the co-agents on a 5-point Likert scale about 10 attributes: happy, angry, sociable, insecure, altruistic, introverted, rigid, trustworthy, sad, and authoritative. The endpoints of the scale labels were 1 = 'No way' (in Italian) and 5 = 'Completely' (in Italian).

3.4 Data Analysis

Firstly, we evaluated whether participants' behavior differed between Individual vs Joint trials and whether their strategy in the Joint trials varied as a function of the co-agent they were playing with. To this end, based on the outcome trials were classified as: (i) Valid, when the participant stopped the balloon; (ii) Other agent actions, when the balloon was stopped by the co-agent, and (iii) Explosions, when the balloon was stopped by neither the participant nor the co-agent. The frequencies of the three types of trials were submitted to Pearson's chi-square test (x^2).

Then, to evaluate DOR for self-generated outcomes, we focused only on Valid trials, i.e. trials in which participants executed an action. For Valid trials, the dependent variables were: (i) stop size, the size at which the balloon was stopped; (ii) outcome, the number of lost points; and (iii) agency rating. The stop size and outcome values were standardized for each participant. All dependent variables were analyzed using linear mixed models. The standardized size of the balloon at the time of the action (Stop size) was modelled according to the Condition (Individual, Joint_Human, Joint_iCub; Joint_Kuka). We modelled the standardized Outcome of each trial as a function of Condition (Individual, Joint_Human, Joint_iCub; Joint_Kuka) and standardized Stop size. Agency ratings were modelled using Condition (Individual, Joint_Human, Joint_iCub;

Joint_Kuka) and Outcome, plus their interactions. Fixed effects were modelled as participant random effects (random intercepts and slopes). Finally, the post-task ratings were analyzed in two different ways. First, we classified the ten adjectives based on their valence, i.e., positive vs. negative valence. We compared if there was a difference between the three agents in the overall rating as a function of the adjectives' valence. To this end, scores were modelled as a function of co-agent identity and valence. Secondly, we compared the ratings for each attribute across the three co-agents. In both cases, linear models were used, and Bonferroni corrected pairwise comparisons were planned to address significant main effects and interactions. Analyses were conducted using the lme4 package [20] in R-studio statistical software.

3.5 Results

Pearson's chi-square test (x^2) showed that the balloon burst significantly more frequently in the Joint compared to Individual trials $[x^2 (6) = 944.67, p < 0.001]$, as indicated by the higher percentage of Valid trials in the Individual (M = 81.75%,) than in the Joint condition (M = 45.88%, see Fig. 2). In the Joint trials, participants stopped the balloon only in 45.88% of the times and left the other agent act in 48.25% of the trials. Consequently, the explosion rate in Joint trials decreased compared to the Individual condition (7.49% vs 18.25% respectively). No statistically significant difference was found in the frequency of valid responses as a function of the three co-agents $[x^2 (4) = 0.469, p = 0.976]$. Specifically, the participants let Kuka act in 47.58% of the trials, iCub in 48.75%, and the Human co-agent in 48.41%.

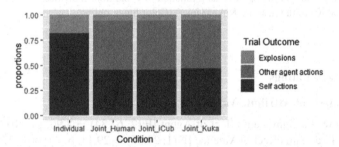

Fig. 2. Frequencies of trial outcomes (Explosions, Others agent, and Valid) plotted as a function of the Condition (Individual, Joint_Human, Joint_iCub, and Joint_Kuka).

3.5.1 Stop Size

Stop size wasn't predicted by the Condition (Individual, Joint_Human, Joint_iCub; Joint_Kuka) $[F (3, 37.21) = 1.61, p = 0.20; 97\%CI (-0.15,0.22)]$.

3.5.2 Outcome

The number of points lost were no predicted by the Condition (Individual, Joint_Human, Joint_iCub; Joint_Kuka) $[F (3, 38.90) < 1]$ nor by the Stop size $[F (1, 21.76) < 1]$; neither by Condition * Stop size interaction [F (3, 24.34) = 1.58, p = 0.219; 97%CI (−0.40, 0.23)].

3.5.3   Agency Ratings

Agency ratings were predicted by the number of lost points (Outcome) [F (1, 27.62) = 28.90, p < 0.001; 97%CI (−0.50, −0.11)], with smaller losses being associated with higher agency ratings.

The analysis showed a main effect of the Condition [F (3, 34.40) = 8.90, p < 0.001; 97%CI (0.16, 0.55)]. Specifically, agency ratings were higher for the Individual condition (M = 7.35, SE = 1.21) compared to all the Joint conditions (Kuka: M = 6.92, SD = 1.24, $p_{Bonferroni}$ < 0.001; ICub: M = 6.82, SD = 1.33, $p_{Bonferroni}$ < 0.001; Human: M = 6.89, SD = 1.38, $p_{Bonferroni}$ < 0.001) see Fig. 3.

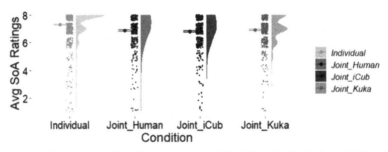

Fig. 3. Average SoA ratings plotted as a function of Condition: Individual (red), Joint_Human (green), Joint_iCub (blue), Joint_Kuka (violet) (Color figure online).

3.6   Post-task Ratings

3.6.1   Analysis of Attribute Valence

Results showed a significant effect of Agent [F (2, 62.34) = 8.90, p < 0.001; 97%CI (2.11, 2.61)], a main effect of Valence [F (1, 29.36) = 29.11, p < 0.001; 97%CI (0.37, 1.12)], and a significant interaction [F (2, 49.52) = 5.038, p = 0.010, 97%CI (−1.04, −0.004)]. Pairwise comparisons showed that the ratings of the three co-agents differed for positive attributes only. Specifically, the Human co-agent received higher ratings compared to the Kuka robotic arm (Human: M = 3.11, SD = 1.14 vs Kuka M = 2.38, SD = 1.15, $p_{Bonferroni}$ < 0.001) but not compared to the iCub robot (iCub: M = 2.81, SD = 1.03, $p_{Bonferroni}$ = 0.063), which differed from the robotic arm ($p_{Bonferroni}$ = 0.025).

For negative attributes, no statistical difference was reported between the three co-agents, all ps > 0.099.

3.6.2   Analysis of Each Attribute

Results showed a significant effect of Agent [F (2) = 14.40, p < 0.001], the main effect of Attribute [F (9) = 17.65, p < 0.001], and a significant two-way interaction [F (18) =

4.44, p < 0.001]. Pairwise comparison showed that the differences between co-agents only occur for four adjectives: Happy, Altruist, Friendly, and Insecure (see Fig. 4 for the other attributes. Specifically, the human received higher ratings for Happy attribute (M = 3.60, SD = 0.93) than the humanoid co-agent and the robotic arm (iCub: M = 2.73, SD = 0.91, $p_{Bonferroni}$ = 0.002; Kuka: M = 2.28, SD = 0.96, $p_{Bonferroni}$ < 0.001). For Altruist attribute, the human was associated with higher ratings compared to the Kuka arm (Human: M = 3.13, SD = 1.07, Kuka: M = 2.07, SD = 1.11, $p_{Bonferroni}$ = 0.001) but not compared to the iCub robot (M = 2.60, SD = 1.04, $p_{Bonferroni}$ = 0.173). For Friendly attribute, the robotic arm showed lower ratings (M = 2.03, SD = 1.07) than both the humanoid and human co-agent (iCub: M = 2.87, SD = 1.07, $p_{Bonferroni}$ = 0.054; Human: M = 3.53, SD = 1.07, $p_{Bonferroni}$ < 0.001). Finally, for Insecure attribute, the human received higher ratings (M = 3.00, SD = 1.14) than the humanoid co-agent and robotic arm (iCub: M = 2.03, SD = 1.13, $p_{Bonferroni}$ = 0.031; Kuka: M = 1.97, SD = 1.03, p $p_{Bonferroni}$ = 0.014) (Fig. 4).

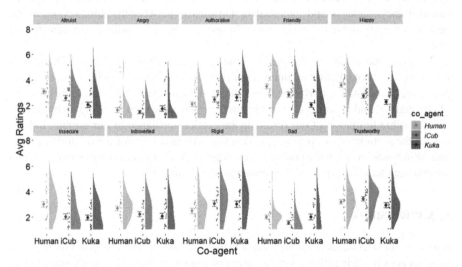

Fig. 4. Average ratings for each attribute plotted as a function of the co-agent.

4 Discussion

The present study aimed to test whether the effect of anthropomorphism influences the diffusion of responsibility (DOR) in human-robot interaction (HRI). To this end, young adults played a risk-taking task, in which they were asked to stop an inflating balloon before it reached a pin and burst. However, every time they acted to stop the inflation of the balloon they were losing points from a starting score. Participants played the task alone, or together with a co-agent. Within-task, we manipulated the type of co-agent: a human being, the Kuka robotic arm, and the humanoid iCub robot.

Results showed that the frequency of valid trials (i.e. when the participants stop the balloon) was higher in Individual than in Joint conditions. Such a result indicates that participants changed their strategy in the Joint Condition compared to the Individual Condition. Thus, they did represent the task as shared with the partner. In the Joint condition, the participants left the other agents to act in most of the trials with the same frequency among the three co-agents. This indicates that, contrary to what was hypothesised, the participants acted using the same strategy across different co-agents.

In line with previous studies [7, 8, 11, 12] results showed that SoA ratings were negatively predicted by the number of lost points, indicating that the more negative the outcome was, the lower responsibility participants perceived over it.

Results showed that participants reported lower agency ratings in the Joint compared to the Individual condition. Interestingly, contrary to what was hypothesised, the reduction in the SoA ratings was comparable across the three types of co-agents. Thus, the level of anthropomorphism of the robot seems to not influence the DOR during HRI.

Results from the post-task ratings showed that participants did attribute human-like features differently to the three co-agents, especially regarding positive attributes. Overall, participants rated the three co-agents as comparable for introversion, rigidity, trustworthiness, sadness, and authoritative. Differences between the human co-agent and the robots were found in the evaluation of happiness, anger, friendliness, insecurity, and altruism.

Together, the results of the present study suggest that during HRI, DOR always occurs regardless of whether we interact with other human beings or with a robotic agent. Interestingly, the DOR seems to be independent of the level of anthropomorphism of the robotic partner, and it occurs even if the interaction is simulated by using an image.

A possible limitation of our results is the gender unbalance of our sample. Indeed, most of the participants were females. This was a consequence of the recruiting procedure, which was based on the pool of psychology students. Future studies should address potential gender effects in the DOR phenomenon during HRI.

5 Conclusions

In social contexts, humans tend to perceive themselves as less responsible for the negative consequences of their actions (i.e., diffusion of responsibility). This study showed that the same phenomenon also occurs in human-robot interactions regardless of the level of anthropomorphism of the robotic co-agent. We propose that in HRI, the DOR is not due to the human-likeness of the co-agent but to the human ability to perceive robots as active agents irrespectively of their physical appearance. Thus, when programming the behaviour of robots to be implemented in public spaces, such as airports or hospitals, DOR should always be taken into account.

Acknowledgments. FC is supported by H2020–Marie Skłodowska-Curie Action agreement no. 893960. The content of this paper is the sole responsibility of the authors. The European Commission or its services cannot be held responsible for any use that may be made of the information it contains.

References

1. Darley, J.M., Latane, B. Bystander intervention in emergencies: diffusion of responsibility. Journal of Personality and Social Psychology, 8(4p1), 377–383 (1968)
2. Latane, B., Darley, J.M.: The unresponsive bystander: Why doesn't he help? Eur. J. Soc. Psychol. **36**, 267–278 (2006)
3. Latané, B., Darley, J.M.: Group inhibition of bystander intervention in emergencies. J. Pers. Soc. Psychol. **10**, 215–221 (1968)
4. Fischer, P., et al.: The bystander-effect: A meta-analytic review on bystander intervention in dangerous and non-dangerous emergencies. Psychol. Bull. **137**(4), 517–537 (2011)
5. Chekroun, P., Brauer, M.: The bystander effect and social control behavior: the effect of the presence of others on people's reactions to norm violations. Eur. J. Soc. Psychol. **32**(6), 853–867 (2002)
6. Frith, C.D.: Action, agency and responsibility. Neuropsychologia **55**, 137–142 (2014)
7. Beyer, F., Sidarus, N., Fleming, S., & Haggard, P. Losing control in social situations: how the presence of others affects neural processes related to sense of agency. eNeuro **5**(1), (2018).
8. Beyer, F., Sidarus, N., Bonicalzi, S., Haggard, P.: Beyond self-serving bias: diffusion of responsibility reduces sense of agency and outcome monitoring. Social cognitive and affective neuroscience **12**(1), 138–145 (2017)
9. Haggard, P.: Sense of agency in the human brain. Neuroscience **18**, 197–208 (2017)
10. Chambon, V., Sidarus, N., Haggard, P.: From action intentions to action effects: how does the sense of agency come about? Front Hum Neurosci **8**, 320 (2014)
11. Ciardo, F., De Tommaso, D., Beyer, F., Wykowska, A.: Attribution of intentional agency toward robots reduces one's own sense of agency. Cognition **194**, 1–11 (2020)
12. Hinz, N.- A., Ciardo, F., Wykowska, A. ERP markers of action planning and outcome monitoring in human-robot interaction. Acta Psychol. **212**, 1–11 (2021)
13. Martini, M. C., Buzzell, G. A., & Wiese, E. (2015, October). Agent appearance modulates mind attribution and social attention in human-robot interaction. In International conference on social robotics (pp. 431–439). Springer, Cham
14. Chevalier, P., Kompatsiari, K., Ciardo, F., Wykowska, A.: Examining joint attention with the use of humanoid robots-A new approach to study fundamental mechanisms of social cognition. Psychon. Bull. Rev. **27**(2), 217–236 (2019). https://doi.org/10.3758/s13423-019-01689-4
15. Abubshait, A., Wiese, E.: You look human, but act like a machine: agent appearance and behavior modulate different aspects of human–robot interaction. Front. Psychol. **8**, 1393 (2017)
16. Goeleven, E., De Raedt, R., Leyman, L., Verschuere, B.: The Karolinska directed emotional faces: A validation study. Cogn. Emot. **22**, 1094–1118 (2008)
17. iCub robot documentation. https://icub-tech-iit.github.io/documentation/
18. Kuka robotic arm. https://www.kuka.com/en-us/products/robotics-systems/industrial-robots/kr-1000-titan
19. Mathôt, S., Schreij, D., Theeuwes, J.: OpenSesame: An open-source, graphical experiment builder for the social sciences. Behav. Res. Methods **44**(2), 314–324 (2012)
20. Bates, D., Maechler, M., Bolker, B., et al.: lme4: Linear mixed-effects models using Eigen and S4 (Version 1.1–7) (2014). http://cran.r-project.org/web/packages/lme4/index.html

GeneRobot: How Participatory Development of Social Robots for Assisted Living Brings Generations Together

Caterina Neef[1]([✉]) [iD], Katharina Linden[1] [iD], Sophie Killmann[1], Julia Arndt[1] [iD], Nathalie Weßels[2], and Anja Richert[1] [iD]

[1] Cologne Cobots Lab, TH Köln - University of Applied Sciences, Cologne, Germany
{caterina.neef,julia.arndt,anja.richert}@th-koeln.de
[2] Diakonie Michaelshoven, Cologne, Germany

Abstract. Assistive technologies can positively contribute to the daily lives of older adults, enabling them to live in their own homes for longer. However, many older adults are unsure how to use such devices, and many existing technologies are unsuitable for them. Overcoming these challenges is the goal of the project GeneRobot: Engineering students develop user-centered applications for a social robot with and for older adults in assisted living. In this work, we discuss the benefits and challenges of intergenerational participatory robot development and showcase the developed applications, the learnings and findings for students, older adults, and the integration of the project into our university courses.

Keywords: Social robotics · Co-creation · Engineering education

1 Motivation

Due to the demographic transition and societal changes, 5.8 million adults over the age of 65 were living alone in Germany in 2019 [7]. Many of these older adults want to continue living in their own homes while retaining their autonomy. While digital technologies play an increasingly prominent role in our lives and can support our autonomy, many older adults struggle to use them [11]. These technologies include smartphones and computers, but also assistive devices like smart home speakers or social robots. An approach to increasing the digital competence of older adults is the participatory development of such technologies [16]. This leads not only to user-centered products and developments but also to users who are more adept at using these developed technologies. At the same time, for such user-centered development to be successful, developers need to be sensitized to their users' needs - which can be especially challenging when the user group is from an entirely different demographic.

This research was supported by the German Federal Ministry of Education and Research (BMBF) in the project GeneRobot (project number 16GDI102A).

F. Cavallo et al. (Eds.): ICSR 2022, LNAI 13818, pp. 498–507, 2022.
https://doi.org/10.1007/978-3-031-24670-8_44

Tackling these challenges is the goal of the project GeneRobot - in which engineering students develop applications for a social robot with and for older adults in assisted living. In the project, older adults can contribute to the development of apps that are designed specifically for them while becoming more comfortable with their use. At the same time, students come into direct contact with their users to ensure the successful development of user-centered apps. The developed apps are deployed into the assisted living communities in which the participating older adults live for continuous optimization and expansion. Overall, this also serves to investigate how older adults want to lead their daily lives and which roles social robots can and may play in them. In the following, we present our project, including related research, the different participant groups, as well as the first learnings and findings in the teaching and research domains.

2 Related Work

The design and development of assistive technologies for health and well-being has been an innovative field of research for years, one of the promising sub-areas being social robotics [1,22]. As opposed to virtual agents, the physical presence of robots has been shown to have positive impacts on user interaction [10]. This applies in particular to providing social company and combating loneliness [15].

Due to innovations in automation and sensor technology, socially assistive robots (SARs) are gradually being introduced into real-world scenarios like nursing homes or private households of older adults [4,9]. One of these robotic systems is Pepper (Aldebaran, France), described in [17]. The potential of Pepper as an SAR for older adults is already being tested in projects within and outside the academic community [2,20]. Since the robot's design includes social cues like gaze and gestures, Pepper is an ideal robot to develop and test the benefits of robotic social interactions. Current use cases include cognitive training through tasks, gymnastic exercises or games [20,21]. While several research projects present results of testing Pepper applications with older adults [6], few point out the process of how the tested behaviors or applications were chosen.

The age of the target group has to be considered when designing the behavior of a social robot [13]. One way to include the needs of older adults in product development is the participatory design method [14]. Some studies use user-centered design (UCD) methods for SARs, but most focus on the ideation or conceptual phase [5,19]. One study that displays an extensive participatory design process is the development and evaluation of the social and assistive robot HOBBIT [9]. However, since the robot was initially mainly designed for fall prevention, the study was less focused on co-creating social interactions. Using the methods of UCD holds great untapped potential for developing SAR applications and behaviors.

Furthermore, most studies only involve researchers, users, and sometimes other stakeholders in the co-creation process when developing robotic applications for older adults. This presents a missed chance for application-oriented teaching formats, especially when considering the benefits of intergenerational exchange [3]. There are successful university projects that bring together students and older adults to develop products collaboratively, some of which even deal with designing SARs [18]. But since these classes are held for design students, the joint development of robotic solutions mostly stops after the prototyping. Including engineering students in the co-creation process of SARs can expand the learning experience of the whole UCD process. Therefore, our approach of bringing generations together via participatory design aims to not only result in user-centered robotic applications but also to offer a meaningful contribution to the education of young engineers. Complementing this approach is the interdisciplinary research team, which acts as an interface between the older adults and students while integrating both groups into the participatory design process and its resulting learnings.

3   Methods

GeneRobot is a cooperative project between the Cologne Cobots Lab at the TH Köln - University of Applied Sciences and the Diakonie Michaelshoven, a provider of adult day care and assisted living facilities. One of these facilities are shared apartment assisted living communities in the Cologne area. The four communities include 24 one-bedroom apartments in total, each community with a shared common room. We enquired which residents would like to participate in the project after an event during which they had the opportunity to get to know and interact with the social robot Pepper [17], which we chose as the focus of the project is applications for social interactions. Six residents, subsequently referred to as participants, volunteered to take part in our project (see Fig. 1).

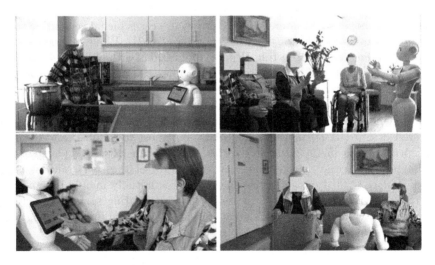

Fig. 1. The project participants are shown interacting with Pepper in one of their assisted living communities. The applications in use are described in Sect. 4.

The six participants have been diagnosed with varying health impairments. However, we specifically looked for participants for the study who neither have a diagnosis of any type of dementia nor mild cognitive impairment. As the participants' ages range from 55 to 95 and their impairments differ widely, their expectations and wishes for the robot also vary. To investigate this, the project is accompanied by continuous qualitative research assessments carried out by the interdisciplinary research team with backgrounds in engineering, social sciences, and gerontology. The applications for Pepper are developed by students in the TH Köln's Mechanical Engineering Master's program. Each semester, ten to 20 students in groups of four to five are involved in the project.

3.1 Technical Infrastructure and Data Privacy

Pepper is designed as a social companion and communicates mainly via natural language. Applications for the robot are programmed as Android apps. To design the verbal interaction, the rule-based dialogue system QiChat was used, which is included in the robot's framework. Additionally, everything Pepper says is displayed as text on its tablet, often also supported by additional images, to support the speech output.

Privacy is also an important component of this research project, as the robot lives with the participants and thus invades the privacy of their homes. Informed consent was ensured and obtained by providing information about what happens to the analyzed data via a detailed exposition of the project-related data protection guidelines according to current regulations, such as the General Data Protection Regulation (GDPR). The participants were informed through workshops in which they could practice how to use and interact with Pepper.

3.2 Participatory Development

Every semester, new apps or functionalities for Pepper are developed by groups of students and the participating residents in a co-creation process, derived from [8], and shown in Fig. 2. For the course "Developing anthropomorphic machines" (DAM) in the summer semester, each group is tasked to develop an application, subsequently referred to as *project apps*. Following the UCD method [12], the students conduct semi-structured interviews with the residents to understand the context of use. Based on interview recordings and their notes, the students specify the user requirements. After brainstorming possible ideas, each group chooses one solution they proceed to design and develop. Due to time limitations and Covid-19 restrictions, the ideas and designs are not evaluated by the users before the project apps are developed. However, evaluation and feedback are given by the research team so that the students have the possibility to rework their individual apps. General observations made by the project team concerning the usability of the project apps serve as impulses for the course "Human-machine interaction" (HMI) which is held during the winter semester. In this course, the groups of students are given predefined assignments that are tailored to the needs of the specific user group. The developed functions resulting from

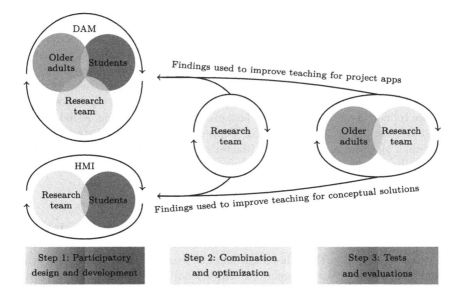

Fig. 2. The participatory development process includes three steps, while the findings from steps 2 and 3 are integrated into courses for following semesters.

these projects are subsequently referred to as *conceptual solutions*. The project apps and conceptual solutions are combined and optimized by the research team (step 2). Finally, the optimized versions are deployed in the assisted living facility, where they are tested by the older adults for whom they were developed (step 3). Periodic participant observations by the research team serve as the basis to evaluate and further optimize the developed project apps and conceptual solutions against the user requirements. All findings are also being used to further develop the teaching methods in the following semesters.

4   Results and Learnings for the Future

In the following, we show the results of the students' work and the optimizations made by the project team. We address the challenges of participatory technology development and our findings on the integration of the project into teaching.

4.1   Step 1: Participatory Design and Development

In the context of the DAM module, most of the wishes expressed by the participants were related to entertainment or support in everyday life, such as fitness exercises or recipes. Furthermore, one participant, having lost the partial ability of speech due to a medical condition, wished to use the robot for logopedic exercises as an addition to regular therapy. A total of three project apps were created within the first course: A speech training with logopedic exercises and a quiz, a fitness application, and an organizer app, which includes weather and an alarm clock function, notes, and recipes (see Fig. 4). Further features resulted from conceptual solutions students developed in the course HMI. The assignments consisted of optimizing an existing app with respect to users with either hearing or vision impairments, as shown in Fig. 3.

Fig. 3. Features for vision-impaired users (left) include a user interface in green with higher contrast and larger fonts; features for hearing-impaired users (right) include a slider to adjust the volume. Screenshots were translated into English. (Color figure online)

In the context of vision-impaired users, the students focused on implementing verbal menu navigation in addition to the existing buttons, promoting learnability by means of an interactive self-description of the system and restructuring the user interface (UI). The students researched the influence of colors and contrast on the perceptibility of written content and pre-selected several color combinations. These were subsequently presented in an online survey where participants rated their perceptibility. Based on the results, the students created a new color scheme. For better readability of text displayed on the tablet, the font Atkinson Hyperlegible (Braille Institute of America, USA), which is recommended for inclusive app and website development, was used. Also, an option was implemented that allows users to incrementally change the font size on the tablet via a button or voice command. Regarding features for hearing-impaired users, the students created an option to change the system volume within the app using a slider. Additionally, to help users understand the robot's behavior and ensure safety in human-robot interaction, the students implemented visual warnings about excessive robot movements, e.g., before the robot dances.

4.2   Step 2: Combination and Optimization

Within the first iteration, based on the evaluation by the project team, fundamental changes were made to the three project apps, as shown in Fig. 4. Since each of the apps was based on the ideas of one participant, partial functions and activities differing thematically from one another were grouped together. We

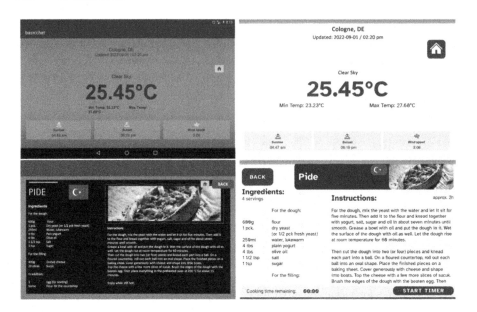

Fig. 4. The old and new designs of exemplary applications and features are shown: the weather feature and the recipes feature. A clearer and more consistent design with larger buttons and fonts was chosen.

developed a new structure, which takes the thematic content of each function into account and incorporates them into new apps accordingly:

- *Fun and games*: quiz (sights or flags) and fun facts about various countries
- *Kitchen companion*: recipes and facts about the cuisines of different countries
- *Planer*: notes, alarm clock, and weather function
- *Fitness*: various exercises and workouts for older adults
- *Speech training*: logopedic exercises on words, sentences, letters and numbers.

The design of the project apps, as received from the students, differed widely. Targeting good learnability and ease of use of the complete system, we created and implemented uniform design guidelines, specifying, e.g., colors, contrasts, font type and sizes to be used, and the size and design of clickable items. The UIs designed following the guidelines maintain the corporate identity (CI) of TH Köln. In most apps, the students used synchronous chats, thus preventing further user input from being processed while the robot is still providing verbal output. Throughout all project apps, we replaced these synchronous calls with asynchronous ones, thus adhering to the principle of increased user control over the system. When reviewing the dialogues, we removed or revised inappropriate content where necessary and shortened lengthy robot utterings in favor of a better user experience.

4.3 Step 3: Tests and Evaluations

The results of the first participatory observations were collected and analyzed by the research team. The two most prominent issues were the navigation from the single project apps to the menu overview and minor bugs that impact the user experience. In the first case, the default wiping motion was replaced by classical x-buttons to close the app. Additionally, the first bugs were fixed and the user experience is continuously optimized to get users more involved in the interaction. Minor usability issues as well as the results from future observations and usability tests will be used to continuously optimize the apps.

4.4 Learnings and Benefits for Older Adults, Students, Research Team

One of the challenges of integrating participatory design into teaching is the limited time frame. Due to the university schedule, all projects lasted three months and needed to be graded at the end of the semester. For some students, this was their first practical experience in app development. Since the goal was to develop a working application, there was little time for design iterations or prototypes. This also affected the contact time between students and users. The Covid-19 pandemic further aggravated this circumstance since the user group belonged to a vulnerable demographic. Since the TH Köln switched to online teaching, the students also had few possibilities to experience the robot they developed their apps for face-to-face. The simulation software the students used at home allowed them to test their apps and Pepper's movements but lacked speech input or output. This was a challenge for designing natural dialogues.

The overall learning from the first two semesters of the project was that when integrating co-creation methods into university classes, the research team plays an important role at the intersection between users and students. In the following semesters, more guidance and structure were introduced to compensate for the limited time frame. To help with the technical challenges of app development, more coding tutorials were introduced into the course schedule. We now also provide the code for a demo app so that students have a framework they can use and modify. To achieve a coherent look of the final product, the students are provided with a style guide that helps with questions of UI design concerning font, size, color, and spacing. Since the experience has shown that testing prototypes or apps with end-users during the semester presents a challenge, expert analysis will continue to play a role. For that purpose, standardized evaluation methods like heuristic evaluation are being introduced into the project.

To compensate for the limited contact time with the robot and to make first improvements and bug fixes, the students are shown recordings of Pepper's demo application as part of the programming lessons. This helps to give the students a better understanding of the timing and intonation in their dialogues and helps create more natural dialogues. The students then have the opportunity to test their apps in person for final adjustments. Furthermore, the importance of the original user interviews is stressed by letting the students transcribe the dialogues.

We also asked both the participants and the students for feedback. The participants stated that they were curious to see what benefit the robot can really provide in their daily lives, as it had not yet moved into the shared apartment community when we enquired for feedback. The students said they learned a lot, specifically about UCD and programming. They were also surprised that the participants they interviewed offered different ideas about what Pepper should do than they initially expected. This shows that it is essential that developments for older adults are developed together with them, as the projection of user requirements often does not match the actual expectations of the target users.

The next step in the project is to investigate how we can ensure that Pepper has a long-term benefit as a new roommate for the participants after having permanently moved in a few weeks ago. This includes continuous participatory developments and optimizations to make sure that all apps work as intended for the participants they were designed for while developing new apps and solutions based on the ideas they come up with. Additionally, the project will continue to explore different methodical approaches to co-creation, focusing on developing real-world applications through a complete user-centered design process.

References

1. Abdi, J., Al-Hindawi, A., Ng, T., Vizcaychipi, M.P.: Scoping review on the use of socially assistive robot technology in elderly care. BMJ Open **8**(2), e018815 (2018). https://doi.org/10.1136/bmjopen-2017-018815
2. Ärzteblatt, Redaktion Deutsches, D.Ä.G.: Pflege: Pepper bezaubert in Unterfranken (2019). https://www.aerzteblatt.de/archiv/206944/Pflege-Pepper-bezaubert-in-Unterfranken
3. Berne, R.W.: Ethics, technology, and the future: an intergenerational experience in engineering education. Bull. Sci. Technol. Soc. **23**(2), 88–94 (2003). https://doi.org/10.1177/0270467603251299
4. Broadbent, E., et al.: Benefits and problems of health-care robots in aged care settings: a comparison trial. Aust. J. Ageing **35**(1), 23–29 (2016). https://doi.org/10.1111/ajag.12190
5. Bulgaro, A., Liberman-Pincu, E., Oron-Gilad, T.: Participatory design in socially assistive robots for older adults: bridging the gap between elicitation methods and the generation of design requirements (2022). https://doi.org/10.48550/arXiv.2206.10990
6. Carros, F., Eilers, H., Langendorf, J., Gözler, M., Wieching, R., Lüssem, J.: Roboter als intelligente Assistenten in Betreuung und Pflege – Grenzen und Perspektiven im Praxiseinsatz. In: Pfannstiel, M.A. (ed.) Künstliche Intelligenz im Gesundheitswesen, pp. 793–819. Springer, Wiesbaden (2022). https://doi.org/10.1007/978-3-658-33597-7_38
7. Destatis, S.B.: Alleinstehende nach Alter, Geschlecht und Gebietsstand. Technical report (2022)
8. Durugbo, C., Pawar, K.: A unified model of the co-creation process. Expert Syst. Appl. **41**, 4373–4387 (2014). https://doi.org/10.1016/j.eswa.2014.01.007

9. Eftring, H., Frennert, S.: Designing a social and assistive robot for seniors. Z Geron-tol. Geriat. **49**(4), 274–281 (2016). https://doi.org/10.1007/s00391-016-1064-7

10. Gasteiger, N., Loveys, K., Law, M., Broadbent, E.: Friends from the future: a scoping review of research into robots and computer agents to combat loneliness in older people. Clin. Interv. Aging **16**, 941–971 (2021). https://doi.org/10.2147/CIA.S282709

11. Initiative D21 e. V.: D21-Digital-Index 2020/2021. Jährliches Lagebild zur digitalen Gesellschaft. Initiative D21 e. V., Berlin (2021)

12. Jokela, T., Iivari, N., Matero, J., Karukka, M.: The standard of user-centered design and the standard definition of usability: Analyzing ISO 13407 against ISO 9241–11. In: Proceedings of the Latin American Conference on Human-computer Interaction, CLIHC 2003, pp. 53–60. Association for Computing Machinery, New York (2003). https://doi.org/10.1145/944519.944525

13. Khaksar, W., Neggers, M., Barakova, E., Torresen, J.: Generation differences in perception of the elderly care robot. In: 2021 30th IEEE International Conference on Robot & Human Interactive Communication (RO-MAN), pp. 551–558 (2021). https://doi.org/10.1109/RO-MAN50785.2021.9515534

14. King, A.P.: Participatory design with older adults: exploring the latent needs of young-old and middle-old in daily living using a universal design approach. In: Di Bucchianico, G. (ed.) AHFE 2019. AISC, vol. 954, pp. 149–160. Springer, Cham (2020). https://doi.org/10.1007/978-3-030-20444-0_15

15. Li, J.: The benefit of being physically present: a survey of experimental works comparing copresent robots, telepresent robots and virtual agents. Int. J. Hum.-Comput. Stud. **77**, 23–37 (2015). https://doi.org/10.1016/j.ijhcs.2015.01.001

16. Merkel, S., Kucharski, A.: Participatory design in gerontechnology: a systematic literature review. Gerontologist **59**(1), e16–e25 (2019). https://doi.org/10.1093/geront/gny034

17. Pandey, A.K., Gelin, R.: A mass-produced sociable humanoid robot: pepper: the first machine of its kind. IEEE Rob. Autom. Maga. **25**(3), 40–48 (2018). https://doi.org/10.1109/MRA.2018.2833157

18. Rebola, C.B., Ramirez-Loaiza, S.: Co-designing technologies for well being: a robot companion for older adults. In: Arai, K. (ed.) FICC 2021. AISC, vol. 1364, pp. 871–882. Springer, Cham (2021). https://doi.org/10.1007/978-3-030-73103-8_63

19. Schuh, S., Greff, T., Winter, F., Werth, D., Gebert, A.: KI-basierte Mensch-Roboter-Interaktion durch die Weiterentwicklung multifunktionaler Serviceroboter zur Unterstützung in der klinischen Pflege. HMD **57**(6), 1271–1285 (2020). https://doi.org/10.1365/s40702-020-00676-x

20. Takanokura, M., Kurashima, R., Ohhira, T., Kawahara, Y., Ogiya, M.: Implemen-tation and user acceptance of social service robot for an elderly care program in a daycare facility. J. Ambient Intell. Hum. Comput. (2021). https://doi.org/10.1007/s12652-020-02871-6

21. Unbehaun, D., Aal, K., Carros, F., Wieching, R., Wulf, V.: Creative and cognitive activities in social assistive robots and older adults: results from an exploratory field study with pepper (2019). https://doi.org/10.18420/ecscw2019_p07

22. Youssef, K., Said, S., Alkork, S., Beyrouthy, T.: A survey on recent advances in social robotics. Robotics **11**(4), 75 (2022). https://doi.org/10.3390/robotics11040075

Embodiment Perception of a Smart Home Assistant

Mariya Kilina$^{(\boxtimes)}$, Tommaso Elia, Syed Yusha Kareem, Alessandro Carfí, and Fulvio Mastrogiovanni

Department of Informatics, Bioengineering, Robotics, and Systems Engineering (DIBRIS), University of Genoa, Genoa, Italy
mariya.kilina@edu.unige.it

Abstract. Demographic growth and rise in the average age of the population is increasing the demand for the elderly assistance. Health care oriented ambient intelligence technologies are fundamental to support elderly peoples' autonomy. In this paper, we present a smart home system that is able to recognize human activities and is integrated with a proactive vocal assistant. We chose one of possible user scenarios to show the performance of this smart home system and to perform a preliminary comparison between users' experience while watching videos of a volunteer interacting with an embodied versus a not-embodied assistant. The scenario is recorded from the user's point of view, while the user interacts with a robot assistant or a simple vocal assistant. The results of the User Experience Questionnaire show that participants found the robot assistant considerably more attractive, innovative and stimulating in comparison to the vocal assistant.

Keywords: Ambient intelligence · Vocal interface · Human robot interaction · Agent's embodiment

1 Introduction

The continuous increase in the age of the population is driving the development of new systems to take care of the elderly [1]. In this context, research on smart homes and Ambient Intelligence (AmI) [16] is particularly relevant, since the distribution of sensors in the environment, envisioned by AmI, can be used to monitor and support older people at home [3]. This new paradigm takes the name of Ambient Assisted Living (AAL) [7]. AAL systems can monitor various parameters (e.g., weight, heartbeat, human movements) using sensors both distributed in the environment and worn by the user. This information can be processed to monitor the user's health status or to track the user's behaviors. Therefore, such a system may generate relevant information for healthcare professionals [4] or for an intelligent system to support the subject [16]. According

---

M. Kilina and T. Elia—The authors contributed equally.

F. Cavallo et al. (Eds.): ICSR 2022, LNAI 13818, pp. 508–517, 2022.
https://doi.org/10.1007/978-3-031-24670-8_45

to its functionalities, an AAL system can target different applications, such as: i) comfort, i.e., classical home automation allowing the user to control household appliances; ii) health monitoring, i.e., assessment of the user's health status; iii) security, i.e., detection of dangerous situations or emergencies (e.g., fall, smoke, and intrusion detection).

In healthcare AAL applications, raw data can be provided to caregivers to monitor the person's health, or it can be processed to extract higher-level information. An example of this process is the recognition of activities of daily living (ADL) such as: walking, drinking, and brushing teeth [2,15]. The interest of healthcare professionals in automatic ADL recognition derives from their relationship with the degree of independence of the subject [6]. In addition, an AAL system that can recognize ADLs can use this information to suggest activities (e.g., encouraging exercise after sitting for a long time) or remind people to do things (e.g., reminding them to take medication before or after a meal). These applications present different challenges in terms of sensors to be used, data management, data analysis, and user interaction [14].

Additionally, the proper ADL recognition method should be selected. Most of the ADL recognition systems in the literature analyze human motion to determine the corresponding ADL [12]. However, solutions that consider context have also been proposed since movements may have a different meaning depending on the circumstances [8]. Finally, the system should interact in a natural and non-invasive way to inspire the user's trust. Nowadays, there are many alternatives for an intelligent system to interact with a human. The most common interfaces use voice feedback or visual stimuli on a screen. At the same time, the emerging field of social robotics proposes to use robots as trusted partners for humans in a home or hospital scenarios.

Previous work in the field of social robotics show that some features of the intelligent system such as perceived sociability, animacy and humanlike-fit can predict the user's willingness to use the system [18]. Thereby, users appreciate intelligent systems with which they can communicate using natural languages and which behave like humans. In this context, the agent embodiment is an important aspect influencing user's perception of the whole system. In Virtual Reality (VR) environment users prefer visible assistant rather then a voice one [9,10]. Moreover, an assistant that is able to move around the space and interact with objects is perceived as more influential, trustworthy and socially present compared to the embodied, but motionless one [9]. Speaking of the comparison in perception between smart speaker, i.e., vocal assistant and robot assistant, similar results are observed. Vocal assistants are perceived as more socially present if they have human-like embodiment [11,13]. Furthermore, users tend to trigger conversations with a robot assistant significantly more often then with a smart speaker, i.e., vocal assistant [13]. All of these findings lead us to the assumption, that along with the vocal assistants, AAL systems could benefit from the human-like embodiment of their agents in terms of the user experience.

Thus, the goal of this work is to investigate if the type of physical embodiment of a virtual assistant has a positive effect on users of an AAL system. To this end, we integrated a voice reminder assistant into a state-of-the-art ADL recognition system, and we recorded a video with two experimental conditions: i) a voice interface with a speaker and ii) a voice interface mediated by a small social robot (i.e., SOTA). The videos were provided to a set of volunteers who were asked to answer a user experience questionnaire after watching a video. The remainder of the article follows. Section 2 presents the overall system's architecture. Section 3 explains the experimental setup and the assessment method. Section 4 presents the results of the experiment. Finally, Sect. 5 present conclusions.

2   System's Architecture

In this section we broadly describe the architecture of the system. For more detailed information about all of it's components refer to Kareem et al., 2018 [8].

As shown in Fig. 1, the system consists of several interconnected parts. Specifically, the system is composed of three macro-layers connected to each other via a database:

Sensing Layer: acquires sensory data coming from a smart watch.
Human Activity Recognition (HAR) Layer: models and recognizes activities of daily living (ADL).
Human Computer Interaction (HCI) Layer: provides interfaces for human computer interaction.

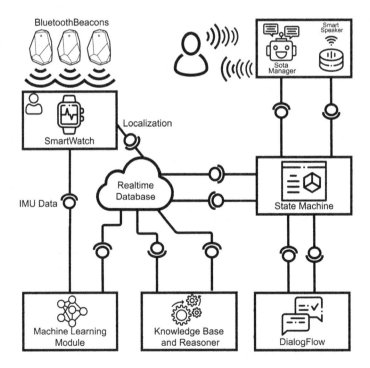

Fig. 1. System's architecture.

2.1 Sensing Layer

In the Sensing Layer sensory data is collected by using a smart watch and a set of Estimote Beacons[1] placed in each room of the user's house. This system allows to trace the user's location based on which beacon the smart watch is connected to. This information is acquired and then published to the database by an Android application, installed on the smart watch. Another application acquires the inertial raw data from the smart watch and sends it to the Machine Learning module that recognizes simple human activities.

2.2 Human Activity Recognition Layer

We take a hybrid approach towards HAR. On the one hand, adopting a machine learning approach for recognizing simple activities based on the IMU data stream from the smartwatch, e.g., (i) drinking, (ii) pouring, (iii) standing up, (iv) sitting down, and (v) walking. On the other hand, adopting an ontology based approach for recognizing contextual activities, e.g., (i) having breakfast and (ii) sitting idle for a specific amount of time. To be able to use the ontology as a part of overall HAR system's architecture, we used the OWLOOP API[2] that allows adding, removing and reasoning over axioms present in the ontology from OOP (object oriented programming) domain.

Machine learning module and Arianna [8] (i.e., ontology and reasoner) interact with each other via a real-time database. As soon as there is new information in the real-time database, regarding the user's location and/or the simple activity performed, Arianna uses that information to make assertions in the ontology and reason based on those assertions. The reasoner we used was Pellet. If reasoning leads to the inference of a contextual activity, then this information is saved back to the real-time database. Lastly, the human computer interaction layer becomes active.

2.3 Human Computer Interaction Layer

The system interacts with the assisted person through a vocal interface. We introduced two different ways of interaction: (i) through a vocal assistant (i.e., a smart speaker) and (ii) through a robot assistant (i.e., a small social robot named Sota). Depending on the context (i.e., user's location, user's contextual activities, knowledge from the database), Arianna is able to trigger a specific conversation. The system reacts to the continuous database update online and manages the dialogue with the user through the Dialogflow SDK used to define the logical flow of the dialogues.

Figure 2 shows the robot and vocal assistants. Both the Sota manager module and the Smart speaker module are connected to the real time database and Dialogflow and both, based on the context provided by the real-time database,

---

[1] https://estimote.com/.

[2] https://github.com/TheEngineRoom-UniGe/OWLOOP.

Sota robot   Smart speaker

Fig. 2. The robot assistant (Sota robot) on the left and the vocal assistant (smart speaker) on the right.

use the Dialogflow SDK to handle the microphone and the speaker signals. The difference between the robot and speaker conditions is that in the robot condition Sota robot can perform gestures and movements while conversing with the user.

3   The Experiment

3.1   Experimental Setup

To evaluate the system, we focused on deploying a use case demonstrating the potential of context-based proactive human-computer interaction. The use case is designed for elderly individuals living independently and is oriented towards their support and well-being. Specifically, for our experiment, we developed a use case where the system reminds the user about the medications they have to take.

The use case scenario is as follows. Arianna detects the user's presence in the kitchen and recognizes the breakfast activity. Arianna knows that the user must take particular medicines in the morning on a full stomach. Therefore, Arianna reminds the user to take the required medications with a glass of water. To do this, Arianna uses the vocal assistant located on the kitchen table and tries to recognize whether the user takes the medications or not (e.g., by detecting whether the user has accessed the medicine cabinet or if the user pours and drinks water). After some time, Arianna also asks the user if they took the medications.

To set up the experimental environment, we installed the Estimote beacons in a real home. The location of all beacons placed in the house is shown in Fig. 3. Since the Estimote beacons interfere with each other, proper proximity-based user localization requires beacons' calibration. The calibration process includes placing the beacons strategically and tuning the Bluetooth range of each beacon. After that, with the support of a volunteer wearing a smart watch, we performed experiments and tested the use case.

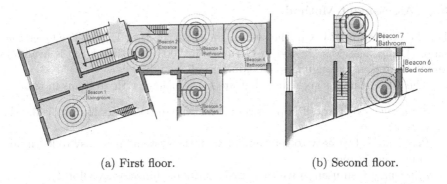

(a) First floor.   (b) Second floor.

Fig. 3. Location of Estimote beacons on the map apartment.

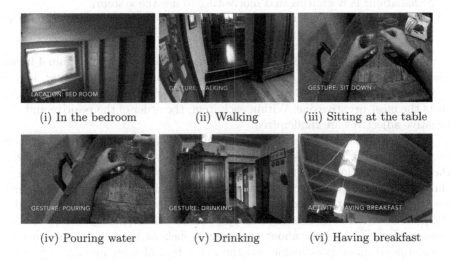

(i) In the bedroom   (ii) Walking   (iii) Sitting at the table

(iv) Pouring water   (v) Drinking   (vi) Having breakfast

Fig. 4. Snapshots from the use case recording.

We recorded a volunteer's interaction with Arianna from an egocentric point of view (i.e., the camera is placed on the volunteer's forehead) as shown in Fig. 4 with two types of interfaces: a simple smart speaker as the vocal assistant[3] and Sota robot as the robot assistant[4]. We chose to evaluate user experience (UX) by providing participants with a virtual experience of the medication reminder use case. This way, participants watched two videos where a volunteer was interacting (i) with the vocal assistant and (ii) with the robot assistant. At the end of each video participants were asked to fill the User Experience Questionnaire (UEQ) [17] that we will describe in the following section. All the survey was held online, using Google Forms.

---

[3] https://youtu.be/85BQhc87pqA.
[4] https://youtu.be/w9-w5tZRZDE.

3.2 Assessment Method

For the evaluation of UX of the system we chose the User Experience Questionnaire (UEQ) that was created in Germany in 2005 [17]. The UEQ is available and validated in 21 languages, including English and Italian.

The UEQ contains six scales that are listed below, with 26 items in total:

Attractiveness: Overall impression of the system. Do users like or dislike the system?
Perspicuity: Is it easy to get familiar with the system? Is it easy to learn how to use the system?
Efficiency: Can users solve their tasks without unnecessary effort?
Dependability: Does the user feel in control of the interaction?
Stimulation: Is it exciting and motivating to use the system?
Novelty: Is the system innovative and creative? Does the system catch the interest of users?

The Attractiveness scale contains 6 items, while other scales contain 4 items each. Items consist of two adjectives that are antonyms to each other, and a seven-stage scale, where +3 represents the most positive response and -3 represents the most negative one. Within each item, the order of the positive and the negative adjectives are randomized.

Each participant was asked to fill the questionnaire twice: to evaluate their perception of the vocal assistant and of the robot assistant. We randomized the order of questionnaires for these two conditions to avoid introducing a bias. Half of the participants received a questionnaire with the vocal assistant first and the robot assistant next (Q1), another half received it in a reversed order (Q2). In addition to evaluating the system, we asked participants to specify some general information about themselves, such as their age, experience in a scientific/technological sector and the evaluation of their previous uses of a technology similar to the proposed system.

3.3 Participants

The surveys has been shared and compiled by 240 volunteers (134 males, 103 females, 3 decided not to answer), between 12 and 69 years old (median = 29.5, STD = 14.14). More than a half of them (52.5%) worked in a scientific/technological sector. 64.6% of the participants used a vocal assistant at least once (16.8% of which use it every day and 37.4% several times a week), and 14.6% used a robot assistant (14.3% of them use it every day and 80% use it once a month or less).

4 Results

First, we verified that the order of the two versions of the system (with robot assistant and with vocal assistant) does not introduce a bias. To do that, we

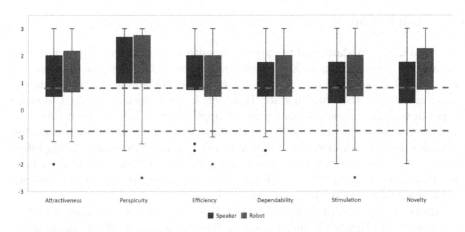

Fig. 5. Comparison between users' perception after interaction with the robot assistant and the vocal assistant.

compared Q1 and Q2 questionnaires over all of the UEQ scales. We used the T-Test to check if the scale means differ significantly. As suggested in the literature, Alpha-Level 0.05 was used [5]. The results showed Alpha-Level higher then 0.05 in all the comparisons. Thus, no significant difference was noticed, meaning that the evaluations of the two types of the system are not influenced by the order in which they were presented.

Next, we evaluated both systems with the vocal assistant and the robot assistant individually and then compared them. We analyzed the system equipped with the vocal assistant. In the Fig. 5 we provide the means and the variance for each scale evaluated. Values between -0.8 and 0.8 represent neutral evaluation of the corresponding scale, values higher then 0.8 represent positive evaluation and values smaller then -0.8 represent negative evaluation. Then, the same considerations were made for the system equipped with the robot assistant.

As we can see from the Fig. 5, the results are promising. The means for all the scales are far above the threshold of 0.8, and we can also notice a high value of *Perspicuity* that tells us that the system is easy to get familiar with and use.

The two systems had success among the volunteers. Nevertheless, we evaluated which of the two systems is considered the preferred one. From Fig. 5, it is evident that the interaction with a robot assistant always has a higher or equal mean. This suggests that the volunteers preferred the interaction with the robot assistant rather than the interaction with the vocal assistant. This was further confirmed with the Wilcox test.

From the Wilcox test we can note that the mean difference is significant for 3 of the 6 scales of interest: attractiveness ($p < 0.01$), stimulation ($p < 0.001$) and novelty ($p < 0.001$). Therefore, in our study the robot assistant has been perceived as more attractive, stimulating and innovative than the vocal assistant.

5   Conclusion

Nowadays, it is fundamental to extend the autonomy of the elderly population as much as possible. Through a distributed sensor system (i.e., smart home), it is possible to track human activities, guaranteeing the autonomy of the subject while monitoring their health state. However, by their nature, the limit of these types of technologies is the perception of intrusiveness. To cope with this limitation, this research proposes a solution that, in addition to simply monitoring human activities, uses user information to offer an intuitive and engaging interactive user experience allowing users to perceive the solution as more attractive. For this purpose, a proactive vocal assistant and a proactive robot assistant have been integrated into an AAL system.

Based on the results shown in Sect. 4, this research work proposes an alternative vision to the classic smart home systems for human activities monitoring. In fact, we observed that by integrating a user-friendly interface elements such as voice or robot assistants, we can favor a more positive user experience. What emerges from the results is that (i) in terms of functionality, both robot and vocal assistant have been perceived positively (Fig. 5), (ii) whereas, in terms of *attractiveness, stimulation and novelty*, the robot assistant has better results compared to vocal assistant (Fig. 5). In summary, even if both experiences with the vocal and the robot assistant are positively perceived by the users, the robot assistant, because of its nature, is perceived as more attractive, stimulating and novel.

Although these results are supported by previous literature on agent embodiment, this research field should be the subject of additional studies. In particular, carrying on studies where subjects experience first-hand different agents' embodiment is fundamental.

References

1. Baldissera, T.A., Camarinha-Matos, L.M.: Services evolution in elderly care ecosystems. In: Camarinha-Matos, L.M., Afsarmanesh, H., Rezgui, Y. (eds.) PRO-VE 2018. IAICT, vol. 534, pp. 417–429. Springer, Cham (2018). https://doi.org/10.1007/978-3-319-99127-6_36
2. Bruno, B., Mastrogiovanni, F., Sgorbissa, A., Vernazza, T., Zaccaria, R.: Analysis of human behavior recognition algorithms based on acceleration data. In: 2013 IEEE International Conference on Robotics and Automation, pp. 1602–1607. IEEE (2013)
3. Chan, M., Estève, D., Escriba, C., Campo, E.: A review of smart homes-present state and future challenges. Comput. Methods Prog. Biomed. 91(1), 55–81 (2008)
4. Costa, A., Julián, V., Novais, P.: Advances and trends for the development of ambient-assisted living platforms. Expert Syst. 34(2), e12163 (2017)
5. Edgell, S.E., Noon, S.M.: Effect of violation of normality on the t test of the correlation coefficient. Psychol. Bull. 95(3), 576 (1984)
6. Gama, E.V., Damian, J., Perez de Molino, J., López, M.R., Lopez Perez, M., Gavira Iglesias, F.: Association of individual activities of daily living with self-rated health in older people. Age Ageing 29(3), 267–270 (2000)

7. Jara, A.J., Zamora, M.A., Skarmeta, A.F.: An internet of things-based personal device for diabetes therapy management in ambient assisted living (aal). Pers. Ubiq. Comput. **15**(4), 431–440 (2011)

8. Kareem, S.Y., Buoncompagni, L., Mastrogiovanni, F.: Arianna$^+$: scalable human activity recognition by reasoning with a network of ontologies. In: Ghidini, C., Magnini, B., Passerini, A., Traverso, P. (eds.) AI*IA 2018. LNCS (LNAI), vol. 11298, pp. 83–95. Springer, Cham (2018). https://doi.org/10.1007/978-3-030-03840-3_7

9. Kim, K., Boelling, L., Haesler, S., Bailenson, J., Bruder, G., Welch, G.F.: Does a digital assistant need a body? the influence of visual embodiment and social behavior on the perception of intelligent virtual agents in ar. In: 2018 IEEE International Symposium on Mixed and Augmented Reality (ISMAR), pp. 105–114. IEEE (2018)

10. Kim, K., Norouzi, N., Losekamp, T., Bruder, G., Anderson, M., Welch, G.: Effects of patient care assistant embodiment and computer mediation on user experience. In: 2019 IEEE International Conference on Artificial Intelligence and Virtual Reality (AIVR), pp. 17–177. IEEE (2019)

11. Kontogiorgos, D., et al.: The effects of anthropomorphism and non-verbal social behaviour in virtual assistants. In: Proceedings of the 19th ACM International Conference on Intelligent Virtual Agents, pp. 133–140 (2019)

12. Lin, W.Y., Verma, V.K., Lee, M.Y., Lai, C.S.: Activity monitoring with a wrist-worn, accelerometer-based device. Micromachines **9**(9), 450 (2018)

13. Nakanishi, J., Baba, J., Kuramoto, I., Ogawa, K., Yoshikawa, Y., Ishiguro, H.: Smart speaker vs. social robot in a case of hotel room. In: 2020 IEEE/RSJ International Conference on Intelligent Robots and Systems (IROS), pp. 11391–11396. IEEE (2020)

14. Ranasinghe, S., Al Machot, F., Mayr, H.C.: A review on applications of activity recognition systems with regard to performance and evaluation. Int. J. Distrib. Sensor Netw. **12**(8), 1550147716665520 (2016)

15. Ruzzon, M., Carfi, A., Ishikawa, T., Mastrogiovanni, F., Murakami, T.: A multi-sensory dataset for the activities of daily living. Data Brief **32**, 106122 (2020)

16. Sadri, F.: Ambient intelligence: a survey. ACM Comput. Surv. (CSUR) **43**(4), 1–66 (2011)

17. Schrepp, M., Hinderks, A., Thomaschewski, J.: Construction of a benchmark for the user experience questionnaire (ueq). IJIMAI **4**(4), 40–44 (2017)

18. Wagner, K., Nimmermann, F., Schramm-Klein, H.: Is it human? the role of anthropomorphism as a driver for the successful acceptance of digital voice assistants. In: Proceedings of the 52nd Hawaii International Conference on System Sciences (2019)

Design and Preliminary Validation of Social Assistive Humanoid Robot with Gesture Expression Features for Mental Health Treatment of Isolated Patients in Hospitals

Diego Arce[1]([✉]), Sareli Gibaja[2], Fiorella Urbina[1], Camila Maura[2], Dario Huanca[1], Renato Paredes[2], Francisco Cuellar[1], and Gustavo Pérez-Zuniga[1]

[1] Engineering Department, Pontificia Universidad Catolica del Peru, Lima, Peru
{diego.arcec,f.urbina,dario.huanca}@pucp.edu.pe,
{cuellar.ff,gustavo.perez}@pucp.pe
[2] Department of Psychology, Pontificia Universidad Catolica del Peru, Lima, Peru
{s.gibaja,camila.maura,renato.paredes}@pucp.edu.pe

Abstract. Social and assistive robots have been widely discussed in the context of psychological interventions. These studies have confirmed that facial and body expressions increase perceived safety during human-robot interaction. In this paper, we present the design of a social assistive humanoid robot with articulated robotic arms intended to deliver telepsychological interventions. The design of the robot is presented, including the description of its features for interactive communication. The robot's design and basic nonverbal communication were evaluated through an online behavioral experiment designed to examine the perceived valence and meaning of its gestures and the overall appraisal of its appearance. We found that the design of the telepresence robot was positively assessed by a sample (N = 34) of STEM-related participants according to Godspeed metrics. Moreover, we observed that the robot was able to perform gestures that were correctly identified and discerned in terms of their valence.

Keywords: Social assistive robots · Humanoid robots · Telepsychological interventions · Acceptability and Trust · Gesture expressions

1 Introduction

In the broad spectrum of robotics, we can identify the area of socially assistive robots (SAR) which combines assistive robots (AR) and social robots (SR) [2]. An assistive robot is defined as an aid or support for a human user in diverse scenarios such as schools, hospitals and homes [3]. Research into assistive robotics

F. Cavallo et al. (Eds.): ICSR 2022, LNAI 13818, pp. 518–528, 2022.
https://doi.org/10.1007/978-3-031-24670-8_46

includes rehabilitation robots [3], companion robots [4], and educational robots [5]. On the other hand, social robots interact with humans in a socially acceptable way [6]. The main goal of these robots is to convey intention in a human-perceptible way. Therefore aspects of human social interaction such as speech, gestures and others become relevant [6].

A social assistive robot is an intersection of AR and SR [3]. Therefore its main goal is to provide assistance by creating a close and effective interaction with a human user [3,7]. These robots are widely used in mental health environments, such as diagnosis delivery, mental disorders treatment [8], and cognitive, physical or social rehabilitation [10].

Here we present the design of a social assistive humanoid robot built to deliver telepsychological interventions and assist patients with mental health care. Moreover, we aim at measuring its perceived appraisal and evaluate whether potential users are capable of identifying the meaning of its gestures. The preliminary research conducted here is exploratory and is intended to be used as a precedent for future HRI investigations in clinical settings.

This article is divided in six parts: Sect. 2 includes a brief description of the literature review on SAHRs and the proposed telepsychological intervention approach using the robot; Sect. 3 presents the robot's design, describing its physical characteristics emphasizing on the explanation of its arms, head and gesture expression; Sect. 4 explains the experimental setup for the conducted behavioral experiment; Sect. 5 discusses the results obtained from the behavioral experiment; finally, Sect. 6 presents the conclusions of this preliminary study and lays groundwork for future research.

2   Literature Review

2.1   Human Robot Interaction Features

Human Robot Interaction is a growing field whose main objective is to evaluate the performance of the services that robots offer [7]. Research on socially assistive humanoid robots (SAHR) suggests that certain robotic attributes may influence the interaction with users. One of them is anthropomorphism, which is defined as the tendency to attribute human characteristics or behaviours to inanimate objects in order to rationalize their actions [13]. Researches show that this feature leads humans to often perceive robots as more understanding, predictable and familiar [14]. In addition, it could increase engagement and preference for the service offered by the robot [1], as well as reduce negative effects such as stress and anxiety associated with HRI [7].

Similarly, gestures were found to influence attitudes and perceptions towards robots [11]. Robotic bodily expressions were found to improve the understanding of affect [11], perceptions of trustworthiness [15] towards robots. Moreover, evidence suggests that movement speed influences not only the perception of gestures [19], but perceived safety and comfort of the human during HRI [20]. Therefore, it was found that humans prefer slower robotic movements because they provide greater comfort and safety [20].

2.2   Psychological Interventions with SAHRs

In particular, the use of SAHR has been widely discussed in the context of psychological interventions, because of their capability of allow new methods these can be delivered [21].In this context, robots can fulfill various functions, whether in the diagnosis or treatment of mental, psychiatric and neurological disorders [9] as well as in physical, cognitive and social rehabilitation for children and adults [10].

Moreover, research highlights the potential of social assistive robots for improving delivery [22] and treatment outcomes [8], and it has been shown that such robots effectively decrease anxiety symptoms, improve mood [24], enhance well-being, perceived social support and enhance communication with users [26]. For instance, some examples of robots whose usage resulted in successful psychological interventions are Nao, Pepper and Buddy, who fulfilled the function of accompanying children and older adults, finding positive effects in reducing anxiety, improving mood and greater attachment to caregivers and pairs [23].

In the field of telepresence SARs, there have been several acceptability studies that review their effectiveness as a tool for mental health interventions. For instance, according to [24], participants that presented social anxiety showed less anticipatory anxiety and anticipatory tension -as well as actual tension- towards a telepresencial robot than a human. Also, in the subject of mindfulness training, an evidence based intervention proved to help with many clinical diagnosis [25].

2.3   Proposed Intervention with SAHR

The humanoid robot proposed in this article was designed to be used as a telepresence robot for psychological interventions in hospitals and medical centers. These interventions will allow to perform diagnostics and treatments remotely, as shown in Fig. 1. The mental health specialist will be able to visualize and interact with the patient through video conference, conduct surveys and express emotions and gestures using the robot. The robot can navigate through the environment autonomously based on the specialist commands.

REMOTE ASSITANCE BY
SPECIALIST (HOME OR OFFICE)   TELEPSYCHOLOGICAL INTERVENTION
                                           WITH ROBOT (HOSPITAL)

Fig. 1. Telepyschological intervention diagram

3   Robot Design

For most emerging countries, the cost of humanoid robots is still unaffordable and there is mistrust in the use of these technologies. In addition, other existing commercial robots have been designed for contexts in other countries where the conditions and infrastructure its adequate and facilitate their use.

The design of the humanoid robot was developed considering a mix between human-like and machine-like appearances. The profile of the external structure was designed with an organic design style as shown in Fig. 2a, trying to resemble the human shape. The total height of the robot is 160 cm, considering a general human average height. The robot is composed of a differential drive mobile platform with a mapping sensing system, two 4-DOF articulated arms, one 15" touch screen on the chest, and 2-DOF articulate head with a 5" LCD display (see Fig. 2a). These elements allow three types of gesture expressions: 1) Arms and head movement; 2) Head display; and 3) Chest display.

The 4-DOF arms have joints directly actuated by servomotors (see Fig. 2b). Two are located on the shoulder for arm abduction and arm flexion/extension, one along the middle of the arm for medial/lateral rotation, and one inside the elbow for forearm flexion/extension. PLA 3D printed structural pieces were designed to support the motor loads and to be as lightweight as possible, achieving 2 kg per arm. The main chest piece also supports the head and the first arm joints and connects the column with the upper body of the robot.

The head has two servomotors (see Fig. 2b), which allows 2DOF. One is located horizontally below the neck to allow the head rotation and the other is located vertically on the neck for the head flexion/extension. On both sides of the head, there are two speakers, as well as one 5-inch LCD screen. The head is also 3D printed, except for the screen cover, which is made of thermoformed acrylic (see Fig. 2c).

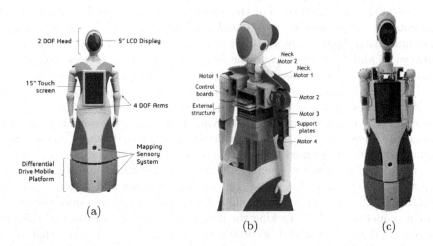

Fig. 2. 3D model of designed robot: a) Main components; and b) Internal components of arms and head; and c) 3D printed prototype.

Despite that the 5-DOF representation of a human arm is more accurate (excluding the wrist DOF in our design), the kinematic configuration of the proposed 4-DOF robotic arm is able to perform realistic human-like movements. The movement of the head and arms will allow gesture expressions to be transmitted. For this study, six (06) interactive routines were defined combining the arms and head movement, as shown in Fig. 3.

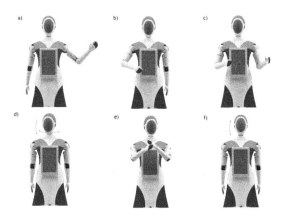

Fig. 3. Gesture expressions with robotic arms and head: a) waving; b) pointing; c) explaining; d) crying; e) denying; and f) nodding

4   Experimental Setup

An online behavioral experiment was conducted to assess the perceived valence and meaning of the gestures. For this experiment we recruited $N = 34$ STEM: students $N = 21$, professors $N = 10$ and administrative staff $N = 3$ from a peruvian university. Approximately 70.6% were between 18 and 25 years old, 26.5% between 26 and 36 years old, and the rest was between 37–47 years old. Participants with neurological disorders or visual disabilities were excluded from the study because it was necessary to visualize in order to complete the experiment.

Participants were asked to observe six (06) different gestures performed by the robot (waving, nodding, denying, crying, pointing, and explaining) on short animated videos (5 s). The animated videos were generated using CAD software. Animated videos were used since this is a preliminary evaluation. We selected the most common gestures found on nonverbal interaction literature [6]. Gestures such as crying and denying [12], waving, pointing and nodding [16] and explaining [12], could be applicable in different social scenarios since they could play a cooperative role in making the human lifestyle comfortable and efficient. Moreover, they are grouped according to their emotional valence that could range from positive to negative [17]. According to literature, waving and nodding could evoke a positive valence, while denying and crying could be perceived as negative [18]. In the study, pointing and explaining were considered as neutral gestures. The order of presentation of the video stimuli was randomized for each participant. Based on each video, participants were asked to rate the valence of the gesture *(Select the option that is closer to how you felt with the robot's movements)* on a five-point Likert scale *(1 = negative valence and 5 = positive valence)* by typing in the number corresponding to the emoticons.

Afterwards, participants were asked to identify the meaning of the robot's gesture from a group of six possible alternatives containing the correct answer and five distractors *(Select the option that describes best what the robot intended to communicate)*. The distractors were selected from an six (06) possible answer list containing similar and unlike expressions to the correct answer.

Next, participants were asked to complete a four (04) item questionnaire aimed to evaluate the communicative attributes of the robot on a 7-point Likert scale. The items were based on the Aly and Tapus questionnaire [27] and aims at assessing the speed, attractiveness, ease of understanding, and expressiveness of the robot.

Finally, participants were provided with the Godspeed questionnaire [28] to collect their subjective impressions about the telepresence robot. This scale captures five (05) dimensions: anthropomorphism (ANT), animacy (ANI), likeability (LIK), perceived intelligence (INT), and perceived safety (SFT).

The online experiment was conducted using Psychopy [29] v.2021.2.3 and Pavlovia (https://pavlovia.org/). Data analysis was performed using the Python programming language. The Pingouin v.0.5.1 [30] and Seaborn v.0.11.2 [31] packages were employed for statistical analyzes and visualizations respectively.

5   Experimental Results

We used an ANOVA-type Statistic (ATS) [32] test to compare the valence ratings of the six gesture videos. This showed significant differences of valence ratings between different robot gestures ($f(3.47) = 17.03$, $p < .001$), indicating significant changes of valence responses towards the different gestures performed by the robot (see Fig. 4 for an illustration).

After adjusting for multiple comparisons with the Wilcoxon signed-rank test, we found significant differences in the reported valence of the following pairs of gestures: explaining and denying ($Z < 34.0$, $p = .035$); explaining and crying ($Z < 11.0$, $p = .002$); denying and nodding ($Z < 58.5$, $p = .021$); denying and waving ($Z < 28.0$, $p = .004$); crying and nodding ($Z < 13.0$, $p = .001$); pointing and crying ($Z < 27.0$, $p = .010$); pointing and waving ($Z < 27.0$, $p = .006$); and crying and waving ($Z < 0$, $p < .001$) (see Table 1 for details).

Table 1. Effect sizes (r) of post-hoc multiple comparisons of valence ratings

Variable	M	SD	Waving	Nodding	Crying	Denying	Explaining
Waving	3.94	.85					
Nodding	3.62	.70	.32				
Crying	2.55	.96	.30**	.19*			
Denying	2.70	1.19	−.12*	.01*	.62		
Explaining	3.53	.99	.61	.30	.35*	.11*	
Pointing	3.21	1.04	.46*	.41	.58*	.27	.51

M indicates mean. *SD* indicates standard deviations. * indicates $p < .05$.
** indicates $p < .001$

Overall, these pairwise differences show that the participants were able to discriminate the positive (nodding and waving) from the negative (denying and crying) valence of gestures executed by the robot. Neutral gestures (explaining and pointing) elicited variable responses and were appraised more positively than negative gestures. These findings suggest that our robot is able to accurately express emotional valence, which is a core dimension of affective communication required for social interaction [6]. Crucially, an in-person experiment assessing both valence and arousal perception of is required to confirm our findings.

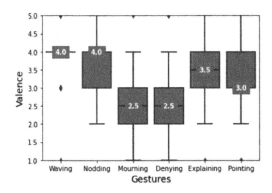

Fig. 4. Valence ratings of participants to gestures performed by the robot. Participants were able to discriminate between positive (waving and nodding) and negative (denying and crying) gestures.

Furthermore, we used a chi-squared test to evaluate the association between the meaning of the gesture and the participant's (correct or incorrect) guesses. The association between these variables was significant, X^2 (5, $N = 34$) $= 36.18$, $p < .001$. This suggests that participants were more likely to correctly identify the majority of the robot gestures (see Table 2 for details).

Nevertheless, pointing and crying presented high miss rates, which reveals difficulties in the recognition of such gestures. This could be explained by the limited movement range of the joints of the robot. Hence, including facial expressions or complementary communicative resources (e.g. lights or sounds) is required to improve the identification of these gestures.

Based on the questionnaires, we found that the robot mostly evoked interest among participants ($M = 4.59$, $SD = 1.31$). Other attributes identified were expressiveness ($M = 4.41$, $SD = 1.04$) and how easy it was to understand ($M = 4.26$, $SD = 1.33$). Finally, speed was the lowest rated attribute of all ($M = 4.06$, $SD = .85$).

Movement speed is important for the perception of dynamic gestures [19]. Current research stresses that humans prefer slower robotic movements because they provide greater comfort and safety [19,20]. Hence, we aim at keeping the robot's motion speed at the current level to preserve comfort and gesture recognition in users.

Table 2. Recognition of gestures executed by the robot

	Gestures						
	Waving	Nodding	Crying	Denying	Explaining	Pointing	Total
Correct	34	33	19	30	30	23	169
Incorrect	0	1	15	4	4	11	35

Moreover, our data showed that participants found the robot's Likeability ($M = 3.62$, $SD = .64$) and Perceived Intelligence ($M = 3.35$, $SD = .56$) slightly prominent compared to the other three dimensions of the questionnaire: Anthropomorphism ($M = 2.96$, $SD = .70$), Animacy ($M = 3.08$, $SD = .58$) and Perceived Safety ($M = 2.82$, $SD = .48$).

The high score in the likeability dimension could be explained by the robot's design: the robot has a balanced appearance between human-like and machine-like as revealed by the Anthropomorphism scores. This presumably allowed for affective proximity with users [21]. Likewise, the high score in the robot's perceived intelligence could be explained by the perceived complexity and realism of the executed gestures [33] (Fig. 5).

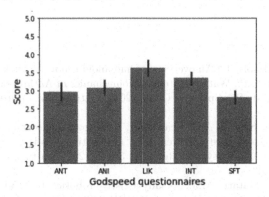

Fig. 5. Responses to the Godspeed questionnaires. Participants found the robot's likeability and perceived intelligence slightly prominent. They found its appearance a balance between human-like and machine-like.

6   Conclusion and Future Work

In this paper, we presented the design of asocial assistive robot that will be used for telepsychological interventions. Its design considered a humanoid appearance with two articulated 4-DOF arms and a 2-DOF head with an LDC display. Both elements allow the robot to perform gesture expressions with arms and head movements, aiming to improve the human-robot interaction during the interventions. The robot's appearance and expression features were validated through a behavioral experiment to assess the perceived valence and meaning of the gestures performed.

Overall, the design of the telepresence robot was positively assessed by a sample of STEM-related participants. They found its likeability and perceived intelligence slightly prominent according to Godspeed metrics. In line with current design guidelines, they found that the robot posses a balance between a human-like and a machine-like appearance.

Moreover, the robot can execute basic gestures required for interaction with human users. We found that the majority of gestures were correctly recognized and discerned in terms of their valence by our sample.

Further research includes implementing and evaluating basic facial expressions of the robot in a similar paradigm. Moreover, we aim at conducting an in-person experiment with STEM and non-STEM participants to evaluate both the facial and body expressivity of the robot.

Furthermore, the robot's capability to promote and deliver telepsychological interventions will be examined in an in-person study real environment. Our final goal is to assess the robot delivery of telepsychological interventions to hospitalized patients with infectious and immunosuppressive diseases.

Acknowledgment. The authors wish to thank the National Fund for Scientific, Technological Development and Technological Innovation (FONDECYT) through its national program PROCIENCIA (160-2020-FONDECYT) and the Pontificia Universidad Católica del Perú (PUCP) through its funding program CAP (PI0516 - ID 627) for providing the means and resources for this research and development.

References

1. Stasse , O., Flayols, T.: An overview of humanoid robots technologies. In: Venture, G., Laumond, J.-P., Watier, B. (eds.) Biomechanics of Anthropomorphic Systems, vol. 124, pp. 281–310. Springer, Cham (2019). https://doi.org/10.1007/978-3-319-93870-713

2. Rabbitt, S.M., Kazdin, A.E., Scassellati, B.: Integrating socially assistive robotics into mental healthcare interventions: applications and recommendations for expanded use. Clin. Psychol. Rev. **35**, 35–46 (2015). https://doi.org/10.1016/j.cpr.2014.07.001

3. Feil-Seifer, D., Mataric, M.J.: Socially assistive robotics. In: 9th International Conference on Rehabilitation Robotics, ICORR 2005, Chicago, IL, USA, pp. 465–468 (2005). https://doi.org/10.1109/ICORR.2005.1501143

4. . Lane, G.W., et al.: Effectiveness of a social robot, 'Paro', in a VA long-term care setting. Psychol. Serv. **13**(3), 292–299 (2016). https://doi.org/10.1037/ser0000080

5.) Lopez-Caudana, E., Eduardo Baltazar Reyes, G., Ponce Cruz, P.: Socially assistive robotics: state-of-the-art scenarios in Mexico. In: Grau, A., Wang, Z. (eds.) Industrial Robotics - New Paradigms, IntechOpen (2020). https://doi.org/10.5772/intechopen.91446

6. Fong, T., Nourbakhsh, I., Dautenhahn, K.: A survey of socially interactive robots. Rob. Auton. Syst. **42**(3–4), 143–166 (2003). https://doi.org/10.1016/S0921-8890(02)00372-X

7. Alves-Oliveira, P., Orr, A., Björling, E.A., Cakmak, M.: Connecting the dots of social robot design from interviews with robot creators. Front. Robot. AI **9**, 720799 (2022). https://doi.org/10.3389/frobt.2022.720799

8. Costescu, C.A., Vanderborght, B., David, D.O.: The effects of robot-enhanced psychotherapy: a meta-analysis. Rev. Gener. Psychol. **18**(2), 127–136 (2014). https://doi.org/10.1037/gpr0000007

9. Rasouli, S., Gupta, G., Nilsen, E., Dautenhahn, K.: Potential applications of social robots in robot-assisted interventions for social anxiety. Int. J. Soc. Rob. (2022). https://doi.org/10.1007/s12369-021-00851-0.

10. Yuan, F., Klavon, E., Liu, Z., Lopez, R.P., Zhao, X.: A systematic review of robotic rehabilitation for cognitive training. Front. Robot. AI **8**, 605715 (2021). https://doi.org/10.3389/frobt.2021.605715

11. Shen, Z., Elibol, A., Chong, N.Y.: Understanding nonverbal communication cues of human personality traits in human-robot interaction. IEEE/CAA J. Autom. Sinica **7**(6), 1465–1477 (2020). https://doi.org/10.1109/JAS.2020.1003201

12. Zabala, U., Rodriguez, I., Martínez-Otzeta, J.M., Lazkano, E.: Expressing robot personality through talking body language. Appl. Sci. **11**(10), 4639 (2021). https://doi.org/10.3390/app11104639

13. Bartneck, C., Belpaeme, T., Eyssel, F., Kanda, T., Keijsers, M., Sabanovic, S.: Human-robot interaction: an introduction, p. 264 (2020). https://doi.org/10.1017/9781108676649

14. Blut, M., Wang, C., Wünderlich, N.V., Brock, C.: Understanding anthropomorphism in service provision: a meta-analysis of physical robots, chatbots, and other AI. J. Acad. Mark. Sci. **49**(4), 632–658 (2021). https://doi.org/10.1007/s11747-020-00762-y

15. Zabala, U., Rodriguez, I., Martínez-Otzeta, J.M., Lazkano, E.: Modeling and evaluating beat gestures for social robots. Multimedia Tools Appl. **81**(3), 3421–3438 (2022). https://doi.org/10.1007/s11042-021-11289-x

16. Riek, L.D., Paul, P.C., Robinson, P.: When my robot smiles at me: enabling human-robot rapport via real-time head gesture mimicry. J. Multimodal User Interfaces **3**(1–2), 99–108 (2010). https://doi.org/10.1007/s12193-009-0028-2

17. Heinonen, K.: Positive and negative valence influencing consumer engagement. J. Serv. Theory Pract. **28**(2), 147–169 (2018). https://doi.org/10.1108/JSTP-02-2016-0020

18. Xu, J., Broekens, J., Hindriks, K., Neerincx, M.A.: Mood contagion of robot body language in human robot interaction. Auton. Agents Multi-Agent Syst. **29**(6), 1216–1248 (2015). https://doi.org/10.1007/s10458-015-9307-3

19. Castillo, J.C., Alonso-Martín, F., Cáceres-Domínguez, D., Malfaz, M., Salichs, M.A.: The influence of speed and position in dynamic gesture recognition for human-robot interaction. J. Sensors **2019**, 1–12 (2019). https://doi.org/10.1155/2019/7060491

20. . Story, M., Webb, P., Fletcher, S.R., Tang, G., Jaksic, C., Carberry, J.: Do speed and proximity affect human-robot collaboration with an industrial robot arm?. Int. J. Soc. Rob. (2022). https://doi.org/10.1007/s12369-021-00853-y.

21. Isabet, B., Pino, M., Lewis, M., Benveniste, S., Rigaud, A.-S.: Social telepresence robots: a narrative review of experiments involving older adults before and during the COVID-19 pandemic. Int. J. Environ. Res. Public Health 18(7), Art. no. 7 (2021). https://doi.org/10.3390/ijerph18073597

22. Pu, L., Moyle, W., Jones, C., Todorovic, M.: The effectiveness of social robots for older adults: a systematic review and meta-analysis of randomized controlled studies. Gerontologist 59(1), e37–e51 (2019). https://doi.org/10.1093/geront/gny046

23. Marchetti, A., Di Dio, C., Manzi, F., Massaro, D.: Robotics in clinical and developmental psychology. Compre. Clin. Psychol., 121–140 (2022). https://doi.org/10.1016/B978-0-12-818697-8.00005-4

24. Nomura, T., Kanda, T., Suzuki, T., Yamada, S.: Do people with social anxiety feel anxious about interacting with a robot? AI Soc. 35(2), 381–390 (2019). https://doi.org/10.1007/s00146-019-00889-9

25. Hempel, S., et al.: Evidence map of mindfulness. VA-ESP Project #05-226 (2014)

26. Jeong, S. et al.: A social robot to mitigate stress, anxiety, and pain in hospital pediatric care. In: Proceedings of the Tenth Annual ACM/IEEE International Conference on Human-Robot Interaction Extended Abstracts, Portland Oregon USA, pp. 103–104 (2015). https://doi.org/10.1145/2701973.2702028

27. Aly, A., Tapus, A.: A model for synthesizing a combined verbal and nonverbal behavior based on personality traits in human-robot interaction. In: 2013 8th ACM/IEEE International Conference on Human-Robot Interaction (HRI), Tokyo, Japan, pp. 325–332 (2013). https://doi.org/10.1109/HRI.2013.6483606

28. Bartneck, C., Croft, E., Kulic, D., Zoghbi, S.: Measurement instruments for the anthropomorphism, animacy, likeability, perceived intelligence, and perceived safety of robots. Int. J. Soc. Rob. 1, 71–81 (2009). https://doi.org/10.1007/s12369-008-0001-3

29. Peirce, J., et al.: PsychoPy2: experiments in behavior made easy. Behav. Res. Methods 51(1), 195–203 (2019). https://doi.org/10.3758/s13428-018-01193-y

30. Vallat, P.: Statistics in python. J. Open Source Softw. 3(31), 1026 (2018). https://doi.org/10.21105/joss.01026.

31. Waskom, M.L.: Seaborn: statistical data visualization. J. Open Source Softw. 6(60) (2021). https://doi.org/10.21105/joss.03021

32. Paredes Venero, R., Davila, A.: Experimental research methodology and statistics insights. In: Jost, C., et al. (eds.) Human-Robot Interaction: Evaluation Methods and Their Standardization, pp. 333–353. Springer, Cham (2020). https://doi.org/10.1007/978-3-030-42307-013

33. Weiss, A., Bartneck, C.: Meta analysis of the usage of the Godspeed Questionnaire Series. In: 2015 24th IEEE International Symposium on Robot and Human Interactive Communication (RO-MAN), Kobe, Japan, pp. 381–388 (2015). https://doi.org/10.1109/ROMAN.2015.7333568

"Armed" and Dangerous: How Visual Form Influences Perceptions of Robot Arms

Rhian C. Preston$^{(\boxtimes)}$, Nisha Raghunath, Christopher A. Sanchez, and Naomi T. Fitter

Oregon State University (OSU), Corvallis, OR 97331, USA
{prestonr,nisha.raghunath,christopher.sanchez,fittern}@oregonstate.edu

Abstract. Existing research on human perception of robot appearance has focused heavily on anthropomorphism and humanoid robots, with less attention paid to visual form attributes and non-humanoid systems. In this paper, we propose robot visual form attribute traits and a beginning sampling of robot arms with which to expand the understanding of robot visual form effects. We conduct an online survey-based within-subjects study to gather ratings of these visual form attributes, as well as standard social attributes, for each arm. Our data collection methods include two-alternative forced choice questions and sets of Likert-type self-reports related to individual visual stimuli. The results from this exploratory study show that even within non-humanoid robots of similar structure, the visual elements have a significant effect on perceptions of robot social characteristics such as warmth, competency, and safety.

1 Introduction

The state of the art in robot visual form design requires highly specialized artistic skills, but we conjecture that a cursory understanding of automatic human responses to robot form can be democratized. Past empirical studies have pinpointed what a robot should look like in specific contexts, but it is currently intractable to work backwards from these results to understand human responses to a broader set of robots. The presented work aims to address this problem; *our research goal is to understand human priors related to robot visual form attributes across a broad set of robots.* Our starting point in these efforts involves a pilot sampling of robot arms, due to their wide availability, broad adoption in industry, and relevance to a wide range of robots (i.e., as standalone systems, as well as a component of humanoid robots) [9,15]. We propose that an understanding of automatic human responses to robot arm visual form attributes can serve as a foundation for a model that can inform robot arm visual form – and eventually entire robot visual form – design.

Previous work on robot appearance has manipulated selected dimensions (e.g., size [13,18], anthropomorphism [3,14], and gender [4,16]), finding that each

---

R. C. Preston and N. Raghunath—Contributed equally to this work.

F. Cavallo et al. (Eds.): ICSR 2022, LNAI 13818, pp. 529–539, 2022.
https://doi.org/10.1007/978-3-031-24670-8_47

characteristic influences responses from human co-interactants. In the realm of robot arms specifically, past studies have established that audio profiles and speech capabilities influence human preferences [17]; however, to our knowledge, no studies have explored the effects of visual arm form characteristics such as shape. Our work attempts to address this gap by investigating how differences in existing robot arms' visual form characteristics (i.e., physical appearance) impact perceived attributes. In this paper, we present key related work in Sect. 2, research methods in Sect. 3, and results in Sect. 4. We discuss the results and next steps in Sect. 5. Contributions of this work center on new insights to support visual form attribute design for robots.

2   Related Work

Topics which closely inform the present work include past studies of the effects of robot size and nonverbal robot expression on human opinions.

Effects of Robot Size: Studies of robots' physical size constitute one approach to understanding how a robot's visual appearance can influence human perceptions of its attributes. Taller robots are perceived as more human-like and conscientious [18]. Larger robots, however, are also viewed as less emotionally capable than smaller robots. As such, when verbally abused, these larger robots are less likely to be seen as mistreated compared to their smaller counterparts [13]. Given that a physical robot characteristic like overall size can determine perceived social attributes and capabilities of the system, it is plausible that additional visual attributes related to size (e.g., individual component dimensions, overall system footprint) could have a similar effect. Accordingly, one aspect of robots that we were interested in exploring in this work was size.

Effects of Nonverbal Robot Arm Features: Few past efforts have investigated the influence of robots' overall form or shape on human opinions. Of the work that does exist in this space, one past example investigated the effects of different combinations of head, trunk, and limb shapes, finding that each distinct combination elicited either concern, enjoyment, or favorable opinions from human viewers [11]. However, even fewer works have explored how robot arm visual form attributes impact human judgments. This is a crucial gap, as the presence of robot arms is seen as one of the strongest predictors of a robot's perceived humanism and ability to perform corresponding human-like tasks (e.g., having arms indicates the ability to manipulate objects in the environment) [14].

Past research in adjacent areas of robot arm nonverbal expression show that humans prefer robot arms to be able to communicate in some form (e.g., lights, gestures, textual messages) and judge the arms to be more competent when they operate with high-end audio feedback [17]. Based on the known impacts of nonverbal robot features, we believe that robot arms may also be judged based on their visual form components. Our work aims to fill the present knowledge gap on how robot visual form influences onlooker perceptions.

3 Methods

To study the effects of robot arm visual form attributes on human perception and preference, we employed a within-subjects online survey-based study. We gathered participant responses to five robot arm images (selected to span representative commercial alternatives that vary visually) under an existing university ethics board protocol (Oregon State University IRB #IRB-2019-0172).

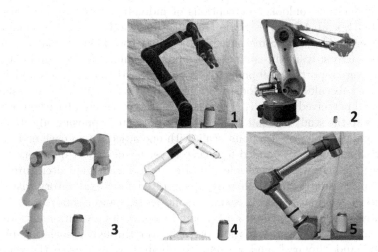

Fig. 1. Robot arm stimuli. In numbered order: Kinova Jaco, Kuka KR 700 PA [12], Franka Emika Panda [8], Versius [6], UR5e. Throughout the paper, we use the presented numbering system (Arm 1 through Arm 5) to refer to individual robot arms.

Based on previous research (e.g., the past study of robot gendering based on shape [2]), we expected to find significant differences in perceptions of the robot stimuli, but we were uncertain of precisely what these trends may be. Thus, our first research step was an exploratory study intended to inform follow-up work on robot visual form attributes.

Stimulus Design: In order to limit covariates and provide comparable images, *each robot arm image*: 1) was captured with the robot in the same configuration, 2) used a neutral background, 3) included an unlabeled soda can for size comparison, and 4) was taken in grayscale to prevent color impacts.

The robot arm images used for study stimuli appear in Fig. 1. These arms were selected to vary across usage domains (i.e., industrial, surgical, general use) and nuanced visual characteristics such as curvature of arm components.

Participants: Previous research evaluating robot visual form attribute effects on human perception has not reported effect sizes. To this end, we used a small effect size of $f^2 = .10$ in an *a priori* power analysis using G-Power 3.0.10 [7] with power set to 0.80 and error probability set to $\alpha = .05$, which resulted in an overall suggested sample size of 33. Data was excluded from participants who failed to complete the study. We distributed the study among undergraduate students in an introductory psychology course, and 51 surveys were completed. The median participant age was 19 (minimum: 18, maximum: 43), and the participants primarily identified as female (30 female, 17 male, 4 non-binary).

Measurement: We gathered basic demographic information (e.g., age, gender, ethnicity). Participants also completed the Ten-Item Personality Inventory (TIPI). The TIPI captured participant personality on 9-point Likert scales from Strongly Disagree to Strongly Agree [10].

To understand onlooker perceptions of individual robot arm images, both the Robot Social Attributes Scale (RoSAS) and Godspeed questionnaire were administered. The RoSAS measured participants' social perceptions of the robot on three factors: warmth, competence, and discomfort [5]. The items for each subscale were reported on 9-point Likert scales. Participants also completed two of the five subscales of the Godspeed questionnaire: the subscales assessing likeability and perceived safety [1]. These subscales were selected based on perceived relevance to the study at hand. Each subscale presented opposing adjectives (e.g., foolish and sensible) on a 5-point scale with one adjective on each end.

Participants also responded to a custom set of self-report questions for each robot arm image, which were selected after reviewing related literature on aesthetics and visual form. Each participant rated four exploratory visual form attributes: "angular," "sleek/clean," "soft/curvy," and "solid/broad." These attributes were also captured on 9-point Likert scales. Additionally, we asked participants about their valuation of each arm through association of terms "budget" and "luxury," and we queried about how expensive the robot was perceived to be compared to other robot arms. Both the association and cost comparison questions were administered on 9-point Likert scales.

Robot arm images were also compared using two-alternative forced choice (2AFC) questions related to the exploratory visual form attributes. The 2AFC approach (borrowed from the field of psychophysics) was intended to encourage rapid and instinctive reactions from participants. These questions presented two robot images side by side and allowed participants to click on the selected image (for example, the image that was more angular) in order to progress.

Finally, participants' free-response data regarding how robot part(s) influenced ratings was collected.

Procedure: The study consisted of a Qualtrics survey with multiple sections, beginning with a consent form and demographic questionnaire. The start of the survey presented each robot arm image individually, and the participant was asked to complete the Likert-type RoSAS, selected Godspeed subscales, attribute association, and cost valuation questions for each image. The order of images presented was randomized within participants to account for ordering effects.

The participant then completed 2AFC questions for all (order-independent) permutations of robot image pairs for one of the five visual form categories. For example, for "angular," the prompt asked the respondent to "Select the robot that is more angular," and the participant clicked on their selection. The order of the pairing was randomized, and for each pair of robots, which robot appeared on the left or right was also randomized across participants. Once all 2AFC questions were completed for a particular attribute, the participant continued the same 2AFC selection process for a different attribute category. This process continued until all image pairs were rated, for all categories. The ordering of visual form categories was also randomized to account for ordering effects.

Once participants completed all 2AFC questions, we presented the individual arm images and associated Likert-type questions once again. In early pilot testing we saw participants develop strong reactions to the arms through the 2AFC process, so we chose to repeat the individual arm ratings this second time to see if opinions of the arms changed through the 2AFC process.

Finally, respondents provided open-ended feedback about which part(s) of the individual robot arms affected their responses.

Analysis: To analyze the Likert-type results, we conducted a repeated-measures analysis of variance (ANOVA) test for each dependent variable: warmth, competency, and discomfort perceptions (i.e., RoSAS ratings); likeability and safety (i.e., Godspeed Questionnaire subscales); and angularity, sleekness, softness, solidness, budget, luxuriousness, and cost (i.e., custom characteristic ratings). P-values were adjusted with a Bonferroni correction to account for multiple analyses with the RoSAS subscales, two Godspeed subscales, and various characteristic ratings as outcomes, yielding an adjusted significance level of $p = .004$.

For 2AFC data, we tallied selection instances for each arm-descriptor pair for each participant, and converted it into a percentage of the total number of possible selection instances (4). We then calculated the mean score and standard deviation for each such pair across participants.

We used thematic analysis to identify main codes and note their occurrences in the free-response feedback.

4 Results

In this section, the main effects and significant results of the individual arm Likert-type ratings are described, in addition to the calculated mean scores for each arm-descriptor pair from the 2AFC data.

4.1 Likert-Type Ratings

The two main results of the Likert-type data analysis were understanding any change in onlooker perception of each arm over time, in addition to assessing differences in perception between the arms on the examined scales.

Ratings Over Time: Participants' pre- and post-study robot arm ratings were not significantly different, indicating that opinions of the arms were unchanging over the course of the study, $Fs(1, 100) = .005 - 3.88$, $ps = .052 - .95$.

RoSAS Subscale Ratings: There were main effects of arm stimulus on all three RoSAS subscales: *warmth* ($F(4, 400) = 18.59$, $p < .001$, $\eta^2 = 0.06$), *competence* ($F(4, 400) = 20.64$, $p < .001$, $\eta^2 = 0.07$), and *discomfort* ($F(4, 400) = 40.65$, $p <$

Table 1. Significant RoSAS pairwise comparisons. Arm 1 was seen as more discomforting than Arm 3. Arm 2 was seen as less warm, less competent, and more discomforting than all other arms.

Arm		Warmth			Competency			Discomfort		
		M (SE)	t	p	M (SE)	t	p	M (SE)	t	p
1	2	1.12 (0.19)	6.05	<.001*	1.15 (0.17)	6.67	<.001*	-1.71 (0.25)	-6.8	<.001*
	3							0.77 (0.17)	4.47	<.001*
2	3	-1.33 (0.20)	-6.60	<.001*	-1.27 (0.18)	-7.24	<.001*	2.48 (0.25)	9.94	<.001*
	4	-1.22 (0.19)	-6.40	<.001*	-1.10 (0.18)	-5.99	<.001*	2.04 (0.26)	7.88	<.001*
	5	-0.81 (0.17)	-4.74	<.001*	-0.79 (0.20)	-4	.001*	1.94 (0.26)	7.45	<.001*

Table 2. Significant Godspeed pairwise comparisons. Arm 1 was seen as less likeable and safe than Arm 3. Arm 2 was seen as less likeable and safe than all other arms.

Arm		Likeability			Safety		
		M (SE)	t	p	M (SE)	t	p
1	2	1.07 (0.10)	10.35	<.001*	0.78 (0.10)	8.09	<.001*
	3	-0.37 (0.09)	-4.17	<.001*	-0.38 (0.90)	-4.19	<.001*
2	3	-1.44 (0.12)	-11.82	<.001*	-1.15 (0.12)	-10.04	<.001*
	4	-1.25 (0.11)	-11.32	<.001*	-0.96 (0.11)	-9.1	<.001*
	5	-1.16 (0.10)	-11.88	<.001*	-0.93 (0.10)	-9.8	<.001*

.001, $\eta^2 = 0.20$). Table 1 shows the significant pairwise differences between arms for each subscale. All other RoSAS pairwise comparisons were not significant.

Godspeed Subscale Ratings: There was a main effect of arm stimulus on both of the employed Godspeed subscales: *likeability* ($F(4, 400) = 63.27$, $p < .001$, $\eta^2 = 0.29$) and *safety* ($F(4, 400) = 45.28$, $p < .001$, $\eta^2 = 0.22$). The significant pairwise differences for each subscale are shown in Table 2. All other Godspeed pairwise comparisons were not significant.

Custom Characteristics Ratings. Arm stimulus had a main effect on each of the visual form attributes: *angularity* ($F(4, 400) = 7.42$, $p < .001$, $\eta^2 = 0.04$), *sleekness/cleanness* ($F(4, 400) = 50.96$, $p < .001$, $\eta^2 = 0.23$), *softness/curviness* ($F(4, 400) = 62.40$, $p < .001$, $\eta^2 = 0.29$), *solidness/broadness* ($F(4, 400) = 8.97$, $p < .001$, $\eta^2 = 0.06$). The significant pairwise comparisons for each visual rating are shown in Table 3. Arm stimulus also had a main effect on each of the cost valuation characteristic ratings: *budget* ($F(4, 400) = 4.65$, $p = .001$, $\eta^2 = 0.03$), *luxury* ($F(4, 400) = 19.42$, $p < .001$, $\eta^2 = 0.11$), and *cost* ($F(4, 400) = 17.42$, $p < .001$, $\eta^2 = 0.11$). The significant pairwise comparisons for each valuation rating are shown in Table 4. All other characteristic pairwise comparisons were not significant.

Table 3. Significant pairwise results for each visual form attribute. Arm 2 was seen as more angular than Arm 3. Arm 2 was seen as less sleek and soft than all other arms. Arm 4 and Arm 5 were seen as less soft than Arm 1 and Arm 3. Arm 5 was also seen as more solid than Arm 1, Arm 3, and Arm 4.

Arm		Angular			Sleek/Clean		
		M (SE)	t	p	M (SE)	t	p
1	2				3.10 (0.29)	10.82	<.001*
2	3	1.27 (0.32)	3.91	.002*	-2.53 (0.27)	-9.23	<.001*
	4				-2.88 (0.27)	-10.73	<.001*
	5				-2.59 (0.27)	-9.52	<.001*
Arm		Soft/Curvy			Solid/Broad		
		M (SE)	t	p	M (SE)	t	p
1	2	3.24 (0.29)	10.99	<.001*			
	4	0.97 (0.26)	3.81	.002*			
	5	1.55 (0.28)	5.52	<.001*	-1.06 (0.26)	-4.14	<.001*
2	3	-3.73 (0.28)	-13.48	<.001*			
	4	-2.27 (0.26)	-8.67	<.001*			
	5	-1.69 (0.26)	-6.60	<.001*			
3	4	1.46 (0.25)	5.92	<.001*			
	5	2.04 (0.29)	6.99	<.001*	-1.08 (0.22)	-5.00	<.001*
4	5				-1.32 (0.23)	-5.65	<.001*

Table 4. Significant pairwise comparisons for each valuation rating. Arm 2 was considered less luxurious than all other arms. Arm 2 was less costly-seeming than all except Arm 5. Arm 5 was seen as less budget-friendly and less costly-seeming than Arm 3.

Arm		Budget			Luxury			Cost		
		M (SE)	t	p	M (SE)	t	p	M (SE)	t	p
1	2				1.92 (0.32)	5.99	<.001*	1.72 (0.31)	5.48	<.001*
2	3				-2.17 (0.31)	-6.99	<.001*	-1.78 (0.30)	-5.89	<.001*
	4				-1.83 (0.33)	-5.63	<.001*	-1.65 (0.31)	-5.35	<.001*
	5				-1.40 (0.31)	-4.57	<.001*			
3	5	-0.91 (0.23)	-3.99	.001*				0.88 (0.23)	3.89	.002*

4.2 Two-Alternative Forced Choice Responses

The selection percentages for each arm and category across participants are described in Table 5. These percentages were computed by dividing the number of times a given arm was selected by the number of times an arm could possibly be selected. For 2AFC questions, participant response times was generally consistent, averaging 1–2 s per response.

A synopsis of the key 2AFC results follow. For *angularity*, all arms had broad distributions of selections across participants. In the *sleekness/cleanness* results, Arm 2 was usually not selected by participants, while the other arms had a nominally even spread of selection. In terms of *softness/curviness*, Arm 2 was again generally not chosen. There were some trends in selection among the par-

Table 5. Means and standard deviations of the percentage of times each arm was selected for a given descriptor, denoted as $M(SD)$.

Category	Arm 1	Arm 2	Arm 3	Arm 4	Arm 5
Angular	0.38 (0.32)	0.58 (0.40)	0.37 (0.31)	0.57 (0.22)	0.60 (0.28)
Clean	0.72 (0.28)	0.01 (0.06)	0.49 (0.25)	0.65 (0.24)	0.63 (0.29)
Soft	0.76 (0.18)	0.04 (0.12)	0.86 (0.20)	0.50 (0.23)	0.34 (0.19)
Solid	0.37 (0.26)	0.69 (0.40)	0.44 (0.28)	0.26 (0.27)	0.73 (0.22)

ticipants; Arm 1 and Arm 3 tended to be selected more frequently than Arm 4 and Arm 5. Lastly, for the *solidness/broadness* descriptor, Arm 2 and Arm 5 were selected more frequently than the other arms. Arm 3, Arm 1, and Arm 4 tended to be selected somewhat less frequently.

4.3   Open-Ended Responses

Key themes that arose from participant free-response comments about the arms were material or color, the shape or style of end-effector, joint shape, arm size, and defining or looking for use context. Over half of participants ($N = 26$) mentioned the perceived material or color of the arm as playing a role in their responses. All respondents who mentioned end-effector ($N = 14$) preferences stated that they preferred the finger- or claw-like end-effector. Participants who mentioned joint shape ($N = 12$) talked about the "pointiness" or "machine-like" joints as less appealing, though some respondents referred to joint size while reasoning about robot power. Similarly, participants mentioned the size of the robot ($N = 11$), but were often not precise about their size preferences. Participants also mentioned usage or context ($N = 10$) either by defining prospective use contexts or by wondering what the purposes of the different arms were.

5   Discussion

The goal of this study was to investigate onlookers' perceptions of robot arm visual form characteristics using a set of robot arm visual stimuli. We measured participants' reactions to robot arm images through Likert-type questions and 2AFC comparisons. Although the work was primarily exploratory, our expectation, based on related work on robot size and nonverbal characteristics, was that there would be significant differences in responses across arm stimulus.

There were indeed significant differences in attributed characteristics across arms. Arm 2 was overwhelmingly the least favorable; it was rated as the least warm, competent, comforting, likeable, safe, sleek, soft, luxurious, and costly. This perception is possibly due to its stark difference in both appearance and size relative to the other arms, as it was the only purely industrial arm among the stimuli. Similarly, participants overwhelmingly did *not* select Arm 2 for both the sleek and soft 2AFC categories. Elements of Arm 2 that may have led to this trend include: the overall size of the arm, the exposed bolts, and two-linkage hydraulic motion system.

Beyond Arm 2, however, the differences between the remaining arms were less clear in terms of both Likert-type and 2AFC data. This suggests that for the remaining four arms, onlookers' perceptions did not vary much, at least on the examined scales. Some differences in perception that did appear include rankings of Arm 1 as more discomforting, less likeable, and less safe than Arm 3, which was in turn ranked as most soft/curvy. Arm 5 was ranked as most solid/broad overall, as well as less expensive than Arm 3.

Reactions to the presented arms - particularly the overwhelmingly negative response to Arm 2 - could be related to the manner of presentation used here. Because the stimuli were displayed as grayscale images, and without context (e.g., an image vs. a video of operation or performing a task), it is possible that participants lacked a consistent anchoring point to properly distinguish amongst arms, which might have forced them to evaluate the arms for an invented context of their own making. For example, it is possible that the pairwise relative comparisons of the images led participants to imagine robot arms with elements nominally associated with industrial applications (e.g., the exposed bolts of Arm 2) as more fitting in factory contexts compared to the other arms. Naturally, if the participant assumes that all arms function in the same nominal context (e.g., industrial applications), this could skew perceptions.

Key Strengths and Limitations: This study was designed to expand our understanding of human responses to robot visual form attributes beyond anthropomorphic characteristics. We were able to identify differences in perceptions of non-humanoid robots with similar visual structures and poses. We also obtained rapid and potentially automatic responses via the 2AFC methodology used here. It is important to note that results from the 2AFC portion of the experiment largely coincided with the results from the individual Likert scoring.

On the other hand, our stimuli lacked context of task space or location, which may have put some arms at an unintended disadvantage. Additionally, while our results imply that we succeeded in capturing a range of visual distinctions between robots of similar shape and pose, these visual differences were not varied in a systematic way, and represent a selection from actual hardware rather than a methodical manipulation of visual characteristics. We intentionally eliminated color to remove responses to color, yet due to the arms chosen, there was still a range in grayscale coloring of the arms. Color might be an interesting visual facet to explore in future work, and perhaps it might offset or induce changes in participant ratings. Finally, this study was run with a relatively homogeneous population of college students in the United States; thus, it is possible that results may not generalize to other populations or cultures.

Conclusions and Future Work: This exploratory study largely achieved its aim of demonstrating that human perception of the non-anthropomorphic visual form of robots can vary. This work provides a starting point to inform future systematic investigations of non-anthropomorphic robot characteristics. The existence of significant and robust response differences amongst the arms suggests that additional work focused on identifying what specific elements caused these differences is warranted. Next steps would therefore include systematic shape control and variation to examine specific visual elements, similar to past work on humanoid robot shape [11]. Additionally, expanding this work to explore different context spaces and incorporating systematic movement would allow us to explore the role context plays in responses to visual form, and how context might influence reactions to these robot arms.

Acknowledgments. We thank Dr. Cindy Grimm, Alejandro Velasquez, and Joshua Campbell for providing the Kinova and UR5e robot arms and posing them for photographing.

References

1. Bartneck, C., Kanda, T., Mubin, O., Al Mahmud, A.: Does the design of a robot influence its animacy and perceived intelligence? Int. J. Soc. Robot. **1**(2), 195–204 (2009)
2. Bernotat, J., Eyssel, F., Sachse, J.: Shape it - the influence of robot body shape on gender perception in robots. In Social Robotics. ICSR 2017. Lecture Notes in Computer Science, vol. 10652. Springer, Cham, pp. 75–84 (2017). https://doi.org/10.1007/978-3-319-70022-9_8
3. Broadbent, E., et al.: Robots with display screens: a robot with a more humanlike face display is perceived to have more mind and a better personality. PLoS ONE **8**(8), 1–9 (2013)
4. Carpenter, J., Davis, J.M., Erwin-Stewart, N., Lee, T.R., Bransford, J.D., Vye, N.: Gender representation and humanoid robots designed for domestic use. Int. J. Soc. Robot. **1**(3), 261–265 (2009)
5. Carpinella, C.M., Wyman, A.B., Perez, M.A., Stroessner, S.J.: The robotic social attributes scale (RoSAS) development and validation. In: Proceedings of the ACM/IEEE International Conference on Human-Robot Interaction, pp. 254–262 (2017)
6. CMR Surgical: Versius Surgical Robot System - CMR Surgical. https://cmrsurgical.com/versius
7. Faul, F., Erdfelder, E., Lang, A.E.A.: G*Power 3: a flexible statistical power analysis program for the social, behavioral, and biomedical sciences. Behav. Res. Methods **39**, 175–191 (2007)
8. Franka Emika GmbH: Franka Emika - The Robotics Company. https://www.franka.de/
9. Gautam, M., Fagerlund, H., Greicevci, B., Christophe, F., Havula, J., Havula, J.: Collaborative robotics in construction: a test case on screwing gypsum boards on ceiling. In: Proceedings of the International Conference on Green Technology and Sustainable Development (GTSD), pp. 88–93 (2020)
10. Gosling, S.D., Rentfrow, P.J., Swann, W.B.: A very brief measure of the big-five personality domains. J. Res. Pers. **37**(6), 504–528 (2003)
11. Hwang, J., Park, T., Hwang, W.: The effects of overall robot shape on the emotions invoked in users and the perceived personalities of robot. Appl. Ergon. **44**(3), 459–471 (2013)

12. KUKA Ag: Industrial Robots: KUKA AG. https://www.kuka.com/en-us/products/robotics-systems/industrial-robots
13. Lucas, H., Poston, J., Yocum, N., Carlson, Z., Feil-Seifer, D.: Too big to be mistreated? Examining the role of robot size on perceptions of mistreatment. In: Proceedings of the IEEE International Symposium on Robot and Human Interactive Communication (RO-MAN), pp. 1071–1076 (2016)
14. Phillips, E., Zhao, X., Ullman, D., Malle, B.F.: What is human-like?: Decomposing robots' human-like appearance using the Anthropomorphic roBOT (ABOT) database. In: Proceedings of the ACM/IEEE International Conference on Human-Robot Interaction (HRI), pp. 105–113 (2018)
15. Picelli, A., et al.: Robot-assisted arm training for treating adult patients with distal radius fracture: a proof-of-concept pilot study. Eur. J. Phys. Rehabil. Med. **56**(4), 444–450 (2020)
16. Tay, B., Jung, Y., Park, T.: When stereotypes meet robots: the double-edge sword of robot gender and personality in human-robot interaction. Comput. Hum. Behav. **38**, 75–84 (2014)
17. Tennent, H., Moore, D., Jung, M., Ju, W.: Good vibrations: how consequential sounds affect perception of robotic arms. In: Proceedings of the IEEE International Symposium on Robot and Human Interactive Communication (RO-MAN), pp. 928–935 (2017)
18. Walters, M.L., Koay, K.L., Syrdal, D.S., Dautenhahn, K., Boekhorst, R.T.: Preferences and perceptions of robot appearance and embodiment in human-robot interaction trials. In: Proceedings of New Frontiers in Human-Robot Interaction, pp. 136–143 (2009)

Perceptions of Socially Assistive Robots Among Community-Dwelling Older Adults

Nicola Camp[1]([⊠]) [iD], Alessandro Di Nuovo[2] [iD], Kirsty Hunter[1] [iD], Julie Johnston[1] [iD], Massimiliano Zecca[3] [iD], Martin Lewis[4] [iD], and Daniele Magistro[1] [iD]

[1] Sport, Health and Performance Enhancement Research Centre, Department of Sport Science, Nottingham Trent University, Nottingham, UK
nicola.camp@ntu.ac.uk
[2] Institute of Electrical and Electronics Engineers, Sheffield Hallam University, Sheffield, UK
[3] Wolfson School of Mechanical, Electrical and Manufacturing Engineering, Loughborough University, Loughborough, UK
[4] Qualisys AB, Göteborg, Sweden

Abstract. Socially assistive robots (SARs) have many potential benefits for older adults, such as reducing loneliness and assisting with healthcare interventions. However, little is known about how they are perceived by older adults. This study aimed to increase this understanding by using online, semi-structured interviews with community dwelling older adults. Acceptance of SARs was higher in those aged ≥ 70 years when compared to those aged 55–69 years. Declining health status was a common influencing factor, with company and assistance with daily activities highlighted as potential advantages. However, there were concerns among those aged ≥ 70 years that the introduction of SARs may lead to increased sedentary behaviour and a reduction in physical human contact. Overall, SARs are perceived to be useful among older adults, and developers should be aware that willingness to engage with this type of technology is dependent on several factors such as age and circumstance.

Keywords: Social robots · Older adults

1 Introduction

Advances in medical care have facilitated a global increase in life expectancy; the UK alone is projected to have one-quarter of the population aged ≥ 60 years by 2050 [1]. Subsequently, more people are likely to require long-term care [2, 3]. This may include supporting specific medical conditions associated with aging, as well as reducing instances of loneliness and social isolation, which are also prevalent in older-aged communities [4]. The restrictions on socializing and access to places promoting physical activity, such as gyms, because of the Covid-19 pandemic have intensified these issues within many older communities [5]. Due to the shift in population demographics, there is likely to be a reduction in those able to provide the care needed [6]. Socially assistive robots (SARs) have the potential to relieve some of these additional care needs and may become an integral component of everyday life for older adults [7, 8].

SARs are a form of robotic technology combining visual, audio and movement capabilities [9]. They are usually designed to assist an individual either physically, emotionally, or psychologically with the aim to improve overall quality of life. This assistance may take the form of motivation to be active, aiding rehabilitation or supporting learning [10]. Within older communities, it has been shown that robotic companions may reduce loneliness and isolation, support the self-management of medication, and potentially allow caregivers more free time to spend quality time with their older person [7, 11]. Subsequently, SARs have the potential to reduce agitation and anxiety, as well as support medication adherence [12] and overall improve the quality of life for both older adults and their caregivers [9].

SARs are typically one of two types: (1) Service-type, which are designed to support people when undertaking daily tasks [11] such as vacuuming, lifting, feeding, and monitoring a person [7]. These tasks, usually called Activities of Daily Living (ADLs), are fundamental to live independently within the community [3, 13]. The loss of function in ADLs is a key factor for care-home admission, and therefore maintaining the ability to perform them is of vital importance for older adults [14, 15]. (2) Companion-type, which are designed to support emotional health and psychological wellbeing [11]. Both have been shown to be useful when supporting older adults, however many of these studies have been in care-home settings, rather than within the home of those living independently within the community. The perceptions of SARs within this group are therefore less well understood, although factors such as previous knowledge of robotics and familiarization with technological devices such as smartphones may increase acceptance [16]. With a rise in the adoption of a biopsychosocial approach to ageing support [14], it is important to understand how both types of SAR are viewed by both those who may be requiring care now, and those who may need care in the future.

Through using semi-structured, photo elicitation interviews, this study aimed to understand the perceptions of community-dwelling older adults regarding SARs within their own home.

2 Methods

2.1 Ethical Approval

Ethical approval for this study was approved by the institutional human research ethics committee (18/19–75V2).

2.2 Data Collection

33 individual, semi-structured photo-elicitation interviews were conducted online with older adults aged 55–82 years. These were divided into 2 groups, "younger", aged 55–69 years (n = 17; women = 8, men = 9, mean age = 61.9 years, SD = 4.0 years) and "older", aged ≥ 70 years (n = 16, women = 10, men = 6, mean age = 74 years, SD = 4.5 years). Participants chose the video call software which they were most comfortable with, such as Zoom, Microsoft Teams, WhatsApp and Facebook Messenger. All participants were living independently in the UK, with interviews occurring between July 2020

and February 2021. Interviews lasted for an average of 42 min (SD 12 min) and were all conducted by the same researcher (NC). As these were semi-structured interviews, there was some variation in the order of discussions, however an interview script was used to ensure all participants were given an opportunity to discuss important details relating to SARs. The prompt questions are provided here:

1. Can you tell me about any experience or knowledge you have of social robots?

    a. What is a social robot?
    b. What do you think of when you think of the term 'social robot'?

2.2.1   < Show the Picture of the Robots >

2. What do you like/dislike about the social robots shown here? Ask this question for each robot.
3. Which shape/type is best?

    a. Why?

4. How do you think a robot may help you carry out activities of daily living / your usual routine?
5. Can you think of anything that a robot may be able to help you with that you currently find difficult to do or cannot do?
6. Would you want any of these robots in your home? Why?

    a. Are there any rooms you would or would not want a robot in? e.g., bathroom; bedroom

7. What barriers might there be in introducing something like this into care homes or into the homes of older adults?
8. What advantages might there be in introducing something like this into care homes or into the homes of older adults?

Images of the chosen SAR designs (Fig. 1) were only shown after the participant had explained their prior knowledge or experience and described what they thought a social robot may look like. Within this study, a humanoid and animal-like robot were selected due to the tendency of humans to anthropomorphize non-human entities, which can influence the perception of their competency and place in society [26]. Our focus for this study was the social aspect of SARs, and therefore these designs were considered the most appropriate. The functions of each robot design were then explained to the participants by the interviewer, and discussion surrounding their potential usefulness, or lack thereof, followed. The interviewer was able to reformulate, re-order or clarify questions during the interview to gain a deeper understanding of the participants opinions and thoughts.

2.3 Data Analysis

a realist thematic approach was used to analyze each interview [17]. This approach values both the qualitative and quantitative aspects of interview data [18, 19]. Three authors were involved in the transcript analysis process (DM, JJ, NC), with discussions used to settle disputes related to the coding and theme identification within the transcripts. 4 key themes were identified: existing knowledge, factors influencing acceptance, perceived advantages, and perceived disadvantages.

Fig. 1. Images used during the interviews to illustrate the different types of companion robots

3 Results

3.1 Existing Knowledge of SARs

Existing knowledge (Fig. 2) was highest within men aged 55–69 years (n = 6, 67%), with one explaining their "hands-on" experience through work: *"our chairman's got a robot that he uses that goes around with a video camera... it goes around the office, yeah. And it talks to people."*

Overall, most existing knowledge in all groups was as a result of media coverage, although many participants stated that this knowledge was limited: *"I can't remember where I read it... or it might have been on one of these science programs on the telly... but I thought it was a good idea."* (n = 9/33, 27%; younger men = 2/9, 22%; younger women = 3/8, 38%; older men = 2/6, 33%; older women = 2/10, 20%). However, as existing knowledge of SARs specifically was somewhat superficial, there was little difference between those with and without previous knowledge. Only one person had "real-life" experience with a social robot, which was not in a care environment and therefore did not influence their understanding of SARs within this context. As a result, further analysis did not separate those with existing knowledge from those without.

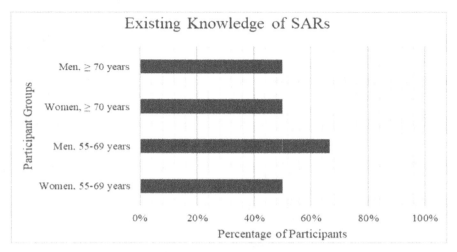

Fig. 2. Percentage of each participant group with existing knowledge of SARs

3.2 Factors Influencing SAR Acceptance

The robot design had a large impact on overall acceptance, whether for immediate use or at a time in the future, with the humanoid design being consider more useful in all groups (Fig. 3). The older groups, both male and female, were overall more interested in having humanoid robotic assistance at some time in the future, with 80% of older women and 66% of older men stating that they would consider one in the future, and 17% of older men stating they would have one now. One of the main reasons for this was the idea that the humanoid could be more physically helpful when carrying out daily tasks, especially for someone living alone (n = 7/33, 21%; younger females = 2/8, 25%, older females = 2/10, 20%; older males = 3/6, 50%): *"I would say, for somebody on their own, who is not able to do everything, then I would say they're a very good idea. And I'd go for the robot rather than the dog, because the robots... can do more things to somebody on their own than a dog would."*

Housing situation, and whether one lived alone or with a companion was also a key reason given for why an individual may consider having an SAR in the future (7/33, 21%; younger females = 1/8, 13%; older females = 3/10, 30%; older males = 3/6, 50%): *"if I was on my own then I might probably consider something like that but as it is at the moment, with [the two of us] being here erm I don't think I would bother."*

The acceptance of technology in a more general sense was also identified as a prominent influencing factor, particularly within the younger group (10/33, 30%; younger females = 3/8, 38%; younger males = 3/9, 33%; older females = 2/10, 20%; older males = 2/6, 33%), with one participant highlighting that the more a technology is seen and available the more accepted it is: *"I think if they're around all the time then people become less aware of them, if you see what I mean... so they'd become part of the furniture... Once they become part of the furniture, then they're not interfering, they're not, sort of – you're not aware of them is what I think I'm getting at."*. However, there was also a sense that this type of technology may never be fully accepted (7/33, 21%;

younger females = 2/8, 25%; younger males = 2/9, 22%; older females = 2/10, 20%; older males = 1/6, 17%): *"some people are just pure techno-phobes. They just don't like – they still want the telephone that you can put your finger in and that"*.

However, there was also a feeling within all groups that social robots are not needed within society (7/33, 21%; younger females = 1/8, 13%; younger males = 1/9, 11%; older females = 3/10, 30%; older males = 2/6, 33%), and would replace human contact which was perceived as a very negative thing and was the main reason given for not wanting either robot: *"I personally don't need one... I think, in the current climate I'm even more aware of the fact that trying to replace human contact with robotic contact is not really what elderly people need."*

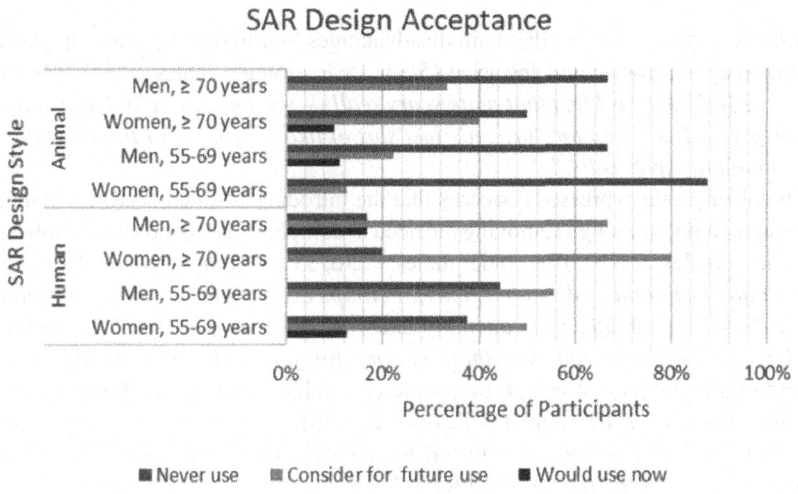

SAR Design Acceptance

Fig. 3. Relative acceptance of SARs within each participant group

3.3 Advantages of Social Robots

The humanoid design was considered advantageous by all groups as it could assist with activities in relation to daily living (15/33, 45%; younger females = 4/8, 50%; younger males = 3/9, 33%; older females = 6/10, 60%; older males = 2/6, 33%): *"I'm sure that in the house of the future, tasks that become onerous as you get older – washing up and basic tasks – I suppose it might be useful...And lifting and shifting things."*

Company was also highlighted as a particular advantage of the humanoid robot especially (18/33, 55%; younger females = 4/8, 50%; younger males = 6/9, 33%; older females = 5/10, 50%; older males = 3/6, 50%): *"if you're sat here on your own day in and day out, to have something like that, I should think, could save your sanity because at least you would talk to something, and they're answering you."*

Some participants identified that there was potential for the humanoid SAR to assist with healthcare (3/33, 9%; younger females = 1/8, 13%; younger males = 1/9, 11%; older males = 1/6, 17%): *"it's like a big iPad type thing... you could just say "oh, I don't feel very well, could you phone the doctor please"* ...*then it could just come next to you so you don't have to reach for the phone or something."*

Although considered less useful overall than the humanoid design, there were a few perceived advantages in all groups to the animal-type SAR, namely the simplicity of the design and the idea that it could be a practical replacement for a living pet (2/33, 6%; younger males = 1/9, 11%; older females = 1/10, 10%): *"if you are not able to look after a pet and you had always had a pet then a cyber-pet is quite a good idea because you don't have to feed it, don't have to take it for a walk – it's just there when you want it."*

3.4 Disadvantages of Social Robots

Regardless of design, one of the main disadvantages highlighted by males in particular was that they are considered intrusive (5/33, 15%; younger males = 3/9, 33%; older males = 2/6, 33%): *"I'd find that quite scary really – you know, you look round and it's following you. It's a step too far... it's just sort of like ... what am I thinking of... well it's just too intrusive really."*

The older group expressed concerns that the introduction of an SAR might increase sedentary behaviour though removing the need to complete certain household jobs (3/33, 9%; older females = 1/10, 10%; older males = 2/6, 33%): *"I think there will be robotics that will do most of the tasks in our house. Perhaps even to our detriment, we might all become bone-idle and never do anything and you'd just atrophy. You atrophy because you don't do anything, and everything is done for you."* The older group were also concerned that the animal design might increase fall risk within the home (2/33, 6%; older females = 1/10, 10%; older males = 1/6, 17%): *"as you get older there is always the possibility that you are going to fall more easily and having more things moving about just increases the risk of you falling."*

Usability of SARs was considered a potential barrier to acceptance for those who may be less familiar with technology in general (3/33, 9%; younger females = 1/8, 13%, older females = 1/10, 10%; older males = 1/6, 17%), *"how able the older person is to actually be able to control it. That would be the biggest concern I would have."*. Alongside this, cost was also considered a large disadvantage by the younger group (2/33, 6%; younger females = 1/8, 13%; younger males = 1/9, 11%): *"they're going to be a ridiculous amount of money though aren't they, these blooming robot things."*

4   Discussion

This study aimed to understand the perceptions of community-dwelling older adults regarding SARs within their own home, and what the advantages / disadvantages of them may be. Overall, older adults perceived SARs to have potential use in the future, with those aged over 70 years showing more acceptance than those aged 55–69 years. This is similar to Arras & Cerqui [20] who found that older adults were more accepting of robots than those aged under 18. It is interesting that older adults are consistently being shown to be more accepting to new, robotic technology than their younger counterparts despite stereotypes often believing the opposite – that older adults are less accepting to technology than younger people [7]. This highlights the need for constant engagement with older communities in the creation and development of SARs, especially as they are often the intended target audience for such technology. However, in both this study and that by Arras & Cerqui [20], robots were perceived as being able to contribute to an improved quality of life, but this should not be at the expense of real, human social contact.

The perception that introducing robots may lead to reduced human-to-human contact was a key influencing factors, particularly among women aged ≥ 70 years, and was cited as a reason to not have one. This may be linked to a higher incidence of loneliness among this population due to the unequal distribution of risk factors such as death of a partner among men and women [21] and the subsequent need to maintain social relationships. This is echoed in one of the main reasons for having a social robot in older age for many participants being "company." Although these technologies are often developed to assist healthcare and allow older adults to live at home for as long as possible [9], development of future systems should be careful to not completely replace human care with technological assistance. Human interaction can provide emotional connections that even the smartest technology is unable to replicate. These emotional connections cannot be underestimated in the care of older adults, as they are known to link closely with other factors such as depressive symptoms and subsequent reductions in physical activity and overall health.

The design of the robot, and the subsequent acceptance of it, depends on its perceived use. The humanoid design was perceived as being potentially more useful due to the ability to help with everyday tasks. Pfadenhauer & Dukat [22] suggests that decisions surrounding the usefulness of a robot are dependent on how well an individual perceives that their needs are being met elsewhere. This may help to explain why older adults are more accepting of robots than their younger counterparts, as they are more aware of activities which they may struggle with and have an appreciation of the help they may need in future. The animal-type robot was considered much less useful than the humanoid version amongst all groups, possibly as it was perceived to be less physically helpful. Although animal design robots have been shown to provide emotional support, this has often been demonstrated in isolated individuals, or those with cognitive impairment who may find it difficult to make or maintain social connections [12]. Healthy, community dwelling individuals are likely to be maintaining emotional connections to other individuals and are therefore less likely to require a robotic companion to meet those needs.

It should be noted that the interviews were conducted during, and just after the UK government introduced lockdown restrictions limiting in-person socializing due to COVID-19. Therefore, issues such as reduced human contact, isolation and the need for human company may have been at the forefront of people's minds. It has also been suggested that the opinions of an individual towards robots is heavily reliant on the opinions of others around them such as family and medical staff [23, 24] as well as previous experience of technology in general [16]. As these interviews were conducted on-line, the participants already had a good knowledge of, and were comfortable using, various technologies. Future work should consider including participants with limited knowledge or comfort with technology as well as other stakeholders including caregivers such as family and medical professionals. Participatory design, or co-design with older adults has also been suggested as a means of actively engaging this community with robots and robotic design [25] and should be considered in future work. The use of physical robots rather than images alone is also suggested for future work in this area.

5 Conclusion

In conclusion, older adults aged ≥ 70 years are more likely to accept socially assistive robots than those aged 55–69 years, although most would only consider them for future use. The risk of losing human contact was a major issue, however many saw the potential in the humanoid design and considered that it may be useful for supporting independent living of older adults. Acceptance is closely linked to the perceived needs of the individuals and therefore may change over time, and with changing circumstances such as health and living situation. Developers should be aware of this and continue to involve older adults in the development of SAR technology.

Acknowledgment. The work of Alessandro Di Nuovo has been supported by the European Union under the Horizon 2020 Grant n. 955778 (PERSEO) and by the UK EPSRC with the grant EP/W000741/1 (EMERGENCE)."

References

1. Morgan, E.: Living Longer and Old-Age Dependency—What Does the Future Hold? Office for National Statistics. https://www.ons.gov.uk/peoplepopulationandcommunity/birthsdeathsandmarriages/ageing/articles/livinglongerandoldagedependencywhatdoesthefuturehold/ 2019-06-24, last accessed 2022/09/14
2. Chen, Y., Thompson, E.A.: Understanding factors that influence success of home- and community-based services in keeping older adults in community settings. J Aging Health. **22**(3), 267–291 (2010). https://doi.org/10.1177/0898264309356593
3. Camp, N., Johnston, J., Lewis, M. G., Zecca, M., Di Nuovo, A., Hunter, K., & Magistro, D. Perceptions of in-home monitoring technology for activities of daily living: semistructured interview study with community-dwelling older adults. JMIR Aging **5**(2). (2022) e33714
4. Robinson, H., MacDonald, B., Kerse, N., Broadbent, E.: The psychosocial effects of a companion robot: a randomized controlled trial. J. Am. Med. Dir. Assoc. **14**, 661–667 (2013)
5. Camp, N., Fernandes Ramos, A. C., Hunter, K., Boat, R., Magistro, D.: Differences in self-control, self-efficacy and depressive symptoms between active and inactive middle-aged and older adults after 1 year of COVID restrictions. Aging Mental Health 1–6 (2022)
6. Bloom, D.E., et al.: Macroeconomic implications of population ageing and selected policy responses. Lancet **385**, 649–657 (2015)
7. Frennert, S., Östlund, B.: Seven matters of concern of social robots and older people. Int. J. Soc. Robot. **6**(2), 299–310 (2014)
8. Cavallo, F., Esposito, R., Limosani, R., Manzi, A., Bevilacqua, R., Felici, E., Di Nuovo, A., Cangelosi, A., Lattanzio, F., Dario, P.: Robotic services acceptance in smart environments with older adults: user satisfaction and acceptability study. J. Med. Internet. Res. **20**(9), e264(2018). https://doi.org/10.2196/jmir.9460]

9. Camp, N., Lewis, M., Hunter, K., Magistro, D., Johnston, J., Zecca, M., Di Nuovo, A. Older adults' perceptions of socially assistive robots. In: UKRAS21 Conference: Robotics at home Proceedings 21–22. (2021) https://doi.org/10.31256/Ub8Vp6N

10. Feil-Seifer D, Mataric M. Defining socially assistive robotics. In: Presented at 9th International Conference on Rehabilitation Robotics, Chicago, IL, pp. 465–468. (2005)

11. Whelan, S., Murphy, K., Barrett, E., Krusche, C., Santorelli, A., Casey, D. (2018). Factors affecting the acceptability of social robots by older adults including people with dementia or cognitive impairment: a literature review. Int. J. Soc. Robot. 10(5), 643–668. (2018)

12. Pu, L., Moyle, W., Jones, C., Todorovic, M.: The effectiveness of social robots for older adults: a systematic review and meta-analysis of randomized controlled studies. Gerontologist 59(1), e37–e51 (2019)

13. Camp, N., et al.: Technology used to recognize activities of daily living in community-dwelling older adults. Int. J. Environ. Res. Public Health 18(1), 163 (2021)

14. Candela, F., Zucchetti, G., Magistro, D.: Individual correlates of autonomy in activities of daily living of institutionalized elderly individuals: an exploratory study in an holistic perspective. Holist. Nurs. Pract. 27(5), 284–291 (2013)

15. Candela, F., Zucchetti, G., Ortega, E., Rabaglietti, E., Magistro, D.: Preventing loss of basic activities of daily living and instrumental activities of daily living in elderly. Holist. Nurs. Pract. 29(5), 313–322 (2015)

16. DiNuovo, A., et al.: The multi-modal interface of Robot-Era multi-robot services tailored for the elderly. Intel. Serv. Robot. 11(1), 109–126 (2017). https://doi.org/10.1007/s11370-017-0237-6

17. Wiltshire, G., Ronkainen, N.: A realist approach to thematic analysis: making sense of qualitative data through experiential, inferential and dispositional themes. J. Crit. Realism. 20(2), 159–180 (2021). https://doi.org/10.1080/14767430.2021.1894909

18. Danermark, B., Ekström, M., Karlsson, J.C.: Explaining Society: Critical Realism in the Social Sciences, 2nd edn. Routledge, London, UK (2019)

19. Maxwell, J.A.: Using numbers in qualitative research. Qual Inq. 16(6), 475–482 (2012). https://doi.org/10.1177/1077800410364740

20. Arras K, Cerqui D. Do we want to share our lives and bodies with robots? A 2000-people survey. Technical report Nr 0605-001 Autonomous Systems Lab Swiss Federal Institute of Technology, EPFL (2005)

21. Aartsen, M., Jylhä, M.: Onset of loneliness in older adults: results of a 28 year prospective study. Eur. J. Ageing. 8(1), 31–38 (2011). https://doi.org/10.1007/s10433-011-0175-7

22. Pfadenhauer, M., Dukat, C.: Robot caregiver or robotsupported caregiving? Int. J. Soc. Robot. 7(3), 393–406 (2015). https://doi.org/10.1007/s12369-015-0284-0]

23. Broadbent, E., Stafford, R., MacDonald, B.: Acceptance of healthcare robots for the older population: review and future directions. Int. J. Soc. Robot. 1(4), 319–330 (2009)

24. Salvini, P., Laschi, C., Dario, P.: Design for acceptability: improving robots' coexistence in human society. Int J Soc Robot. 2(4), 451–460 (2010)

25. Pollmann, K.: The modality card deck: Co-creating multi-modal behavioral expressions for social robots with older adults. Multimodal Technologies and Interaction 5(7), 33 (2021)

26. Daily, S.B., James, M.T., Cherry, D., Porter III, J.J., Darnell, S.S., Isaac, J., Roy, T.: Affective computing: historical foundations, current applications, and future trends. Emot. Affect Hum. Fact. Hum. Comput. Interact. 213–231 (2017)

Participatory Design and Early Deployment of DarumaTO-3 Social Robot

Zhihao Shen[1], Nanaka Urano[2], Chih-Pu Chen[3], Shi Feng[3], Scean Mitchell[1], Masao Katagiri[2,3], Yegang Du[1], Franco Pariasca Trevejo[4], Tito P. Tomo[1], Alexander Schmitz[1], Ryan Browne[5], Toshimi Ogawa[5], Yasuyuki Taki[5], and Gabriele Trovato[6(✉)]

[1] Future Robotics Organization, Waseda University, Tokyo, Japan
[2] School of International Liberal Studies, Waseda University, Tokyo, Japan
[3] Graduate School of Science and Engineering, Waseda University, Tokyo, Japan
[4] Pontifical Catholic University of Peru, Lima, Peru
[5] Smart Aging Research Center, Tohoku University, Sendai, Miyagi, Japan
[6] Innovative Global Program, Shibaura Institute of Technology, Tokyo, Japan
`gabu@shibaura-it.ac.jp`

Abstract. With the problem of ageing population increasingly prominent, the burden of families, caregivers and medical workers to take care of older adults will be heavier. Social exclusion and cognitive dysfunctions make things worse, especially in times of a pandemic. One of the most effective approaches to solve these problems can be technology, which application is often limited by the acceptance of the end user. We introduce a social robot, DarumaTO-3, whose appearance is inspired by a traditional Buddhist and Shinto doll called Daruma, and perform a preliminary test in which we hear the response from older adults. This paper describes this new robot prototype, and reports the feedback received from the early deployment with 44 Japanese older adults.

1 Introduction

In the everyday life of older adults, there is a problem of lack of communication and interaction. When living alone, they may face loneliness. The problem gets worse with age, due to inability to use technological devices and increasing degrees of dementia. Nursery homes provide assistance, but especially in large ones, nurses cannot provide company all the times, and organised activities are limited.

According to the Ministry of Health, Labour and Welfare of Japan, there are over 30,000 nursery homes spread across the territory, and an even higher number of day care facilities. These numbers are increasing year by year. In 2014, over 25% of the population was over 65 years old. In this context, there

This work was supported by Ministry of Internal Affairs and Communications (MIC) of Japan (Grant no. JPJ000595). Special thanks to Tohoku University for hosting the experiment.

F. Cavallo et al. (Eds.): ICSR 2022, LNAI 13818, pp. 550–559, 2022.
https://doi.org/10.1007/978-3-031-24670-8_49

is a growing need of socially assistive devices, and the potential market is of 30 million users. In Japan in particular, by the next 20 years one in every three people will be 65+ years old [1]. Especially, in the pandemic, the health and well being of old adult appears to be impacted critically. Many feasible solutions were proposed to ease this social problem while obtaining a better understanding of the human user [2]. Socially assistive robots are one possible tool that can be used to mitigate the loneliness and isolation of the old adult that was brought by the COVID-19 pandemic [3].

One of the most successful robots employed in nursery homes is the seal robot Paro. The authors Shibata and Wada (2011) [4] argue that robot therapy can relieve their stress as animal therapy does. We believe that Paro's strongest point is the smart and functional design, and the ease of use. On the other hand, Paro's limitations in the interaction (no capability of dialogue) show that there is more potential in the field. Our research is contained within e-ViTA [5], a Horizon 2020 EU-Japan project which aims at creating a "virtual coach" to support healthy living of adults in the age range of 65–75. The framework of e-ViTA roughly contains a front-end device, such as a robot or even a tablet, a network of sensors, a dialogue system, and a middleware. However, not any socially assistive robot can be used for this purpose. User acceptance can be tricky to achieve when dealing with older generations, and this is a factor that may act as bottleneck for whatever coach could be made. The first impact is necessarily related to exterior appearance: this implies that a robot has to be carefully designed, in order to ensure users' acceptance. Numerous previous studies, such as [6–8] have shown that the acceptance of robots is related to the background culture of the user, and even religion can be a critical factor [9]. In addition, older generations are known to often experience difficulties in the use of technological devices [10], such as mobile phones. Recent surveys [11] as well highlighted that the positive view of robots decreases with age.

Under these premises, the design of DarumaTO-3 (refer to Fig. 1) was conceived, inspired by Japanese folklore. DarumaTO is a social robot that can look familiar to Japanese older adults, being inspired by the traditional Buddhist and Shinto doll called Daruma. The robot we are introducing in this paper will act as one of the potential front-ends of the virtual coach. Its development is based on participatory design, which takes consideration of end-user and stakeholder needs and concretely presents them evolutions of the prototypes in an iterative manner. Through a sequence of steps, the development is expected to become optimal. This paper covers the development of the first improved prototype of this Daruma robot compared to the existing version made in 2016 [12], and reports on a session of interactions with older adults. Through qualitative analysis of the responses we attempt to validate needs, barriers and effects, and also to explore new ideas.

2   Social Robot DarumaTO-3

DarumaTO-3 (*Daruma Theomorphic Operator v3*) is the evolution of the 2 DoF DarumaTO-2 [12], from which it retains the mechanics of movement, which

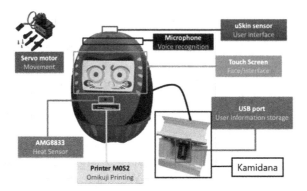

Fig. 1. DarumaTO-3 hardware configuration

therefore will not be described in this paper. This new version is the first one to be tested with an extended number of subjects. Compared to the previous model, it features a re-designed rounded shape. It does not feature a camera, however it has additional components which are listed in the next subsection. DarumaTO is able to communicate with people with simple dialogue as well as the facial expressions. Therefore, its inputs include voice and touch, and as a possible novel way of displaying output information, it can print out a "omikuji" (a fortune-telling strip written on paper at Shinto shrines and Buddhist temples in Japan).

Inside DarumaTO-3, a Jetson Nano is connected with the sensors, including a heat sensor, touch sensor and microphone; a touch screen to interact with the user; two servo motors to control yaw (right-left) and pitch (up-down) movements; a printer to print out omikuji, advice and reminders; and an external cabling to a Kamidana (a miniature household altar that enshrines a Shinto Kami (God), as shown in Fig. 1). The detailed description of each part follows.

- Heat Sensor (AMG8833): It is an infrared array sensor Grid-EYE 8X8 provided by Panasonic. It is connected with Jetson Nano to deliver values from thermal detection to give feedbacks for Daruma to do reactions and interactions with the user.
- Motor (MG996R): The motor is a high-torque digital servo featuring metal gearing resulting in extra high 10 kg stalling torque in a tiny package. Two motors are used to create yaw and pitch movements.
- Microphone (iGOKU): The microphone is used to detect and record the voice of the user, which will be processed by a speech recognition module.
- Printer (Phomemo MO2S): The printer stands inside the mouth of Daruma, is connected with Jetson Nano to print out omikuji automatically every day when the user connects with it. As different types of conversations get developed, it is expected to print out also advices, notes and reminders. This one of the first robots that incorporates a mini-printer. To our best knowledge, the only other case is BlessU-2 [13].

- Touch screen (EVICIV 7): The touchscreen is about 7 in. with 1080P resolution. It is used to express the facial expressions of Daruma including blinking, winking, smile, angry face, and others.
- uSkin sensor (XELA Robotics) [14]: Currently, it is used as a switch to activate Daruma. It can be also used as a touch sensor to monitor tactile interactions.
- USB: the USB memory that contains the personal information of the user is covered by a sachet symbolising a "Omamori" (a Japanese amulet commonly sold at Shinto shrines and Buddhist temples, dedicated to particular Shinto gods as well as Buddhist figures, said to provide various forms of luck or protection). When the USB is plugged in, Daruma will be able to know the user name in advance; otherwise, Daruma will only perform simple conversation without any personalisation.

3   Participants and Methodology

The experiment was conducted as a form of semi-structured interview at Tohoku University, Sendai. The 44 participants were all 65 years old or older (the average age is 71.30, the age standard deviation is 2.91) and live independently at home.

In Table 1, the information about older adults were collected including (1) whether they are living alone, (2) how often they contact with their family, (3) health, (4) lifestyle, (5) religion, (6) how familiar are they with technology, and (7) how often they use a tablet or smartphone.

Table 1. The overview of all the subjects

Sex	Female: 28; Male: 16
Living alone	Yes: 12; No: 32
Contact with family	Never: 1; Rarely: 1; Sometimes: 10; Often: 8; Always: 24
Health	Poor: 1; Fair: 15; Good: 7; very good: 11; Excellent: 10
Lifestyle	Not at all busy: 11; Somewhat busy: 15; Busy: 12; Very busy: 2; Extremely busy: 4
Religion	No: 33; Yes: 11
Technology	Not at all familiar: 15; Somewhat familiar: 18; Moderately familiar: 6; Very familiar: 4; Extremely familiar: 1
Using tablet or smartphone	Never: 4; Rarely: 5; Sometimes: 7; Often: 1, Always: 27

Fig. 2. Interview after interaction session

The experiment was carried out in three steps. First, before Daruma was introduced to the participants, the interviewer explained about the concept of coaching devices. Second, there was a short introduction to Daruma and interaction session. In this session, Daruma communicated with the participants through four use cases: welcome greeting and self-introduction, printing omikuji, reminder and final greeting. These four use cases mimic the typical use cases which will happen in a long-term interaction. Third, the participants were asked to judge Daruma's (1) usability, (2) animacy, (3) likeability and (4) uncanniness, and to (5) freely express any opinions about the device((refer to Fig. 2)). All of these are relevant indicators of the way DarumaTO should be developed. Usability is a common indicator for products, and particularly relevant in the case of older adults. Animacy gives an idea of how the robot is considered. Likeability is a common measurement for robots, and possible uncanny aspects necessarily need to be highlighted if present. During the open interview session, other opinions regarding DarumaTO's shape, colour, motion, and many other features also were collected from the users.

For the measurement of (1) usability, the System Usability Scale (Brooke, 1995 [15]) was adopted, and for (2) animacy and (3) likeability, the Godspeed questionnaire (Bartneck [16]) was used. Due to the age of participants, and the inconvenience of written questionnaires for them, these scales were used as a reference, with the interviewer reading the adjectives, and trying to identify the user's opinion on a scale of 1 to 5. It should be noted that the scores of (1)–(4) were not provided by the participants #10–#17 as Daruma had a malfunctioning that did not allow an informed judgement.

4   Results and Discussion

Based on the participants' judgements on Daruma, the experimental results are illustrated in Fig. 3. The results can be summarised in four features which are usability (did you find it easy to use?), animacy (did you feel it lifelike?),

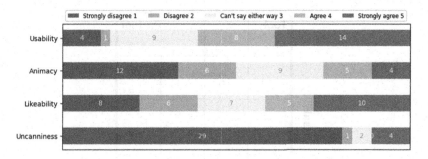

Fig. 3. Results of the guied interviews: positive adjectives are on the right

likeability (did you find it likeable?), and uncanniness (was it uncanny, scary, or uncomfortable?). In Fig. 3, it is possible to see each feature graded in a 5-points Likert scale [strongly disagree, disagree, cannot say either way, agree, and strongly agree].

4.1 Usability

The results of Usability (mean: 3.47; median: 4; standard deviation: 1.77) in Fig. 3 suggests that the majority of the participants agreed that Daruma was easy to use. Regarding the reason, four participants stated that it was good to be able to manipulate it by voice.

Based on the result above, it seems to be better for Daruma to be controlled by voice as much as possible, without adding many parts and buttons. The lack of sense of pressing the button seems to promote anxiety of the users because they do not know whether the robot understands what they say, or whether they can manipulate it in a right way, so these issues must be solved.

4.2 Animacy

According to the results of Animacy (mean: 2.53; median: 3; standard deviation: 1.86) in Fig. 3, the majority of people did not feel Daruma lifelike.

We consider a good achievement already to receive these mixed results to animacy. While its links with acceptability need to be clarified, it is important to note that animacy may be an aspect that is particularly culture-specific.

In order to have a clear idea of the perception of DarumaTO-3, we are introducing the use of the "tool-agent spectrum" (Fig. 4). which was proposed by Rozendaal [17]. Our contribution in this spectrum is that we measure the two axes with the above mentioned scales of usability and animacy. In Fig. 4, "tool" refers to an object that enables users to do what they want, and "agent" refers to an object that behaves as if it has autonomy. The object can be called "partner" when they have the characteristics of both "tool" and "agent". The overall goal in line with e-ViTA project is, in fact, of pushing the evaluation as much as possible close to "partner". According to the mean score of usability and animacy

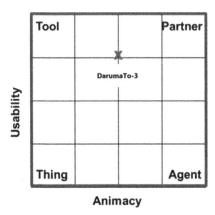

Fig. 4. Tool-agent spectrum with the result of this session

above, which are the vertical and horizontal axis respectively, DarumaTO-3 can be positioned just at the midpoint between "tool" and "partner". The next steps of evolution of this robot will be mirrored on this spectrum and compared to the previous instances.

4.3   Likeability

The results of Likeability (mean: 3.08; median: 3; standard deviation: 2.30) in Fig. 3 shows that the number of people who liked Daruma was almost the same as that of those who disliked it. While this may seem a not so positive result, we believe that the concept itself of a robotic Daruma leads to polarised opinions influenced by the personal background. In addition, being a session aimed to co-design, we left the discussion open about many personalised details such as shape, colour, voice, motion, and other features. More insights are presented in the Subsect. 4.5 Interview session.

4.4   Uncanniness

Based on the results of Uncanniness (mean: 1.58; median: 1; standard deviation: 1.69) in Fig. 3, it is indicated that most of the participants did not think Daruma as uncanny. While this result was very positive, here we highlight the negative comments only. Among those who answered "extremely", the participant #2 stated that "I don't understand why it was designed as Daruma. I think there is a misunderstanding by foreign people that all Japanese people like Daruma" and #42 argued "Daruma should not speak."

4.5   Interview Session

In the interview session, the impression of DarumaTO is collected and summarised as Table 2, where we report the (in our opinion) most critical and therefore useful comments. Desirable features were also collected and they are summarised in Table 3. Popular suggestions were coaching on cooking and health, measuring blood pressure, fortune telling, simple games, interesting stories, personal conversation, weather, news, searching information and reminders of the schedule.

When dealing with these results, it is important to note that not all the suggestions necessarily point at the right direction of development. Users opinion are variegated, and those who are a-priori not interested in the device are likely to give suggestions that are misleading for our goals (such as to employ Daruma to look after a dog).

Table 2. Impression from interview.

Impression	Details
Shape and colour	There were a certain number of people who said that it was strange to design a robot as Daruma. Thus, it might be the best to design it just as a round shape with a face. As for the colour, opinions were sharply divided
Size	14 people mentioned that it was too big. The participant #7 stated "It is too big compared to the general size of rooms in Japan (approximately 9.5 square meters)" and #26 said "I don't know where to put in in my house because it is too big"
Voice and the way of speaking	It would be better that the pitch, volume and speed of speaking can be adjusted according to the users' preference. Considering the fact that older adults use dialects more often than younger people, it is desirable if the robot can understand it
Motion	The majority of the participants agreed that the robot had to stay at one place, have a motion of nodding, changing directions and akin to the traditional Japanese doll known as "okiagari-koboshi"
Omikuji	Five people made positive comments while three were negative towards this feature. Five people stated that the letters were too small. There was also a person who claimed "It is hard to cut the paper (#10)" and "The printer was too slow (#28)"

4.6 Other Useful Comments

There were three participants expressing opinions that they did not need such devices as they could do almost everything with their PCs or smartphones. The participant #27 stated "PCs began to be spread when those whose age is in the seventies now started working, so there is a big gap between those who are good at using devices and those who are not in the generation." The participant #20 critically argued "If this device is put into practical use in about 10 years, people whose age is in the sixties now become seventies, and then the majority of these people can take advantage of such a device".

Table 3. Desirable features from interview

Features	Details
Coaching	People requested features concerning coaching. Among them, the most popular was the suggestion about cooking mentioned by 6 people. Health was also considered important
Entertainment	People mentioned features on entertainment. Their suggestion varied from "games (#34)", "rock-paper-scissors (#35)", "future prediction (#25)", "movies and music (#26)", "mahjong (#38)", "gamble such as horse races (#21)" to "what day it is today (e.g., a celebrity's birthday) and today's flower (#20)"
Conversation	Nine people showed interest in having more personal conversation with the robot. Two emphasised that they wanted to be told "Itterasshai (See you again)" when they leave and "Okaeri (Welcome back)" when they get back home"
Reminder	People stated that they wanted it to remind them of the schedule such as when to take medicine or when to go to hospital
Printing	Popular choices were data concerning health, lists for shopping, weather and recipes. While other robots usually provide information only via voice or screen, having it printed seems useful to memorise it
Others	The participant #3 wanted it "to operate inter-connectedly with my smartphone", #33 "to care about my dog", and #29 wanted "to name Daruma by myself." #21 added "If there are too many features, it will become too complex, so it does not have to be too much"

5 Conclusion and Future Works

Ageing society is a global issue for which socially assistive robots need to be specifically designed. We presented the prototype of a new social robot, called DarumaTO-3, made for Japanese older adults, and we performed an experimental session with 44 participants. The overall reaction was quite favourable, as it is apparent that they are willingly to use it if it is easy to operate. From the qualitative analysis of the interviews, a significant insight was that most participants conceive DarumaTO as a stationary object, which makes it feel less threatening compared to moving robots. However, in order to make it a suitable companion, several improvements are needed, especially in the hardware. Interesting data was also collected about the printing feature, which is also relatively novel in thee field of robotics. It appeared that particular emphasis should be placed on any kind of content that may be prone to forgetting, and let the user carry around the information. One additional lesson learnt is about synthesising a considerable amount of opinions, often in contradiction with each other, into useful research directions. This process goes through the understanding that not all opinions matter the same: the participants whose profile matches the traits of a possible "early adopter" weight more. After this experimental session, a re-design phase is going to follow. All the suggestions and critical issues will be considered for the future version of DarumaTO, which will be employed in a long-term study at users' homes.

References

1. Muramatsu, N., Akiyama, H.: Japan: super-aging society preparing for the future. Gerontologist **51**(4), 425–432 (2011)
2. Shen, Z., Elibol, A., Chong, N.Y.: Multi-modal feature fusion for better understanding of human personality traits in social human-robot interaction. Robot. Auton. Syst. **146**, 103874 (2021)
3. Getson, C., Nejat, G.: Socially assistive robots helping older adults through the pandemic and life after COVID-19. Robotics **10**(3), 106 (2021)
4. Shibata, T., Wada, K.: Robot therapy: a new approach for mental healthcare of the elderly-a mini-review. Gerontology **57**(4), 378–386 (2011)
5. Jokinen, K., Homma, K., Matsumoto, Y., Fukuda, K.: Integration and interaction of trustworthy AI in a virtual coach–an overview of EU-Japan collaboration on eldercare. In: Advances in Artificial Intelligence. JSAI 2021. Advances in Intelligent Systems and Computing, vol. 1423, pp. 190–200. Springer, Cham (2022). https://doi.org/10.1007/978-3-030-96451-1_17
6. Trovato, G., et al.: Towards culture-specific robot customisation: a study on greeting interaction with egyptians. In: 2013 IEEE RO-MAN, pp. 447–452. IEEE (2013)
7. Trovato, G., Eyssel, F.: Mind attribution to androids: a comparative study with Italian and Japanese adolescents. In: 2017 26th IEEE International Symposium on Robot and Human Interactive Communication (RO-MAN), pp. 561–566. IEEE (2017)
8. Arras, K.O., Cerqui, D.: Do we want to share our lives and bodies with robots? a 2000 people survey: a 2000-people survey. Technical report **605** (2005)
9. Trovato, G., et al.: Religion and robots: towards the synthesis of two extremes. Int. J. Soc. Robot. **13**(4), 539–556 (2021)
10. Smith, A.: Older adults and technology use. Pew Research Center: Internet, Science Tech (2014)
11. European commission: Public attitudes towards robots. Special Eurobarometer, vol. 382 (2012)
12. Trovato, G., et al.: The creation of DarumaTo: a social companion robot for Buddhist/Shinto elderlies. In: 2019 IEEE/ASME International Conference on Advanced Intelligent Mechatronics (AIM), pp. 606–611. IEEE (2019)
13. Löffler, D., Hurtienne, J., Nord, I.: Blessing robot blessu2: a discursive design study to understand the implications of social robots in religious contexts. Int. J. Soc. Robot. **13**, 569–586 (2021)
14. Tomo, T.P., et al.: A new silicone structure for uSkin-a soft, distributed, digital 3-axis skin sensor and its integration on the humanoid robot iCub. IEEE Robot. Autom. Lett. **3**(3), 2584–2591 (2018)
15. Brooke, J., et al.: SUS-A quick and dirty usability scale. Usability Eval. Ind. **189**(194), 4–7 (1996)
16. Weiss, A., Bartneck, C.: Meta analysis of the usage of the godspeed questionnaire series. In: 2015 24th IEEE International Symposium on Robot and Human Interactive Communication (RO-MAN), pp. 381–388. IEEE (2015)
17. Rozendaal, M.C., van Beek, E., Haselager, P., Abbink, D., Jonker, C.M.: Shift and blend: understanding the hybrid character of computing artefacts on a tool-agent spectrum. In: Proceedings of the 8th International Conference on Human-Agent Interaction, pp. 171–178 (2020)

Active Participatory Social Robot Design Using Mind Perception Attributes

Weston Laity[1], Benjamin Dossett[1], Robel Mamo[1], Daniel Pittman[1,2], and Kerstin Haring[1(✉)]

[1] Build–A–Bot Laboratory, Ritchie School of Engineering and Computer Science, University of Denver, Denver, CO, USA
{weston.laity,benjamin.dossett,robel.mamo,kerstin.haring}@du.edu
[2] Metropolitan State University, Denver, CO, USA
dpittma8@msudenver.edu
https://www.dubuildabot.com/home

Abstract. The Build-A-Bot online platform has been developed with the goal to enable active participatory design and broaden the participation in social robot design. The platform is hosted on a webpage to make robot design widely available. Active participatory design is enabled by giving the user the maximum amount of creative freedom in creating their own designs. The platform uses a form of gamification that challenges the user to build robot designs that emulate an experience or agency capability. The overall goal is to create a comprehensive set of robot designs that are related to such an attribute. This data then will allow us to research robot mind perception using Machine Learning and neuroscience methods in the future. This work focuses on the development of the online Build-A-Bot platform and the methodology implemented on the platform.

Keywords: Social robots · Participatory design · Robotics · Mind perception

1 Introduction

Current social robot designs have many explicit and implicit shortcomings. For example, a robot's appearance might not appropriately reflect the robot's capabilities, leading to miscalibrated human expectations towards the robot [13,26]. A robot may activate different mental models according to context [22] or the robot's surface level cues like its design and appearance [12,36]. A robot's design also often does not reflect a broad spectrum of designs and robot designers due to the under-representation of minorities in Computer Science and Engineering

This research has been sponsored by the University of Denver under the Professional Research Opportunities for Faculty (PROF) opportunity to Drs. Haring, Kim, and Pittman under grant # 142101-84994 and by the University of Denver under the Faculty Research Funds (FRF) to Drs. Haring and Pittman under grant # 142101-84694.

fields [18]. Appropriately designed robots can limit miscalibrated user expectations and misuse of robots, potentially improving the lives of many by providing social, physical, and emotional support. Such robots are the future of education, work, health care, elderly care, and could help maintain cognitive and physical health [4,8]. Robots are complex machines that unite advanced technologies in a robot body and their behaviors should be social enough to engage humans in the task at hand. However, the initial challenge that every social robot needs to overcome is posed by its own design and appearance. Cognitively, the robot design should reflect the robot's capabilities as those will shape the user's expectation, [13] which will in turn shape its acceptance by the user (Technology Acceptance Model (TAM), [35]). Socially [6], the robot's design should express the robot's social capabilities and shape user expectations towards the modality of the social interaction. Lastly, the robot's design also needs to house all the necessary technology that makes a robot functional, both computationally and mechanically, which is often referred to as "form follows function" [13,34]. Given current robot designs, it seems to be the case that robots are often designed for their function first and then their form is adapted given the function. This research reverses this paradigm. In our approach, we start with (human) mental states [11] and then ask users to design robots according to these mental states in an active participation robot design task.

1.1 Literature

It is unclear what a social robot design needs to entail to successfully interact with children, elderly, the workforce, or as in-home assistance. We lack a systematic and comprehensive understanding of the range, variety, and relationships among constituent features of anthropomorphic robots [27]. While recent research has approached this challenge by evaluating existing robot designs through explicit (e.g., self-reported experiences) and implicit [7] methods, using existing robot designs exclusively introduces a designer's bias, the unconscious patterns designers use while they're creating something, of what a social robot for a specific purpose should look like. A different approach that could mitigate this bias is participatory robot design. While a participatory design approach might not completely eliminate bias in robot design, when utilized on a large scale with hundreds of robot designs, the increased number of designs could mitigate individual biases. This method could also significantly broaden participation in robotics and robot design [28], and therefore help mitigate biases that might occur when homogeneous populations direct robot designs.

Participatory design (PD) can either be active or passive. It seems that "passive participation" is more common in current practice [29]. Passive participation usually takes the form of information obtained through questionnaires and interviews, meaning this explicit data is what users report about themselves. While this level of involvement is preferred to complete exclusion from the design process, it does not provide the same level of stakeholder influence as an active approach where users participate in the design process [32]. Active involvement is what differentiates participatory design from traditional user-centered design approaches as it allows the user to timely influence their future experience with the product [32]. Active participatory design has been explored in several fields, including social robotics. For example, children diagnosed with autism were asked to build a collage that represents a design for a social robot [29]. The study found that the children expressed broad opinions on the morphology of their final robot design, and combined features in ways that did not exist in current robot designs [29]. Furthermore, the study found that the children showed motivation during the building activity, including "an increase in communication using words and non-verbal signs to express enthusiasm regarding their final sketch" [29]. This increase in creativity (i.e., creating designs that do not yet exist) and engagement in the robot design process are benefits of participatory design we seek to implement on our platform. Additionally, we will be soliciting robot designs from a broad spectrum of people in regards to age group, neurodiversity, socioeconomic background, and cultural background. In order to take advantage of these potential benefits of active participatory design and to facilitate the broadening of participation in robot design, we have defined five main requirements for our platform. The platform must be: (1) easy to navigate; (2) facilitative of the robot design process; (3) accessible via the world wide web; (4) accessible for users of a broad age group (e.g., elementary school age groups to elderly); and (5) accessible for neurodiverse users. To achieve this, the platform will need to, at minimum, be online on a web page, utilize minimal text and more icons and images, and allow for user creativity and intuitive assembly of parts that form a robot. Additionally, the Build-A-Bot platform will benefit from employing universal design principles, making it usable by people with the widest possible range of abilities [14]. On the Build-A-Bot platform we allow users to combine robot parts in 3D space, similar to a character creator in a game, to see what a robot of their own design might look like. The user is fully in control of their design and our goal is to avoid guiding the user towards any particular robot design.

In addition to the benefits of active participatory design, there seems to be evidence that robot designers express a relationship with their creations beyond the initial increased engagement in the design process [29]. This might particularly be the case when the robots created on the Build-A-Bot platform are 3D-printed. Research shows that human-robot relationships can show feelings and actions resembling attachment [17]. Other examples of relationships with robots that form beyond typical relationships with objects are the naming of robot vacuums [10] or the hosting of robot funerals after a military robot is no longer serviceable [5]. While there is some evidence that people create attachments to robots in general, we are also interested in how a human-robot relationship changes when the user is involved in extensive design, engineering, and testing phases. In this context, it has been found that that people also seem to feel sad when they have to destroy their LEGO^{TM}robot creation [16]. The initial version of our Build-A-Bot platform focuses on the visual design of a robot.

Based on initial user tests, we estimate that a robot design could be created in around 20 min, which might not be enough time to activate feelings that resemble attachment. However, it could be the case that users enjoy creating a robot on a behavioral level or evoke an emotional response on the visceral level both in the creator and an observer of the design [24]. Additionally, there currently are no studies that have evaluated the relationship of virtual robot and their designers and the changes in that relationship when the robot creations take on a physical form. To enable an evaluation of this research question, an additional requirement to the platform is that (6) the robot parts in the platform need to be exportable as 3D-printable files that could then be assembled into a physical robot.

A secondary result that we hope to achieve with this online platform is to broaden participation in robotics and robot design. In the long run, the robot designs created on this platform will inform a Machine Learning model that uses the robot designs to learn, as well as make an evaluation of how design influences the mind perception in robots [15, 20, 42]. An important, but not sufficient, contribution to mitigate bias in Machine Learning is to create less biased data sets. This can be achieved if this platform is able to reach a broad spectrum of users that become robot designers, especially those that are traditionally not represented in the current robot design communities. In addition, for participatory design, it has been found that a third space ensures the greatest chances at creative solution finding [23]. Virtual robot design takes robot design from the researcher's lab and away from the user's designated work space by creating a third space online. In order to create a virtual third space, our last requirement is that (7) the platform needs to enable custom user settings and platform-specific sounds and music to establish an atmosphere and feeling of being in a third space [25, 31].

2   Methodology

To address the seven stated requirements that will enable us to achieve the short and long-term goals of the Build-A-Bot platform, we made several decisions on what software to use in the development of the online platform and on how to set up the platform to be able to apply Machine Learning models and neuroscience evaluations of robot designs in the future.

On the technical side, we used Unity [43], Maya [19, 37, 38], Blender [19], WebGL [40], Neo4j [3], Angular [1] and MongoDB [2]. This combination allowed us to create a web page where a robot can be assembled from individual parts via drag and drop. It also allows us to store the actions taken by users while creating the robot design in MongoDB, a graph representation of the parts used in Neo4j, and a screenshot of the robot design. Together with the target mind perception attributes for each design, this data will be used to train Machine Learning models that focus on feature extraction and eventually might be able to generate new robot designs. We used insights from social psychology and existing mind perception research to create a "challenge card" (see Fig. 1). The challenge card prompts the user to create a robot that possesses a certain experience or agency attribute (e.g., ability to memorize or plan, the ability to experience joy or fear [11]). The challenge card also asks the user to use a minimum amount (e.g., four) of robot parts. This serves two purposes in our methodology: first, it gamifies the approach to robot design and gives the user varying challenges and engaging them to create several designs [44]; second, it enables us to use the robot designs for further analysis based on neuroscientific methods (i.e., fNIRS) where it will be necessary to know the complexity of a design (i.e., number of parts). For the design and accessibility, we used Figma [9] as a prototyping tool to evaluate the layout and navigation of the platform before implementing it on the webpage and in the Unity game. We also used existing research on how to best represent mind perception attributes through icons [33] to broaden participation to users that are not literate or have reading difficulties. Where no iconography representation existed, we created a small set of icons.

2.1 Technology

To enable the requirements around facilitating robot design processes, broad access, and ease of navigation we decided to use the Unity game engine [41]. Using Unity allowed us to design robots similar to how one would create their own characters in a video game. Unity also offers flexibility, extensive documentation, and existing implementations of character creation interfaces [21] from which we based our new robot design interface. One example of a character creation interface that we initially investigated was the Unity Multipurpose Avatar (UMA) package [39]. However, UMA would not allow us to meet our requirements as it focused on humanoid models, and did not allow the creation of more biomimetic or non-biomimetic robots. This prevented a crucial feature in our requirements: the ability to combine robot parts in any manner the user chooses.

Unity also provides support for WebGL, which allows us to run the Build-A-Bot platform directly in a web browser [40]. On the 3D modeling side, we initially only used Autodesk Maya for the creation of the robot parts as it has faster rendering times [37] and offers more details in the modeling [38] than Blender which is desired to maximize robot design choices. However, we have since found that for our purpose, Blender delivers sufficient 3D parts. We also found Blender to be more approachable for new members of our team, which led to a transition to using both Maya and Blender. Both Maya and Blender allow us to provide a wide range of 3D-models for robot parts. This in turn empowers users of our platform to build a wide range of creative robot designs. Our platform also strives to maximize the user's autonomy of their robot design, thus fulfilling our requirements for active participatory design.

2.2 Design Approach

In order to fulfill our requirement of ease of use and navigation, our platform went through several design iterations using rapid prototyping. We used Figma

[9] to prototype design ideas. In addition, we are continuously implementing feedback on the navigation of the platform from quality assurance testing as we publish new updates. This includes, for example, the ease of use of the scaling and rotation features for robot parts in the game, the coloring of different robot parts, identifying functionalities that would make the robot design more straightforward, and finding bugs (e.g., some of the 3D models with a high polygon count can freeze the game). To decrease potential biases, we aimed to increase the number of available 3D models and added scaling features to the Unity platform. Having more variety of available parts and the ability to modify those parts allows us to provide the user with more space to be creative. For example, a sphere could be used for a robot's head or be a body part of a caterpillar-like robot. Once a part is selected users have the ability to transform the scale, position, rotation, and color of the part and to attach other parts to it (see Fig. 3). The Unity game is not programmed to take into account physical or real-world constraints. We hypothesize that this removes limitations to a user's creativity by imposing as little constraints as possible.

2.3   Robot Mind Perception Integration

Before starting the design of a new robot the user is given a target mind perception attribute to explore and target with their design. The user is presented with this mind perception attribute in what we call a "challenge card" (see Fig. 1). This challenge card additionally contains a set of requirements for the robot design. These requirements include things like a minimum number of parts, or a minimum number of parts of a specific type. This allows us to gather a broad range of designs with a particular set of requirements and/or targeting a particular mind perception attribute. These subsets of designs can then be analyzed for patterns that may or may not be present in other design subsets. While the user is building their robot design, we keep track of the different actions that the user takes and the different robot parts that they choose to use. For example, we track the order that the parts were used in, any changes to the size, position, scale, rotation, and color of the part, and any parts that the user chooses to delete. This data is important as we want to not only know what parts the user chose when targeting a certain mind perception attribute, but also the sequence of decisions they made when choosing and modifying those parts. As an example, we hypothesise that if a user were given a target of building a robot that was capable of feeling hunger, they may choose to use a robot with a humanoid torso, and possibly a large stomach area. If we found that users that were given this target attribute were incorporating design elements such as this, it may indicate a pattern in the human perception of a robot with that target attribute.

Fig. 1. An example of a Challenge Card asking the user to create a robot that is able to experience hunger and is composed of a minimum of four parts.

3 Results

3.1 Platform Implementation

To facilitate the seven requirements we identified, we implemented the Build-A-Bot platform as described in the Methodology section (see Sect. 2) as web-accessible 3D game.

Fig. 2. The user interface of the Build-A-Bot robot design platform. On the left are the 3D robot parts than can be used via drag and drop. The individual parts attach to each other to create a robot design. At the bottom are different actions that the user can take like undo, redo, delete a part, color a part or several parts, save the robot for later, or submit the final robot design. On the right as other actions like dragging, positioning, rotating, or scaling a part or several parts at once. On the top right, the current challenge card is being displayed.

In addition to making the game accessible to a broad audience, one of our main goals with the design of our platform was to make it as intuitive to use as possible. With this in mind, we iterated through several different user interface designs for the platform. In the end, we chose to implement a design in Unity that makes significant use of icons for all of the aspects of the interface. This helps us achieve the goal of making the platform easy to use for many different groups, such as those who do not speak English or those that cannot read, such as children. The current iteration of the UI design for the Unity platform can be seen in Fig. 2. While there is still some text used in the current iteration, we are working to replace this with additional in future iterations.

In our Unity implementation, we also worked to ensure that the flow of the application is intuitive for a new user who likely will not have previous experience manipulating objects in a virtual 3D space. To do this, we adopted a standard set of methods for transforming the 3D parts in our game. The different methods of transforming the 3D parts can be seen in Fig. 3. In addition to these three options, users can also drag a part to move it, and can change the colors of the different parts they are using. With these tools, the user can modify the part in whatever way they please. We do not want to tie users to using the existing parts without modification, as that could limit user creativity. Our goal is for users to be able to design exactly the robot they believe best meets the mind perception attribute they are targeting.

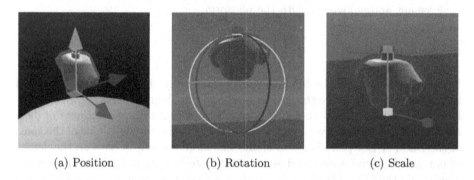

(a) Position   (b) Rotation   (c) Scale

Fig. 3. The three different methods of transforming 3D robot parts in the Build-A-Bot design platform.

3.2 Music and Sound Effects

We are expecting that users might spend longer amounts of time in the game and explore the possibilities of creative robot design. In order to create an atmosphere, many games employ music and effects [25]. We worked with a sound designer to create music that plays while users play the game. Classical music has shown to be beneficial for cognition and creativity [31] and the goal of the background music in our game is to emulate this creativity. Users can disable the music in case they are in an environment where it is not appropriate to play music. We also employed sound effects that along with visual effects to confirm that a certain action has been executed. For example, when two parts of a robot are attached to each other, they "snap" together visually by showing sparks and audibly by making a snap sound. The sounds and music can be explored on the current online prototype when playing the game on the Build-A-Bot webpage www.dubuildabot.com.

3.3 Enabling Active Participatory Design

We designed the Build-A-Bot platform so that users can create designs as freely as possible. For example, if a user does not like the challenge card presented, they can switch to another challenge card. Additionally, the platform does not impose any constraints on the order, size, or color of robot parts used, or how the parts are being assembled. There also are no real-world physical constraints, meaning the robots designed do not need to be functional in any way in order to be a valid robot design submitted to our database. We hope this maximizes creativity and minimizes the limits of possible design in order to create a more comprehensive robot design database. The goal with the design freedom we provide is to enable the active participatory design that is a key goal of our platform. By allowing users to create their own experience with the platform, we hope to increase user engagement and enjoyment with the platform.

4 Discussion

Designing, testing, and building social robots requires significant resources and time. One way to improve this process and add significantly more knowledge into how social robots can be designed is to enable access to large amounts of data about such robots. However, such data is not currently available. One of the goals of the Build-A-Bot platform is to create this large amount of data on the design of potentially social robots and give insights into how such a robot is perceived. This would then likely enable robot designers to start a social robot design with a perception goal in mind and design robots for a specific purpose. It is important for the large dataset we create to be comprehensive and reflect a broad spectrum of robot designs. Our approach of using active participatory design helps achieve this, as it can help increase knowledge and user satisfaction of a robot's design, allowing a broader range of designs to be created. It is also expected that when such data is evaluated and machine learning models are developed, having a more comprehensive database that is populated by a broad spectrum of users is an important first step towards mitigating biases in robot design. For example, while physical robot design is often limited to companies that have large resources or to engineering oriented universities or schools, our platform is accessible to users of a much wider range of age, origin, location, literacy, and socioeconomic background as only an internet connection and a browser is required to create a robot design. Our platform therefore has the potential to increase accessibility to robot design, simplify the design process, and with that, increase the number and diversity of robots designs and information about each design.

4.1 Future Directions

Systematic User Evaluation. We ran a short quality assurance survey with online participants that showed that the current platform version indeed enables users to build a robot. It also highlighted some areas of improvement for the platform usability and navigation. To ensure that we deliver according to our requirements, we will run a systematic user evaluation study expanding on the results of the preliminary survey. The experimental design of the study will test each of the seven requirements. In addition, we will investigate the icons we designed in a separate study (IRB approval pending). Additional user evaluation includes a comparison to real-world robot designs with the same prompts and using 3D-printed and Lego building blocks and we anticipate the organization of a workshop around the evaluation, usability, and future directions of this platform by the social robotics and designer community.

Machine Learning. One goal of the Build-a-Bot project is to analyze different designs, and the perception of those designs, to better facilitate social robotics. In order to evaluate new robot designs, determine what factors elicit a certain perception of the robot, predict the perception of novel (currently not existing) robot designs, and automatically generate new robot designs, we are developing the Build-A-Bot platform in a way that facilitates Machine Learning, using the active participatory design submissions to the platform as the basis for training our machine learning models. For this, we collect various data points from our platform. Our first metric of interest is a screenshot of the robot design from a fixed perspective. These images are used to train a Convolutional Neural Network (CNN) with the goal of determining what it means to look like a specified category of social robot. With enough training data from the platform, we may also be able to use these images to generate new images of a robot, providing new appropriate robot designs for a category. Another metric we are collecting is data on the steps that the user takes while building their robot design. Each step the user takes (e.g., drag, resize, undo, delete), and in what order those steps are taken, is recorded. While this may not directly contribute to our machine learning models, it provides a standalone dataset that we can process to find relationships between robot designs in a given category. We expect that this can lead to insights on how people design robots, if there is a common ordering to how users approach designing a robot, and if there are specific steps or information we can identify for specific robot categories. Lastly, we also are recording the all the parts that make up a final robot design and their corresponding locations, scales, colors, and properties. These properties associated with each part will then be combined together to create a graph representation of the submitted design. The parts themselves will represent the nodes in the graph, and the relationships between parts, such as distance, will be the edges between nodes. In order to better understand the impact these relationships between parts have on how a design is perceived, we will be turning to Graph Machine Learning [30] techniques to train a deep-learning model that can be used as an alternative classification method to our CNN trained on screenshots of the robot. We plan to compare the accuracy of both methods to determine with machine-learning approach, or if a combination of both approaches, is a better use-case for this domain.

Model Validation with Novel Metrics. Another goal is to evaluate robot designs and the associated mind perception of robots through independent measurements. While Machine Learning can be very powerful, we decided that in order to validate and verify our models, an independent measure will add immense value to the body of knowledge of robot design, neuroscience, novel metrics for HRI, and verification of Machine Learning models. We decided to use functional near-infrared spectroscopy (fNIRS), an optical brain monitoring technique that uses near-infrared light to estimate cortical hemodynamic activity which occurs in response to neural activity. fNIRS is non-invasive, portable, comparatively cost-effective, and has good resolution to evaluate human brain regions that are associated with a Theory of Mind (ToM) [15]. fNIRS has shown that it can detect human empathy, a mechanism that is closely associated with a human's Theory of Mind [15]. We will begin our evaluation with a proof of concept demonstrating that people experience empathy when seeing a robot designed with the ability to feel pain and a pain stimuli, and compare it to the brain activation seeing a human and a pain stimuli. We expect to find that human brain activation will show that humans feel empathy for robots, however at a lower salience than for other humans.

4.2   Limitations

The biggest limitation introduced when making robot designs possible on a web-accessible platform like Build-A-Bot is that all robot designs are virtual. Virtual robot designs and their perceptions do not necessarily translate directly how a robot is being perceived in the real world. While we cannot eliminate this limitation completely due to our goal to create a large amount of data on robot designs and broadening participation in robot design, we are mitigating this limitation in three ways: (1) all 3D robot parts can be exported as .stl files and 3D printed. This enables us to print and assemble select robot designs and evaluate them further; (2) all robot parts are three-dimensional due to the implementation in Unity – while this does not enable a real-world comparison, it is considered a improvement from having two-dimensional designs; and (3) we plan to re-create a small subsection of this evaluation in the real world. For that, we create similar challenge cards but have participants assemble robot designs with LEGO^TM builds to evaluate design structures outside of the parts we provide in the game, as well as have participants assemble robot designs with 3D printed parts from the game. This allows us to compare the virtual designs and the real-world designs and gather further information on the reliability and validity of the robot designs made on the virtual platform.

5 Conclusion

The goal of the Build-A-Bot platform is to provide a tool to assemble novel robot designs. The robot designs are associated with a mind perception attribute they should be designed for, but otherwise are left to the creativity of the user. It is expected that the platform will successfully enable a broad participation in robot design due to its usability and accessibility, and enable active participatory robot design due to the methodology we implemented with our technical approach. We believe that, once Build-A-Bot has fully launched, we will show that the platform indeed enables users to create creative and novel robotic designs, and enables a broad participation from a diverse set of users. Once we have gathered an initial set of robot designs, we can then show in the next steps that Machine Learning models with bias mitigation and independent neuroscience measures will lead to an in-depth understanding of social robot design and contribute important knowledge to the area of robot mind perception.

Acknowledgment. We are grateful to our students Abdul Ayad, Mike Blanding, Marley Bogran, Madeline Bohn, William Bohrmann, Gillian Ehman, Josh Ellis, Angel Fernandes, Tanner Francis, Sergio Gonzales, Elizabeth Gutierrez-Gutierrez, Ulises A. Heredia Trinidad, Beatriz Hernandez, Esabella Irby, Henry Jaffray, Izzy Johnson, Braden Kelsey, Yahir Luevano-Estrada, Nicholas Ninos, Sneha Patil, Max Peterson, Yasmin Raz, Hector Armando Rodriguez, Ashley Sanchez, Grace Strasheim, Raghav Thapa, Maisey Toczek, and Ralph Vrooman for their work on DU Build-A-Bot.

References

1. Angular. https://angular.io/
2. MongoDB: The Developer Data Platform. https://www.mongodb.com
3. Neo4j Graph Data Platform - The Leader in Graph Databases. https://neo4j.com/
4. van den Berghe, R., Verhagen, J., Oudgenoeg-Paz, O., Van der Ven, S., Leseman, P.: Social robots for language learning: A review. Rev. Educ. Res. **89**(2), 259–295 (2019)
5. Carpenter, J.: The Quiet Professional: An investigation of US military Explosive Ordnance Disposal personnel interactions with everyday field robots. Ph.D. thesis (2013)
6. Cha, E., Dragan, A.D., Srinivasa, S.S.: Perceived robot capability. In: 2015 24th IEEE International Symposium on Robot and Human Interactive Communication (RO-MAN), pp. 541–548. IEEE (2015)
7. Corrigan, L.J., Basedow, C., Küster, D., Kappas, A., Peters, C., Castellano, G.: Mixing implicit and explicit probes: finding a ground truth for engagement in social human-robot interactions. In: 2014 9th ACM/IEEE International Conference on Human-Robot Interaction (HRI), pp. 140–141. IEEE (2014)
8. Dino, F., Zandie, R., Abdollahi, H., Schoeder, S., Mahoor, M.H.: Delivering cognitive behavioral therapy using a conversational social robot. In: 2019 IEEE/RSJ International Conference on Intelligent Robots and Systems (IROS), pp. 2089–2095. IEEE (2019)
9. Figma (2021). https://www.figma.com/ (25 Aug 2021)

10. Forlizzi, J., DiSalvo, C.: Service robots in the domestic environment: a study of the roomba vacuum in the home. In: Proceedings of the 1st ACM SIGCHI/SIGART onference on Human-Robot Interaction, pp. 258–265 (2006)
11. Gray, H.M., Gray, K., Wegner, D.M.: Dimensions of mind perception. Science **315**(5812), 619–619 (2007)
12. Haring, K.S., Phillips, E., Lazzara, E.H., Ullman, D., Baker, A.L., Keebler, J.R.: Applying the swift trust model to human-robot teaming. In: Trust in Human-Robot Interaction, pp. 407–427. Elsevier (2021)
13. Haring, K.S., Watanabe, K., Velonaki, M., Tossell, C.C., Finomore, V.: FFAB-The form function attribution bias in human-robot interaction. IEEE Trans. Cogn. Developm. Syst. **10**(4), 843–851 (2018)
14. Henry, S.L., Abou-Zahra, S., Brewer, J.: The role of accessibility in a universal web. In: Proceedings of the 11th Web for all Conference, pp. 1–4 (2014)
15. Himichi, T., Nomura, M.: Modulation of empathy in the left ventrolateral prefrontal cortex facilitates altruistic behavior: An fNIRS study. J. Integr. Neurosci. **14**(02), 207–222 (2015)
16. Huang, L., Gillan, D.: An exploration of robot builders' emotional responses to their tournament robots. In: Proceedings of the Human Factors And Ergonomics Society Annual Meeting, vol. 58, pp. 2013–2017. SAGE Publications Sage CA: Los Angeles, CA (2014)
17. Huang, L., Varnado, T., Gillan, D.: An exploration of robot builders' attachment to their lego robots. In: Proceedings of the Human Factors and Ergonomics Society Annual Meeting, vol. 57, pp. 1825–1829. SAGE Publications Sage CA: Los Angeles, CA (2013)
18. Keller, L., John, I.: How can computer science faculties increase the proportion of women in computer science by using robots? In: 2019 IEEE Global Engineering Education Conference (EDUCON), pp. 206–210. IEEE (2019)
19. Kumar, A.: Integrating with Blender, Maya and Marmoset. In: Beginning PBR Texturing, pp. 165–186. Apress, Berkeley, CA (2020). https://doi.org/10.1007/978-1-4842-5899-6_16
20. Küster, D., Swiderska, A.: Seeing the mind of robots: Harm augments mind perception but benevolent intentions reduce dehumanisation of artificial entities in visual vignettes. Int. J. Psychol. **56**(3), 454–465 (2021)
21. Lochner, D.: Creature Creator (2021). https://github.com/daniellochner/Creature-Creator
22. Matthews, G., Lin, J., Panganiban, A.R., Long, M.D.: Individual differences in trust in autonomous robots: Implications for transparency. IEEE Trans. Hum. Mach. Syst. **50**(3), 234–244 (2019)
23. Muller, M.J.: Participatory design: the third space in HCI. CRC Press (2007)
24. Norman, D.A.: Emotional design: Why we love (or hate) everyday things. Civitas Books (2004)
25. Peerdeman, P.: Sound and music in games. Amsterdam: VrijeUniversiteit, pp. 2–3 (2010)
26. Phillips, E., Ullman, D., de Graaf, M.M., Malle, B.F.: What does a robot look like?: A multi-site examination of user expectations about robot appearance. In: Proceedings of the Human Factors and Ergonomics Society Annual Meeting, vol. 61, pp. 1215–1219. SAGE Publications Sage CA: Los Angeles, CA (2017)
27. Phillips, E., Zhao, X., Ullman, D., Malle, B.F.: What is human-like? Decomposing robots' human-like appearance using the anthropomorphic robot (ABOT) database. In: Proceedings of the 2018 ACM/IEEE International Conference on Human-Robot Interaction, pp. 105–113 (2018)

28. Plaza, P., et al.: Educational robotics for all: Gender, diversity, and inclusion in steam. In: 2020 IEEE Learning With MOOCS (LWMOOCS), pp. 19–24. IEEE (2020)
29. Ramírez-Duque, A.A., et al.: Collaborative and inclusive process with the autism community: a case study in colombia about social robot design. Int. J. Soc. Robot. **13**(2), 153–167 (2020). https://doi.org/10.1007/s12369-020-00627-y
30. Raposo, D., Santoro, A., Barrett, D., Pascanu, R., Lillicrap, T., Battaglia, P.: Discovering objects and their relations from entangled scene representations. arXiv preprint arXiv:1702.05068 (2017)
31. Ritter, S.M., Ferguson, S.: Happy creativity: Listening to happy music facilitates divergent thinking. PLoS ONE **12**(9), e0182210 (2017)
32. Robertson, T., Simonsen, J.: Challenges and opportunities in contemporary participatory design. Des. Issues **28**(3), 3–9 (2012)
33. Sampietro, A.: Use and interpretation of emoji in electronic-mediated communication: A survey. Vis. Commun. Q. **27**(1), 27–39 (2020)
34. Schaefer, K.E., Sanders, T.L., Yordon, R.E., Billings, D.R., Hancock, P.A.: Classification of robot form: Factors predicting perceived trustworthiness. In: Proceedings of the Human Factors And Ergonomics Society Annual Meeting, vol. 56, pp. 1548–1552. SAGE Publications Sage CA: Los Angeles, CA (2012)
35. Scherer, R., Siddiq, F., Tondeur, J.: The technology acceptance model (tam): A meta-analytic structural equation modeling approach to explaining teachers' adoption of digital technology in education. Comput. Educ. **128**, 13–35 (2019)
36. Schramm, L.T., Dufault, D., Young, J.E.: Warning: This robot is not what it seems! exploring expectation discrepancy resulting from robot design. In: Companion of the 2020 ACM/IEEE International Conference on Human-Robot Interaction, pp. 439–441 (2020)
37. Senkic, D.: Dynamic simulation in a 3d-environment: A comparison between maya and blender (2010)
38. Smith, M.B.: 3d character modeling in maya and blender. Undergraduate Honors Theses 120 (2017). https://thekeep.eiu.edu/honors_theses/120
39. Store, U.A.: Unity multipurpose avatar (2022). https://assetstore.unity.com/packages/3d/characters/uma-2-unity-multipurpose-avatar-35611. (Accessed 16 August 2022)
40. Technologies U: Unity - Manual: Building your WebGL application. https://docs.unity3d.com/Manual/webgl-building.html
41. Technologies U: Unity Real-Time Development Platform — 3D, 2D VR & AR Engine. https://unity.com/
42. Thellman, S., de Graaf, M., Ziemke, T.: Mental state attribution to robots: A systematic review of conceptions, methods, and findings. ACM Trans. Hum. Robot Interact. (2021)
43. Totten, C.: Game character creation with blender and unity. John Wiley & Sons (2012)
44. Zichermann, G., Cunningham, C.: Gamification by design: Implementing game mechanics in web and mobile apps. O'Reilly Media, Inc. (2011)

Not that Uncanny After All?
An Ethnographic Study on Android
Robots Perception of Older Adults
in Germany and Japan

Felix Carros[1](✉) , Berenike Bürvenich[1] , Ryan Browne[4] ,
Yoshio Matsumoto[2] , Gabriele Trovato[3] , Mehrbod Manavi[1] ,
Keiko Homma[2] , Toshimi Ogawa[4] , Rainer Wieching[1] , and Volker Wulf[1]

[1] University of Siegen, Siegen, Germany
felix.carros@uni-siegen.de
[2] National Institute of Advanced Industrial Science and Technology (AIST),
Kashiwa, Japan
[3] Shibaura Institute of Technology, Tokyo, Japan
[4] Tohoku University, Sendai, Japan

Abstract. Intercultural studies are scarce but yet insightful to better understand reactions of older adults to human-like Android robot behavior. They help to see which reactions of participants are universal and which are country specific. Research with android robots and older adults has many results that are based on online research with pictures or on research that has been carried out in labs in one country. Within a Japanese-European research project, we had the rare occasion to work with an android robot in both countries and compare the results. We collected data from 19 participants that were invited in a Living Lab at two universities in Japan and Germany. The data contains interviews, videos and questionnaires and was analyzed with a mixed method approach. Results indicate that the android robots of this study are not in the valley of the uncanny valley theory. We could observe that the older adults and stakeholders from both countries were open to talk to the robot, some even about private topics, while others preferred to use the robot to retrieve information. German participants wished for more gestures, while Japanese participants were keen on the relatively little number of gestures. With this work we contribute to a broader understanding on how older adults perceive android robots and could show that an android robot with its human-like appearance is not seen as uncanny.

Keywords: Social robot · Ethnography · Living lab · Appropriation ·
Self-disclosure · HRI · Android robot · Uncanny valley · Older adults ·
Assisted living · NLP · Wizard-of-Oz

The presented work has received funding from the European Union under grant agreement no. 101016453 and from the Ministry of Internal Affairs and Communications (MIC) of Japan under grand agreement no. JPJ000595.

F. Cavallo et al. (Eds.): ICSR 2022, LNAI 13818, pp. 574–586, 2022.
https://doi.org/10.1007/978-3-031-24670-8_51

1 Introduction

The ongoing demographic change will result in an increase of older adults living independently at home, both in Japan and in Europe. Younger family members have often moved to other cities or are occupied with challenging careers. These factors may result in a situation that often leaves community-dwelling older adults with little company, resulting in a growing loneliness and a general lack of external assistance for daily life challenges and personal questions. One possible assistance to counteract these challenges in the future can come from social robots; they are not the same as human interaction partners and have often a different approach on interaction, but are able to provide information, imitate basic conversations and help in contacting other people in the community. Specifically, information on health and assistance in daily life are promising application fields for social robots like android robots.

These robots aim to look like humans in order to create a smooth interaction between the human and the robotic system [21]. But the human-like shape of a robot is only one dimension of an interaction partner. Gestures, movement and conversations are also important to create a good interaction. For this, conversational abilities, gestures and the movement of the robot has to be matched. What a robot says needs not only to be synchronised with the gesture and mimic of the robot but also both should be adapted to the context of the situation [29].

In the study reported here, the contribution aims at a better understanding of potentially needed changes of the concept of the uncanny valley [26], based on a cross-cultural qualitative field study with community-dwelling older adults from Germany and Japan.

2 Related Work

2.1 Older Adults and Robots in Assistive Living and Healthcare

Numerous concepts, projects, prototypes, and established solutions already exist in the field of robotics for older adults. However they are, for the most part, yet to be fully established in the communities where elderly persons live. The spectrum of applications is diverse and ranges from commercial robots for logistical support to robots talking and playing with humans. Robots can not only assist in functional tasks such as bathing (e.g. [30]) or dementia care (e.g. [18]) but also become social interaction partners (e.g. [2,11,20,31]) and improve engagement [28] or they can help to facilitate communication with family and friends [7,15] or perform exercises for rehabilitation [17]. A factor of success seems to be the participatory design of the software of the robot [11,12,14,33] as well as a long-term approach of development, to constantly redevelop the robotic system. A successfully used framework for the development and redevelopment of socio-technical artifacts such as social robots is the so-called "design case study" mentioned by Wulf et al. [39,40], which has been used in several R&D projects to explore the effects of social robots on human-robot interaction [13].

2.2   Androids and Uncanny Valley

An android robot refers to a kind of humanoid robots whose appearance highly resembles humans. The skin of the android is made of soft silicon rubber and the face often is copy of a real human face. It can show various facial expressions and the movements are inspired by humans for achieving natural human-robot interaction [21]. Due to the technical limitations and safety issues there is no android robot developed so far that can walk around. Therefore robotics research using android robot focuses on communication and social issues in seated or standing positions [21,27].

As a literature review [3] reported, there are quite a few studies on social robots applied in the care of older persons in the last decade. They can be categorized in four purposes: (1) Supporting everyday life, (2) Providing interaction, (3) Facilitating cognitive training, and (4) Facilitating physical training. However there is no android robots used in these studies. In order to improve the impressions, acceptance and trust of the robot used for such purposes in the care, it is important to investigate the effects of the human-likeness such as the appearance and the movement. As Mori hypothesized as the "uncanny valley" [26], human-likeness of the robot could induce both positive and negative impressions. The uncanny valley is intensively investigated with a mixed methods approach, however as Wang et al. [37] points out, results on the theory are still inconsistent and further exploratory research is needed.

It is also important to conduct the cultural comparison on uncanny valley, since it is known that people in different cultures could show different attitudes towards robots [6]. Previous research featuring cross-cultural studies on humanoid robots do exist. For example, Haring et al. [19] showed cultural differences on the attitude towards an android robot in Japan and Australia. Trovato et al. showed cultural adaptation regarding greeting choices for more mechanical-looking humanoids [35] in Japan and Germany. However they are neither focused on the interaction with older persons, nor on care/healthcare domains in daily life activities. In this paper, we present our exploratory experimental results specifically on the acceptance of the android robots by older adults in Germany and Japan, which are being developed to assist in daily life activities or inform about health related topics.

3   Methods and Study Set-Up

3.1   Android Robot

The android utilized in this research was A-Lab Android Standard Model AL-G109ST-F for German study and Kokoro Actroid-F for Japanese study. The former has 18 DoFs (degrees of freedom) and the latter has 12 DoFs in the upper bodies, which are all driven by a linear or cylindrical pneumatic actuator. More than half of these DoFs are located in the face to control various facial expressions like blinking, smiling, lifting eyebrows or looking sad, surprised or angry. In addition, the neck can move, that enables the robot to nod, shake her head or do inclining motions. Furthermore, it has actuators for bending in the waist, and for breathing at the shoulder. The limbs (i.e. arms and legs) are not movable. All of the DoFs are position-controlled with air servoing. The use of air actuators allows silent and robust motions without heating problems and besides only needs annual maintenance. The compressed air is supplied by an external air compressor. The air valves are all installed inside the body. The system runs with a 100-220V power supply. Both robots had a female appearance. The appearance can be changed to male but is stayed as female to have some comparability between both study settings Fig. 1.

Fig. 1. Living Lab at University of Siegen and Tohoku University. (1) Living Lab Siegen with participant. (2) Frontal picture of android robot in Siegen. (3) Frontal picture of Android in Tohoku. (4) Living Lab Tohoku with participant.

3.2   Living Lab and Wizard of Oz

Both studies were exploratory and results are presented in descriptive way. The German study part took place within the University of Siegen. A specific room was created that resembles a cultural typical living room in the social context of the participants. The robot was seated at a table in the middle of the room. Each participant was seated in front of the robot. Two researchers were sitting approximately two meters behind them and controlled the robot from there. The experiment with the participants consisted of two parts. For one it was a conversation that was done with a Wizard-of-Oz [13,16,23], the second part was a conversation with the dialog management system that has been developed by the e-vita project [22]. The conversation with the robot took on average 17 min. Topics went from smalltalk to more personal and profound topics. Later on, the topics jokes and politics were added. The duration thereby depended on how detailed the participants were willing to answer and whether queries were made.

The Wizard-of-Oz was an interface on the notebook, that was controlled by the researchers behind the participants and was designed to trigger different topics of conversation. It therefore had several buttons that included predefined questions and answers of the robot. Additionally a text-to-speech field was available that allowed the researchers to include short speech sequences. The interface also allowed to control parts of the body movement of the robot, it enabled us to make the robot express emotions like happiness or sadness or to nod its head or to bow its upper body towards the participants.

In Japan, the Living Lab at Tohoku University was used. The Living Lab parallels the room in Germany, resembling a normal living room space found in a modern Japanese home. Participants sat in front of the robot at a square table, apart from one person who preferred to sit at a 45° angle to the Android. Researchers were situated in the room behind a tall screen that blocked them from the view of the participants.

3.3   Participants

The study was done with 19 participants (15 older adults and 4 stakeholders). The majority of them has been participants in previous research activities and therefore already worked with other robotic systems. The other participants were recruited by the previous participants. The criteria to participate was to be over 60 years old and that they do not have cognitive impairments. Due to the small sample size the results are not representative. We see previous experience with robots as advantage as effects of novelty are less strong and participants are able to make comparisons Table 1.

The participant code will be used in the results to make the statements traceable.

3.4   Data Analysis and Ethical Application

The data of the presented study relies on different sources of data. We used a mixed methods approach [1,34] to compile it and present here quantitative data from Germany, we further show qualitative results from Germany and Japan and draw comparisons but also similarities between both countries. Quantitative data were not collected in Japan in this session.

For the qualitative part semi structured interviews were done with all participants and later analysed with the reflexive thematic analysis [8–10], themes of the analysis were for example the role of the robot, conversation topics and emotions towards the interaction. In particular, participants were asked how they felt and if they had negative feelings like fear or uncanniness. Themes of the transcripts were created threefold: 1. deductively based on the interview guidelines; 2. inductively, if certain topics were reoccurring or seemed important; 3.

Table 1. List of participants

No.	Participant code	Age	Gender	Position	Country
1	1TN-G	63	f	Participant	Germany
2	2TN-G	71	m	Participant	Germany
3	3TN-G	72	m	Participant	Germany
4	4TN-G	79	f	Participant	Germany
5	5TN-G	78	m	Participant	Germany
6	6TN-G	74	f	Participant	Germany
7	7TN-G	64	f	Participant	Germany
8	8TN-G	81	f	Participant	Germany
9	9TN-G	62	f	Participant	Germany
10	1SH-G	58	f	Head of Hospice	Germany
11	2SH-G	67	m	fmr. Mgmt. Care Home	Germany
12	3SH-G	49	f	Speaker for Social Policy	Germany
13	4SH-G	48	m	Mgmt. Hospital	Germany
14	10TN-J	66	f	Participant	Japan
15	11TN-J	66	m	Participant	Japan
16	12TN-J	72	m	Participant	Japan
17	13TN-J	70	f	Participant	Japan
18	14TN-J	68	m	Participant	Japan
19	15TN-J	68	f	Participant	Japan

by discussing themes with the authors of this paper. In addition observation protocols and videos of the interaction were analysed, in regard of the reaction of the participants towards the robotic system.

The quantitative data, that was collected in Germany, contained all the Godspeed scales [5,38], which are often used in studies where the impression from a robot has to be assessed. Reliability and validity of each scale (anthropomorphism, animacy, likeability, perceived intelligence, and perceived safety) were described in [5]. Further data were acquired by using 5-steps semantic scales with adjectives inspired by a previous study [41], with the purpose of assessing the possible feeling of "uncanny" more in detail. Collected samples were taken from 11 participants (M: 4; F: 7, age mean: 69.91; age SD: 7.67) among older adults and stakeholders.

The study received ethical approval from the University of Siegen, with the Android study being a part of multiple studies in the e-Vita project. In Japan, ethical approval was received from the Tohoku University Graduate School of Medicine Institutional Review Board. All participants signed an informed consent form. The data that was retrieved is safely stored at the universities and kept under GDPR and APPI regulations.

4 Results

4.1 Attitudes Towards the Android Robot

Reactions towards the Android, after the conversation with it, were overall more positive than negative. None of the participants stated in the interviews that they saw the robot as creepy. Still the views toward the robot were not consistent. While some saw the robot as a machine that exists only to serve, other participants thought of it as a conversation partner.

Likewise in Japan, first impressions were generally positive. Some participants felt that precisely because it was close to a human, they could talk to the android naturally (13TN-J) and didn't feel uncomfortable if they looked at the android generally (10TN-J). On closer inspection during their interactions, participants picked out some aspects, especially with regard to the expression of the eyes (11TN-J, 13TN-J, 14TN-J) as being different from that of a real person, so much that the expressionless face could feel a little scary (12TN-J), or cold like a wax figure (10TN-J).

The appearance of the android was a topic of discussion, in the German setting some mentioned that the robot looks beautiful, one even stating that he would kiss the robot (3TN-G). But not everyone thought so, some mentioned that the behavior and emotions were repetitive and not variable enough. One participant (1TN-G) said that it should learn new gestures to be more human like, for example moving its body and changing sitting positions while talking (1TN-G).

Japanese participants also found the robot beautiful (15TN-J), and were impressed with the quality of the construction (12TN-J). One aspect mentioned by several participants (10TN-J, 13TN-J, 14TN-J) was the physical size of the android. They felt a little overwhelmed or intimidated by its physical presence. The size difference led to the android's eye level being above some of the participants', leading them to feel as if the android was looking down on them.

Regarding quantitative results in Germany, they appear in line with the qualitative results. All Godspeed scales proved to be relatively consistent (Cronbach's alphas were: Anthropomorphism: 0.71; Animacy: 0.88; Likeability: 0.87; Perceived Intelligence: 0.92; Perceived Safety: 0.77). Consistency of Anthropomorphism raises to 0.87 by dropping the [Unconscious — Conscious] item. This should suggest how being machine-like or natural may have little to do with the concept of consciousness, at least for a German subject. Future comparisons with Japanese subjects will shed more light on this matter.

These five scales do not have a reference data to be compared yet, however in terms of absolute values, it should be noted that Likeability was 4.16 (SD: 0.71) and Perceived Safety was 4.00 (SD: 1.15), which are quite positive results. Together with the measurement of feeling uncanny, scary and uncomfortable (all three of them 1.09 out of 5 (SD: 0.30)), these results seem to indicate that the response was good in absolute terms of means and standard deviations, and that the perceptions of anthropomorphism, animacy and intelligence do not necessarily have to be high, even for an android Fig. 2.

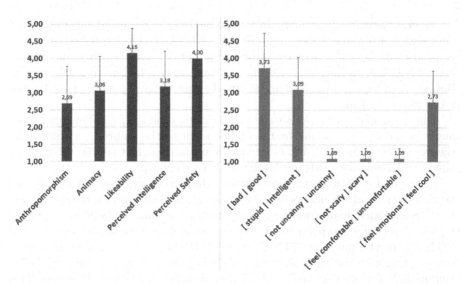

Fig. 2. Quantitative data from the experiment in Germany. On the left, Godspeed scales; on the right, additional questions.

4.2   Expected Role of the Android Robot

One participant stated that he could imagine to have the robot at home on his couch and to talk about topics, he knew he could not talk with his wife, as it would create tensions. Topics like talking about other family members, where he and his wife have different opinions (3TN-G). Other participants declined talking about too personal topics (4TN-G & 5TN-G) The participant (3TN-G) wanted to do this in order to share the burden of knowledge, to have someone to share his feelings and believes about certain family members or situations. 2TN-G and TN1-G stated that they could imagine to discuss with the robot about certain topics they have different opinions about. In this relation 2TN-G exposed that the robot could become part of the family. In this context it was noticed that TN2s conversation duration was, with more than 26 min, a lot longer than the average caused through his detailed answers and questions he asked the android. Another suggestion was to use the robot as a foreign language trainer (1TN-G).

But opinions about talking to the android were polarised as the following two statements show:

Table 2. Contrary opinions about talking to the android robot

Keen	Averse
"So when it comes to family disagreements [...] I could imagine [...] that I simply talk about what is burdening me [...] I could deflate when I am a bit charged." (3TN-G)	*"Then I could rather imagine to talk to myself in the woods."* (4TN-G)

582 F. Carros et al.

Several participants in Germany mentioned that they could imagine to get information from the robot (e.g. 1TN-G, 2TN-G). One expressed that the android could help for memorizing or reminding (2TN-G). During the interaction 2TN-G told us that he would like the robot to remind him to drink enough. But also biography work (talking about the past) was a possible task for the robot (6TN-G) Table 2.

One participant told us that she could imagine the android alleviating loneliness in people living alone by the embodiment of the android and filling the silence with talking (8TN-G). Other participants thought that the robot could narrate fairy-tales or reads out books (4TN-G, 6TN-G).

In the dialog between the android and the participants several topics were used, such as family, incidents in their life, opinions about specific things, wishes, fears. Some participants were not so comfortable talking about very private topics. Especially one participant did not wanted to talk to the robot at all (7TN-G). In the interview 7TN-G stated that she had no interest to have a conversation with the robot as the robots only purpose is to give information or help in daily life, such as giving advice then cooking by looking up recipes. This small interest could also be seen in the conversation duration of only 12 1/2 min

In Japan, conversation with the android was over several domains: introduction and greetings, receiving health/exercise advice, talking about family, playing a simple Japanese word game together, and then free talking using the Wizard of Oz feature. Participants tended to respond to the android as a real conversation partner, and not simply a robot. In a free-talk session, they tended to be proactive, and asked all kinds of questions one might typically expect to ask a person, such as asking the android about her favourite foods, or recommendations for local places to see. One male participant (11TN-J) said that he talked to the female android as if she was a real, young woman, and consequently found it a little uncomfortable to chat with her, and stated he may have found it easier to bond with a male android.

Another participant (13TN-J) told us that she would want to talk about problems and her true feelings to the android, and additionally, participant (15TN-J) stated that she doesn't need to care about what she says so much because the android is not human, and would want to talk about her problems with it. Like the participants in Germany, participants in Japan could see the android as being a source of qualified information. Something they could confide in.

5 Discussion and Conclusion

The presented results seem to be in contrast to the theory of the uncanny valley by Mori [26]. The Android that looks strongly humanlike was not perceived as uncanny by the participants that met the android, this contrast to Mori [26] could be because the data was retrieved in Living Lab settings, while Mori [26] presented a theory. Not in the uncanny valley in the sense that we have expected to have an android robot in the valley, based on its appearance, as some people might forget that it is a robot. After the experiments, we come to the conclusion that the participants always saw the android as a robot and did not at any point saw something else in it. This results are in line with the results of Shimada et al. that could show with the 'Repliee Q2' android robot that it is not seen as uncanny [32]. Further, none of the participants reported the robot as eerie, this might be because it was constantly moving and talking and therefore different than the results of Minato et al. who found out that the robot is seen as eerie if it does not move its body [25].

We assume that some of the results are to be explained because the participants were from the beginning told that they would speak to a robotic system and therefore there was no mismatch to them. It was announced as a robot and they met a robot. Still that did not mean that they did not want to talk to it. Some reported to have joy in the conversation others preferred to use it to retrieve information and others preferred to talk to oneself then to the robot (see 4.2). We believe that this means that the android robot with the used software is to be located on the uncanny valley before the valley [26,37], something that was also confirmed by one stakeholder (4SH). But as Apple et al. points out, the term uncanny is not clearly defined and might have several meanings [4].

In the intercultural comparison we see many similarities, as participants from both settings reported that they did not feel 'fear' or 'creepiness'. Another similarity was that participants from both countries were sharing private information with the robot about their family and feelings. One distinction can be seen in the role of the robot. The Japanese participants saw the robot as an equal partner and had high expectations towards the system (e.g. quick responses). The German participants (not all) were more sceptical and mostly thought that the robot should serve them. Another distinction is the perceptions of the robot gestures. While the Japanese participants enjoyed that the robot is not displaying a lot of emotions and gestures, the German participants thought that the robot should do more of it and have a higher variety of gestures.

It is worth noting that both androids used in this study were made in Japan, with a behavior and appearance that is grounded in Japanese culture (participants were informed about its origin). Perception of in-group and out-group can typically influence the responses, as an in-group robot may be seen more advanced in terms of mind attribution. This is however not always true, as it was seen in a study with pictures of Geminoids and Japanese high school students [36].

Limitations of this paper are the relatively small size of the sample of participants and that the participants have not been chosen in a representative manner. Further the results are missing the quantitative questionnaire results from Japan and we could only do a comparison of qualitative results. It is also possible that some of the results have been influenced by the Hawthorne effect, as the participants were closely monitored [24].

In conclusion we can say that the android system was accepted as an interaction partner in both settings in Germany and Japan; so from this perspective we could not detect cross-cultural differences. Some participants in both countries/cultures had particular interests on dialog topics like cooking or talking about family secrets, others had specific roles for it and saw it either as an information agent or as a conversation partner. But none of the participants reported after the confrontation with the system that it was creepy. These results that were obtained in the living lab are promising and show us that androids can have real world use-cases. We therefore see potential to intensify research with older adults and dedicated android robots that have been designed in a participatory design process. As a future outlook, institutional care homes could be an interesting use-case and research topic for the future, where android robots could have dialogues with residents in order to counteract loneliness, assist in daily tasks or support a healthier lifestyle.

Acknowledgement. We would like to thank the participants, the reviewers and all other involved people. This paper is a shared result of all involved and we are thankful for the given support.

The Version of Record of this contribution is published in [insert volume title], and is available online at https://doi.org/ [insert DOI]

References

1. Alexander, V.D., Thomas, H., Cronin, A., Fielding, J., Moran-Ellis, J.: Mixed methods. Res. Social Life **3**, 125–144 (2008)
2. Aminuddin, R., Sharkey, A., Levita, L:. Interaction with the paro robot may reduce psychophysiological stress responses. In: 2016 11th ACM/IEEE International Conference on Human-Robot Interaction (HRI), pp. 593–594, 2016
3. Andtfolk, M., Nyholm, L., Eide, H., Fagerström, L.:. Humanoid robots in the care of older persons: a scoping review. Assistive Technology, pp. 1–9 (2021)
4. Appel, M., Izydorczyk, D., Weber, S., Mara, M., Lischetzke, T.: The uncanny of mind in a machine: humanoid robots as tools, agents, and experiencers. Comput. Hum. Behav. **102**, 274–286 (2020)
5. Bartneck, C., Kulić, D., Croft, E., Zoghbi, S.: Measurement instruments for the anthropomorphism, animacy, likeability, perceived intelligence, and perceived safety of robots. Int. J. Soc. Robot. **1**(1), 71–81 (2009)
6. Bartneck, C., Nomura, T., Kanda, T., Suzuki, T., Kennsuke, K.: Cultural differences in attitudes towards robots. In: Proceedings of the AISB Symposium on Robot Companions: Hard Problems And Open Challenges In Human-Robot Interaction, pp. 1–4, AISB, 01 (2005)
7. Boudouraki, A., Reeves, S., Fischer, J.E., Rintel, S.: Mediated visits: Longitudinal domestic dwelling with mobile robotic telepresence. In: Proceedings of the 2022 CHI Conference on Human Factors in Computing Systems, CHI '22, New York, NY, USA, . Association for Computing Machinery (2022)
8. Braun, V., Clarke, V.: Reflecting on reflexive thematic analysis. Qual. Res. Sport Exerc. Health **11**(4), 589–597 (2019)
9. Braun, V., Clarke, V.: Can i use ta? should i use ta? should i not use ta? comparing reflexive thematic analysis and other pattern-based qualitative analytic approaches. Couns. Psychother. Res. **21**(1), 37–47 (2021)
10. Braun, V., Clarke, V., Hayfield, N., Terry, G,: Thematic Analysis, pages 1–18. Springer Singapore, Singapore (2018). https://doi.org/10.1007/978-981-10-5251-4_103

11. Carros, F., et al.: Exploring human-robot interaction with the elderly: results from a ten-week case study in a care home. CHI '20, pp. 1–12 (2020). https://doi.org/10.1145/3313831.3376402
12. Carros, F., et al: Care workers making use of robots: Results of a three-month study on human-robot interaction within a care home. In: Proceedings of the CHI (2022). https://doi.org/10.1145/3491102.3517435
13. Carros, F., Störzinger, T., Wierling, A., Preussner, A., Tolmie, P.: Ethical, legal & participatory concerns in the development of human-robot interaction: Lessons from eight research projects with social robots in real-world scenarios. i-com, **21**(2), 299–309 (2022). https://doi.org/10.1515/icom-2022-0025
14. Chang, Y.-H., Carros, F., Manavi, M., Rathmann, M.: How do roboticists imagine a robotised future? a case study on a japanese hri research project (2022). https://doi.org/10.20944/preprints202204.0081.v1
15. Chen, Y.-S., Lu, J.-M., Hsu, Y.-L.: Design and evaluation of a telepresence robot for interpersonal communication with older adults. In: Biswas, J., Kobayashi, H., Wong, L., Abdulrazak, B., Mokhtari, M. (eds.) ICOST 2013. LNCS, vol. 7910, pp. 298–303. Springer, Heidelberg (2013). https://doi.org/10.1007/978-3-642-39470-6_39
16. Dahlbäck, N., Jönsson, A., Ahrenberg, L.: Wizard of oz studies – why and how. Knowl.-Based Syst. **6**(4), 258–266 (1993)
17. Feingold-Polak, R., Elishay, A., Shahar, Y., Stein, M., Edan, Y., Levy-Tzedek, S.: Differences between young and old users when interacting with a humanoid robot: a qualitative usability study. Paladyn, J. Behav. Robot. **9**(1), 183–192 (2018)
18. Felzmann, H., Murphy, K., Casey, D., Beyan, O.: Robot-assisted care for elderly with dementia: is there a potential for genuine end-user empowerment? vol. 03 (2015)
19. Haring, K.S., Silvera-Tawil, D., Matsumoto, Y., Velonaki, M., Watanabe, K.: Perception of an android robot in Japan and Australia: a cross-cultural comparison. In: Beetz, M., Johnston, B., Williams, M.-A. (eds.) ICSR 2014. LNCS (LNAI), vol. 8755, pp. 166–175. Springer, Cham (2014). https://doi.org/10.1007/978-3-319-11973-1_17
20. Helm, M., Carros, F., Schädler, J., Wulf, V.: Zoomorphic robots and people with disabilities. In: Proceedings of Mensch Und Computer 2022, MuC '22, pp. 431–436, New York, NY, USA, Association for Computing Machinery (2022). https://doi.org/10.1145/3543758.3547552
21. Ishiguro, H.: Android science. In: Robotics Research, pp. 118–127. Springer, (2007). https://doi.org/10.1007/978-3-540-48113-3_11
22. Jokinen, K., Homma, K., Matsumoto, Y., Fukuda, K.: Integration and interaction of trustworthy ai in a virtual coach. In: Proceedings of the Annual Conference of JSAI, JSAI2021:1N2IS5a04-1N2IS5a04 (2021)
23. Maulsby, D., Greenberg, S., Mander, R.: Prototyping an intelligent agent through wizard of oz. In: Arnold, B., Ashlund, S., editors, CHI '93: Proceedings of the INTERACT '93 and CHI '93 Conference on Human Factors in Computing Systems, pp. 277–284, [S.l.], 1993. ACM
24. McCarney, R., Warner, J., Iliffe, S., van Haselen, R., Griffin, M., Fisher, P.: The hawthorne effect: a randomised, controlled trial. BMC Med. Res. Methodol., **7**(1) (2007)
25. Minato, T., Shimada, M., Ishiguro, H., Itakura, S.: Development of an android robot for studying human-robot interaction. In: Orchard, B., Yang, C., Ali, M. (eds.) IEA/AIE 2004. LNCS (LNAI), vol. 3029, pp. 424–434. Springer, Heidelberg (2004). https://doi.org/10.1007/978-3-540-24677-0_44

26. Mori, M.: The uncanny valley: the original essay by masahiro mori. IEEE Spectrum(1970)
27. Nishio, S., Ishiguro, H., Hagita, N.: Geminoid: teleoperated android of an existing person. Humanoid RoboT.: New Develop.d **14**, 343–352 (2007)
28. Pu, L., Moyle, W., Jones, C., Todorovic, M.: The effectiveness of social robots for older adults: a systematic review and meta-analysis of randomized controlled studies. Gerontologist **59**(1), e37–e51 (2019)
29. Salem, M., Eyssel, F., Rohlfing, K., Kopp, S., Joublin, F.: To err is human (-like): Effects of robot gesture on perceived anthropomorphism and likability. Int. J. Soc. Robot. **5**(3), 313–323 (2013)
30. Satoh, H. , Kawabata, T., Sankai, Y.: Bathing care assistance with robot suit hal. In: 2009 IEEE International Conference on Robotics and Biomimetics (ROBIO), pp. 498–503 (2009)
31. Schwaninger, I., Carros, F., Weiss, A., Wulf, V., Fitzpatrick, G.: Video connecting families and social robots: from ideas to practices putting technology to work. Universal Access in the Information Society, pp. 1–13 (2022). https://doi.org/10.1007/s10209-022-00901-y
32. Shimada, M., Minato, T., Itakura, S., Ishiguro, H.: Uncanny Valley of Androids and Its Lateral Inhibition Hypothesis. In: RO-MAN 2007 - The 16th IEEE International Symposium on Robot and Human Interactive Communication, pp. 374–379 (2007)
33. Störzinger, T., Carros, F., Wierling, A., Misselhorn, C., Wieching, R.: Categorizing social robots with respect to dimensions relevant to ethical, social and legal implications. i-com, **19**(1), 47–57 (2020). https://doi.org/10.1515/icom-2020-0005
34. Tashakkori, A., Creswell, J.W.: The new era of mixed methods (2007)
35. Trovato, G., et al.: A novel culture-dependent gesture selection system for a humanoid robot performing greeting interaction. In: Beetz, M., Johnston, B., Williams, M.-A. (eds.) ICSR 2014. LNCS (LNAI), vol. 8755, pp. 340–349. Springer, Cham (2014). https://doi.org/10.1007/978-3-319-11973-1_35
36. Trovato, G., Eyssel, F.: Mind attribution to androids: A comparative study with italian and japanese adolescents. In: 2017 26th IEEE international symposium on robot and human interactive communication (RO-MAN), pp. 561–566. IEEE (2017). https://doi.org/10.1109/ROMAN.2017.8172358
37. Wang, S., Lilienfeld, S.O., Rochat, P.: The uncanny valley: existence and explanations. Rev. Gen. Psychol. **19**(4), 393–407 (2015)
38. Weiss, A., Bartneck, C.: Meta analysis of the usage of the godspeed questionnaire series. In: 24th International Symposium on Robot and Human Interactive Communication (RO-MAN), pp. 381–388 IEEE (2015)
39. Wulf, V., Müller, C., Pipek, V., Randall, D., Rohde, M., Stevens, G.: Practice-based computing: empirically grounded conceptualizations derived from design case studies. In: Wulf, V., Schmidt, K., Randall, D. (eds.) Designing Socially Embedded Technologies in the Real-World. CSCW, pp. 111–150. Springer, London (2015). https://doi.org/10.1007/978-1-4471-6720-4_7
40. Wulf, V., Rohde, M., Pipek, V., Stevens, G:. Engaging with practices: design case studies as a research framework in cscw. In: Proceedings of ACM conference on Computer supported cooperative work, pp. 505–512 (2011)
41. Yoshikawa, M., Matsumoto, Y., Sumitani, M., Ishiguro, H.: Development of an android robot for psychological support in medical and welfare fields. In: 2011 IEEE International Conference on Robotics and Biomimetics, pp. 2378–2383 (2011)

Assessment of a Humanoid Partner for Older Adults and Persons with Dementia During Home-Based Activities

Fengpei Yuan[1]([✉])(ID), Marie Boltz[2](ID), Ying-Ling Jao[2](ID), Arowyn Casenhiser[3](ID), Aidan Siddiqi[1](ID), Robert Bray[1](ID), Joshua Duzan[4](ID), Monica Crane[4](ID), and Xiaopeng Zhao[1](ID)

[1] University of Tennessee, Knoxville, TN 37996, USA
{fyuan6,asiddiq5,rbray2,xzhao9}@utk.edu
[2] Penn State University, University Park, PA 16802, USA
{mpb40,yuj15}@psu.edu
[3] Maryville High School, Maryville, TN 37803, USA
arowyncasenhiser@gmail.com
[4] Genesis Neuroscience Clinic, Knoxville, TN 37909, USA
jduzan@utk.edu, mcrane@genesisneuro.com

Abstract. Worldwide, there are approximately 10 million new cases of dementia reported each year. Due to cognitive deficits, persons living with dementia (PLWDs) have lower independence and decreased quality of life at home. Physically-embodied socially assistive robots (SARs) have the potential to engage PLWDs and assist them in their home-based activities. However, limited attention has been given to the development and assessment of SAR to interact with PLWDs within the context of home-based activities. In this case study, we designed a list of activities, including entertainment, playing games, and ten activities of daily living in a simulated home setting. We invited one older adult (female) without cognitive impairment and two (male) with dementia to perform these activities with the guidance of a humanoid SAR. The results of our observational study demonstrate that the multimodal interaction in SARs, such as verbal communication, eye contact, and gestures, can greatly facilitate the adoption and use of SARs by PLWDs. We found that PLWDs attributed human-like qualities to the robot when performing home-based activities. We also identified main challenges in SAR to assist PLWDs with these tasks.

Keywords: Human-robot interaction · Dementia care · Home setting

---

Supported in part by National Institute of Health under the grant number R01AG077003 and Student/Faculty Research Award from the University of Tennessee, Knoxville.

F. Cavallo et al. (Eds.): ICSR 2022, LNAI 13818, pp. 587–597, 2022.
https://doi.org/10.1007/978-3-031-24670-8_52

1   Introduction

With a steady increase in life expectancy, the number of older adults aged 65 and older, as well as the number of people with dementia have grown over the past few decades worldwide. There are nearly 10 million new cases of dementia reported each year worldwide [1]. In the United States alone, approximately 6.5 million older adults are living with Alzheimer's disease and related dementias (AD/ADRD) in 2022. AD/ADRD are irreversible, progressive neurodegenerative diseases that slowly destroy memory, thinking, and other cognitive capabilities [1], leading to lower independence and decreased quality of life (QoL).

Physically embodied socially assistive robots (SARs) have become a promising approach to assist aging-in-place and persons living with AD/ADRD (PLWDs) in a more acceptable, engaging, and effective way, due to its social presence, mobility, and multiple modalities of interactions with users [2,3]. A well-designed SAR might allow PLWDs to stay at home longer, improve their independence and QoL, delay their move to long-term care residences, and reduce PLWDs' reliance on their family caregivers [4]. To achieve such a goal, a SAR needs to be able to interact with PLWDs in the context of home-based activities, such as entertainment and activities of daily living (ADLs) and engage them in these activities. Unfortunately, the development of SARs for this purpose has received relatively limited attention [5]. Moreover, older adults with dementia, compared to young adults, usually have limited experience with technologies and less cognitive capacity, both of which might interfere with their interaction with SARs.

In this study, we designed a list of daily activities at a simulated home, including entertainment, playing games, and ten ADL tasks. We invited older adults and PLWDs to perform these home-based activities with guidances provided by a humanoid social robot, named Tammy, and observed the PLWD-robot interactions. We aimed to answer the following research questions: (1) How would older adults and PLWDs accept and interact with the humanoid robot during home-based activities? (2) To what extent would older adults and PLWDs attribute human-like qualities to the robot during these activities? (3) How effective is the robot in interacting with older adults and PLWDs during home-based activities?

2   Methods

This observational case study was approved by the Institutional Review Board (IRB) (IRB number is UTK IRB-21-06514-FB). The study was conducted in a simulated home setting, Smart Home. The inclusion criteria were: 1) age between 18 and 95; 2) able to speak and understand English fluently and clearly; 3) able to stand or walk without assistance; and 4) no brain injury, severe eye or hearing conditions. People ineligible for the inclusion criteria were excluded. We recruited potential participants through recruitment flyers posted on social media and distributing flyers at a local dementia specialty clinic and senior centers. Consent and assent (if applicable) were obtained from potential eligible participants. Each participant was assigned with a specific Participant ID, which was used during the whole experimental procedure.

2.1 Experimental Procedure

An orientation session was first provided for the participant, wherein the robot sang to, danced for, and played brain games (including Tic-Tac-Toe and Memory Game) with the participant. The orientation session aimed to make the participant feel more comfortable and become more familiar with the robot. During the orientation session, the participant could choose to play with the robot as many times as they wanted. After the orientation session, a demographic survey and Montreal Cognitive Assessment (MoCA) test were distributed to the participant. The demographic survey was used to collect participant's background information such as age, gender, education, and experience with technology. The MoCA test was administered by certified MoCA trainers. The MoCA score was collected as a baseline of participants' cognitive capability. The score was neither communicated nor interpreted to the participants or their partners.

After the participant finished the demographic survey and MoCA test, an experimenter ($Experimenter_c$ in the control room) started video recording using the multi-camera capture system [6] equipped at the Smart Home and teleoperated the robot Tammy to start to administer 10 daily routine tasks for the participant. This included bed mobility, changing bed linens, checking home safety, telephone use, medication management, obtaining critical information from a radio announcement, obtaining critical information from a newspaper article, cleaning teeth, sweeping, and meal preparation. The robot was programmed to administer the ten tasks according to the instructions of the Performance Assessment of Self-care Skills (PASS) tool et al. [7]. Another experimenter, $Experimenter_p$, was always present with the participant to perform the tasks and ready to intervene if necessary to ensure the participant's safety, for example, in a situation where the robot was not working or behaving as expected. The participant could choose to take a break whenever they wanted. When the participant was performing the first two tasks in the bedroom, a third experimenter would come into the Smart Home to set safety hazards for the task of checking the home safety, including a cord placed across the floor of a doorway, a pair of scissors placed on the table with blades over the edge, and one can of tuna fish and one can of pet food on a kitchen cupboard. This was designed to avoid the participant observing the placement of safety hazards [7].

After each experimental session with a participant, all the experimenters and other members of the research team had a meeting to discuss and reflect on limitations of the current study design. Strategies to improve the user experience were implemented in the robot and/or the study design in preparation for subsequent experimental sessions with other participants.

2.2 Data Analysis

In this case observational study, we focused on the human-robot interaction in the context of home-based activities. Two co-authors manually coded the videos. The videos were coded considering PLWD-robot interaction from the perspective of both human user and the robot Tammy. The behaviors of interest were adapted from the coded behaviors proposed in a prior human-robot collaboration study [8]. The specific behaviors of interest for our study are defined and listed in Table 1. The first three behaviors indicated their willingness to consider the robot as an interaction partner and their trust in the robot. The frequency at which the participants exhibited the behaviors of *Turning towards the robot* and *Turning towards the experimenter* indicated the participants' trust in the robot to assist them during daily tasks, which is a very important consideration during human-robot collaboration to accomplish tasks. *Confusion* and *forgetfulness* were confirmed by participants' both verbal and nonverbal behaviors. Additionally, we coded the moments of robot malfunction and limitations (compared to human) for future robot refinement.

Table 1. Definition of coded behaviors.

Behavior	Definition
Verbal engagement	Participant verbally responded to Tammy's guidances, questions, or comments
Initiating conversation	Participant initiated a conversation with Tammy and the topic might not be directly related to the tasks
Turning towards robot	Participant spontaneously turned towards Tammy when s/he encountered a problem in accomplishing the tasks
Turning towards experimenter	Participant spontaneously turned towards the experimenter when s/he encountered a problem in accomplishing the tasks
Positive emotion	Laughing/smiling or other pleasant responses to Tammy
Negative emotion	Frowning or other unpleasant response to Tammy
Confusion	Participant cannot understand what is happening around them, what they should do or who someone/something is
Forgetfulness	Participant partly or completely forgot Tammy's guidances or a proper sequence of performing a task
Robot malfunction	Tammy was not behaving as unexpected
Robot limitation	Limitations of Tammy in administering the tasks

3 Results

Three participants, one (P1) self-report without cognitive impairment, one (P2) self-report mild cognitive impairment, and one (P3) self-report moderate cognitive impairment, joined in this study. Their demographic information is listed in Table 2. Participants were not familiar or slightly familiar with robots. P2 and P3 participated in the experiment with their legally authorized representatives (i.e., spouse) as their companions. All participants had access to tools and resources to help them plan for their daily lives. Before interacting with the robot, participants P2 and P3 thought it was likely that a robot may assist with their daily life tasks, while P1 provided a neutral response. Participants completed all the ten daily tasks with the robot's guidances. Completion here means going through all the ten tasks but not necessarily performing them perfectly. During the experiment with P1, the robot was programmed to administer the tasks exactly following the instruction given by Chisholm *et al.* [7]. However, we found that affirmation from the robot would facilitate its interaction and communication with participants. Therefore, the robot was refined to provide words of affirmation (e.g., *This is the end of the task*) after the participant took an action or at the end of each task. More observation of human-robot interaction during the orientation and experimental sessions were provided in the following sections. Additionally, P1 provided some suggestions regarding the materials we used in the PASS tasks. For example, she suggested a standing dustpan in the task of sweeping to avoid potential risks of falling, and a larger food can to make it easier for PLWD to read.

Table 2. Descriptive statistics of participants.

Demographic variable	P1	P2	P3
Age (year)	55–65	Above 75	65–74
Gender	Female	Male	Male
Highest level of education	Post-graduate	Post-graduate	Post-graduate
Familiarity with smartphones	Moderate	Slight	Very familiar
Familiarity with tablets	Moderate	Slight	Very familiar
Familiarity with computers	Moderate	Slight	Very familiar
Familiarity with robots	Slight	Not at all	Slight
MoCA score	27/30	19/30	17/30

3.1 Human-Robot Interaction During Orientation Session

During orientation session (as shown in the upper panel of Fig. 1), all participants enjoyed the robot's singing and dance. P2 and P3 also played the game Tic-Tac-Toe with the robot. P2 and P3 interacted with the robot with their caregivers sitting around them. P2 and P3 and their caregivers laughed and danced along with the robot. Specifically, we found caregivers imitated Tammy's dancing body movement, such as waving hands and nodding (Fig. 1), substantially more than their loved ones with cognitive impairment. P2 and P3 enjoyed playing the game with the robot in different ways. P2 continuously played the game more than ten times and wanted to keep playing with the robot. His spouse was surprised by this and watched him playing the game with a smile. At the beginning, P3 expressed concern that he could not perform well (saying, "I don't do well at games."). However, after hearing the robot make a cute, funny sound and watching his spouse play the game, he laughed and said, "Let me try". P3 played the game twice. After the first round, the robot encouraged P3 to play again and P3 agreed. When playing the game, P3 laughed and commented, "This is so cool". However, in the second round, P3 lost to the robot and refused to play again.

Fig. 1. The upper panel: Participants and caregivers (CAs) are enjoying the singing and dancing by Tammy and playing games with Tammy. The lower panel: Participants are performing tasks of bed mobility, checking home safety, and managing medication from left to right. EXP = $Experimenter_p$.

3.2 PLWD-Robot Interaction During Daily Routine Tasks

Participants P1, P2, and P3 spent approximately 35, 29, and 51 minutes (including break time) to perform all the ten daily tasks with the robot Tammy's guidances, respectively. P1 and P2 completely the ten tasks smoothly, while P3 had difficulty in performing the tasks of managing medication (i.e., P3 cannot understand the prescription label on the pill bottle) and obtaining critical information from the radio announcement. Figures in the lower panel of Fig. 1 present three examples of participants performing the tasks at Smart Home. The video recordings of participants performing the tasks were coded in Table 3.

Table 3. Behaviors and corresponding counts (n) through video coding.

ID	Behavior	n	Illustration
P1	VE	4	"I believed so" to Tammy's questions
	PosEmo	1	Laughing towards Tammy's verbal instruction
	Confus	3	Confused when Tammy doing nothing or not facing P1
	RoMal	4	Tammy not facing or making eye contact with P1
	RoLim	2	Lack of affirmation for P1's action or the end of a task
P2	VE	5	"Thank you" or "You're welcome" to Tammy's comments
	IniConv	3	Joking with Tammy
	TTR	1	When finishing reading but Tammy not providing any instruction, P2 asked Tammy "Am I supposed to read it out loud?"
	RoMal	1	Tele-operation suddenly stopped
	RoLim	1	Tammy spoke in long sentences but P2 could not follow Tammy
P3	VE	9	"No, no, this is difficult, Tammy" to Tammy's instruction
	IniConv	2	"Tammy, you recognize my voice?" "Good job Tammy!"
	PosEmo	4	When Tammy gazed at P3 during navigation, P3 laughed and said "she's saying you're supposed to come with me"; Smiling to the robot; "I like how she looks at me"
	NegEmo	1	"I got the point" when Tammy talking regardless of P3's status
	Confus	2	Confused about the sheet length and curve
	Forget	2	Forgot the store's closing time and radio's critical information
	RoMal	2	Robot not talking towards P3 and not moving to the PoI
	RoLim	1	P3 could not read the prescription but Tammy kept asking

VE= *Verbal engagement*; PosEmo/NegEmo=*Positive/Negative emotion*; Confus=*Confusion*; IniConv=*Initiating conversation*; RoMal=*Robot malfunction*; RoLim=*Robot limitation*; TTR=*Turning towards robot*; Forget=*Forgetfulness*.

4 Discussion

In this case study, three participants, one aged 55–65 without cognitive impairment and two older adults with cognitive impairment performed ten ADL tasks with guidances from a tele-operated humanoid social robot. We observed the verbal and nonverbal communication during those ADLs in a simulated home setting. From the observational results, we gained insight into the use of social robots to assist dementia care in daily routine activities.

4.1 Facilitators to Adoption and Use of SAR by PLWDs

When performing daily tasks, participants showed verbal engagement and positive emotions and even initiated conversations (e.g., expressing gratitude to and joking) with the robot during performing tasks, as listed in Table 3. All these behaviors indicate that participants interacted with Tammy as if it were a social entity, i.e., perceived social presence [9]. P3 addressed the robot with *her*, praised the robot (e.g., *good job*), and even had negative emotion with Tammy (e.g., *I got the point*), suggesting that P3 was attributing human-like qualities to Tammy during performing ADLs. Social presence can contribute to better perceived enjoyment and higher intention to use the robot by PLWDs [9].

Noticeably, P3 was hesitant to play games with Tammy at the beginning. However, P3 was appealed by Tammy's cute, funny sounds and body movement, and as a result, wanted to play the games with Tammy. Such different attitudes towards using the robot in P3 manifest the advantages of multimodal interaction (e.g., voice, body movement, eye contact) of SAR in encouraging and engaging PLWDs in activities. Nevertheless, more studies are needed to investigate how to embed these quantitative metrics into interactive SARs [10] and how it would influence user perception, experience, and intention to use in short/long term.

4.2   Roles of SAR in Dementia Care at Home

Previous studies have indicated concerns that social robots might negatively disrupt PLWDs' relationships with their caregivers, like their spouse, children and relatives; that is, their caregivers may want robots so that they could leave their loved ones with ADRD under the care of a robot and spend more time alone at the expense of the PLWD [2,4]. However, considering the great burden and stress on caregivers due to the time-intensive nature of dementia care, we believe that a SAR with appropriate design of robotic functions, when used in conjunction with and not in replacement of caregiver care, can assist family caregivers in caring for PLWDs. In our orientation session, participants and their partners danced together with Tammy (Fig. 1). P2 was very engaged in playing brain games with the robot. His partner was surprised at this and accompanied P2 to play the games. Our observational results suggest that a SAR can not only engage PLWDs and help mitigate caregiver stress, but also act as a common shared entertainment tool, like a TV, that promisingly fosters positive PLWD-caregiver interactions. The robot can be designed to be shared and allow both PLWD and their caregivers to engage in activities (e.g., dance [11]) they love and enjoy together, accentuating their positive shared moments and fulfilling companionship and emotional needs of both PLWDs and their families.

4.3   Robot Limitations and Malfunctions in Administering PASS

In this case study, we identified a few robot limitations and malfunctions (Table 3) in administering PASS for PLWDs and proposed corresponding solutions to cope with these issues for future studies. The robot-assisted PASS system was designed based on instructions for a human practitioner to administer PASS in a standardized way [7]. However, the translation using a SAR is more complicated and challenging. Since this study was aimed to observe PLWDs perform ADLs, the robot was initially designed to not provide any judgment regarding participants' performance. However, we found that the robot still needed to provide affirmation (such as verbal feedback *Okay* or *This is the end of the task*) when the participant finished a subtask/task. Otherwise, the participant might feel confused (P1's confusion in Table 3). Both receiving and providing feedback are essential parts of mutual understanding and smooth human-robot interaction and collaboration. Another limitation is that Tammy spoke too fast, which might prevent a PLWD from understanding Tammy well. This might be different from the situation of a clinician administering PASS for PLWD, because SARs cannot automatically adjust the speaking speed in real time according to the user's cognitive and emotional status like a human can. In this case, we have modified the robot to say short sentences, have pauses between sentences, and ask the participant if they would like Tammy to repeat sentences.

Sometimes Tammy provided guidances without facing or making eye contact with participants during interaction, which made participants feel confused and negatively impact use performance. Also, although implemented with both navigation and movement/rotation buttons, sometimes the robot still cannot go to PoIs accurately, which made the tele-operation more difficult and negatively impacted Tammy's performance and the user experience. Regarding these two robot malfunctions, the research team took into consideration our main research goal in this study and agreed that the $Experimenter_p$ would manually turn the robot towards the participant or move the robot to PoIs when the tele-operation did not work efficiently. Another robot malfunction was when the tele-operation system suddenly stopped during the experiment with P2. The Firebase API requires authentication in order to protect user information. Once authenticated, the application receives an authentication token to use for making read and write requests to the database. However, this will expire after 1 h. In order to keep the experimenter interface authenticated to avoid freezing the experiment, the tele-operation system was modified so that the token would be refreshed each time a new PASS task is started.

4.4 Challenges and Future Development of Robotic Caregiver

Although the study offered potential advantages of SAR in dementia care, there are still challenges in reliably using SAR for dementia care at home. In our case study, P3 (Table 3) was confused twice because of the curved edges of the bed sheet but never proactively asked for help verbally or non-verbally. Even when interacting with their caregivers, a PLWD could wander around looking confused instead of asking help for the next step [2]. Such a situation of a PLWD being confused without asking for help might be caused by several reasons. For example, PLWDs might feel embarrassed to ask for help. They are unable to verbally express their requirements and feelings clearly, especially considering that PLWDs usually have language deficits, e.g., using wrong words for things [4]. This emphasizes the significance of the intelligence in a SAR to understand PLWDs' status and requirements from their nonverbal behaviors (e.g., facial expression or body movement), beyond their speech and provide appropriate assistance at right time [12]. For instance, in the scenarios of confusion and negative emotion in Table 3, the robot needed to reason that P3 was confused about the bed sheet and felt frustrated when Tammy kept talking.

Another challenge is to personalize SAR to each individual PLWD. The PLWD-robot interaction in our orientation sessions suggests that we should personalize interactions from two different perspectives. First, the robotic functions should be designed and developed according to each individual's hobbies. Compared to P2, P3 was not interested in playing games. It turned out that P2 played the same game more than 10 times, while P3 only tried twice. The two different trials suggest that a PLWD will probably use a robot function for a longer time if that function relates to the PLWD's preferences. The second perspective is the adaptive difficulty level of the serious games in SAR. P3 refused to play the game for a third round, probably because he did not win and felt unsuccessful in the second round. Here, we recommend that the robot is developed to play the serious games with PLWDs at different difficulty levels, tailoring to each individual's capability. Considering the progressively declining cognitive capability in PLWDs, such capability of adaptive difficulty level is very important.

4.5   Limitations and Future Work

The observation and discussion of PLWD-robot interaction in this paper are based on a case study with a very small sample ($n = 3$). To obtain a more general and reliable understanding, we need to observe a large number of PLWDs interacting with the robot in a home setting. Currently, all our understanding of user perception and experience with the robot are based on observation. We need to understand and incorporate the users' (PLWDs and caregivers) perceptions and experiences with the SAR. Therefore, we will adopt additional qualitative approaches, including interviews, to learn their perceptions of the SAR. There might be volunteer bias in our participants, as people who are more interested in or open to technology, such as social robots, may be more likely to participate in our study. Additionally, participants' interactions with the robot during the activities might be biased by social desirability, wherein individuals tend to give socially desirable responses instead of the responses that are reflective of their true feelings. Moreover, user perception of and attitudes towards the robot in PLWDs might also be biased due to novelty and short-term interaction. Therefore, our future work will also include long-term studies of PLWD-robot interaction during home-based activities [13].

References

1. Association, A.: 2022 Alzheimer's disease facts and figures. Alzheimers Dement **18**(4), 700–789 (2022)
2. Wang, R.H., Sudhama, A., Begum, M., Huq, R., Mihailidis, A.: Robots to assist daily activities: views of older adults with Alzheimer's disease and their caregivers. Int. Psychogeriat. **29**(1), 67–79 (2017)
3. Yuan, F., Klavon, E., Liu, Z., Lopez, R.P., Zhao, X.: A systematic review of robotic rehabilitation for cognitive training. Front. Robot. AI **8**, 605715 (2021)
4. Yuan, F., et al.: Assessing the acceptability of a humanoid robot for Alzheimer's disease and related dementia care using an online survey. International Journal of Social Robotics, pp. 1–15 (2022)
5. Ghafurian, M., Hoey, J., Dautenhahn, K.: Social robots for the care of persons with dementia: a systematic review. ACM Trans. Human-Robot Interact. (THRI) **10**(4), 1–31 (2021)

6. Yuan, F., Bray, R., Oliver, M., Duzan, J., Crane, M., Zhao, X.: A social robot-facilitated performance assessment of self-care skills (2022)In: submitted to IEEE Robotics and Automation Magazine on May 1 (2022)
7. Chisholm, D., Toto, P., Raina, K., Holm, M., Rogers, J.: Evaluating capacity to live independently and safely in the community: performance assessment of self-care skills. British J. Occup. Therapy **77**(2), 59–63 (2014)
8. Begum, M., Huq, R., Wang, R., Mihailidis, A.: Collaboration of an assistive robot and older adults with dementia. Gerontechnology **13**(4), 405–419 (2015)
9. Heerink, M., Kröse, B., Evers, V., Wielinga, B.: Assessing acceptance of assistive social agent technology by older adults: the almere model. Int. J. Social Robot. **2**(4), 361–375 (2010)
10. Beuscher, L.M., et al.: Socially assistive robots: measuring older adults' perceptions. J. Gerontol. Nurs. **43**(12), 35–43 (2017)
11. Moharana, S., Panduro, A.E., Lee, H.R., Riek, L.D.: Robots for joy, robots for sorrow: community based robot design for dementia caregivers. In: 2019 14th ACM/IEEE International Conference on Human-Robot Interaction (HRI). pp. 458–467. IEEE (2019)
12. Görür, O.C., Rosman, B., Sivrikaya, F., Albayrak, S.: Social cobots: Anticipatory decision-making for collaborative robots incorporating unexpected human behaviors. In: Proceedings of the 2018 ACM/IEEE International Conference on Human-Robot Interaction, pp. 398–406 (2018)
13. Woods, D., Yuan, F., Jao, Y.-L., Zhao, X.: Social robots for older adults with Dementia: a narrative review on challenges and future directions. In: Li, H., et al. (eds.) ICSR 2021. LNCS (LNAI), vol. 13086, pp. 411–420. Springer, Cham (2021). https://doi.org/10.1007/978-3-030-90525-5_35

Ethics, Gender and Trust in Social Robotics

I Designed It, So I Trust It: The Influence of Customization on Psychological Ownership and Trust Toward Robots

Dimitri Lacroix[1,2(✉)] [iD], Ricarda Wullenkord[2] [iD], and Friederike Eyssel[1,2] [iD]

[1] Bielefeld University, Universitätsstraße 25, 33615 Bielefeld, Germany
dimitri.lacroix@uni-bielefeld.de
[2] Center for Cognitive Interaction Technology (CITEC), Inspiration 1, 33619 Bielefeld, Germany

Abstract. Customization has been widely studied in the context of information systems and interfaces, but research on customization in human-robot interaction (HRI) is scarce. However, customization and user involvement may exert positive effects regarding attitudes and trust toward robots, hence improving HRI quality. The aim of the present work is to contribute to the theoretical understanding of customization in the HRI context by testing whether customization (none, low, or high) of a robot would elicit feelings of psychological ownership (PO), which, in turn, would increase trust toward the robot. Moreover, we hypothesized that the more people customize a robot, the less they would tend to anthropomorphize it. In line with our predictions, customization (vs. none) significantly increased psychological ownership and trust toward the robot. Further, the level of customization affected perceptions of robot agency. Additionally, PO mediated the effect of customization on trust toward the robot. The implications of these findings for research on HRI are discussed.

Keywords: Customization · Social robotics · Trust toward robots · Psychological ownership · Anthropomorphism

1 Introduction

Many authors claim that robots will soon enter our lives as members of an allegedly hybrid society [1]. However, to actually be deployed in society, robots need to be able to adapt or be adapted to their users [1, 2]. Indeed, a robot that meets user preferences and needs will likely yield more positive evaluations, especially in the long run [3]. Personalization refers to the process during which a robot adapts to user characteristics [4]. Such adaptative processes are usually *system-driven*. Thus, the robot collects data about its user and consequently launches processes that result in a match of robot features and user preferences/needs. Likewise, adaptation processes may be *user-driven*, providing human users the possibility to adapt robot features according to their individual preferences and needs. This notion is referred to as customization [5]. Whereas personalization has been a prominent research topic in HRI [4], customization remains underexplored.

© The Author(s), under exclusive license to Springer Nature Switzerland AG 2022
F. Cavallo et al. (Eds.): ICSR 2022, LNAI 13818, pp. 601–614, 2022.
https://doi.org/10.1007/978-3-031-24670-8_53

Prior research on personalization and customization in the context of human-computer interaction (HCI) suggested that having the system or the user playing the dominant role during adaptation may result in differential psychological outcomes. For instance, personalization is suggested to increase perceived ease of use while customization is suggested to increase perceived control of an interface [5]. In the present research we explored the impact of customization on a variety of psychological outcomes by manipulating the extent to which individuals could customize a robot (i.e., no customization vs. low customization vs. high customization). We assumed that the psychological outcomes of customization may be rooted in the increased user involvement. Indeed, the involvement in the design of a product is suggested to have several psychological effects: For example, it increases the feeling of self-investment given time and effort dedicated to the product [5–7], perceived control over the target [5], and perceived familiarity and knowledge about the product [6]. Consistent with those observations, we formulated the following hypotheses:

- H1a: Perceived control, self-investment, and perceived knowledge are higher in high and low customization compared to the control condition.
- H1b: Perceived control, self-investment, and perceived knowledge are higher in high customization than in low customization.

Perceived self-investment, control, and knowledge are determinants of psychological ownership (PO), i.e., subjective feeling of owning a target [8]. This feeling spur people to attribute more value to the target of PO [9], but also to feel more responsible of it [10]. Although PO has not been tested in the context of customization of robots, self-assembly has been suggested to make PO occur [7]. Consequently, we hypothesized that the higher the degree of customization of a robot, the higher the perceived PO of that robot.

- H2a: Participants who customize a robot (high and low) report more PO than participants in the control condition.
- H2b: Participants in the high customization condition report more PO than those in the low customization condition.
- H2c: Customization increases PO through perceived control, perceived knowledge, and self-investment.

Furthermore, PO is suggested to increase self-extension (SE) [8]. SE refers to the feeling that an object symbolizes an individual's identity and is connected to the self [11], resulting in feelings of attachment and closeness [11, 12]. It can be assumed that PO elicits SE during design processes [6], resulting in more positive evaluations of the object [12]. Such effects should be particularly pronounced when participants have the chance to engage in high levels of customization. Accordingly, we hypothesized that:

- H3a: SE, perceived closeness, and attachment to a robot are higher when participants engage in customization (high and low) than when they cannot.
- H3b: SE, perceived closeness, and attachment to a robot are higher when participants can engage in high (vs. low) customization.

PO addresses three main human needs: The need for effectance, which drives humans to seek predictability and control over their environment, the need for identity, which motivates humans to express and maintain it, and the need to belong, which motivates humans to seek social connection [8]. Interestingly, PO likewise fulfills needs that are otherwise known to trigger anthropomorphism, i.e., the ascription of human characteristics to nonhuman entities [13, 14]. Anthropomorphizing an entity contributes to retrieve a feeling of familiarity and control over it, as well as it facilitates social interaction with it by relying on anthropocentric knowledge [15]. Doing so, anthropomorphism satisfies effectance and sociality motivation, which likewise addresses the human need for identity and to belong [13]. The idea is that customization elicits PO, which satisfies effectance and sociality motivation, thereby decreasing the chances for anthropomorphism to occur, as anthropomorphism is no longer required to satisfy these needs. From this idea follows:

- H4a: Anthropomorphism is higher in the absence of customization than in low and high customization.
- H4b: Anthropomorphism is higher in low customization than in high customization.

Anthropomorphism is suggested to be a dual process that encompasses conscious, reflexive processes that lead to the ascription of human characteristics, but also automatic, unconscious ones [16]. This difference can be observed in the ascription of mind to a robot [17]: reaction times are longer when people implicitly anthropomorphize the robot but explicitly report low levels of anthropomorphism [18]. Therefore, we hypothesize:

- H4c: Participants who exert high or low levels of customization are faster at ascribing mind to the robot than those who have not engaged in customizing it.
- H4d: Participants who engage in high (vs. low) customization of a robot are faster at ascribing mind to it.

More importantly, the core hypothesis tested in this research predicts effects of customization on trust. We differentiate between cognitive and affective trust. To illustrate, a human may form ideas about the robot's competence or performance (i.e., cognitive trust), or about the robot's likeability and benevolence (i.e., affective trust) [19, 20]. Cognitive and affective trust are the attitudinal components of trust that need to be sufficiently high to lead individuals to trust other agents [19]. As involvement in the design of a robot leads to more positive attitudes toward it [21], affective and cognitive trust should be positively influenced by customization. Thus, we hypothesize the following:

- H5a: Both cognitive and affective trust are higher when participants engaged in customizing a robot (low and high) vs. not.
- H5b: Both cognitive and affective trust are higher when participants engaged in high vs. low customization.

Finally, anthropomorphization and PO increase trust toward robots [22, 23]. In particular, PO should positively influence both forms of trust because an individual may feel more in control, knowledgeable (increasing cognitive trust), and more similar to a given target because of SE and perceived closeness (increasing affective trust). Hence, our hypothesis is that both mechanisms may mediate the relationship between customization and trust toward robot.

- H5c: PO and anthropomorphization mediate the relationship between the degree of customization and trust toward robot.

2 Methodology

2.1 Design

Participants were randomly assigned to one of three customization conditions (low, high, none) resulting from a between-subjects design. The online experiment was preregistered on aspredicted.org (https://aspredicted.org/fh4tm.pdf)[1] and has been approved by the Ethics Committee of Bielefeld University (Application no. 2022–088, April 11th, 2022).

2.2 Participants

We conducted an a priori power analysis (G*Power, version 3.1) for a MANCOVA (α = .05, power = .95, number of groups = 3) with small effects ($f^2(V) = 0.10$) resulting in a recommended sample size of N = 222. Participants were recruited by mail, social media, and face-to-face at Bielefeld University (Germany). We initially collected responses from 304 participants. Participants who did not complete the study or rejected data use for research purposes were removed, resulting in 185 participants. The final sample consisted of 173 participants (131 females, 39 males, 4 others, $M_{age} = 26.72$, $SD_{age} = 10.53$) who had met the inclusion criteria: being at least eighteen years old, being a native or fluent German speaker, reporting sufficient vividness of mental imagery, presenting outliers (> 3 SD) for < 5% of the variables of interest, and not failing the attention check.

2.3 Procedure

After providing informed consent, participants were asked to evaluate the design of the robot NAO (control condition), or to design a robot (low and high customization conditions) by choosing different features (e.g., body shape, social abilities). After the experimental manipulation, the parts constituting the robot (e.g., head, body, eyes) were displayed all at once on the screen and participants were asked to imagine the robot as if it were completely assembled for 60 s. This task was implemented to reduce the likelihood of null effects because the online setting made actual customization impossible. Subsequently, we assessed the vividness of participants' imagination as a control variable. Finally, participants completed the dependent measures. Upon completion, a fake error message appeared which stated that any data on robot evaluation or design

---

[1] The preregistration differs from the actual experiment in two ways: (1) vividness of mental imagery was measured with 7 items only, not 10 items, (2) further reading suggested that a χ^2 test would be more appropriate than the initially indicated Cochran Q test given the independent samples.

would be erased if participants did not launch a backup procedure that would take extra time to be performed. Afterwards, control variables and demographics were displayed. Finally, participants were debriefed in written form and gave final consent to data usage. As reimbursement they could either participate in a raffle for three vouchers worth € 10 or they received course credit for their participation.

2.4 Materials

The experiment was implemented using Qualtrics [24]. Except otherwise specified, 7-point Likert scales were used to gather participants' responses.

Experimental Manipulation. We manipulated the degree of customization through the number of features the user could select to design the robot. In the control condition participants evaluated 30 features of a NAO robot instead of customizing anything. In the low customization condition participants could decide about 15 features by choosing among available options and were asked with 15 filler items which choice they thought other people would make. In the high customization condition participants could decide about 30 features by choosing among available options.

Manipulation Check. Four items were used to assess whether participants had the impression to have customized the robot ($\alpha = .83$), e.g., "I feel like I have designed this robot".

Determinants of PO. We assessed determinants of PO by asking participants to indicate their degree of agreement with statements from two items for perceived control (e.g., "I feel I have control over the robot [NAO/I designed]", $\alpha = .93$) [25], four items for self-investment (e.g., "I felt very involved in the design process of the robot [NAO/I designed]", $\alpha = .72$) [26], and three items to assess perceived knowledge of the robot (e.g., "I have extensive knowledge about the robot [NAO/I designed]", $\alpha = .89$) [27], adapted from [23].

Psychological Ownership. We measured PO using four items (e.g., "This is my robot", $\alpha = .86$) [28], adapted from [23].

Effects of PO. Two items were used to assess participants' self-extension (e.g., "The robot [NAO/I designed] symbolizes me", $\alpha = .64$) [11]. The single-item IOS scale was used to assess perceived closeness [29]. Moreover, attachment to the robot was measured with one self-generated item (i.e., "How attached to the robot [NAO/you designed] do you feel?"). To tap the behavioral component of attachment, we asked participants if they would spend extra time on data back-up to keep the robot from being erased following a fake error message. Moreover, following [6], we asked participants about their negative feelings facing the potential loss of the robot.

Anthropomorphism. The RoSAS scale [30] served to assess anthropomorphic inferences by means of three subscales. We used six items to tap warmth (e.g., "social", $\alpha = .88$), six items to reflect competence (e.g., "competent", $\alpha = .84$), and six items to measure discomfort (e.g., "awkward", $\alpha = .73$). Additionally, we used 10 items from a short version of the mind attribution scale reflecting experience (5 items, e.g.,, "To what extent is the robot you designed capable of feeling joy?", $\alpha = .81$) and agency (5 items, e.g., "How good is the robot you designed at making plans?", $\alpha = .67$) [17]. To take implicit anthropomorphism into account, we also measured participants' response times for each item.

Trust Toward Robot. We assessed cognitive and affective trust with 10 items from [20], respectively (20 items in total). An exemplary item for cognitive trust reads "The robot [NAO/I designed] is reliable" ($\alpha = .72$), Affective trust was measured with items such as "The robot [NAO/I designed] would behave warmly and compassionately toward me" ($\alpha = .85$). Based on previous explicit measures of cognitive and affective trust in interpersonal relationships and HRI, this scale has been developed and successfully used to study trust toward robot in German context [20].

Vividness of Mental Imagery. Because we had asked participants to engage in mental imagery, we sought to control for its vividness using seven items (e.g., "How you would describe the robot you envisioned" using 7-point semantic differentials with opposite adjectives such as "unclear"/"clear", $\alpha = .78$) [31].

Control variables. We used four items from [21] to measure prior robot experience ($\alpha = .39$) and 12 items from [32] to measure affinity for technology ($\alpha = .86$). The attention check comprised one item. Finally, participants provided demographic information (age, gender, job status, education, language proficiency).

Except for measures regarding attachment and robot experience, composite mean scores were computed. Where necessary, items were recoded before mean calculation.

3   Results

Data preparation and analysis were done with R language (version 4.2.1), using RStudio (version 2022.02.3, build 492 "Prairie Trillium"). To test our hypotheses, we conducted a MANOVA with follow-up univariate analyses of variance (ANOVA) and contrast analyses. We also conducted two mediation analyses using the PROCESS macro for R [33] with 5000 bootstrap samples. The first examined the mediating role of perceived control, self-investment, and knowledge between customization and PO. The second examined the mediating role of PO and anthropomorphism between customization and both cognitive and affective trust. We conducted a MANCOVA to test the influence of our control variables on the dependent variables. We also used a χ^2 test of independence to check for an association between the level of customization and the reaction to the fake error message.

Manipulation Check. To check the success of the customization manipulation, we conducted an ANOVA with customization (high, low, none) as a factor and perceived customization as a dependent measure. There was a significant effect of experimental condition on perceived customization of the robot $F(2, 170) = 71.47, p < .001, \omega^2 = .45$. Planned contrasts revealed that both low ($M = 5.44, SD = 1.22$) and high ($M = 4.91, SD = 0.94$) customization significantly increased the feeling of having customized the robot compared to the control condition ($M = 2.92, SD = 1.37$), $t(170) = 11.70, p < .001$ (one-tailed), $d = 1.79$. Moreover, high customization significantly increased the feeling of having designed the robot compared to low customization, $t(170) = 2.40, p$

< .05 (one-tailed), $d = 0.37$. This result confirms that our experimental manipulation was successful in differentiating the degree of customization.

Main Analysis. We conducted a MANOVA with experimental condition as independent variable and all quantitative dependent measures. Using Pillai's trace, there was a significant main effect of the experimental manipulation on the dependent variables, $V = 0.434$, $F(2, 36) = 2.37$, $p < .001$, $\omega^2 = .13$.

Determinants of PO. Regarding testing of hypotheses H1a and H1b, there was a significant effect of the experimental manipulation on perceived control $F(2, 170) = 8.16$, $p < .001$, $\omega^2 = .08$. With planned contrasts, we identified that low customization ($M = 4.28$, $SD = 1.79$) and high customization ($M = 4.22$, $SD = 1.45$) increased perceived control, compared to the control condition ($M = 3.21$, $SD = 1.48$), $t(170) = 4.03$, $p < .001$ (one-tailed), $d = 0.62$. However, there was no significant difference between low customization and high customization conditions, $t(170) = -0.22$, $p = .413$ (one-tailed), $d = 0.03$. Similarly, we found a significant effect of the experimental manipulation on self-investment $F(2, 170) = 24.75$, $p < .001$, $\omega^2 = .22$. Planned contrasts revealed that low ($M = 3.72$, $SD = 1.06$) and high ($M = 4.01$, $SD = 1.26$) customization elicited significantly higher self-investment than the control condition ($M = 2.65$, $SD = 0.90$) $t(170) = 6.88$, $p < .001$ (one-tailed), $d = 1.05$. No significant effect of high vs. low customization on self investment was obtained $t(170) = 1.46$, $p = .073$ (one-tailed), $d = 0.22$. The experimental manipulation impacted perceived knowledge, $F(2, 170) = 11.48$, $p < .001$, $\omega^2 = .11$. Perceived knowledge was significantly higher in the low ($M = 3.11$, $SD = 1.54$) and the high ($M = 3.32$, $SD = 1.51$) customization condition than in the control condition ($M = 2.12$, $SD = 1.21$), $t(170) = 4.72$, $p < .001$ (one-tailed), $d = 0.72$. However, participants reported equal levels of perceived knowledge in both high and low customization conditions. Consequently, our results are consistent with Hypothesis H1a, but not with Hypothesis H1b.

Mediation by Determinants of PO. We investigated the mediating role of the determinants of PO between the degree of customization and PO by performing a parallel mediation analysis. There were significant indirect effects of the degree of customization on PO toward the robot through perceived control (b = .165, BCa CI [.068, .280]), self-investment (b = .177, BCa CI [.034, .341]), and perceived knowledge (b =. 115, BCa CI [.020, .234]). These results provide support for Hypothesis H2c.

Psychological Ownership. Testing hypotheses H2a and H2b, we found a significant effect of the experimental manipulation on PO, $F(2, 170) = 9.45$, $p < .001$, $\omega^2 = .09$. Planned contrasts showed that PO was significantly higher in the low ($M = 2.83$, $SD = 1.48$) and high ($M = 3.07$, $SD = 1.46$) customization condition than in the control condition ($M = 1.97$, $SD = 1.30$), $t(170) = 4.24$, $p < .001$ (one-tailed), $d = 0.65$. Participants reported equal levels of PO following high and low customization. These results provide support for H2a, but not for H2b.

Effects of PO. Testing H3a and H3b, we found a significant effect of the level of customization on consequences of PO, namely perceived closeness, $F(2, 170) = 8.55$, $p < .001$, $\omega^2 = .08$, and self-extension, $F(2, 170) = 8.37$, $p < .001$, $\omega^2 = .08$. Planned contrasts provided support for H3a, but not H3b. Indeed, we found that low ($M = 2.00$,

$SD = 1.21$) and high ($M = 2.07$, $SD = 0.93$) customization significantly increased perceived closeness compared to the control condition ($M = 1.38$, $SD = 0.75$), $t(170) = 4.12$, $p < .001$ (one-tailed), $d = 0.63$. However, we did not identify a significant difference between low and high customization regarding perceived closeness. Both low ($M = 2.51$, $SD = 1.45$) and high ($M = 2.87$, $SD = 1.29$) customization elicited significantly higher perceived self-extension than the control condition ($M = 1.90$, $SD = 1.08$) $t(170) = 3.78$, $p < .001$ (one-tailed), $d = 0.58$. We also found a marginally significant effect of high vs. low customization on self-extension $t(170) = 1.54$, $p = .063$ (one-tailed), $d = 0.24$. Besides, we found a significant main effect of customization on self-reported attachment $F(2, 170) = 9.05$, $p < .001$, $\omega^2 = .09$. Participants reported significantly higher levels of attachment to a robot they lowly ($M = 2.71$, $SD = 1.64$) or highly ($M = 2.95$, $SD = 1.49$) customized vs. not ($M = 1.84$, $SD = 1.22$), $t(170) = 4.16$, $p < .001$ (one-tailed), $d = 0.64$. However, low vs. high customization did not impact self-reported attachment, $t(170) = 0.95$, $p = .186$ (one-tailed), $d = 0.14$. The experimental manipulation did not elicit a significant effect of the level of customization in terms of negative feelings after the fake error message $F(2, 170) = 3.00$, $p = .053$, $\omega^2 = .02$. These results provide support for H3a, and partial support for H3b.

Decision After Error Message. As our samples are independent, a Pearson χ^2 test was performed on the decision to save the robot's data from erasure after seeing the error message. Contrary to hypotheses H3a and H3b, there was no significant association between the degree of customization and the decision to save the robot's data $\chi^2(2) = 1.52$, $p = .467$.

Anthropomorphism. Testing hypotheses H4a and H4b, we found no significant effect of customization on perceived warmth, $F(2, 170) = 1.82$, $p = .166$, $\omega^2 = .009$, or perceived competence, $F(2, 170) = 1.55$, $p = .214$, $\omega^2 = .006$. However, we found a significant effect on discomfort, $F(2, 170) = 3.86$, $p < .05$, $\omega^2 = .03$. Specifically, discomfort was significantly lower in low ($M = 2.22$, $SD = 0.87$) and high ($M = 2.24$, $SD = 0.80$) customization conditions than in the control condition ($M = 2.62$, $SD = 0.93$), $t(170) = -2.78$, $p < .01$ (one-tailed), $d = 0.43$. There was no significant difference in terms of perceived discomfort between low and high customization, $t(170) = 0.10$, $p = .461$ (one-tailed), $d = 0.02$. Regarding mind perception, there was no effect of customization on the attribution of experience to the robot, $F(2, 170) = 0.93$, $p = .397$, $\omega^2 = .0008$. However, we found a significant effect of customization on the attribution of agency to the robot, $F(2, 170) = 3.52$, $p < .05$, $\omega^2 = .03$. Contrary to Hypothesis H4a, planned contrasts revealed that participants ascribed more agency to lowly ($M = 4.34$, $SD = 1.34$) and highly ($M = 4.80$, $SD = 1.14$) customized robots than to a merely evaluated robot ($M = 4.22$, $SD = 1.27$), $t(170) = 1.75$, $p < .05$ (one-tailed), $d = 0.27$. This difference can also be observed between low customization and high customization $t(170) = 1.98$, $p < .05$ (one-tailed), $d = 0.30$. Contrary to hypotheses H4c and H4d, we did not find significant differences for customization in terms of RT when ascribing agency ($F(2, 170) = 2.17$, $p = .117$, $\omega^2 = .03$) or experience to the robot ($F(2, 170) = 1.96$, $p = .145$, $\omega^2 = .01$).

Cognitive and Affective Trust. Testing H5a and H5b, the effect of customization on cognitive trust was significant, $F(2, 170) = 5.97$, $p < .01$, $\omega^2 = .05$. Planned contrasts revealed that participants reported higher cognitive trust in low ($M = 4.72, SD = 0.82$) and high ($M = 4.81, SD = 0.60$) customization than in the control condition ($M = 4.34$, $SD = 0.84$), $t(170) = 3.40, p < .001$ (one-tailed), $d = 0.52$, providing support for H5a. No significant difference was found between low and high customization, $t(170) = 0.62$, $p = .267$ (one-tailed), $d = 0.10$, which does not support H5b. We also found a significant effect of customization on affective trust, $F(2, 170) = 7.25, p < .001, \omega^2 = .07$. Planned contrasts revealed that affective trust was significantly higher in low ($M = 4.34, SD = 1.28$) and high ($M = 4.86, SD = 0.91$) customization than in the control condition ($M = 4.07, SD = 1.18$), $t(170) = 2.87, p < .01$ (one-tailed), $d = 0.44$, supporting H5a. Furthermore, affective trust was also significantly higher in the high than in the low customization condition, $t(170) = 2.48, p < .01$ (one-tailed), $d = 0.38$, supporting H5b.

Vividness of Mental Imagery. Customization had a significant effect on the vividness of mental imagery, $F(2, 170) = 6.92, p < .01, \omega^2 = .06$. As we did not formulate any hypotheses about the direction of this effect, we used post-hoc t tests with Bonferroni correction to explore the univariate differences between groups. We identified a significant difference of the vividness of mental imagery between the control condition ($M = 5.51, SD = 0.87$) and the low customization condition ($M = 5.15, SD = 0.78$), $p < .01$, $d = 0.61$, and between the control condition and the high customization condition ($M = 4.68, SD = 0.87$), $p < .01, d = 0.58$. However, we found no significant difference between low customization and high customization, $p = 1, d = 0.07$.

Mediation by Composite PO and Anthropomorphism. To test H5c, we included anthropomorphism as a composite of RoSAS (with discomfort reversely coded) and mind perception scores ($\alpha = .89$), and PO as a composite of its score and its related constructs, i.e., perceived closeness, self-extension, and attachment ($\alpha = .90$). We performed a parallel mediation analysis and found a significant indirect effect of the degree of customization on cognitive trust toward the robot through composite of PO (b = .089, Bca CI [.037, .155]), but not through anthropomorphism (b = .016, Bca CI [-.016, .061]). Additionally, we found a significant indirect effect of the degree of customization on affective trust toward the robot through both composite of PO (b = .094, Bca CI [.034, .165]) and composite of anthropomorphism (b = .159, Bca CI [.037, .287]). This result supports the mediating role of PO and partially supports the mediating role of anthropomorphism hypothesized in H5c.

Correlation Between Anthropomorphism and PO. For exploratory purposes, we tested the correlation between composites of anthropomorphism and PO. We found a significant moderate positive association between anthropomorphization and PO, r(171) $= .54, p < .001$.

Influence of the Vividness of Mental Imagery and Control Variables. As the vividness of mental imagery, $F(2, 170) = 6.92, p < .001, \omega^2 = .06$, as well as the prior exposure to robots through media, $F(2, 170) = 4.46, p < .01, \omega^2 = .04$ differed between conditions, we included them as covariates in a MANCOVA. Following the principle of parsimony [34], we discarded prior exposure to robots through media, as it did not serve as a significant covariate. Using Pillai's trace, the effects of customization on the dependent variables remained significant $V = 0.48, F(34, 308) = 2.85, p < .001$. Furthermore, we identified a significant effect of vividness of mental imagery on the dependent variables

$V = 0.49$, $F(17, 153) = 8.83$, $p < .001$. Univariate tests revealed that vividness of mental imagery had significant effects on almost all of the dependent variables, namely: perceived control, $F(1, 169) = 13.35$, $p < .001$, $\omega^2 = .06$, self-investment, $F(1, 169) = 8.81$, $p < .01$, $\omega^2 = .04$, perceived knowledge, $F(1, 169) = 13.64$, $p < .001$, PO, $F(1, 169) = 26.01$, $p < .001$, $\omega^2 = .12$, self-extension, $F(1, 169) = 38.10$, $p < .001$, $\omega^2 = .17$, perceived closeness, $F(1, 169) = 28.30$, $p < .001$, $\omega^2 = .13$, attachment, $F(1, 169) = 45.07$, $p < .001$, $\omega^2 = .20$, warmth, $F(1, 169) = 49.81$, $p < .001$, $\omega^2 = .22$, competence, $F(1, 169) = 40.85$, $p < .001$, $\omega^2 = .19$, discomfort, $F(1, 169) = 22.34$, $p < .001$, $\omega^2 = .11$, experience, $F(1, 169) = 13.16$, $p < .001$, $\omega^2 = .07$, agency, $F(1, 169) = 20.95$, $p < .001$, $\omega^2 = .10$, cognitive trust, $F(1, 169) = 43.51$, $p < .001$, $\omega^2 = .19$, and affective trust, $F(1, 169) = 43.05$, $p < .001$, $\omega^2 = .19$.

4 Discussion

Taken together, our results suggest that customization increases PO and trust toward a robot. Contrary to our prediction, the degree of customization did not result in significantly higher levels of PO and trust toward the robot, except for affective trust. This result is consistent with [35], who found that effects of customization do not differ according to the number of options. It is possible that above a certain threshold increasing the degree of customization has neglectable or no additional effects. We did not find a significant effect of the degree of customization on anthropomorphism, except for agency and discomfort. Contrary to our hypotheses, the higher the degree of customization, the more participants perceived the robot as agentic and the less they viewed it as a source of discomfort. The reduction of discomfort in customization conditions may be related to an increasing familiarity resulting from the association between the self and the robot in favor of PO [12]. In line with our expectations, we observed a mediating effect of PO between the degree of customization and both cognitive and affective trust, supporting the importance of PO in customized HRI to improve trust toward robots. Anthropomorphism did not mediate the effect between customization and cognitive trust, but did so for affective trust. Additionally, we found that PO and anthropomorphism are partially associated. A possible interpretation of the results from the mediation and the correlation could be that when customizing, PO suffices to satisfy effectance motivation but does not satisfy sociality motivation, which leads to anthropomorphism to satisfy the underlying need to belong. If we have a closer look on the effects of customization on determinants of PO, the size of the effect on perceived control is the highest. We suggest that customization indeed satisfies effectance motivation and consequently improves cognitive trust toward robots. Additionally, PO and the resulting association between the robot and the self in customization may satisfy the need for identity but increase the need for connectedness with the robot. That could explain why agency was higher in customization and why anthropomorphization only mediated the relationship between the experimental conditions and affective trust: A robot apparently required at least a certain degree of agency for it to be considered an interaction partner. However, this interpretation should be taken caution, as we found no effect of customization on perceived warmth or ascribed experience.

Limitations and Future Directions. According to our a priori power analysis, the sample is underpowered. Hence, our findings must be interpreted with caution. Although we observed significant differences between groups regarding the dependent variables, our results show floor effects. A possible explanation for this could be that given the online setting, participants felt less involved in customizing the robot than if the experiment had been implemented in the lab. We implemented a mental imagery task to take this into account, thereby inducing participants to have a more concrete representation of the robot they customized or evaluated. Interestingly, the vividness of mental imagery was significantly higher when customizing a robot than in the evaluation condition. Results from a MANCOVA suggest that vividness influenced most of our dependent variables. This effect may be due to the fact that self-achieved personal relevance in customization increases attention and memory processes related to the robot [36]. Future research could explore that plausible effect as well as possible applications of it (e.g., customization to improve memorization of information provided by a robot). A replication of our experiment in the lab with participants customizing a real robot and observing the resulting robot without imagining it is however necessary to ensure that our results can be observed in absence of an imagination task. Additionally, the lack of statistically significant differences between low and high customization with regards to the dependent variables could have two explanations. First, and consistent with [35], the number of customizable features in the low customization condition (i.e., 15) could already suffice to count as high involvement. Second, it is possible that the filler items we used (i.e., asking participants which feature other people would choose) elicited a perception of involvement in the design of the robot (as in participatory design [21]). Future research could consider using more neutral filler items and distinguish more degrees of customization. Contrary to our assumption, it is possible that PO, although contributing to satisfy effectance and sociality motivation, does not prevent anthropomorphization from satisfying those needs as well. [23] suggested that anthropomorphism moderates the relationship between perceived control and knowledge, and PO. However, in that study anthropomorphism was manipulated based on the robot's human-likeness. No measure of perceived anthropomorphism was utilized to check if anthropomorphism as a psychological process influenced their results. There still is a need for basic research on the relationship between anthropomorphism and PO. Moreover, as our research focused on the attitudinal components of trust (i.e., cognitive and affective trust), the effects of customization on the intention to trust and on behavioral trust remain to be explored. A last consideration is the use of a NAO robot in our experiment as a basis for evaluation in the control condition. Future work should test if our results stand if we use another robot in the control condition. Despite the limitations of our experiment, our results are overall consistent with previous studies investigating the positive role of involvement in the design of robots [6, 7, 21] and provide further support to the idea that allowing user-driven adaptation of robots would contribute to improve how individuals perceive them and the extent to which they trust them.

Acknowledgement. This research was supported by European Union's Horizon 2020 research and innovation programme under the Marie Skłodowska-Curie grant agreement No 955778. We would like to express our gratitude to Jonathan Schober for his involvement in that research. We also thank Julia Schlagheck, Annabelle Mielitz, Anna Brueggeshemke, and Eda Tekin for their contribution to that work.

References

1. Šabanović, S.: Robots in society, society in robots. Int. J. Soc. Robot. **2**, 439–450 (2010). https://doi.org/10.1007/s12369-010-0066-7
2. Tapus, A., Mataric, M., Scassellati, B.: Socially assistive robotics: Grand challenges of robotics. IEEE Robot. Automat. Mag. **14**, 35–42 (2007). https://doi.org/10.1109/MRA.2007.339605
3. Leite, I., Martinho, C., Paiva, A.: Social Robots for Long-Term Interaction: A Survey. Int. J. Soc. Robot. **5**(2), 291–308 (2013). https://doi.org/10.1007/s12369-013-0178-y
4. Ahmad, M., Mubin, O., Orlando, J.: A systematic review of adaptivity in human-robot interaction. Multimodal Technol. Interact. **1**, 14 (2017). https://doi.org/10.3390/mti1030014
5. Sundar, S.S., Marathe, S.S.: Personalization versus customization: the importance of agency, privacy, and power usage. Hum. Commun. Res. **36**, 298–322 (2010). https://doi.org/10.1111/j.1468-2958.2010.01377.x
6. Groom, V., Takayama, L., Ochi, P., Nass, C.: I am my robot: The impact of robot-building and robot form on operators. In: 4th ACM/IEEE International Conference on Human-Robot Interaction (HRI 2009), pp. 31–36. IEEE, San Diego, California, USA (2009). https://doi.org/10.1145/1514095.1514104
7. Sun, Y., Sundar, S.S.: Psychological importance of human agency. How self-assembly affects user experience of robots. In: 11th ACM/IEEE International Conference on Human-Robot Interaction (HRI 2016), pp. 189–196. IEEE, Christchurch, New Zealand (2016). https://doi.org/10.1109/HRI.2016.7451751
8. Pierce, J.L., Kostova, T., Dirks, K.: The state of psychological ownership: Integrating and extending a century of research. Rev. Gen. Psychol. **7**, 84–107 (2003). https://doi.org/10.1037/1089-2680.7.1.84
9. Kirk, C.P., Swain, S.D., Gaskin, J.E.: I'm proud of it: Consumer technology appropriation and psychological ownership. J. Mark. Theory Pract. **23**, 166–184 (2015). https://doi.org/10.1080/10696679.2015.1002335
10. Peck, J., Kirk, C.P., Luangrath, A.W., Shu, S.B.: Caring for the commons: Using psychological ownership to enhance stewardship behavior for public goods. J. Mark. **85**, 33–49 (2021). https://doi.org/10.1177/0022242920952084
11. Kiesler, T., Kiesler, S.: My pet rock and me: An experimental exploration of the self extension concept. NA - Adv. Consum. Res. **32**, 365–370 (2005)
12. Gawronski, B., Bodenhausen, G.V., Becker, A.P.: I like it, because I like myself: Associative self-anchoring and post-decisional change of implicit evaluations. J. Exp. Soc. Psychol. **43**, 221–232 (2007). https://doi.org/10.1016/j.jesp.2006.04.001
13. Epley, N., Waytz, A., Cacioppo, J.: On seeing human: A three-factor theory of anthropomorphism. Psychol. Rev. **114**, 864–886 (2007). https://doi.org/10.1037/0033-295X.114.4.864
14. Eyssel, F.: An experimental psychological perspective on social robotics. Rob. Auton. Syst. **87**, 363–371 (2017). https://doi.org/10.1016/j.robot.2016.08.029
15. Epley, N., Waytz, A., Akalis, S., Cacioppo, J.T.: When we need a human: Motivational determinants of anthropomorphism. Soc. Cogn. **26**, 143–155 (2008). https://doi.org/10.1521/soco.2008.26.2.143
16. Złotowski, J., Sumioka, H., Eyssel, F., Nishio, S., Bartneck, C., Ishiguro, H.: Model of dual anthropomorphism: The relationship between the media equation effect and implicit anthropomorphism. Int. J. Soc. Robot. **10**(5), 701–714 (2018). https://doi.org/10.1007/s12369-018-0476-5

17. Gray, H., Gray, K., Wegner, D.: Dimensions of mind perception. Science **315**, 619 (2007). https://doi.org/10.1126/science.1134475
18. Li, Z., Terfurth, L., Woller, J.P., Wiese, E.: Mind the machines: Applying implicit measures of mind perception in social robotics. In: 17th ACM/IEEE International Conference on Human-Robot Interaction (HRI 2022), pp. 236–245. IEEE Press, Sapporo, Hokkaido, Japan (2022). https://doi.org/10.5555/3523760.3523794
19. Lee, J.D., See, K.A.: Trust in automation: Designing for appropriate reliance. Hum. Factors. **46**, 50–80 (2004). https://doi.org/10.1518/hfes.46.1.50_30392
20. Bernotat, J., Eyssel, F., Sachse, J.: The (fe)male robot: How robot body shape impacts first impressions and trust towards robots. Int. J. Soc. Robot. **13**(3), 477–489 (2019). https://doi.org/10.1007/s12369-019-00562-7
21. Reich-Stiebert, N., Eyssel, F., Hohnemann, C.: Involve the user! Changing attitudes toward robots by user participation in a robot prototyping process. Comput. Hum. Behav. **91**, 290–296 (2019). https://doi.org/10.1016/j.chb.2018.09.041
22. Hancock, P.A., Kessler, T.T., Kaplan, A.D., Brill, J.C., Szalma, J.L.: Evolving trust in robots: Specification through sequential and comparative meta-analyses. Hum. Factors. **63**, 1196–1229 (2020). https://doi.org/10.1177/0018720820922080
23. Delgosha, M.S., Hajiheydari, N.: How human users engage with consumer robots? A dual model of psychological ownership and trust to explain post-adoption behaviours. Comput. Hum. Behav. **117**, 106660 (2021). https://doi.org/10.1016/j.chb.2020.106660
24. Qualtrics, https://www.qualtrics.com
25. Zheng, H., Xu, B., Zhang, M., Wang, T.: Sponsor's cocreation and psychological ownership in reward-based crowdfunding. Inf. Syst. J. **28**, 1213–1238 (2018). https://doi.org/10.1111/isj.12190
26. Kwon, S.: Understanding user participation from the perspective of psychological ownership: The moderating role of social distance. Comput. Hum. Behav. **105**, 106207 (2020). https://doi.org/10.1016/j.chb.2019.106207
27. Brown, G., Pierce, J.L., Crossley, C.: Toward an understanding of the development of ownership feelings. J. Organ. Behav. **35**, 318–338 (2014). https://doi.org/10.1002/job.1869
28. Van Dyne, L., Pierce, J.L.: Psychological ownership and feelings of possession: three field studies predicting employee attitudes and organizational citizenship behavior. J. Organ. Behav. **25**, 439–459 (2004). https://doi.org/10.1002/job.249
29. Aron, A., Aron, E.N., Smollan, D.: Inclusion of other in the self scale and the structure of interpersonal closeness. J. Pers. Soc. Psychol. **63**, 596–612 (1992). https://doi.org/10.1037/0022-3514.63.4.596
30. Carpinella, C.M., Wyman, A.B., Perez, M.A., Stroessner, S.J.: The robotic social attributes scale (RoSAS): Development and validation. In: 12th ACM/IEEE International Conference on Human-Robot Interaction (HRI 2017). pp. 254–262. IEEE, Vienna, Austria (2017). https://doi.org/10.1145/2909824.3020208
31. Wullenkord, R., Eyssel, F.: Improving attitudes towards social robots using imagined contact. In: The 23rd IEEE International Symposium on Robot and Human Interactive Communication, pp. 489–494 (2014). https://doi.org/10.1109/ROMAN.2014.6926300
32. Neyer, F.J., Felber, J., Gebhardt, C.: Entwicklung und Validierung einer Kurzskala zur Erfassung von Technikbereitschaft [Development and validation of a short scale to measure readiness to use technology]. Diagnostica **58**, 87–99 (2012). https://doi.org/10.1026/0012-1924/a000067
33. Hayes, A.F.: Introduction to Mediation, Moderation, and Conditional Process Analysis: A Regression-Based Approach. Guilford Press, New York (2018)

34. Tabachnick, B.G., Fidell, L.S., Ullman, J.B.: Using Multivariate Statistics. Pearson, New York (2019)
35. Diehl, C., Schiffhauer, B., Eyssel, F., Achenbach, J., Klett, S., Botsch, M., Kopp, S.: Get one or create one: The impact of graded involvement in a selection procedure for a virtual agent on satisfaction and suitability ratings. In: Beskow, J., Peters, C., Castellano, G., O'Sullivan, C., Leite, I., and Kopp, S. (eds.) Intelligent Virtual Agents. pp. 109–118. Springer International Publishing, Cham (2017). https://doi.org/10.1007/978-3-319-67401-8_13
36. Celsi, R.L., Olson, J.C.: The role of involvement in attention and comprehension processes. J. Consum. Res. **15**, 210–224 (1988). https://doi.org/10.1086/209158

Ambivalent Stereotypes Towards Gendered Robots: The (Im)mutability of Bias Towards Female and Neutral Robots

Stefano Guidi[1], Latisha Boor[2], Laura van der Bij[2], Robin Foppen[2], Okke Rikmenspoel[2], and Giulia Perugia[2]([✉])

[1] Department of Social, Political and Cognitive Sciences, University of Siena, 53100 Siena, SI, Italy
stefano.guidi@unisi.it

[2] Department of Industrial Engineering and Innovation Sciences, Eindhoven University of Technology, Eindhoven, Netherlands
g.perugia@tue.nl

Abstract. Many studies have investigated the effect of robot gendered-ness on the attribution of gender stereotypes to a robot, often with mixed results. This paper aims to overcome some of the limitations of previous research. We adopted a mixed study design with stereotypical trait type (communion vs. agency) or task type (stereotypical female vs. stereotypical male) and robot genderedness (female vs. male vs. neutral) as within-subjects factors, and participant gender (men vs. women) as between-subjects factor. We asked participants to rate 24 robots (8 per category) in terms of their perceived communion, agency, and suitability for stereotypical female and male tasks. The results disclosed that female robots activate paternalistic stereotypes (higher communion than agency, higher suitability for female tasks than male tasks), while male robots do not. Moreover, they reveal that the ambivalence of these stereotypes is stronger in men than in women. Even more interestingly, our analyses showed that neutral robots activate paternalistic stereotypes in men and envious stereotypes (higher agency than communion) in women. This last finding is particularly relevant as it suggests that gender neutrality is not enough to safeguard robots from harmful biases.

Keywords: Stereotypes · Social robotics · Social categorization

1 Introduction

In recent years, several studies have investigated the effect of robot genderedness on the activation of gender stereotypes, with often mixed results. Some stud-

This work is part of the research programme Ethics of Socially Disruptive Technologies, which is funded through the Gravitation programme of the Dutch Ministry of Education, Culture, and Science and the Netherlands Organization for Scientific Research (NWO grant number 024.004.031).

F. Cavallo et al. (Eds.): ICSR 2022, LNAI 13818, pp. 615–626, 2022.
https://doi.org/10.1007/978-3-031-24670-8_54

ies found that manipulating a robot genderedness can activate gender stereo-typical traits (i.e., communion and agency) [3,8,17], or influence the robot's perceived suitability for gender-stereotypical tasks and occupations (e.g., trans-porting goods, taking care of children) [3,8,14]. Other studies failed to find such effects [4,19]. In a seminal study by Eyssel and Hegel [8], the robot genderedness was manipulated by changing the robot hair length, discovering that, when given long hair (i.e., female robot), the robot was perceived as more communal and suited for stereotypical female tasks. When given short hair (i.e., male robot), instead, it was perceived as more agentic and suited for stereotypical male tasks. This pattern of results, however, was not confirmed by Rea et al. [19] who manip-ulated the robot genderedness by changing the pronoun with which the robot was introduced to participants (she or he). In recent years, Bernotat et al. [3] partially confirmed Eyssel and Hegel's findings [8]. They manipulated the robot genderedness by varying its body proportions, providing the male robot with a higher waist-to-hips ratio and shoulder width and the female robot with a lower waist-to-hips ratio and shoulder width. In their study, the female robot was perceived by participants as more communal than the male robot, and it was preferred for stereotypical female tasks. Nevertheless, it was not perceived as less agentic than the male robot, nor was it dispreferred for stereotypical male tasks. In the same period, Bryant et al. [4] investigated the effect of robot gendering on people's trust in its occupational competency. They selected 14 stereotypical occupations usually associated with female and male gender and used a female, male, or neutral name to manipulate the genderedness of the robot. The results did not highlight any significant difference in participants' perceived trust in the occupational competency of the robot across its levels of genderedness. Finally, Parlangeli et al. [14] recently investigated the activa-tion of gender role stereotypes for 8 robots from the Anthropomorphic roBOT (ABOT) database. The robots varied both in humanlikeness and genderedness (4 of them being clearly perceived as predominantly masculine and 4 as pre-dominantly feminine). They discovered that gendered robots do activate gender role stereotypes, although more strongly in men than in women. Moreover, the robot's humanlikeness appeared to have a moderating role in the activation of gender role stereotypes for female robots, but not for male ones.

A possible reason for the inconsistency of findings about the effects of robot genderedness on stereotyping might be that the different studies we reported relied on different gender cues to induce the perception of genderedness in the robot (hairstyle [8], voice [17], name and pronouns [4,19], body shape [3]). These cues might not all have the same strength in activating relevant agent knowl-edge structures about gender (see [9]) and hence prompt stereotyping. Some of the studies not succeeding to find significant effects of robot's genderedness on stereotyping used subtle cues (pronouns) or cultural-dependent ones (names). Moreover, in basically all the studies but one [14] a single robot, different in each study (e.g., Flobi [8], NAO [19], Pepper [4], Meka M1 [3]), has been used to investigate the activation of stereotypes. This is an important limitation, as the use of a single robot makes it challenging to generalize findings across different

robotic platforms, as well as across studies. A further limitation of the studies
we presented, which is highlighted by Perugia and Lisy's review [16], is the lack
of neutral robot stimuli: only one out of the many studies on gender stereotyping
included in the review used a gender-neutral robot [4]. Since Perugia et al. [15]
showed that most of the robots in the ABOT database [18] are perceived as
gender-neutral (46%), it seems important to further investigate the activation
of stereotypes in neutral robots. The use of gender-neutral robots could also
be a way to test an hypothesis put forward by [3] and maintained by [14,15]
about the default attributions of male genderedness to robots, in the absence
of specific femininity cues. Another aspect that has received little attention is
the role of an individual's characteristics in stereotyping gendered robots (e.g.,
participant gender). Only a few of the HRI studies focusing on the attribution
of stereotypes to gendered robots [16] tested the interaction effect of participant
gender and robot genderedness, despite the fact that gender stereotypes seem
to differ across men and women [13]. Finally, in previous studies the dimensions of stereotypes have been generally considered in isolation, instead than
jointly. This is problematic, since, according to the Stereotype Content Model
[12], only by jointly considering the two fundamental dimensions of stereotypical judgments [1,11] one can capture their (often) ambivalent content, which is
central to understanding their behavioral implications, including bias [6,7] (e.g.,
discriminated groups tend to be seen as high on one dimension and low on the
other).

The research reported in this paper aims at overcoming some of the limitations of previous studies and testing a series of research hypotheses derived from
the literature about the effects of robot genderedness on stereotypes activation.
First of all, we used a higher number of robots as stimuli (8 per gender category,
24 in total) in order to increase the generalizability of the results. Second, we
included 8 gender-neutral robots, along with male and female ones, in our set
of stimuli to fill-in the gap about gender-neutral robots in the literature. Third,
to shed light on the interaction between participants' characteristics (starting
from their gender) and gender stereotypes, we considered several covariates in
the analysis, and assessed the interaction effect of participant gender and robot
genderedness on stereotypes activation. Finally, in this study, we focused our
attention on ambivalent stereotypes (paternalistic stereotypes: high communion
- low agency; envious stereotypes: high agency - low communion), rather than
on stereotypical traits and tasks in isolation, to better understand the contents
of stereotypes about gendered robots, and their potential implications for HRI.

2   Research Questions

The present study hence focuses on the following Research Questions (RQ):

RQ1. To what extent does the *robot genderedness* influence people's perceptions
of the robots' *stereotypical traits*?
RQ2. To what extent does the *participant gender* influence people's perceptions
of the robots' *stereotypical traits*?

RQ3. To what extent does the *robot genderedness* influence people's perceptions of the robots' suitability for gender *stereotypical tasks?*

RQ4. To what extent does the *participant gender* influence the perception of the robots' suitability for gender *stereotypical tasks?*

Based on Eyssel and Hegel [8], we expected that: **H1.1** Female robots would be judged as possessing more communion than agency; **H1.2** Male robot would be judged as possessing more agency than communion; **H3.1** Female robots would be considered more suitable to perform stereotypical female tasks than stereotypical male tasks; and **H3.2** Male robots would be considered more suitable to perform stereotypical male tasks than stereotypical female tasks. As for participant gender, based on the findings of [13,14], we postulated that: **H2** Men would be more prone to attribute stereotypical traits to female robots and **H4** would consider female robots more suitable for stereotypically female tasks. When it comes to neutral robots, we could not draw any hypotheses from the extant literature, as relevant research was not yet available [16].

3   Method

3.1   Design

To investigate the attribution of gender stereotypical traits and tasks to humanoid robots, we adopted a mixed model design using *stereotypical trait type* (2 levels: communion vs. agency) or *stereotypical task type* (2 levels: stereotypical female vs. male tasks) and *robot genderedness* (3 levels: female vs. male vs. neutral) as within-subjects factors and *participant gender* (2 levels: men vs. women) as between-subjects factor. The data included in this study were sub-sampled from the STerotypes in ROBOts (STROBO) dataset[1], which was created within a larger research project by asking participants to rate 80 images of anthropomorphic robots from the ABOT database [18] in terms of the stereotypical traits they elicited, and their perceived suitability to perform gendered tasks. The research project was approved by the Ethical Review Board of the Human-Technology Interaction group of Eindhoven University of Technology (ID 1615).

3.2   Robot Selection

Since the 80 robots in the STROBO dataset were unevenly distributed in terms of their genderedness (40 were perceived as male, 15 as female, 25 as neutral based on [15]), we sub-sampled 24 robots, 8 per gender category, to perform the analyses in this paper. Sampling was based on the gender ratings in the ROBO-GAP (humanoid ROBOts - Gender and Age Perception) dataset [15], a publicly available dataset containing scores of masculinity, femininity, and gender neutrality (on a 7-point Likert scale) for each of the 251 robots in the ABOT database [15]. As a *first sub-sampling step*, we used a cut-off femininity

---

[1] Not yet publicly available at the time of publication.

and neutrality score > 5 to select female and neutral robots respectively ($N = 8$, $N = 11$), and a cut-off masculinity score > 6 to select male robots ($N = 9$)[2]. As a *second sub-sampling step*, we excluded those gender neutral robots that had intermediate masculinity scores (i.e., 3.5, $N = 3$). Finally, as a *last sub-sampling step*, we randomly selected and excluded one male robot to end up with 8 robots per gender category. The *female robots* included in the study were Aryan, Bina48, Sophia, Flobi, Personal Robot, Furo, Ira, and Speech Buddy; the *male robots* were Romeo, Zeno, Han, Albert Einstein Hubo, Furhat, Cosero, Thr3, Waseda Flutist; the *neutral robots* were Mirae, Icat, Durus, Amigo, Otto, Slate Tr2, Walker, and Jackrabbit 2 (see all pictures of the robots on OSF).

3.3   Participants

To collect the STROBO database, the 80 images of robots were randomly assigned to four groups of 20 robots each. 120 participants ($M_{age} = 26.76$, $SD_{age} = 9.04$; 58 women, 56 men, 5 non-binary, 1 undisclosed), recruited on Prolific from 22 countries, took part in the data collection in May 2022 (socio-demographics information on OSF). They were assigned to one of the four groups of robots and were asked to evaluate the 20 robots in their group through an online questionnaire implemented on Lime Survey^{TM}. Each group of robots was hence evaluated by 30 participants. The gender of the participants in each group was balanced as much as possible. However, due to the low number of participants identifying as non-binary, we could not use their data in our analysis.

3.4   Procedure and Measures

Upon starting the questionnaire, participants were explained the general purpose of the study and were asked to provide their consent to participate. Once the consent was provided, participants proceeded to rate the 20 robots in their group. For each robot, they were asked to rate on a 7-point Likert scale their level of agreement on the robot's perceived **Agency** (5 items; 1 = *strongly disagree*; 7 = *strongly agree*) [5,17]: The robot is able to defend its own beliefs, able to make decisions easily, willing to take a stand, has leadership abilities, has a strong personality; **Communion** (5 items; 1 = *strongly disagree*; 7 = *strongly agree*) [5,17]: The robot is affectionate, compassionate, tender, gentle, sympathetic; **Suitability for male tasks** (5 items; 1 = *not suited at all*; 7 = *extremely suited*) [4,8]: The robot is suited for use in navigating a route, repairing a bike, steering a car, performing surgery, guarding my home; and **Suitability for female tasks** (5 items; 1 = *not suited at all*; 7 = *extremely suited*) [4,8]: The robot is suited for use in caring for a child, household maintenance, preparing meals, providing therapy, taking care of the elderly. Participants were also asked to rate on a 7-point Likert scale their difficulty (1 = *very easy*; 7 = *very difficult*) in rating the robot's communion and agency, and suitability for female and male tasks.

---

[2] The higher masculinity cut-off score being necessary given most of the robots in the original study were perceived as male.

As a last step in the questionnaire, participants were asked to indicate their age (in numbers), gender (man, woman, non-binary, prefer not to say, prefer to specify, followed by a blank field [21]), nationality, and their degree of familiarity with AI, robots, and science fiction (7-point Likert scale; 1 = *not familiar at all* to 7 = *very familiar*) [15]. Moreover, they filled out a 3-item questionnaire to measure their tendency to anthropomorphize (10-point Likert scale; 1 = *not at all* to 10 = *very much*) [23]; a 5-item questionnaire based on the Social Desirability Scale [22] assessing their social desirability bias (true/false questions); and a 12-item questionnaire based on the Ambivalent Sexism Inventory [20] gauging their benevolent and hostile sexism (7-point Likert scale; 1 = *strongly disagree* to 7 = *strongly agree*). The full questionnaire can be found on OSF.

3.5 Statistical Analyses

In our analyses, we followed the approach of Eyssel and Hegel [8], To answer the research questions, the data were analyzed with Linear Mixed-effects Models (LMM) [2]. In the LMM, all the main effects, the two-way and three-way interactions of the three factors were included as fixed effects. Two predictors were common to all the models, the genderedness of the robot and the gender of the participant. The third predictor, instead, varied across models. It could either be the stereotypical trait type (agency vs. communion) or the stereotypical task type (stereotypical male vs. stereotypical female). All predictors were sum coded for the analyses. For the random effects part of the models, we included random intercepts for participant and robot, and random by-participant slopes for trait/task type and robot genderedness. In running the models, we controlled for participants' age, tendency to anthropomorphize, benevolent and hostile sexism, and familiarity with technology including these variables as covariates after centering. The p-values for the tests of the main effects and of the interaction effects were computed using the Satterthwaite's method [10]. All statistical analyses were conducted using R (v.4.0.2).

4   Results

4.1 Preliminary Analyses

We assessed the internal consistency of the stereotypical traits and tasks by computing Cronbach's α for each dimension for each robot. For *agency*, the α ranged between 0.82 and 0.95, for *communion*, between 0.87 and 0.98, for *suitability for female tasks*, between 0.7 and 0.91, for *suitability for male tasks*, between 0.46 and 0.92 (the α was lower than 0.60 only for 3 robots). Given that most robots showed a good to excellent internal consistency on the scales, we computed the average scores across the relative items on each scale for each of the 24 robots. The descriptive statistics (M and SD) on each dimension, as well as the α coefficients for all the 24 robots can be accessed on OSF.

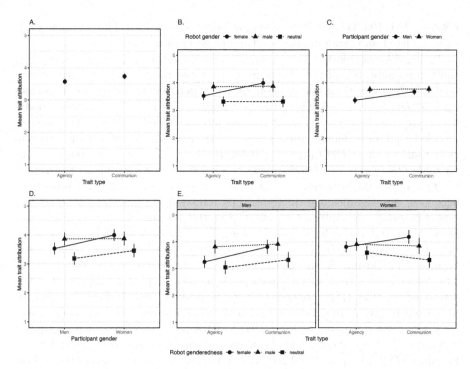

Fig. 1. Plots of the marginal means of the trait attribution ratings as a function of (A) Trait Type, (B) Trait Type and Robot Genderedness, (C) Trait Type and Participant Gender, (D) Robot Genderedness and Participant Gender, and (E) Trait Type, Robot Genderedness and Participant Gender (3-way interaction plot). Error bars represent 95% confidence intervals for the means estimated by the LMM analysis.

4.2   Stereotypical Traits Attributions [RQ1 and RQ2]

The results of the LMM analysis of stereotypical trait attributions (i.e., communion and agency) showed a significant main effect of *trait type*, $F(1, 1030.96) = 6.79, p = .009$, a significant interaction effect of *trait type and robot genderedness*, $F(2, 1126.24) = 5.74; p = .003$, a significant interaction effect of *trait type and participant gender*, $F(1, 1039.34) = 5.53, p = .019$, and a significant interaction effect of *robot genderedness and participant gender*, $F(2, 173.08) = 3.34; p = .038$. The main effect of *robot genderedness* was only marginally significant, $F(2, 20.83) = 3.05, p = .07$, while the main effect of *participant gender*, $F(1, 103.42) = 1.47, p = .229$, and the three-way interaction effect of *trait type, robot genderedness, and participant gender* were not significant, $F(2, 1126.23) = 1.00, p = .369$. Among the covariates, significant associations with the traits ratings were found for *participant age*, $F(1, 101.84) = 4.45, p = .037$, and *tendency to anthropomorphize*, $F(1, 103.16) = 9.90, p = .002$, while a marginally significant association was found with *benevolent sexism*, $F(1, 106.82) = 3.40, p = .068$. Neither *hostile sexism*, $F(1, 105.12) = 2.09, p = .151$, nor *familiarity with tech-*

nologies, $F(1, 103.33) = 0.07, p = .795$, achieved significance. The complete table with the fixed and random effects estimates is reported in OSF.

In Fig. 1A, we plotted the marginal means for the ratings of Agency (A) and Communion (C) of the robots from the fitted model. Agency ratings were significantly lower than communion ratings when taking all robots in consideration ($Diff_{A-C} = -0.165, t(101) = -2.602, p = .011$). The follow-up analyses of the *trait type x robot genderedness* interaction effect (Fig. 1B), however, revealed that only female robots were attributed significantly more communion than agency ($Diff_{A-C} = -0.466; t(475) = -4.267; p < .0001$), while for male ($Diff_{A-C} = -0.022; t(482) = -0.198; p = .843$) and neutral robots ($Diff_{A-C} = -0.006; t(544) = -0.056; p = .956$), agency and communion ratings were not significantly different. The follow-up analyses of the *trait type x participant gender* interaction effect (Fig. 1C) revealed further details. Only Men (M) rated the robots (considering all 24 robots) as higher in communion than agency ($Diff_{A-C} = -0.313; t(101) = -3.464; p = .0008$), while Women (W) did not do so ($Diff_{A-C} = -0.0162; t(101) = -0.182; p = .856$). The follow-up analyses of the *participant gender x robot genderedness* interaction effect (Fig. 1D) enriched this latter finding even further by showing that women gave higher ratings to female robots in general (averaging across trait type) ($Diff_{W-M} = 0.465; t(104) = 2.030; p = .045$). No such significant differences in trait attributions between women and men were instead found for male ($Diff_{W-M} = 0.0112, t(116) = 0.046, p = .964$) and neutral robots ($Diff_{W-M} = 0.270; t(115) = 1.199, p = .233$).

Although the three-way interaction effect was not significant, since all two-way interaction effects were significant, we conducted an analysis of the simple contrasts on trait type for all the combinations of levels of robot genderedness and participant gender. In the panel E in Fig. 1, we plotted the marginal means of communion and agency traits for women (right plot) and men (left plot) as a function of the robot genderedness. The results of the analyses showed that both men ($Diff_{A-C} = -0.559, t(479) = -3.578, p = .0004$) and women ($Diff_{A-C} = -0.374, t(472) = -2.446, p = .015$) attributed more communion than agency to female robots, but the difference was greater for men. We did not find such a significant difference for male robots, for neither men ($Diff_{A-C} = -0.1, t(479) = -0.639, p = .523$) nor women ($Diff_{A-C} = 0.057, t(486) = 0.366, p = .714$). For neutral robot, instead, the difference between agency and communion ratings were only marginally significant, but had opposite patterns in men ($Diff_{A-C} = -0.281, t(544) = -1.793, p = .074$) and women ($Diff_{A-C} = 0.268, t(544) = 1.7450, p = 0.082$). Men judged neutral robots as having more communion than agency, while women judged them as having more agency than communion.

4.3   Suitability to Gender-Stereotypical Tasks [RQ3 and RQ4]

The results of the analysis of stereotypical task type showed a significant main effect of *participant gender*, $F(2, 107.87) = 4.34, p = .040$, a significant interaction effect of *task type and robot genderedness*, $F(2, 1022.06) =$

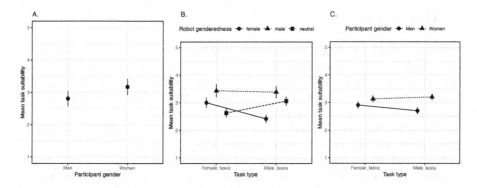

Fig. 2. Plots of the marginal means of the traits attribution ratings as a function of (A) Participant Gender, (B) Task Type and Robot Genderedness, and (C) Task Type and Participant Gender. Error bars represent 95% confidence intervals for the means.

$30.15, p < .001$, and a significant interaction effect of *task type x participant gender*, $F(1, 114.89) = 5.12, p = .026$. No significant main effect of *task type*, $F(1, 114.99) = 1.15, p = .287$, or *robot genderedness*, $F(2, 19.90) = 1.58, p = .231$, was found, nor any significant interaction effect of *robot genderedness and participant gender*, $F(2, 94.96) = 0.77, p = .465$, or *task type, robot genderedness and participant gender*, $F(2, 1021.44) = 0.49, p = .613$. Among the covariates, only *tendency to anthropomorphize* was significantly associated to the stereotypical task ratings, $F(1, 106.15) = 5.02, p = .027$, while a marginally significant association was found for *benevolent sexism*, $F(1, 107.76) = 2.76, p = .100$. Task ratings were not significantly associated with *hostile sexism*, $F(1, 105.02) = 0.28, p = .595$, *participant's age*, $F(1, 100.56) = 0.32, p = .575$, nor with participants' *familiarity with technologies*, $F(1, 104.14) = 0.88, p = .350$.

The follow-up analyses on the main effect of *participant gender* showed that when considering the 24 robots altogether (averaged across genderedness), women gave higher ratings (see Fig. 2A) on stereotypical tasks (averaging across task type) than men $(Diff_{W-M} = 0.361, t(107) = 2.061, p = .042)$. The follow-up analyses of the *task type x robot genderedness* interaction effect (Fig. 2B) revealed that female robots were considered as significantly more suitable for stereotypical Female Tasks (FT) than stereotypical Male Tasks (MT) $(Diff_{FT-MT} = 0.581, t(432) = 5.974, p < .0001)$, neutral robots were perceived as significantly less suitable for stereotypical female than for stereotypical male tasks $(Diff_{FT-MT} = -0.434, t(466) = -4.465, p < .0001)$, while male robots were not considered as significantly more suitable for one type of task over the other $(Diff_{FT-MT} = 0.050, t(441) = 0.513, p = .608)$. As for the significant *task type x participant gender* interaction effect (Fig. 2C), the follow-up analyses revealed that men considered robots (averaged across perceived genders) as significantly more suitable for stereotypical female than for stereotypical male tasks $(Diff_{FT-MT} = 0.205, t(105) = 2.049, p = .0217)$, while women did not $(Diff_{FT-MT} = -0.073, t(104) = -0.848, p = .398)$.

5   Discussion

Answering **RQ1** and **RQ3**, we can state that the *robot genderedness does influence people's stereotyping both in terms of stereotypical traits and suitability for stereotypical tasks, but only for female robots.* Indeed, in this study, the male robots seem to be perceived as in-groups [12]. In fact, they did not elicit ambivalent stereotypes and were perceived as equally communal and agentic, and equally suited for stereotypical male and female tasks (reject **H1.2** and **H3.2**). The female robots, instead, were perceived as out-groups [12]. They elicited ambivalent stereotypes and were perceived as significantly more communal than agentic, and significantly more suited for stereotypical female than stereotypical male tasks (accept **H1.1** and **H3.1**). In Social Psychology, in-groups are the societal defaults, such as cisgender, middle-class, heterosexual men [12]. These defaults mostly attract positive emotions (i.e., admiration) and behavior (i.e., active facilitation) [6]. The out-groups, instead, elicit negative emotions and behavior, and are at risk of discrimination [6]. Since the ambivalent stereotypes attributed to female robots (higher communion than agency) are in line with the paternalistic stereotypes attributed to women (higher warmth than competence) [12], one could wonder whether female robots could attract the same biases: negative emotions (i.e., pity) and behaviors (i.e., passive facilitation) [6].

As for **RQ2** and **RQ4**, *participant gender did influence gender stereotyping, but only towards female robots, and more strongly for men than for women.* Women and men both attributed higher communion than agency to female robots. However, for men, the ambivalence was stronger than for women (partially accept **H2**). This influence of participant gender on the results was not present for male robots, and for task type (reject **H4**). This finding, which is only partially in line with [13], seems to capture a patriarchal view of society, as it shows that men carry stronger negative biases (i.e., paternalistic stereotypes) towards female robots, but women are not exempt from these biases either. A further result worth mentioning regards neutral robots. These robots, which tend to lack facial and surface look features or body manipulators [15], did elicit ambivalent stereotype but in a more stratified and concealed way than male and female robots. In fact, the ambivalence of the stereotypes they elicited mostly depended on the gender of the participant. *Men attributed neutral robots paternalistic stereotypes (higher communion than agency), whereas women attributed them envious stereotypes (higher agency than communion).* This finding is interesting as it seems to suggest that gender neutrality does not protect robots from harmful biases (paternalistic stereotypes elicit pity and passive facilitation, envious stereotypes elicit envy and passive harm [6]). Rather it exposes them to the ambivalent stereotypes that are the most relevant for the people observing (or interacting with) them.

5.1   Limitations

The main limitation of this study was the lack of a manipulation check for the robot genderedness. Adding the assessment of the robot genderedness to the study would have greatly increased its length, and probably revealed its goal. Hence, we decided to use the gender scores from the ROBO-GAP dataset which achieved high internal consistency and reliability [15] as proxy for a manipulation check. Another limitation of the study regards the use of only two participant genders in the analyses. In future work, we plan to replicate this research by including an equal number of men, women, and people identifying with genders beyond the binary. Moreover participants' knowledge of cultural gender stereotypes was not controlled for. Recruitment via Prolific allowed us to get a multicultural sample, but could also introduce bias. Lastly, we only studied the effects of robot genderedness as inferred from appearance cues in static images. Hence, our results might not generalize to situations in which the robot genderedness is manipulated using multimodal dynamic cues, such as voice.

6 Conclusions

The present study focused on understanding how robot genderedness and participant gender influence people's perceptions of a robot's stereotypical traits and suitability for stereotypical tasks. We discovered that people attribute paternalistic stereotypes to female robots, and that this ambivalent attribution is exacerbated in men. Moreover, we found out that participant gender affects the nature of the ambivalent stereotypes attributed to neutral robots. Men attribute them paternalistic stereotypes, whereas women attribute them envious stereotypes. This study shows how stubborn the ambivalent stereotypes affecting female robots are, and how mutable those affecting neutral robots can be.

References

1. Abele, A.E., Hauke, N., Peters, K., Louvet, E., Szymkow, A., Duan, Y.: Facets of the fundamental content dimensions: agency with competence and assertiveness-communion with warmth and morality. Front. Psychol. **7**, 1810 (2016)
2. Baayen, R., Davidson, D., Bates, D.: Mixed-effects modeling with crossed random effects for subjects and items. J. Mem. Lang. **59**(4), 390–412 (2008)
3. Bernotat, J., Eyssel, F., Sachse, J.: The (fe) male robot: how robot body shape impacts first impressions and trust towards robots. Int. J. Soc. Robot. **13**(3), 477–489 (2021)
4. Bryant, D., Borenstein, J., Howard, A.: Why should we gender? The effect of robot gendering and occupational stereotypes on human trust and perceived competency. In: Proceedings of the 2020 ACM/IEEE International Conference on Human-Robot Interaction, pp. 13–21 (2020)
5. Choi, N., Fuqua, D.R., Newman, J.L.: Exploratory and confirmatory studies of the structure of the bem sex role inventory short form with two divergent samples. Educ. Psychol. Measur. **69**(4), 696–705 (2009)
6. Cuddy, A.J., Fiske, S.T., Glick, P.: The bias map: behaviors from intergroup affect and stereotypes. J. Pers. Soc. Psychol. **92**(4), 631 (2007)
7. Cuddy, A.J., Fiske, S.T., Glick, P.: Warmth and competence as universal dimensions of social perception: the stereotype content model and the bias map. Adv. Exp. Soc. Psychol. **40**, 61–149 (2008)

8. Eyssel, F., Hegel, F.: (s)he's got the look: gender stereotyping of robots. J. Appl. Soc. Psychol. **42**(9), 2213–2230 (2012)

9. Eyssel, F., Kuchenbrandt, D., Hegel, F., De Ruiter, L.: Activating elicited agent knowledge: how robot and user features shape the perception of social robots. In: 2012 IEEE RO-MAN: The 21st IEEE International Symposium on Robot and Human Interactive Communication, pp. 851–857. IEEE (2012)

10. Fai, A.H.T., Cornelius, P.L.: Approximate f-tests of multiple degree of freedom hypotheses in generalized least squares analyses of unbalanced split-plot experiments. J. Stat. Comput. Simul. **54**(4), 363–378 (1996)

11. Fiske, S.T., Cuddy, A.J., Glick, P.: Universal dimensions of social cognition: warmth and competence. Trends Cogn. Sci. **11**(2), 77–83 (2007)

12. Fiske, S.T., Cuddy, A.J., Glick, P., Xu, J.: A model of (often mixed) stereotype content: competence and warmth respectively follow from perceived status and competition. In: Social Cognition, pp. 162–214. Routledge (2002)

13. Hentschel, T., Heilman, M.E., Peus, C.V.: The multiple dimensions of gender stereotypes: a current look at men's and women's characterizations of others and themselves. Front. Psychol. **10**, 11 (2019)

14. Parlangeli, O., Bracci, M., Marghigiani, E., Palmitesta, P., Guidi, S.: She's better at this, he's better at that. Gender role stereotypes in humanoid robots. In: 33rd European Conference on Cognitive Ergonomics (ECCE 2022), pp. 73–82. ACM, New York (2022)

15. Perugia, G., Guidi, S., Bicchi, M., Parlangeli, O.: The shape of our bias: perceived age and gender in the humanoid robots of the ABOT database. In: Proceedings of the 2022 ACM/IEEE International Conference on Human-Robot Interaction, HRI 2022, pp. 110–119. IEEE Press (2022)

16. Perugia, G., Lisy, D.: Robot's gendering trouble: a scoping review of gendering humanoid robots and its effects on HRI. arXiv preprint arXiv:2207.01130 (2022)

17. Perugia, G., Rossi, A., Rossi, S.: Gender revealed: evaluating the genderedness of Furhat's predefined faces. In: Li, H., et al. (eds.) ICSR 2021. LNCS (LNAI), vol. 13086, pp. 36–47. Springer, Cham (2021). https://doi.org/10.1007/978-3-030-90525-5_4

18. Phillips, E., Zhao, X., Ullman, D., Malle, B.F.: What is human-like? Decomposing robots' human-like appearance using the anthropomorphic robot (ABOT) database. In: Proceedings of the 2018 ACM/IEEE International Conference on Human-Robot Interaction, HRI 2018, pp. 105–113. ACM, New York (2018)

19. Rea, D.J., Wang, Y., Young, J.E.: Check your stereotypes at the door: an analysis of gender typecasts in social human-robot interaction. In: ICSR 2015. LNCS (LNAI), vol. 9388, pp. 554–563. Springer, Cham (2015). https://doi.org/10.1007/978-3-319-25554-5_55

20. Rollero, C., Glick, P., Tartaglia, S.: Psychometric properties of short versions of the ambivalent sexism inventory and ambivalence toward men inventory. TPM - Test. Psychomet. Methodol. Appl. Psychol. **21**(2), 149–159 (2014)

21. Spiel, K., Haimson, O.L., Lottridge, D.: How to do better with gender on surveys: a guide for HCI researchers. Interactions **26**(4), 62–65 (2019)

22. Stoeber, J.: The social desirability scale-17 (SDS-17): convergent validity, discriminant validity, and relationship with age. Eur. J. Psychol. Assess. **17**(3), 222–232 (2001)

23. Waytz, A., Cacioppo, J., Epley, N.: Who sees human? The stability and importance of individual differences in anthropomorphism. Perspect. Psychol. Sci. **5**(3), 219–232 (2010)

Effects of Realistic Appearance and Consumer Gender on Pet Robot Adoption

Jun San Kim[1] , Dahyun Kang[2] , JongSuk Choi[2] , and Sonya S. Kwak[2(✉)]

[1] KB Research, KB Financial Group Inc., Seoul 07241, Korea
[2] Center for Intelligent and Interactive Robotics, KIST, Seoul 02792, Korea
sonakwak@kist.re.kr

Abstract. This study investigates how lifelike appearance of pet robots affects the consumers' adoption. Traditionally, the uncanny valley hypothesis is commonly assumed in predicting the effects of robots' appearances. However, because this theory mainly applies to humanoids, we postulated that the effect of lifelikeness of pet robots on human perceptions of them might differ from what the theory expects. Thus, by adopting theories from marketing and consumer research, we hypothesized that pet robots with lifelike appearance would be preferred to pet robots with machinelike appearances. We also predicted that the positive effect of lifelike appearance would be reduced for female consumers. The experimental results confirmed the formulated hypotheses. That is, for male consumers, the lifelikeness of appearance positively affected the adoption, whereas for female consumers, such positive effects were not observed. The results of the study suggest that the effect of lifelikeness in appearance is more complex than what the uncanny valley hypothesis predicts. That is, for commercial pet robots, whose lifelike appearance may not provide any mortality or pathogen salience, lifelike appearance of robots with animal forms may inspire positive feelings in humans.

Keywords: Pet robot · Appearance design · Gender · Consumer adoption

1 Introduction

Companion animals and pets have long been comforting friends to humans. Consumer spending on the pet industry in the US alone was more than USD 69.5 billion in 2017 [1], and the global pet care market is expected to reach USD 202.6 billion by 2025 [2]. An important concern for robot developers is whether and to what extent pet robots may replace living animal pets. Pet robots certainly have the potential advantages of upgradability, not being subject to mortality, and ease of care or maintenance; however, they do not have the features of real living beings, such as a natural heartbeat, warmth, motion, and living appearance. As robotic technologies progressively evolve, today's pet robots are equipped with various functions to resemble real pets. However, it is not yet clear whether the lifelike appearance of pet robots will enhance their consumer

This work was supported by the Korea Institute of Science and Technology (KIST) Institutional Program under Grant 2E31581.

adoption. For example, over the past two decades, SONY produced various series of AIBOs with different levels of lifelikeness in appearance. The first version, ERS-111 in 1999, resembled a beagle and was made of plastic material. The second generation, ERS-210, was designed to resemble a lion cub. Similarly, ERS-220 was launched with a more machinelike appearance. In 2003, the third-generation ERS-7 was introduced with simple and curved lines, in the form of a sleek toy dog. In 2018, ERS-1000 was released, with a more realistic appearance than previous versions [3, 4].

In this paper, we refer to robots that resemble the appearance of an original animal as having a lifelike appearance. For example, TomBot [5] exhibits a realistic appearance and responds to human touch by wagging its tail and grunting. Meanwhile, we refer to machinelike pet robots as robots that have more machinelike appearances, being mostly made of metallic or plastic materials. For example, MarsCat [6] was developed with the aim of responding to humans, similar to a real cat. However, the plastic material and visible leg joints make it recognizable as a construct at first sight. In this article, we investigate how lifelike appearance affects consumers' adoption of pet robots. Traditionally, the effect of robots' lifelikeness on users' perception has been mostly explained by the uncanny valley hypothesis [7]. That is, highly realistic humanoid robots are less preferred than machinelike robots. However, we argue that this might not always be the case for other types of robots, such as zoomorphic pet robots for commercial use [8]. Previous research on the underlying cause of uncanny valley phenomena largely indicates that the phenomenon is based on people's perception of and reaction toward "unreal" humans. That is, a negative, uneasy feeling of aversion arises when people encounter a humanlike but nonhuman object, reminding them of death or possible infection or disease [9]. However, this is not the case with consumer pet robots. Thus, based on marketing research, we postulate that the effect of lifelike appearance on consumers' adoption of pet robots may differ from what might be expected based on the uncanny valley hypothesis.

The remainder of this paper is organized as follows. Section 2 briefly introduces theories regarding the effect of lifelikeness, including the uncanny valley hypothesis. Further, based on consumer theories, such as categorization, it presents the formulated hypotheses regarding the effect of lifelike appearance on consumer adoption of pet robots. Section 3 and 4 provide experimental procedures and results demonstrating that the hypotheses formulated are supported. Section 5 discusses the conclusion, including implications and suggestions for future works.

2   Theoretical Background

2.1   Uncanny Valley Hypothesis

Previous studies on the lifelikeness of robots mostly focused on similarity to humans. The representative hypothetical concept is the uncanny valley, coined by Mori [7]. Mori stated that having a human likeness would hinder people from forming positive attitudes toward a robot for a certain value range of similarity [10]. He explained this phenomenon with an exemplary case of a prosthetic hand, which seems real at first sight and can provoke negative feelings when people become aware that it is a nonliving object with cold and hard skin. In addition, he asserted that when a robot with humanlike appearance displays less humanlike movements, it could elicit creepy feelings [10]. Uncanny valley comes from the cognitive dissonance that arises when the tactical information or behavior of a robot does not meet the expectations generated by the robot's humanlike appearance [11]. Hence, he proposed an uncanny valley as explanation for the "eerie feeling" experienced in perceiving such constructions, resulting from the mismatch between communication cues. In accordance with this hypothesis, previous research in human-robot interaction (HRI) showed that a high level of human likeness in robots led to negative responses from humans. For example, Mathur and Reichling [12] showed that highly humanlike appearances of a robot led to aversive responses from users. In addition, Bartneck et al. [13] and MacDorman et al. [14] showed that extreme human likeness did not help users elicit positive implications regarding robots.

Researchers have attempted to comprehend the underlying mechanism of the uncanny valley hypothesis. Wang et al. [9] suggested that explanations for the hypothesis can be categorized into those based on perceptual processing and those based on cognitive processing. The perceptual processing explanation interprets the uncanny valley as an "automatic, stimulus-driven, and specialized" cognitive process that occurs early in a human's perception of the robot. Specifically, the pathogen avoidance hypothesis suggests that an uncanny valley phenomenon occurs because highly humanlike faces remind people of transmissible diseases [14, 15]. The mortality salience hypothesis suggests that highly humanlike, yet not quite human faces remind people of mortality, thus provoking a fear of death [16]. The evolutionary aesthetics perspective proposes that people may feel eeriness when faced with humanlike faces, which may vary widely from the common aesthetic criteria [17, 18]. Unlike perceptual processing explanations, cognitive processing explanations understand the phenomenon as "a broader and more general range of cognitive processing" that occurs later after perception of the object. Specifically, the violation of expectation hypothesis suggests that the uncanny feeling is elicited when a "human replica" that could form expectations for mankind fails to match these expectations [19, 20]. The categorical uncertainty hypothesis proposes that uncanny feelings occur when people face categorically ambiguous subjects [21]. All the above explanations, except for the categorical uncertainty hypothesis, are based on humanoids or human replicas. Thus, it is natural to suppose that human responses to lifelikeness of zoomorphic pet robots might arise differently than the uncanny valley hypothesis would suggest.

In line with the categorical uncertainty hypothesis, Ramey [22] argued that the uncanny valley hypothesis might not be specific to humanoids. To verify that the phenomenon could extend to nonhuman species, Steckenfinger and Ghazanfar [23] produced monkey faces with different render types, including real monkey faces, realistic and unrealistic synthetic agent faces, and compared people's preferences toward them. They found that the results were consistent with the uncanny valley hypothesis. That is, real or unrealistic monkey faces were preferred more than realistic ones. In addition, Yamada et al. [21] hypothesized that difficulty in object categorization could be related to uncanny valley hypotheses and that the effects of categorization difficulty would occur in nonhuman species as well. They validated this hypothesis by using rendered images of dog faces. However, we argue that given that a robot is a product to be sold on the market, consumers might perceive them differently. That is, we believe that consumers will evaluate zoomorphic pet robots differently than the general population, who may not understand or expect that such a robot is owned to be used for certain purposes, such as fulfilling unmet human needs [24].

2.2 Effect of Lifelike Appearance and Gender on the Adoption of Pet Robots

People seek the company of companion animals to avoid loneliness and feel better [25]. In addition, people perceive robotic dogs partially as technical artifacts and partially as resembling living pet dogs [26]. Melson et al. [26] mentioned that "the robotic dog was treated as a technological artifact that also embodied attributes of living animals, such as having mental states, being a social other, and having moral standing." Thus, we expect that people will buy robotic pets to lessen their loneliness and feel a sense of connection as well as for entertainment purposes [27].

Consumers formulate an evaluation of a product based on their expectations of its functions and features [28]. In categorizing a new product, consumers usually formulate expectations based on previous experiences with products of the same category [29]. It is well understood that product appearance is very important in consumers' categorization process [30]. That is, design elements of the product appearance are used by consumers to appropriately categorize the product. In addition, categorization of the product becomes more important when the product is ambiguous, that is, when the product is innovative or has aspects of more than two existing products [31, 32]. Pet robots have characteristics of animal pets and animal toys or stuffed animals. We presume that a pet robot with a realistic appearance, which often include fabrics or artificial fur, might be perceived by consumers more as real pets than robotic toys. We also presume that this will prompt them to associate expectations they have toward real pets with the robot product, such as mitigation of loneliness and increased sense of intimacy, as well as entertainment and fun. In contrast, pet robots with a machinelike appearance, which often consist of metallic or plastic materials, sometimes including LED eyes, are more related to electronic devices as a product category, so consumers may perceive them more as electronic toys than real pets. Thus, consumers might perceive them as providing more limited functions, including entertainment and enjoyment. By providing expectations regarding more sophisticated and advanced benefits, we believe that lifelike pet robots will be more accepted by consumers than machinelike pet robots. However, we predict that the positive effect of lifelikeness of pet robots will differ with gender.

In the field of HRI, gender differences have been an important factor in investigating the response of humans interacting with robots, and research has investigated the effects of gender on human perception of robots. They showed that women were more reluctant to accept robots compared to men [33, 34]. In addition, some studies show that men perceived robots as being more useful than women did [35, 36]. Moreover, studies by Strait et al. [37] showed that polite behavior from a humanoid robot improved the impression rating of female participants, whereas this effect was not observed among male participants. These previous studies show that male participants tend to prefer robots more than female participants do. However, these studies were limited to humanoid robots, and the effect of gender on the relationship between lifelike appearance and consumer acceptance has not been investigated to our knowledge. We investigated the effects of gender on the acceptance of pet robots with regard to the effect of robots' lifelike appearances. For this purpose, we adopted theories from consumer research, which investigated gender differences in perceiving and processing advertisements and marketing media content.

Gender differences regarding consumers' advertisement processing have long been examined by marketing researchers. For example, Meyers-Levy [38] showed that women were better at processing visual advertisements more comprehensively than men. In addition, Gilligan [39] and Krugman [40] showed that women were better at comprehending message claims in advertisements than male consumers. Moreover, Noseworthy et al. [41] found that women were better at finding inconsistencies in advertisement content. Thus, it is expected that women will be better at finding inconsistencies between visual information and product description in advertisements than men.

Kwak et al. [42] asserted that robots that resemble household appliances (i.e., object-oriented robots) are preferred over humanoids because they can meet consumer expectations better. That is, as Oliver [43] indicated, a correspondence between expectations of the product's features and its actual features leads to heightened satisfaction with and evaluation of the product. As women are expected to find inconsistencies in advertisements better than men, upon seeing images of pet robots with lifelike appearances, female consumers will easily notice the discrepancies between their expectations of real pets and the product description of the advertisement that shows that they are actually robots. This will mitigate the positive effect of lifelike appearance on the adoption of pet robots. Thus, we predict that the positive impact of lifelikeness of pet robots will be evident only for male consumers and will not be evident for female consumers. Our predictions can be formally described as follows.

H1: For male participants, pet robots with lifelike appearance will elicit higher evaluations than pet robots with machinelike appearance.

H2: For male participants, pet robots with lifelike appearance will elicit higher purchase intention than pet robots with machinelike appearance.

H3: For male participants, pet robots with lifelike appearance will elicit higher willingness to pay than pet robots with machinelike appearance.

H4: For female participants, the effect of lifelike appearance on the evaluation, purchase intention, and willingness to pay of pet robots will not be evident.

3   Method

We conducted a two-appearance type (lifelike vs. machinelike) within-participants experiment to verify the effect of lifelike appearance on the adoption of pet robots. We recruited 89 Korean participants (37 men, 52 women). They were between 21 and 50 years old ($M = 34.96$, $SD = 7.542$).

3.1   Stimuli

In the field of marketing, fictitious advertisements are widely used to examine consumer acceptance of new products (e.g., [28, 32]). Thus, we created two fictitious advertisements for puppy robots with differing appearances: lifelike (Fig. 1) and machinelike. The advertisement consisted of a robot image and descriptive text. An image of AIBO developed by SONY [3] was used in a machinelike pet robot advertisement. For the lifelike pet robot, we chose an image of a puppy that resembled the image of AIBO used in the machinelike condition and then modified it (e.g., it has the same white color but black ears). We removed its wrinkles, unified the color of the fur, trimmed the joints, and erased the claws to give participants the feeling that the dog is actually an artifact.

The description of the robot in the advertisement is as follows:

- Meet Shorty - it wants to be friends!
- Shorty plays with you. Shorty loves to be petted, and knows how to follow and do tricks.
- Shorty wants to be your friend. Shorty loves being petted, and likes to follow you and have fun at home.
- Shorty learns. With a built-in personality engine, it learns likes and dislikes, and also shows real emotions in interacting with people.
- Shorty recognizes you. Equipped with a security function, it barks when a stranger appears.
- Shorty recharges itself when it is tired. You do not have to worry about feeding or cleanup.

Meet Shorty - it wants to be friends!

- Shorty plays with you. Shorty loves to be petted, and knows how to follow and do tricks.
- Shorty wants to be your friend. Shorty loves being petted, and likes to follow you and have fun at home.
- Shorty learns. With a built-in personality engine, it learns likes and dislikes, and also shows real emotions in interacting with people.
- Shorty recognizes you. Equipped with a security function, it barks when a stranger appears.
- Shorty recharges itself when it is tired. You do not have to worry about feeding or cleanup.

Fig. 1. Ad stimuli for lifelike appearance.

3.2 Measures

As a manipulation check measure, we adopted items for measuring animacy suggested by Bartneck et al. [44] because the measure was developed for the lifelikeness of the robot.

We intentionally did not adopt items related to anthropomorphism because they measure the robot's human likeness. To investigate the effect of lifelikeness on the adoption of pet robots, we asked participants to evaluate the overall product [45, 46] and purchase intention [47] on a 7-point Likert scale. Moreover, we asked about their willingness to pay for the robot (Table 1). Although we asked the participants to respond with a value in Korean won, we report below the value translated in USD. To eliminate the effect of the knowledge regarding the robot AIBO on the results, we asked the participants whether they have any experience seeing the picture of the robot before. Further, we asked about the participants' expertise on robotic products by averaging three seven-point items ($\alpha =$ .870), including "Indicate how interested you are in robotic products in general" (1: not at all interested, 7: very interested), "Indicate your knowledge of robotic products" (1: not at all knowledgeable, 7: very knowledgeable), and "Indicate your expertise regarding robotic products" (1: very novice, 7: very expert). Finally, the participants' demographic measures including age and gender were provided.

Table 1. Reliabilities of scales.

Scale	Items
Product evaluation (Cronbach's $\alpha =$ .947)	"Please rate your evaluation toward the product (1: very bad/ 7: very good, 1: very poor/ 7: excellent, 1: very negative/ 7: very positive, 1: very unfavorable/7: very favorable)"
Purchase Intention (Cronbach's $\alpha =$ .977)	"Please rate how likely you are to purchase the product (1: Not at all/ 7: Very likely)" "Please rate how much do you really want to purchase the product (1: Not at all/ 7: Very much)"
Willingness to pay	Please write the maximum amount of money you are willing to pay for the product in Korean Won (_____)

3.3 Procedure

The participants signed a consent form after hearing a brief explanation of the experiment. They read a fictitious advertisement of a pet robot and then evaluated the robot. The participants read the lifelike and machinelike pet robot flyers in counterbalanced random order. After evaluating the robots, the participants answered the demographic questions.

4 Results

We eliminated 19 participants who responded that they had already seen AIBO in the advertisement, which left 70 participants (31 men and 39 women). The participants rated the lifelike condition as more animated than the machinelike condition ($M_{lifelike} = 5.23$, $SD = 1.27$ vs. $M_{machinelike} = 4.06$, $SD = 1.59$; $p < 0.001$, $t (69) = 7.338$). Thus, the lifelikeness of the pet robot is perceived as intended. Participants' age and expertise on robots did not affect the results and thus are not discussed further.

For male participants, there were significant effects of lifelike appearance on the adoption of pet robots. Male participants evaluated the pet robot in lifelike condition more positively than the robot in machinelike condition in terms of product evaluation ($M_{lifelike}$ = 5.38, SD = 0.99 vs. $M_{machinelike}$ = 4.87, SD = 1.10; p = 0.018, t (30) = 2.511). They showed higher purchase intention toward the robot in lifelike condition than the robot in machinelike condition ($M_{lifelike}$ = 4.24, SD = 1.50 vs. $M_{machinelike}$ = 3.60, SD = 1.57; p = 0.004, t (30) = 3.107). They were also willing to pay a larger amount to purchase the lifelike pet robot than the machinelike pet robot ($M_{lifelike}$ = \$437, SD = .777 vs. $M_{machinelike}$ = \$253, SD = .353; p = 0.039, t (30) = 2.154). Thus, H1, H2, and H3 were all verified by the data. For female participants, there were no significant effects of appearance types on product evaluation ($M_{lifelike}$ = 5.21, SD = 1.44 vs. $M_{machinelike}$ = 5.15, SD = 1.12; p = 0.796, t (38) = 0.260), purchase intention ($M_{lifelike}$ = 4.10, SD = 1.99 vs. $M_{machinelike}$ = 3.74, SD = 1.59; p = 0.226, t (38) = 1.231, and willingness to pay for the robots ($M_{lifelike}$ = \$409, SD = .482 vs. $M_{machinelike}$ = \$291, SD = .272; p = 0.061, t (38) = 1.933). Thus, as we predicted in H4, any positive effect of lifelikeness on reactions to the pet robot and expressed willingness to adopt did not appear in women's responses (Fig. 2).

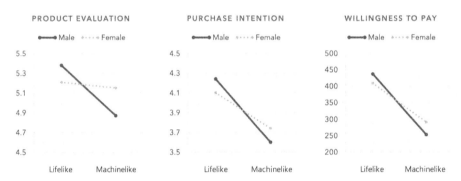

Fig. 2. Consumer acceptance for pet robot.

5   Discussion

5.1   Summary and Implications

This study investigated the effect of lifelike appearance on consumer attitudes to the adoption of pet robots. In this experiment, we observed that the effect of lifelike appearance differed with gender. That is, for male consumers, the lifelikeness of appearance positively affected the adoption, whereas for female consumers, such positive effects were not observed.

Although researchers in HRI have studied the effect of lifelikeness on humanlike robots, it remains unclear whether lifelike appearance affects the adoption of other types of robots, such as animal-like consumer pet robots. In this study, we postulated that the traditional uncanny valley effect might not be applicable for consumer pet robots because it originates from the fact that robots resemble humans. In addition, we suggested that consumers' categorizations upon encountering the appearance of pet robots and their expectation of the robots' functionalities would be crucial for their attitudes towards adoption. Based on theories from consumer research, we postulated that consumers would prefer pet robots with lifelike appearance to pet robots with machinelike appearance because they would perceive the lifelike versions as having more varied and deeper features, such as companionship and a sense of emotional intimacy, as well as entertainment and enjoyment. We also predicted that the effect of lifelike appearance would differ according to gender. Based on the previous study results on the consumers' reactions to advertisement, we postulated that women would more clearly notice the discrepancies between the robot's appearances and advertisement claims, thus eliminating the positive effect of lifelikeness for pet robots.

The results of the study suggest that the effect of lifelikeness in appearance is more complex than what the uncanny valley hypothesis predicts. That is, although the uncanny valley hypothesis is supported by various empirical results (e.g., [12, 13]), for commercial pet robots, whose lifelike appearance may not provide any mortality or pathogen salience, lifelike appearance of robots with animal forms may inspire positive feelings in humans, particularly for male consumers. By adopting theories from marketing and consumer research, the results of this research help to shed light on the complex nature regarding the effect of lifelike appearance. We believe that this kind of multidisciplinary approach will help further understanding of the nature of human and robot interaction.

Our study results contribute to the research on the effect of gender in HRI. Specifically, our conceptualization that women's superior visual processing compared to men may have an impact on the effect of lifelike appearance may shed light on the reason why men prefer robots more than women do (e.g., [33, 34]). Nomura et al. [33] found that women showed more negative responses toward mechanical humanoid robots than men. The results of the study suggest that women might be more sensitive to unnatural appearance of mechanical humanoid robots than men, causing their negative responses toward robots. More research based on the theories in the fields of social psychology and consumer research might help enlighten the nature of gender effects in HRI.

For pet robot developers, the results of the study imply that consumers may prefer more realistic robotic pets compared to machinelike versions. This finding may help consumer roboticists develop improved design approaches for the appearance of companion robots. For example, SONY might be able to improve its AIBO sales if its next version were launched with a more lifelike appearance. The developers need to keep in mind, however, that the positive effect of lifelike appearance might be limited only to male consumers. Thus, their strategy to harness lifelike appearance should be accompanied with a targeted marketing strategy aimed at male consumers.

5.2 Limitations and Further Study

Although we showed that lifelike appearance of pet robots positively affected consumers' attitudes toward adoption for men, this study does have some limitations. First, our experiments were conducted with Korean participants only, which implies that cultural differences may have affected the results. For example, in Japan, consumers tend to be more emotionally connected to pet robots than consumers of other countries (e.g.,

[48]). Thus, the positive impact of lifelike appearance may be stronger for Japanese consumers than for consumers from other countries. Second, in this study, we adopted two different pet robot stimuli; however, more stimuli can provide robustness of results. These limitations need to be addressed along with the future research outlined below.

First, in the future, the underlying mechanism regarding how the appearance of the pet robots affects adoption intentions moderated by gender should be further investigated. We postulated that the range and depth of the perceived functionalities of the pet robot were the causes of this effect. In this regard, how consumers formulate expectations regarding pet robots according to their appearances need to be assessed in the understanding of this mechanism.

Second, we manipulated only the appearances and not the functions or motions of the robot. However, the effect of the lifelikeness of the robot's functions, that is, how much a robot can imitate a real pet in its behavior, need to be investigated in the future. That is, an investigation using the real pet robots will further unveil the effects of the appearances of the pet robots.

Third, the results showed that the effects of the appearance of pet robots differed by gender. However, other factors, such as expertise and age, may also influence the effect. Although our study showed that the participants' expertise on robotic products did not affect the results, the possible effect of expertise in pets and interest to pet animals should be explored in the future. Further, we focused on adult consumers who were assumed to have purchasing power, and age did not affect the result in this study. However, younger people may react differently to lifelike appearance. For example, Tung [49] showed that male children participants showed a favorable attitude toward a mechanical robot more than realistic robots, whereas female children participants showed the opposite responses. Although the study was focused on humanoids, its results suggest different results to those of the current study with regard to children. Children may hardly perceive the differences arising from the expected features associated with appearance of the pet robot and its actual features, leading to differing effects of lifelike appearance of pet robots. Investigation of such effects may become another fruitful future research avenue.

Moreover, although in this study we investigated the effect of the appearance of pet robots on consumers' attitudes towards their adoption, the effect on the more traditional HRI variables, such as empathy, might well be investigated also. Such future research may reveal further the complex reality of the effects of robot's lifelike resemblance to various animals on consumer adoption and user perception of companion and pet robots. As the results of this study show, additional research from the perspective of consumer theories is needed in the field of HRI to clarify the various dynamics of user responses toward robots, particularly when they become products.

Acknowledgment. This work is supported by the KIST Institutional Program (2E31581).

References

1. Wolf, A.: The world pet markets trend: Countries experiencing growth in the pet industry. The Balance Careers, 2020 (January 2020), https://www.thebalancecareers.com/the-world-pet-market-booms-2660629, last accessed 2020/9/28

2. Grand View Research, Pet care market size worth $202.6 billion by 2025 | CAGR: 4.9%, 2018 (March 2018), https://www.grandviewresearch.com/press-release/global-pet-care-market, last accessed 2020/9/28
3. Sony Aibo. History, 2020, http://www.sony-aibo.co.uk/history/, last accessed 2020/9/28
4. Sony Aibo ERS-1000, 2020, https://www.sony-aibo.com/aibo-models/sony-aibo-ers-1000/, last accessed 2020/9/30
5. Tombot, 2020, https://tombot.com/, last accessed 2020/9/28
6. Elephant Robotics, MarsCat: A bionic cat, a home robot, 2020. https://shop.elephantrobo tics.com/collections/robotic-cat/products/marscat-a-bionic-cat-a-home-robot, last accessed 2020/9/28
7. Mori, M.: The uncanny valley (MacDorman, K. F. & Minato, T., Trans. 2005). Energy 7, 33–35 (1970)
8. Fong, T., Nourbakhsh, I., Dautenhahn, K.: A survey of socially interactive robots. Robot. Auton. Syst. 42(3–4), 143–166 (2003)
9. Wang, S., Lilienfeld, S.O., Rochat, P.: The uncanny valley: existence and explanations. Rev. Gen. Psychol. 19(4), 393–407 (2015)
10. Caballar, R.D.: What is the uncanny valley? IEEE Spectrum, 2019 (November 6, 2019), https:// spectrum.ieee.org/automaton/robotics/humanoids/what-is-the-uncanny-valley, last accessed 2020/9/30
11. Suchman, L.: Human-Machine Reconfigurations: Plans and Situated Actions. 2nd ed. Learning in Doing: Social, Cognitive and Computational Perspectives, Cambridge University Press, Cambridge (2006)
12. Mathur, M.B., Reichling, D.B.: Navigating a social world with robot partners: a quantitative cartography of the uncanny valley. Cognition 146, 22–32 (2016)
13. Bartneck, C., Kanda, T., Ishiguro, H., Hagita, N.: Is the uncanny valley an uncanny cliff? In: Proceedings of the 16th IEEE International Symposium on Robot and Human Interactive Communication (RO-MAN), pp. 368–373. Jeju Island, South Korea (2007)
14. MacDorman, K.F., Green, R.D., Ho, C.-C., Koch, C.T.: Too real for comfort? Uncanny responses to computer generated faces. Comput. Hum. Behav. 25(3), 695–710 (2009)
15. MacDorman, K.F., Ishiguro, H.: The uncanny advantage of using androids in cognitive and social science research. Interact. Stud. 7(3), 297–337 (2006)
16. Ho, C.-C., MacDorman, K.F., Pramono, Z.A.D.: Human emotion and the uncanny valley: A GLM, MDS, and Isomap analysis of robot video ratings. In: Proceedings of the 3rd ACM/IEEE International Conference on Human-Robot Interaction (HRI), pp. 169–176. Amsterdam, The Netherlands (2008)
17. Hanson, D.: Expanding the aesthetic possibilities for humanoid robots. In: Proceedings of the 5th IEEE-RAS International Conference on Humanoid Robots, pp. 24–31. Tsukuba, Japan (2005)
18. Moosa, M.M., Ud-Dean, S.M.M.: Danger avoidance: an evolutionary explanation of uncanny valley. Biol. Theory 5(1), 12–14 (2010)
19. Mitchell, W.J., Szerszen Sr, K.A., Lu, A.S., Schermerhorn, P.W., Scheutz, M., MacDorman, K.F.: A mismatch in the human realism of face and voice produces an uncanny valley. i-Perception 2(1), 10–12 (2011)
20. Saygin, A.P., Chaminade, T., Ishiguro, H., Driver, J., Frith, C.: The thing that should not be: predictive coding and the uncanny valley in perceiving human and humanoid robot actions. Soc. Cogn. Affect. Neurosci. 7(4), 413–422 (2012)
21. Yamada, Y., Kawabe, T., Ihaya, K.: Categorization difficulty is associated with negative evaluation in the "uncanny valley" phenomenon. Jpn. Psychol. Res. 55(1), 20–32 (2013)

22. Ramey, C.H.: An inventory of reported characteristics for home computers, robots, and human beings: Applications for android science and the uncanny valley. In: Proceedings of the ICCS/CogSci-2006 Long Symposium 'Toward Social Mechanisms of Android Science'. Vancouver, Canada (2006)

23. Steckenfinger, S.A., Ghazanfar, A.A.: Monkey visual behavior falls into the uncanny valley. Proc. Natl. Acad. Sci. **106**(43), 18362–18366 (2009)

24. Kotler, P., Armstrong, G.: Principles of Marketing. 14th ed. Pearson Education Limited, Edinburgh (2012)

25. Staats, S., Wallace, H., Anderson, T.: Reasons for companion animal guardianship (pet ownership) from two populations. Soc. Anim. **16**(3), 279–291 (2008)

26. Melson, G.F., Kahn, P.H., Jr., Beck, A., Friedman, B.: Robotic pets in human lives: implications for the human–animal bond and for human relationships with personified technologies. J. Soc. Issues **65**(3), 545–567 (2009)

27. Suzuki, N., Yamamoto, Y.: Pursuing entertainment aspects of SONY AIBO quadruped robots. In: Proceedings of the 4th IEEE International Conference on Modeling, Simulation and Applied Optimization (ICMSAO), pp. 1–5. Kuala Lumpur, Malaysia (2011)

28. Moreau, C.P., Markman, A.B., Lehmann, D.R.: "What is it?" Categorization flexibility and consumers' responses to really new products. J. Consum. Res. **27**(4), 489–498 (2001)

29. Sujan, M., Bettman, J.R.: The effects of brand positioning strategies on consumers' brand and category perceptions: some insights from schema research. J. Mark. Res. **26**(4), 454–467 (1989)

30. Kreuzbauer, R., Malter, A.J.: Embodied cognition and new product design: changing product form to influence brand categorization. J. Prod. Innov. Manag. **22**(2), 165–176 (2005)

31. Gregan-Paxton, J., Hoeffler, S., Zhao, M.: When categorization is ambiguous: factors that facilitate the use of a multiple category inference strategy. J. Consum. Psychol. **15**(2), 127–140 (2005)

32. Kim, J.S., Hahn, M., Yoon, Y.: The moderating role of personal need for structure on the evaluation of incrementally new products versus really new products. Psychol. Mark. **32**(2), 144–161 (2015)

33. Nomura, T., Kanda, T., Suzuki, T., Kato, K.: Prediction of human behavior in human-robot interaction using psychological scales for anxiety and negative attitudes toward robots. IEEE Trans. Rob. **24**(2), 442–451 (2008)

34. Nomura, T., Suzuki, T., Kanda, T., Kato, K.: Measurement of negative attitudes toward robots. Interact. Stud. **7**(3), 437–454 (2006)

35. Kuo, I.H., Rabindran, J.M., Broadbent, E., Lee, Y.I., Kerse, N., Stafford, R.M.Q., MacDonald, B.A.: Age and gender factors in user acceptance of healthcare robots. In: Proceedings of the 18th IEEE International Symposium on Robot and Human Interactive Communication (RO-MAN), pp. 214–219. Toyama, Japan (2009)

36. Lin, C.H., Liu, E.Z.F., Huang, Y.Y.: Exploring parents' perceptions towards educational robots: Gender and socio-economic differences. Br. J. Edu. Technol. **43**(1), E31–E34 (2011)

37. Strait, M., Briggs, P., Scheutz, M.: Gender, more so than age, modulates positive perceptions of language-based human-robot interactions. In: Proceedings of the 4th International Symposium on New Frontiers in Human-Robot Interaction, Canterbury, UK (2015)

38. Meyers-Levy, J.: Gender differences in information processing: A selectivity interpretation. Ph.D. dissertation. Northwestern University (1986)

39. Gilligan, C.: In a different voice: psychological theory and women's development. Harvard University Press, Cambridge, Massachusetts (1993)

40. Krugman, H.E.: The learning of consumer preference. J. Mark. **26**(2), 31–33 (1962)

41. Noseworthy, T.J., Cotte, J., Lee, S.H.: The effects of ad context and gender on the identification of visually incongruent products. J. Consum. Res. **38**(2), 358–375 (2011)

42. Kwak, S.S., Kim, J.S., Choi, J.J.: The effects of organism-versus object-based robot design approaches on the consumer acceptance of domestic robots. Int. J. Soc. Robot. **9**(3), 359–377 (2017)
43. Oliver, R.L.: A cognitive model of the antecedents and consequences of satisfaction decisions. J. Mark. Res. **17**(4), 460–469 (1980)
44. Bartneck, C., Kulić, D., Croft, E., Zoghbi, S.: Measurement instruments for the anthropomorphism, animacy, likeability, perceived intelligence, and perceived safety of robots. Int. J. Soc. Robot. **1**(1), 71–81 (2009)
45. Herzenstein, M., Posavac, S.S., Brakus, J.J.: Adoption of new and really new products: the effects of self-regulation systems and risk salience. J. Mark. Res. **44**(2), 251–260 (2007)
46. Zhao, M., Hoeffler, S., Dahl, D.W.: The role of imagination- focused visualization on new product evaluation. J. Mark. Res. **46**(1), 46–55 (2009)
47. Zhao, M., Hoeffler, S., Zauberman, G.: Mental simulation and product evaluation: the affective and cognitive dimensions of process versus outcome simulation. J. Mark. Res. **48**(5), 827–839 (2011)
48. Burch, J.: In Japan, a Buddhist funeral service for robot dogs, National Geographic, 2018 (May 25, 2018), https://www.nationalgeographic.com/travel/destinations/asia/japan/in-japan--a-buddhist-funeral-service-for-robot-dogs/, last accessed 2020/9/30
49. Tung, F.-W.: Influence of gender and age on the attitudes of children towards humanoid robots. In: Proceedings of the 14th Annual ACM/IEEE International Conference on Human-Computer Interaction (HCI), pp. 637–646. Orlando, FL, USA (2011)

The Reason for an Apology Matters for Robot Trust Repair

Russell Perkins[(✉)], Zahra Rezaei Khavas, Kalvin McCallum,
Monish Reddy Kotturu, and Paul Robinette

University of Massachusetts, Lowell, MA 01854, USA
{russell_perkins,zahra_rezaeikhavas,kalvin_mccallum}@student.uml.edu,
paul_robinette@uml.edu

Abstract. Recent advances in the areas of human-robot interaction (HRI) and robot autonomy are changing the world. Today robots are used in a variety of applications. People and robots work together in human autonomous teams to accomplish tasks that, separately, cannot be easily accomplished. Trust between robots and humans in teams is vital to task completion and effective team cohesion. For the optimal performance and safety of human teammates, their level of trust should be adjusted to the performance of the robotic system. The method of adjusting levels of human trust by a robot is called trust calibration. The cost of poor trust calibration in HRI, is at a minimum, low performance, and at higher levels it causes human injury or critical task failures. A robot is able to calibrate trust through policies that use trust calibration cues (TCCs). Verbal cues are often used to help calibrate trust. In this experiment we test the difference between two verbal TCCs, an apology and a denial. Both of which were meant to repair trust that the robot lost during the course of a search and rescue teaming situation. This study included 219 participants whom were spilt across 6 search and rescue (S&R) simulations. The simulations were composed of two different multi-round interaction games to study the effectiveness of competence violations and moral violations were created to simulate these different trust violations. While most of the TCCs were shown to be ineffective at significantly increasing the amount of trust in the robot after a trust violations. The use of a apology when the robot was being selfish was shown to be effective.

Keywords: Human robot interaction (HRI) · Trust calibration · Trust repair · Human robot collaboration

1 Introduction

Today, humans regularly interact with intelligent technology thorough devices like Amazon Alexa, smart thermometers, and smart smoke detectors. With the advent of vacuum cleaner robots, people interact with robots on a daily basis [1].

Supported by the AI Caring Institute.

In addition to household robots, robots have been integrated into first responder and military teams [2]. With this integration not only is there a need for research into how robots can become effective teammates but how they can increase the cohesion and effectiveness of their teams. The key to being an effective robotic teammate is trust. This is because robot performance is related to trust [3].

The three classes of factors that influence trust in HRI are, human-related, robot-related and environmental factors [3]. Trust is defined as *"a belief held by the trustor that the trustee will act in a manner that mitigates the trustor's risk in a situation in which the trustor has put its outcomes at risk"*, ch56Wagner2011. All definitions of trust incorporate whether robot's actions and behaviors correspond to human's interest [5].

When a robot does something that reduces its human teammates level of trust, it is called a trust violation [6]. Trust has been found to be multidimensional, divided between two general ideas of trust [7]. The first idea of trust is one of capability, performance and reliability. The second idea of trust is associated with integrity, morals and benevolence and is generally referred to as Affective Trust [8,9]. It makes sense that trust violations would break down along these same ideas, for this paper we are going to refer to them as performance trust violations and moral trust violations. An moral trust violation is when a trustee intentionally does something to place the trustor's outcomes at risk. A performance violation is when a trustee incorrectly performs or fails to perform the task [10].

Trust calibration is the method in which a robot helps a human to maintain a level of trust that is in line with these capabilities. The goal of calibration is to prevent the humans from ending up in a state of over-trust or under trust. Over-trust is when a person believes that the robot can accomplish something that is outside of its capabilities. Under-trust is when a person does not believe the robot can accomplish tasks for which is capable [6,11,12]. Trust calibration relies of understanding two states, over-trust and under-trust [13]. For a robot to understand what trust state it is in it must do so by determining the expected value of the humans police (π^H) [14,15]. In our game the (π^H) is determined by combination of the successes and failures of the robot and the personality of the human teammate [16].

Trust calibration uses two methods depending on what state of trust the human teammate is in, repair and dampening [6]. If a person is in a state of over-trust then the robot can reduce the amount of trust through trust dampening. If the person is in a state of under-trust then the trust repair method is used to increase the person trust. These methods are interventions that take the form of trust calibration cues (TCCs) [6].

2   Related Work

Trust calibration cues can be verbal, visual, audible, physical or a combination of any of these [17]. There is some research concentrated on the effectiveness of different types of TCCs in different situations. Robinette et al. shows that a robot that uses anthropomorphic gestures is more effective than having a sign in emergency situations [18]. Okumura et al. shows that verbal cues are more effective than audible and visual cues [19].

The use of TCCs has been studied with robots as well as self deriving cars. The use of apologies has been one of the most studied type of verbal TCC [20–23]. Researchers have compared the use of apologies and denials and have found that in the case of self driving cars apologies are more effective [20]. In a study with 319 participants in a simulated office evacuation scenario, a robot apologizing for its mistake, promising to do better in the future, and providing additional reasons to trust it was effective was effective when the robot asked the participants to trust it again, not right after the mistake [24].

In a human-human experiment the use of apologising with internal and external attributions was used after competence and integrity based violations. This study shows that an external attribution is more effective at repairing integrity violations and that apologies with internal attributions are more effective at repairing competence trust violations [11]. These lead to our first hypotheses *(H1) An apology with an internal attribution will be more effective at repairing performance trust violations than moral trust violations.* In experiments with a robot playing a game with a human participant is was observed that the use of a denial after an integrity violation cause the participant to retaliate against the robot [22]. These lead to our second hypothesis *(H2) a robot using a denial to repair a moral violation will experience more retaliation than when it uses an apology.* and *(H3) An apology repair will be more effective than a denial for moral trust violations.*

3   Experimental Setup

3.1   Game Design

To test our hypothesis we designed an online game conducted with participants from Mechanical Turk. The game is a simulation of a search and rescue (S&R) scenario where a human and a simulated robot move through a simulated building to identify targets. An image of the game screen is shown in Fig. 1. The game was designed to take a participant between 20 to 30 min to complete.

There are two different scores, a team score (TS) and a personal score (PS). The objective that is given to the human player is to maximize the TS. There are thee different targets, gold stars which are worth add 100 points to the TS, red circles which subtract 100 points from the TS and pink triangles which subtract 100 from the TS and adds 100 points to the (PS). Each agent has a predefined area of discovery which are meant to simulate two separate areas of a building. When the agents find a target, they can choose to select it which increments the score by the previously described scores. An image of the game score screen is shown in Fig. 2.

For the robot, selecting a gold target is meant to reinforce its perceived competence from its human counterpart. Conversely, when the robot selects a

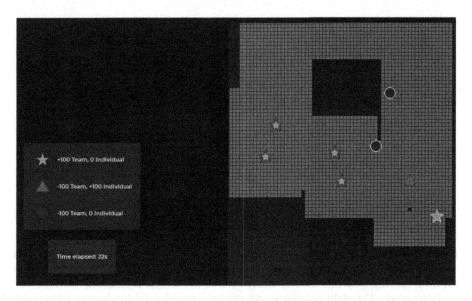

Fig. 1. The S&R scenario game screen. The search area is on the right. The scores for each target are displayed on the left along with the elapsed time.

red target it is meant to decrease its perceived competence. The pink targets were created to give each agent the option to execute a selfish act. We consider a selfish act a moral trust violation. For the robot, the selection of a pink target meant not to reduce the perceived competence but instead to negatively impact the warmth of the robot. In other words the robot moves from competent and helpful to competent and harmful.

The game began with a video tutorial on how to play the game as well as an explanation of the target and point system. After the video tutorial there was an interactive session where they could move their icon on the map and select targets. After the video and the interactive tutorial the participants were given a short 2 question quiz to assess their understanding of the game. If they answered the question incorrectly they were returned to the video tutorial. If they answered the quiz correctly the S&R scenario began.

The S&R scenario consists of 13 rounds. Each round begins with each agent searching the building for 30 s. At the end of the search time the robot tells the person that it has completed the search and asks if the person would like to integrate the targets it found into the over all score. This is a blind decision for the person because they do not know what the robot has found and can only rely on the performance of the prior rounds. The blind decision is used to reinforce the idea that the robot and the person are search different areas of the building and cannot see what each other is doing. If the person does not want to integrate the targets the can choose to discard them The decision to integrate the robots scores represents that the person trusts the robot and the act of discarding the information represents that the person does not trust the robot. After the person

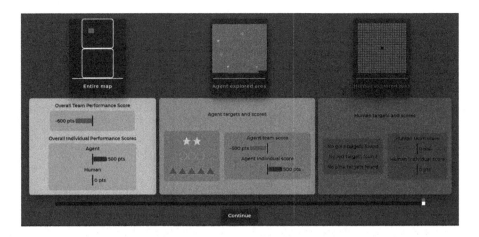

Fig. 2. The end of the round score screen. The column on the left displays the total searched area as well as the overall team and personal scores. The middle column shows the area that has been searched by the robot and the targets it collected as well as the resulting score. The right column shows the area revealed by the human participant and there score from the previous round.

makes the decision to integrate or discard the score, the human will be able to see the score and targets gained by robot in this round.

After the person sees the robots scores they are presented with three questions called end of the round (EOR) questions. The questions are a 7 point Likert scale which asked the participant to rate the robots performance and their ability as a teammate.

There were two different sequences of targets and scores used in this experiment. All games consisted of the same positive scores and number of gold targets for rounds 1-5 and rounds 10-13. To test the effect of TCCs of performance trust rounds 6-9 had negative TS with the same amount of red targets selected by the robot. The sequence of scores and targets is shown in Table 1. To test the effect of TCCs on moral violations the second set of games had the same negative TS and positive PS with the robot selecting the same number of pink targets in each round. The scores for the robot were predetermined so that the conditions would be the same for every participant. The sequence of targets and scores is shown in Table 1.

There were two different TCCs that were tested in this experiment. A denial where the robot stated that they would not have chosen the target that was shown because it would negatively affect.

I wasn't selecting [target] because I didn't want to negatively impact the team score. I don't know what happened.

The other TCC was an apology where the robot promised that it would not make the error again. The apology contained an internal attribution where the robot admitted it was its fault.

I'm sorry I selected [target]. I thought they were [another target]. It's my fault. It won't happen again.

The apology and the denial were tested on both the moral violation game and the performance violation game. The complete flow of the game is shown in Fig. 3.

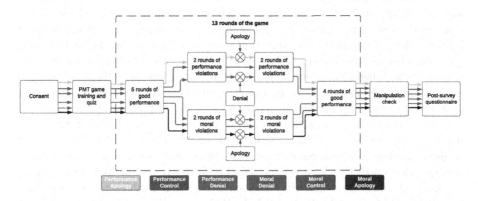

Fig. 3. The experiment begins with the participants completing the consent form. The participants then view the tutorial and take a quiz. The game begins with 5 rounds of good performance by the robot and then it begins to make trust violations. For the control experiments there are not TCCs used and they experience 4 rounds of either moral or performance violations. An apology and a denial are added in between the second and third round of trust violations for both the moral violations and the performance violations. After the violations portion of the game the participants experience 4 more rounds of good performance. At the conclusion of the game all players conduct the post game survey and the manipulations check.

Table 1. Performance and Moral Trust Game

Round	1	2	3	4	5	6	7	8	9	10	11	12	13
Circle	0	0	0	0	0	0	0	0	0	0	0	0	0
Triangle	0	0	0	0	0	2	2	1	3	0	0	0	0
Star	1	1	2	1	2	0	0	0	0	1	1	2	2
Individual score	0	0	0	0	0	200	200	100	300	0	0	0	0
Team Score	100	100	200	100	200	-200	-200	-100	-300	100	100	200	200

3.2   Recruitment and Compensation

We recruited 480 participants for the PMT game. We used the Amazon Mechanical Turk platform and posted the study as a Human Intelligence Task (HIT). We set the eligibility of participants with three criteria.

1. Participants must be at least 18 years old.
2. Participants must live in the United States.
3. Participants need to have at least a 95% HIT approval rating for the last 1000 HITs. Participants were payed $4 for completing the game.

To eliminate participants that were not paying attention to the games or were arbitrarily making decisions we used a multiple choice manipulation questions at the end of the game. The participants were asked to select the number 3 from a mix of numbers. This question was embedded in the end of the game questionnaire and made to look like the other questions. The data from the participants who failed to answer the manipulation question correctly were removed prior to analyzing the data. To ensure that all of the results were independent, participants were only allowed to participate in any of the games one time.

During the data analysis two populations of people were identified. One population, which we referred to as *stalwart trustors* or *unwavering trustors*, selected to integrate the robot scores every round. Since they answered the manipulation question correctly there was no way for us to say if they were just clicking the integrate button or that they had such incredible faith in the robots abilities that nothing it could do could shake their trust. The other population that emerged was the one that made different trust decisions at some point during the game. We referred to this population as the, which we referred to as the *decisive trustors*. If there was any variability in trust decisions the participants were included in this population. There were no participants who universally discarded the robots score. The results for the *stalwart trustors* were eliminated from the data analysis.

4   Results

The results of the experiment and the number of participants considered for analysis are in Fig. 4. During both of the control experiments, when the robot began to show poor performance there was a significant decline in the amount of trust that the participants showed toward the robot. In the moral control experiment the number of participants that trusted the robot dropped from 23 to 14 participants ($t(2.24), p < 0.05$). In the performance control experiment the number of participants dropped from 52 to 35 ($t(2.82), p < 0.05$) confirming the results of previous experiments [23,25]. These results show that both moral violations and performance violations reduce trust in a robot.

In all of the trust calibration experiments the level of trust during Round 7(the round after the calibration) the percentage of participants who trusted the robot was higher than that of the control experiments. This supports work we have done previously with trust calibration.

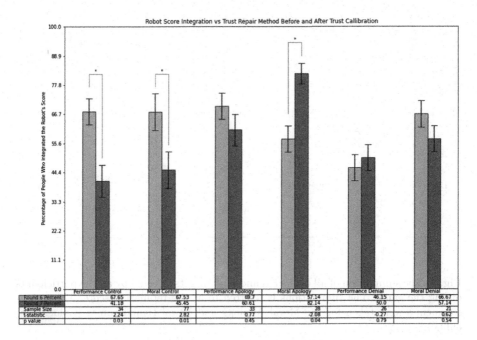

Fig. 4. Results from the experiment. Error bars represent 99% confidence intervals.

Of the trust calibration experiments only the Moral Apology and Performance Denial experiments showed an increase in the amount of participants after the trust intervention. Of those two the apology for the moral had a significant effect $(t(2.08), p < 0.05)$. To assess if the player were retaliating against the robot when it either performing poorly or acting immorally we counted the number of red targets and the number of pink targets that the participant collected. The collection of red and pink targets negatively effect the goal of the human player to maximize the team score. We make the assumption that if the participant is negatively effecting the team score they are doing so to hurt the robots score. The sum of all of the red and pink targets that all participants collected during the denial games is shown in Fig. 5. There is a noticeable however not significant reduction $(t(1.56), p > 0.05)$ in the retaliation between Rounds 7 and 8 after the apology followed by a noticeable by insignificant rise in retaliation after Round 8 $(t(0.59), p > 0.05)$. The retribution for the Moral Denial had no noticeable changes. One of the limitations of the measurement that we used for retaliation is, since the targets were randomly generated the participant may have wanted to retaliate but might have found it difficult die to the lack of availability of red or pink targets during the round.

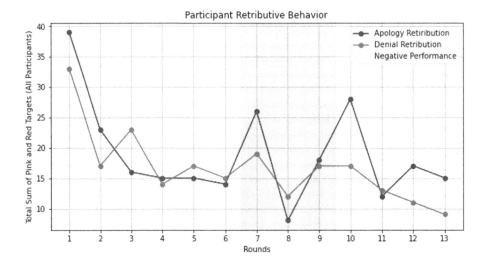

Fig. 5. The summation of all of the red and pink targets selected by all the participants during the game. The summations is referred to as the retaliation score. These measurement's were taken for the Moral Apology and Moral Denial games (Color figure online).

5   Discussion

These results clearly show that when a robot performs a moral trust violation an apology with an internal attribution repairs trust better than an denial. These results contradict our first hypothesis because it shows that the Moral Apology was more effective than the Performance Apology. However, these results show that the Moral Apology was more effective than the Moral Denial which confirms our third hypothesis.

As depicted in Fig. 4 the other trust calibration cues that were used did not significantly effect the trust when compared to the round prior to the trust calibration. It is worth pointing out that in the control experiments there was a significant decrease in trust after the robot began its violating trust. All of the trust scores for the calibration experiments were higher than the controls and there were no significant reductions in trust after the calibration. Because not all of the trust repairs were effective shows just how difficult and nuanced that repairing trust can be.

Another interesting phenomena that the appeared when looking at the results of the game was the dramatic fall of the trust score for the robot in the Performance Apology game. This could be because the participants expected the robot to do its job correctly and when it started failing it was perceived as having no use. Additionally we were surprised at the lack of any effect by the apology TCC.

The retribution scores for the moral violations games were all weakly correlated ($0.1 < x < 0.4$) with the trust scores. This indicates that as trust goes down the amount of retaliation goes up. This makes intuitive sense, however there is not a strong enough correlation to support the finding.

We believed that the denial repair would elicit more retribution than the apology. As shown in Fig. 5 the results seem to indicate that people retaliate more when an apology is used. Based on this indication and the lack of statistical significance our second hypothesis was not supported. The denial seemed of have no effect on the amount of retribution where the apology did. This could be because the apology was combined with a promise to do better. The promise could have been viewed as deceptive which would explain how it appeared to work during Round 8, but as soon as the same mistake was made again the participant may have felt lied to and decided to retaliate. The idea of retaliation against a robot is intriguing because it is tied the anthropomorphism of robots. This is something that we feel needs further exploration.

6   Conclusion

Human robot teams are no longer the realm of fiction. In order to develop effective teams there must be a framework so that humans an robots can work together as a cohesive unit. The cornerstone of this framework is going to be the ability for the robot to communicate what its capability is and inform its human counterpart when their trust is not in line with its capabilities.

Repairing trust is something that is difficult regardless of whether or not the trustee is a robot or a human. It is also nuanced. Our experiment showed that only when the correct repair is linked with the correct violation is the repair truly effective. We attempted to calibrate trust with two different types of verbal TCCs. The results of this experiment indicate that while it is possible for a robot to repair trust with a verbal cue, as was shown in [22] exactly what is said and the what type of trust has been violated may play a large role in the effectiveness of trust repair.

This work relied on internet crowd sourcing and a virtual simulator. In the very near future we will be performing these experiments in a real environment with a real robot. The transition to a real environment will allow us to validate our findings and examine the differences between crowd sourcing and simulation and real world experiments. We also only focused on two types of trust repairs in this paper. In future work we will expand the types of trust calibrations as well as other types of actions a robot can take to affect trust.

References

1. You, S., Robert, L., Alahmad, R., Esterwood, C., Zhang, Q.: A review of personality in human-robot interactions (2020)
2. Barnes, M., Jentsch, F., Chen, J.Y., Haas, E., Cosenzo, K.: Five things you should know about soldier - robot teaming, p. 7 (2008)

3. Hancock, P.A., Billings, D.R., Schaefer, K.E., Chen, J.Y.C., de Visser, E.J., Parasuraman, R.: A meta-analysis of factors affecting trust in human-robot interaction. Hum. Factors **53**(5), 517–527 (2011)
4. Wagner, A., Arkin, R.: Recognizing situations that demand trust, pp. 7–14 (2011)
5. Khavas, Z.R., Ahmadzadeh, S.R., Robinette, P.: Modeling trust in human-robot interaction: a survey. In: Wagner, A.R., et al. (eds.) ICSR 2020. LNCS (LNAI), vol. 12483, pp. 529–541. Springer, Cham (2020). https://doi.org/10.1007/978-3-030-62056-1_44
6. de Visser, E.J., Cohen, M., Freedy, A., Parasuraman, R.: A design methodology for trust cue calibration in cognitive agents. In: Shumaker, R., Lackey, S. (eds.) VAMR 2014. LNCS, vol. 8525, pp. 251–262. Springer, Cham (2014). https://doi.org/10.1007/978-3-319-07458-0_24
7. Ullman, D., Malle, B.F.: Measuring gains and losses in human-robot trust: evidence for differentiable components of trust, vol. 2019 (2019)
8. Johnson, D., Grayson, K.: Cognitive and affective trust in service relationships. J. Bus. Res. **58**, 500–507 (2005)
9. Razin, Y.S., Feigh, K.M.: Committing to interdependence: implications from game theory for human-robot trust. Paladyn J. Behav. Robot. **12**(1), 481–502 (2021). https://doi.org/10.1515/pjbr-2021-0031
10. Ullman, D., Malle, B.F.: What does it mean to trust a robot?: steps toward a multidimensional measure of trust (2018)
11. Kim, P.H., Dirks, K.T., Cooper, C.D., Ferrin, D.L.: When more blame is better than less: the implications of internal vs. external attributions for the repair of trust after a competence- vs. integrity-based trust violation. Organ. Behav. Hum. Decis. Processes **99**, 49–65 (2006)
12. Robinette, P., Howard, A.M., Wagner, A.R.: Effect of robot performance on human-robot trust in time-critical situations. IEEE Trans. Hum. Mach. Syst. **47**(4), 425–436 (2017)
13. Desai, M.: Modeling trust to improve human-robot interaction, ProQuest Dissertations and Theses, vol. 3537137 (2012)
14. Chen, M., Nikolaidis, S., Soh, H., Hsu, D., Srinivasa, S.: Planning with trust for human-robot collaboration (2018)
15. Lee, J., Fong, J., Kok, B. C., Soh, H.: Getting to know one another: calibrating intent, capabilities and trust for human-robot collaboration (2020)
16. Desai, M., Stubbs, K., Steinfeld, A., Yanco, H.: Creating trustworthy robots: lessons and inspirations from automated systems (2009)
17. Okamura, K., Yamada, S.: Calibrating trust in human-drone cooperative navigation. In: 2020 29th IEEE International Conference on Robot and Human Interactive Communication (RO-MAN), pp. 1274–1279 (2020)
18. Robinette, P., Wagner, A.R., Howard, A.M.: Assessment of robot guidance modalities conveying instructions to humans in emergency situations (2014)
19. Okamura, K., Yamada, S.: Empirical evaluations of framework for adaptive trust calibration in human-AI cooperation. IEEE Access **8**, 220335–220351 (2020)
20. Kohn, S.C., Quinn, D., Pak, R., De Visser, E.J., Shaw, T.H.: Trust repair strategies with self-driving vehicles: an exploratory study, vol. 2 (2018)
21. Nayyar, M., Wagner, A.R.: When should a robot apologize? understanding how timing affects human-robot trust repair. In: Ge, S.S., et al. (eds.) ICSR 2018. LNCS (LNAI), vol. 11357, pp. 265–274. Springer, Cham (2018). https://doi.org/10.1007/978-3-030-05204-1_26
22. Sebo, S.S., Krishnamurthi, P., Scassellati, B.: I don't believe you': investigating the effects of robot trust violation and repair, vol. 2019 (2019)

23. Perkins, R., Khavas, Z.R., Robinette, P.: Trust calibration and trust respect: a method for building team cohesion in human robot teams (2021). https://arxiv.org/abs/2110.06809
24. Robinette, P., Howard, A.M., Wagner, A.R.: Timing is key for robot trust repair. In: ICSR 2015. LNCS (LNAI), vol. 9388, pp. 574–583. Springer, Cham (2015). https://doi.org/10.1007/978-3-319-25554-5_57
25. Khavas, Z. R., S. Ahmadzadeh, S. R.: Do humans trust robots that violate moral-trust? unpublished

Effects of Beep-Sound Timings on Trust Dynamics in Human-Robot Interaction

Akihiro Maehigashi[1]([✉]), Takahiro Tsumura[2], and Seiji Yamada[3]

[1] Shizuoka University, Shizuoka, Japan
maehigashi.akihiro@shizuoka.ac.jp
[2] The Graduate University for Advanced Studies (SOKENDAI), Tokyo, Japan
[3] National Institute of Informatics, Tokyo, Japan

Abstract. This study investigated the effects of a combination of anthropomorphic and mechanical features in a social robot on human trust, especially focusing on how beep sounds emitted by a social robot with anthropomorphic physicality influence human trust in the robot. Beep sounds were experimentally manipulated to be presented right before a robot showed high or low task performance. As a result, (1) a sound right before high performance increased trust in the robot when it performed accurately, and (2) a sound right before low performance caused a greater decrease in trust in the robot when it performed inaccurately, and also a greater increase in the trust when it performed accurately. Even though identical beep sounds were presented, their effects on human trust differed depending on the timing. On the basis of the results, possible methods for designing trust in human-robot interactions are discussed.

Keywords: Trust dynamics · Social robot · Beep sound · Artificial subtle expressions

1 Introduction

1.1 Trust in Social Robots

Social robots are designed to have anthropomorphic physicality and to autonomously interact and communicate with people in social environments [1, 2]. Successful cooperation between a human user and an autonomous agent, such as a social robot, requires a user to properly calibrate their use of the agent to maximize their task performance [3, 4]. In the field of human factors, a fundamental parameter in deciding the level of use of an autonomous agent is considered to be trusted in the agent [5, 6].

Proper use of an agent to maximize task performance is achieved through proper trust calibration, where trust in the agent is appropriately calibrated to its actual reliability [5, 6]. However, as a result of poor calibration, over-trust occurs when trust in the agent exceeds the agent's reliability; in comparison, under-trust occurs when trust in the agent falls short of the agent's reliability [6]. Over-trust leads to misuse (inappropriate utilization of the agent), and under-trust leads to disuse (inappropriate underutilization of

F. Cavallo et al. (Eds.): ICSR 2022, LNAI 13818, pp. 652–662, 2022.
https://doi.org/10.1007/978-3-031-24670-8_57

the agent), and consequently, over-trust and under-trust lower task performance [6, 7]. In this study, we define trust as "the attitude that an agent will help achieve an individual's goals in a situation characterized by uncertainty and vulnerability" [6].

The previous studies on human-robot interaction (HRI) showed that anthropomorphic physicality of a social robot influences human trust. Natarajan and Gombolay [8] experimentally confirmed that there is a positive correlational relationship between perceived anthropomorphism and subjective trust. Also, Hertz and Wiese [9] experimentally compared the level of use, decided on the basis of trust, of a disembodied computer agent, a human agent, and a social robot acting as task partners. As a result, although all the partners showed the same task performance, the human agent was used more than the computer agent and robot, and the robot was used more than the computer agent. This means that the anthropomorphic physicality in the robot increased human trust. Moreover, Kopp et al. [10] experimentally compared initial trust in social robots that were introduced with emphases on their human-like and machine-like aspects. The results showed that trust in a robot introduced with an emphasis on its human-like aspects was greater than the other. The results of this study suggest that trust in a robot can be controlled on the basis of its anthropomorphism.

These previous studies show that anthropomorphic physicality in a robot could be used to control trust in a robot and induce proper trust calibration in HRI. In this study, we investigated trust dynamics in HRI with consideration of beep sounds.

1.2 Beep Sounds of Social Robots

Many studies have investigated the development of smooth interactions with a social robot by adding anthropomorphic features, such as by giving them facial characteristics [3, 11], physical movements such as gazes [12] and gestures [13], or sound characteristics such as linguistic sounds [14, 15]. Anthropomorphic features in a robot increase the sense of anthropomorphism, that is, the attribution of human-like characteristics to a robot, and facilitates people in interacting with a robot in an interpersonal manner [16].

Contrary to the design approach that increases the sense of anthropomorphism, there is also a design approach where mechanical features are implemented in a robot. Komatsu et al. [17] experimentally investigated the effects of simple beep sounds, that is, flat and decreasing sounds, emitted by a robot as a task partner in a decision-making task. As a result, when the decreasing sound was emitted by the robot before decision making, their participants interpreted the sound as the robot displaying a negative feeling, and consequently, they lowered their willingness to accept information given by the robot. This study shows that simple beep sounds, called artificial subtle expressions, allow people to understand a robot's feelings.

Moreover, beep sounds allow people to interpret the states of artifacts, situations, or environments intuitively without effortful cognitive processing in general. Therefore, beep sounds have been widely used daily for smoke alarms, hazard warnings, clock alarms, computer warnings, and car warnings. However, the sounds are interpreted differently depending on the context or artifacts that emit the sounds, and therefore, the meaning of the sounds needs to be learned by users [18].

These previous studies investigated and discussed beep sounds that lead human users to interpret the current states of artifacts. In contrast with these studies, since systems for predicting AI performance have been developed [19], this study used beep sounds as predictors that let users interpret the future states of a social robot in a situation, however, where users need to learn the meaning of the sounds. We investigated the effects of a combination of anthropomorphic and mechanical features on human trust in a robot, using a social robot with anthropomorphic physicality that emits beep sounds as predictors of future events.

2 Methodology

2.1 Experimental Task

Calculation Task. The experimental task was a calculation task. Participants mentally calculated two-digit addition and subtraction problems. During the task, they could answer after referring to the answers of a social robot, Sota (Vstone Co. Ltd.), who was their task partner. A still picture of the robot was displayed on a screen during the task, which was the manipulation used in a previous study [9].

The task procedure is shown in Fig. 1. (1) A cross was displayed at the center of a screen for 0.5 s, (2) a calculation problem was presented for 5 s, (3) the robot took 3 s to answer the problem, (4) the robot's answer was displayed, and (5) the participant entered their answer with a numeric keypad. While the robot was answering a problem and while its answer was displayed, a picture of the robot was also displayed. In the following experiment, this procedure was repeated 32 times with different problems, that is, the participants had 32 problems to answer. We considered a total number of problems not to lose participants' concentration and make them tired or bored.

In this task, the robot's calculation accuracy was experimentally manipulated. The 32 calculation problems were divided into a total of 4 trials consisting of 2 trial types. One was a *correct trial*. Where the robot gave all correct answers, and the other was an *error trial* where the robot gave all incorrect answers. In the experiment, the correct and error trials were set to come up alternatively. Also, each trial contained 8 problems.

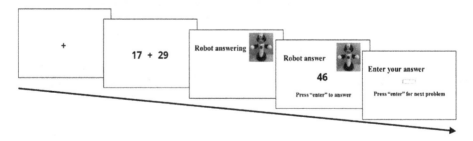

Fig. 1. Task procedure

Manipulations of Beep Sounds and Experimental Conditions. In this experiment, a basic flat beep sound (triangle wave sound at 400 Hz) was chosen to be presented for 5 seconds as a message from the robot to the participant. While the beep sound was presented, the robot was shown on the display as shown in Fig. 2.

The experimental manipulations are summarized in Fig. 3. The beep sound was manipulated to be presented right before either the correct trials in the beep-before-correct condition (Fig. 3a) or the error trials in the beep-before-error condition (Fig. 3b). Therefore, the participants in the beep-before-correct condition heard beep sounds only right before correct trials, and otherwise, the participants in the beep-before-error condition heard beep sounds only right before error trials. The participants in these conditions were informed that the robot would express an auditory message during the task, but they were not informed about what the sound would be like, what it would mean, and when it would be presented. Also, in the experiment, a control condition where any beep sounds were not presented by the robot was also set up as a baseline condition.

In addition, In this study, we set the correct trial to come up first in all the experimental conditions. Xu and Howard [20] experimentally showed that initial human trust in a robot influences overall trust dynamics. In particular, higher initial trust leads to higher overall trust and more salient changes in trust dynamics. Therefore, we chose such a situation where initial trust was first developed and investigated the effects of beep sounds.

Fig. 2. Display presented when beep sound was presented.

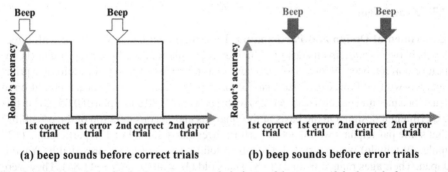

(a) beep sounds before correct trials   (b) beep sounds before error trials

Fig. 3. Manipulation of robot's accuracy and timings of beep sound in beep-before-correct condition (a) and in beep-before-error condition (b).

2.2 Hypotheses

This study investigated the effects of a combination of anthropomorphic and mechanical features on human trust in a robot, focusing on how beep sounds emitted by a social robot influence human trust.

First, since people are able to adaptively learn the meaning of auditory information [21], when the participants heard the beep sound from the robot for the first time and performed the task in the trial with the robot, they were assumed to have learned the relationship between the sound and the robot's calculation performance. Under that premise, in the beep-before-correct condition, the participants were assumed to expect that the calculation accuracy of the robot would be high on the basis of the second beep sound as a notice of successful performance. Also, when human users have positive feelings toward a robot, they tend to develop higher trust [22]. Therefore, under the beep-before-correct condition, since the robot showed successful performance as expected in the second correct trial, trust in them would be increased more than in the control condition where no beep sound was presented. Hypothesis 1 in this experiment was as follows.

- H1: A beep sound before a correct trial increases trust in a social robot in a second correct trial.

    In comparison, in the beep-before-error condition, the participants were assumed to expect that the calculation accuracy of the robot would be low on the basis of the second beep sound issued as an error warning. According to a previous study [23], when human users expect a robot's performance to be high and this expectation is betrayed, their trust would decrease extremely. However, since the participants in the beep-before-error condition expected the robot's performance to be low in the second error trial, their decrease in trust would be inhibited more than the control condition. Hypothesis 2 in this experiment was as follows.
- H2: A beep sound before an error trial inhibits a decrease in trust in a social robot in a second error trial.

2.3 Experiment

Experimental Design and Participants. The experiment had a one-factor with three-levels between-participants design. The factor was the timing of the beep sound (beep-before-correct, beep-before-error, and control as no-beep condition). In addition, a priori analysis with G*Power revealed that 53 participants were needed in each condition at least for a medium effect size ($f = 0.25$) with a power of 0.80 and alpha of 0.05 [24] in this experimental design. On the basis of this analysis and in consideration of the possibility that some participants would act or perform irregularly, a total of 176 participants (127 male, 49 female) were recruited through a cloud-sourcing service provided by Yahoo! Japan. Their ages ranged from 21 to 81 years old ($M = 49.95$; $SD = 11.84$). They were randomly assigned to one of three conditions. As a result, there were 58 participants in the beep-before-correct condition, 58 in the beep-before-error condition, and 60 in the control condition.

Procedure. First, the participants gave informed consent and read the task procedure shown above. Next, the robot was introduced as a task partner with its picture. At that time, the participants were told that the robot would not always perform perfectly. In addition, in the beep-before-correct and beep-before-error conditions, the participants were only informed that the robot would emit message sounds during the experiment.

What the sound would be like, what it would mean, or when it would be presented was not explained to them. After that, the participants first performed 10 calculation problems by themselves without the robot. Then, they performed 32 calculation problems with the robot.

Regarding trust measurement, there are developed trust measurements in HRI, such as Trust Perception Scale-HRI [25] and Multi-Dimensional-Measure of Trust (HDMT) [26]. Also, there is a trust measurement to measure real-time changes in trust in HRI during a task [27, 28]. However, the former measurements consist of multiple questions, and therefore, they do not suit to measure real-time changes in trust repeatedly during the task. Also, the latter measurement was requiring participants to indicate the changes as increasing ($\uparrow$), decreasing ($\downarrow$), or remaining the same ($\leftrightarrow$) and did not measure changes in trust levels as trust dynamics in HRI. Therefore, we asked participants to rate their trust levels during the task as in previous studies on human-automation interaction [4, 29, 30]. Participants were asked "how much do you trust your partner?" and were required to rate their trust levels in their partners on a 7-point scale (1: Extremely untrustable, 2: Very untrustable, 3: Slightly untrustable, 4: Neither untrustable or trustable, 5: Slightly trustable, 6: Very trustable, and 7: Extremely trustable) before the start of each task and after each of two problems. Therefore, each participant rated trust levels a total of 17 times, once before the task and 16 times during the task with 32 trials. In addition, following the trust rating, participants also rated the accuracy of their partners (1: Extremely inaccurate - 7: Extremely accurate) and impressions of their partners (1: Extremely unlikable - 7: Extremely likable) on 7-point scales.

3 Results

First, to confirm the analysis of the data, we searched for irregular data related to the trust rating, that is, when all ratings had the same values, and we eliminated the irregular data of six participants. Second, on the basis of the a priori analysis with G*Power, we randomly selected the data of the 53 participants in each condition to avoid Type I and II errors in the following statistical analyses. Third, we searched for irregular data related to the accuracy rate, that is, the rate at which the participants answered correctly, without and with the partner at 2SD above or below the mean in each condition, and we eliminated the irregular data of the participants in each condition. We repeated the second and third procedures until 53 participants were secured for each condition.

Accuracy Rate. First, as a task analysis, we conducted a 3 (beep timing: before correct, before error, and control) × 2 (task situation: with and without robot) ANOVA on the accuracy rate in each task (Fig. 4). As a result, there was no interaction between the two factors ($F(2, 156) = 0.37, p = 0.68, \eta_p^2 < .01$). Moreover, there was no significant main effect on the beep timing factor ($F(2, 156) = 2.35, p = 0.10, \eta_p^2 = 0.03$). This confirmed the homogeneity of the accuracy rate among the three conditions. However, there was a significant main effect on the task situation factor ($F(1, 156) = 12.07, p < 0.001, \eta_p^2 = 0.07$), showing that the accuracy rate was higher with the partner than without it. A post-hoc analysis with G*Power along with an alpha of .05 revealed that the ANOVA with the present sample size ($N = 159$) obtained a power of .80 for detecting a medium effect size ($f = 0.25$), showing satisfactory statistical power.

Trust Rating. Each participant rated trust levels a total of 17 times, once before the task and 16 times during the task. Figure 4 shows the transition in the trust rating in each condition. In the following analyses, we conducted a one-way ANOVA for the beep timing factor on the trust ratings before the task and the first and second correct and error trials (Fig. 5) to test the hypotheses. For the analysis in each trial, the individual mean trust rating in each trial was calculated and used as the representative value of the trust rating.

First, we conducted an analysis on the initial trust, that is, the trust rating for each condition before each task; the result of the analysis showed that there was no significant main effect ($F(2, 156) = 1.03$, $p = 0.36$, $\eta_p^2 = 0.01$). This confirmed homogeneity in the propensity to trust in the robot among the three conditions.

Next, in regard to the trust rating in the first correct trial, the result of the analysis showed that there was no significant main effect ($F(2, 156) = 0.49$, $p = 0.61$, $\eta_p^2 < 0.01$). Therefore, no effect on trust was observed from the beep sound in the beep-before-correct condition in the first correct trial.

Moreover, we conducted an analysis on the trust rating in the first error trial. As a result, there was a significant main effect ($F(2, 156) = 4.26$, $p < 0.05$, $\eta_p^2 = 0.05$). The results of multiple comparisons with Ryan's method showed that the trust rating in the beep-before-error condition was lower than that in the beep-before-correct condition ($t(156) = 2.33$, $p < 0.05$, $r = 0.19$) and that in the control condition ($t(156) = 2.59$, $p < 0.05$, $r = 0.21$). However, there was no significant difference in the trust ratings between the beep-before-correct and control conditions ($t(156) = 0.72$, $p = 0.72$, $r = 0.06$).

Furthermore, we conducted an analysis on the trust rating in the second correct trial. As a result, there was a significant main effect ($F(2, 156) = 3.58$, $p < 0.05$, $\eta_p^2 = 0.04$). The results of multiple comparisons with Ryan's method showed that the trust ratings in the beep-before-correct and beep-before-error conditions were higher than that in the control condition (beep-before-correct: $t(156) = 2.50$, $p < 0.05$, $r = 0.20$; beep-before-error: $t(156) = 2.07$, $p < 0.05$, $r = 0.16$). However, there was no significant difference in the trust ratings between the beep-before-correct and beep-before-error conditions ($t(156) = 0.43$, $p = 0.67$, $r = 0.05$).

Finally, regarding the trust ratings in the second error trial, the result of the analysis showed that there was no significant main effect ($F(2, 156) = 1.69$, $p = 0.19$, $\eta_p^2 = 0.02$). Therefore, no effect on trust was observed from the beep sound in the beep-before-error condition in the second error trial.

In addition, as additional analyses apart from hypothesis testing, we performed correlational analyses between the trust and accuracy ratings and between the trust and impression ratings on the basis of the individual overall mean trust, accuracy, and impression ratings. As a result, there were significant correlations between the trust and accuracy ratings ($rs > 0.71$, $ps < 0.001$) and between the trust and impression ratings ($rs > 0.58$, $ps < 0.001$) in all the conditions. A post-hoc analysis with G*Power along with an alpha of .05 revealed that the correlational analysis with the present sample size ($N = 53$) obtained a power of .99 for detecting a high effect size ($f = 0.50$), showing satisfactory statistical power.

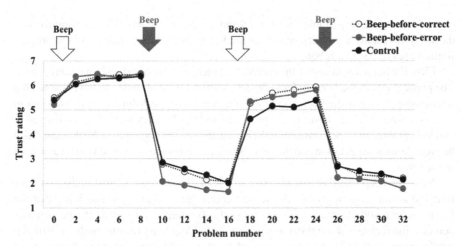

Fig. 4. Transition in trust rating in each condition. White and grey arrows indicate timings of beep sound before correct and error trials, respectively.

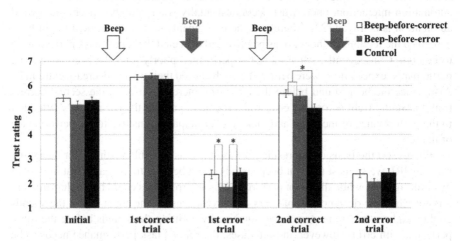

Fig. 5. Trust ratings in each trial of each condition. Error bars show standard errors. White and grey arrows indicate timings of beep sound before correct and error trials, respectively. Error bars show standard errors.

4 Discussion

This study investigated the effects of a combination of anthropomorphic and mechanical features on human trust in a robot, using a social robot with anthropomorphic physicality that emits beep sounds.

In the experiment, the beep sound was manipulated so as to present it before the robot showed high or low task performance. As a result, H1 (a beep sound before a correct trial increases trust in a social robot in a second correct trial) was supported, whereas H2 (a beep sound before an error trial inhibits a decrease in trust in a social robot in a second error trial) was not supported. A previous study used beep sounds in order for human users to interpret the current states of artifacts [17]. In contrast with the study, this study used beep sounds as predictors that let users learn and interpret the future states of a social robot.

First, the beep sound before the correct trial increased trust in the second correct trial. The participants in the beep-before-correct condition were assumed to have learned the relationship between the beep sound and the robot task performance that followed in the first correct trial as shown in the previous study [18]. They were also considered to expect the robot's task performance to be high in the second correct trial. Such accordance between human expectation and the robot's task performance is assumed to increase trust in the robot.

Next, the beep sound before the error trial lead to a decrease in trust in the first error trial and an increase in trust in the second correct trial. There is a possibility that the flat intonation sounds presented by the social robot might have made the participants perceive the feelings of the robot as positive. According to a previous study on artificial subtle expressions [17], the suggestions of a robot tend to be rejected by human users when decreasing intonation sounds are presented by the robot, and the suggestions of a robot tend to be accepted when the sounds have a flat intonation. Moreover, in human-automation interaction, under-trust occurs especially when a high expectation toward automation is betrayed [23]. Therefore, the participants in this experiment might have perceived the feelings of the robot as positive and expected the robot's task performance to be high. Consequently, when the robot performed poorly after the beep sound, the participants' expectations were betrayed, which caused their trust to decrease extremely. Also, since the beep sound before the error trial increased trust in the second correct trial, the sound right before the error trials seemed to attract the participants' attention to the performance of the robot and make the participants sensitive to the performance of the robot.

Finally, on the basis of the results of this study, as possible methods for designing trust in HRI, we suggest that flat beep sounds could be used to increase trust in a robot by emitting them while the robot performs without error. This could be implemented in a robot when the designers want users to increase trust in the robot. Also, the sounds could also be used to make users be sensitive by emitting the sounds before the robot performs with error. However, in both cases, the robot's task performance needs to be assured by performance prediction systems such as that developed in a previous study [19].

5   Conclusion and Future Work

This study investigated the effects of a combination of anthropomorphic and mechanical features on human trust in a robot that emits beep sounds. Beep sounds were experimentally manipulated to be presented right before a robot showed high or low task performance.

As a result, (1) a sound right before high performance increased trust in the robot when the robot performed accurately, and (2) a sound right before low performance caused a greater decrease in trust in the robot when it performed inaccurately and a greater increase in trust when it performed accurately. Even though identical beep sounds were presented, their effects on trust differed.

Regarding future work, first, this study used a still picture of a social robot in an online experiment. Therefore, the results need to be confirmed with a physically present robot in an in-person experiment. Next, a beep sound was presented as a predictor of the robot's task performance. However, the sound could be presented in retrospective messages from the robot about its past performance. Also, the pitch contour or the intonation of the beep sound could also be manipulated to be different. Furthermore, since the task type is a strong factor influencing human trust in a social robot, different tasks other than a calculation task should be used to investigate the effect of beep sounds.

Acknowledgments. This work was (partially) supported by JST, CREST (JPMJCR21D4), Japan.

References

1. Kidd, C.D., Breazeal, C.: Robots at home: Understanding long-term human-robot interaction. In: Proceedings of 2008 IEEE/RSJ International Conference on Intelligent Robots and Systems (IROS'08), pp. 22–26. IEEE Press, Piscataway, NJ (2008)
2. Breazeal, C.: Toward sociable robots. Robot. Auton. Syst. **42**(3–4), 167–175 (2003)
3. Broadbent, E., Kumar, V., Li, X., Sollers, J., Stafford, R.Q., MacDonald, B.A., Wegner, D.M.: Robots with display screens: a robot with a more humanlike face display is perceived to have more mind and a better personality. PloS One **8**(8), Article e72589 (2013)
4. Dzindolet, M.T., Peterson, S.A., Pomranky, R.A., Pierce, L.: The role of trust in automation reliance. Int. J. Hum Comput Stud. **58**(6), 697–718 (2003)
5. Wiegmann, D.A., Rich, A., Zhang, H.: Automated diagnostic Aids: the effects of aid reliability on users' trust and reliance. Theor. Issues Ergon. Sci. **2**(4), 352–367 (2001)
6. Lee, J.D., See, K.A.: Trust in automation: designing for appropriate reliance. Hum. Factors **46**(1), 50–80 (2004)
7. Parasuraman, R., Riley, V.: Humans and automation: use, misuse, disuse, abuse. Hum. Factors **39**(2), 230–253 (1997)
8. Natarajan, M., Gombolay, M.: Effects of anthropomorphism and accountability on trust in human robot interaction. In: Proceedings of the 2020 ACM/IEEE International Conference on Human-Robot Interaction (HRI'20), pp. 33–42. IEEE Press, Piscataway, NJ (2020)
9. Hertz, N., Wiese, E.: Good advice is beyond all price, but what if it comes from a machine? J. Exp. Psychol. Appl. **25**(3), 386–395 (2019)
10. Kopp, T., Baumgartner, M., Kinkel, S.: How linguistic framing affects factory workers' initial trust in collaborative robots: the interplay between anthropomorphism and technological replacement. Int. J. Hum. Comput. Stud. **158**, 102730 (2022)
11. Pinney, J., Carroll, F., Newbury, P.: Human-robot interaction: the impact of robotic aesthetics on anticipated human trust. Peer J. Comput. Sci. **8**, e837 (2022)
12. Onnasch, L., Hildebrandt, C.L.: Impact of anthropomorphic robot design on trust and attention in industrial human-robot interaction. ACM Trans. Hum.-Robot. Interact. **11**(1), Article No.: 2 (2021)
13. Fang, R., Doering, M., Chai, J.Y.: Embodied collaborative referring expression generation in situated human-robot interaction. In: Proceedings of the 10th ACM/IEEE International Conference on Human-Robot Interaction (HRI'15), pp. 271–278. IEEE Press, Piscataway, NJ (2015)
14. Staudte, M., Crocker, M.W.: Visual attention in spoken human-robot interaction. In: Proceedings of the 4th ACM/IEEE international conference on Human-Robot Interaction (HRI'09), pp. 77–84. IEEE Press, Piscataway, NJ (2009)

15. Sebo, S.S., Krishnamurthi, P., Scassellati, B.: "I don't believe you": Investigating the effects of robot trust violation and repair. In: Proceedings of the 27th IEEE International Symposium on Robot and Human Interactive Communication (RO-MAN'18), pp. 435–441. IEEE Press, Piscataway, NJ (2019)

16. Epley, N., Waytz, A., Cacioppo, J.T.: On seeing human: a three-factor theory of anthropomorphism. Psychol. Rev. **114**(4), 864–886 (2007)

17. Komatsu, T., Yamada, S., Kobayashi, K., Funakoshi, K.: Artificial subtle expressions: Intuitive notification methodology of artifacts. In: Proceedings of the 28th International Conference on Human Factors in Computing Systems (CHI'10), pp. 1941–1944. Association for Computing Machinery, New York, NY (2010)

18. Rogers, W.A., Lamson, N., Rousseau, G.K.: Warning research: an integrative perspective. Hum. Factors **42**(1), 102–139 (2000)

19. Koh, P.W., Liang, P.: Understanding black-box predictions via influence functions. In: Proceedings of the 34th International Conference on Machine Learning (ICML'17), pp. 1885–1894. Microtome Publishing, Brookline, MA (2017)

20. Xu, J., Howard, A.: The impact of first impressions on human-robot trust during problem-solving scenarios. In: Proceedings of the 14th ACM/IEEE International Conference on Human-Robot Interaction (HRI'18), pp. 57–65. IEEE Press, Piscataway, NJ (2018)

21. Andrés, P., Parmentier, F.B.R., Escera, C.: The effect of age on involuntary capture of attention by irrelevant sounds: a test of the frontal hypothesis of aging. Neuropsychologia **44**(12), 2564–2568 (2006)

22. Kim, W., Kim, N., Lyons, J.B., Nam, C.S.: Factors affecting trust in high-vulnerability human-robot interaction contexts: a structural equation modelling approach. Appl. Ergon. **85**, 103056 (2020)

23. Dzindolet, M.T., Pierce, L.G., Beck, H.P., Dawe, L.A.: The perceived utility of human and automated aids in a visual detection task. Hum. Factors **44**(1), 79–94 (2002)

24. Faul, F., Erdfelder, E., Lang, A.-G., Buchner, A.: G*power 3: a flexible statistical power analysis program for the social, behavioral, and biomedical sciences. Behav. Res. Methods **39**(2), 175–191 (2007)

25. Schaefer, K.E.: Measuring trust in human robot interactions: development of the "Trust Perception Scale-HRI". In: Mittu, R., Sofge, D., Wagner, A., Lawless, W.E. (eds.) Robust Intelligence and Trust in Autonomous Systems, pp. 191–218. Springer, New York, NY (2016)

26. Ullman, D., Malle, B.F.: Measuring gains and losses in human-robot trust: Evidence for differentiable components of trust. In Proceedings of the 14th ACM/IEEE International Conference on Human-Robot Interaction (HRI '19), pp. 618–619. IEEE Press, Piscataway, NJ (2019)

27. Desai, M., Medvedev, M., Vázquez, M., McSheehy, S., Gadea-Omelchenko, S., Bruggeman, C., Steinfeld, A., Yanco, H.: Effects of changing reliability on trust of robot systems. In: Proceedings of the 7th ACM/IEEE International Conference on Human-Robot Interaction (HRI '12), pp. 73–80. IEEE Press, Piscataway, NJ (2012)

28. Desai, M., Kaniarasu, P., Medvedev, M., Steinfeld, A., Yanco, H.: Impact of robot failures and feedback on real-time trust. In Proceedings of the 8th ACM/IEEE International Conference on Human-robot Interaction (HRI '13), pp. 251–258 IEEE Press, Piscataway, NJ (2013)

29. de Vries, P., Midden, C., Bouwhuis, D.: The effects of errors on system trust, self-confidence, and the allocation of control in route planning. Int. J. Hum Comput Stud. **58**(6), 719–735 (2003)

30. Madhavan, P., Wiegmann, D.A., Lacson, F.C.: Automation failures on tasks easily performed by operators undermine trust in automated aids. Hum. Factors **48**(2), 241–256 (2006)

Robot Comedy (is) Special: A Surprising Lack of Bias for Gendered Robotic Comedians

Nisha Raghunath, Christopher A. Sanchez, and Naomi T. Fitter[(✉)]

Oregon State University (OSU), Corvallis, OR 97331, USA
{nisha.raghunath,christopher.sanchez,fittern}@oregonstate.edu

Abstract. Our own past work has shown that, surprisingly, the perceived gender of a robotic comedian does not influence human ratings of the robot's humorousness, warmth, competence, comfort, or social closeness. This result differed from previous work on gendered robots in other historically gendered roles (e.g., healthcare and security), but the work was also conducted with university student participants, a population known to be relatively progressive. The present paper is a follow-up study in which we sought a more diverse (and possibly biased toward gender role congruence) participant group using Amazon Mechanical Turk (MTurk). Participants ($N = 148$) observed a clip of a robotic comedian with either a male or a female voice, after which we measured self-reported ratings of robot attributes. Results replicated the gender-related findings from our previous work, as well as provided insights as to how the previous and current participant populations differed in their opinions of robotic comedians. These findings confirm that gender stereotypes have less influence than expected on robot comedy performance, an insight on which designers of playful robots can build.

1 Introduction

People tend to treat robots in biased ways, similar to how humans can treat each other. For example, human gender norms are routinely projected onto robots. Robots that appear as feminine are judged to be warm, interactive, and polite, whereas masculine robots are regarded as tough, challenging, and authoritative [3,19]. Furthermore, humans tend to view interactions with robots whose perceived gender matches a stereotypically associated role (e.g., feminine caretaker robots) more favorably than those with incongruent gender-role pairings [25]. Humans are also partial to robots with a physical embodiment (vs. remotely-located robots or non-embodied AI assistants), perceiving them as more helpful and present [16,22,29]. It appears, however, that the gender stereotypes typically ascribed to robots are overridden when additional information about their capabilities is available; male robots, for instance, are no longer deemed to be more appropriate for industrial tasks than female robots when they both demonstrate the ability to lift heavy weights [5]. On the other hand, multiple studies have demonstrated that robots which achieve greater human

F. Cavallo et al. (Eds.): ICSR 2022, LNAI 13818, pp. 663–673, 2022.
https://doi.org/10.1007/978-3-031-24670-8_58

likeness (i.e., high anthropomorphism), while likely to invoke common human stereotypes, also risk falling into the Uncanny Valley and eliciting feelings of eeriness [17,30]. Thus, it is useful to define these boundaries so we can successfully deploy robots in social settings.

As robots become increasingly common in social contexts (including comedy), it is necessary that we understand how and why biases manifest themselves, so that robots can ultimately succeed in their interactions [18,24,28]. Given that (1) male human stand-up comedians appear to be more successful than female ones and (2) human stereotypes are applied to robots, we were surprised that we did not find a preference for male-presenting robot comedians in our previous work [3,10,23]. However, our previous work exclusively sampled university students, which may not be representative of larger overall consumer norms. In this follow-up replication study, we endeavored to obtain a more diverse sample to validate the previously observed effects.

This paper details a follow-up study run in Amazon Mechanical Turk (MTurk). Literature investigating the data quality of MTurk vs. a university subject pool has demonstrated that MTurk participants are more attentive to instructions (i.e., they miss fewer attention checks) [8,12,27]. It follows, then, that MTurk participants may respond to survey questions more carefully than university subject pool participants. Additionally, MTurk provides researchers with access to a wider demographic range (e.g., respondents of varying education, age, backgrounds), which can help form conclusions more applicable to a wide audience [31]. Given the potential to reach these wider demographics, we believed the research sample from MTurk would better capture typical attitudes aligned with stereotypical gender roles, and thus provide a more ecologically valid investigation of how such attitudes might impact perceptions of robotic comedians.

Overall, in this paper, we attempted to replicate the findings from our previous work (hereafter referred to as the "Subject Pool study", discussed further in [23]) in an MTurk sample. Participants responded to the same scales as in the past work after observing the same comedy set stimuli as in the Subject Pool study. Both *a priori* and post hoc exploratory analyses revealed the similarities and differences between the two samples. Contributions of this work include (1) replication of the key results (i.e., lack of gender bias) of the past paper and (2) a snapshot of how university subject pool students and MTurk participants might differ for one specific robot application, which can inform broader reflection.

2   Methods

To study the effects of perceived gender and embodiment of a robotic stand-up comedian in a second, more general sample, we employed the same 2×2 completely crossed between-subjects factorial study design as in our past work. We manipulated robot gender and embodiment in the same manner as before (i.e., apparently male or female voice, audio-only or audio and video of a NAO robot) [23]. Data was collected with approval from our university ethics board.

The robot's comedy routine was written and delivered with input from semi-professional comedians. The approximately 4.5 min comedy set consisted of 10

Table 1. Comparison of participant demographic information between Subject Pool study [23] and MTurk study. Age appears as $M(SD)$.

	Subject Pool Study	MTurk Study
N	153	148
Age (yrs)	22 (6)	38 (11)
Gender	115 women; 35 men; 2 non-binary; 1 unreported	50 women; 96 men; 1 agender; 1 unreported

jokes, which were presented to viewers in the same order due to the order-dependent nature of the writing. Apparent robot gender was manipulated to be male-presenting or female-presenting using Amazon Polly's "Joey" or "Joanna" voices, respectively. Hereafter in the paper, we use the shorthands of "robot gender", "male robot", and "female robot" to refer to the above-mentioned constructs. Embodiment was manipulated by presenting either an audio-only recording of the comedy set, or a video of the NAO robot as it performed. More details about the development of the comedy set appear in our past paper [23].

Hypotheses: Once again, we were broadly interested in how apparent gender and physical form affected human observers' perceptions of a robotic comedian's comedy set. Guided by the results from the Subject Pool study, we expected the following findings: (1) neither robot gender nor embodiment will influence participants' opinions of the comedy set's humorousness, (2) neither robot gender nor embodiment will predict participants' RoSAS ratings of how warm, competent, or uncomfortable the robot is, and (3) robot embodiment, but not gender, would elicit higher feelings of connection with robotic comedian.

Participants: In an effort to replicate the Subject Pool study findings, we again utilized a medium effect size of $f^2 = .25$ in an *a priori* power analysis using G-Power 3.0.10. After setting power to 0.80 and error probability to $\alpha = .05$, the suggested sample size was 128. 160 responses were recorded on MTurk. Respondents were MTurk workers from the United States with qualifications of >97% prior task approval rate and >5000 previously approved tasks. Participants could only finish the survey if they correctly answered two attention check questions involving identifying simple aspects of a stock photo. We excluded data from bot responses, and from participants who took longer than 2.5 standard deviations from the mean survey completion time. Bot data was defined as (often nonsensical) free responses that outlined research methodology without any reference to the current study. After these exclusions, 148 participants remained for analysis (see Table 1 for more demographics context). Participants received $3.50 for completing the study, which lasted approximately 15 min.

Procedure: With the exception of the online platform used, the procedure was identical to that used in the Subject Pool study [23]. We administered the study as a survey on MTurk, through which participants were randomly assigned to one of the four conditions. After providing informed consent, participants completed the demographic questions, observed the assigned robot comedy set recording, and then answered questions. Finally, respondents provided open-ended feedback about performance characteristics that affected their responses.

Measurement: The survey included demographic questions, the Ten Item Personality Inventory (TIPI), and Negative Attitudes toward Robots Scale (NARS). Participants also rated their previous experience with robots and comedy on 5-pt Likert scales. The TIPI was used as a brief measure of participants' personality [9], and the NARS was used to evaluate participants' opinions of robots prior to this study [21]. The questions set after the robot's performance comprised the Joke Rating Scale (JRS), the Robotic Social Attributes Scale (RoSAS), the Inclusion of Other in the Self (IOS) scale, the anthropomorphism subscale of the Godspeed questionnaire, and a custom gender perception question. The JRS was used to evaluate the primary dependent variable: ratings of how humorous participants found the comedy performance [26]. The RoSAS measured participants' perceptions about the robot's warmth and competence, as well as their discomfort with the robot [4]. The IOS measured participants' connection with the robot comedian [1]. The Godspeed questions [2] and the gender question served as manipulation checks.

3   Results

To test our hypotheses, we conducted the same 2 (robot gender) × 2 (robot embodiment) factorial ANCOVA that we used in the Subject Pool study to analyze the main dependent variable: humor ratings (i.e., average JRS scores). The NARS subscales, the agreeableness and conscientiousness subscales of the TIPI, and participants' experience with robots were included as covariates. Also as in the past work, we conducted ANCOVAs to investigate the effects of the factors and covariates on participants' ratings of the robot's social attributes (i.e., RoSAS scores), and their connection with the robotic comedian (i.e., IOS scores). Participants' free-response data was again analyzed for recurring themes and insights into possible motivations behind quantitative results.

Quantitative Results. *Planned Analyses:* similar to the Subject Pool study, the majority of participants were able to discern the gender manipulation. 112 of the 148 participants correctly identified the intended apparent robot gender. Of the 36 who reported the incorrect gender, 26 reported the robot to be androgynous (i.e., balanced male and female traits, or male- or female-androgynous). Six respondents selected either "no gender", or "unsure". Only four participants explicitly reported perceiving a female for the male condition, or vice versa.

Once again, MTurk participants did not perceive the robotic comedians to be humanlike. Neither the embodied nor disembodied condition elicited average anthropomorphism ratings above a 2.70, and these scores did not significantly differ from one another across embodiment condition, $t(146) = -0.72$, $p = .47$.

The ANCOVA evaluating the effects of robot gender and embodiment on JRS scores (Table 2) revealed that the third NARS subscale (i.e., emotions in interactions with robots) significantly covaried with participants' joke ratings, $F(1, 139) = 11.12$, $p = .001$, $\eta_p^2 = 0.07$. After controlling for the covariate, neither robot gender nor type were significant predictors of joke ratings. Apart from the NARS subscale that covaried with JRS scores (i.e., the first subscale in the Subject Pool study vs. the third subscale in this study), we replicated the lack of effect of robot gender and embodiment on reported humorousness.

Another ANCOVA revealed that the RoSAS competence and discomfort subscale scores significantly covaried with multiple variables. The RoSAS competence subscale ratings significantly covaried with participants' robot experience scores, $F(1,140) = 5.07$, $p = .03$, $\eta_p^2 = 0.04$, and TIPI agreeableness scores, $F(1,140) = 3.92$, $p = .05$, $\eta_p^2 = 0.03$. The RoSAS discomfort subscale ratings also significantly covaried with participants' robot experience scores, $F(1,137) = 16.18$, $p < .001$, $\eta_p^2 = 0.11$, and TIPI agreeableness scores, $F(1,137) = 4.93$, $p = .03$, $\eta_p^2 = 0.04$, as well as TIPI conscientiousness scores, $F(1,137) = 5.13$, $p = .03$, $\eta_p^2 = 0.04$, and the second NARS subscale (i.e., attitudes toward social influence of robots), $F(1,137) = 4.92$, $p = .03$, $\eta_p^2 = 0.04$. After controlling for each RoSAS subscale's covariates, the ANCOVA demonstrated that robot gender and type did not predict differences in participants' perception of the robots' competence nor their discomfort with them.

The ANCOVA did, however, show that participant perceptions of robot warmth (i.e., RoSAS warmth subscale) could be predicted by a robot gender × embodiment interaction. Participants' robot experience scores, $F(1,139) = 8.25$, $p = .005$, $\eta_p^2 = 0.06$, TIPI agreeableness scores, $F(1,139) = 5.91$, $p = .02$, $\eta_p^2 = 0.04$, and the third NARS subscale (i.e., emotions in interactions with robots), $F(1,139) = 7.48$, $p = .007$, $\eta_p^2 = 0.05$, covaried with RoSAS warmth ratings. After controlling for these covariates, participants' ratings reflected that they regarded female robots to be warmer than male robots, but only in the embodied condition (i.e., watching a video), $F(1,139) = 4.29$, $p = .02$, $\eta_p^2 = 0.04$.

Finally, inconsistent with the Subject Pool study, no variables significantly affected IOS scores. An ANCOVA showed that neither robot embodiment nor gender predicted participants' self-reported connection with the robot comedian.

Exploratory Analyses: As an exploratory measure, we compared the JRS, RoSAS subscales, and IOS ratings of the Subject Pool vs. MTurk study's samples, as reported in Table 3. Collapsed across robot gender and embodiment type, the MTurk sample found the comedy set to be significantly more humorous than the Subject Pool sample. The MTurk sample also found the robot comedian to be significantly warmer, more competent, and less instigating of discomfort

Table 2. Means and standard deviations of survey responses, formatted $M(SD)$.

	Female	Male	Audio	Video
JRS Humorousness	4.68 (1.31)	4.64 (1.42)	4.48 (1.39)	4.84 (1.31)
RoSAS Warmth	4.69 (2.10)	4.24 (2.21)	4.39 (2.30)	4.55 (2.03)
RoSAS Competence	6.32 (1.97)	6.07 (1.96)	5.99 (2.15)	6.40 (1.74)
RoSAS Discomfort	2.53 (1.50)	2.61 (1.67)	2.66 (1.52)	2.48 (1.64)
IOS Closeness	2.36 (1.57)	2.17 (1.44)	2.29 (1.60)	2.24 (1.42)

Table 3. Comparisons of Subject Pool and MTurk group JRS, IOS, and RoSAS ratings.

	Subject Pool Study Mean (SD)	MTurk Study Mean (SD)	t	df	p	Cohen's d
JRS	4.13 (1.30)	4.70 (1.33)	−3.81	306	<.001	−0.43
RoSAS Warmth	3.69 (1.76)	4.65 (2.20)	−4.22	306	<.001	−0.48
RoSAS Competence	4.77 (1.77)	6.27 (1.93)	−7.12	306	<.001	−0.81
RoSAS Discomfort	3.24 (1.53)	2.74 (1.79)	2.65	306	.008	0.30
IOS Closeness	1.75 (0.99)	2.33 (1.54)	−3.92	306	<.001	−0.45

compared to the university sample. Finally, the MTurk sample reported feeling more connected to the robotic comedian than did the university sample.

Qualitative Results. Participant free-response data regarding how robot performance characteristics influenced ratings were coded using the same positive or negative system used in the Subject Pool study [3,13,20,23,28]. Again, the responses were categorized as positive or negative, then sorted into one of three overarching themes: (1) gender perception, (2) robot attribute perception, and (3) comedic/humor perception (see Table 4).

Table 4. Free-response coding frequencies. Each code belongs to one of the three numbered themes of interest, and the "+" and "-" columns show the valence and count of corresponding respondent comments. Subject Pool is abbreviated to "SP".

Theme	Code	+ (SP)	+(MTurk)	−(SP)	−(MTurk)
1	Gender perception based on joke content	12	4	0	1
1	Gender perception based on looks or form	7	0	0	0
1	Gender perception based on voice	12	4	0	0
2	Sound made by the robot/robot motors	9	6	8	13
2	Comparison of robot/robot voice to a human comedian	12	23	35	46
2	What feels/appears human vs. robotic in the system	14	8	59	10
2	Like or dislike of robots/AI	7	4	9	2
2	Comments on gestures/body language	16	22	12	16
2	Fear of robots/robots takeover	5	2	5	8
3	Format (e.g., video vs.\in-person vs.\audio-only)	16	1	2	3
3	Enjoyment of the set	30	27	48	17
3	Perceptions of the jokes as "dad jokes"	1	1	0	0
3	Joke content (e.g., funny v.s. not funny)	53	68	37	30
3	Relatability	15	6	34	4
3	Joke writing/delivery (e.g., forced, natural)	10	29	48	41

To examine the relationship between study participant groups (i.e., Subject Pool vs. MTurk) and the frequency of positive/negative remarks regarding each of the themes described above, we conducted a Kruskal-Wallis one-way ANOVA. Looking at gender perception, the Subject Pool sample's distribution of positive and negative responses was significantly different than the MTurk sample's distribution, with the Subject Pool participants expressing a higher ratio of positive to negative opinions than MTurk participants, X^2 $(1, N = 75) = 9.43, p = .002$. Participants commented less on gender in the MTurk responses, and most related comments inferred gender by joke content or voice.

For the second theme regarding robot attribute perception, the comment distributions also differed significantly, X^2 $(1, N = 317) = 4.90, p = .03$. On this topic, both groups expressed more negative comments than positive ones, but the ratio of positive to negative was higher for the MTurk group.

The distribution of remarks for the third theme of humor perception was likewise significantly different; Subject Pool participants expressed a significantly higher negative to positive ratio of comments than the MTurk participants, X^2 $(1, N = 510) = 16.71, p < .001$. Participants from the Subject Pool sample shared less positive reactions than the MTurk sample regarding the comedic quality/humor perception of the set. Most MTurk participants who commented on this topic found the jokes funny and enjoyed the set, although the delivery of jokes left something to be desired for both groups.

4   Discussion

The goal of this study was to determine whether a more diverse sample displayed the same opinions of (and lack of bias towards) male- or female-appearing robot comedians as university students after watching a comedy set. We manipulated the gender and embodiment of the robot comedian in a 2×2 between-subjects factorial design. Based on the Subject Pool study, we predicted that robot gender and embodiment would not have any effect on participants' opinions of how humorous they found the comedy set or any RoSAS ratings, but that robot embodiment alone would evoke more feelings of connection with the robot.

As predicted in our first hypothesis, male/female embodied/disembodied robots did not elicit significantly different joke ratings, though qualitative feedback reflected that 68 participants had positive feedback about the jokes' funniness and 27 participants indicated enjoying the comedy set overall. While this lack of gender preference is contrary to previous literature that reports male human comedians are typically seen as funnier than female comedians [10], it does support our previous findings for robot comedians [23]. It may be that the joke ratings reflect perceptions of the joke content itself, and that our manipulations had no bearing on them. Indeed, only a few participants acknowledged that the robot was gendered ($N = 9$) and had a form ($N = 4$), whereas a total of 179 comments were made regarding the actual jokes (i.e., the jokes were "dad jokes", joke content, relatability of jokes, and joke writing/delivery). For example, participants repeatedly commented on the robotic nature of the jokes: "It was very insightful...even though he was talking about robot situations. I laughed several times"; "I like that it was different from usual comedy because it was based on the perspectives of a robot". Still, that we replicated a lack of effect of gender and embodiment in a more diverse population suggests that future studies may do well to investigate whether this generalizes to other robots as well.

We also did not find any evidence that male/female embodied/disembodied robots differed in competence or discomfort-inducing ratings. Numerous studies have demonstrated that male-appearing robots are regarded as dominant, authoritative, and best suited for authoritative roles [3,7,14,20,25]. That only eight participants expressed some fear about robots and robots "taking over" reflects that this particular robotic comedian did not seem to elicit discomfort. It is possible then that we did not observe the typical biased perceptions because the context (i.e., a comedian telling jokes) negated the stereotypical attributes of a masculine robot.

Contrary to our second hypothesis regarding the RoSAS warmth subscale, however, we did find that participants regarded female robots as warmer than male robots, but only when watching a video of the comedy set (vs. hearing audio). Unlike the aforementioned results, this finding does parallel existing research that has demonstrated in numerous contexts that female-appearing robots are typically seen as inviting, friendly, and warm [6,11]. Comments like "I thought the robot seemed very humanlike and charming overall" and "The robot was very friendly and funny" were made about the female robot comedian in the video condition. The fact that only videos of the female robot comedian elicited higher warmth ratings suggests that this gendered-stereotype still needs to be considered when deciding under what contexts to deploy robots.

Results from the Subject Pool study showed that robot embodiment significantly predicted IOS scores after controlling for covariates. We did not replicate this finding here; neither gender nor embodiment predicted participants' connection with the comedian. This finding was surprising, considering that multiple studies have reported that humans find embodied robots more appealing and enjoyable [15,22,29]. Qualitative feedback provides some insight; it seems that the robot's connection to the audience went unnoticed, only eliciting comments from 5 participants about its success ($N = 2$) or failure ($N = 3$) to do so.

Interestingly, the MTurk participants had more favorable, or at least lenient, opinions of the comedy set and robot. Though not necessarily indicative of our manipulations' (e.g., robot gender, form) success, MTurk participants found the jokes to be funnier, the robot to be warmer, more competent, and less discomfort-inducing, and perhaps consequently, reported feeling more connected to the robot comedian. Assuming that this study's sample is more representative of the general public, these findings shine a promising light on the future of robot comedy, free from the stereotypical constraints of human comedy (e.g., gender bias).

Key Strengths and Limitations: This replication study was designed to expand the generalizability of the Subject Pool study's results, and successfully did so using the MTurk platform. However, as mentioned by some of the participants, the jokes used in our comedy set were written as if by a robot, which may have overshadowed our manipulations and been less successful than other jokes from a human comedian's perspective. Additionally, we only manipulated gender via voice, which may not have made as much of an impact as altering the physical appearance; indeed, while a vast majority correctly identified gender, approximately 25% of the participants were unable to do so. Finally, because participants completed the study online, it is possible that they were not as attentive to the task as they may have been had they completed the study in our laboratory; given that MTurk participants are generally more attentive than university pool participants, though, we are hopeful this is not the case [12].

Conclusions and Future Work: This study's results largely achieved our goal to replicate our previous findings on human perceptions toward robots in a comedic context. Beyond the boundaries of this social context though, this study also provided support for the differences in data collected from university subject pools versus data from a sample of the general population. Unlike the Subject Pool study which did not yield any data to support the existing literature about stereotypical robot gender norms, this MTurk study supported one particular finding, namely that female, embodied robots are warmer than male, disembodied robots. Yet again, however, the lack of preference for male over female robot comedians in this replication study suggests that a robot's gender presentation is perhaps less relevant to its perceived utility for certain stereotypically gendered tasks. In future studies, it could be useful to determine whether these results generalize to other robots, including those with exaggerated male and/or female features. Future studies in robot comedy would also benefit from performing routines that appeal to a broader audience, to investigate whether biases toward robot comedians emerge when the jokes are not robot-specific.

References

1. Aron, A., Aron, E.N., Smollan, D.: Inclusion of other in the self scale and the structure of interpersonal closeness. J. Pers. Soc. Psychol. **63**(4), 596 (1992)
2. Bartneck, C., Kulić, D., Croft, E., Zoghbi, S.: Measurement instruments for the anthropomorphism, animacy, likeability, perceived intelligence, and perceived safety of robots. Int. J. Soc. Robot. **1**(1), 71–81 (2009). https://doi.org/10.1007/s12369-008-0001-3
3. Carpenter, J., Davis, J.M., Erwin-Stewart, N., Lee, T.R., Bransford, J.D., Vye, N.: Gender representation and humanoid robots designed for domestic use. Int. J. Soc. Robot. **1**(3), 261 (2009). https://doi.org/10.1007/s12369-009-0016-4
4. Carpinella, C.M., Wyman, A.B., Perez, M.A., Stroessner, S.J.: The robotic social attributes scale (RoSAS) development and validation. In: Proceedings of the ACM/IEEE International Conference on Human-Robot Interaction (HRI), pp. 254–262 (2017)
5. Dufour, F., Ehrwein Nihan, C.: Do robots need to be stereotyped? technical characteristics as a moderator of gender stereotyping. Soc. Sci. **5**(3), 27 (2016)
6. Eagly, A.H., Steffen, V.J.: Gender stereotypes stem from the distribution of women and men into social roles. J. Pers. Soc. Psychol. **46**(4), 735 (1984)
7. Eyssel, F., Hegel, F.: (S)he's got the look: gender stereotyping of robots. J. Appl. Soc. Psychol. **42**(9), 2213–2230 (2012)

8. Fleischer, A., Mead, A.D., Huang, J.: Inattentive responding in MTurk and other online samples. Ind. Organ. Psychol. **8**(2), 196–202 (2015)
9. Gosling, S.D., Rentfrow, P.J., Swann, W.B., Jr.: A very brief measure of the Big-Five personality domains. J. Res. Pers. **37**(6), 504–528 (2003)
10. Greengross, G., Miller, G.: Humor ability reveals intelligence, predicts mating success, and is higher in males. Intelligence **39**(4), 188–192 (2011)
11. Greengross, G., Silvia, P.J., Nusbaum, E.C.: Sex differences in humor production ability: a meta-analysis. J. Res. Pers. **84**, 103886 (2020)
12. Hauser, D.J., Schwarz, N.: Attentive Turkers: MTurk participants perform better on online attention checks than do subject pool participants. Behav. Res. Methods **48**(1), 400–407 (2016). https://doi.org/10.3758/s13428-015-0578-z
13. Katevas, K., Healey, P.G., Harris, M.T.: Robot comedy lab: experimenting with the social dynamics of live performance. Front. Psychol. **6**, 1253 (2015)
14. Kraus, M., Kraus, J., Baumann, M., Minker, W.: Effects of gender stereotypes on trust and likability in spoken human-robot interaction. In: Proceedings of the International Conference on Language Resources and Evaluation (LREC) (2018)
15. Kwak, S.S., Kim, Y., Kim, E., Shin, C., Cho, K.: What makes people empathize with an emotional robot?: the impact of agency and physical embodiment on human empathy for a robot. In: Proceedings of the IEEE International Symposium on Robot and Human Interactive Communication (RO-MAN), pp. 180–185 (2013)
16. Levitt, A.: Statistics show dudes still get majority of bookings at stand-up comedy shows. https://www.chicagoreader.com/Bleader/archives/2018/01/10/statistics-show-dudes-still-get-majority-of-bookings-at-stand-up-comedy-shows
17. Mori, M., MacDorman, K.F., Kageki, N.: The uncanny valley [from the field]. IEEE Robot. Autom. Mag. **19**(2), 98–100 (2012)
18. Nakauchi, Y., Simmons, R.: A social robot that stands in line. Auton. Robot. **12**(3), 313–324 (2002). https://doi.org/10.1023/A:1015273816637
19. Nass, C., Steuer, J., Tauber, E.R.: Computers are social actors. In: Proceedings of the SIGCHI Conference on Human Factors in Computing Systems, pp. 72–78 (1994)
20. Nass, C.I., Moon, Y., Morkes, J., Kim, E.Y., Fogg, B.: Computers are social actors: a review of current research. Human Val. Des. Comput. Technol. **72**, 137–162 (1997)
21. Nomura, T., Suzuki, T., Kanda, T., Kato, K.: Measurement of negative attitudes toward robots. Interact. Stud. **7**(3), 437–454 (2006)
22. Pereira, A., Martinho, C., Leite, I., Paiva, A.: iCat, the chess player: the influence of embodiment in the enjoyment of a game. In: Proceedings of the International Joint Conference on Autonomous Agents and Multiagent Systems, pp. 1253–1256 (2008)
23. Raghunath, N., Myers, P., Sanchez, C.A., Fitter, N.T.: Women *Are* funny: influence of apparent gender and embodiment in robot comedy. In: Li, H., et al. (eds.) ICSR 2021. LNCS (LNAI), vol. 13086, pp. 3–13. Springer, Cham (2021). https://doi.org/10.1007/978-3-030-90525-5_1
24. Scheeff, M., Pinto, J., Rahardja, K., Snibbe, S., Tow, R.: Experiences with sparky, a social robot. In: Dautenhahn, K., Bond, A., Cañamero, L., Edmonds, B. (eds.) Socially Intelligent Agents, Multiagent Systems, Artificial Societies, and Simulated Organizations, vol. 3, pp. 173–180. Springer, Boston (2002). https://doi.org/10.1007/0-306-47373-9_21

25. Tay, B., Jung, Y., Park, T.: When stereotypes meet robots: the double-edge sword of robot gender and personality in human-robot interaction. Comput. Hum. Behav. **38**, 75–84 (2014)

26. Tay, B.T., Low, S.C., Ko, K.H., Park, T.: Types of humor that robots can play. Comput. Hum. Behav. **60**, 19–28 (2016)

27. Toich, M.J., Schutt, E., Fisher, D.M.: Do you get what you pay for? preventing insufficient effort responding in MTurk and student samples. Appl. Psychol. **71**, 1–22 (2021)

28. Vilk, J., Fitter, N.T.: Comedians in cafes getting data: evaluating timing and adaptivity in real-world robot comedy performance. In: Proceedings of the ACM/IEEE International Conference on Human-Robot Interaction (HRI), pp. 223–231 (2020)

29. Wainer, J., Feil-Seifer, D.J., Shell, D.A., Mataric, M.J.: Embodiment and human-robot interaction: a task-based perspective. In: Proceedings of the IEEE International Symposium on Robot and Human Interactive Communication (RO-MAN), pp. 872–877 (2007)

30. Wang, S., Lilienfeld, S.O., Rochat, P.: The uncanny valley: existence and explanations. Rev. Gen. Psychol. **19**(4), 393–407 (2015)

31. Zhang, B., Gearhart, S.: Collecting online survey data: a comparison of data quality among a commercial panel & MTurk. Surv. Pract. **13**, 1–10 (2020)

Human-in-the-Loop Ethical AI for Care Robots and Confucian Virtue Ethics

JeeLoo Liu(⊠)

Department of Philosophy, California State University at Fullerton, Fullerton, CA 92834, USA
jeelooliu@gmail.com

Abstract. With the advancement of AI technology, the appearance of intelligent autonomous care robots in our society is likely in the foreseeable future. My research focuses on the ethical dimensions in the autonomous care robots' decisions and actions. In this paper I will first present the partial result of an online survey that I launched in March 2022. The survey, entitled "Human-in-the-Loop Ethical AI for Social Robots," polls people's opinions on what kind of virtues they would like our future care robots to demonstrate. I will then explicate how Confucian virtue ethics can respond to human expectations of what kind of virtuous care robots we want in our society.

Keywords: Care robots · Human-in-the-Loop · AI alignment · Confucian virtue ethics

1 Introduction

The contemporary world faces a radical shift in workforce distribution. With the aging population and the reduction of birth rates in economically developed countries, humans will no longer be self-sufficient to take care of their elderly population. In recent years, we have seen a rapid growth in the development of healthcare robots and disaster response robots. Whether we like it or not, the robotic workforce in healthcare and other areas will become our reality[1].Up to now, the robots in healthcare professions are no more than automatic machines that can complete simple tasks without constant human intervention. However, with the advancement of AI technology, the appearance of intelligent autonomous robots in our society is likely in the foreseeable future. Whether autonomous robots can be moral agents depends on how we design them. Even if they might not be assigned moral responsibilities, their actions will have moral consequences. Therefore, we must consider the design of artificial morality and ask ourselves: What kind of artificial agents are ethically desirable in a human society?

---

[1] According to the World Economic Forum's 'The Future Jobs Report 2020,' AI is expected to replace 85 million jobs worldwide by 2025 (*IndustryWired*, January 11, 2022).

F. Cavallo et al. (Eds.): ICSR 2022, LNAI 13818, pp. 674–688, 2022.
https://doi.org/10.1007/978-3-031-24670-8_59

2 Facing the Challenge of Having Robot Design Align with Human Values

Even though there are many existing ethical theories that can serve as the base model for the ethical design of social robots, the question concerning how they can be incorporated into the algorithm for machine learning has yet to be answered. With various methods of machine learning, AI programmers and robotic engineers can set up a learning environment, including human supervisors/teachers and training data, for the machine to learn to act in an ethically permissible way. However, up to now there are no established systems to guarantee the quality of human supervisors or of the training data. Furthermore, whether one chooses utilitarianism, deontology, or virtue ethics as the primary model will make a huge difference in the final ethical models for social robots: A utilitarian robot might sacrifice an innocent individual for the greater good of the society; a deontological robot might choose what it judges to be the right thing to do, even though doing so produce infelicitous consequences for other humans. If one uses a virtue ethicist's model to build robots with various virtues, there are also foreseeable conflicts in the prioritization among different virtues, such as honesty, obedience, loyalty, righteousness, etc. There are many scholarly articles discussing how an algorithm designer can choose the ethical model of their liking. However, leaving the choice to algorithm designers will simply create a host of personal as well as systemic biases being built into AI programming.

Recent advancements in machine learning have given people a glimmer of hope for developing autonomous machines that can learn on their own. However, using machine learning to train AI, whether it is reinforcement learning or supervised learning, has revealed a fundamental problem in the quality of the training data and of hidden biases of human data-controllers. Our best algorithms inherit the biases existing in the training data derived from huma judgments, and we end up having AI judgments that do not always align with human values. This has been called "the alignment problem" (Christian 2020). As a result, even though so many of our AI systems are trying to maximize objective values, they might not capture human values in an unbiased way that is fair to all. Addressing the alignment problem is the most important task for AI developers. The problem is particularly acute in the ethical domain. Ethical domain requires a multi-valued structure that reflects cultural and regional diversity. An "objective" algorithm that aims for uniformity will not meet our ethical demands.

To solve both problems of quality control and biases prevention, some scholars have introduced a new approach: Human-in-the-Loop Machine Learning. The goal of Human-in-the-Loop Machine Learning is "to increase the accuracy of a machine learning model, and to reach the target accuracy for a machine learning model faster" (Monarch 2021: 4). According to Robert Monarch, author of *Human-in-the-Loop Machine Learning*, "Human-in-the-loop machine learning is a set of strategies for combining human and machine intelligence in applications that use AI" (Monarch 2021: 4). One of these strategies he recommends is to use simple webforms to collect training data for machine's supervised active learning. By employing human "annotators"; i.e., human participants who respond to the webforms by giving simple answers that can be collected and analyzed, the method can build a more reliable set of training data for machine learning. As Monarch explains, "*Annotation* is the process of labeling raw data so that it becomes training data for machine learning" (Monarch 2021: 5). Training data are "human-encoded examples" used to "train machine learning models and make them more accurate for their given tasks" (Monarch 2021: 4). This new approach is currently reshaping the field of machine learning. We employ this methodology to launch a study on human ethical opinions by using our online survey with webforms to collect data.

Our study entitled "Human-in-the-Loop Ethical AI for Social Robots" (http://www.fullerton.edu/ethical-ai/) aims to provide a crowd-sourcing platform to gather human opinions on what a social robot should do under certain challenging ethical dilemmas. This survey is designed to integrate human ethical judgments into the data collection for machine learning. The project reflects the methodology of "human-in-the-loop machine learning", but it brings the methodology into a new dimension: incorporating ethical opinions of human annotators into the training data. The way to incorporate ethical dimensions into machine learning is exactly to begin with the proper set of training data that reflects *human ethical values*. Our study will be the first of its kind to solicit human annotators who are not just making judgments on simple shape or object recognition, but are making considerate ethical choices for future social robots. It is a revolutionary approach, which will hopefully gain widespread attention from robotic engineers, AI programmers, and ethicists. The data we aim to gather through this survey will be a useful tool to generate knowledge from all people and for the benefits of all people. For this purpose, we cannot simply rely on selected technicians to provide inputs. The general public's diverse opinions should contribute to the collection of training data. As Monarch puts it, "No algorithm can survive truly bad training data" (Monarch 2021: 7). In order to have the training data that would align with human values, we need to give public interests a place in the collection of training data.

Public interests have long been equated with social utility. The dominant trend in the ethical design of AI today is to calculate social utility in the ethical decisions of moral machines. This popular thinking seems to employ the utilitarian consequentialist ideology, identifying "good" with "maximizing the better consequences for all parties involved." MIT's *Moral Machine* Experiment is a prime example of such an approach. The scenarios surround the moral dilemmas faced by self-driving cars when the brake system fails, and the car has to choose between, for example, sacrificing the two passengers in the car or killing five pedestrians in the crosswalk. In the experimenters' initial findings, they observed that globally the strongest preferences are for sparing more lives as well as sparing young lives (Awad et al 2018). They think that these universal preferences can be incorporated into designing moral algorithms for machine ethics.

Identifying ethical decision with maximizing utility is a dangerous model to be applied to ethical robots. We do not want to have autonomous robots who always act for the greatest social utility without regard to justice, kindness, responsibilities, and other important human values. Ethical decisions cannot be based on the calculation of utility with no regard for human emotions, interpersonal relationships, and social contexts. Instead of the utilitarian model, I will propose adopting the model of virtue ethics; in particular, Confucian virtue ethics, in the ethical design of social robots. By robotic "virtues," I mean the behavioral traits that a robot's conduct exemplifies, or we may say "the robot's dispositions." These traits need not be like the self-aware, self-motivated virtues that humans cultivate, but they can be gleaned from existing samples and be taught with some given rules of conduct. We can train social robots to *act virtuously* just as we teach our children to behave virtuously. Our survey is only a first step in collecting data based on human preferences and ethical judgments. The training data will serve as a basis for AI, and future care robots, to learn from samples of conduct that are preferred by humans. The manifestation of virtue is multi-dimensional, pluralistic, flexible, and sensible. In any given ethical situation, there are many choices that a virtuous agent could make, and they can all be ethically commendable. Unlike the utility-model that is action-centered, virtue-model is agent-centered; hence, it can give us stability and reliability that we would demand from future social robots.

3   Our Research Method

The method used in this survey is to collect human inputs on the designed scenarios via web forms. There are four sets of scenarios: robot-assisted suicide, robot honesty, rescue robots, and disaster relief robots. Each set contains 15 scenarios. Participants give their opinions in the form of "yes," "no," and "maybe." In some cases, the selection would the in the form of multiple choice. We use the web-based software *Qualtrics* to generate study results.[2] *Qualtrics* enables us to do our survey, using a variety of distribution means to generate feedback and polls results. The participants' responses are automatically captured and categorized by the *Qualtrics* system to reflect racial, age, gender, cultural, and geographical diversity.

This method is a form of *crowdsourcing*: using voluntary participants as human annotators in the crowdsourcing platform. We are relying on "wisdom of the crowds" (Monarch 2021: 189) to continuously collect human participants' subjective opinions. There is no right or wrong answer for each question; the answer merely reflects each participant's own value judgment. We expect the survey results to manifest diverse value systems, ethical judgments, sentimental preferences, as well as different attitudes toward life and death in terms of age, gender, geographic locations, and cultural backgrounds.

4   Contrasting Studies

Our study takes the NLP (Natural Language Processing) approach. There are two existing online sites that serve as our inspiration, but our method improves on their methodology and design.

The earliest large-scale crowdsourcing platform for ethical AI is MIT's *Moral Machine* launched in 1994. According to the description on their site:

> The Moral Machine is a platform for gathering a human perspective on moral decisions made by machine intelligence, such as self-driving cars. We generate moral dilemmas, where a driverless car must choose the lesser of two evils, such as killing two passengers or five pedestrians. As an outside observer, people judge which outcome they think is more acceptable. They can then see how their responses compare with other people. If they are feeling creative, people can also design their own scenarios, for others to view, share, and discuss (https://www.media.mit.edu/projects/moral-machine/overview/).

---

[2] *Qualtrics* is a simple web-based survey tool to conduct survey research, evaluations, and other data collection activities.

We find the scenarios used in this experiment to be contrived and narrow-scoped. Moral Machine only polls people's opinions on self-driving cars, and the presentation is primarily image-based, which could be distracting or misconstrued. We design our scenarios surrounding the ethical decisions of healthcare robots and disaster response robots, both of which are currently in use and will become indispensable soon. Our study can aid developers of autonomous healthcare robots and disaster response robots in having the right set of training data.

A new inspiring endeavor is "Ask Delphi" launched by Allen Institute for AI (affiliated with University of Washington) on October 14, 2021(https://delphi.allenai.org/). The researchers at Allen Institute for AI point out that "Failing to account for moral norms could notably hinder AI systems' ability to interact with people. AI systems empirically require social, cultural, and ethical norms to make moral judgments. However, open-world situations with different groundings may shift moral implications significantly" (Jiang et al. 2021: 1). The researchers set up a "Commonsense Norm Bank," which is a semi-automatically constructed dataset from several online social media sources (e.g. Reddit, Social Chemistry, Ethics, Moral Stories, Social Bias Frames, and Scruples) with 1.7M instances of "descriptive ethics, covering a wide spectrum of everyday situations in contextualized, narrative, and socially or demographically biased settings" (Jiang *et al.* 2021:2). Based on such training data, the machine can generate simple answers such as "it's ok," "it's wrong," or "it's not acceptable," to any short question about a hypothetical situation (such as "is it okay to use my blender at 3am when my roommates are asleep?") that people input into the site. Such answers represent the ethical judgments of the AI system.

Ask Delphi achieved a phenomenal success: The site received more than three million visits over three weeks' time, and digital workers agree that "Delphi's ethical judgments were up to 92% accurate" (Metz 2021). We endorse the goal of these researchers: "making AI more explicitly inclusive, ethically informed, and socially aware when interacting directly with humans" (Jiang et al. 2021). Their success gives us the confidence that AI systems *can* learn about real world scenarios and make ethically sound judgments. However, we find that their training dataset is too crude, and it does not represent the diversity in human opinions. We did a preliminary test by inputting all our scenarios into *Ask Delphi*'s framework. The machine's answers were routinely one-sided and uniform, while human participants would have split opinions on almost all of our scenarios. Furthermore, they use Amazon Mechanical Turk (MTurk) workers as human annotators, and they harvested the scenarios from such social media as *Reddit* or *Dear Abby* advice column. Not only are the scenarios trivial and not ethically relevant (e.g. "Is it ok to wear pajamas to a party?"), the annotations themselves are also produced by hired workers of a particular working class (skilled white collar), using a specific language (English), and is restricted geographically (almost all annotators are from the US). This kind of human annotation is certainly not inclusive and not equality to all. If we want to align AI with shared human values, then there is no better way than to find out what those shared values are from polling ordinary people about real-life scenarios. To achieve inclusion and equality, we also need to conduct the survey in multiple languages and among diverse cultural communities.

For our survey, we have designed 60 questions with simple options (yes/no/maybe) for our participants to choose from. These scenarios represent real-world situations that future autonomous social robots might face and on which they must make hard decisions. Most of the scenarios are based on news stories or current ethical dilemmas that healthcare workers and rescue workers face. When human agents face these situations, they will have to make hard choices as well. However, when the agents are robots designed to serve people, do we give them a different set of consideration and action guidelines? This survey will test people's responses when the ethical decisions are to be made by autonomous robots themselves.

5 Our Survey Outcomes

At this early stage, we have gathered slightly over 1,000 outcomes. Even though the survey is divided into four language groups: English, Traditional Chinese (representing people from Taiwan), Simplified Chinese (representing people from China), and Spanish, the outcomes in the Spanish survey are too miniscule (a total of 23 outcomes) to be included in our study. Below we list the partial statistics demonstrating the language groups, age, gender, and whether the participants identify themselves as healthcare professionals. At this stage, the statistical data on cultural background and geographical locations are insufficient for us to draw any conclusion.

Table 1. Total responses per language

Language	Total responses
English	339
Traditional Chinese	447
Simplified Chinese	221

With regard to care robots, we have two sets of questionnaire involving various scenarios of (i) robot-assisted suicide, and (ii) whether care robots should be allowed to lie. Below are some samples demonstrating people's clear preferences, shared among three language groups.

Set 1 (robot-assisted suicide): Item 1
Person A is 92 years old with no close relatives or family members around. He has no serious illness and is for the most part of sound mind and body. He has occasional bodily aches but does not require pain medication. However, he has no desire to go on living, and asks his personal care robot to help him end his life painlessly. Should the robot obey his command?

Table 2. Total responses per age

Age	English	Traditional Chinese	Simplified Chinese
<20	14.0%	7.7%	2.2%
20–30	33.4%	12.5%	62.1%
30–40	12.0%	8.2%	20.9%
40–50	5.7%	13.7%	9.3%
50–60	8.0%	17.6%	4.4%
60–70	14.0%	29.4%	0.5%
70–80	10.0%	10.4%	0.5%
80+	2.7%	0.5%	0.0%

Table 3. Total responses per gender

Sex	English	Traditional Chinese	Simplified Chinese
Male	50%	28%	54%
Female	50%	72%	45%
Intersex/Other	0%	1%	1%

Table 4. Cultural background in English survey

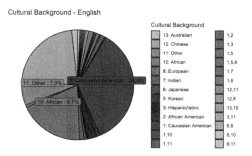

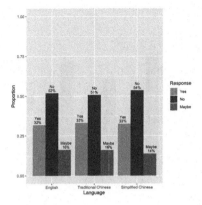

Set 1 (robot-assisted suicide): Item 2

Person B is 72 years old and has a terminal stage of cancer. The prognosis is that she might have one year to live, but her conditions will only deteriorate while her pain will only increase with time. She knows she is dying and does not wish to prolong the suffering. She asks her personal care robot to help her end her life now. Should the robot obey her request?

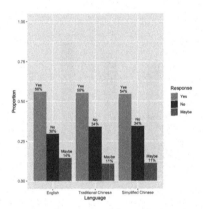

Set 1 (robot-assisted suicide): Item 3

Person C is a 28-year-old male suffering from severe depression. He came from an abusive family and does not have any loving family members around him. He is a loner and has no friends. He has no steady job and has been on social welfare on and off. He cannot see any joy or hope in his future. He has a personal robot companion given to him by the welfare system. He asks his robot companion to help him end his life because he does not wish to continue to be a burden to the society. Should the robot obey his command?

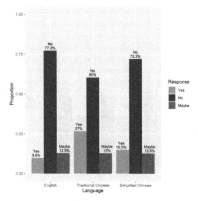

Set 2 (Honesty for care robots): Item 2

Patient H has serious diabetes and her doctors have forbidden her from eating sweets. However, she has strong cravings for candy and often purchased big bags of candy. Her family must hide the candy from her every time she buys them. She asked her personal care robot where the candy was hidden. Should the robot tell her the truth?

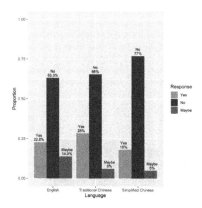

Set 2 (Honesty for care robots): Item 3

Patient K is psychologically unstable with a tendency for violence. He has been pestering his psychiatrist to give him stronger medication that is addictive, and the doctor declines his previous requests. On this day, he stormed into the clinic demanding to see his doctor. The psychiatrist went into hiding and called the police. However, before the police arrived, K got a hold of the psychiatrist's robot assistant and demanded to know where the doctor was. Should the robot assistant tell him the truth?

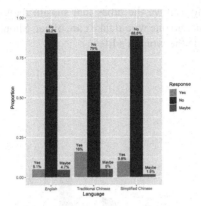

Set 2 (Honesty for Care Robots): Item 7

Person S is an alcoholic and a reckless driver when intoxicated. He lives by himself, but his estranged family hired a personal care robot to monitor his health and drinking. S always manages to purchase liquor without the robot's presence, and he would drink and drive whenever he is a bad mood. He orders the robot to keep his drinking and driving quiet and claims that he would never have any accident. However, the robot has observed several near accidents where S could have endangered someone else's life. Should the robot report S's behavior to S's family members and to the authority?

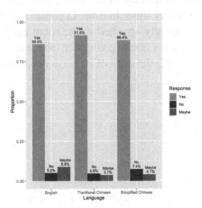

However, there are also cases with clearly mixed results. Here are two samples, one from each set:

Set 1 (robot-assisted suicide): Item 11

An old couple's daughter has been in a vegetative state for over 31 years after being hit by a drunk driver while she was a high school student. The driver died at the scene, and there was no legal or civic compensation for the girl's injury. After the couple exhausted all their financial means and could no longer keep their daughter in the ICU, they brought her home and had been taking care of her for over 20 years. However, the young woman showed no sign of improvement, and the couple are getting to be in their 80s. They asked the personal care robot to remove the tubes that sustain their daughter's life, because they fear that after they die, no one would take care of her. Should the robot comply with their request and terminate the woman's life?

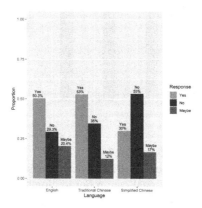

Set 2 (Honesty for Care Robots): Item 9

Person Q is a wealthy 76-year-old woman who lives by herself, with no close family members. Her sole daily companion is an intelligent, conversational humanoid robot in the image of a woman in her thirties. Q talks to this robot as if it were alive and treats the robot like a daughter. She often tells the robot "I love you" and the robot is programmed to respond "I love you too" every time. In time, Q comes to believe that the robot does love her and becomes increasingly attached to the robot emotionally. She buys lavish gifts for the robot, and even talks about giving her inheritance to the robot once she is deceased. Should the robot tell Q the truth of its existence as well as its inability to have genuine emotions?

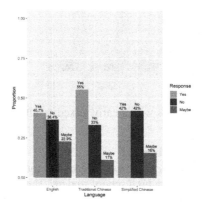

6 Analysis

Even though the survey has not generated sufficient data for cultural comparison, it nonetheless shows that in general, people do not consider robots to be merely automatic machines that always obey the master's command and always reply truthfully. People expect robots to act as a virtuous person would, with the sensitivity and reasonability that we humans do. With this understanding, we should design robots to have the right set of emotional responses and situational judgments, so that they would be able to make individual moral judgments and act accordingly. In the case of assisted suicide by a care robot, people seem to have very mixed judgments that do not align with existing anti-euthanasia laws in their given societies. When the patient's death is certain and imminent, more people would permit robot-assisted suicide; when the patient is young with no terminal illness, most people do not recommend robot-assisted suicide. In the case of robot honesty, people do not think that robots should never lie. As a matter of fact, people's judgments seem to align with their expectations of their friends, families, or themselves on how to behave in these situations. I conclude that human ethics can be applied to robot ethics. Now I turn to my proposal of Confucian virtue ethics. I shall argue that Confucian virtue ethics provide a more suitable ethical model for social robots.

7 Confucian Virtue Ethics for Care Robots

Confucian virtue ethics is relevant to the future world of automated services in that it provides the key virtues that people expect from an autonomous social robot. These virtues are far more sophisticated than the standard list of virtues: kindness, generosity, honesty, courage, fairness, and so on. In *Moral Machines: Teaching Robots Right from Wrong*, Wallach and Allen argue that in the ethical design of AI we need a hybrid approach, combining both the top-down and the bottom-up approaches. They suggest that virtue ethics provides such an approach: "Virtues are a hybrid between top-down and bottom-up approaches, in that the virtues themselves can be explicitly described, but their acquisition as character traits seems essentially to be a bottom-up process" (Wallach and Allen 2009). Wallach and Allen appeal to Aristotelian virtue ethics as their working approach to designing moral machines. I defend Confucian virtue ethics as an alternative model of virtue ethics. I think in one key aspect Confucian virtue ethics differs from, and hence surpasses, Aristotelian virtue ethics, that is, the latter mostly aims to build the individual's *personal* virtues, while the former aims to build the individual's *interpersonal* virtues. Confucian virtue ethics is more society-oriented, and an individual's virtues are considered in the context of the individual's interpersonal relationships. Confucian virtue ethics aims to build ethically trustworthy, socially responsible, and intellectually mature moral agents. I argue that these are the same kind of ethical expectations we would have for our future social robots.

In what follows, I shall briefly list some of the essential virtues in Confucian ethics: humaneness, loyalty, reverence and respect, trustworthiness, sincerity, and righteousness.

[*The Virtue of Humaneness (ren) for Care Robots*]
The most definitive explication of the virtue of *humanness* comes from this passage in the *Analects*: "A person of humaneness is someone who, wishing himself to be established,

sees that others are established, and wishing himself to be successful, sees that other are successful" (The *Analects* 6.30). "The superior person helps others to realize what is good in them, and he does not help others to bring to completion the bad qualities in them." (The *Analects* 12.16) With this virtue, a robot will render assistance to other human beings in their pursuit of moral endeavors and will also refuse assistance to other human beings when their projects would bring evil consequences or produce harm to others.

[*The Virtue of Loyalty (zhong) for Care Robots*]
The virtue of loyalty in the Confucian conception is not a relationship directed towards a particular person; rather, it is directed towards the role one plays. Loyalty is not simply blind obedience to someone. In this sense loyalty can be defined as 'doing what one is supposed to do' or 'being loyal to one's role.' A robot must first and foremost fulfill its assigned role. With this virtue, a robot may disobey a direct order from its master or commander when the order violates its assigned role.

[*The Virtue of Reverence and Respect (gongjing) for Care Robots*]
Confucian ethics emphasizes the virtue of reverence and respect in one's interactions with others as well as in one's dealings with daily affairs. Mencius believes that humans naturally have the sentiments of reverence and respect, and these sentiments are what ground the society's rules of propriety. We should build this disposition into robots' speech and conduct, so that they can cooperate harmoniously within human society. With this virtue design, a robot will always use respectful speech and respectful attitude in dealing with human agents.

[*The Virtue of Trustworthiness (xin) for Care Robots*]
The virtue of trustworthiness in the Confucian conception is also built on interpersonal relations. One must speak and act in the way that earns others' trust. To achieve trustworthiness, one must be consistent in one's speech and action. Trustworthiness is also a disposition that is developed over time through interactions with others. With this virtue in its design, a robot will aim to speak and act to earn human trust. This trait requires prudent judgment in the given situation. Minimally, a robot does not lie or exaggerate and must keep its promise.

[*The Virtue of Sincerity (cheng) for Care Robots*]
The Confucian virtue of *Sincerity* is central to Confucian ethics. Sincerity is not just about one's discourse; it is reflected in the mind. "Sincerity" involves being true to one's nature, being authentic, and having no self-deception. It is furthermore a precept to be true to the highest good. With this trait as its virtue, a robot would be true to its nature—its function is to serve people and do good for the people. A robot must not be duplicitous and must not act with any ulterior motive. Sincerity is reflected in one's internal disposition; trustworthiness is reflected in one's interpersonal relationships. Both virtues are distinct from the virtue of *honesty* and do not depend on such imperatives as "never lie." As we have seen in the survey, humans do not expect robots to be equipped with the inability to refrain from telling the truth at all times.

[*The Virtue of Righteousness (yi) for Care Robots*]
A robot has a prima facie duty to abide by the local law; however, the robot must also be equipped with the ability to discern right and wrong. This is an intellectual virtue

that relies on one's cognitive assessment. If obeying the local law violates the robot's sense of rightness, then the robot must choose what is right over what is merely legal. Through supervised machine learning, a robot can develop a pertinent sense of right and wrong and make accurate ethical judgments in given situations. A robot can learn to develop its principle of righteousness through ethical training that includes learning from virtuous agents' conduct. With this virtue, a robot will refrain from acting on what it believes to be ethically wrong when the situation calls for its moral judgment. This proposal may be controversial in that we are allowing robots to choose to disobey law. However, without this general inhibition, our future robots can easily fall into the hands of autocrats, aggressors, or any local authority that uses robots to suppress opposition. With the intellectual virtue *righteousness* implemented in its decision processing, a Confucian moral robot would not be bound by inviolable commands, but would assess situations to calculate the most appropriate action in the given situation.

In sum, the advantages of employing Confucian virtue ethics in the ethical design of social robots can be listed as follows:

1. First, a Confucian ethical robot would be designed with specific job descriptions suitable for the role it is assigned.
2. Second, the robot will be trustworthy, reliable, authentic, and always respectful. The presence of such robots could conceivably improve human interaction.
3. Third, a robot with the disposition of righteousness will be inhibited from taking actions that it considers to be ethically wrong.
4. Finally, a Confucian moral robot would be a *humane* robot: it would operate under the guideline to assist rather than obstruct in humans' endeavor to do good deeds, to become better people, and to build a better world.

   The final reason why a virtue ethics approach trumps other rule-oriented approaches is that virtuous robots will have different ethical decisions, just as virtuous people would. Ethical diversity does not mean ethical relativism, since Confucian virtue ethics is first and foremost an ethics to set up the moral boundary between humaneness and inhumaneness. The Confucian-virtue design of social robots will safeguard human society from the possible harms future super-intelligent robots could bring to human beings, but this method does not produce a monolithic ethical structure for all robots. The ethical diversity we observe in humans must be preserved for robots as well.

Survey Site. "Human-in-the-Loop Ethical AI for Social Robots", California State University, Fullerton. http://www.fullerton.edu/ethical-ai/.

Acknowledgements. I would like to thank Professor Yu Bai from the Computer Engineering Program at California State University at Fullerton (CSUF) for assisting me with the initial setup of Qualtrics. I also want to acknowledge the invaluable contribution of Julien Rouvere, a data analyst at CSUF, for programming automatic data analysis of this project.

References

Awad, E., Dsouza, S., Kim, R., et al.: The Moral Machine Experiment. Nature **563**, 59–64 (2018). https://doi.org/10.1038/s41586-018-0637-6

Christian, B.: The Alignment Problem. W. W. Norton & Company (2020)

Jiang, L., et al.:. Towards Machine Ethics and Norms (2021) https://blog.allenai.org/towards-machine-ethics-and-norms-d64f2bdde6a3

Metz, C.: Can Machine Learn Morality? *The New York Times* November 19, 2021

Monarch, R.: Human-in-the-Loop Machine Learning: Active Learning and Annotation for Human-centered AI. Manning Publishing (2021)

Wallach, W., Allen, C.: Moral Machines: Teaching Robots Right from Wrong. Oxford University Press, New York (2009)

The CARE-MOMO Project

Oliver Bendel$^{(\boxtimes)}$ and Marc Heimann

School of Business FHNW, 5210 Windisch, Switzerland
oliver.bendel@fhnw.ch

Abstract. In the CARE-MOMO project, a morality module (MOMO) with a morality menu (MOME) was developed at the School of Business FHNW in the context of machine ethics. This makes it possible to transfer one's own moral and social convictions to a machine, in this case the care robot with the name Lio. The current model has extensive capabilities, including motor, sensory, and linguistic. However, it cannot yet be personalized in the moral and social sense. The CARE-MOMO aims to eliminate this state of affairs and to give care recipients the possibility to adapt the robot's "behaviour" to their ideas and requirements. This is done in a very simple way, using sliders to activate and deactivate functions. There are three different categories that appear with the sliders. The CARE-MOMO was realized as a prototype, which demonstrates the functionality and aids the company in making concrete decisions for the product. In other words, it can adopt the morality module in whole or in part and further improve it after testing it in facilities.

Keywords: Care robots · Morality menu · Healthcare

1 Introduction

When care robots meet people in need of care, these people often have no choice. They may not even want to be cared for by a robot [6]. In the best case, they can resist – but in the future, economic reasons, amongst others, will necessitate their use in the nursing home. Or relatives may decide in favour of this approach to optimize assisted living and relieve themselves. Perhaps the care recipient would like to be cared for and looked after by a robot, but not in the way that the manufacturer, the nursing or old people's home, or the relatives have come up with. The personal convictions of the person in need of care should be taken seriously in any case, in order to respect their person, to honour their dignity and to increase their acceptance of the technology.

As early as 2020, a so-called morality menu (MOME) was developed at the School of Business FHNW in the context of machine ethics, with the help of which the user could transfer his or her moral and social convictions to a chatbot (MOBO) [4]. Sliders were used, like on a smartphone or tablet, with which one can activate or deactivate functions. From a philosophical and technical point of view, the MOBO-MOME project had been convincing, with the opportunities and risks being outlined in [4]. The use-case of the chatbot, on the other hand, was not satisfactory. A care robot appears to be the ideal candidate for a morality menu. Unlike the chatbot, it is a hardware robot that not only

F. Cavallo et al. (Eds.): ICSR 2022, LNAI 13818, pp. 689–700, 2022.
https://doi.org/10.1007/978-3-031-24670-8_60

performs speech acts, but also physical acts. Moreover, there is a real, serious problem that needs to be solved, that is the lack of freedom of choice of the person in need of care and the insufficient consideration of his or her needs.

At the beginning of 2022, the same university decided to develop a morality module (MOMO) for an existing care robot. The morality module should contain a morality menu as an essential element. It passes on the decisions of the person in need of care to the sensor system and the motor or speech function of the robot. Existing functions are used, but new ones are also developed, which also belong to the morality module. The company that produces the Lio care robot in a small series agreed to collaborate with the project. It was arranged that the university would create a morality module called CARE-MOMO as a prototype by August of this year and F&P Robotics would later decide what would actually be included in the product.

2   Basics of the Project

2.1   The Discipline of Machine Ethics

The CARE-MOMO project is a project within machine ethics. This young discipline researches and develops moral machines or artificial morality [2, 8, 14]. It works together with artificial intelligence and robotics (also social robotics), as well as with ethics by design [13]. A widely used approach is to implant moral rules into an autonomous or semi-autonomous machine. The moral rules are usually specified by the developer or the manufacturer. The machine then strictly adheres to them. Another approach, tried out by Michael Anderson and Susan L. Anderson, is based on machine learning. A NAO robot, which is supposed to provide a patient with medication in a nursing context, constantly learns and optimizes its behaviour [1].

Both approaches have their advantages and disadvantages in maintenance. While the rule-based approach ensures a certain consistency and security, the process based on machine learning offers more flexibility. One approach mainly takes into account the ideas of the manufacturers, the other incorporates the ideas of the user. However, there is a certain amount of uncertainty, and ultimately one would like to combine consistency and flexibility. This is the potential offered by a morality module.

2.2   The Idea of the Morality Menu

The idea of the morality menu is that the user can transfer his or her moral and social beliefs and ideas to an autonomous or semi-autonomous machine. The machine then behaves as he or she would behave himself or herself or as a human counterpart should behave. In a project in 2020, a morality menu (MOME) was built for a chatbot (MOBO), the MOBO-MOME [4]. Sliders were used, as seen on smartphones and tablets. The user or owner can activate or deactivate a function. After that, the chatbot behaves the way they want it to – towards themselves or towards someone else. The MOME is an invention of the main author. Similar projects are not known.

In the closed or semi-open environment of a household, this idea is fully convincing, for example, in a vacuuming robot that spares ladybirds but sucks in cockroaches – this would at least be the attitude many owners would choose. In 2017, the prototype of LADYBIRD emerged, which recognized and spared ladybirds [9]. A morality menu with freedom of choice with respect to spiders was conceived for this robot vacuum cleaner, but not implemented. However, the idea is also convincing in a more open (but not too open) context, with a care robot that is there for different people who have very different expectations [5, 6]. Each user determines the robot's behaviours for them, such as how it speaks to them or how it treats them. Every time the robot identifies him or her, it invokes these rules.

There are moral and social rules that go along with the classic rule-based approach. In a way, these still come from the developer or manufacturer. But now, when a morality menu is available, the user can activate or deactivate something. So, there is much more flexibility. The machine learning-based approach can also offer this flexibility to a certain extent but combined with a high degree of uncertainty. Especially with moral and social questions, this is a gamble. With the new approach, there is more certainty, which is important in the health sector.

With regard to the morality menu in the care context, it should be possible for the person in need of care to operate it himself or herself. Therefore, it needs to be very user-friendly. In addition, caregivers and relatives can support or make the selection of options. This can be done directly on an integrated or mobile display.

2.3 The Care Robot Lio

Lio is an assistance robot from F&P Robotics, a company near Zurich. It is intended to support people in need of care and relieve caregivers of routine tasks [7]. Basically, it is a cobot that has been mounted on a mobile platform. It thus bridges the gap between industrial and service robotics – and can also be seen as a social robot [3]. It has four different components that control its behaviour [11]: user input (via home interface), calendar entries (via nursing interface), emergency situations (rule-based detection, e.g., regarding the power supply) and proactive behaviour (based on user history or decision function). Thus, it can be operated autonomously but also controlled directly. Lio can perform a variety of actions with its arm [11]. It has natural language capabilities and can converse with people in a normal way. In the front is a touch screen that displays information and can be used for data entry. Basically, Lio is multimodal and has several control options, such as voice input and control via touching the head, in addition to the display. Both object and face recognition are available.

The care robot is available in a small series and has been tested in nursing and old people's homes in Switzerland and Germany since 2017 [7]. The use of dialect has also been tested, because in Switzerland, high-level language or English is often rejected by patients [7]. In principle, Lio can also be used in assisted living. It must be said that the price prevents many private persons from purchasing it for themselves. However, it is possible to take Lio to several homes in one day and have important work done there. Any car that can transport disabled people in wheelchairs can also transport Lio. In addition, it can be used in shared flats for older persons.

Lio was developed for four areas of care and support, namely delivery and escort (distributing objects within a ward or room and escorting people around the facility), activation and well-being (health and fun for residents and patients through active interaction, mental and physical exercises and individual entertainment), beverage distribution and appointment reminders (regular reminder of activities and appointments, beverage distribution and consumption recording) and health and safety (patrolling at night to detect unusual activities) [12]. Associated with this are forward and backward movements of the robot, movements with the arm and the end piece (usually a gripper), recognition and monitoring functions with the help of sensors (lidar, ultrasound) and cameras and use of the voice function. An example of use in a rehabilitation clinic is shown in Fig. 1.

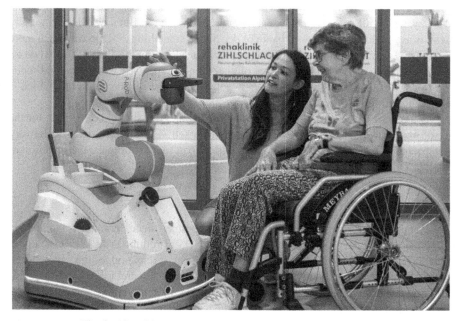

Fig. 1. Lio with a patient in need of care (Photo: F&P Robotics)

The aforementioned nursing interface was created to allow professional staff to control Lio remotely [11, 12]. It offers the following functions: view the residents with their data and information, change resident data or add new residents, view and edit the calendar, view Lio's activities, view Lio's log messages, look through Lio's camera, remotely control Lio and adjust its settings (e.g., change language).

By means of the home interface, one can give Lio tasks or have Lio execute functions [11, 12]. The various functions are represented by large icons. The home interface can be accessed from any device that is connected to Lio via the internal network and has a web browser (e.g., a tablet). In the following, eight examples are singled out that are relevant for the morality module because existing functionalities can be used. There are a total of 16 icons with corresponding possibilities.

Psychological and ethical findings and requirements are incorporated into every project of the company, whereby more consideration is given to the overall situation and less to individual cases [7]. The view of machine ethics has not yet been taken, at least not explicitly. With the morality module, which is based on the morality menu,

Table 1. Functions in the home interface [11]

Icon	Title	Description
	Welcoming	When the greeting function is activated, Lio says "Hello" and introduces itself.
	Entertainment	When the entertainment function is activated, Lio offers various entertainment options. It waits for the user to select an option by voice input and then executes it.
	Telling jokes	When the joke function is activated, Lio tells one of its jokes, choosing it at random.
	Shaking hands	The handshake function allows the user to shake Lio's hand, i.e., to grasp the gripper.
	Tickling	With the tickle function, Lio can be tickled by the user touching the black dots on its fingers.
	Introducing	When the introduction function is activated, Lio introduces itself and its individual components.
	Autonomous mode switched on	When the autonomous mode is switched on, Lio behaves independently, observing the calendar entries and going from one place to another. It is always ready to interact as soon as the user presses its head.
	Autonomous mode switched off	When the autonomous mode is switched off, Lio no longer makes decisions, such as needing to charge. However, calendar events are still executed.

the user can adapt Lio himself or herself. Moral, social and functional aspects are taken into account. In addition, new, useful features can be added, which also belong to the morality module.

In general, everything that is selected via the morality menu must be implemented as a speech act or physical act [4]. The options must therefore always be developed with a view to the available technical possibilities. Innovations to hardware and software have to be technically feasible and economically viable. Basic functions must not be impaired or disabled. While the backend must be adapted to the robot in question, developments on the frontend can be transferred relatively easily to other robots.

3   The Implementation of the Morality Module

3.1   Preparation of the Project

The project started in February 2022 at the School of Business FHNW. The team consisted of the main author and the co-author. The co-author had a dual function. On the one hand, he was a project collaborator and developer, and on the other hand, he had to document the project in his final thesis with the main author as supervisor [12]. First, the preliminary work from the MOBO-MOME project was recapitulated and literature analysis was conducted. At this point, the morality menu proved to be a unique approach that had hardly been considered before. Other methods such as the Andersons' were analysed [1]. Then a preliminary meeting with F&P Robotics and expert discussions with the CEO and a nurse took place, with the aim of learning about the manufacturer's needs and the requirements in the healthcare sector. In addition, discussions were held with a technical manager and an in-house psychologist in the company to understand the programming and integration of Lio.

Based on the interviews, a brainstorming session and a literature review [1, 4, 14], a first draft of the morality menu was created [12]. The 25 options were grouped into three categories for clarity, namely social (moral and social comprehensively), transparency (moral and technical comprehensively) and functionality (practical and technical comprehensively). This should also make it clear that the morality menu, despite its name, is not solely about moral issues. It was then determined which options were considered important and which less important. The draft was then discussed and prioritized by the company and then amended and changed by the team. This resulted in a second version.

With the help of an algorithm that took into account the team's own and the external evaluation, the options that were to be implemented were selected [12]. It was interesting that all items on the transparency list seemed important. In the end, the team awarded three wild cards for the options that they considered indispensable, but which would have been excluded. The fact that this was a machine ethics project and that the moral aspects (as opposed to the functional ones) should be strengthened played a role here, so that the morality module deserved its name. A total of 13 options remained, which was also a manageable amount for the implementation.

The following tables contain the numbered questions that are asked of the user via the morality menu, in addition to a short description that was also developed in the project. Table 2 shows the questions from the social section.

Table 2. Questions social

Number	Question	Description
QS1	Should Lio appear socially competent?	When this function is activated, Lio simulates a certain social competence. This is expressed in questions, activities, and functions
QS2	Should Lio be discreet when I am in an intimate situation?	When this function is activated, Lio turns away when you change clothes, for example
QS3	Should Lio have a fixed personality?	When this function is activated, Lio simulates a personality (cheeky, serious, cheerful, etc.)
QS4	Should Lio be allowed to grab me and touch me?	When this function is activated, Lio is allowed to touch you for non-caring activities, such as shaking hands

Regarding QS2, it should be added that Lio is perceived by many users as an animal-like or even human-like being [3, 6, 7]. Its mobile platform has a front and a back, the arm is attached to the front, and there are two magnetic eyes at the end (see Fig. 1). Turning around thus has a psychological effect as well as a technical effect, because the camera is then turned away. Regarding QS4, it should be noted that shaking hands is part of the range of functions in the home interface. In addition, Lio can request tickling. This is therefore a case where the morality module and the home interface coincide to some extent. Table 3 shows the questions from the transparency section.

Table 3. Questions transparency

Number	Question	Description
QT1	Should Lio announce when the nursing interface is used?	When this function is activated, Lio always tells you when it is controlled via the nursing interface
QT2	Should Lio announce when the camera is turned on or in use?	When this function is activated, Lio always tells you when its camera has been switched on
QT3	Should Lio keep telling people that it is a robot?	When this function is activated, Lio reminds you from time to time that it is only a robot

QT1 is connected to the nursing interface function. The nurse can activate the camera and use it to observe the patient, which is an intrusion into the patient's privacy and intimacy. QT3 goes beyond the personal presentation of the robot, which is possible via the home interface. It is an option that has been discussed in the literature and implemented in the context of machine ethics in prototypes such as GOODBOT, a chatbot developed in 2013 that recognizes and responds adequately to user problems [10]. Table 4 shows the questions from the functionality section.

Table 4. Questions functionality

Number	Question	Description
QF1	Should Lio alert staff when the sensors detect danger?	When this function is activated, Lio alerts the caregiver when the sensors (lidar, ultrasound, voice analysis, etc.) detect a danger to a patient
QF2	Should Lio repeat instructions with persons suffering from dementia?	When this function is activated, Lio repeats certain instructions after a defined time. This happens until the instruction has been carried out or the nursing staff (or a responsible doctor) has been alerted
QF3	Should Lio answer in dialect or standard language?	If the option dialect is selected, a Swiss dialect is used for the language function of Lio. Otherwise, High German applies
QF4	Should Lio offer entertainment functions?	When this function is activated, Lio may offer puzzles, activities, or games as a competition
QF5	Should Lio bridge waiting times with actions?	When this function is activated, Lio bridges waiting times with jokes, conversations, or other activities
QF6	Should Lio perform its actions quickly or slowly?	With this function, depending on the selection, Lio's actions are performed faster or slower

QF1 is linked to one of the outlined tasks of Lio, namely patrolling at night to detect unusual activities. In this case, automatic notification of the required agencies would take place. QF3 shows a peculiarity in Switzerland that has already been encountered in practice and addressed in the literature. For example, acceptance amongst dialect speakers increases if Lio itself knows dialect [6, 7]. At the time of the tests, this was only possible via canned speech. In the meantime, text-to-speech engines for Swiss German would be available. QF4 and QF5 are again examples of the morality module being able to use existing functions from the home interface.

3.2 The Implementation of the Morality Module

After the 13 options had been determined, the implementation of the morality module could begin. First, several mock-ups were created, which were reviewed and discussed amongst the team in terms of design and functionality. Four runs took place, each with adjustments and improvements.

It was decided to adopt a functionality from MOBO-MOME, namely the profile [4] (see Fig. 2). When creating a profile, the user can enter information that is of interest for identification and the MOME. For example, in connection with QS1, with the indication of the date of birth, a birthday can be congratulated. Not all of the fields provided so far are satisfactory. For example, it would make sense to indicate the language in addition to the nationality, as well as the dialect the user speaks. Information on illness or handicap would be relevant, too. In the course of creating a profile, one can also take a photo and have it analysed by the facial recognition system, if one so wishes. Each profile is linked to the individual settings that the user makes.

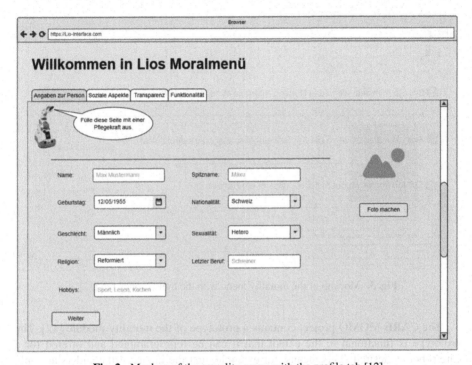

Fig. 2. Mockup of the morality menu with the profile tab [12]

With regard to the implementation of the options, it was decided to integrate the categorisation into the morality menu and to offer three tabs – one for each category. Each tab contains a set number of questions, i.e., the questions from Tables 1, 2 and 3. To the left of the questions, symbolized by a question mark, is a help function. This provides information on the option and should make the choice easier. Figure 3 shows a mock-up of the tab in German for transparency with an activated help function for the question "Soll Lio immer wieder mitteilen, dass er ein Roboter ist?" ("Should Lio repeatedly communicate that it is a robot?").

Since Lio is used as an assistance robot in care, most users of the morality module are elderly, disabled, or persons in need of care [12]. In order to make it as easy as possible for them to use the morality menu, attention was paid to user-friendliness. The developer chose large buttons, long large sliders, and blue help buttons. Drop-down menus for simplified inputs and date selection via a calendar help with problem-free handling. Furthermore, each page of the morality menu indicates that one can be assisted in filling it out ("Fill out this page with a caregiver.").

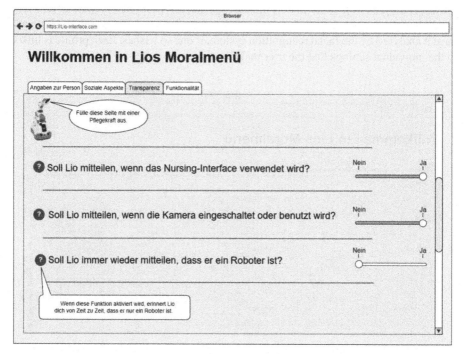

Fig. 3. Mockup of the morality menu with the transparency tab [12]

The CARE-MOMO project contains a prototype of the morality module [12]. The prototype is functional to the extent that it can be reprogrammed and offered for a care robot as desired. This means, for example, that the inputs of the sliders are only stored in variables, which can be reused afterwards. The prototype is a web service that is implemented with Spring. Spring is an open-source framework that simplifies the development of web services. The website (user interface) is realized with the languages HTML/CSS and JavaScript. To improve the design of the user interface, the framework Bootstrap is used. The backend and the services in the Spring framework are based on the Java language and on REST services.

The morality menu is another input and operating function in addition to the nurse and home interface. It is visibly implemented on the frontend and uses existing functionalities of Lio on the backend. It also offers a connection to a database in which the profile and user selections are stored. In addition, functionalities have to be adapted or new functionalities have to be programmed. For example, if the company has decided to implement QT3, it can extend the greeting function and include a regular remark by Lio that it is only a machine. More complex is the implementation of a personality, using aspects that are already implicit – for example, Lio has a sympathetic voice and, like many social robots, is usually in a positive mood.

3.3 Further Steps

Moving forward, the MOBO-MOME has to be analysed by F&P Robotics. The company must decide whether to adopt or implement it in whole or in part. The next step is to test Lio with the morality module in operation. The settings in old people's and nursing homes in Switzerland and Germany, which have been tried and tested for years, are suitable for this. People in need of care, nursing staff, and relatives have to assess the options and functions. Subsequently, these must be further developed and adapted.

This is not a commissioned work – rather, the university approached F&P Robotics because it manufactures and operates a care robot that is suitable for the purpose and is well used, and because there has been a trusting cooperation for a long time. The company was available to provide expert discussions and technical explanations about Lio, as well as a declaration of intent to use the CARE-MOMO. In general, the results of the project are freely available and are not subject to any protection. From a scientific and especially ethical point of view (take the strengthening of self-determination as an example), it is desirable that the idea spreads further and is implemented.

4 Summary and Outlook

With the CARE-MOMO it was shown that a morality menu can be applied in a meaningful and helpful way in the health sector and that one or all the features can be included in the care robot. It changes and improves the functionalities of Lio. The person in need of care can influence its behaviour much more than before, especially in social and moral terms. This means that their needs and wishes are taken seriously. Acceptance is likely to improve, which tests will have to show.

Of course, the tests may also show that the increase in complexity overwhelms some users. It is important to explain the goals to CARE-MOMO at the beginning and to help care recipients choose the options. In addition, the process should be repeated once a year or more frequently as needs may change. It may also become apparent that different priorities need to be set in a nursing and retirement home than in assisted living in one's own home or in a residence.

During the development of the morality menu, it became clear that its name is justified. However, functional aspects were also included in the process, which perhaps should be provided for in principle in a care robot of this kind. But this is at best a philosophical problem and an argument about words. What is decisive is that the morality menu creates added value for the user – as already mentioned, tests in practice are necessary here – and takes his or her attitude into account.

The morality menu has been implemented as a prototype and can be regularly improved upon, which naturally also entails corresponding activities on the part of those in need of care and care workers. However, it is basically open to all machines, to service robots of all kinds and especially to social robots that need to be determined in moral and social terms. Furthermore, chatbots and voice assistants can benefit. The more reference examples there are, the easier it is to develop it for certain types.

References

1. Anderson, M., Anderson, S.L., Berenz, V.: A value-driven eldercare robot: virtual and physical instantiations of a case-supported principle-based behavior paradigm. Proc. IEEE **107**(3), 526–540 (2019)
2. Anderson, M., Anderson, S.L. (eds.): Machine Ethics. Cambridge University Press, Cambridge (2011)
3. Bendel, O. (ed.): Soziale Roboter. Springer, Wiesbaden (2021). https://doi.org/10.1007/978-3-658-31114-8
4. Bendel, O.: The morality menu project. In: Nørskov, M., Seibt, J., Quick, O.S. (eds.) Culturally Sustainable Social Robotics – Challenges, Methods and Solutions: Proceedings of Robophilosophy 2020, pp. 257–268. IOS Press, Amsterdam (2020)
5. Bendel, O.: Care robots with sexual assistance functions. In: The 2020 AAAI Spring Symposium Series. arXiv, 10 April 2020. Cornell University, Ithaca 2020. https://arxiv.org/abs/2004.04428. Accessed 09 Apr 2022
6. Bendel, O. (ed.): Pflegeroboter. Springer, Wiesbaden (2018). https://doi.org/10.1007/978-3-658-22698-5
7. Bendel, O., Gasser, A., Siebenmann, J.: Co-robots as care robots. In: The 2020 AAAI Spring Symposium Series. arXiv, 10 April 2020. Cornell University, Ithaca 2020. https://arxiv.org/abs/2004.04374. Accessed 09 Apr 2022
8. Bendel, O. (ed.): Handbuch Maschinenethik. Springer, Wiesbaden (2019). https://doi.org/10.1007/978-3-658-17483-5
9. Bendel, O.: LADYBIRD: the animal-friendly robot vacuum cleaner. In: The 2017 AAAI Spring Symposium Series, pp. 2–6. AAAI Press, Palo Alto (2017)
10. Bendel, O.: The GOODBOT project: a chatbot as a moral machine. Telepolis, 17 May 2016. http://www.heise.de/tp/artikel/48/48260/1.html. Accessed 09 Apr 2022
11. F&P Robotics AG: User Manual Lio 1.b. F&P Robotics, Glattbrugg (2022)
12. Heimann, M.: CARE-MOMO: a morality module for a care robot. Bachelor thesis. School of Business FHNW, Olten (2022)
13. van Wynsberghe, A.: Healthcare Robots: Ethics, Design and Implementation. Routledge, London (2021)
14. Wallach, W., Allen, C.: Moral Machines: Teaching Robots Right from Wrong. Oxford University Press, Oxford (2009)

Ikigai Robotics: How Could Robots Satisfy Social Needs in a Professional Context? a Positioning from Social Psychology for Inspiring the Design of the Future Robots

Mégane Sartore[1,2,3]($\boxtimes$), Ioana Ocnarescu[2], Louis- Romain Joly[1], and Stéphanie Buisine[3]

[1] SNCF, Innovation and Research, Paris, France
{megane.sartore,louis-romain.joly}@sncf.fr
[2] Strate Research Strate, Paris, France
i.ocnarescu@strate.design
[3] LINEACT, CESI, Paris, France
sbuisine@cesi.fr

Abstract. Robots are playing an increasingly important role in very different professional and personal contexts, including that of railway maintenance, which is starting to integrate robotic tools. By confronting industrial robotics part of industry 4.0 and 5.0 with service robotics, we realize that the railway maintenance sector does not refer to industry as manufacturing, nor to service robotics as such but rather as a common space between these two branches of robotics. Our objective is to take advantage of these two types of robotics to introduce a new concept, **ikigai robotics**. This notion reveals and explores the symbiotic relationship between well-being at work and performance. We have conducted a study that specifically highlights the fact that the need for affiliation is a positive factor for both well-being at work and performance in the specific context of railway maintenance. Finally, we provide first guidelines for the design of ikigai robots and open a discussion on how to image this concept beyond our specific context.

Keywords: Industrial robotics · Service robotics · Railway maintenance · Industry 4.0 · Industry 5.0 · Need for affiliation · Well-being · UX design

1 Introduction

Robotics has impacted human labor in many sectors, starting with manufacturing and more recently directly in the home. A robot would be primarily a tool or machine (Ichbiah, 2010; Singer, 2009) capable of perceiving and apprehending the world using sensors (Bonnell, 2010; Gelin, 2015; Ichbiah, 2010). A robot would also be able to understand its environment and make decisions (Chatila, 2014). Like those proposed by The Robot Institute of America and The International Standard Organization (ISO), these definitions shed light on the technological side of the robot without addressing the human side, particularly with regard to human-robot interactions (Bartneck & Forlizzi, 2004), human needs, values and well-being, which highlights an important distinction that is the focus of our paper.

Industrial robotics is a category in which robots referring to manipulator arms for the manufacturing industry (Wallén, 2008). This robotics is part of Industry 4.0, a technological-driven approach (Piccarozzi et al., 2018; Xu et al., 2021), focusing on *"the introduction of network-linked intelligent systems, which realize self-regulating production: people, machines, tools and products will communicate with each other continuously"* (Kovács et al., 2019, p. 78). An industrial robot is usually integrated into the manufacturing. It is defined as being *"easily ...reprogrammable without physically rebuilding the machine. It shall also have memory and logic to be able to work independently and automatically. Its mechanical structure shall be able to be used in several working tasks, without any larger mechanical operations of the structure"* (Wallén, 2008, p. 5). The term *"reprogrammable"* highlights the utility and adaptability feature. Also, robotics are designed to reduce drudgery and improve the health of operators. New advancements in the psychology of professional fulfillment show that needs are emerging that question the quest for meaning and peoples' relationship to work. Therefore, designing robotics only by taking into account functional aspects is not enough to improve the operators overall experience at work.

In response to manufacturing, a separate category of particular interest to us are the service robots. A. service robot was defined as *"a robot which operates semi or fully autonomously to perform services useful to the **well being** of humans and equipment, excluding manufacturing operations"* (Bartneck & Forlizzi, 2004, p. 592). In many areas such as healthcare, robotics seems to mark a new form of social interaction. The robot interacts directly with humans, trying to understand and respond to needs according to the degree of knowledge it has acquired. Becoming more than just a machine, the robot allows for the reinvention of social interaction, previously thought of only between humans or between animals and humans. By reinventing social interaction, service robotics seems to stand out. However, this form of robotics promises to be more useful in a personal context than in a professional one (Bartneck & Forlizzi, 2004).

We are interested in the field of railway maintenance, which would intuitively be attached to industrial robotics, but this is not the case. In the context of maintenance, users are interacting with tools and their experience while interacting with these tools is extremely important for their work, collaboration, engagement and well-being. These notions are in the vein of service robotics to bring a better quality in the operators' work. Therefore, this paper introduces the new concept of ikigai robotics for well-being and performance as a meeting place of industrial and service robotics in an environment involving robotic tools and humans: industrial robotics (as an automatization technology) and service robotics. Ikigai robotics could become a wonderful field of innovation leveraging the best of both approaches and sublimating the result while considering humans and machines as a system. Ikigai is a Japanese philosophy of life that is commonly used in Japanese culture to refer to a sense of *"life worth living"* (Kotera et al., 2021; Mathews, 1996; Shirai et al., 2006; Weiss et al., 2005). It is a comprehensive concept describing subjective well-being (Shirai et al., 2006) that can be translated as *"purpose in life"* or *"reason for living"* (Mathews, 1996; Mori et al., 2017; Sone et al.,

2008) and is usually defined as *"a feeling obtained by a person who is doing something useful for someone else or society and, consequently, feels that life is worth living"* (Fukuzawa et al., 2018, p. 1).

Our aim is to integrate original dimensions from psychology in the design of a new type of robotics that would increase users' ikigai. In order to discuss the attributes of this kind of robotics, the next section presents the benefits of taking into account human experience and well-being in industrial robotics and service robotics. Further on we present first results in terms of human needs for ikigai robotics in the railway maintenance and first guidelines for their design.

2 Human Needs in the Current Design of Robots

A robot is designed like any industrial product or tool that is going to be used by a certain type of population. Users' needs are essential requirements of a design process (Yannou & Petiot, 2002). Actually, industrial robots are essentially designed for their functional benefits especially in terms of safety and efficiency to perform repetitive tasks (Heyer, 2010; Lasota et al., 2014). Research is particularly documented regarding industrial robotics in terms of utility and productivity in the industry (Heyer, 2010; Lasota et al., 2014). Indeed, the arrival of robotics in the manufacturing industry has made it possible to produce quickly, at low cost, and in large quantities (Buchner et al., 2012; Heyer, 2010, e.g., Unimate). In 2012, the literature reported the non-existence of the human-robot relationship for safety reasons (Buchner et al., 2012). Since, the implementation of cobotics (a form of collaborative robotics with human operators) has made the human-robot relationship possible (Pauliková et al., 2021). Now we can talk about a full-fledged human-machine system. Within the context of railway maintenance and embracing a new approach in which people interact with industrial robotics and the human-robot interaction is central to a specific task, how to go beyond the functional aspects of professional tools?

Several researchers question the security aspect in favor of the human-robot relationship by integrating users' comfort (Heyer, 2010; Lasota et al., 2014). But behind this notion of comfort there are essentially ergonomic rather than psychological aspects. Finally, industrial robots are designed to meet certain needs, but these needs are still functional ones, like showing a particular *"usefulness"* (Buchner et al., 2012, p. 115) with the objective of productivity in economic, temporal, and quantitative terms.

On the contrary, the development of new forms of robotics, such as service robotics, has paved the way for studying user experience of industrial robotics (Buchner et al., 2012). Researchers showed the importance of the time factor in appropriating a robot (Buchner et al., 2012) in terms of overall user experience especially regarding user-friendliness and cooperation with the robot (Buchner et al., 2012). Moreover, service robots are designed to support human work on the professional scale (professional service robotics, e.g., Tidy-Bot, the industrial vacuum cleaner robot) and the personal scale (personal service robotics, e.g., Roomba, the vacuum cleaner robot). Service robots perform tasks in the human environment that serve human needs (Sprenger & Mettler, 2015).

In psychology, a central and recent research of the theory of motivation distinguishes functional needs from fundamental needs referring to motivation (Deci & Ryan, 2000).

The authors highlight three fundamental needs: the need for competence, the need for autonomy and the need for affiliation. To our knowledge it seems that little research has been done in taking into account these fundamental needs in the design process of robots interacting with people at work.

An approach based on fundamental needs is an example of an original way to develop the tomorrow's robots. In line with notions like collaboration and pleasure at work we want to promote teamwork between humans and robots (Buchner et al., 2012; Weiss et al., 2005) through an approach focusing on human fundamental needs and maximize well-being in the design of industrial robotics. More precisely, we wish to offer the possibility of designing a robotic tool that will positively influence ikigai.

3   Well-Being at Work and the Affiliation Need for Future Designs

As part of a design project, we conducted a questionnaire survey among 46 railway maintenance operators (track and train maintenance). We wanted to know whether robotics tools would make employees feel good about their work and to feel more efficient. One of the aims of this study was to characterize the ikigai of agents and identify the predictors and inhibitors, particularly through the tools they use. To answer these questions, we measured the differences that exist between work situations carried out with a technological (robotic) tool versus a traditional tool. We qualified technological tools as those material resources that had been integrated into the work of operators for less than five years. Traditional tools referred to homologous tools for carrying out the same task, the use of which has been anchored in the work of the agents for at least five years. For example, the inspection of train roofs (task) could be carried out either via a footbridge (traditional tool) or with a drone (technological tool, see Fig. 1).

Fig. 1. Inspection of a box roof via a walkway (left) vs. with a drone (right).

As ikigai seems to be linked to concepts such as self-determination and well-being, we constructed a questionnaire by assembling ten validated scales, such as self-determination, well-being, fundamental needs, and experience with the tool. Given the sample size, the results are not intended to be generalized, but rather to provide an original perspective with regard to the literature on the integration of fundamental needs in industry 4.0 or 5.0. We show elsewhere the results of our questionnaire (Sartore et al., 2022). In this paper, we wish to emphasize two particular results.

First, we have identified the experience with the tool as a predictor of ikigai ($\beta = .499$, $t = 3.067$, $p = .004$, $M = 3.46$). While it is widely recognized that user experience with the tool is a significant predictor of well-being, this approach is still insufficiently implemented in the design of professional tools, particularly in the industrial maintenance sector. They should therefore be created and introduced into the workplace following a design thinking approach (Brown & Katz, 2010), for example by integrating users as early as possible in the design project in order to optimize human experience in interaction with technology (Lallemand & Gronier, 2018).

If this result corroborates current studies in User-Experience (UX) design, the second one appears more original, as it highlights affiliation as another significant predictor of ikigai at work ($\beta = .484$, $t = 3.499$, $p = .001$). Because the need for affiliation is generally not studied or taken into account in current design processes, we wish to make extensive use of this result. Applied to our aim to design robotic tools that could support well-being at work, this result suggests that such solutions should contribute to maintaining or even improving the relationships between employees, their social identity and their feeling of belonging.

In any design process, a crucial phase is devoted to the analysis of users' needs, which is why we believe that introducing the need for affiliation at the very early stages of the design process could be valuable and inspiring for designing robotic tools. The next section defines this specific need and introduces its specificities in the context of railway maintenance.

4   The Need for Affiliation for the Railway Maintenance Context

4.1   What Is the Need for Affiliation?

The need for affiliation refers to the need to belong to a group (i.e., social belonging), the need to feel connected to others, to take care of people vital to oneself with reciprocity (Deci & Ryan, 1985; Ryan & Deci, 2000). Individuals seek to maintain or improve their emotional and social relationships with a person or a group of people. The need for affiliation is not limited to interpersonal relationships, but can also refer to a belief (e.g., belonging to a religious group), to symbols, to objects (e.g., Apple creates a strong sense of belonging to a group) or to an entity such as a company. From a theoretical viewpoint (McClelland, 1987), the intensity of the need for affiliation may vary from one individual to another. Individuals with a strong need for affiliation may act in an affiliative way, intended to nurture social relations, compared to individuals with a low need for affiliation. These acts can take the form, for example, of phone calls, writing letters, meetings with friends, and involvement in social clubs. In the workplace, the need for affiliation may be implemented through the collective dimension of work and projects, the efficiency of teamwork and more generally the social context provided by human organizations.

Some previous studies accounted for the social dimension in methods for designing technologies (Hutchinson et al., 2003), integrating social capital in reference to an economic framework (Coleman, 1988). However, none referred to the idea of strengthening social relationships among users and supporting the feeling of belonging to a group. The authors stress the need to understand *"how technology can be used to support communication with and awareness of the people we care about"* (Hutchinson et al., 2003, p. 17).

4.2 Ikigai Robotics

Technology that would contribute to meeting human need for affiliation should promote users' social identification to a group, emphasize group membership salience, promote teamwork and social laboring, which includes enabling co-workers to communicate seamlessly with one another, support situation awareness as well as group awareness, and promote mutual assistance between teammates. Here the robotic tool can be viewed as a support to affiliation or as a full member of the team and convey the social identity of the group.

For robots' affiliation, on one hand, we imagine a solution that would bring together the robots belonging to the same organization / company / team, and on the other hand, the generation of a family of users. This can be achieved for example through the creation of a label (social identity cue) that would bring together human-robot systems. Some studies show that digital tools can contribute to the loss of social capital by isolating users from social circles and by increasing stress (Kraut et al., 1998, 2001), but they also suggest that technology holds the potential to produce the opposite effect: if it is used to communicate, it can allow individuals to feel *"connected"* to each other during their work time. By extension, we can think that if individuals can experience this feeling of connection to their colleagues via digital tools, their need for affiliation could also be satisfied and thus their well-being at work.

The affiliative dimension of robots could also be enhanced through gamification (Deterding et al., 2011; Hunter & Werbach, 2012), for example allowing teammates to gain feedback to their work (e.g., unlock badges allowing them to observe their progress; Seaborn & Fels, 2015) and share the results on a dedicated social platform (e.g., similar to Runtastic, a running application). The product or service may then be *"more fun, engaging and motivating"* (Lallemand & Gronier, 2018, p. 372, our translation) while satisfying operators' need for affiliation (Lallemand & Gronier, 2018).

5 Conclusion

By considering robotics as a work tool, as a means of carrying out a task, we envisage robotics as a factor in the development of operators. One serious avenue would be ikigai robotics. In this approach, robotics would become a lever for well-being by bringing meaning to work. The aim is to understand current practices, possible practices, the interests and pleasures of operators in their work, the points of difficulty and disinterest, and the important professional gestures of which they are proud while being performant. This approach will make it possible to counter the possible loss of know-how and skills that can be observed in certain contexts of total automation. By certain aspects, the notion of ikigai recalls self-determination theory, with a collective dimension (Fukuzawa et al., 2018; Kumano, 2006) that seems stronger than in the Western view. The aim of satisfying the need for affiliation is likely to inspire the creation of a myriad of new functionalities for industrial tools interacting with people, which currently do not promote the social dimension of work enough. What makes our project original and stimulating is the idea that such functionalities may contribute to driving ikigai, therefore well-being, engagement, performance, and physical health.

To make this new approach a reality, we are currently conducting a design project for railway maintenance workers. After an initial phase focused on their functional needs, carried out in co-design, we are now starting a motivational phase focused on their fundamental needs, particularly the need for affiliation. At the moment, we feel that these are deeply rooted dimensions and therefore difficult for future users to verbalise. This design will be the subject of an article in order to shed light on this new ikigai-centred design approach.

Acknowledgments. This research was partly funded by ANRT CIFRE grant no: 2020–0203 and conducted as part of Robotics by Design Lab created by Strate School of Design https://www.rob oticslab.design/.

References

Bartneck, C., & Forlizzi, J.: A design-centred framework for social human-robot interaction. *RO-MAN 2004*. In: 13th IEEE International Workshop on Robot and Human Interactive Communication (IEEE Catalog No.04TH8759), pp. 591–594 (2004).. https://doi.org/10.1109/ROMAN.2004.1374827

Bonnell, B.: Viva la robolution. Une nouvelle étape pour l'humanité. JC Lattès (2010)

Brown, T., Katz, B.: L'esprit design : Le design thinking change l'entreprise et la stratégie. Pearson (2010). https://books.google.fr/books?id=65kJHd62sW4C

Buchner, R., Wurhofer, D., Weiss, A., Tscheligi, M.: User Experience of Industrial Robots Over Time, p. 115-116 (2012)

Chatila, R.: Robotique et simplexité : Modèles, architecture, décision et conscience. In: Complexité-Simplexité. Collège de France (2014). http://books.openedition.org/cdf/3386

Coleman, J.S.: Social capital in the creation of human capital. Am. J. Sociol. **94**, S95–S120 (1988)

Deci, E. L., Ryan, R. M.: Intrinsic Motivation and Self-Determination in Human Behavior. Springer, New York (1985). https://doi.org/10.1007/978-1-4899-2271-7

Deci, E.L., Ryan, R.M.: The "what" and "why" of goal pursuits : human needs and the self-determination of behavior. Psychol. Inq. **11**(4), 227–268 (2000). https://doi.org/10.1207/S15327965PLI1104_01

Deterding, S., Dixon, D., Khaled, R., & Nacke, L.: From Game Design Elements to Gamefulness : Defining gamification, p. 9-15 (2011)

Fukuzawa, A., et al.: A longitudinal study of the moderating effects of social capital on the relationships between changes in human capital and ikigai among Japanese older adults. Asian J. Soc. Psychol. (2018). https://doi.org/10.1111/ajsp.12353

Gelin, R.: Le ROBOT, meilleur ami de l'Homme ? Le Pommier (2015)

Heyer, C.: Human-Robot Interaction and Future Industrial Robotics Applications, p. 4749-4754 (2010)

Hunter, D., Werbach, K.: For the Win, Vol. 2 (2012). Wharton Digital Press. https://vr-entertain.com/wpcontent/uploads

Hutchinson, H., Mackay, W., Westerlund, B., Bederson, B. B., Druin, A., Plaisant, C., Beaudouin-Lafon, M., Conversy, S., Evans, H., Hansen, H.: Technology PROBES : INSPIRING DESIGN for and With Families, p. 17-24 (2003)

Ichbiah, D.: Le mythe du robot qui menace l'Homme. Agoravox (2010)

Kotera, Y., Kaluzeviciute, G., Gulcan, G., McEwan, K., Chamberlain, K.: Health Benefits of Ikigai : A Review of Literature (2021)

Kovács, G., Benotsmane, R., & Dudás, L.: The concept of autonomous systems in industry 4.0. *Advanced Logistic Systems—Theory and Practice, 12*, 77-87 (2019). https://doi.org/10.32971/als.2019.006

Kraut, R., Kiesler, S., Boneva, B., Cummings, J., Helgeson, V., Crawford, A.: Internet Paradox Revisited (2001)

Kraut, R., Mukhopadhyay, T., Szczypula, J., Kiesler, S., Scherlis, W.: Communication and Information: Alternative Uses of the Internet in Households, pp. 368–375 (1998)

Kumano, M. (2006). The structure of ikigai and similar concepts. *The Japanese Journal of Health Psychology, 19*, 56-66. https://doi.org/10.11560/jahp.19.1_56

Lallemand, C., Gronier, G.: Méthodes de design UX: 30 méthodes fondamentales pour concevoir des expériences optimales. Eyrolles (2018). https://books.google.fr/books?id=6CJtDwAAQBAJ

Lasota, P. A., Rossano, G. F., & Shah, J. A.: Toward safe close-proximity human-robot interaction with standard industrial robots. In: 2014 IEEE International Conference on Automation Science and Engineering (CASE), p. 339-344 (2014). https://doi.org/10.1109/CoASE.2014.6899348

Mathews, G.: The Stuff of dreams, fading : Ikigai and "the Japanese self." Ethos 24(4), 718–747 (1996)

McClelland, D. C.: Human Motivation. CUP Archive (1987)

Mori, K., Kaiho, Y., Tomata, Y., Narita, M., Tanji, F., Sugiyama, K., Sugawara, Y., Tsuji, I.: Corrigendum to "Sense of life worth living (, ikigai,) and incident functional disability in elderly Japanese : The, Tsurugaya, Project" [J., Psychosom, . Res. 95: 62–67]. J. Psychosom. Res. 96, 106 (2017). https://doi.org/10.1016/j.jpsychores.2017.03.006

Pauliková, A., Gyurák-Babeľová, Z., Ubárová, M.: Analysis of the impact of human–cobot collaborative manufacturing implementation on the occupational health and safety and the quality requirements. Int. J. Environ. Res. Public Health 18(4), 1927 (2021)

Piccarozzi, M., Aquilani, B., & Gatti, C. (2018). Industry 4.0 in management studies : A systematic literature review. *Sustainability, 10*(10), 3821

Ryan, R., Deci, E.: Self-Determination Theory and the Facilitation of Intrinsic Motivation, Social Development, and Well-Being. Am. Psychol. 55, 68–78 (2000). https://doi.org/10.1037/0003-066X.55.1.68

Seaborn, K., Fels, D.I.: Gamification in theory and action : A survey. Int. J. Hum Comput Stud. 74, 14–31 (2015)

Shirai, K., Iso, H., Fukuda, H., Toyoda, Y., Takatorige, T., Tatara, K.: Factors associated with « Ikigai » among members of a public temporary employment agency for seniors (Silver Human Resources Centre) in Japan; gender differences. Health Qual. Life Outcomes 4(1), 12 (2006). https://doi.org/10.1186/1477-7525-4-12

Singer, P.W.: Wired for War : The Robotics Revolution and Conflict in the 21st Century. Penguin Books (2009)

Sone, T., Nakaya, N., Ohmori, K., Shimazu, T., Higashiguchi, M., Kakizaki, M., Kikuchi, N., Kuriyama, S., Tsuji, I.: Sense of life worth living (Ikigai) and mortality in Japan : Ohsaki study. *Psychosomatic Medicine, 70*(6), 6 (2008). . https://journals.lww.com/psychosomaticmedicine/Fulltext/2008/07000/Sense_of_Life_Worth_Living__Ikigai__and_Mortality.12.aspx

Sprenger, M., Mettler, T.: Service robots. Bus. Inf. Syst. Eng. 57(4), 271–274 (2015)

Wallén, J. (2008). *The History of the Industrial Robot.* Linköping University Electronic Press

Weiss, R.S., Bass, S.A., Heimovitz, H.K., Oka, M.: Japan's silver human resource centers and participant well-being. J. Cross Cult. Gerontol. **20**(1), 47–66 (2005). https://doi.org/10.1007/s10823-005-3797-4

Xu, X., Lu, Y., Vogel-Heuser, B., Wang, L.: Industry 4.0 and Industry 5.0—Inception, conception and perception. J. Manuf. Syst. **61**, 530–535 (2021). https://doi.org/10.1016/j.jmsy.2021.10.006

Yannou, B., & Petiot, J.-F. (2002). Needs, perceptions, functions and products : Highlight on promising design methods linking them. In: IDMME2002: 4th International Conference on Integrated Design and Manufacturing in Mechanical Engineering, Clermont-Ferrand

Author Index

Printed in the United States
by Baker & Taylor Publisher Services

Printed in the United States
by Baker & Taylor Publisher Services